Drivers of Authoritarianism

ELGAR STUDIES IN LAW AND POLITICS

This series examines the infrastructure of collective governance: the legal regulation of the political realm and political catalysts for legal change. Its depth of focus expands and contracts with the subject of each volume, from the micromechanics of local electoral struggles to the rise and fall of constitutional democracy. With expert and interdisciplinary analysis drawing on law, political science, history, and social psychology, the series aims to interrogate the actors, institutions, and structures of political engagement. The series highlights new modes of mobilization and contestation as well as new perspectives on familiar but enduring controversies. Both monographs and edited collections are welcomed.

For a full list of Edward Elgar published titles, including the titles in this series, visit our website at www.e-elgar.com.

Drivers of Authoritarianism

Paths and Developments at the Beginning of the 21st Century

Edited by

Günter Frankenberg

Emeritus Professor of Public Law, Philosophy of Law and Comparative Law, Institute for Public Law, Goethe University Frankfurt am Main, Germany

Wilhelm Heitmeyer

Emeritus Professor of Sociology, Centre for Interdisciplinary Research, University of Bielefeld, Germany

ELGAR STUDIES IN LAW AND POLITICS

Edward Elgar PUBLISHING

Cheltenham, UK • Northampton, MA, USA

Cover image: El Anatsui, The Beginning and the End, 2015, Dimensions, Variable.
Photo by Maximilian Geuter, 2019. © El Anatsui.

Published by
Edward Elgar Publishing Limited
The Lypiatts
15 Lansdown Road
Cheltenham
Glos GL50 2JA
UK

Edward Elgar Publishing, Inc.
William Pratt House
9 Dewey Court
Northampton
Massachusetts 01060
USA

A catalogue record for this book
is available from the British Library

Library of Congress Control Number: 2024930580

This book is available electronically in the **Elgar**online
Law subject collection
http://dx.doi.org/10.4337/9781035324705

ISBN 978 1 0353 2469 9 (cased)
ISBN 978 1 0353 2470 5 (eBook)

Contributors

Brigitte Bargetz holds a habilitation in political science and is a principal investigator of the research project "New Charity Economy Through the Lens of Affective Statehood: Volunteering for Food Banks and Social Supermarkets in Austria" (with Markus Griesser) at Vienna University of Economics and Business. She is also member of the International Populism Research Network at Kiel University and and co-editor of "Femina Politica. Journal for Feminist Political Science". Her research interests include affect theory as political theory, theories of the political, the relationship between affect, populism and democracy, and feminist, queer and postcolonial theory. Selected publications on the topic: *The Complexity of Populism: New Approaches and Methods*, New York 2024 (eds. with Paula Diehl); "Affektive Narrative des Rechtspopulismus: zur Mobilisierung von Männlichkeit" (with Nina Elena Eggers), in: Kim, Seongcheol & Selk, Veith (eds): *Wie weiter mit der Populismusforschung?*, Baden-Baden 2021, 247–270.

Kai Biermann is an editor in the joint Investigative Research and Data department of the weekly newspaper *DIE ZEIT* and *ZEIT online*. There he focuses primarily on IT security and surveillance, but also terrorism and the work of intelligence services and police. He is the author of several non-fiction books. Together with Thomas Wiegold, he wrote a book on *Drohnen – Chancen und Gefahren einer neuen Technik* (Ch. Links 2015). He has been awarded various prizes for his work, including the Grimme Online Award, the Reporter Award and the American George Polk Award. In 2021, he was a member of the Pegasus Project. The participants received the EU Parliament Prize in 2021 in honour of Daphne Caruana Galizia, who was murdered in Malta.

Oliver Decker, Prof. Dr. phil., Dipl.-Psych., holds the Chair of Social Psychology and Intercultural Practice at the Sigmund Freud University in Berlin. He is director of the Else-Frenkel-Brunswik Institute and the Centre for Research on Right-Wing Extremism and Democracy, both located at the University of Leipzig. Since 2005 he has organised a series of conferences with Christoph Türcke: "Critical Theory – Psychoanalytic Practice". Together with Elmar Brähler, he has led the Leipzig Authoritarianism Studies on extreme right-wing attitudes in Germany since 2002 (until 2018 Leipziger "Mitte-Studien"). Selection of recent book publications: *Psyche und Gesellschaft in Zeiten der Pandemie* (2021 Psychosozial-Verlag/Gießen, with

Steffen Elsner and Julia Schuler), *Demokratie in Sachsen - Das EFBI-Jahrbuch* (Edition Überland/Leipzig 2022, with Fiona Kalkstein and Johannes Kiess) and *Escape into Authoritarianism* (2022, Routledge/New York, with Elmar Brähler and Johannes Kiess).

Paula Diehl is Professor of Political Theory, History of Ideas and Political Culture at the Christian-Albrechts-Universität in Kiel. Her research focuses on democratic theory, political culture, the political imaginary, political representation and performativity, populism, right-wing populism and totalitarianism. She is a board member of the DVPW working groups "Politics and Culture" and "Constructivist Theology". Selected publications: "For a Complex Definition of Populism", in: *Populism Concepts and Methods*, Polity 2022; with W. Bergem and H. Lietzmann, eds, *Politische Kulturforschung Reloaded*, Bielefeld 2019. "The Populist Twist. The Relationship Between the Leader and the People in Populism", in: Pollak, Johannes & Castiglione, Dario (eds), *Making Present. Theorizing the New Politics of Representation*, Chicago 2019.

Klaus Dörre has been Professor of Labour, Industrial and Economic Sociology at Friedrich Schiller University in Jena since 2005. From 2011 to 2021, he was one of the directors of the DFG research group Post-Growth Societies, is responsible for the Centre for Digital Transformation Thuringia (ZeTT) together with Prof. Heike Kraußlach and is co-editor of the *Berliner Journal für Soziologie* and *Global Dialogue*. His work focuses on the theory of capitalism, precarisation of work and employment, labour relations, social consequences of digitalisation and right-wing populism. Recent publications on the topic: Dörre, Klaus et al, "Arbeiterbewegung von rechts?", in: *Berliner Journal für Soziologie* 2018, 28, 55–90. "'Take Back Control' – Marx, Polanyi and Right-Wing Populist Revolt", in: *Österreichische Zeitschrift für Soziologie*, 2019, 44, 225–243; and *In der Warteschlange. Arbeiter*innen und die radikale Rechte*, Münster 2020.

Nina Elena Eggers, Dipl.-Pol., is a Political Scientist and a Doctoral Candidate at the University of Bremen. Her research focuses on contemporary political theories, political narratives, theories of (right-wing) populism, ideologies of the New Right, and gender politics. She researches and teaches in the field of political theories, history of ideas and political culture with a focus on narrative and politics, theories of collective and national identity and right-wing populism. Latest publications: "Affektive Narrative des Rechtspopulismus: zur Mobilisierung von Männlichkeit" (with Brigitte Bargetz), in: Kim, Seongcheol & Selk,Veith (eds): *Wie weiter mit der Populismusforschung?*, Baden-Baden 2021, 247–270; "Narrative Identität und kulturelle Differenz. Eine erzähltheoretische Perspektive auf Konstruktionen des Anderen", in: Bizeul, Yves &

Rudolf, Dennis B. (eds) *Gibt es eine kulturelle Identität?*, Baden-Baden 2020, 177–196.

Günter Frankenberg, Dr. phil. and Dr. jur., Emeritus Professor of Public Law, Comparative Law and Philosophy of Law at Goethe University in Frankfurt am Main since 1992; Senior Professor from 2013 until 2022. From 1978 to 2018, he was co-editor of the journal Kritische Justiz. His work focuses on legal and constitutional theory, methods of comparative law, security law and the constitutions of authoritarian regimes. Recent publications: *Authoritarianism. Constitutional Perspectives*, Berlin: Suhrkamp 2020. "Legal Transfer", in: Foblets, Marie-Claire et al. (eds) *Oxford Handbook of Law and Anthropology*, Oxford 2021, 333–351. "Constituting the Negative Globality of Fear", in: *International Journal of Constitutional Law*, 21, 5–13 (2023).

Klaus Günther is Professor of Legal Theory, Criminal Law and Criminal Procedure at the Goethe University Frankfurt am Main, where he is a member of the Normative Orders Research Network, the Research Institute for Social Cohesion (FGZ) and the Institute for Social Research. Historical and systematic research on the philosophy of law (including the discourse theory of law, legal trust) and on the foundations of criminal law. Publications among others: "Pays réel, pays légal, patria naturae, patria iuris. Vom Sinn und Unsinn einer begriffspolitischen Unterscheidung", in: Bung, Jochen & Kuhli, Milan (eds), *Volk als Konzept in Recht und Politik*, Berlin/Boston 2020, 63–72; "Legalität als Waffe? Kommentar zur Dialektik von Entlegitimierung und Relegitimierung von Legalität bei Schmitt und Kervégan", in: *Rechtsphilosophie – Zeitschrift für die Grundlagen des Rechts*, 2021, 141–157.

Wilhelm Heitmeyer, Emeritus Professor of Sociology, Dr., was the founder and from 1996 to 2013 the director of the Institute for Interdisciplinary Research on Conflict and Violence at the University of Bielefeld. Most recently, he was a senior professor. From 2008 to 2014, he was Editor-in-Chief of the *International Journal of Conflict and Violence*. With John Hagan, he edited the *International Handbook of Violence Research* in 2002. His research focuses on the theory of social disintegration, violence, group-focused enmity and right-wing extremism. He was editor of the 10-volume series *Deutsche Zustände 2002–2012*, Frankfurt am Main/Berlin: Suhrkamp. Most recently he published Autoritäre Versuchungen, Berlin: Suhrkamp, 2018; and, together with M. Freiheit and P. Sitzer, *Rechte Bedrohungsallianzen*, Berlin: Suhrkamp 2020.

Maximilian Pichl, Dr. phil., Dr. jur., is Professor at the Rhein-Main University of Applied Sciences in Wiesbaden. His research focuses on: critical legal theory, state theory, asylum law, and migration law. Recent publications: *Rechtskämpfe. Eine Analyse der Rechtsverfahren nach dem Sommer der*

Migration, Frankfurt am Main: Campus, 2021. His dissertation in law: *Untersuchung im Rechtsstaat. Eine deskriptiv-kritische Beobachtung der parlamentarischen Untersuchungsausschüsse zur NSU-Mordserie*, Weilerswist: Velbrück 2022, was awarded two distinguished prizes.

Lars Rensmann, Prof. Dr., is Professor of Political Science with a focus on Comparative Government at the University of Passau. Main research interests: comparative politics in a global context; American and European party and government systems; populism, authoritarianism, right-wing extremism, anti-Semitism and racism; democracy and democratic crisis research; comparative political culture research; international political theory and critical theory. Publications on the topic include *Authoritarianism and Democracy: Studies on Political Culture in Global Modernity* (Wochenschau Verlag, 2011, with Hajo Funke & Steffen Hagemann).

Dieter Rucht, Dr. rer. pol., is Emeritus Professor of Sociology, Research Fellow at the Social Science Research Center Berlin and member of the Institut für Protest- und Bewegungsforschung in Berlin. His research focuses on political participation, the public sphere, social movements and political protest. Publications: Rucht, Dieter & Neidhardt, Friedhelm, "Soziale Bewegungen und kollektive Aktionen", in: Joas, Hans & Mau, Stefan (eds), *Lehrbuch Soziologie*, 4th completely revised and expanded edition, Frankfurt am Main: Campus, 2020, 831–864.

Birgit Sauer is Professor of Political Science at the University of Vienna. Her research focuses on right-wing populism and gender, politics and gender, political representation of women, affects and politics. Recent publications include: Mojca Pajnik and Birgit Sauer, *Populism and the Web. Communicative Practices of Parties and Movements in Europe*, London: Routledge (2017), "Authoritarian Right-Wing Populism as Masculinist Identity Politics. The Role of Affects", in: Dietze, Gabriele & Roth, Julia (eds), *Right-Wing Populism and Gender. European Perspectives and Beyond*, Bielefeld: transcript Verlag, 2020, 23–40. "Cultural war 2.0? The relevance of gender in the radical populist-nationalist right", in: Atzmüller, Roland et al. (eds), *Capitalism in Transformation. Movements and Countermovements in the 21st Century*, Cheltenham: Edward Elgar, 2019, 169–182.

Bernd Stegemann is Professor of Dramaturgy at the Ernst Busch Academy of Dramatic Arts in Berlin and dramaturge at the Berliner Ensemble. Numerous monographs on the art of theatre and the dramaturgy of public speaking: *Die Kritik des Theaters*, Berlin 2013; *Lob des Realismus*, Berlin 2015; *Das Gespenst des Populismus*, Berlin 2017; *Die Moralfalle. Für eine Befreiung linker Politik,* Berlin 2018; *Die Öffentlichkeit und ihre Feinde*, Stuttgart 2021; and *Wutkultur*, Berlin 2021. Publications in *DIE ZEIT*, *SPIEGEL*, *Frankfurter*

Allgemeine Zeitung, *Süddeutsche Zeitung*, *WELT*, *Lettre international,* and *Cicero.*

Natascha Strobl is a Political Scientist, Magistra, Diploma Studies in Political Science and Scandinavian studies, Magistra in Vienna. Her research focuses on the Identitarian Movement and the rhetoric of the New Right. Publications: (with J. Bruns and K. Glösel) *Die Identitären. Handbuch zur Jugendbewegung der Neuen Rechten in Europa*, Münster 2014; (with J. Bruns and K. Glösel) *Rechte Kulturrevolution. Wer und was ist die die Neue Rechte von heute?*, Hamburg 2015; *Radikalisierter Konservatismus. Eine Analyse*, Berlin 2021.

Volker Weiß holds a doctorate in history and researches mainly on the history and present of the extreme right in Germany. His work has been translated into several languages. *The study The Authoritarian Revolt. The New Right and the Decline of the Occident* was nominated for the 2017 Leipzig Book Fair Non-Fiction Prize and is now considered a standard work. In 2019, he commented on the first publication of the lecture "Aspekte des neuen Rechtsradikalismus" (Aspects of the New Right-Wing Radicalism) by Theodor W. Adorno. Weiß is a fellow at the Centre for Research on Antisemitism at the Technical University of Berlin, a member of the Working Group on Antisemitism Research in the German Sociological Association (DGS) and the Villigst Research Forum on National Socialism, Racism and Antisemitism e.V. In 2021, he was a visiting professor at the Institute for Contemporary History at the University of Innsbruck.

Michael Zürn is Director of the Department of Global Governance at the Social Science Research Center Berlin (WZB) and Professor of International Relations at the Free University of Berlin. Since 2019, he has been the spokesperson for the DFG-funded Cluster of Excellence "Contestations of the Liberal Script" (SCRIPTS). His research focuses in particular on the emergence and functioning of inter- and supranational institutions and organisations and their impact on political orders. His publications cover, among others, the legitimacy and effectiveness of international institutions. His most recent publication is "Die demokratische Regression" (with Armin Schäfer), published by Suhrkamp Verlag, 2021.

Preface

Due to past and current crises, authoritarian temptations have become increasingly visible among sections of the population in Western societies as well over the past two decades. At the same time, authoritarian movements and parties have emerged and gained influence in numerous countries. Finally, authoritarian activities – even beyond the boundaries of law – can be detected in state institutions. Accordingly, serious threats to pluralistic societies and modern democracies can be identified across the globe. It is the goal of this book to trace and explain the advance of authoritarianism. Its varieties can only be understood through multi- and interdisciplinary approaches which pursue different lines of research and pose different questions that are laid out in this volume: How empirically evident and enduring are the manifestations of authoritarian developments in modern societies? Which historical and economic backgrounds contribute to the explanation of current development processes? Which sociological, political science, jurisprudence, social psychology, philosophy, and media studies findings can be used to uncover the diverse authoritarian mechanisms that affect social life and spill over into labor relations and gender relations? What are the correspondences in the various subsystems of politics, law, culture, media, education, economy, psychology, etc.?

On the part of political regimes, authoritarian mechanisms come to bear in statecraft, repression, and rhetoric; on the part of social movements, in agendas and strategies; and on the part of populations, in their patterns of thought, orientations to action, their attitudes towards minorities and strangers, and their readiness to follow and submit to leader figures. The contributions to this book are guided by the question who or which forces are driving authoritarian developmental thrusts. We assume that social, economic or political crises are the main drivers of authoritarian developments. This assumption can be tested promisingly only with the above-mentioned interdisciplinary interest in research and with a view to international comparative perspectives. Despite all analytical efforts, the picture will remain incomplete in the end. The expected criticism will have to be accepted and dealt with.

The theme of the book also applies to the events that have held us all spellbound since Russia's attack on Ukraine ordered by Vladimir Putin in February 2022. At the time of the research event preparing this volume, in September 2021, and in the final stages of writing the (German) manuscripts, it could not have been foreseen that the Russian president would wage a criminal war revealing basic features of a fascist system. So, instead of a detailed analysis only fragments of a critical interpretation could be provided.

This volume focuses on the drivers of authoritarian developments in pluralistic societies and modern democracies, in particular the various crises (climate, COVID-19, poverty/inequality, etc.) – analyzed from the vantage point of various scientific perspectives, notably political science, sociology, media theory, political economy, analysis of social movements, history, feminism, etc.). In consequence, the volume is genuinely interdisciplinary product as regards its preparation (research event and discourse among the authors) and completion. As far as it necessary, some of the chapters will be updated for the English publication.

Neither the former Soviet Union nor today's Russia could ever be counted among the pluralist societies. It has long been a commonplace that Russia is an authoritarian state and society. This commonplace now needs to be revised. Since the beginning of the war against Ukraine in February 2022, there have been numerous essays on what might have been the preceding and present domestic and social developments of the system that drove the realization of this criminal war of aggression. Some authors emphasize the transition from an authoritarian to a totalitarian state. Others classify it as a development from a "spin dictatorship" to a repressive police-state dictatorship. The transition from the system of Putinism to a new form of Stalinism has also been described and has been qualified more recently as an authoritarian system that has turned into fascism.

Although some of the contributions in this book also make references to the dramatic course of events, for obvious reasons of time we will not be able to present our own, sufficiently well-founded assessments of these events and developments. Where considerations and classifications are implied, they will have to be substantiated in later analyses.

We thank Ulrike Rogat who helped us to technically manage the drafting of this volume, and Charlie Zacharoff for his thorough and thoughtful editing of most of the articles.

Frankfurt am Main & Bielefeld
Günter Frankenberg & Wilhelm Heitmeyer

PART I

On the theory and empiricism of authoritarianism

1. Authoritarian developments as a threat to democracy and pluralism

Günter Frankenberg and Wilhelm Heitmeyer

1. THE FOCUS

Over the last two decades, societies in both the Global North and South have witnessed an authoritarian trend that is represented by social movements, political parties, and regimes whose anti-democratic agenda has gained political and cultural influence worldwide. Globally, different parts of the population have given in to authoritarian temptations. Authoritarianism is a current and highly relevant topic that particularly emerges in conjunction with crises, such as the climate catastrophe, the corona pandemic, and recurrent labour disputes and distribution conflicts; by the same token, it makes itself heard time and again, albeit less visibly and more insidiously, outside of crisis-ridden situations – most recently the war of aggression waged by Russian dictator Vladimir Putin against the Ukraine since February 2022. Both overt facets and covert traces of authoritarian agendas, aspirations, and attitudes can be detected at various levels: in strategic alliances between organisations and states; in networks and associations that operate as collective actors, such as political parties and social movements; and in communities, workplaces, and families.[1]

In view of the broad and uneven field of authoritarianism and its country-specific manifestations, we limit ourselves in this book to phenomena in the right-wing and extreme right-wing authoritarian spectrum. An appropriate extension to left-wing authoritarian manifestations would go beyond the scope of this concept, because overlaps and distinctions would have to be made.

[1] Usually, organizations, actors, and relationships are assigned to the macro, meso, or micro level.

2. CONTEMPORARY HISTORY: OUTLINING A PROBLEM

Authoritarian developments in the twenty-first century have not come out of nowhere.[2] They are embedded in contemporary historical and current contexts. From which contemporary historical spaces, events, processes, and actors can clarifications of these ongoing processes be expected?

The world history of the twentieth century as the 'age of extremes' (Hobsbawm 1998) was characterised by violence, wars, and authoritarian social and political conditions in which modernity and barbarism were interconnected (Miller & Soeffner 1996). After the 'rupture of civilization' (Diner 1988) and the end of National Socialist rule, it took a long time for a pluralistic society and liberal democracy to successively emerge in Germany (Rensmann et al. 2011), fostered by the structures and civil rights of the newly created Basic Law and its 'naturalization' (Rödel et al. 1989) – flanked and safeguarded by developments in the legal system, the media, the education system, and an economic system in which capital interests and workers' interests were 'balanced' by political interventions over longer periods of time.

Several developments have contributed to instabilities in the statics of this architecture. The first was the collapse of the communist system and, with it, of the politically stabilising 'system competition'. In the West, these led to euphoric and ideological statements celebrating the 'end of history', which found expression in the alleged 'universalization of Western democracy as man's final form of government' (Fukuyama 1992). Later, after a look into the 'posthuman future' (Fukuyama 2003) little of the 'end of history' would remain. On the contrary, the topic of a 'new authoritarian system competition' has been on the agenda for quite some time. It is closely linked to the question of how to answer the major questions of the future, especially the climate crisis, sustainable growth, and, of course, pandemics. At the same time, it is linked to the authoritarian development paths of societies, their economic and political systems, together with the constitutional relations of freedom and security. One cipher for this is the talk of the 'Chinese century' (Stiglitz 2014; Aust & Geiges 2012).

Second, the architecture changed due to the rapid acceleration and expansion of economic globalisation, whose diffusion into the realm of culture as well as its social consequences for societies and political systems affected

[2] Putin's war will probably have to be excluded, because most experts and politicians have long agreed that the time of wars of aggression should be over in Europe (and thus also the military strategy of territorial national defence). See Herfried Münkler, *The New Wars,* Polity: 2004.

parliamentary democracy and undercut the primacy of politics. The shift to neoliberal economic policies, characterised by far-reaching political deregulation and austerity measures, diminished the power of democratically legitimised politics vis-à-vis an increasingly anonymous global financial capitalism. Gains in control and land grabs by capital were associated with losses of control of politics, especially the nation-state version, and with processes inaccurately described as privatisation and economisation (Biebricher 2021). More striking, though unnecessarily apocalyptic, are statements such as those of the American sociologist Birnbaum (1997): where market orthodoxy triumphs, democracy dies. Dahrendorf (1997) was quick to point out the tense relationships between capitalist economy, social integration or disintegration, and democracy in the age of neoliberal globalisation. He spoke of a 'squaring of the circle'. In his diction, this metaphor means that considerable tensions exist between, first, maintaining competitiveness in the raging competition of the global economy; second, ensuring social solidarity and cohesion, i.e. integration; and third, being able to do so within the framework of institutions of democratic societies.

In view of the 'new' control relations, the aforementioned metaphor leads to the question: Who is harmed by this development? Especially when more and more social inequalities, phenomena of the authoritarian, however, were already pronounced in the twentieth century and long before (Arendt 1951). Contrary to Dahrendorf's prediction and comparable assessments, this 'age of extremes' (Hobsbawm 1998) tends – or at least tended – to be credited to human rights and liberal democracy. Nonetheless, there is no lack of empirical evidence that political authoritarianism, borne by social movements, political parties, and/or (consolidated) regimes, has been on the rise over the past twenty years of the twenty-first century (Heitmeyer 2018; Bertelsmann Stiftung 2018, 2020, and 2022; Lauth et al. 2020; Schäfer & Zürn 2021: 24–58). Regardless of whether terms like 'renaissance of the authoritarian' or 'democratic regression', 'new authoritarian international' or 'globalisation of authoritarianism', or the combination of 'democratic, hybrid, and authoritarian regimes' (as chracterised by International IDEA 2021) accurately describe the development, it is indisputable that, according to estimates, the population in autocracies grew from 2.3 to 3.3 billion from 2003 to 2017, and more than half of 137 states worldwide can be characterised as autocracies (Bertelsmann Stiftung 2022; Heitmeyer 2018: 177–196; Diamond et al. 2016). According to the Bertelsmann Stiftung BTI Index (2022) and International IDEA data, authoritarian governance patterns have steadily increased over the past decade and more 'defective democracies' (Merkel et al. 2003 and 2006) have descended into autocracy than have risen to become functioning democracies. As a result, many autocracies have become significantly more repressive, while fundamental rights of participation and the rule of law are being challenged in democracies that previously appeared to be consolidated. The trend of a worldwide erosion of the quality of democracy or 'democratic regression' (Schäfer & Zürn 2021: 24–58; Zürn in this volume) thus continues unabated. The apocalyptic tone of numerous publications on the state and future of democracy is not very helpful from an analytical point of view, but it is hardly surprising in view of these findings (Luce 2017; Levitsky & Ziblatt 2018; Mounk 2022).

If the time frame of the 'young' twenty-first century is chosen here for an analysis of drivers and paths of authoritarian developments, the 'old' twentieth century must still be taken into account. What characterises 'the authoritarian' in this century as compared to the previous one? Has the authoritarian toolkit been modernised, including the agendas, dispositions, and mentalities? Indeed, there are numerous indications for this. If one looks at the developments in the new communication media, it is easy to see that they open up completely new, effective possibilities for mass manipulation and mobilisation as well as 'instruments for unbounded repression' (Biermann, in this volume). In this way, militarised fighting units with uniforms are no longer absolutely necessary to insidiously advance new, authoritarian standards of normality. Likewise, the anti-democratic elites have changed their strategies. In Western Europe and elsewhere, the undisguised and brutal rejection of the constitutional state that marked the twentieth century has given way to covert ideological flexibility, such as a 'cult of immediacy' in communication geared toward fantasies of an imagined community (Frankenberg 2020: 200–238), which can subtly fill the voids created by the erosion of the quality of democracy (Heitmeyer 2001: 517). Political alienation and loss of trust in parts of the population are magnets for authoritarian offers by movements and parties.

Authoritarian developments in the 'shadow of globalisation' (Loch & Heitmeyer 2001) have become visible for a while. In some of the states with authoritarian tendencies or already fully established autocracies, one factor is particularly striking: the urban–rural divide. To take only a few examples: Trump found considerable success with voters in the election of 2016, especially in the disconnected rural areas of the Midwest with its moribund coal and steel districts, while Hillary Clinton, with the arrogance of the East Coast elite, had denigrated these areas and their people as a 'basket of deplorables'.[3] In the United Kingdom, with its structures of enormous inequality, many Britons who voted for Brexit in 2016 lived in the countryside or in small towns. In Hungary, Prime Minister Viktor Orbán's landslide victory in the 2022 national elections came mainly from the rural population. Similarly, in Poland, the PiS (Law and Justice Party) has sprung up and grown in the countryside and has positioned itself against 'those in Warsaw' with the help of the Catholic

---

3 *Time*, 10 September 2016.

Church. In France's centralist, Paris-centred political system, the rural population, or rather the regions that have been left behind by economic development, also gave the far-right candidates Marine Le Pen and Eric Zemmour substantial vote gains in the first round of the 2022 elections compared to 2017 and before. Zemmour additionally made particular gains (relative to his overall result) in cities with wealthy, upper-class neighbourhoods. In the runoff, Le Pen found the bulk of her supporters in rural areas.

The picture of the rural–urban partition is both more complex and simpler in Germany when one looks at the socio-geographic structure. In the western states of the 'old' republic, there is no such sharp division, except in a few isolated areas. Socio-geography in eastern Germany is rather different. There, small communities and small towns dominate. In the logic of the societies mentioned so far, with the political consequences of sharp urban–rural differences in material prosperity, opportunities to participate in social goods, social recognition, future prospects, etc., it does not come as a surprise that the authoritarian national radicalism of the party *Alternative für Deutschland* (AfD) is particularly successful in eastern Germany.

Even when different traditions, social milieus and voting behaviour are taken into account, the factor of social inequality still stands out, with the consequences of social disintegration that propel authoritarian political proposals. Since processes of comparison always take place between social groups in society in order to identify and classify one's own social status – and as a result, recognition – these massive urban–rural differences give rise to perceptions of relative deprivation, i.e. in comparison to other groups. These feelings of deprivation are perceived as injustice. They can be easily mobilised in politics when particular groups can be readily blamed. Empirical studies based on Relative Deprivation Theory[4] have repeatedly shown that such feelings often centre around anger that is frequently directed at certain groups. This situation is often instrumentalised by right-wing authoritarian movements and parties against two target groups: migrants and refugees in the countryside on the one hand and ruling elites in the metropolises on the other. The motivations and slogans vary from country to country: 'Make America [Austria, Brazil, Italy ...] Great Again',[5] 'Take Back Control', 'We're Taking Back Our Country', etc. These examples show how dangerous such urban-rural differences can be

---

[4] If not meant to emphasize the individual experience of discontent, relative deprivation is characterized by the comparative lack of resources to sustain the diet, lifestyle, activities and amenities that an individual or group is accustomed to or that are, according to social norms, widely encouraged or approved in the society one belongs to (Runciman 1966).

[5] 'Make America Great Again' was introduced by Ronald Reagan (1980), adopted by Bill Clinton (1991) and others, then most successfully popularized by Donald Trump

politically: when social inequality triggers processes of political disintegration, the ground becomes fertile for authoritarian movements.

3. PROFILES OF THE AUTHORITARIAN

The erosion of democracy and democratic regression are among the many phenomena that are registered under the rubric of democracy and law-rule caused by practices of corruption or institutional defects, generating deviant or deficient institutionalisations of democracy, or symptoms of the decay of representation or pathological symptoms of participation (post-democracy, post-politics, etc.) or of the disciplinary state (Yongshun 2015). They extend over a broad horizon (Crouch 2004 and 2021; Brown 2019; O'Donnell 2007; Przeworski 2019; Democracy Index 2020). Conceptually prepared and theoretically interpreted, these phenomena are generally divided into three camps that are not always easy to delineate from each other. Protagonists of these camps are currently drawing the demarcation lines that characterise the topography of what is considered authoritarian, autocratic, or anti-democratic.[6] The profiles of populism, illiberalism and authoritarianism are to be identified here (in the brevity required by the format of an introduction). They claim, not in combination but each separately, the interpretive authority over the phenomena labelled as 'global retreat of democracy' or 'retreat of western liberalism' (Luce 2017), 'third wave of autocratisation' or 'renaissance of authoritarianism' (Frantz 2018; Przeworksi 2020; Lührmann & Hellmeier 2020). Depending on the theoretical perspective, these trends are attributed to political crises or national 'fatigue (or stress) fractures'[7] in the structures of democracy, the rule of law and the welfare state; to signs of democratic exhaustion, a dramatic weakness of democracy as a form of government and life; to economic and social crisis tendencies, such as capitalist land grabs and loss of control on the part of the citizens; or else to the consequences of globalisation (Zürn 2018 and in this volume; Best et al. 2011). Whether narrowly political-institutional or more

---

(2016), and copied by authoritarian politicians in other countries. The slogan is usually meant to invoke an imaginary glorious (or better) past.

[6] Just as diverse as their perspectives may be, they all echo the classic formula: 'History will teach us ... that of the men who overthrew the liberties of the republics, most began their careers courting the people in servility; they began as demagogues and ended as tyrants' (Alexander Hamilton, *The Federalist Papers,* 1787, No 1). See Frantz 2018; Sajo 2021; F. Decker 2021; Appletree 2021; Kauth & King 2021; Lührmann & Hellmeier 2020.

[7] Fatigue fractures (and distortions) have been a topic in the social and economic sciences for quite some time – Winfried Süss (2006), 'Ermüdungsbrüche im Wohlfahrtsstaat' in 3 *Zeithistorische Forschungen*, 470–74; Claus Offe (2007), 'Der bedrängte Wohlfahrtsstaat' in 47 *Archiv für Sozialgeschichte*, 95–126.

broadly economic and social, crises or emergencies are overwhelmingly held responsible for driving new qualitative forms, movements, agendas, and mentalities of political authoritarianism. We will return to this point (see chapter 7).

First of all, the rise of authoritarian regimes and agendas, aspirations and attitudes calls for conceptual clarification. In this introduction, attention is therefore directed to whether and to what extent the scholarly vocabulary and interpretive lenses of 'populism', 'illiberalism' and 'authoritarianism' take account of the specific techniques and ideologies, attitudes and practices of authoritarianism, and how they solve the obvious definitional difficulties in view of the diverse phenomena and introduce plausible demarcations.

3.1 Populism

Established and practised for more than two decades, the interpretive lenses of populism studies are unable to offer a truly coherent pattern of interpretation, even after both in-depth and impressive empirical studies of populist movements and parties as well as analyses of structures and guiding ideas.[8] One could think, for example, of the conceptual combination of a popular programme with an appeal to the imagined community of the people (Anderson 2005) as a source of legitimacy. What is widespread, however, are predominantly controversial, definitional set pieces of populism. They contour a basic political stance that, in radical opposition to the ruling elites in politics, economics, culture, and society, claims for itself to recognise and represent the authentic will of the people (Müller 2016; Mudde & Kaltwasser 2019; Diehl 2020), or which presents a Manichean worldview populated by the true, virtuous people and the self-serving establishment, elsewhere the oligarchs – a faint echo of Robespierre's thesis of the decent people and corrupt magistrate.[9]

Nevertheless, the use of the term 'populism' – driven by the media (hardly interested in conceptual precision) and the political class (attuned to the repetition of what is often said) – remains popular, albeit highly indeterminate. Despite thorough research and in-depth discussion, the social sciences have not succeeded in gaining a sharp profile for the phenomena behind the collective singular. As a semantic umbrella, populism can be stretched over movements and regimes that promote democracy (inclusionary) as well as those that undermine it (exclusionary), over movements and aspirations on

---

[8] E.g. Canovan 1981; De la Torre 2015; Moffitt 2016; Mudde & Kaltwasser 2017; Priester 2017; Schäfer & Zürn 2021: 59–88; Möller 2022.

[9] 'Tout institution qui ne suppose pas le peuple bon et le magistrat corruptible est vicieuse.' Art XIX of Robespierre's proposed declaration of human rights (1793), *Discours et rapports*, 10 May, 256.

the right-wing or left-wing fringes, or even in the centre of the conventional political coordinate system. Under this umbrella, demagogues and tyrants, as well as racist, ethnocentric, xenophobic, misogynist, homophobic, popular and unpopular heads of state and parties and groups gather (in the hardly manageable field of publications).

In the steadily swelling discourse on populism, one sometimes misses the willingness to adjust the grammar of populism to better reflect its different political levels, contexts of use, and conjunctures. To begin with, it would be necessary to differentiate between movements, parties, and regimes, because it can be safely assumed that oppositional lifeworlds, party organisations, and governmental responsibility shape different forms of populist programming. Thus, although populism is located in the political coordinate system, its practices and rhetoric are not addressed with adequate distinction. A helpful contrast, without reducing the phenomena to this (Priester 2011 and 2017; Norris & Inglehart 2019), could be: populism as a style of mobilisation that targets marginalised groups (such as early Peronism, Chavismo, or Podemos in Spain) and can turn into a Machiavellian strategy to gain or defend power (exemplified by the Danish 'People's Party', the Swiss People's Party, Fidesz in Hungary, the Rassemblement National, the Lega in Italy, the Alternative for Germany, or even Trump's election campaigns). This practice is supported by rhetoric too often labelled populist and interpretations of the world which, however simple, are effectively designed to activate resentment (against elites, 'the system', minorities, foreigners, the 'lying press', etc.) in order to conjure up an imaginary, collective identity in the phantasm of the authentic people or nation.

It is striking that the varieties of populism, which can be roughly characterised as either dangerous or positively corrective deviations from democratic 'normality', predominantly operate without a concept of the constitution and therefore mostly demand 'rights' of the people – the latter linked in substantial unity, not by social contract or as individuals. These rights do not function as defensive rights against unlawful state encroachments, but as expressions of a 'sovereignty' of the imagined common will or of the nation (invoked situationally and selectively in protests) which overcomes politics and as a rejection of constitutional institutions.

This applies primarily to the term 'right-wing populism', which stands out in the discourse on populism due to its particularly frequent use, bereft of a somewhat uniform definition, allegedly operating as a form of authoritarianism with a 'thin ideology' and an orientation towards the past. The widely held thesis of a thin ideology must be countered by the fact that populist (or more precisely: authoritarian) aspirations are not only distinguished by their political style and strategies aimed at gaining power, but also by a 'set of ideas' and a 'specific understanding of politics and democracy' (Schäfer & Zürn 2021:

64–73; Zürn, in this volume) or a 'pattern model for interpreting the social situation' (Zürn, in this volume) not limited to anti-elitism and the rejection of parliamentary democracy (Frankenberg 2020: 123–33; Urbinati 2019: 49–51). Robespierre's dichotomy of good people and corrupt magistrate thus no longer suffices to grasp the gist of the populist worldview. With the ideological combination and political programme of anti-elitism and anti-pluralism, a culture of immediate communication, a xenophobic nationalism and the phantasm of imaginary communality, an adequate description of populism needs to move far away from democratic grass roots and Robespierre's dichotomy. Hence, we should feel invited to accept the interpretation offered by the camp of authoritarianism.

According to a series of surveys and studies analysed, among others, in a meta-study by Cambridge University, a decline in support for democracy can be observed in Germany, Austria, Switzerland, in Southern European countries and in so-called 'maturing democracies' in Latin America (Centre for the Future of Democracy 2022). In these countries the performance of democracy as a form of government and life is doubted, while elsewhere the democratic euphoria of the transition years has faded, leaving behind the unresolved challenges of corruption, inter-group conflict and urban violence. Paradoxically, as dissatisfaction with democratic governance has risen since the beginning of the pandemic, populist leaders and parties have seen their poll numbers fall and have lost elections.[10]

3.2 Illiberalism

Compared to the populism crescendo, the 'illiberalism' discourse comes along quietly. This may be because its dissemination is a bit recent and therefore has yet to assure itself of its academic position and media acceptance.[11] An article by Fareed Zakaria on 'illiberal democracy' is widely regarded as the publication that opened the current debate. It signalled a changed perception of populism, now linking it to the constitution. Zakaria observed that democratically elected regimes routinely ignore the constitutional limits of their power

[10] Declining poll ratings were recorded, for example, by Donald Trump, Jair Bolsonaro, Viktor Orbán, Recep Tayyip Erdoğan, Andrej Babiš, Boris Johnson and Andrés Manel Lopéz Obrador (Mexico), who are widely listed as 'populists'. Benjamin Netanyahu lost the (re-)election, then had a come-back. In Chile, the populist and ultra-conservative José Antonio Kast lost in the run-off to Gabriel Boric in 2021. See Centre for the Future of Democracy, *The Great Reset*, 16.

[11] As distinct from 'illiberalism', the term 'illiberal' is not of recent origin. See Hugo von Hofmansthal (1979) 'Der Dichter und diese Zeit' [1906] in *Gesammelte Werke* I, Frankfurt, 54.

and deprive the citizenry of their fundamental rights and freedoms (Zakaria 1997: 22).

Meanwhile, the methodologically very different surveys of the (authoritarian) world of governance and democracy count about 80 illiberal democracies, whose classification can shift towards the category of 'weak' or 'deficient' democracies, 'hard' or 'moderate' autocracies, or 'backsliding countries' depending on their development and the authors' matrix (Bertelsmann 2020; International IDEA 2021; Lauth et al. 2020; Schlenkrich 2021). In political science, the accent has been placed somewhat differently with the theory and regional analysis of 'defective democracies' (Merkel 2004; Merkel et al. 2003 and 2006). Starting from the normatively demanding concept of an institutionally 'embedded democracy', authors examine the conditions of functionality and stability in democratic systems (beginning with former state-socialist states) to identify their defects. The characteristics of such defects in terms of separation of powers, political liberties and the rule of law then justify the qualification as 'illiberal'.

While the ageing frame of populism, proliferating in the academic world and supported by the media, can calmly face the storm of ever-new categories, illiberalism will still have to defend its status and field of research. The fact that Hungarian Prime Minister Viktor Orbán promoted the agenda of building an 'illiberal state' within the European Union in his Băile Tuşnad speech in 2014 is unlikely to further the category's academic career. However, in a number of recent publications and the *Journal of Illiberalism Studies*, the discussion on illiberalism may now be gaining momentum, but also a diversity of interpretations (Kauth & King 2021).

The *Routledge Handbook on Illiberalism* (Sajó et al. 2022) brings together in its more than 60 contributions a considerable plurality of theoretical perspectives and impressive diversity of illiberal phenomena from theocracy to military regimes, from elective democracies to those based on Bonapartist referendums. Without a doubt, these will present a more multi-faceted, but also more confusing picture of illiberalism, especially since no coherent theoretical outline will unite them into a single paradigm. One of the editors, András Sajó, has presented a concentrated introduction and committed defence of the term and agenda with 'Ruling by Cheating' (Sajó 2021). He examines the constitutional structures of illiberal democracies as well as illiberal phenomena in 'mature', consolidated democracies (a distinction that is not really strictly enforced) and tries to show that the global trend towards 'mild despotism' should not be characterised as authoritarianism but as an abuse of constitutionalism. Clearly, Sajó has in mind the Orbán regime in Hungary and Jarosław Kaczyński, who dominates politics in Poland, and probably also Jair Bolsonaro when he was president in Brazil. Sajó also tries to validate his thesis of a conservative, plebeian and patriotic constitutional state including elements of the rule of law by taking the example of 'illiberal democracies' in Latin America (especially Chavismo in Venezuela).

The definitional problem faced by all advocates of illiberalism as a plausible interpretative category is obvious: they have to ask themselves how to separate the systematically linked twins of liberalism and illiberalism and make illiberalism an analytically free-standing object of analysis and critique. One is tempted to recall the unequal brothers Cain and Abel in the biblical creation story which, as is well known, did not end well for either of them. Cain would be, as it were, the representative of the dark 'illiberalism' on which Abel's (liberal) light of goodness always cast a gloomy shadow. According to political scientist Thomas J Main, illiberalism is a fundamental rejection of liberalism based on a rejection of democratic elections, the rule of law, human rights and tolerance (Main 2022), which hardly distinguishes illiberalism from authoritarianism. In addition, Main also calls on the racist Ku Klux Klan and the reactionary movements of the Alt-Right and Dark Enlightenment as key witnesses and advocates of illiberalism, although they can hardly be uniformly labelled as false prophets. Rather, they find their unity in the fact (and to the extent) that they give in to fascist temptations. A more convincing solution is presented by Marlène Laruelle, who orders the conceptual field by highlighting several ideological components of illiberalism: in particular, the update of conservative views (nationalism) and of far-right ideologies (the belief in meta-politics) and the intensified critique of, or rather polemic against, elements of political liberalism (anti-parliamentarism, critique of minority rights). Moreover, Laruelle (2022) moves further away from conceptual labelling by identifying 'different semantic spaces' in which the term 'illiberal' is or can be operationalised: 'the world of politics/think tanks, the political sphere and the academic spheres'.

The toxic political ideology and practice of illiberalism lack the very things that distinguish a reasonably functioning constitutional democracy: political freedoms, separation of powers and rule-of-law institutions and procedures such as, above all, an independent judiciary. So, 'illiberal democracy' might not be an alternative in the end, but rather an oxymoron (Lührmann & Hellmeier 2020) and echo of Francis Fukuyama's erroneously and hastily declared 'end of history'. In almost all relevant studies illiberalism owes its existence as a category to a combination of four factors. These are, first, the formalistic reduction of democracy to elections; second, the decoupling of such electoral democracy from basic, institutional preconditions (especially freedom and equality of choice, protection of minorities, and post-judicial control); third, the criticism of liberal concepts of freedom and liberty because of their alleged hypertrophic individualism and protection of minorities and their 'decadent' ways of life; and fourth, the counterfactual (self-)labelling of 'illiberal' regimes as somehow democratic after all.

In academic debates, this combination of factors is consistently described as an abuse of democracy, which consists primarily in the fact that the rules that apply to everyone are not adhered to by the government, that above all the meta-rules intended for such changes are not heeded (Sajó 2021). Rules matter not as rules *in abstracto*, but because they ensure government accountability, limitation and judicial review (Przeworski 1995; O'Donnell 2004; Lührmann et al. 2018; Sajó 2021). In addition to the aforementioned Orbán and Kaczynski, current examples of 'illiberal democracies' might also include the governance practices of Erdoğan (Turkey), Fujimori (Peru), Evo Morales (Bolivia), Bolsonaro (Brazil), Chávez (Venezuela), and Trump (USA) – most of them also classified as populists in academia and the media.

These disparate case studies, as well as the diverse and vague definitions of illiberality, indicate why the concept of 'illiberal democracy' cannot be distinguished from alternative offerings such as semi- or pseudo-democracy, truncated or defective democracy, hybrid democracy or 'soft autocracy' (Levitsky & Way 2002) without considerable difficulty. In essence, critiques of political illiberalism primarily invoke the essential Anglo-European elements of law-rule and civil liberties. According to the central argument, these are violated by leaders/officials and regimes who pretend to follow a rule but break or circumvent it to gain undeserved advantages (Sajó 2021).

3.3 Authoritarianism

In contrast to the neologism illiberalism, authoritarianism presents itself as an established, if likewise contested concept, not as a scholarly term of art. It requires definition and delimitation, but not introduction. Both everyday language and conceptual history accommodate a fairly comprehensible understanding of authoritarianism – the former, admittedly, with meagre explanations. Another difference: the history of the term does not begin in the twenty-first century but, via the 'age of extremes' in the twentieth century, goes back at least to the long nineteenth century, in which authoritarianism is repeatedly associated with Bonapartism (Marx 1963; Rémond 1954). Bonapartism was recently also introduced by authors to single out the authoritarian core of protagonists often described as populist or illiberal, notably Hugo Chávez or Donald Trump (Beck & Stützle 2018) and remembered as a legacy of French authoritarian constitutionalism (Mérieau 2019).

Authoritarianism shares with populism and illiberalism the dual nature of an empirical as well as a normative concept. As explained above, populism is assigned various attributes and a basic political stance in the (social) academic debates which, in the end, usually remain controversial. With regard to authoritarianism, several levels of analysis are to be distinguished – especially the attitudes, practices, and programmes of individuals, groups/social movements, political parties, and regimes. However, the phenomena of authoritarianism are 'departmentalised' (Gessenharter 1983) in the approaches of the interested sciences and reappraised according to their respective specific logic and methodology. The reduction of authoritarian complexity to the dualism of a form of state (Linz 2003), not based on a specific or differentiated ideology, and an educational style that generates the development of the 'authoritarian character' (Adorno et al. 1950 and 1995) would be a first approach to the debates, rather than the final stage. Admittedly, this does not do justice to the plurality of approaches in research nor to the theoretical perspectives on various driving forces of authoritarianism brought together in this volume, such as social disintegration, alienation, discrimination, capitalist land grabbing (Dörre 2009), globalisation, migration and religion. Moreover, the reduction is clearly not up to date with the theory debates and does not take into account the results of empirical studies, especially in comparative regime theory and political science[12] (Zürn and Rensmann in this volume). It fails to take sufficient note of historical arguments (Günther in this volume) and economic processes and political consequences in authoritarian capitalism (Dörre 2009 and in this volume; Heitmeyer 2018), the socio-psychological and sociological research on parent-child relationships and 'the authoritarian character' (O. Decker et al. 2010 and Decker in this volume) as well as political attitudes (Decker & Brähler 2018 and 2020) and gender-specific attitudes (Sauer in this volume; Bargetz & Eggers in this volume), as well as the studies of authoritarian politics (Pichl in this volume) and phenomena in political culture (see the contributions of Diehl, Stegemann and Weiß in this volume).

The analysis of authoritarianism cannot be approached with a Cain/ Abel comparison, as it does not need to rely on liberalism or any other counter-concept as its *definiens*. Nevertheless, authoritarianism does not stand completely unchallenged and free as the designation of an isolated phenomenon in the world. Rather, analysts must work through a difficult and more than conceptual relationship to authority and also distinguish it from totalitarianism (Linz 2003; Lams et al. 2014; Frankenberg 2020: 40–44). As a legitimation and structural pattern of political power, authoritarianism refers to a relationship between those in power (office-holders, functionaries and agents in either formally defined or informal positions) in governments, parties and other organisations on the one hand and those subject to power (members, followers, supporters) on the other.

---

[12] Geddes 1999; Geddes et al. 2018; Rensmann et al. 2011; Frankenberg 2020; Applebaum 2020; Schäfer & Zürn 2021; and Costa Pinto & Morlino 2011.

Depending on the theoretical paradigm, power is grounded in language, will, or violence.[13] In the social practice in which it is constituted and enacted, this relationship is always dependent on the authority of the power holder and the reaction of those who enter into a power-based relationship. When authority is freely 'credited' – whether out of admiration, respect, reverence, enthusiastic support, or cool acquiescence – it is grounded in recognition that initially constitutes a symmetrical relationship between rulers and ruled. In this relationship someone is a ruler/leader because he/she relates to others as their subjects/followers and these, conversely, believe themselves to be followers/subjects of the person whom they regard as their ruler/leader (Marx 1967). With the recognition of authority an asymmetry is established. However, it differs from a totalitarian or enforced one in that it is entered into voluntarily. Authority thus comes about casually in the social practice of mutual recognition:

> Authority depends on the willingness of others to listen and be persuaded. No governor has any other authority than that which others see in him. He has the authority he is able to extract from those he wants to lead and which they are willing to award him. Authority enables governors to get others to do for them, but at the same time the governor is at the mercy of those same others for the authority he needs in order to lead. Authority, then, although appearing to belong to the governor, is really a gift from those he wants to exercise authority over … (Ringen 2011)

In authoritarian constellations, such recognition fails and the symmetrical relationship between those who govern/decide and those who are governed/decided upon is distorted. Thus, no (liberal) counter-image is required to be able to identify authoritarian leaders or regimes, an authoritarian programme or attitude as their silhouette. According to Max Weber, power consists in 'the chance to assert one's own will within a social relationship even in the face of opposition, regardless of what this chance is based on' (Max Weber 1978: 28). Weber's action-theoretical approach to domination as finding obedience for a command can be easily connected with the considerations on authority. Authority becomes authoritarian when compliance is imposed, submission is induced by deception and obedience is compelled by threat or physical force. Authority is then based on the sheer 'power to get things done' (Ringen 2013). In this power to get things done (also the desire to have such power), the asymmetry of authoritarian relations takes effect and develops a dynamic in which violence can emerge. This is what we need to come back to when we establish a connection (necessarily abbreviated here) between authoritarianism, power and violence.

[13] For different perspectives see Arendt 1970 and 2017; Weber 2002; Luhmann 1982; Rudolph 2017; and Ringen 2011.

Authoritarianism suffers from the relationship to its brother run amok, totalitarianism. The suffering can be conceptually and theoretically overcome, or at least alleviated, through demarcation. The conventional view of the intensified techniques of repression in totalitarian systems may be plausible as a necessary condition of such demarcation (Linz 2003). Admittedly, further characteristics must be added: Hannah Arendt sees this intensified form of authoritarianism in a hermetic, totalising ideology and in terror:

> The iron shackle of terror constitutes the totalitarian body politic and makes it an incomparable instrument for accelerating the movement of the natural or historical process'. (Arendt 1951: 205)

In terror, the social control and subjugation that encompasses everyone and everything and strangles every form of system criticism and opposition, regimes show their totalitarian face drastically and clearly. The propagation of a closed ideology, executed by eventual terror, is in the service of a secularised 'political religion' (Aron 1965). This is the approach to define total or totalitarian regimes not only by their state technique, but also to understand them as bearers of an 'anonymous intentionality' (Lefort 1988; Gauchet 1990). This intentionality aims at the phantasm of a society in which all are of the same mind and which is transparent to itself. The desolate nightmare of a like-minded and like-governed society does not allow for political pluralism, diversity of visions of the good life, or opposition of interests. A regime must shield this nightmare, this secret of the totalitarian, at all costs. Apart from institutionalising terror, it must authority ande slightest questioning of authority, and declare those who dare to do so to be enemies (Rödel et al. 1989) and deprive them of their freedom and life; indeed, of their lives.

The Russian President Putin, supported by the power apparatus and the arsenal of violence of his repressive, police-state dictatorship (Guriev & Treismann 2022), provides an object lesson in totalitarianism. This has long since exceeded the limits of mere authoritarianism or a 'controlled democracy' (Mommsen & Nußberger 2007). Especially since the war of aggression on Ukraine, authors have noted a development from an authoritarian to a totalitarian state or a new form of Stalinism, in which lies are protected by criminal law and violence triumphs. Michael Khodarkovsky characterises the regime as pure fascism:

> Like all such regimes, it is about imperial nostalgia, restoration and expansionism. Fascist regimes rely on perceived humiliations at the hands of foreign countries and

on a national leader whose masculinity, will and determination promise to restore past relevance and greatness.[14]

The phenomena of the authoritarian are obviously as complex as they are disputed. Consequently, neither an 'agreement on a uniform terminology' (Virchow 2017: 17) nor a uniform description of the phenomena can be expected. With authoritarianism, too, a proposal is made here that we hope will enable connections and lend itself to further discussion. This also applies, for example, to the at least temporary renaissance of technocratic authoritarianism (Zürn, in this volume). According to recent studies, especially the meta-study by the Centre for the Future of Democracy (2022), the disenchantment with democracy, as explained above, has also infected so-called populism and, in turn, caused faith in the expertise of technocrats to mushroom. Whether technocratic authoritarianism can be based on a change in values is not a foregone conclusion. It remains to be seen whether it can 'hold on to power' beyond the time of the pandemic, once the momentum of economic globalisation, currently slowing down, picks up again; and whether it can hold its own against a return to democracy or other authoritarian temptations.

The conjunctures and manifestations of authoritarianism point to the fact that 'work on the concept' is just as indispensable as the sharpening of interpretative profiles. However, we think that it would be helpful for the media treatment of the authoritarian, as well as for academic dialogue, if conceptual preferences and interpretative approaches were made explicit and thus accessible for discussion. This task will be served by the certainly incomplete profiles presented here, which will be supplemented in a next step by logics and practices of authoritarianism and then by references to its relationship to violence.

4. BASIC NARRATIVES OF AUTHORITARIANISM: DISCOURSE LOGICS AND CONFLICT PRACTICES

The basic narratives that play a dominant role in the development of authoritarianism primarily include the threat to order, the destruction of hierarchies and dominance, the dissolution of identities, a victim status due to the actions of hostile powers both internally and externally, and fantasies of the demise of the people (*Untergang des Volkes*). These narratives have, among other things, the function of stirring up collective fears and, at the same time, setting mobi-

---

[14] Michael Khodarkovsky (2022) 'Putin's Faschismus' in *Die Welt* 29. March, p. 14: https://www.welt.de/kultur/plus237843197/Putins-Faschismus-Es-geht-um-mehr-als-den-Krieg-in-der-Ukraine.html/. Concerning the 'politics of the past': Costa Pinto & Morlino, eds (2011).

lisations in motion and driving authoritarian movements and aspirations. It can be seen from the narratives that the concept of authoritarianism carries with it a not-inconsiderable ambivalence. It refers to the different contexts in which authoritarianism is deployed and acquires resonance and requires clarification of its discursive logic, concepts of conflict and its relationship to power and violence.

4.1 Discursive Logic

The discursive logic of authoritarianism is expressed in political rhetoric. It appears above all in programmatic statements and electoral propaganda. As the following tableau shows (Figure 1.1), these have a dichotomous structure and tend to construct Manichean worldviews; frequently encountered are the aforementioned opposition of the true people ('body of the people') dominated by aloof, corrupt elites and narratives of a society whose homogeneity is threatened by foreign infiltration (*Überfremdung*). In authoritarian narratives, the metropolis functions as a cipher for corrupt elite rule: in Italy, the Lega (Nord) takes pleasure in referring to the government in Rome as 'Roma Ladrona' (Rome, the robber). In the USA, authoritarian discourse pits the 'real America' against Washington; in the 'storming of the Capitol' (see Diehl in this volume), it stepped up to subversive action after the authoritarian national radical Trump had been ousted. In Germany, the capital Berlin and the EU capital Brussels take on the role of a 'totem of elite critique' in the pronouncements of authoritarian organisations, which makes it possible to plausibly describe political opponents as irresponsible, distant from the people, egoistic, or – in the case of Bundestag members, for example – as vegan cyclists and cosmopolitans (Haffert 2018).

4.2 Conflict Concepts and Practices

The rhetoric of authoritarian leaders and the programme of authoritarian organisations and regimes gain sharpness in political conflicts, election campaigns and mobilisation campaigns. The dichotomous structures and Manichean worldviews mentioned above, with 'corrupt elites' standing in absolute opposition to 'the good people' and their self-appointed representatives, shape a logic that defines and facilitates controversies as either/or disputes (Hirschman 1994). They are characterised by an all-or-nothing structure beyond negotiation and compromise (Frankenberg 2000). In such confrontations, the idea of self-commitment and self-restraint cannot come into play in the conflict between equals before the law, insofar as the parties to the dispute struggle 'for the whole' as, for example, truth or identity which cannot be translated into a distributional conflict according to the rules of more

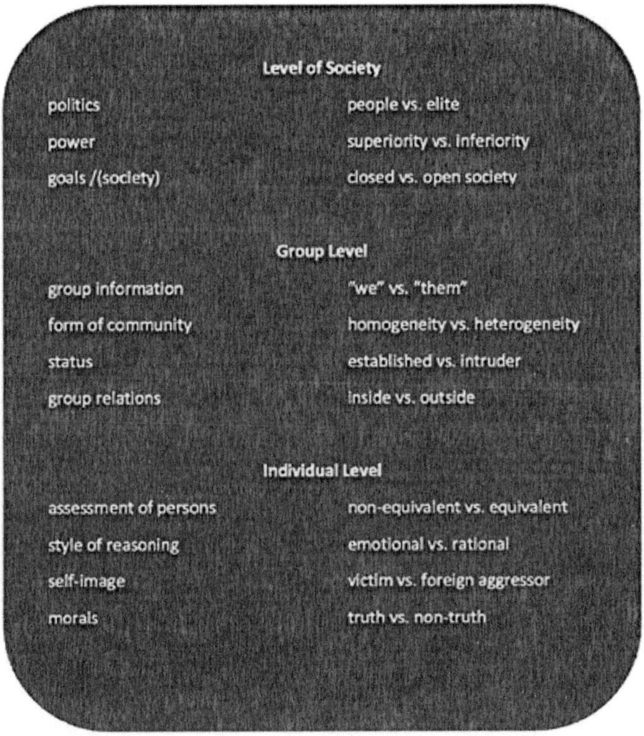

Source: Heitmeyer 2018: 248.

Figure 1.1 Discursive logic of authoritarianism

or less. 'For the whole' or 'all or nothing' implies antagonistic constellation: 'The very idea of finding oneself in this substantially heterogeneous other appears pointless from the outset' (Gauchet 1980).

In the conflicts led by authoritarian movements, organisations and regimes, it is not a matter of compromise or negotiation, but rather of decisions in favour of a rigid assertion of power and a seizure of the most comprehensive possible control of behaviour in all areas of life in society and the institutions of the political system. The authoritarian structures and the overspilling, authoritarian tendency of such disputes are particularly evident in the way indivisible demands and interests are to be enforced. Typically, although not always, this is done by resorting to methods of dispute that 'go the whole hog', not accepting tolerance and self-restriction to civil/democratic forms of dispute. Such methods of conflict cannot be restrained by procedures and rules that come into play in conflicts over distribution. Demands put forward on the battlefields of ethnicity, identity, and religion show their crude authoritarian face when they claim unconditional allegiance or exclusivity in the medium of politics (such as ethnic purity, rejection of foreigners, or a 'leading national culture'). Those who dissent must fear hatred to be the answer and that they will be denied the right to exist in public space on an equal footing. The model of exclusion displaces the model of competition (Frankenberg 2000: 11).

5. AUTHORITARIANISM IN RELATION TO POWER AND VIOLENCE

The practice of political rhetoric and conflict as well as the model of exclusion, are in particular need of clarification when and insofar as they concern the relationship between authoritarianism, power and violence. For obvious reasons, the broad and far-reaching scholarly debate on the concept and phenomena of power, also narrowed to political domination (Imbusch 2012) and of violence[15] cannot be adequately recapitulated here. Both power and violence, even when confined to the perspective of action theory, are highly indeterminate, controversial, but internally connected concepts; while power and violence are quite different phenomena, they usually occur together (Arendt 1970).

In the profile of authoritarianism above, a relational understanding of authority was introduced to emphasise the social asymmetry in power relations that takes centre stage in the violent exercise of power and fully displaces moments of understanding, persuasion and consent. In the context of authoritarianism and violence, the aspect of control becomes ascendant in society and the state, which also results in different standards of legitimacy than in the context of the political concept of domination. In the context of violence, the above-mentioned power of accomplishment can be differentiated into four types of power if one follows Popitz (2017): action power as power to violate; instrumental power as power to subjugate; authoritative power as power to control behaviour; and power as objectified power of technical action (Imbusch 2012: 16). Both violation and subjugation power refer to violent forms and practices of exercising power. Beyond the conceptual ambiguity, the relationship of such variants of power to violence begs the question as to when violence begins to develop 'inconspicuous' forms rather insidiously. In addition, the different versions of violence must be factored in, i.e. individual acts of violence, violence in gender relations, collective violence, structural violence or state violence.

[15] Heitmeyer & Hagan 2002: 16 ff.; Heitmeyer 2004; Galtung 1975; Riches 1986; Koher 2007.

In the analyses of this volume, forms of political violence are the central theme to express that the question of power arises centrally in every political behaviour and in every act of political violence. In other words, every form of violence is always a demonstration of power (Popitz 2017; Giddens 1985). This also applies to all forms of individual violence in domestic contexts or in public, to collective violence between youth groups or between criminal gangs. However, these forms of violence each have a limited radius and are usually of limited duration, unless violent structures develop as in mafia networks. Nevertheless, in a constitutional democracy, these forms are always under the (more or less effective) monitoring of controlling institutions and the judicial system with its law enforcement apparatus.

Political violence in the understanding of authoritarianism applied here has other spheres of action and validity into which the controlling institutions and the judicial system have also to be integrated. It must be extended to other social and administrative contexts where further distinctions are necessary. Riots, pogroms and non-peaceful mass protests are specific examples of collective political violence and should be distinguished from state violence. Nevertheless, dynamics of violence can drive one or the other reciprocally into escalation. Alternatively, collective outbreaks of violence can be driven, condoned or tolerated by state power. The state gives the mob a free hand and then punishes the victims.

6. FORMS OF DISCOURSE AND ACTIONS OF THE RIGHT-WING AUTHORITARIAN AND RIGHT-WING EXTREMIST SPECTRUM

For the 'translation' of the concept of authoritarianism into current social and political conditions and developments, a focus on right-wing authoritarianism and the extreme right-wing spectrum is appropriate. Virchow (2016) shows the considerable range of conceptual, theoretical and empirical approaches in his differentiated and broad presentation of terms, research fields and controversies. Accordingly, no agreement on a uniform approach can be expected; however, this need not be a shortcoming for further debates and research. Nonetheless, it makes sense to have points of reference against which one can 'work through' one's own approaches by agreeing to, modifying or rejecting them. This begins at a conceptual level if the consequences of rejecting the democratic constitutional state and its fundamental values are to be examined.

Attempts from political science have been launched with a so-called 'consensus definition' of right-wing extremism (Virchow 2017: 17; Kreis 2007: 13–15). However, this attempt at consensus has a serious shortcoming, if seen from a sociological point of view. The dimension of violence remains hidden from the concept at the attitudinal level. Such an accentuation is found in Heitmeyer et al. (1992: 13 f.) with the core connection of ideology of inequality and acceptance of violence. The ideology of inequality contains two central dimensions. The first is group-based inequality. Later, it has been conceptualised and studied as 'group-focused enmity' (Heitmeyer 2002). It manifests itself in facets such as nationalist or ethnic self-exaggeration; racist classification; sociobiological assertion of natural hierarchies; social Darwinist emphasis on the right of the strongest; totalitarian understandings of norms with regard to the devaluation of 'being different' and the emphasis on cultural homogeneity versus heterogeneity.

The second dimension is related to living conditions and aims at demands for exclusion in the form of socially, economically, culturally, legally, and politically unequal treatment of strangers and 'others'. Acceptance of violence manifests itself in four increasingly escalating variants: the conviction of the unalterable existence of violence, approval of private and repressive state violence, one's own willingness to use violence and actual acts of violence. This is based on the fundamental assumption that violence is legitimate as a 'normal' form of action for settling conflicts. This is where the rejection of rational discourse comes from: the emphasis on the everyday struggle for existence; the rejection of democratic forms of regulating social and political conflicts; as well as the emphasis on authoritarian and militaristic manners and styles.

In addition to this definitional extension, political science research on right-wing extremism, with its fixation on party programmes, electoral successes, political symbols, and historical-political references, needs to be expanded. Political science's focus solely on the party system cannot explain the rise of right-wing and far-right forces in society (Pirro 2022). Therefore, explicitly sociological research on right-wing extremism opens up a view of the connections between economic, social, and political structural developments, individual and collective processing, and the political consequences of action (cf. pattern of analysis in Heitmeyer 2018: 43–48), if a corresponding range of action is available. This includes a variety of forms of militant protests that can be located as resolute hostility, often with an affinity to dictatorship and readiness to use violence, in the triangle of cultural liberalisation, economic deprivation, and political alienation (Rucht 2018). This also means no longer focusing on individual aspects or events in a parcelled manner, but rather making visible the 'right-wing threat-alliances' that reach into the middle of society with the help of the 'concentric escalation continuum' (Heitmeyer et al. 2020: 58 ff). This is also a plea to include the qualitative changes of right-wing threat alliances in the analysis. These include, among other things, the modernisation of historical ideologies; the expansion of resonances in the political sphere through the differentiation of manifestations with progressive connectivity for 'crude bourgeois behaviour' ('rohe Bürgerlichkeit');

more flexible forms of communication with increased mobilisation capacity; escalation-orientated forms of action such as attacks not infrequently leading to terror.

6.1 Identity Politics

The qualitative changes leading to authoritarian developments cannot be understood without awareness of identity politics. This widespread political debate (Sauer 2020, and in this volume; Stegemann in this volume) has become increasingly charged in the last 10 years as a question of power in the vein of indivisible 'either/or' conflicts (see Chapter 4). It is all about the whole. The core is found in essentialist cultural attributions of ethnic affiliations and hardened group boundaries of 'us' versus 'them'. These promote the ideology of inequality and the consolidation of hierarchies and dominance in a cultural homogeneity of the (respective) people. Exclusion is the programme.

The 'identitarians' (*die Identitären*) are the political implementation of this as a social movement; they originated in France, spread to Austria and have offshoots in Germany and England (Lazaridis et al. 2016); their political echo can be heard in Viktor Orbán's Hungary, the Austrian Freedom Party (FPÖ), the AfD in Germany, and Vox in Spain. Their core message is 'ethnopluralism': each ethnic group in its own social or state space. Thus, the central goal is set against globalism, migration and an open and thus pluralistic – not to mention multicultural – society and is aggressively propagated to the public with innovative forms of presentation in order to appeal to the young generation in particular. The 'identitarians' are part of an authoritarian revolt (Weiß 2017). Their identity politics – like that emerging from the left – has socially destructive consequences. The form described here fits in perfectly with right-wing threat alliances.

Threat alliances, terror frequency and militant protests, including those of the 'identitarians', bring the emergence of escalation dynamics into the field of vision, with which the approving or silently tolerating participation of considerable parts of the population can be grasped. The role of the population as accomplices or silent partners of the regime (Frankenberg 2020: 171–99) points to the fact that authoritarian elites are also dependent on legitimacy and participation as long as they want to maintain a formal Western-style democratic system or are forced to do so by political, economic and social counterforces. This can be shown with the help of the model of the 'concentric escalation continuum' mentioned above. In the 'onion model' with five levels, the starting point is the attitude patterns of group-based misanthropy in parts of the population that give in to authoritarian temptations and, in this way, the authoritarian national radicalism of, for example, the AfD in Germany, the Freiheitliche Partei (FPÖ) in Austria or Fidesz in Hungary.

This way, attitudes can be forged into catchy political slogans such as ethnic reset (*Umvolkung*) or foreign infiltration, for instance, by refugees (*Überfremdung*), 'corona dictatorship' or even hate speech, such as 'We will hunt them down. We will hunt down Frau Merkel or whomever ...' (Gauland, AfD, on election night 2017 on the German public broadcaster ARD), which then serve as 'bridges of legitimacy' for a 'right of self-defence' that includes violence and is directed at movement-based, violent right-wing extremism. This 'philosophy of action' (*Philosophie der Tat*) in turn functions as an escalating 'legitimisation bridge' for clandestine, right-wing terrorist planning and support networks. These networks provide the perpetrators of assassinations and arson attacks on refugee homes with logistics, recognition, etc., to save the 'German people'. Those parts of the population, for example in European societies (Zick et al. 2011), who display attitudes of group-based misanthropy or explicit authoritarian attitudes (Decker & Brähler 2018; also Decker and Weiß, in this volume) are thus involved in political violence via various, escalating stages of legitimation – not as perpetrators in the legal sense, but as political accomplices and legitimation helpers.

The dichotomous image of society that was often created politically and in the media after the murders of the (German) National Socialist Underground (NSU) were uncovered, with the clear distinction between 'humane society' on the one hand and the 'gang of murderers' on the other, is deliberately false. It represents an attempt to spread a calculated social and political ideology of self-relief. This also means that looking solely at political elites as drivers of authoritarian development is short sighted and does not go any further in illuminating the hidden paths of 'normalised' authoritarian development in society.

The model outlined here is only one example of the attempt to precisely name the drivers of and the actors behind such developments and not to let the necessary analyses be blurred by abstract and vague terms like 'structural shifts'. In order to clarify the dynamics and escalations of authoritarianism, the focus in this volume is on actors: parties; members of social, media and economic elites; political movements and networks; charismatic individuals with the corresponding media armament, who set out to undermine and delegitimise democratic institutions – among other methods by filling them with hierarchical ideas and concepts of inequality, at the same time creating new dependencies, transforming a society that is open to diverse forms of life and demands into one which is hermetically closed. In the twenty-first century, authoritarian developments continue to rely on combinations of the instruments of power, control and violence. Nevertheless, attention must always be paid to the way their forms and manifestations differ from developments in the twentieth century.

7. CRISES PROPELLING AUTHORITARIAN DEVELOPMENTS?

The contributions to this volume direct a special spotlight, from different academic perspectives, on the crisis events and developments since the beginning of the twenty-first century, which have given us 'insecure decades' (Heitmeyer 2018: 89–95), a 'post-national constellation' (Habermas 1998), and a 'global risk society' (Beck 2008 and 2016; Rensmann et al. 2011; Bertelsmann Stiftung 2016), to which societies do not react uniformly but with gradations of collective, 'learned helplessness' (Munich Security Conference 2022). We assume that developments and events that come to a head in crises are drivers of authoritarian developments: because of their dynamics, the visibility of disappointed expectations as well as anxieties are triggered more intensively than in normal situations. According to the data published in the Munich Security Index 2022, it can be presumed that in crises, such as the pandemic in particular, authoritarian regimes are popular because they promise or are expected to provide security and help regain control. Whether this also applies to the war and geopolitical crisis set off by Vladimir Putin's war of aggression remains to be seen.

7.1 The Concept of Crisis

When speaking of crisis events as drivers of authoritarian development, the first step is to give contour to the indeterminate concept of crisis (Koselleck 1982; Mergel 2012; Luhmann 1982). We refrain from dramatising culture and apocalyptic visions and instead apply three criteria that denote an *open horizon of possibilities* (Makropoulos 2013; Oevermann 2016). Accordingly, a crisis presupposes that, first, the previous political, social and economic routines for coping with events are no longer effective and the existing knowledge stocks are not sufficient to solve the problem. Second, the conditions before these events cannot be restored. Third, in crisis situations that can neither be fully cognitively controlled nor preventively resolved, different possibilities of realisation compete with each other, generating behavioural uncertainty and insecurity of orientation, releasing collective fears, and, as can currently be observed, preparing the breeding ground for delusions and conspiracy theories (Butter/Knight 2020; Butter 2018; Douglas 2021), which usually have an ideological character that emerges in political protests and struggles for political power. The combination of these three criteria suggests that situations with an emergency-like character, at the same time 'moments of a crisis of freedom' (Günther 2021), correspond with the experience of loss of control. Acts of terror (intensified by the official rhetoric of fighting and announcements of danger), economic threats, budget cuts affecting the social system, or the catastrophic mood repeatedly heated up by the media (globalisation, climate, pandemic, inflation, refugees, war, China): these 'event complexes' or code words for problematic situations are processed differently according to the degree to which they affect people and their resilience, and are translated into individual fears and collective anxieties with varying intensity and sustainability. Nevertheless, taken as a whole, they can generate notions of loss of control and destabilisation (Heitmeyer 2018: 94–109), which can be identified as promoting authoritarian tendencies.

Within this conception of crisis, we distinguish between two types that differ in terms of scope (Heitmeyer in this volume). The first type is geared to crises that affect one or more different spheres of life and functional systems of a society abruptly and result in massive dysfunctions. In the 'insecure decades' of the twenty-first century, such sectoral crises include, above all, three intensified danger situations in the 'post-9/11' era: from the beginning of the century, many countries, including the United States, went through a *sectoral* social crisis in 2008/2009, the global banking and financial crisis shook the 'system-relevant' financial sector of the economy, with spillover effects across the entire European Union.[16] In 2015/2016, the refugee movement was construed by politics and the media as a crisis, above all a social-cultural one, with effects on the political-administrative system (see Pichl in this volume). Characteristics of this type of sectoral crisis are their disparate occurrence over time and the aforementioned localisation in different sub-sectors of society, however they may be associated with the spread of status fears into the middle classes – i.e, their exposure to social decline (unemployment, poverty).[17] At the same time, society and politics had various instruments at hand to 'contain' these dysfunctions and to prevent serious destructive effects on the system as a whole.

In contrast, the second type of crisis affects the entire social system, i.e. it is a *systemic* crisis. This includes slowly escalating danger situations, such as the crisis still referred to as 'climate change' and the COVID-19 pandemic, which

---

[16] Since the sub-prime crisis in the USA in 2007, banks, companies, infrastructures, or professions that play such a significant economic or infrastructural role in the state and society that their insolvency or a serious malfunction is unacceptable ('too big to fail') and must be prevented by state intervention have been described as systemically important. See only Andrew Ross Sorkin (2009) *Too Big to Fail,* Viking Press; Adam Tooze (2018) *Crashed: How a Decade of Financial Crises Changed the World*, New York.

[17] For an overview see www.gisreportsonline.com/r/europe-economy-crises/; https://philanthropynewsdigest.org/features/commentary-and-opinion/america-s-growing-poverty-crisis; and https://time.com/4504004/men-without-work/.

'rapidly' moved towards a recognisably catastrophic state of emergency. In the 'rapid' crisis, the potential for authoritarian developments becomes particularly apparent because numerous 'containment instruments' do not take effect and thus individual-biographical, collective and political losses of control occur in combination; these are linked to conspiracy theories and delusions and are instrumentalised politically.

Against this conceptual background, some of the current danger situations can be fanned out and linked to the question of whether crises and the associated 'spillover effects' and opportunities for instrumentalisation are prone to propel authoritarian developments and on which paths this could happen.

7.2 Crisis Through Terrorism

What crisis-like events and developments does a survey of the first two decades of the twenty-first century reveal? Do they indicate that the world has 'come apart at the seams' and societies are 'in search of lost security' (Beck 1999 and 1992; Heitmeyer 2018)? The century of crises, if it can be called such to date, opened in 2001 with the mass murder of 9/11, the 'birth of the present' (Weidner 2021), when terrorist Islamism pitted itself against the West on the world stage, putting the USA in a state of emergency and bringing the terrorism of the 1990s and before (Frankenberg 2014: 185–220; Gassert 2021; Hoffman 2001) to a head as a religious-political political crisis. In the years since, the crisis history of security threats, centred around terrorism and 'organised crime', has been perpetuated globally and nationally (Waldmann 2005; Jäger 2015) and has taken shape in ever-expanding surveillance systems. In military operations such as 'Enduring Freedom' in Afghanistan, Somalia/Djibouti, Northern Mali and Iraq, attempts to manage crises have been carried out in a cross-border and border-violating manner.

7.3 Crises Through Financial Crimes as a System

Nevertheless, the crisis registry increasingly focused its attention on the sphere of authoritarian financial capitalism (Heitmeyer 2001; Piketty 2017; Dörre 2012; Steg 2019). Here, the increase, perceived simultaneity and interdependence of crisis-related events allowed other danger situations to fade into the background. The dotcom bubble (2000), subprime loans (2007/2008), and Euro crisis (2009) as a combination of sovereign debt, banking and currency crisis have become memorable as keywords of these emergency situations (Erceg et al. 2005; Arestis & Sawyer 2013). They drove societies such as Greece, Portugal and Italy to the brink of bankruptcy, endangered their social cohesion and, to the extent that they existed, wore away the cushions of solidarity in the European Union. At the same time, the crises produced instruments of regulation, in particular the 'rescue funds' of the European Stability Mechanism (ESM), the European Financial Stabilisation Mechanism (EFSM), and the European Financial Stability Facility (EFSF), which both loosened legal ties and reduced the density and efficiency of parliamentary control.

7.4 Crisis Through Climate Catastrophe

Behind the trivialising term 'climate change', which suggests meteorological regularity, lies a climate crisis that has been steadily worsening since the beginning of this century, not just in a linear fashion (Ripple et al. 2021). With its ecological, political and social dimensions, it essentially results from human-made global warming, which threatens the existence of all societies from the Marshall Islands in the Pacific to Greenland, each in a different way, but with comparable force (Klein 2015; Overpeck & Conde 2019; Kegel 2021). Natural disasters such as forest fires, floods, hurricanes, and droughts bring the horror of the climate catastrophe into the collective consciousness at ever-shorter intervals. The nuclear disaster at Fukushima must also be considered. Scientifically elaborated scenarios of the end of the world contrast with the ritually adopted resolutions of the UN climate summits, which do little more than clothe the inaction of the world community in pious wishes and organise the uncertainty of possible solutions year after year (Przeworski 1991). Not only is much of the damage that has already occurred irreversible but, according to scientific calculations, the dynamics of warming can only be slowed down over an extraordinarily long period of time.[18] The climate damage register, which according to the Federal Environment Ministry is to systematically bundle long-term damage and damage costs caused by climate change in the future, refers to this against its official design. Recently, the Federal Constitutional Court of Germany could not escape the dramatic nature of the climate catastrophe and in its sensational 'climate decision' assigned fundamental rights the task of the 'intertemporal safeguarding of freedom'.[19] The climate catastrophe is becoming a driver of authoritarianism in several respects: it promotes strategies of denial and, in the case of further policy failure, the ecological state of emergency. It exacerbates global tensions and social inequality and with them, inevitably, political reactions (Günther 2021: 341).

---

[18] IPCC Working Group I Report (2021) Climate Change 2021: the Physical Science Basis, 6 August. Susan Solomon et al. (2009), 'Irreversible climate change due to carbon dioxide emissions' in 106 *PNAS* 1704–09.

[19] Federal Constitutional Court of Germany (2021).

7.5 Crisis Through Policy Failure on Migration

Wars and climate are extremely important (if not the only) causes of global migration movements (Luft 2017; in detail Pichl, in this volume). Where weapons speak and work is lacking, where violence and poverty prevail, where minorities are persecuted and harassed, where the development of 'failed states' is favoured, people take flight. Their fate of persecution and their search for an adequate existence become a crisis when they cross the border at home – simply because they arrive in large numbers (BAMF 2021; European Commission 2022). Colonial histories, arms supplies, prior climate damage attributable to the host country, moral, political or economic responsibility, or even the glaring deficiencies of the European Union's asylum concept (Dublin Procedure, Frontex) and national refugee policies are not included in the diagnosis of crisis (Bade 2017; Meier-Braun 2018). The situation for state and society created by the entry of more than one million refugees, migrants and other protection seekers into Germany in 2015 and 2016 is regularly referred to as a 'refugee crisis', although many things point to a (long-term) policy failure rather than a temporary loss of control. The main fears are the destabilisation of the state, the disintegration of society, an increase in crime and the overburdening of social systems. According to the criteria for a crisis discussed above, it can be assumed that immigration can no longer be reversed. Migration cannot be managed at will with recruitment agreements and recruitment stops, return bonuses and deportations (Finotelli 2007; BMI 2018): 'People set themselves in motion, leave their homes, build an existence in another country, reinvent themselves and their environment, circumvent state rules, gain access to economic and social resources, change politics, the economy and society' (Ayata 2021).

7.6 The COVID-19 Pandemic as a Systemic Crisis

Beginning in the Spring of 2020, the COVID-19 pandemic has plunged the social, political and economic systems of many countries into a crisis that was virulent for at least three years and is still plaguing some countries, notably China. Despite repeated influenza epidemics and pandemics in the past and this century (Vasold 2015), notably avian flu (H5N1) in 2003, SARS (SARS-CoV) in 2004/2005, and swine flu (A/H1N1) in 2009, states had neither developed infection control routines nor taken adequate preventive measures (Alviar & Frankenberg 2021). In December 2019, corona virus (SARS-CoV-2), initially misdiagnosed as simple influenza or pneumonia in Wuhan, was then identified as a contagious viral infection. Since then, COVID-19 has gone through several waves of infection worldwide and the virus has mutated several times. After the shock events in China, then in Lombardy and the USA, in Brazil and India, each with exorbitant death tolls and numerous serious courses of disease, the momentum of the pandemic in most countries seems to have slowed down at least temporarily, albeit not completely neutralised. Apart from the COVID-19 incidence, mortality, infection rate, hospitalisation incidence and mutations have abated significantly in most societies. That conditions prior to the onset of COVID-19 cannot be completely restored is demonstrated by those who, devoid of any practical reason, have persistently demonised state infection control, from mandatory masks to lockdown and, most recently vaccination, as a 'dictatorship' (Kleffner/Meisner 2021; Reichardt 2021). Politicians, who are still looking for solutions and certainties should the pandemic return, only recently warned the population of a 'loss of control' and prepared them for an (irreversible) change of circumstances. During the crisis, epidemic fears have taken root in societies (Frankenberg 2023 and in this volume; Naumann/Kamann 2021; Hepfer 2021). In the camps of corona resistance that cannot be reached with arguments, these fears are accompanied and covered up by conspiracy theories and delusions. Since diffuse fears of contagion and state measures have no precise target, they can be activated in any crisis situation. This is precisely what is to be expected when, as in the past, new so-called 'zoonoses' appear, i.e., when infection crosses the species barrier between animals and humans, was presumably the case in SARS-CoV-2.

Legislators worldwide have not remained inactive in their many attempts to 'combat' crises. Examples from the beginning of the century include a myriad of counter-terrorism acts and further amendments (Roach 2015); more recently climate protection acts and 'climate change laws';[20] immigration laws (some praised as 'milestones' regulating residence, immigration, integration, work permits and protection against deportation); as well as the many infection protection acts and their frequent modifications (Alviar & Frankenberg 2021). The feverish activity suggests that parliaments, in cooperation with governments, are providing rescue plans for ways out of the crisis. Seen in the light of day, however, the legislative and executive reaction patterns do not suggest that legislation and politics have everything under control and that a return to the normal routines could succeed: the serial amendments to anti-terror laws and immigration and asylum law, along with the hectic adjustments of infection control law to the course of the pandemic (as well as the expected revisions of the 'most comprehensive climate protection package to date'), testify to legislative activity – and search strategies – in the field of security law but do not prove that everything is under control. On the contrary, the crises and their dynamics follow the rules of a grammar that does not bow to the logic of state regulations and the rhetoric of control that accompanies them. If the return

---

[20] https://www.lse.ac.uk/GranthamInstitute/tag/cclw/.

to the status quo ante is postponed, new routines must be established under conditions of uncertainty and new knowledge has to be developed.

7.7 Authoritarian Mobilisation Opportunities: Collective Crisis Fears

Crises whose damaging effects come to light via dramatic events or poison social relations over time do not leave the public uninvolved, but, depending on the danger, trigger individual and collective fears that can condense into the notion of 'collective helplessness' mentioned above. In the relevant context here, the question is whether and how crisis fears can become drivers of authoritarian development. There is no question that the crisis-like events outlined here, as external events, internally generate a connection between specific cue stimuli and their possible harmful consequences – a connection which is learned through experience, observation of foreign behaviour or instruction. Although the types of concern are just as diverse as the risks of a pandemic and dangers from a progressive climate catastrophe, it can nevertheless be assumed that fears as object-directed warnings of actual dangers can be distinguished from undirected (neurotic) or abstract fears (Neumann 1967; Frankenberg 2023). This distinction is helpful insofar as it sheds light on the connection between crisis, conflict and affective response. Fears of the consequences of climate catastrophe and migration movements, of contagion risks, renewed financial crises and, currently, of the expansion of the war Putin is waging against Ukraine, whether imagined or realistic, whether based on knowledge, ignorance, or deception, can hardly be intercepted by a political class that 'drives by sight' and elites that follow the primacy of the market and of corporate interests. The more danger situations repeat, change or become perpetuated, and the more perceptions of loss of control as well as uncertainties (regarding the causes of the crisis and possible solutions) develop which cannot be neutralised by science, the law fails as a medium of normative orientation. In such situations, even real fears that warn of tangible, concrete dangers mutate into free-floating, contingent fears that prevent any risk assessment and awaken irrational rescue needs. These are exploited by authoritarian movements and organisations, which first resort to stoking fears (of Islam and immigrants, of Europe and the elites and their experts) in order to then provide their followers with delusional rescue fantasies. Donald Trump promised in 2015, after criticising illegal immigration: 'Don't worry, we'll take our country back.'[21] Likewise, Alexander Gauland (AfD) pledged to the

[21] Elizabeth Chuck, *NBC News*, 11 July 2015.

'disenfranchised subjects': 'We will take back our country and our people.'[22] Boris Johnson's Brexit slogan 'We'll take back control' obeys the same logic.[23] It's all about the politics of the past, charged with fear (Wodak 2021) filled with soothing promises about restoring control.

8. AUTHORITARIAN ATTITUDES IN THE POPULATION AS POWER MATERIAL

If the thesis is pursued that crises must be seen as propelling authoritarian development, then it is also necessary to look at the patterns of attitudes and behaviour in populations, because authoritarianism does not just find its expression in political movements, parties and governments. Such developments depend on authoritarian attitudes and behaviour as sources of legitimacy and loyalty.

8.1 What Theoretical Conceptions Exist to Analyse How Authoritarian Attitudes Emerge in Social Structures?

As is well known, the origins go back to the theory of the 'authoritarian personality' (Adorno et al. 1950) to explain the overt or covert approval behaviour in the population towards the National Socialist system. A close connection is established between a repressive early childhood socialisation and the willingness to follow in the civilisational catastrophe. The theoretical basis was the psychoanalytic approach, elaborated by Oliver Decker in this volume (see also Decker & Brähler 2020: 15–26).

For many years, numerous newer social-scientific (i.e. sociological and social-psychological) approaches have emerged that no longer follow the original psychoanalytic tradition, as the differentiated overview analysis by Seipel et al. (2022) shows. Two developments become clear here. On the one hand, the development of authoritarian attitudes is no longer attributed to the early childhood experiences of a repressive family socialisation that produces submissiveness because a massive change in educational processes has unmistakably taken place in recent decades. Nevertheless, during this change, new variants have emerged that can also foster such attitudes. These include the 'release' from value and norm references, which can create anomie, a disorientation that leads to 'authoritarian temptations' under the pressure of social uncertainties.

---

22 During the party with which the AfD celebrated their parliamentary mandates.
23 Dörre (2019).

On the other hand, it becomes clear in the newer conceptions that socialisation theories (instead of personality characteristics) and social structural conditions are gaining greater importance. Genuinely sociological categories such as social inequality, social and political disintegration, anomie and loss of control, among others, are included in the explanation of conditions of emergence and political consequences of authoritarianism.

Four of these approaches are relevant to the issues discussed here. One of the most influential is the conception of Altemeyer (1981), who first explicitly emphasises the socialisation theory of social learning in adolescence, because he could not empirically find a connection between repressive parenting styles and authoritarian attitudes. Second, he reduces the classical authoritarianism scale to three dimensions: conventionalism, authoritarian aggression and authoritarian submissiveness.

Oesterreich presented an influential conceptualisation and introduced the category of threat early on. His study 'Flucht in die Sicherheit' (Escape to Security) (1996) also looks at socialisation theories, especially situational factors in everyday social life that provoke authoritarian reactions.

Another influential theory comes from Sidanius & Pratto (1999). It is the 'social dominance theory' (SDO), which focuses on intergroup conflicts and the safeguarding of social hierarchies. Seipel et al. (2022: 182) point out that this approach was not developed in the narrower context of classical authoritarianism research, but nevertheless overlaps when the defence of entrenched hierarchies is related to authoritarian attitudes. Sidanius and Pratto's introduction of 'authoritarian dominance' is also a fruitful complement to Altemeyer's category of 'authoritarian submissiveness'.

Finally, Duckitt (1989) who focuses on collective and intergroup action should be mentioned. Duckitt takes Altemeyer's approach and redefines it for his concern: 'Conventionalism now means orientation to the norms of one's own group, authoritarian submissiveness means submission to the authorities of one's own group, and authoritarian aggression is aggression towards all those who do not submit to the norms of one's own group' (Seipel et al. 2022: 183).

In consideration of the social science approaches presented, which were usually implemented in empirical studies using quantitative methods, our focus will be on what empirical evidence they offer for correlations in two directions: for support for authoritarian movements as well as parties and for antipathy against various groups in society. The diverse analyses differ, also due to different operationalisations, in some respects that cannot be listed here. However, they all have a common core.

There is empirical evidence for both lines of questioning. Above all, authoritarian attitudes have a high predictive value for the devaluation of and discrimination against different groups in society (see, among others, Meloen 1993 for a meta-analysis).

An example from the Bielefeld Longitudinal Study on Group-Related Xenophobia (Heitmeyer 2002) can illustrate this. Based on a representative population survey, Heitmeyer & Heyder (2002: 59–70) used the Altemeyer scale and the dimensions 'authoritarian aggression' and 'authoritarian submissiveness' to examine the correlations with elements of group-related misanthropy. The more clearly someone holds authoritarian convictions, the more likely they are to agree with xenophobic (.52) and racist (.46) statements. In a weakened form, this also applies to anti-Semitism (.32), heterophobia (.31), and classic sexism (.28). Also striking is the claiming of established prerogatives (.41), i.e. recourse to social dominance to secure established hierarchies in the sense of the theory of Sidanius and Pratto.

These contexts constitute the power material for authoritarian movements and parties to establish or secure authoritarian social and political power structures.

This gives rise to broader questions in the wake of the social and political crises already outlined, which primarily concern threats and losses of control. There are a large number of studies on this that show the connections between authoritarian attitudes and contexts perceived as threatening (numerous references in Seipel et al. 2022: 185).

The aforementioned approaches by Duckitt and Oesterreich also make special reference to this. Two models can be distinguished (Seipel et al., ibid.): 'On the one hand, authoritarianism could be activated by threats, but on the other hand, existing authoritarianism could also be the cause for situations being perceived as threatening.'

Both mechanisms of action have been demonstrated by Rippl and Seipel (2012). Furthermore, Onret et al. (2013) have pointed out that two levels, i.e. the threat to personal circumstances and the social order with authoritarianism, are connected.

Both levels always play a role in the crises referred to above. There and in Heitmeyer's work on crises and loss of control (in this volume), authoritarian attitudes are linked to Oestereich's conception of the 'flight into security'. It is then a matter of restoring authoritarian-led control, so that against this background the classical conception of authoritarianism proves inadequate. Decker (in this volume) also refers to this with regard to the changed role of the capitalist economy.

At the same time, it is necessary to provide differentiated conceptualisations of authoritarianism for future differentiated crisis developments to capture the 'authoritarian temptations' more precisely. A first proposal has been formulated for this purpose. It contains the differentiation into submissive authoritarianism, which is a product of rigid socialisation practices that increase the willingness to follow. The second variation is anomic authoritarianism, which feeds on disorientation and loss of control. The third variety is self-conscious authoritarianism, which is geared towards acting with power and control (Heitmeyer 2018: 85–88). This area needs conceptual development and empirical research.

This is especially true for comparative analyses to other societies, because the study on the concept of group-related misanthropy in eight European countries (Zick et al. 2011: 60–76 and 88) more than a decade ago showed how devaluations of and discriminations against certain groups were the widespread results of authoritarian attitudes. This applies to Poland and Hungary in particular for numerous indicators. The simultaneous success of authoritarian parties and governments in elections in these countries once again prove the postulated connections.

9. AUTHORITARIAN CONTEXTS AND STRATEGIES IN DIFFERENT SOCIETIES

For the analysis of authoritarian developments, the state of democracies of varying quality and history, predominantly in Europe and North America, was selected as the central frame of reference. This excludes explicitly and thoroughly authoritarian societies such as Russia or China, even though they formally present themselves as democratic and constitutional, in particular with elections (however manipulated), an (at least basic) system of political institutions based on the separation of powers, and (outwardly liberal) constitutions. The leading assumption here is that 'authoritarian developments' as dangers or threats to society and democracy can only be spoken of in societies that are not completely structured along authoritarian lines. It does not make sense to seek out institutional developments as long as political authoritarianism is already fully developed and firmly established, which holds true not only for North Korea or Belarus but also for Russia.[24] Especially in Putin's system of a 'managed democracy' supported by a 'vertical of power' (Mommsen 2007), the unsurprisingly manipulative extension of his presidential mandate is not an 'authoritarian development' but merely a continuation of the long-trodden path of a 'defective democracy' (Merkel et al. 2003 and 2006). The fact that China's Communist Party abandoned the principle of collective leadership in favour of an (at least temporary) return to the principle of a strong leader (in

---

[24] In the face of hardened structures and institutions that entrench the involuntary asymmetry in the relationship between subjects and rulers, at best climatic improvements ('thaw') or the replacement of personnel can be observed. On the change of tyranny in Russia: Guriev & Treismann 2022.

the person of General Secretary Xi Jinping) or that it introduced new systems of social scoring and political monitoring did not change the basic structure of 'inclusive authoritarianism' and the freedom of the collective in the 'disciplinary state'.[25]

Thus, this book concentrates on societies whose political structures, institutions and practices provide space for processes of authoritarian development that are striking because they deviate from the routines. However, a distinction must be made between the specific institutional contexts or public discourses into which authoritarian strategies penetrate and reshape the institutional system, infiltrate state practice, and find expression in political rhetoric. The following (rather cursory) comparative notes, while not representative, illustrate exemplarily and sufficiently clearly the diversity of authoritarian strategies. The strategic starting points provide information about the specific areas and institutions that are susceptible to authoritarian attacks or are considered susceptible and are therefore targeted and taken up as bridgeheads by power-holding or power-seeking groups in various historical contexts and political constellations.

Regardless of their context-specificity, authoritarian strategies are characterised by the fact that they are designed to eliminate institutional mediations and controls on communication from the leadership to the led and to thereby establish immediacy (Frankenberg 2020: 200–219). In accordance with this calculation, authoritarian efforts almost universally aim to eliminate procedures and controls that distance the rule of law from the government, to bypass parliaments and courts, notably constitutional courts, and to neutralise all media and organisations in the social sphere (especially parties, unions, and social movements) that are based on pluralism and competition. As will be shown, this basic pattern allows for considerable strategic variation but, in many regimes, it leads to tactics of disempowering the judiciary as an authoritarian state technique. Former US President Donald Trump focused his authoritarian judicial strategy on public (Twitter) attacks against judges he disliked and the less conspicuous, but consequential, appointments of judges to federal courts, including the Supreme Court. In just one term, he appointed a total of 221 predominantly white, conservative men to judgeships.[26]

Since 2015, the Polish government, supported by the national conservative PiS party, has set out to radically restructure the judiciary to its liking (Kovács

---

[25] See Sebastian Weise (2020) 'Invented in China – Hochtechnologie im Dienste des Illiberalismus', Konrad-Adenauer-Stiftung, ed., Auslandsinformationen, 16 March; Thomas Heberer & Armin Müller (2020), 'Entwicklungsstaat China', Friedrich-Ebert-Stiftung, ed., Bonn.

[26] One-fifth of all 890 federal judges were thus nominated by Trump, NZZ, 25 August 2020.

& Scheppele 2018). It aims to guarantee a handwringing, conservative-Catholic supreme judiciary. In July 2017, the government adopted a new retirement scheme that resulted in the majority of the previous Constitutional Tribunal judges retiring earlier and being replaced by judges politically close to PiS. This attack on the independence of the judiciary was completed by the government's influence on appointments also to lower courts and the installation of a disciplinary chamber at the Supreme Court, which can review any judicial procedure and, in case of doubt, take disciplinary action against the personnel involved – up to and including the dismissal of judges or prosecutors. The success of this authoritarian politicisation was exemplified by a new abortion law, the rejection of a decision of the European Court of Justice (ECJ) on Polish judicial policy as 'ultra vires' and a violation of the Polish constitution and, most recently, the decision that the right to a fair criminal trial before an independent court, guaranteed in the European Convention on Human Rights (Art. 6), violates the Polish constitution.[27]

Hungary's Orbán government was more skilful and hardly less rigorous than Poland in restructuring the judiciary (Scheppele 2018). A first attempt to make room for lawyers loyal to the regime by forcibly retiring judges failed in 2012 due to the resistance of the ECJ. In another decision, the ECJ ruled that the EU could withdraw funds from Member States if their proper use could not be ensured due to systematic violations of the rule of law.[28] The establishment of 'parallel administrative tribunals', to be appointed by the Minister of Justice, was also later abandoned due to opposition from the Council of Europe.[29] Most recently, the Hungarian government initiated a 'national survey' on the 'people's perception of justice' which they planned to use to reform the judiciary. Apart from strengthening victim protection and the expansion of prisons, concrete measures of judicial reform are still pending, but it is certain that they are intended to serve the construction of an 'illiberal state'.[30] The keystone of the authoritarian judicial policy under Orbán, however, is the constitutional bracket that encloses the currently prevailing conditions and structurally hardens them through increased majority requirements for constitutional changes and reforms (Arato/Sájo 2021).

---

[27] See the report from the internal perspective of a Polish judge by Dariusz Mazur, Süddeutsche Zeitung 12 November 2021, 6; and the ECJ decision in November 2019 (Case C 192/18).

[28] ECJ, 16 February 2022 (C-156/21 and C-157/21) – Dismissal of the claims by Poland and Hungary.

[29] The Venice Commission published several critical evaluations of developments in Poland and Hungary.

[30] *Neue Züricher Zeitung,* 19 February 2020.

Turkish President Erdoğan's grip on the judiciary began drastically, backed by the far-right organisation 'Grey Wolves' (Bozay 2017), with the intensified persecution of the Kurdish population, the 'cleansing' of the state apparatus, and the arrest of 4,000 judges accused of being involved in the 'Pelican coup' of 2016. Irrespective of his already far-reaching powers under exceptional law, Erdoğan then pursued the 'autocratisation of the state apparatus' with a strategic bundle that has been compared to Stalin's 'Great Terror' (Yenigun 2021). Priority was given overall to the repression of the opposition, including opposition NGOs and media, the control of universities, and the disciplining of the judiciary. This was first attempted top-down with a law that gave the Minister of Justice the power to initiate disciplinary investigations against the Turkish High Council of Judges. This law was declared unconstitutional by the Turkish Constitutional Court in November 2021. Secondly, a law was passed in November 2022 (with prior approval from the judiciary committee) that, while officially supposed to bring about 'more democracy', in fact facilitated the splitting of the bar associations, which had been a haven of opposition to the Erdoğan regime for 18 years, especially in Turkey's big cities (Yenigun 2021; Tahiroglu 2020). After sharp protests from the legal profession, the Constitutional Court will probably be challenged again to prove its resilience in Erdoğan's system of 'competitive authoritarianism' (Esen/Gümüşcü 2016).

In a dramatic move, Israel's coalition of the conservative Likud and extremist right-wing parties, representing the radically nationalist and orthodox religious movements, using their strong showing in the elections as blackmailing power, set out in January 2023 to dismantle the administration of justice, primarily the courts. The judicial overhaul, played down in the media as a 'reform', would give the Israeli parliament, the Knesset, and therefore the majority of the parties in power, more control over Israel's judiciary, notably the appointment of judges and the competencies of the Supreme Court.[31] Israel's parliament, that is the governing majority, will have the power to overturn Supreme Court decisions. While Israel's founding compact was designed to include the Jewish religion in the state, the coalition of extremist factions of the Knesset appears to pursue the inverted project of including the Israeli state in the religion. Since January 2023, hundreds of thousands of Israelis have taken to the streets to protest the intended far-reaching changes to the legal system that some say threaten the country's democratic foundations.

---

[31] Hadas Gold (2023) 'A threat to democracy or a much-needed reform? Israel's judicial overhaul explained', CNN 27 March, https://edition.cnn.com/2023/03/25/middleeast/israel-judiciary-netanyahu-explainer-intl/index.html/.

The protests seem to have prompted Prime Minister Netanyahu to 'delay' the overhaul for 'further dialogue'.[32]

On the state side, it is obvious that authoritarianism can be consolidated by combining the dismantling of the rule of law with interventions in the right to vote and the institution of democratic elections. Autocrats let people vote, or, in elective democracies, have to let people vote, willy-nilly. However, they regularly exclude the democratic risk of defeat by manipulating the election results (Schedler 2006). Particularly conspicuous were the authoritarian abuses of Nicolás Maduro, elected in 2013 with a narrow majority as successor to the charismatic Venezuelan President Hugo Chávez. After a resounding electoral defeat, he ousted the elected parliament in 2015 and replaced it two years later with the hand-picked members of a 'Constituent Assembly'. Maduro won the 2020 election, which was boycotted by parts of the opposition because of fears of manipulation, with about 68 per cent; in the 2021 regional elections, Maduro's ruling party won most of the states.

The USA is currently ranked last among 'Western' countries in terms of electoral freedom. Contrary to the Voting Rights Act of 1965 and encouraged by the jurisprudence of the US Supreme Court, the shaping of electoral law was delegated to the states and since then has been systematically restricted by the authoritarian wing of the Republican Party in the states governed by it (most recently in 19 individual states) to the detriment of minorities, the majority of whom vote for the Democratic Party:[33] traditional gerrymandering, i.e., the tailoring of electoral districts to give unfair advantages to one party (McGee 2020), was supplemented by harassment such as the introduction of compulsory identification and other regulations to make voter registration more difficult; the obstruction of 'early voting' and also of the actual voting process through waiting times of up to 10 hours; the closure of polling stations in districts with a high proportion of Democratic voters (in residential areas of the African-American population, on college campuses); the withdrawal of the right to vote, among other things in the case of debt; the 'purging' of voter lists, i.e. the deletion of voters who did not participate in the last election or who were falsely registered as non-voters; and 'cracking', i.e. the splitting of the electorate in certain districts in order to prevent 'voting blocks'.[34] In the climate of political smears and lies (the campaigns of Trump and his aides against alleged 'voter fraud'), the measures are designed to corrode

---

[32] 'Israeli protests reignite as PM pushes on with justice system overhaul'. The Guardian, 8 July 2023.

[33] See *Shelby County v. Holder* 570 U.S. 529 (2013).

[34] Detailed reports on this in FAZ.online, 20 October 2020; *NZZ* 01 July 2021; ZEIT.online 1 November 2020. As of January 2022, 34 restrictions on voting rights have been registered since 2020.

democratic rules, to abet a racist agenda and style of politics dictated by authoritarian manipulative power (in favour of the return of the failed Trump). While these 'rules' are reminiscent of the Jim Crow laws that aimed to deprive African-Americans in the southern states of the US of their modest rights and few economic and political gains gained during Reconstruction (1863–1877),[35] today's authoritarianism (Parker & Towler 2019) increasingly relies on more contemporary tools, especially on data analytics companies such as Cambridge Analytica or its successor Emerdata, and commissions analyses with the aim of influencing behaviour in elections (Trump in 2016) or votes (Brexit) through individually tailored messages and misinformation (microtargeting) (Kaiser 2020; Biermann in this volume).

Insofar as authoritarian regimes, parties, or aspirations pursue the intention of halting the risky free run of unhindered public communication and preventing the mediatisation of their relationship with the followers or population ('the people'), the control, if not the neutralisation, of the media is naturally a particularly important strategic goal. This applies to both the classic print and visual media as well as the digital media. The Hungarian Prime Minister Orbán was quick to pursue the gradual enforced conformity (*Gleichschaltung*)[36] and control of the media. Unimpressed by criticism from the other EU Member States and from the Commission, he had a media law passed as early as 2010 with a two-thirds majority in the Fidesz parliament, with which he installed the National Media and Infocommunications Authority as a supervisory institution and created the basis for the takeover of the media and the advertising market (Deutscher Bundestag – Wissenschaftliche Dienste 2011). He ordered the dismissal of journalists critical of the government and the closure of newspapers and sanctioned opposition reporting. In conjunction with his judicial policy, Orban's media policy reveals the basic features of a comprehensive, systemic conception of the authoritarian, which is summed up in the 'illiberal democracy' he celebrates and the envisaged national 'community' as a model for Europe, at least for the former socialist states. It is casually associated with fantasies of a 'Greater Hungary', reclaiming territory lost in the Treaty of Trianon concluded in 1920 between Hungary and the Allied and Associated Forces. These fantasies have now been set in stone with the 'monument of national togetherness'.[37] The critique of the 'degenerated way of life' of liberal individualism has justified far-reaching intrusions into social and cultural

---

[35] Brenda Alvarez (2022) 'Are Today's Voter Suppression Laws the New Jim Crow?' in neaToday 17 January; and Gillian Brockell (2021) *The Washington Post*, 2 July.

[36] The banning of opposition and competition.

[37] The concept of a Greater Hungary is also connected to the rehabilitation of the controversial war-time governor Miklos Horty, *Balkan Insight*, 24 October 2022.

life by the Hungarian government. This 'politics with fear' (Wodak 2021: 231–255) is carried out in the persecution of lesbians and gays, the expulsion of the European University (promoted by Soros) from Budapest to Vienna and the rigorous sealing off against any migration and cultural diversity.

In 1958, France's Fifth Republic was given a semi-authoritarian structure by the constituted presidential democracy (Mérieau 2019), which was translated into competences, the state of siege (*état de siège*), and the emergency law (*Loi N°55–385* on the *état d'urgence*) and normalised in the law on internal security.[38] Since the attack in Nice in July 2016, the *état d'urgence* has been repeatedly extended. Terrorist attacks have repeatedly provoked French presidents Sarkozy and Macron into declarations of war in the Schmittian sense (Oberndorfer 2016). Like an echo of the official government declarations (Macron: '*Nous sommes en guerre!*'), public discourses in France have revolved around terrorism and Muslim migration since the attacks on the Bataclan, Charlie Hebdo, in Nice on the Promenade and later in the Basilica, then also the beheading of the teacher Samuel Paty in the run-up to the presidential elections in April 2022. By all appearances, an authoritarian consensus is developing, proclaimed by the president but driven by the spokespersons of the extreme right, Marine Le Pen and, more recently, Eric Zemmour. They use Islamist terror as a driver of the 'increased desire for authoritarian measures ... and ... [the] longing for authoritarian figures' to further poison the public climate.[39]

In Italy's fragmented party landscape, a widely shared anti-parliamentary tendency can be discerned in the confusing pool of far-right, fascist and authoritarian radical nationalist organisations, which moreover are internally divided and have always been unable to agree on a common agenda (Delledonne et al. 2021). Some, such as the Lega (Nord), also cultivate an authoritarian etatism (Stiede 2012). Eye-catching are the repeated attempts to bundle the 'right-wing forces', such as the Alleanza Nazionale and the Fratelli d'Italia (Ben-Ghiat 2022) that emerged from it, the Lega, Forza Nuova, and Casa Pound. The only things that can be widely agreed on are a substantial degree of EU scepticism and a racially motivated, restrictive migration regime. This agenda helped the leader of the Fratelli d'Italia, Giorgia Meloni, to become the first female prime minister of Italy in October 2022 with the support of a right-wing nationalist coalition government.

---

38 See Arts 5,11, 12, 15 and 16 of the French Constitution (1958/2008).

39 'Eric Zemmour: A French Trump or a French Farage?' in Politico v. 16 September 2021; Wieviorka, Michel (2017), 'Eine neue Spaltung Frankreichs?' in Mannheimer, Olga ed., *Blau, weiß, rot. Frankreich erzählt,* München 2017, 104–21.

A current look at Great Britain shows that the development path of British democracy also points in an authoritarian direction. Behind the clownish façade, the former Johnson government systematically dismantled democracy with five legislative projects.[40] Under Tory auspices, it instituted an 'elective dictatorship',[41] which ensured the prerogative of the executive (on the prerogative see Frankenberg 2020: 80–88). In March 2022, the Dissolution and Calling of Parliament Act largely removed the dissolution of parliament by the prime minister and the interpretation of laws by the government from judicial review. In its authoritarian grip on electoral law, the Tory majority, similar to some Republican Party-dominated individual states in the USA, introduced compulsory identification when voting and subjected a hitherto independent Electoral Commission to executive control. Two other laws, also passed in April 2022, the Nationality and Borders Act and the Police, Crime, Sentencing and Courts Act, drastically reduced protections for fugitives and migrants attempting to cross the English Channel and gave the police free rein to break up gatherings and criminalise participants. Taken together, these laws fit into a comprehensive executive control programme designed to revoke reforms of the Blair years and to normalise authoritarian structures and powers under the table.

10. COUNTEREVIDENCE?

An analysis of authoritarianism should be wary of unnecessary discouragement and refrain from spreading apocalyptic visions or yet another tale of decay of modern democracy. An antidote to excessive pessimism might be to include possible counterevidence in the balance. Therefore, it should be asked whether there are signs of a reversal of the 'democratic regression' (Schäfer & Zürn 2021) and the corresponding progression of authoritarianism. Of course, one could only speak of counterevidence if trends and events indicated that both the thesis of an increasing internal weakness of consolidated democracies and the observation that authoritarian regimes are advancing inexorably had to be revised; that, for example, the 'storming of the Capitol' (Diehl in this volume), the trucker blockade[42] of Canada's capital Ottawa in February 2022 and the

---

40 See Ferdinand Mount, *Frankfurter Allgemeine Zeitung*, 24 May 2022, 12.

41 A term coined by Lord Hailsham to characterize the domination of the Westminster system by the government, (1976), 'Elective dictatorship', The *Richard Dimbleby Lecture*, BBC.

42 The truckers' blockade during February 2022 consisted of occupation actions and roadblocks that paralysed Canada's capital and, according to the leaders, were intended to overthrow the democratically elected government. Ostensibly disguised as a vaccination protest, the protest coalition of Alt-Right groups, White Supremacists,

coup-like riots in Brasilia, staged by supporters of former President Bolsonaro after he had lost the elections in 2022,[43] would remain singular, atypical events and the swelling national-radical discourse in a number of European states would be irrelevant.

10.1 Renaissance of the Social Democratic Parties?

To proclaim a 'social democratic spring' would probably be too emphatic, but developments in recent years have nevertheless been remarkable. It would still have to be shown, however, that they are trends and not just singular events. Two such developments seem remarkable for the time being and will be outlined below: the electoral successes of social democratic parties at the expense of authoritarian competitors and the loss of popularity of populist politicians and parties.

From a German perspective and with a view to some Member States of the European Union, it is striking that, surprisingly, social democracy is on the upswing these days. In the Federal Republic, after years of low approval ratings, the SPD has at least won enough votes to lead the coalition government and appoint the chancellor. Thanks to the ideological fragmentation of the right-wing authoritarian parties, the Danish Social Democrats have formed a minority government after increasing their approval rating among the population by 6.8 per cent. After their election victory in 2021, the Norwegian Labour Party will lead a centre-left alliance. Sweden has been governed by a social democratic prime minister since 2014, as has Finland since 2019, where pragmatic (i.e. moderate ideological) parties form a coalition with the Social Democrats (Krell et al. 2018). In Slovakia, the social liberal candidate Zuzana Čaputová won the presidency in 2019. In Italy, the Partito Democratico surprisingly bypassed the populist Cinque Stelle movement and the authoritarian national-radical Lega in the last local elections in many big cities in June 2022. Only three months later, the right-wing coalition won the next national election in 2022. In contrast to the fickle situation in Italy, the socialist parties in Spain and Portugal stand out in that they were spared both unexpected defeats and a political implosion like their comrades in the Netherlands and France.

On balance, it would be just as premature to proclaim a 'social democratic century' for Europe than to predict the social democrats' demise. A closer look at election results, issues, and coalitions reveals that the Scandinavian and Western European countries, Spain, and Portugal do not present the

---

neo-Nazis, anti-Semites and libertarians made right-wing extremism visible in the 'model country', Edward Alden, *CFR*, 11 February 2022.

[43] Heinrich-Böll-Stiftung ed. (2023), *Chronicles of a Frustrated Coup*, Berlin.

unclouded picture of a social democratic triumph or even a pivot away from authoritarianism. With regard to the turnaround in Germany and Norway, it should be noted that the West German Social Democratic Party (SPD) had its third-worst election result of the post-war period and the Norwegian Labour Party its second-worst since 1924. With an average loss of votes in Western Europe of 10–15 per cent, social democratic electoral successes are usually based on keeping their losses lower than the conservative parties. Aside from these results and changes, four aspects speak against a secular, anti-authoritarian tendency.

First, social democratic parties benefited from the disenchantment of the Greens once they were in government.

Second, social democrats were favoured by the COVID-19 pandemic insofar as it pushed issues that endangered their popularity – migration in particular – into the background.

Third, when assessing the success of social democratic parties, it is important to take into account the price – or more precisely, the programmatic and political concessions to authoritarian-nationalist parties – for participating in government coalitions. For example, the Danish Social Democrats bought the tolerance of the 'moderately extreme right-wing' Dansk Folkeparti (according to Stöss 2006 and 2017) with considerable political concessions, especially an extremely hard line on immigration and asylum policy. Other parties in Scandinavia that are predominantly labelled as right-wing populist, with a consistently authoritarian-nationalist and xenophobic agenda, and which have been able to consolidate themselves even in the face of social democratic successes, include Sverigedemokraterna and Fremskrittpartiet in Norway as well as Perussuomalaiset and Sannfinländera in Finland (Jungar & Jupskås 2014).

Fourth, the most important aspect that speaks against a social democratic tendency on a broad front in Europe is probably the interplay between government participation and opposition, which is not unusual for established democracies. However, it is striking that changing majorities in elections and government reshuffles in almost all the democracies mentioned have hardly reduced the influence of authoritarian, radical nationalist, and xenophobic parties in the long run, apart from cyclical fluctuations.

Fifth, France is a special case not only from the point of view of social democratic counterevidence and resilience. In April 2022, incumbent Emmanuel Macron was able to defend his presidency. In 2027, therefore,[44] a new candidate will have to emerge to keep Marine Le Pen and her radical authoritarian, nationalist Rassemblement National in check. More than 40 per cent of the

[44] Art 6, para 2 of the 1958/2008 French Constitution allows for only two consecutive terms of office.

electorate – the majority of blue- and white-collar workers – cast their ballots for Le Pen, representing an increase of about 8 per cent since 2017. The Socialists, torn between far-right and far-left currents, are not to be counted on as majority leaders after the parliamentary elections in the summer of 2022 nor seriously in the next presidential elections. The electoral system, the deepening of the boundary between rich and poor evident in the 2022 election results and the trend indicating a preference for political movements such as Macron's La République en marche and Le Pen's Rassemblement National over traditional parties favour authoritarian impulses and agendas.

10.2 Resurgence of the Left in Latin America?

Comparable to the (weak) renaissance of social democracy in Europe, there was talk of a 'resurgence of the left' (Levitsky & Roberts 2011) in Latin America during the first phase of the rule of a few charismatic, initially non-authoritarian presidents. In this phase, Juán Perón's rise in Argentina – at least from 1946 to 1949 – and the Peronist 'Partida Justicialista' as an attempt to embark on a third way between communism and capitalism with social reforms can be included as an ideological model. The image of presidents in Latin America in the first decades of this century who are social democratic in the broadest sense and labelled as populist is shaped by Hugo Chávez, President of Venezuela from 2002 to 2013, Luiz Inácio Lula da Silva, one of the founders of the Workers' Party and President of Brazil from 2003 to 2011 and again since 2023, José Alberto Mujica Cordano, leader of the Movimiento de Participación Popular and president of Uruguay from 2010 to 2015, and finally Evo Morales, leader of the Bolivian Socialist Party and president of Bolivia from 2006 to 2019. Surprisingly, the head of the Partida Convergencia Social, Gabriel Boric, won the presidential election in 2021 against the ultra-conservative António Kast, but failed to gain a majority for his constitutional project.

With the fading of the popularity and charisma of popular leaders – after their deselection, resignation, death, or else with the resistance of unsolved social problems (especially poverty, unemployment, crime, unequal distribution) – the 'virus of authoritarianism' spread (again) from Mexico, Nicaragua, Venezuela, and Colombia to Argentina in the second decade (Maihold 2020). This spread began with the restriction of democratic rights and procedures and ended in some countries, especially Nicaragua and Brazil, with the normalised state of emergency (Do Alto 2008). Apart from the singular alliance of left parties in Uruguay (the Frente Amplio), established social democratic parties also got caught in the maelstrom of authoritarianism (Lanzaro 2007; Thiery 2010). However, with the election of the candidate of the Apruebo Dignidad coalition, Gabriel Boric, as president of Chile, there is at least the possibility that the extreme neoliberal social and economic model can be overcome by building a social democratic welfare state and a new constitution (2022). Colombia, on the other hand, increasingly became a laboratory of 'competitive authoritarianism' (Levitsky & Way 2010), where the national government and elites delegate the social and political control of marginalised regions to local elites, giving them the regional monopoly on the use of force, along with access to the population and a wide range of resources (land, state finances, drugs).

According to the 'Democracy Index' for the years 2021 and 2022 of the magazine *The Economist*, considerable declines are recorded for Latin America (as well as for Europe), measured by the criteria of electoral process and pluralism, civil liberty, functioning of government, political participation, and political culture. Compared to the countries of the continents of Africa and Asia, the 'Democracy Index' registers a conspicuous downward trend for Latin America from a comparative perspective.[45] Even after the retreat of the military regimes (Zürn, in this volume), poverty and corruption, transnationally organised crime, deficient political institutions, and presidentialism continue to play into the hands of authoritarianism in Latin America.[46] The counter evidence of the recent past has therefore not proven stable. *The Economist* sees Latin America 'under authoritarian threat' based on the 2022 Democracy Index.[47]

10.3 The Dawn of 'Populism'?

As mentioned above, a large number of surveys and studies evaluated, among others, in the meta-study by Cambridge University, suggest that there is a decline in approval not only for democracy but also for (populist) authoritarian parties and regimes in Germany, Austria, Switzerland, in Southern European countries and in so-called 'maturing democracies' in Latin America – a decline that is also noticeable at the ballot box. While in many countries of the European Union the performance of democracy as a form of government and life is doubted, elsewhere, demonstrably in Latin America, the euphoria

---

45 'Latin America's average regional score fell for a sixth consecutive year, from 6.09 in 2020 to 5.83 in 2021. This was not only the steepest decline recorded in the index by any region of the world in 2021, it was also the biggest downgrade recorded by any region since we launched the Democracy Index. The region's score across all categories of the index worsened in 2021, led by a sharp decline in the political culture score.' Economist Intelligence Unit (2022), *Democracy Index 2021. The China Challenge*, London, 38–51.

46 O'Donnell 1994; O'Donnell et al. 1983; Nohlen & Fernández 1998; Smith & Ziegler 2008.

47 *The Economist*, 15 February 2023.

of the democratic transition years has faded. At the same time, the unresolved challenges of poverty, corruption, inter-group conflict, and urban violence remain.

What is remarkable is that, despite the rising dissatisfaction with the democratic form of government since the beginning of the pandemic, the poll ratings for authoritarian-populist leaders and parties are falling at the same time, and they are losing or are in danger of losing elections. That even populism is falling into disrepute at a time when support for democracy is waning seems like a paradox at first glance. However, on reflection these are two sides of the same coin: according to the Cambridge meta-study, the inability of elected politicians – and especially elected populists such as Orbán in Hungary – to offer solutions to the pandemic and to remedy the risk anxiety and 'learned helplessness' of the population explains why enthusiasm for democratic governments has waned and why populists have fallen out of favour.[48]

The fate of populist authoritarianism is thus by no means a foregone conclusion and it stands to reason to wait and see how things develop after COVID-19. Nevertheless, the aforementioned meta-study, which analyses several thousand surveys and studies, provides clear indications that authoritarian leaders, movements and parties, at least in electoral democracies, are not 'self-perpetuating' and are not exempt from the risk of defeat in elections or loss of popularity.

10.4 Resilience of Democratic Attitudes?

The question of counterevidence to rampant authoritarianism would not be adequately answered by the consolidation of (democratic) party milieus or the resilience of democratic institutions alone, even if it came to more pleasing results. Rather, the question must be posed more deeply and begin at the level of the actors, that is, by looking at the political attitudes and mentality of the citizenry, which is expected to have sovereignty. This includes their resistance to authoritarian temptations (Heitmeyer 2018), their defence against authoritarian escapes (O. Decker 2018: 15–63), and the motives for voter migration. The findings collected by various research groups, in particular the Leipzig studies on authoritarian and far-right attitudes in Germany (Decker & Brähler 2018), give little cause for democratic optimism. However, it must be consid-

[48] 'That populism has become discredited at a time of eroding support for democracy may initially seem to present us with a paradox. In reality, these are two sides of the same coin. It is precisely the inadequacy of elected politicians – including, above all, elected populists – to offer solutions to the pandemic that explains why enthusiasm for democratic government has waned, and why populists have fallen from favour' Centre for the Future of Democracy, *The Great Reset.*

ered that in the majority of European states only a minority of the population gives in to the authoritarian temptation. Moreover, civil societies react quite defensively and spontaneously, without waiting for authoritarian leadership, to challenges such as the influx of refugees in 2015 and 2022, in the latter case by helping those who fled the war in Ukraine. Nevertheless, it should be borne in mind that group-based misanthropy and conspiracy mentalities, resentments and fears of decline are inculcated over time through readjustment, external direction and loss of control.[49] As a rule, they appear more difficult to change than, for example, the popular opinion of authoritarian politicians – who, as mentioned before, promise solutions and ways out of insecurity but in the end have none to offer, thus prompting a reversal of voter migration. The 'externally directed character' (Dubiel 1986: 265), marked by readjustment and insecurity, surrenders to the fear of freedom and diversity and compensates for the loss of self-determination with a conformist orientation to the (apparent) security of others. Erich Fromm's concept of 'prosthetic security' (1936: 179) is still instructive for understanding this relationship of authority. It not only determines external behaviour but also imprints itself on the 'psychic inside' (O. Decker 2018: 44 and 53) and, when certain stimuli are set, activates the authoritarian syndrome. External steering – such is the democratic hope – could be deflected by structural change in the (analogue and digital) public spheres and the containment of anti-democratic tendencies, especially in the capital-driven digital media, insofar as this change is directed towards a willingness to accept diversity and to deal with conflicts openly.

11. DRIVERS OF THE AUTHORITARIAN: PATHS OF DEVELOPMENT

Without giving in to a tendency to tell stories of decay and apocalypse, the first two decades of the twenty-first century present a picture that gives little cause for optimism about further democratic progress. The picture does not change significantly if the counterevidence just discussed is included in the balance nor if it is considered that the unfulfilled security promises of authoritarian regimes are capable of undermining their legitimacy, attractiveness and 'populism' and reactivating the resilience of the citizenry against authoritarian temptations. In summary, it remains to be observed in Western societies that different parts of the population – across age groups and regardless of social situation – have given in to authoritarian temptations in a statistically significant and conspicuous manner. They have allowed themselves to be influenced

[49] Fromm 1941; O Decker 2018; Heitmeyer 2018; Löwenthal 1982; Nachtwey 2016; Frankenberg 2022.

by national radical movements, that is, where they have not accommodated these movements of their own free will. They have allowed group-based misanthropy against minorities and, above all, foreigners to be expressed – and acted upon. Part of the overall picture is that authoritarian parties and regimes in Europe and worldwide have gained political and cultural influence, which has contributed to the development labelled above as 'democratic regression', 'global retreat of democracy', 'third wave of autocratisation', or 'renaissance of authoritarianism' (Frantz 2018; Przeworksi 2020; Lührmann & Hellmeier 2020; Schäfer/Zürn 2021).

In this framework, we have attempted to identify and focus on crisis events in the first two decades of the twenty-first century as drivers of authoritarian development, on the one hand to sharpen the vague concept of crisis such that it captures these very developments and on the other hand to substitute it for more metaphorical concepts such as national 'fatigue fractures' and to examine the narratives and practices of the authoritarian. In the early twenty-first century, as explained, a series of crises have driven the standard narratives of authoritarianism, especially the threat to order and the dissolution of identities by 'enemy forces' (such as elites, foreigners and refugees), and set in motion their mobilisation within authoritarian agendas. In these narratives and their implementation in politics, the authoritarian internal tendency is particularly conspicuous: in the crises (such as financial crime, climate catastrophe, policy failure in migration and corona), the ethnic, social and other minorities are rejected and excluded as 'foreigners' wherever possible – and excluded from democratic conflicts.

We have defined authoritarian *developments* as dangers or threats to society and democracy to emphasise that they can only be meaningfully detected in societies that are not completely structured along authoritarian lines. Consequently, the inevitably cursory investigation in this chapter concentrated on societies whose political structures, institutions and practices give room for the insight that there are deviations from democratic routines towards authoritarianism. Such trajectories can be seen in the above-mentioned political-legal interventions of the Republicans in US electoral law or the discrimination directed against the Muslim population by the Hindu nationalist government in India. They can focus on individual events where trajectories and structures initially remain in the background, but authoritarian attitudes emerge, as in the storming of the Capitol building in Washington DC on 6 January 2021, the trucker blockade in Ottawa, or the self-staging of *Querdenker* ('lateral thinkers') as victims of the corona dictatorship. Finally, authoritarian courses also find expression in linguistic assaults in which, for example, 'right-wing populist' politicians make use of the arsenal of Fascist rhetoric and programmes ('*Umvolkung*', '*Überfremdung*') (Reisigl 2012) to stir up hatred against minorities.

In all these processes, however, a distinction must be made between the specific institutional contexts or public discourses into which authoritarian strategies and verbal messages penetrate so as to reshape the institutional system, shaping state practice, or infiltrating the consciousness of the followers. Regardless of the different perspectives, the strategic variants and the diverse courses of the crisis scenarios, it is striking that authoritarian movements always attack two components of the basic liberal order: on the one hand, they are directed against the recognition of diversity in a pluralistic society and tolerance; on the other hand, they despise the democratic rules for the resolution of social conflicts.

REFERENCES

Adorno, Theodor W., Frenkel-Brunswik, Else, Levinson, Daniel, and Sanford, Nevitt (1950) *The Authoritarian Personality*, New York.

Alviar, Helena & Frankenberg, Günter (2021), 'Paying for the Consequences. How Privatization and Austerity Disabled Infection Protection Law' in 54 *VRÜ/World Comparative Law*, 27–54.

Anderson, Benjamin (2016) *Imagined Communities. Reflections on the Origin and Spread of Nationalism*, New York.

Applebaum, Anne (2020) *Twilight of Democracy. The Temptation of Authoritarianism*, New York.

Arendt, Hannah (1951) *The Origins of Totalitarianism,* New York.

Arendt, Hannah (1970) *Macht und Gewalt*, München.

Arendt, Hannah (2016 [1963]) *On Revolution*, London.

Arestis, Philip & Sawyer, Malcolm C. (2012) *The Euro Crisis*, London.

Aron, Raymond (1965) *Démocratie et totalitarisme*, Paris.

Aust, Stefan & Geiges, Adrian (2012) *Mit Konfuzius zur Weltmacht: Das chinesische Jahrhundert*, Hamburg.

Ayata, Imran (2021), 'Nur für geladene Gäste' in *Frankfurter Allgemeine Sonntagszeitung* Nr 42, 33.

Bade, Klaus (2017) *Migration – Flucht – Integration*, Karlsruhe.

BAMF (2021), 'Statistik Asyl und Flüchtlingsschutz', hrsg v Bundesamt für Migration und Flüchtlinge, *Aktuelle Zahlen*, 9/2021, Bremen.

Beck, Martin & Stützle, Ingo (2018) *Die neuen Bonapartisten. Mit Marx den Aufstieg von Trump & Co. verstehen*, Berlin.

Beck, Ulrich (1992) *The Risk Society. Towards a New Modernity*, Newbury Park.

Beck, Ulrich (1999) *World Risk Society*, Cambridge/Oxford.

Beck, Ulrich (2016) *The Metamorphosis of the World*, Cambridge.

Ben-Ghiat, Ruth (2022), 'The Return of Fascism in Italy', *The Atlantic*, 23 September.

Bertelsmann Stiftung (2016) *Krisenmanagement. Einflussfaktoren auf Bedrohungen und Mechanismen der Bewältigung von Krisen*, Gütersloh.

Bertelsmann Stiftung (2018) *Transformationsindex BTI 2018*, Gütersloh.

Bertelsmann Stiftung (2020) *Transformation Index*, Gütersloh.

Bertelsmann Stiftung (2022) *Demokratie weltweit weiter unter Druck: Zahl der autoritären Regierungen steigt weiter*, 23 February, Gütersloh.

Best, Steven, Kahn, Richard, Nocella II, Anthony J., & McLaren, Peter (2011) *The Global Industrial Complex: Systems of Domination*, New York.
Birnbaum, Norman (1997) 'Siegt die Marktorthodoxie, stirbt die Demokratie' in 12 *Blätter für deutsche und internationale Politik*, 1443–1456.
BMI (Bundesministerium des Innern) (2018) *Maßnahmen zur Steuerung, Ordnung und Begrenzung der Zuwanderung*, Berlin.
Bozay, Kemal (2017) 'Graue Wölfe – die größte rechtsextremistische Organisation in Deutschland' in *Bundeszentrale für politische Bildung* Bonn, 24 November.
Brown, Wendy (2019) *In the Ruins of Neoliberalism: The Rise of Antidemocratic Politics in the West*, New York.
Butter, Michael (2018) *'Nichts ist, wie es scheint'. Über Verschwörungstheorien*, Berlin. Canovan, Margaret (1981) *Populism*, New York.
Butter, Michael & Knight, Peter (eds.) (2020) *Routledge Handbook of Conspiracy Theories*, Abingdon
Castañeda, Jorge G (2007) 'Latin America's Left Turn' in 85 *Foreign Affairs*, 5–6.
Centre for the Future of Democracy (2022) *The Great Reset: Public Opinion, Populism and the Pandemic*, Cambridge UK, January 2022.
CEPAL (2006), *Anuario estadístico de América Latina y el Caribe*, Santiago de Chile.
Costa Pinto, António & Morlino, Leonardo (2011), *Dealing with the Legacy of Authoritarianism. The 'Politics of the Past' in Southern European Democracies*, Milton Park.
Crouch, Colin (2004) *Post-Democracy*, Hoboken NJ.
Crouch, Colin (2021) *Postdemokratie revisited*, Berlin.
Dahrendorf, Ralf (1997) 'Die Quadratur des Kreises. Ökonomie, sozialer Zusammenhalt und Demokratie im Zeitalter der Globalisierung' in 9 *Blätter für deutsche und internationale Politik*, 1060–71.
Decker, Frank (ed.) (2006) *Populismus. Gefahr für die Demokratie oder nützliches Korrektiv?*, Wiesbaden.
Decker, Frank (2021) 'Populismus', in Uwe Andersen, Uwe/Wichard Woyke (Hg.), *Handwörterbuch des politischen Systems der Bundesrepublik Deutschland*, 776–782.
Decker, Oliver (2018) *Flucht ins Autoritäre*, in Oliver Decker/Elmar Brähler, *Flucht ins Autoritäre. Rechtsextreme Dynamiken in der Mitte der Gesellschaft*, Gießen, 15–63.
Decker, Oliver & Brähler, Elmar (2020) *Autoritäre Dynamiken – Neue Radikalität – alte Ressentiments*, Gießen.
Delledonne, Giacomo (2021) *Challenges to Democracy in the 21st Century*, London.
Deutscher Bundestag (2011) *Wissenschaftliche Dienste – Stellungnahme zum ungarischen Mediengesetz*, Berlin, WD 10 – 3000 – 008/11.
Diamond, Larry & Plattner, Mark (2015), *Democracy in Decline?*, Baltimore.
Diamond, Larry, Plattner, Mark & Walker, Christopher (2016) *Authoritarianism Goes Global*, Baltimore.
Diehl, Paula (2020) 'Populism' in Oberreuther, Heinrich (ed.), *Staatslexikon der Görres-Gesellschaft*, Freiburg.
Diner, Dan (ed.) (1988) *Zivilisationsbruch. Denken an Auschwitz*, Frankfurt am Main.
Dörre, Klaus (2009) 'Die neue Landnahme. Dynamiken und Grenzen des Finanzmarktkapitalismus' in Dörre, Klaus, Lessenich, Stephan & Rosa, Hartmut (eds.), *Soziologie – Kapitalismus – Kritik*, Frankfurt am Main, 21–86.
Dörre, Klaus (2012) 'Landnahme, das Wachstumsdilemma und die 'Achsen der Ungleichheit'' in 22 *Berliner Journal für Soziologie*, 101–128.

Douglas, Karen M. (2021) 'COVID-19 Conspiracy Theories', 24 *Group Processes & Intergroup Rel.* 270.
Dubiel, Helmut (1986) 'Autonomie oder Anomie. Zum Streit über den nachliberalen Sozialcharakter' in *Soziale Welt – Sonderband 4: Die Moderne – Kontinuitäten und Zäsuren*, 263–81.
Economist Intelligence (2022) *Democracy Index 2021. The China Challenge*, London.
Erceg, Christopher u.a. (2005) 'Expansionary Fiscal Shocks and the Trade Deficit', in *International Finance Discussion Paper No 2005–825*, (ed.) Board of Governors of the Federal Reserve System, Washington DC.
Esen, Berk & Gümüşçü, Sebnem (2016) 'Rising Competitive Authoritarianism in Turkey' in 37 *Third World Quarterly*, 1581–1606.
European Commission (2022) *Statistics on Migration to Europa*, Brussels, 1 January.
Finotelli, Claudia (2007) *Illegale Einwanderung, Flüchtlingsmigration und das Ende des Nord-Süd-Mythos,* Münster.
Frankenberg, Günter (2000) 'Tocqueville's Question. The Role of a Constitution in the Process of Integration' in 13 *Ratio Juris* 1–30.
Frankenberg, Günter (2014) *Political Technology and the Erosion of the Rule of Law. Normalizing the State of Exception*, Cheltenham.
Frankenberg, Günter (2020) *Authoritarianism. Constitutional Perspectives*, Cheltenham.
Frankenberg, Günter (2023) 'Constituting the Negative Globality of Fear' in *I.CON*, 1–9.
Frantz, Erica (2018) *Authoritarianism: What Everyone Needs to Know*, Oxford.
Fromm, Erich (1936) 'Studien über Autorität und Familie. Sozialpsychologischer Teil' in id., *Gesamtausgabe Bd. 1*, Stuttgart, 139–187.
Fukuyama, Francis (1989) 'The End of History' in 16 *The National Interest*, 3–18.
Fukuyama, Francis (2002) *Our Posthuman Future: Consequences for the Biotechnology Revolution*, London.
Gassert, Philipp (2021) *Der 11. September 2001*, Stuttgart.
Gauchet, Marcel (1980) 'Tocqueville, l'Amérique et nous', in *Libre* No 7, 75–84.
Gauchet, Marcel (1990) 'Die totalitäre Erfahrung und das Denken des Politischen' in Ulrich Rödel, (ed.), *Autonome Gesellschaft und libertäre Demokratie*, Frankfurt am Main, 207–238.
Geddes, Barbara (1999) 'What Do We Know About Democratization After Twenty Years?' in 2 *Annual Review of Political Science*, 115–144.
Geddes, Barbara, Frantz, Erica, & Wright, Joseph (2018) *How Dictatorship Works. Power, Personalization, and Collapse*, Cambridge.
Gessenharter, Wolfgang (1983) 'Autoritarismus' in Lippert, Ekkehard/Wakenhut, Roland (Hg.), *Handwörterbuch der Politischen Psychologie. Studienbücher zur Sozialwissenschaft*, Wiesbaden, 39–48.
Günther, Klaus (2021) 'Krisenmomente der Freiheit' in 107 *Archiv für Rechts- und Sozialphilosophie*, 330–355.
Guriev, Sergei & Treismann, Daniel (2022) *Spin-Dictators: The Changing Face of Tyranny in the 21st Century*, Princeton.
Habermas, Jürgen (1998) *Die postnationale Konstellation*, Frankfurt am Main.
Habermas, Jürgen (2021) 'Überlegungen und Hypothesen zu einem erneuten Strukturwandel der Öffentlichkeit' in Seeliger, Martin & Sevignani, Sebastian (eds.) *Ein neuer Strukturwandel der Öffentlichkeit?, Sonderband Leviathan*, 37, Baden-Baden, 470–500.

Haffert, Lukas (2018) 'Metropole des Populismus – Berlin als Totem der Elitenkritik' in 72 *Merkur*, 30 January, 71–76.
Hall, Stuart (1985) 'Authoritarian Populism: A Reply' in 151 *New Left Review*, 115–124.
Heitmeyer, Wilhelm (1992) *Die Bielefelder Rechtsextremismus-Studie*, Weinheim.
Heitmeyer, Wilhelm (2001) 'Autoritärer Kapitalismus, Demokratieentleerung und Rechtspopulismus. Eine Analyse von Entwicklungstendenzen' in Loch, Dietmar & Heitmeyer, Wilhelm (eds.) *Schattenseiten der Globalisierung. Rechtsradikalismus, Rechtspopulismus und separatistischer Regionalismus in westlichen Gesellschaften*, Frankfurt am Main, 497–534.
Heitmeyer, Wilhelm (2018) *Autoritäre Versuchungen. Signaturen der Bedrohung 1*, Berlin.
Heitmeyer, Wilhelm, Freedom, Manuela & Sitzer, Peter (2020) *Rechte Bedrohungsallianzen*, Berlin.
Heitmeyer, Wilhelm & Hagan, John (2002) 'Gewalt. Zu den Schwierigkeiten einer systematischen internationalen Bestandsaufnahme' in Heitmeyer, Wilhelm & Hagan, John (eds.) *Internationales Handbuch der Gewaltforschung*, Wiesbaden, 15–25.
Hepfer, Karl (2021) *Verschwörungstheorien. Eine philosophische Kritik*, 3rd edn, Bielefeld
Hirschman, Albert O. (1994) 'Wieviel Gemeinsinn braucht die liberale Gesellschaft?' in 22 *Leviathan*, 293–304.
Hobsbawm, Eric (1998) *Das Zeitalter der Extreme. Weltgeschichte des 20. Jahrhunderts*, München.
Hoffman, Bruce (2001) 'Change and Continuity in Terrorism' in 24 *Studies in Conflict & Terrorism*, 417–428.
International IDEA (2021) *The Global State of Democracy. Report 2021*. See https://www.idea.int/.
Jäger, Thomas C, (ed.) (2015), *Handbuch der Sicherheitsgefahren*, Wiesbaden.
Kauth, Jasper T. & King, Desmond (2021) 'Illiberalism' in 61 *European Journal of Sociology*, 365–405.
Kegel, Bernhard (2021) *Die Natur der Zukunft*, Köln.
Klein, Naomi (2015) *This Changes Everything: Capitalism vs. The Climate*, New York.
Kovács, Kriszta & Lane Scheppele, Kim (2018) 'The Fragility of an Independent Judiciary: Lessons from Hungary and Poland – and the European Union' in 51 *Communist and Post-Communist Studies*, 189–200.
Kreis, Joachim (2007) *Zur Messung von rechtsextremer Einstellung: Probleme und Kontroversen am Beispiel zweier Studien*, Otto-Stammer-Zentrum: Berlin.
Krell, Christian, Möllers, Henri & Ferch, Niklas (2018) *Reclaiming Action. Strategien progressiver Parteien in Zeiten des wachsenden Rechtspopulismus in Dänemark, Norwegen, Schweden und Deutschland*, Friedrich-Ebert-Stiftung, Stockholm.
Lams, Lutgard, Crauwels, Geert & Anisoara Serban, Henrieta (2014) *Totalitarian and Authoritarian Discourses – A Global and Timeless Phenomenon*, Frankfurt am Main.
Lanzaro, Jorge (2007) 'Gobiernos socialdemócratas en América Latina' in *Revista Nexos* Nr 354.
Laruelle, Marlène (2022) 'Illiberalism: A Conceptual Introduction', 38 East European Politics, 303–327.
Lauth, Hans-Joachim (2020) *Demokratiematrix Gesamtwertindex* 2020, Würzburg.
Lazaridis, Gabriella, Campani, Giovanna & Benveniste, Annie (2016) *The Rise of the Far Right in Europe – Populist Shifts and 'Othering'*, London.

Lefort, Claude (1988) 'The Concept of Totalitarianism' in ders., *Papers in Social Theory*, Warwick University: Coventry UK, 166–186.
Levitsky, Steven & Roberts, Kenneth M (2011) *The Resurgence of the American Left*, Baltimore.
Levitsky, Steven & Way, Lucien A (2002) 'Elections Without Democracy' in 13 *Journal of Democracy*, 51–61.
Levitsky, Steven & Way, Lucien A (2010) *Competitive Authoritarianism: Hybrid Regimes after the Cold War*, Cambridge.
Levitsky, Steven & Ziblatt, Daniel (2018) *How Democracies Die*, New York.
Linz, Juan (2003) *Totalitäre und autoritäre Regime*, Berlin.
Loch, Dietmar & Heitmeyer, Wilhelm (2001), *Schattenseiten der Globalisierung. Rechtsradikalismus, Rechtspopulismus und separatistischer Regionalismus in westlichen Demokratien*, Frankfurt am Main.
Löwenthal, Leo (1982) 'Falsche Propheten' in Dubiel, Helmut, *Leo Löwenthal, Schriften 3: Zur politischen Psychologie des Autoritarismus*, Frankfurt am Main, 255–273.
Luce, Edward (2017) *The Retreat of Western Liberalism*, London.
Luft, Stefan (2017) *Die Flüchtlingskrise. Ursachen, Konflikte, Folgen*, 2nd edn, München.
Lührmann, Anna & Hellmeier, Sebastian (2020) 'Populism, Nationalism and Illiberalism: A Challenge for Democracy and Civil Society' in Heinrich Böll–Foundation, (ed.), *A Companion to Democracy*, February, Berlin.
Lührmann, Anna, Tannenberg Marcus & Lindberg, Staffan I. (2018) 'Regimes of the World: Opening New Avenues for the Comparative Study of Regimes' in 6 *Politics and Governance*, 60–77.
Luhmann, Niklas (1982), *Trust and Power*, Hoboken NJ.
Luhmann, Niklas (1984) 'The Self-Description of Society: Crisis Fashion and Social Theory' in 25 *Int'l Journal of Comparative Sociology*, 59–68.
Maihold, Günther (2020) 'Das Virus des Autoritarismus breitet sich in Lateinamerika aus' in *SWP–Aktuell* 2020/35, 13 May.
Main, Thomas (2022) *The Rise of Illiberalism*, Washington DC.
Marx, Karl (1963) *The Eighteenth Brumaire of Louis Bonaparte*, New York.
Marx, Karl (1967) *Capital. A Critique of Political Economy*, I, Moscow.
Meier-Braun, Karl-Heinz (2018) *Schwarzbuch Migration,* München.
Mergel, Thomas (2012) *Krisen verstehen. Historische und kulturwissenschaftliche Annäherungen*, Frankfurt am Main.
Mérieau, Eugénie (2019) 'French authoritarian constitutionalism and its legacy' in Alviar, Helena & Frankenberg, Günter (eds.), *Authoritarian Constitutionalism. Comparative Analysis and Critique*, 185–208.
Merkel, Wolfgang (2004) 'Embedded and defective democracies' in 11 *Democratization*, 33–58.
Merkel, Wolfgang (2021) 'Neue Krisen. Wissenschaft, Moralisierung und die Demokratie' in Bundeszentrale für politische Bildung, (ed.), *Zustand der Demokratie*, 25 June, Bonn.
Merkel, Wolfgang, Puhle, Hans-Jürgen, Croissant, Aurel, Eicher, Claudia & Thiery, Peter (2003) *Defekte Demokratie. Bd. 1: Theorie*, Wiesbaden.
Merkel, Wolfgang, Puhle, Hans-Jürgen, Croissant, Aurel, Eicher, Claudia & Thiery, Peter (2006) *Defekte Demokratie. Bd. 2: Regionalanalysen*, Wiesbaden.

Miller, Max & Soeffner, Hans-Georg (1996) 'Modernität und Barbarei. Eine Einleitung' in Miller, Max & Soeffner, Hans-Georg (eds.) *Modernität und Barbarei*, Frankfurt am Main, 12–27.
Möller, Kolja (2022) *Populismus. Ein Reader*, Berlin.
Moffitt, Benjamin (2016) *The Global Rise of Populism*, Stanford.
Mommsen, Margareta (2007) 'Putin's 'gelenkte Demokratie': ‚Vertikale der Macht' statt Gewaltenteilung' in Buhbe, Matthes & Gorzka, Gabriele (eds.) *Russland heute – Rezentralisierung des Staates unter Putin*, Wiesbaden, 235–252.
Mommsen, Margareta & Nußberger, Angelika (2007) *Das System Putin: gelenkte Demokratie und politische Justiz in Russland*, München.
Mounk, Yascha (2022) *The Great Experiment. Why Democracies Fall Apart and How They Can Endure*, London/New York.
Mudde, Cas (2010), 'The Populist Right: A Pathological Normalcy' in 36 *West European Politics*, 1167–1186.
Mudde, Cas (1996) 'The War of Words Defining the Extreme Right Party Family' in 19 *West European Politics*, 225–248.
Mudde, Cas & Kaltwasser, Rovira Cristóbal (2017) *Populism: A Very Short Introduction*, Oxford.
Mudde, Cas & Kaltwasser, Rovira Cristóbal (2019) *Populismus. Eine sehr kurze Einführung*, Bundeszentrale für politische Bildung: Bonn.
Müller, Jan-Werner (2016) *Was ist Populismus? Ein Essay*, Berlin.
Naumann, Annelie & Kamann, Matthias (2021) *Corona–Krieger. Verschwörungs-Mythen und die Neuen Rechten*, Berlin.
Nachtwey, Oliver (2016) *Die Abstiegsgesellschaft. Über das Aufbegehren in der regressiven Moderne*, Berlin.
Neumann, Franz (1967) 'Angst und Politik' in id., *Demokratischer und autoritärer Staat. Studien zur politischen Theorie*, Frankfurt am Main, 261–291.
Nohlen, Dieter & Fernández, Mario (1998) *El Presidencialismo renovado: Instituciones y cambio político en América Latina*, Caracas.
Norris, Pippa & Inglehart, Ronald (2019) *Cultural Backlash – Trump, Brexit, and Authoritarian Populism*, Cambridge.
Oberndorfer, Lukas (2016) 'Europa und Frankreich im Ausnahmezustand? Die autoritäre Durchsetzung des Wettbewerbs' in 46 *PROKLA*, 561–581.
O'Donnell, Guillermo (1994) 'Delegative Democracy' in *Journal of Democracy*, Jg. 5, 55–69.
O'Donnell, Guillermo (2004) 'The Quality of Democracy: Why the Rule of Law Matters' in 15 *Journal of Democracy*, 32–46.
O'Donnell, Guillermo (2007) 'The Perpetual Crises of Democracy' in 18 *Journal of Democracy*, 5–11.
Oesterreich, Detlef (1966) *Flucht in die Sicherheit*, Opladen.
Oevermann, Ulrich (2016) ''Krise und Routine' als analytisches Paradigma in den Sozialwissenschaften' in Becker–Lenz, Roland, Franzmann, Andreas, Jansen, Axel, Jung, Matthias (eds.), *Die Methodenschule der Objektiven Hermeneutik*, Wiesbaden, 43–114.
Overpeck, Jonathan T & Conde, Cecilia (2019) 'A Call to Climate Action' in 364 *Science*, 807.
Parker, Christopher S & Towler, Christopher C (2019) 'Race and Authoritarianism in American Politics' in 22 *Annual Review of Political Science*, 503–519.
Piketty, Thomas (2017) *Capital in the Twenty-first Century*, Cambridge MA.

Pirro, Andrea (2022) 'Far right: The Significance of an Umbrella Concept'' in 29 *Nation and Nationalism*, 101–112.
Popitz, Heinrich (2017) *Phenomena of Power* (1986) New York.
Priester, Karin (2017) 'Rechtspopulismus – ein umstrittenes theoretisches und politisches Phänomen' in Virchow, Fabian, Langebach, Martin & Häusler, Alexander, *Handbuch Rechtsextremismus*, Wiesbaden, 533–560.
Przeworski, Adam (1991) *Democracy and the Market. Political Reforms in Eastern Europe and Latin America*, Cambridge.
Przeworski, Adam (1995) *Sustainable Democracy*, Cambridge.
Przeworski, Adam (2019), *Crises of Democracy*, Cambridge.
Quent, Matthias (2016), *Rassismus, Radikalisierung, Rechtsterrorismus. Wie der NSU entstand und was er über die Gesellschaft verrät*, Weinheim/Basel.
Reichardt, Sven (2021) *Die Misstrauensgemeinschaft der 'Querdenker': Die Corona–Proteste aus kultur- und sozialwissenschaftlicher Perspektive*, Frankfurt am Main.
Reisigl, Martin (2012), 'Rechtspopulistische und faschistische Rhetorik: ein Vergleich' in 9 *Totalitarismus und Demokratie*, 303–323.
Rémond, René (1954), *Les droits en France*, Paris.
Rensmann, Lars, Funke, Hajo & Hagemann, Steffen (2011) *Autoritarismus und Demokratie. Politische Theorie und Kultur in der globalen Moderne* (*Wochenschau Wissenschaft*), Schwalbach.
Ringen, Stein (2011) 'It's about authority, stupid! Having power is not enough to get things done' in *WZB Mitteilungen* Nr 133.
Ringen, Stein (2013) *Nation of Devils. Democratic Leadership and the Problem of Obedience*, New Haven.
Ripple, William, Wolf, Christopher, Gregg, Jillian W, Levin, Kelly, Rockström, Johan, Newsome, Thomas M, Betts, Matthew G, Huq, Saleemul, Law, Beverly E, Kemp, Luke, Kalmus, Peter & Lenton, Timothy M (2021) 'World Scientists' Warning of a Climate Emergency' in 20 *BioScience*, 1–5.
Roach, Kent (2015) *Comparative Counter-Terrorism Law*, Cambridge
Rödel, Ulrich, Frankenberg, Günter & Dubiel Helmut (1989) *Die demokratische Frage*, Frankfurt am Main.
Röhner, Cara (2019) *Ungleichheit und Verfassung. Vorschlag für eine relationale Rechtsanalyse*, Weilerswist.
Rucht, Dieter (2018) 'Right-wing populism in context: A historical and systematic perspective' in Fitzi, Gregor, Mackert, Juergen & Turner, Bryan (eds.) *Populism and the crisis of democracy*, London, 67–84.
Rudolph, Enno (2017) *Wege der Macht*, Weilerswist.
Sajó, Andras (2021) *Ruling by Cheating*, Cambridge.
Sajó, Andras, Uitz, Renáta & Holmes, Stephen (eds.) (2022) *The Routledge Handbook of Illiberalism*, Abingdon.
Sauer, Birgit (2020) 'Authoritarian Right-Wing Populism as Masculinist Identity Politics. The Role of Affects' in Dietze, Gabriele & Roth, Julia (eds.), *Right–Wing Populism and Gender. European Perspectives and Beyond*, Bielefeld, 22–39.
Schäfer, Armin & Zürn, Michael (2021) *Die demokratische Regression*, Berlin.
Schedler, Andreas (Hg.) (2006) *Electoral Authoritarianism. The Dynamics of Unfree Competition*, Boulder/London.
Scheppele, Kim Lane (2019) 'Autocratic Legalism' in 85 *The University of Chicago Law Review*, 545–583.
Schubert, Klaus & Klein, Martina (2020) *Das Politiklexikon*, 7th edn, Bonn.
Steg, Joris A (2019) *Krisen des Kapitalismus*, Frankfurt am Main.

Stegemann, Bernd (2021) '*Identitätspolitik ist für die Linke ein Irrweg*' in *SPIEGEL. Online*, 11 January.

Stiede, Anna-Franziska (2012) 'Autoritäre Tendenzen und Geschlechterverhältnisse in Italien' in 1 *Femina Politica*, 51–62.

Stiglitz, Joseph E (2014) 'China Has Overtaken the U.S. as the World's Largest Economy', *Vanity Fair*, 4 December.

Stöss, Richard (2006) 'Rechtsextreme Parteien in Westeuropa' in Niedermayer, Oskar, Stöss, Richard & Haas, Melanie (eds.), *Die Parteiensysteme Westeuropas*, Wiesbaden, 521–563.

Stöss, Richard (2010) *Rechtsextremismus im Wandel*, Friedrich-Ebert-Stiftung, (ed.), Berlin.

Stöss, Richard (2017) *Trade Unions and Right-wing Extremism in Europe*, Friedrich-Ebert-Stiftung, (ed.), Berlin.

Strobl, Natascha (2021) *Radikalisierter Konservatismus*, Berlin.

Tahiroglu, Merve (2020) 'How Turkey's ÖLeaders Dismantled the Rule of Law', 44 *Rule of Law Throughout the World*, 67–96.

Thiery, Peter (2010) 'Autoritarismus und Demokratie in Lateinamerika' in Albrecht, Holger & Frankenberger, Rolf (eds.), *Autoritarismus Reloaded*, Baden-Baden, 295–313.

de la Torre, Carlos (ed.) (2015) *The Promise and Perils of Populism: Global Perspectives*, Lexington.

Vasold, Manfred (2015) *Grippe, Pest und Cholera. Eine Geschichte der Seuchen in Europa*. Stuttgart.

Virchow, Fabian (2016) 'Rechtsextremismus: Begriffe – Forschungsfelder – Kontroversen', in Virchow, Fabian, Langebach, Martin & Häusler, Alexander (eds.), *Handbuch Rechtsextremismus*, Wiesbaden, 6–41.

Waldmann, Peter (2005) *Terrorismus. Provokation der Macht*, München.

Weber, Max (1978) *Economy and Society*, I, Berkeley.

Weiß, Volker (2017) *Die autoritäre Revolte. Die Neue Rechte und der Untergang des Abendlandes*, Stuttgart.

Weiß, Volker (2021) 'Vom elitären Zirkel zur Massenbewegung? Die Neue Rechte in Pandemiezeiten' in Kleffner, Heike & Meisner, Matthias (eds.), *Fehlender Mindestabstand. Die Corona-Krise und die Netzwerke der Demokratiefeinde*, Freiburg, 158–166.

Weigner, Stefan (2021) *Ground Zero. 9/11 und die Geburtsstunde der Gegenwart*, München.

Wodak, Ruth (2021) *Politik mit der Angst: Die schamlose Normalisierung rechtextremer und rechtspopulistischer Diskurse*, Wien/Hamburg.

Yenigun, Halil I. (2021) 'Turkey as a Model of Muslim Authoritarianism' in Sajó, Andras, Uitz, Renáta & Holmes, Stephen (eds.), *Routledge Handbook of Illiberalism*, New York/Abingdon, S. 840–85.

Yongshun, Cai (2015) *State and Agents in China: Disciplining Government Officials*, Stanford CA.

Zakaria, Fareed (1997) 'The Rise of Illiberal Democracy' in *Foreign Affairs*, November/ December, 22–43.

Zakaria, Fareed (2007) *The Future of Freedom. Illiberal Democracy at Home and Abroad*, New York.

Zürn, Michael (2018) 'Autoritärer Populismus vs. offene Gesellschaft – eine neue Konfliktlinie?', Heinrich-Böll-Stiftung, (ed.), Berlin.

Zúquete, José Pedro (2018) *The Identitarians. The Movement Against Globalism and Islam in Europe*, Notre Dame.

PART II

Threats to democracies and authoritarian system competition

2. Authoritarian forms of rule in the twenty-first century[1]

Michael Zürn

1. INTRODUCTION: DEMOCRACY ON THE DEFENSIVE

A look at the data of the currently best measurement of the development of democracy – from the "Varieties of Democracy" project (V-Dem) (Coppedge et al. 2011) – shows that the democratic form of rule has gone on the defensive. No matter which conception of democracy we follow,[2] there is a downward trend in the spread of democracy at the beginning of the new millennium, the extent of which now shows similarities to the 1930s.

The turning point was probably the year 2001. Only three months after 9/11, the Al-Qaeda attack on the Twin Towers in New York's financial district and the Pentagon, John O'Neill of Goldman Sachs published a paper where he coined the term "BRIC" for the four emerging powers: Brazil, Russia, India and China. In retrospect, this coincidence proved to be symbolic. The surveying of democracy at precisely this time points to a break in a development that many saw as teleological. Instead of a long-term and secular trend of political

[1] I would like to thank Johannes Gerschewski, Lisa Scheuch, Alexandros Tokhi and the editors of the volume in particular for helpful comments and advice.

[2] The trend hardly differs, no matter whether we consider the most important indicators for a purely electoral democracy (free and fair elections, universal suffrage, freedom of expression and association), a liberal democracy (electoral democracy as well as (constitutional) legal review of political decisions, separation of powers), a deliberative democracy (electoral democracy as well as public justification of political decisions, in which recourse is made to the common good; acceptance of counter-arguments and extensive consultation of different groups in the decision-making process), an egalitarian democracy (electoral democracy as well as comprehensive rights of freedom, equal access to decision-making bodies (power) and approximately equal distribution of resources), or a participatory democracy (electoral democracy and extensive involvement of civil society actors in decision-making processes; possibility of referendums and consistent implementation of subsidiarity) (cf. Schäfer and Zürn 2021, 30).

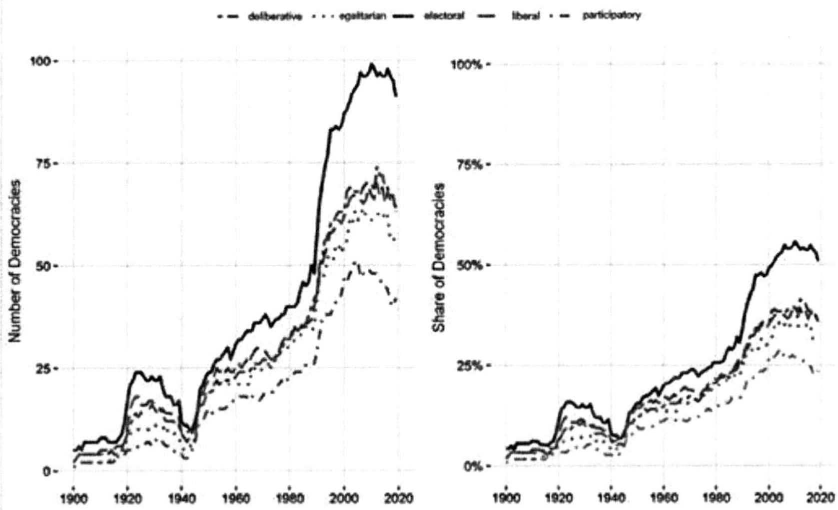

Source: Schäfer and Zürn (2021).

Figure 2.1 Absolute number and proportion of democracies measured by different concepts of democracy

modernization (Inglehart and Welzel 2001; Pinker 2018), the spread of democracy after World War II could also be due to specific historical contextual conditions of the post-war period that no longer exist in the same way today. The democratic form of government would then lose its status as a model without alternatives and could numerically sink again to a significantly lower level. At the very least, however, this development makes it clear why cautionary voices are warning against *backsliding* (Bermeo 2016), *deconsolidation* (Foa and Mounk 2016), or *recession* (Diamond 2015) of democracy.

If democracy and autocracy are understood as the two basic types of political systems of rule, then the decline of democracy automatically conceals an increase in authoritarian temptation (Heitmeyer 2018) and authoritarianism (Frankenberg 2020). However, shifts in the balance of power between the two basic types are mostly viewed one-sidedly from the perspective of democracy. Although there are both (empirical) theories of democracy (Dahl 1991; Lijphart 1999; Schmidt 2019) and theories of autocracy and authoritarianism (Geddes, Wright and Frantz 2018; Svolik 2012), such theories refer, as it were, to the functioning of the respective form of political rule and within the basic type. When it comes to the interaction between the two types of regime and their dynamics, however, an asymmetry becomes apparent. We are familiar with numerous theories of democratization and, more recently, also with theories of how democracies die (Levitsky and Ziblatt 2018; Waldner and Lust 2018). Theories of autocratization, however, are scarce. For the most part, research on authoritarian forms of rule is either about the question of how authoritarian regimes can hold on to power (Gerschewski et al. 2013), about strategies and institutions for securing autocratic rule or about their performance profiles (Kailitz and Köllner 2013). In this respect, the shift in the balance of power between democracy and autocracy is seen as *democratic backsliding*, but hardly as autocratization or a rise of authoritarianism.

In line with the conception of this volume with its focus on the drivers of authoritarianism (Frankenberg and Heitmeyer, this volume), this contribution attempts to take a step towards a theory of autocratization by identifying, within the framework of a typology, two authoritarian forms of rule that have actually gained importance and power in recent decades. The first is *populist authoritarianism*, which is ideologically linked to the upheavals in liberal democracies in the wake of globalization. The second is called *technocratic authoritarianism*, which defines the form of old autocracies that have managed to resist the spread of democracy.

For the purpose of this theoretical sketch, the first section discusses the core of authoritarian systems as distinct from democratic political systems. Four characteristics identified are common to all forms of authoritarian political rule. Against this background, the second section discusses different types of authoritarian rule, preparing the ground for analyzing in the third section why two of these types in particular are proving successful in our times. The chapter concludes with general considerations of a theory of autocratization.

2. CHARACTERISTICS OF AUTHORITARIAN POLITICAL SYSTEMS

A widely used definition from *Lexikon der Politik* (Nohlen 1998) defines authoritarian regimes as "political systems whose basic type differs substantially from democratic and totalitarian forms of rule, according to J.J. Linz (1985), primarily because of three characteristics: (as compared to democracy) by limited pluralism, (as compared to totalitarian regimes) by the absence of a comprehensively formulated ideology and by the lack of both extensive and intensive mobilization" (Ibid., 60).[3] What is striking about this description here

---

[3] Translation by M. Zürn of the German original: "Politische Systeme, deren Grundtyp sich substantiell von demokratischen und totalitären Herrschaftsformen unterscheidet, und zwar J.J. Linz (1985) zufolge v.a. aufgrund von drei Merkmalen: (gegenüber der Demokratie) durch begrenzten Pluralismus, (gegenüber totalitären Regimen) durch das Fehlen einer umfassend formulierten Ideologie sowie durch den Mangel an sowohl extensiver als auch intensiver Mobilisierung" (Nolan 1998, 60).

is that authoritarian forms of rule are defined twice in the negative: authoritarian regimes are neither democratic nor totalitarian.

In contrast, I consider democratic and authoritarian systems as the two basic types of political rule. On the one hand, this only makes sense if anarchy is taken out of the equation with the argument that it aims precisely at the absence of rule. On the other hand, the reduction to two basic types of political rule requires that the diversity and variability of both democratic and authoritarian forms of rule be fanned out. Totalitarianism is then not a third basic form of political rule that, in contrast to authoritarianism, strives to influence all social relations in order to form a "new human being" (Friedrich and Brzezinski 1965; Linz 2000), but rather a specific type of authoritarian form of rule that penetrates particularly strongly into all areas of life (on this also the discussion in Frankenberg/Heitmeyer, in this volume, Chapter 3).

If we reduce the triad of democracy–authoritarianism–totalitarianism to the juxtaposition of democratic and authoritarian forms of rule, then the question arises as to what the opposite of democracy is. The contrast between democracy ("rule of the many") and autocracy ("rule of the one") is common, linguistically clean and focuses strongly on the question of the number of those exercising rule. The distinction between democratic and authoritarian forms of rule is, of course, based on a whole bundle of characteristics. In this respect, authoritarianism could also be used as an alternative term to democracy. In this usage, the term authoritarianism also includes a totalitarian variant (Frankenberg 2020). In the following, I will mostly use the term autocracy when referring to the ideal-typical antithesis to democracy. I use authoritarianism plus an adjective to describe certain types of authoritarian rule.

If one follows this conceptualization and considers democracy and autocracy as the two basic types of political rule, then a negative definition of autocracy as "everything that is not democracy" is not sufficient. Therefore, with the help of recent authoritarianism research,[4] authoritarian political systems should be defined in the positive. This is done using four general characteristics that are common to autocracy, but whose concrete implementation varies depending on the regime type. Only if all four characteristics are fulfilled should one speak of an authoritarian form of rule. In hybrid regimes, at least one or two characteristics are present (also Levitsky and Ziblatt 2018).

In autocracy, first, the political leadership makes a "far-reaching claim to power" in a double sense. On the one hand, it can arbitrarily undermine the autonomy of other sectors of society. The scope of the claim to power varies, however, and can range from all-pervasive totalitarianism to a mild

[4] See, among others, Bank (2010); Frankenberg (2020); Gandhi (2008); Geddes et al.(2018); Kailitz et al. (2013); Svolik (2012).

authoritarianism that generally leaves the autonomy of other sectors of society unmolested. On the other hand, autocracy knows hardly any *checks and balances* and generally has a clear center of power – although this is not always easily identifiable due to the tendency for secrecy (Svolik 2012) – to which all other power holders are hierarchically subordinate. However, the center of power can look very different depending on the type and it can change over time. It can be individualized in the form of a claim for leadership or perceived through a party; it can be largely personalized or highly bureaucratized. Such a center of power may be headed by a monarch, a religious or military leader or a charismatic politician. Thus, for example, one can distinguish between party dictatorships, military dictatorships and personalist dictatorships on the basis of their supporters (Geddes et al. 2018).

Secondly, autocracy claims to have "no alternative." It knows of no free and institutionalized opposition that can legitimately and equally compete for power. Accordingly, opposition groups are either co-opted, obstructed or suppressed. Thus, there may be a pseudo opposition, which may also sit in parliament and have no claim to power. Such groups that are important for safeguarding their function and existence are often co-opted (Gandhi and Przeworski 2006). Opposition groups that neither limit themselves to a pseudo opposition nor allow themselves to be co-opted, on the other hand, are suppressed and not infrequently terrorized.

Thirdly, autocracy is linked to an "anti-pluralist or homogeneous understanding of representation." The rulers represent the people as a whole. This is associated with justifications of rule or legitimation narratives that are mostly community based and anyhow only recognize individual rights to a limited extent. Depending on the variant, traditional, populist, salvation-promising and technocratic legitimation narratives dominate (Gerschewski 2018).

Finally, authoritarian forms of rule are characterized by a "one-sided or pre-democratic relationship between the rulers and those subject to rule." Subordination and willingness to follow are demanded of those who are subject to rule, without the rulers being subject to accountability or the possibility to be replaced. Authoritarianism is thus characterized by an understanding of political authority that is based on the claim of "unconditional" obedience. A possessive understanding of authority prevails, which sees itself as a characteristic of the incumbent and not as an interactive relationship of recognition that is reversible as such.

The distinction between possessive and interactive understandings of authority is accompanied by the premise that political and epistemic authorities can also play a central role in democratic forms of rule. If, following Weber (2013 [1921–1922], 451), authority is understood to mean that certain decisions or interpretations find obedience among an identifiable group of people, then political and epistemic authorities belong to all types of political rule (Zürn 2018). Weber even used authority and rule more or less interchangeably (Simmerl and Zürn 2016). The constitution of authority is therefore the decisive factor in distinguishing democracy from authoritarianism. If it is based on a mutual recognition process in which authority is delegated, as it were, by those affected by decisions and interpretations and, conversely, those exercising authority recognize the delegation as reversible, then political and epistemic authority is compatible with the democratic exercise of rule. Authority – understood as a characteristic of those exercising rule that insists on unconditional obedience – is the form of political and epistemic authority that often accompanies authoritarianism (Frankenberg & Heitmeyer in this volume). Thus, pointedly formulated, one can distinguish between an interactive-democratic and a possessive-authoritarian understanding of authority.[5]

The one-sided understanding of authority in authoritarian systems of rule can be internalized based on mobilization. Obedience as part of a mobilizing ideology characterizes totalitarian authoritarianism in particular. In this extreme case, paradoxically, internalization is "forced." Other forms of authoritarianism are less thorough in this respect. They refrain from mobilization and achieve obedience through repression and arbitrariness.

With regard to autocracy as a generic term, it can be said that these are political forms of rule in which different types of rulers (1) claim to exercise (depending on the type) far-reaching power and limit or prevent opposition, (2) claim to represent the people as a whole along with different legitimation narratives depending on the variant and (3) insist on a one-sided (or possessive) understanding of public authority, the manner of enforcement of which can vary. These features are common to all forms and types of authoritarianism. Different types of authoritarian rule result from the fact that the concrete design of these four basic characteristics varies depending on the type.

3. TYPES OF AUTHORITARIAN RULE

In the basic understanding of autocracy outlined above, totalitarianism represents a specific type characterized by the combination of the features "all-encompassing and unrestricted claim to power of the ruling elite," "com-

[5] In this respect, the meaning of the adjective "authoritarian" appears to be different from that of the noun authority. This is already inherent in the use of the terms in early critical theory. Adorno et al. (1950) see the *authoritarian personality* as the humus of fascism. Max Horkheimer (1987 [1936], 24) on the other hand, understands authority as *affirmed dependency* which, to cite Georg Simmel (2009, 131) is "a freedom of those subject to the authority [...]" and "not based on coercion and pure resignation alone".

plete repression of the opposition," "promising legitimacy with the aim of mass mobilization" and "enforcing internalized willingness to comply." However, I will not consider totalitarian authoritarianism in any further detail below, as it no longer plays a significant role. Even in the case of North Korea, it no longer seems to be fully valid. However, other types of authoritarian forms of rule show that elements of totalitarianism or totalitarian authoritarianism are regaining in importance.

In general, I will not unfold all conceivable forms of rule in a comprehensive typology. The combinatorics of the four general characteristics of authoritarianism result in 16 (2^4) different types even with purely dichotomous characteristics. In the following, I consider only five types in a rough sketch as examples. Neo-patrimonial regimes (Schlumberger 2008), rentier states (Beck 2007) or the new despotism (Keane 2020) will not be discussed, but they can be subsumed under the typology. In any case, the discussion of five currently relevant types is not intended to imply that other types or subtypes do not currently exist. The consideration of the five types serves as an illustration and intermediate step, in order to then take a closer look at two currently expanding types in the section on the rise of new authoritarian forms of rule. While the existence of other authoritarian regimes primarily acts as brakes on the spread of democracy, I will analyze these two types as drivers of the current *democratic backsliding*.

Even if the classic military dictatorship has lost its significance with the parliamentary elections in Thailand in 2019, it is far from extinct. In sub-Saharan Africa, it seems to be experiencing a *revival* in countries such as Mali, Sudan, Guinea-Bissau and Burkina Faso. Egypt also experienced a quasi-military coup a few years ago and, on 1 February this year, the junta led by General Min Aung Hlaing seized power in Myanmar. Military regimes try to take hold with brutal force. For the sake of conceptual symmetry, such military dictatorships will be referred to here as "military authoritarianism." Historical examples of military authoritarianism in Europe are Spain (1939—1975) and Greece (1967—1974); in Latin America, Argentina (1976—1983) and Chile under Pinochet (1973—1990); in Asia, South Korea (1961—1987) and Indonesia (1965—1998). For a long time, military authoritarianism was, along with socialist states, the type with the highest number of cases (Svolik 2019, 21).

The claim to power of military authoritarianism is borne either by a single person at the top (e.g. Pinochet) or by a clique of generals (junta). It is, therefore, highly individualized. Visible opposition is not permitted. There is partial co-optation of other, primarily economic, elites, but public opposition is suppressed and generally portrayed as a threat to order and security. The dominant legitimation narrative is originally conservative and static. The junta is presented as the guarantor of order and stability. Ideological mobilization of the population is largely dispensed with — it is about order, not a particular order.

Instead of internal mobilization, such regimes like to use the international power constellation to generate external support for internal stabilization. This worked particularly well in the days of the East-West antagonism, when the two superpowers could be played off against each other.

There is some evidence to suggest that military authoritarianism will no longer play a particularly important role. However, other forms of authoritarianism seem to converge with military authoritarianism over time. Belarus under Alexander Lukashenko is a case in point. The example makes it clear that military authoritarianism now often stands for a last-ditch attempt to retain power when the authoritarian system is already in decline. However, military authoritarianism no longer seems to pose an original threat to democracy. It only happens when democracy has long since been lost. Democracies are no longer subject to the armor of the military (Levitsky and Ziblatt 2018).

Stalin's Soviet Union was classified in classical doctrine together with National Socialism as a totalitarian system (Friedrich and Brzezinski 1965). Most socialist countries turned away from Stalinism in the 1950s. As a result, a form of rule emerged that can be described as "socialist authoritarianism" and is often referred to in the literature under the label of *single-party system* (e.g. Geddes 2003). Starting from the Soviet sphere of influence in Eastern Europe and Central Asia, socialist authoritarianism was able to establish itself in individual countries on all continents. The declared bearers of power were the communist parties as the embodiment of the working class. It was not uncommon for these parties to be headed by an all-dominant general secretary who adorned himself with elements of the personalized exercise of power. The complete personalization of rule, however, took place almost exclusively in the special case of the revolutionary leader, who was able to remain at the top for a long time. In the course of power changes within socialist authoritarianism, a bureaucratization of the power apparatus usually took place.

The socialist power apparatus was able to operate largely unrestricted and dominate society. It came across as a profoundly controlling and repressive. Opposition was only allowed pro forma in sham elections. Socialist socialization would create a new person and thus make opposition obsolete anyway. Only on the way to a just and socialist vision of society did some impositions arise, but these were legitimized by the target promise of socialist perfection. Today, socialist authoritarianism has largely died out. Despite some internal reforms, Cuba can still be classified as real socialist. North Korea persists, but still exhibits clear characteristics of totalitarian authoritarianism.

Parallel to the decline of socialist authoritarianism, a new type has established itself: "theocratic authoritarianism." It has gained a foothold primarily in North Africa and in the southwestern parts of Asia. It aspires to be closely associated with radical forms of Islamism. The starting point of its modern form was the Iranian revolution in 1979, but it did not stop there, as has been recently emphatically observed in Afghanistan or by the developments in Egypt and Somalia. In addition, there are more traditional theocracies, such as Saudi Arabia and Morocco, which are always subject to internal pressure to radicalize.

The concrete form of theocratic authoritarianism depends not least on the underlying religion. In general, however, it can be said that power is exercised by a small group of religious leaders. On the top level, this comes close to a personalized form of rule. The way in which the opposition is dealt with varies. In the concrete manifestations of the Islamic State, radical repression takes place, while in Iran, for example, elections are held with a partly open outcome. There, the opposition is intimidated and hemmed in, but not completely eliminated. The legitimation narrative is religious and aims at comprehensive mobilization. In forcing mobilization, theocratic authoritarianism shows a kinship with totalitarian authoritarianism.

"Technocratic authoritarianism" is found primarily in Asia – with China, Vietnam and, to some extent, Singapore being the best-known representatives. Technocratic authoritarianism is based on a strong state and a functional bureaucracy that originates from either a socialist or a colonial past (Singapore was a crown colony) and has been modernized in the course of turning away from this past. At its core, leadership in this type of authoritarianism is depersonalized, with the respective party leader occupying a prominent position (especially Lee Kuan You's family in Singapore). However, the strong position of the person at the top is embedded in the orderly process of transfer of power and it only partially translates into a charismatic narrative of legitimacy.

The central narrative of legitimacy is, rather, based on the performance and (primarily economic) successes of the regime. Technocratic authoritarianism grants the economy a considerable degree of subsystemic autonomy. It has also scored points in recent years with enormous growth rates, outstanding successes in combating poverty and significant increases in the country's status. This orientation towards performance and consumption goes hand in hand with a far-reaching renunciation of ideological mobilization. China's development over time is particularly impressive in this respect. The totalitarian Cultural Revolution under Mao Zedong gave way to a model of society characterized in particular by a private retreat into materialism. The second pillar of rule consolidation consists of repression. Technocratic authoritarianism does not shy away from using politically repressive measures. This includes the suppression of opposition and the use of modern surveillance technologies that target society as a whole.

Authoritarian-populist parties have achieved considerable political success in many electoral political systems in recent decades (Norris & Inglehart 2018; Manow 2018; Schäfer & Zürn 2021). Wherever such parties come to power, they strive for "populist authoritarianism" as a form of rule (Frankenberg &

Heitmeyer, in this volume). Such a regime is supported by a party that is generally led by an unchallenged leader and can therefore be classified as being strongly personalized. This leader has a comprehensive claim to power and dismantles the institutionalized separation of powers. In particular, courts and the entire judicial system are an early field of activity for the establishment of populist authoritarianism.

Authoritarian populist parties come to power through elections. John Keane (2020) describes the logic of gaining power by a "despotic regime" as follows: "Seduction, not repression, is their defining quality. In this sense, the despotisms of our time are state-of-the-art forms of tutelary power, a new type of media-saturated political rule that manages to do something many observers thought impossible: they dominate their country by winning their calculated support and affection by means of top-down, people-friendly techniques of government" (Ibid. 2020, 17). Elections and the will of the majority remain the central basis of legitimacy of populist authoritarianism even after the seizure of power. The will of the majority usually receives an exclusive nationalist interpretation. Elections imply that a certain institutionalization of opposition must be maintained even after the transformation of the regime. In populist authoritarianism, however, elections are no longer free. Through control of the media, manipulation of electoral rules and all kinds of impositions on opposition parties, those in power gain a sufficient degree of control over election results. Repression partly replaces seduction in this process. Opposition is thus limited by a mixture of repression and containment, but it persists.

The more those in power control the outcome of elections, the less important the mobilizing ideology becomes. Ideological mobilization of the population is fundamental to populist authoritarianism as a means of gaining power. Populist ideology is held together by a Manaean juxtaposition of a decent but excluded national population and a draining elite that tends to be global (Mudde 2004; Müller 2016). However, the anti-elite appeal loses significance with each new election with an authoritarian-populist party in power. It dissipates over time.

The excerpt from a comprehensive typology of authoritarianism outlined here results from specific combinations of the manifestations of its general characteristics. The five types envisaged certainly do not cover the entire diversity of types of authoritarianism. However, these five types are of particular importance for an analysis and discussion of authoritarianism at the beginning of the twenty-first century.

Table 2.1 *Types of authoritarianism*

	Bearer of the claim to power	Role of the opposition	Legitimacy narrative	Mobilizing ideology
Military authoritarianism	Small group of military (personalized)	Co-optation or repression	Order (traditional)	Very weak
Socialist authoritarianism	Party (crystal-clear hierarchy, but depersonalized beyond the revolutionary leaders)	Repression	Necessities of the means to a socialist society	Very strong (but decreasing importance over time)
Theocratic authoritarianism	Religious caste (crystal-clear hierarchy, but depersonalized)	Enclosure or repression	Religious	Very strong
Technocratic authoritarianism	Party or state elite (mostly depersonalized)	Repression	Performance and prosperity	Weak
Populist authoritarianism	Party with a personalized leader	Co-optation and enclosure and repression	Nationalism; people's will	Strong (decreasing over time)

Source: Authors.

4. GLOBALIZATION AS A BACKGROUND CONDITION FOR THE NEW AUTHORITARIANISM

If the balance of power between democracy and autocracy is to be understood, it is not enough to analyze only the "absolute" strength and weakness of the democratic form of rule. It is also necessary to look at the dynamics of autocratization that arise independently of the development of democracy. Conversely, the spread or decline of democracy is not only a function of the absolute quality of democracies, but it may also have to do with the state of authoritarian systems of rule. It was perhaps no coincidence, after all, that the perception of an unstoppable spread of democracy dominated precisely in the early 1990s, when authoritarian systems of rule had particularly low mobilization energies. Thus, in addition to the question of how authoritarian regimes can hold on to power, the conditions of success of autocratization must also be considered. In this perspective, different types of authoritarian rule systems are less a passive stock of tradition from prehistoric times whose rate of degradation is determined by the power of new practices, but more an alternative form of rule that itself actively influences the balance of power between democracy and autocracy.

In the remainder of this chapter, I would like to adopt a perspective of this kind and identify two authoritarian forms of rule from the above-outlined typology of authoritarianism that have actually gained in importance and power over the last three decades. The first is "populist authoritarianism," which ideologically docks on to the social upheavals in liberal democracies in the course of globalization and thus enjoys considerable electoral success. The second is a type that can be called "technocratic authoritarianism," which has proved to be, as it were, an evolutionary adaptation of the old (socialist) authoritarianism, able to resist the spread of democracy and build up its own appeal using a globalized economy.

Globalization functions as an important framework for these two forms of authoritarianism. The surge of globalization that began in the 1980s permanently changed the chances of success and consolidation for authoritarianism. The KOF Globalisation Index captures this dynamic. It is based on numerous indicators ranging from tourism and trade to the proliferation of international non-governmental organizations. It captures the legally codified (de jure) and actual (de facto) extent of cross-border interactions. In the sum of all indicators, between 1970 and 2017, the de facto index has increased from 40 to 59 and the de jure value even from 36 to 64 (on a scale of 0 to 100) (Gygli et al. 2019). While the increase in the sub-areas of social and political globalization accelerated from 1990 onwards, the de facto values of economic globalization, in particular, indicate a significant increase from the end of the 1970s.

In the short term, globalization seems to have contributed to the collapse of socialist authoritarianism and to talk of the historic success of democracy (e.g. Fukuyama 1989). Globalization externally increased the economic pressure on socialist authoritarianism and internally strengthened civil society opposition. In addition to the collapse of Soviet-style socialist authoritarianism, military authoritarianism, whose security narrative lost its legitimizing power during the dissolution of the East–West antagonism, also crumbled during this period. In the 1990s and early 2000s, due to the (temporary) disappearance of system competition, it was no longer able to generate external support through skillful tactics between the blocs. In this respect, the short-term effect of globalization on authoritarianism can be classified as negative. This is evident not least in the dramatic increase in democracies between the 1990s and the early 2000s.

The verdict is somewhat different when looking at the medium term. If one compares the situation of authoritarianism today with that at the end of the 1970s, the observation of considerable land losses remains, but at the same time a tectonic shift in the relative strength of different types becomes apparent. While socialist and military authoritarianism have become dramatically

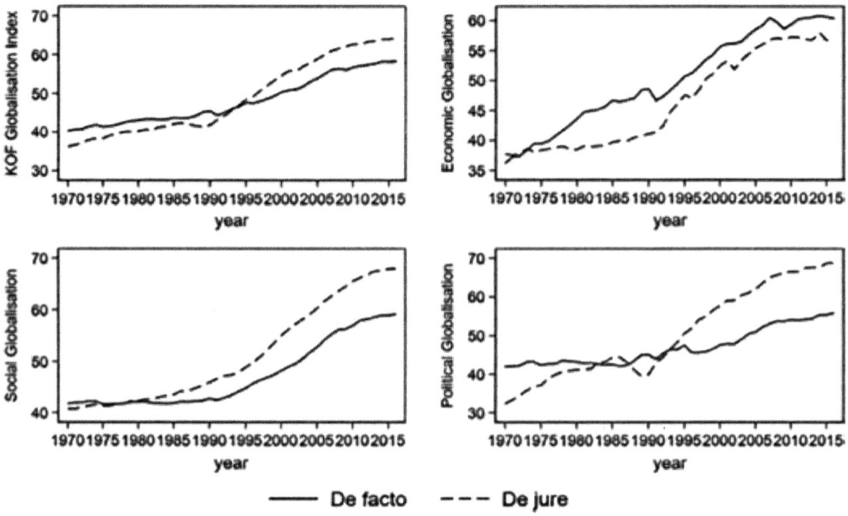

Source: Gygli et al. (2019).

Figure 2.2 Globalization since the 1970s

less popular, theocratic and especially populist and technocratic authoritarianism seem to have become the most important variants. Populist and technocratic authoritarianism are the drivers of current autocratization. What both forms of rule have in common is that they are the consequence of a regular change of government, that is, they represent a kind of executive takeover of power. Milan Svolik (2019) sums it up as follows: "After the 1990s, [...], the relative frequency of executive takeovers surged" (Ibid. 21).

The fact that technocratic and populist authoritarianism have managed to gain in importance in the course of ongoing globalization can first be explained by looking at the elephant curve of income growth in world society (Milanovic 2016). The distribution of global economic growth points to the material conditions that have strengthened the two main forms of new authoritarianism. On the one hand, they illustrate the enormous success story of technocratic authoritarianism. The authoritarian ruling elites in countries like China and Vietnam cannot easily be dismissed as selfish despots. Their policies have a recognizable "common good" component and can point to considerable progress, especially in the fight against poverty. Enormous welfare gains can be observed across the board in these countries. The winner of globalization is the new global middle class, many of whom live in countries of technocratic authoritarianism. These regimes show that social progress is possible without those in power being subject to democratic control.

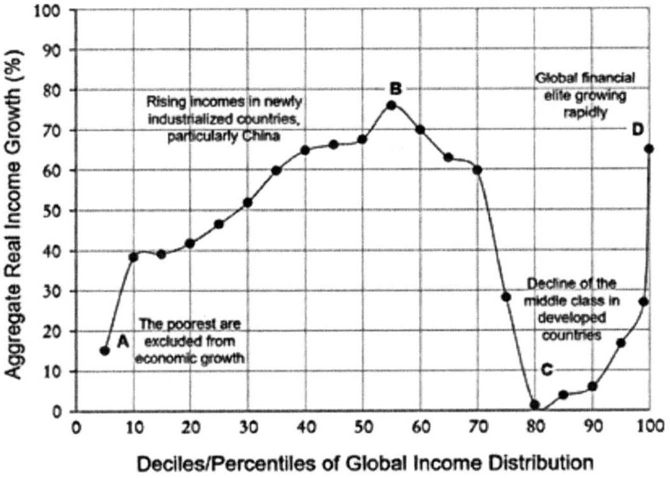

Note: The percentage income increases between 1988 and 2008 are shown for different income groups. The poorest groups are on the far left, the richest on the far right.
Source: Schäfer & Zürn (2021, 7–9) according to Milanović (2016).

Figure 2.3 *The elephant curve of income growth*

On the other hand, the elephant curve points to the growing inequality in the rich democracies of the West. The material basis for supporting democracy is softening. In particular, the income stagnation of the lower middle classes in the rich democracies combined with the obscene income gains of the global elite serve the authoritarian populist critique of liberal democracy. Authoritarian populists reinforce an anti-pluralist, anti-internationalist and decisionist interpretation of the will of the people, which, if they seize power, they often refer to as "illiberal democracy."

In the medium term, economic globalization has thus called into question a lesson of history that was long considered unambiguous: a materially rich life, innovative and convenient products and an efficient political system – all of which only exist in Western democracies. Due to the income development described in the elephant curve, this promise has lost credibility and given rise to two new types of authoritarianism.

5. TECHNOCRATIC AUTHORITARIANISM AS A SUCCESSFUL ADAPTATION

A few months before the Monday demonstrations in Leipzig, hundreds of thousands of people protested for weeks on Tiananmen Square in central Beijing for an accelerated opening and democratization of the political regime in China. The 1989 protests were organized by students, intellectuals and trade union activists. The Chinese military violently suppressed these protests on 3 and 4 June 1989.

The Tiananmen movement was inspired by the reform efforts in the Soviet Union and Eastern Europe, as well as by the reforms initiated by Deng Xiaoping and especially Zhao Ziyang at home. The movement became known worldwide not least through the state visit of Mikhail Gorbachev and the international press that traveled with him. While largely peaceful reform succeeded in the Soviet Union and Eastern Europe, this attempt failed in China. After the protests were suppressed, the "Reforms and Opening-up" program was initially suspended. It was not until 1992 that the new rulers continued the course of economic liberalization, after Deng Xiaoping vehemently called for it during his historic tour of the South.

The result was an authoritarian form of rule that vigorously promoted economic liberalization and opening and assigned the economy a high degree of subsystemic autonomy. Similarly, science – temporarily even parts of the social sciences – has been largely liberated from political dictates and opened up internationally. At the same time, the political system remained highly authoritarian. The dominance of the party was maintained, as was the repression of the opposition. The open repression was complemented by a comprehensive social surveillance system using new technologies. Although the Chinese Communist Party still occupies a central position in the power structure, it has gutted itself ideologically. Its policies are determined less by Marxist or Maoist guidelines than by a dense network of experts who focus on economic growth, political problem-solving ability and the use of long-term strategies. The justification of technocratic authoritarianism is also based on these goals: alleviating poverty, economic growth and prosperity and the restoration of China as a venerable civilization and world power.

Technocratic authoritarianism can be seen as a reaction to the general crisis of autocratism in the 1980s and 1990s, which proved to be evolutionarily successful. The growth rates of China and Vietnam after the systemic adaptation are legendary. From 1992 to 2018, China's annual GDP growth was always at least 7 percent, with peaks above 14 percent. In each of those years, growth was higher than in the United States. Chinese companies are now fighting for world market leadership in various sectors including artificial intelligence, semiconductor technology, space travel and climate protection technology (Sommavilla and Pramer 2021). This economic dynamism is associated with the rise of an urban middle class and the eradication of absolute poverty. According to the national definition of poverty, more than 770 million Chinese were still living below this poverty line in 1990 – about two-thirds of inhabitants. By 2012, when President Xi took office, that number had already fallen to around 100 million and by 2019 it had dropped to 5.5 million (Post 2021).[6] As a result, a domestic market that is central to global economic development and underpins China's global political ambitions has emerged. This ambition is strengthened by a remarkable problem-solving capacity of the political system. The successes in combating COVID-19 are remarkable and much has been achieved in environmental policy in just a few years, even if there is still much more to be done.

This all seems to translate into a level of political support in the country that three decades ago was considered out of the question for authoritarian forms of rule. If the World Value Survey (Wave 7) (Haerpfer et al. 2021) data is to be believed, satisfaction with the functioning of the political system in the country is at 84 percent of the population (rather satisfied to fully satisfied), significantly higher than in the United States or Germany. While these extremely positive readings are not taken at face value, they still reflect a fair amount of popular support for the regime.[7] This is also reflected in the almost palpable pride in their country's successes, which is evident in conversations with Chinese academics – even when clear criticism of the government's human rights policy is voiced.

The effect of technocratic authoritarianism on the retreat of democracy shown in Figure 2.1 is still small. Both China and Vietnam are in the bottom 20 percent on the "liberal democracy" index with extremely poor scores; however, when comparing the values between 2008 and 2018, China has only slightly deteriorated and Vietnam has improved slightly. The two countries therefore do not directly contribute to the decline in average democratic quality on a global scale. Nevertheless, the importance of this type of authoritarianism should not be underestimated in the medium term. This is partly due to a deliberate strategy of diffusing the model through Chinese credit and infrastructure policies, especially (but not only) in Africa. The state-owned Export-Import Bank grants multi-year, low-interest loans that are secured by the borrower's

---

6 The figures are based on data from Deutsche Welthungerhilfe e.V.

7 The question "How satisfied are you with how the political system is functioning in your country these days?" can be answered in the WVS with scale values from 1 ("not satisfied at all") to 10 ("completely satisfied"). Adding the scale values 6–10 yields a value of 32.54% for the United States, 68.21% for Germany and 84.03% for China.

natural resources. In the early 2010s, for example, Angola borrowed $14.5 billion, Ghana $13 billion, Nigeria $8.4 billion, the Democratic Republic of Congo $6.5 billion and Ethiopia $3 billion for infrastructure projects carried out by Chinese construction companies (Grassi 2013). This trend has since accelerated. Added to this are direct investments. In the area of investments too, China has now clearly overtaken the West in Africa. This active diffusion policy makes it likely that technocratic authoritarianism will become a proliferating type of authoritarianism in the medium term, as well as significant in terms of power politics. In essence, it represents an evolutionarily successful type of authoritarianism that emerged during the great crisis of authoritarianism in the 1980s and 1990s. In light of the characteristics discussed here, it is doubtful whether the more recent autocratic hardenings under President Xi already represent a departure from technocratic authoritarianism. However, it is clear that technocratic authoritarianism can also integrate totalitarian elements – particularly in the case of digital surveillance policy.

6. POPULIST AUTHORITARIANISM AND THE WEAKNESS OF GLOBALIZED DEMOCRACIES

The rise of authoritarian populist parties in the consolidated democracies of Western Europe began in the second half of the 1980s when Jean-Marie Le Pen in France and Jörg Haider in Austria achieved their first electoral successes. In 2018, authoritarian populist parties received an average of 22.2 percent of the vote in 33 European countries (TAB 2019). Some of these parties have even made it into government, either as heads of government by taking over from an established party (mostly in first-past-the-post systems, as in the United States) or as part of a coalition government (mostly in proportional representation systems, as in Italy). Outside the group of consolidated democracies in Western Europe and North America, they have been even more successful. In some large countries such as India, Brazil or Turkey, as well as in some Eastern European countries, they are in power but still hold elections in which opposition parties participate. When authoritarian-populist parties come to power, they aim to abolish the regime that made them possible. They want a new political system: populist authoritarianism.

Early cases of contemporary populist authoritarianism are associated with the names Hugo Chávez, Vladimir Putin and Viktor Orbán. All three originally gained government power as a result of their success in largely open and reasonably fair elections. After Hugo Chávez was released from prison following an unsuccessful coup, he founded the Fifth Republic Movement party and was elected president of Venezuela in 1998 with 56.2 percent of the vote. He was re-elected with an absolute majority in 2000, 2006 and 2011. After his death, the previous vice-president Nicolás Maduro came to power (albeit by unconstitutional means). After Boris Yeltsin's resignation, Vladimir Putin temporarily took over his office in Russia; three months later, on 26 March 2000, he won the then open-ended presidential election in the first round with 53 percent of the votes. He has since been re-elected with overwhelming majorities in increasingly less fair elections, as has Dmitry Medvedev, his deputy between 2008 and 2011. Viktor Orbán headed a liberal-conservative coalition government from 1998 to 2002 which promoted Hungary's integration with the West. He served as opposition leader from 2002 to 2010 and was re-elected to office in 2010 as leader of the now strictly authoritarian-populist Fidesz party with an absolute majority.[8]

After taking power, Chávez, Putin and Orbán pursued a system transformation – from an electoral democracy, if you will, to an electoral autocracy in the form of populist authoritarianism. The steps towards this consisted of increasing restrictions on the freedom of the press, the systematic erosion of the independence of the judiciary and the undermining of multi-party democracy through an increasing stranglehold on and suppression of opposition parties. In the meantime, it is no longer possible to speak of free elections in any of these countries. Accordingly, legitimacy also changed. The mobilization of the ordinary population against the established elite lost importance over time. The new elite still presents itself as the embodiment of the people's will, but it relies more on the leader, emphasizes stability and order more strongly and relies more on foreign policy confrontations to play the nationalism card.

The tangible successes of populist authoritarianism are limited. Economic successes are mainly the result of external resource inflows, as it were, due to the sale of raw materials (Russia and Venezuela) or the provision of particularly attractive investment opportunities (Hungary). Russia, for example, had above-average growth rates in the first Putin years, but since 2008, they have been below the United States. Hungary was slightly below the Czech Republic and Poland for a long time. Venezuela's GDP fluctuated strongly due to oil prices. Chavez's expansionary spending policies have since led to Venezuela's disastrous economic situation. The general problem-solving ability of such regimes can also be classified, at best, as medium to low. This has been demonstrated in the fight against COVID-19, as well as in climate policy and the fight against poverty. Accordingly, satisfaction with the political system in these countries is limited. According to the European Value Survey (EVS 2020), 44 percent of the population in Russia are satisfied or fully satisfied (values 6–10 on the scale), while in Hungary this value is only 39 percent. This means they are far from China's values, but also still far away from Germany's. However, both countries are slightly above the United States. Authoritarian

---

8 Erdoğan has also made a similar transition in office in Turkey.

populist parties achieve electoral success in democracies with globalized economies by relying on a non-mediatized form of majority representation and the "cult of immediacy" (Frankenberg 2020, 258–80) and by turning nationalistically against "liberal cosmopolitan elites" (Schäfer and Zürn 2021, 59–88).

Authoritarian populism emphasizes nationalism because, first, it excludes the legitimate interests of other countries by strictly following the topos *our nation first*. Second, it is clear from the outset who belongs to one's own people. The anti-pluralism of authoritarian populism arises from the idea of a homogeneous people with uniform political goals. Those who claim to know the will of the people and to represent it cannot tolerate the existence of other legitimate opinions. That is why authoritarian populists label political opponents as traitors and corrupt power cliques. Third, this specific understanding of politics results in the rejection of established processes of decision making. Fourth, it is primarily about recognizing the will of the people through the political leadership and then implementing it without further ado. Fifth, that is why authoritarian populism is also close to a relativistic truth regime. Speech acts, speeches and campaigns can be completely freed from their reference to the truth claims and instead be used exclusively as weapons in political debates.

When authoritarian populists come to power, they first tamper with the liberal safeguards of democracy, such as a free press and separation of powers, and harass the opposition. The step from a liberal to an electoral democracy is then quick and easy. If the authoritarian populists succeed in staying in power, then with each new election, it becomes less likely that they will be voted out – not because of an increase in the popularity of the authoritarian populist rulers, but because of the manipulation of political competition. With that, the step towards populist authoritarianism is completed. The distinction often used in comparative politics among liberal democracy, electoral democracy and electoral autocracy points in a similar direction, but overlooks the fact that these types can also be regular stages in the authoritarian-populist seizure and consolidation of power. Kim Lane Scheppele (2018) speaks in this context of a "script of autocratic legalists to show precisely how they consolidate power under the cover of law" (p. 549). In the course of this dynamic, the opposition's electoral chances decrease dramatically, as does the anti-elitist mobilization of the population; in contrast, political repression, election manipulations and increasingly outward-looking nationalism increase.

It is this dynamic built into populist authoritarianism that accounts for a significant part of the democratic retreat depicted in Figure 2.1. In each of the best-known cases of authoritarian populist seizure of power, there has been a significant decline in the quality of democracy.

Authoritarian populist parties can come to power in liberal democracies (such as the United States) and in electoral democracies (such as Turkey).

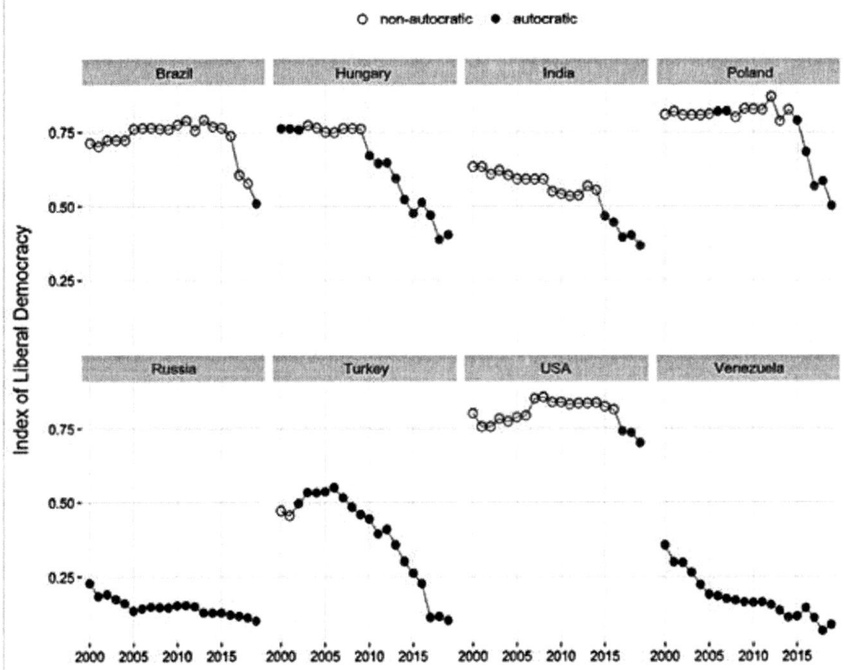

Sources: Schäfer & Zürn (2021, 172); data: V-Dem dataset, version 10 (Coppedge 2020). Quality of democracy under authoritarian-populist rulers. The list includes the eight countries in which particularly well-known authoritarian-populist governments were in office for a longer period of time. Unfilled circles indicate non-authoritarian, filled circles authoritarian heads of government in the period between 2000 and 2019. For Poland, only those years in which the PiS provided the prime minister and president are marked as "authoritarian". This was the case from 2005 to 2007 and has been the case since 2015.

Figure 2.4 *Absolute number and proportion of democracies measured by different concepts of democracy*

The example of Hungary clearly shows that it is possible to go all the way from liberal democracy to electoral authoritarianism; however, the path is not necessarily preordained. The example of the United States shows that the train can be stopped, especially at the first election after an authoritarian-populist seizure of power. However, this does not mean that the retreat of democracy has been permanently averted, as the return of the PiS in Poland shows. The result is a type of authoritarianism whose roots lie in problems of democracy in a globalized world and which, if established, can develop over time and at different stages.

7. CONCLUSION: TOWARDS A THEORY OF AUTOCRATIZATION

The balance of power between democracy and autocracy cannot be understood unilaterally by analyzing the expansion and regression of democracy. Authoritarian forms of rule do not only develop as a negative foil to the waves of democratization; its inherent dynamics must also be considered. Conversely, the decline of democracy may also have something to do with the state of authoritarian forms of rule. Therefore, a theory of the dynamics of autocracy is needed.

This contribution is intended as a corresponding sketch. It starts from the general features of authoritarian forms of rule, according to which authoritarian power-holders lay claim to (depending on the type) far-reaching and likely unlimited powers, oppress or suppress opposition, believe they represent the people as a whole together with different but community-heavy legitimation narratives and insist on a possessive understanding of public authority. On this basis, different types of autocracy can be distinguished. Two of them, technocratic and populist authoritarianism, appear particularly significant in the age of globalization. Technocratic authoritarianism emerged in the 1980s and early 1990s as a variant that proved resilient in the face of the crisis of authoritarian forms of rule at the time and subsequently used the economic opportunities of globalization to secure and strengthen its own existence. Populist authoritarianism, on the other hand, profited from the political weaknesses of globalized democracies. This led to the rise of authoritarian populist parties, which – in the event of a government takeover – can result in a dynamic process to undermine democracy and building populist authoritarianism. The momentum seems to be halted only if these new rulers suffer an electoral defeat before they can fully manipulate the electoral system.

The theory of autocratization in the age of globalization is only complete when it includes the conditions of existence and the conditions of decline in addition to the ones of ascent. Then it would have a similar status and degree of maturity as has now been achieved by empirical theories of democracy and theories of democratization. Only the interplay of these two theories would allow for making reasonably reliable and meaningful statements about the balance of power between democracy and authoritarianism.

REFERENCES

Adorno, Theodor W., Else Frenkel-Brunswik, Daniel J. Levinson & R. Nevitt Sanford (1950) *The Authoritarian Personality*. New York: Harper & Brothers.

Bank andré (2010) 'Die neue Autoritarismusforschung: Ansätze, Erkenntnisse und konzeptionelle Fallstricke', in Holger Albrecht and Rolf Frankenberger (eds.),

Autoritarismus Reloaded: Neuere Ansätze und Erkenntnisse der Autokratieforschung. Baden-Baden: Nomos Verlagsgesellschaft mbH & Co. KG, 19–37.

Beck, Martin (2007) 'Der Rentierstaats-Ansatz und das Problem abweichender Fälle'. *ZIB Zeitschrift für Internationale Beziehungen* 14(1): 43–70.

Bermeo, Nancy. 2016. 'On Democratic Backsliding'. *Journal of Democracy* 27(1): 5–19.

Coppedge, Michael (2011) 'Conceptualizing and Measuring Democracy: A New Approach'. *Perspectives on Politics* 9(2): 247–67.

Coppedge, Michael, Gerring, John, Altman, David, Bernhard, Michael, Fish, Steven, Hicken, Allen, Kroenig, Matthew, Lindberg, Staffan I., McMann, Kelly, Paxton, Pamela, Semetko, Holli A., Skaaning, Svend-Erik, Staton, Jeffrey & Teorellet, Jan (2020) 'V-Dem Dataset 2020'. https://www.v-dem.net/dsarchive.html (May 26, 2023).

Dahl, Robert A. (1991) *Democracy and Its Critics.* New Haven: Yale University Press.

Diamond, Larry (2015) 'Facing Up to the Democratic Recession'. *Journal of Democracy* 26(1): 141–55.

EVS (2020) 'European Values Study 2017: Integrated Dataset (EVS 2017)'. https://search.gesis.org/research_data/ZA7500?doi=10.4232/1.13560 (May 26, 2023).

Foa, Roberto Stefan & Yascha Mounk (2016) 'The Danger of Deconsolidation: The Democratic Disconnect'. *Journal of Democracy* 27(3): 5–17.

Frankenberg, Günter (2020) *Autoritarismus: Verfassungstheoretische Perspektiven.* Erste Auflage. Berlin: Suhrkamp.

Friedrich, Carl J. & Zbigniew Brzezinski (1965) *Totalitarian Dictatorship and Autocracy.* Cambridge, MA: Harvard University Press.

Fukuyama, Francis (1989) 'The End of History?' *The National Interest* (16): 3–18.

Gandhi, Jennifer (2008). *Political Institutions under Dictatorship.* Cambridge, UK: Cambridge University Press.

Gandhi, Jennifer & Adam Przeworski (2006) 'Cooperation, Cooptation and Rebellion under Dictatorships'. *Economics and Politics* 18(1): 1–26.

Geddes, Barbara (2003) *Paradigms and Sand Castles: Theory Building and Research Design in Comparative Politics.* Ann Arbor, MI: University of Michigan Press.

Geddes, Barbara, Joseph Wright & Frantz, Erica (2018) *How Dictatorships Work: Power, Personalization and Collapse.* Cambridge, UK: Cambridge University Press.

Gerschewski, Johannes (2013) 'The Three Pillars of Stability: Legitimation, Repression and Co-Optation in Autocratic Regimes'. *Democratization* 20(1): 13–38.

Gerschewski, Johannes (2013) 'Warum überleben Diktaturen?' in Steffen Kailitz and Patrick Köllner (eds.), *Autokratien Im Vergleich*, Nomos, 111–36.

Gerschewski, Johannes (2018) 'Legitimacy in Autocracies: Oxymoron or Essential Feature?' *Perspectives on Politics* 16(3): 652–65.

Grassi, Sergio (2013) 'China Und Der Wachstumskontinent Afrika'. *Neue Gesellschaft. Frankfurter Heft* 6: 10–14.

Gygli, Savina, Florian Haelg, Niklas Potrafke & Jan-Egbert Sturm (2019) 'The KOF Globalisation Index – Revisited'. *The Review of International Organizations* 14(3): 543–74.

Haerpfer, Christian et al. (2021) 'World Values Survey Wave 7 (2017–2020) Cross-National Data-Set'. http://www.worldvaluessurvey.org/WVSDocumentationWV7.jsp (May 26, 2023).

Heitmeyer, Wilhelm (2018) *Autoritäre Versuchungen. Signaturen Der Bedrohung I.* Originalausgabe, 3. Auflage. Berlin: Suhrkamp.

Horkheimer, Max (1987) 'Theoretische Entwürfe Über Autorität Und Familie. Allgemeiner Teil' in Max Horkheimer, Erich Fromm and Herbert Marcuse (eds.), *Studien Über Autorität Und Familie. Forschungsberichte Aus dem Institut für Sozialforschung*, Schriften des Instituts für Sozialforschung, Lüneburg: Librairie Félix Alcan, 3–76.

Inglehart, Ronald & Christian Welzel (2001) *Modernization, Cultural Change and Democracy: The Human Development Sequence*. Cambridge, UK: Cambridge University Press.

Kailitz, Steffen and Patrick Köllner (2013) 'Zur Autokratieforschung Der Gegenwart: Klassifikatorische Vorschläge, Theoretische Ansätze Und Analytische Dimensionen'. in Steffen Kailitz and Köllner, Patrick (eds.), *Autokratien Im Vergleich*, Baden-Baden: Nomos, 14–39. http://www.nomos-elibrary.de/index.php?doi=10.5771/9783845244655-14 (May 26, 2023).

Keane, John (2020) *The New Despotism*. Cambridge, MA: Harvard University Press.

Levitsky, Steven & Daniel Ziblatt (2018) *Wie Demokratien sterben: und was wir dagegen tun können*. München: Deutsche Verlags-Anstalt.

Lijphart, Arend (1999) *Patterns of Democracy: Fovernment Forms and Performance in Thirty-Six Countries*. New Haven: Yale University Press.

Linz, Juan J (2000) *Totalitarian and Authoritarian Regimes*. Boulder, Colorado: Lynne Rienner Publishers.

Manow, Philip (2018) *Die Politische Ökonomie Des Populismus*. Originalausgabe, Erste Auflage, Sonderdruck. Berlin: Suhrkamp.

Milanovic, Branko (2016) *Global Inequality: A New Approach for the Age of Globalization*. Cambridge, MA: Harvard University Press.

Mudde, Cas (2004) 'The Populist Zeitgeist'. *Government and Opposition* 39(4): 541–63.

Müller, Jan-Werner (2016) *What Is Populism?* Philadelphia: University of Pennsylvania Press.

Nohlen, Dieter (1998) *Lexikon der Politik*. München: C.H.Beck.

Norris, Pippa and Inglehart, Ronald (2018) *Cultural Backlash: Trump, Brexit and the Rise of Authoritarian-Populism*. New York, NY: Cambridge University Press.

Pinker, Steven (2018) *Aufklärung jetzt: für Vernunft, Wissenschaft, Humanismus und Fortschritt: eine Verteidigung*. Frankfurt am Main: S. Fischer.

Post, Ulrich (2021) 'China hat die Armut ausgerottet. Wirklich?' *Welthungerhilfe*. https:// www .welthungerhilfe .de/ welternaehrung/ rubriken/ entwicklungspolitik-agenda-2030/china-erklaert-das-ende-der-armut (May 26, 2023).

Schäfer, Armin & Zürn, Michael (2021) *Die Demokratische Regression: Die Politischen Ursachen Des Autoritären Populismus*. Berlin: Suhrkamp.

Scheppele, Kim L. (2018) 'Autocratic Legalism'. *University of Chicago Law Review* 85(2): 545–83.

Schlumberger, Oliver (2008) *Autoritarismus in Der Arabischen Welt: Ursachen, Trends Und Internationale Demokratieförderung*. Baden-Baden: Nomos.

Schmidt, Manfred G. (2019) *Demokratietheorien: Eine Einführung*. Wiesbaden, Germany: Springer VS.

Simmel, Georg (2009) *Sociology: Inquiries into the Construction of Social Forms*. Leiden/Boston: Brill.

Simmel, Georg & Michael Zürn (2016) 'Internationale Autorität'. *Zeitschrift für Internationale Beziehungen* 23(1): 38–70.

Sommavilla, Fabian & Pramer, Philip (2021) 'Endlich Weltmeister: Sieben Bereiche, die China bis 2030 dominiert'. *Der Standard.* https://www.derstandard.de/story/2000128092713/endlich-weltmeister-sieben-bereiche-die-china-bis-2030-dominiert (May 26, 2023).

Svolik, Milan W. (2012) *The Politics of Authoritarian Rule.* Cambridge University Press.

Svolik, Milan W (2019) 'Polarization versus Democracy'. *Journal of Democracy* 30: 20–32.

TAB (2019) 'The Data – Timbro Authoritarian Populism Index 2019'. *populismindex.* https://populismindex.com/data/ (January 17, 2022).

Waldner, David & Lust Ellen (2018) 'Unwelcome Change: Coming to Terms with Democratic Backsliding'. 21: 93–113.

Weber, Max (2013) 'Wirtschaft Und Gesellschaft' in (eds.) Knut Borchardt, Hanke, Edith and Schluchter, Wolfgang, *Wirtschaft Und Gesellschaft. Soziologie. Unvollendet. 1919–1920*, Max Weber-Gesamtausgabe. Tübingen: Mohr Siebeck.

3. Autocratization as a global process? Authoritarianism and democracy in an international context

Lars Rensmann

1. INTRODUCTION: A NEW GLOBAL WAVE OF AUTOCRATIZATION?

During the last decade, several studies in comparative political science research have noted a development: a far-reaching global "renaissance of authoritarianism" (Frantz 2018). This resurgence of authoritarian political tendencies, ideas, and systems on a global scale seemed hardly conceivable just 20 years ago. Its scope does not just point to the consolidation and, in part, aggressive expansion of autocratic regimes. It also points to a transnational legitimacy crisis of liberal democracy (Przeworski 2020) as a model of government and as a social form. Some have coined this a "democratic recession" (Diamond 2015) or a "global retreat" (Kurlantzick 2013) of constitutional democracy and "Western liberalism" (Luce 2017). Today a thin majority of states still meet at least a minimal definition of democracy. By 2020, however, 68 percent of the world's population lived in autocracies, electoral autocracies or closed authoritarian systems – a dramatic rise of 20 percent from 2010, when only 48 percent of citizens on the planet lived under autocratic rule.

Democracies today find themselves under pressure from authoritarian challenges in several ways. First, democracies are confronted with a rising number of authoritarian political systems and the repressive consolidation of existing ones, which in part take a more self-confident and aggressive position in the international system – think of China or Russia. Autocratic regimes hereby increasingly intervene in democracies' internal affairs through technology, economics, digital communication and – as in the case of the Russian war of aggression in Ukraine – by military means and violent intervention. Second, in recent years we see authoritarian erosions in unstable hybrid regimes. This includes democracies formerly classified as defective democracies. After the turn of the millennium, states which were once considered bearers of hope for further democratization (such as Turkey, Egypt and Tunisia after the "Arab Spring" or, more recently, Zimbabwe and Myanmar) have regressed to (electoral) autocracies (Lührmann & Lindberg 2019). Such accelerated autocratic transition has led to the loss of (potential or actual) allies for democracies at the interstate level.

Third, we can observe a significant erosion of the societal foundations and democratic integration within constitutional democracies, that is: democracies guaranteeing civil and political rights, the separation and dispersion of power, intermediary bodies, free and fair elections, democratic procedures, and a free public sphere – which are the only forms of democracy which can ultimately be considered democracies at all and are sustainable as such (Urbinati 2015). In several national cases, indicators point to the internal erosion of democracy's institutional safeguards and the very conditions of systemic survival, and thus to the danger that democratically legitimated counter-poles against autocracies may collapse. It is not just relatively young and not fully consolidated democracies and former transition societies such as Brazil, Hungary and Poland which are now profoundly threatened by authoritarian challenges within democratic political systems. Long-established and consolidated constitutional democracies – such as France, Italy or the USA, the oldest continuously existing democracy in the world – are challenged as well, namely by new, successful authoritarian (populist) actors, resurgent authoritarianism in the public realm, or even democratic backsliding towards illiberalism. An example is Donald Trump's ascendency and presidency (2017–2021) in the US, when civil institutions were threatened and the executive branch attacked free media as "enemies of the people."

Against this backdrop, the thesis of a "third wave of autocratization" (Lührmann & Lindberg 2019; Boese, Lührmann & Lindberg 2021; Tommi 2021) seems valid,[1] even though after-effects of the third wave of democratization are also still partly discernible (Mechkova, Lührmann & Lindberg 2017).[2] The diagnosis of a third global autocratization wave is based in empirical measurements of democracy indicators (in particular the *Varieties of Democracy Project/V-Dem*, largely analogous to the *Freedom House Index*). These indicators refer to empirical collected data on human rights or civil

---

1 The periodization of democratization waves and counter-waves was originally proposed by Samuel Huntington (1991).

2 It was this third wave of democratization that led Francis Fukuyama at the beginning of the Cold War to make the daring, by now long empirically outdated prognosis that a democratic "end of history" was on its way. He understood this "end of history" as a telos and as the "end point of the ideological evolution of humanity and the universalisation of Western liberal democracy as the final form of human government" (Fukuyama 1991: 1).

rights violations, attacks on the separation of power (including an independent judiciary), threats to free media, or an uneven electoral playing field. Over the last 15 years, in many countries democratic rules and principles as well as individual and collective rights and liberties have been suspended. The diagnosis of a third wave of autocratization especially points to a largely gradual, creeping and seemingly contagious de-democratization process. It affects more and more nation-states in which democratic modes of political integration have been recently replaced by pseudo-democratic electoral mimicry or the significant curtailing of democratic rights. These trends often unfold alongside an increasingly authoritarian allocation, consolidation and concentration of power.

This chapter focuses on the forms and causes of the third wave of autocratization. The chapter will analyze both key internal factors and regime effects of this wave, on the one hand, and on the other hand examine how this wave has changed and partly restructured the relationship between authoritarianism and democracy in the global horizon. I will first offer a comparative look at regime types and subtypes of authoritarian systems, their general characteristics, and the dominant contemporary strategies by which they rule and exercise their power. Second, I will analyze key features and transformations of the globally most powerful authoritarian states today, China and Russia. These real types of consolidated authoritarian regimes combine the internal expansion of their repressive system with external expansionist-imperialist efforts, aiming in particular at a new, neo-imperial system competition with Western liberal democracies. Third, I briefly examine increasingly autocratic systems that emerged from constitutional democracies, namely post-Communist Hungary and post-colonial India. The latter was long considered the most populous democracy in the world. Both are still mostly considered so-called hybrid systems but are now characterized by, and deeply embedded in, processes of large-scale autocratization, which is nurtured by both systemic factors and authoritarian actors. In a fourth step, I will analyze current trends of authoritarian rule and their contemporary enabling conditions in a more comprehensive global perspective. Fifth, authoritarian challenges within liberal democracies are discussed, against the background of theoretical and empirical democracy research and research on *crises of democracy*. The focus is here on the US and Germany, which serve as case studies. Authoritarian-populist actors in government and in parliaments demonstrate how anti-democratic positions have gained legitimacy and, in part, power and leverage within democratic societies. These developments are partly enabled by long-simmering, politically fostered processes of what I call the *precarization of democracy*, or democratic disintegration (Heitmeyer 2018). My contribution will conclude by theoretically conceiving key conditions or factors which may help explain the current third wave of autocratization.

2. THE STABILITY OF AUTOCRACIES: TYPES AND SUBTYPES OF AUTHORITARIAN RULE IN THE GLOBAL CONTEXT TODAY

Conceptualizing a political form of rule and establishing a typology of regimes is, first of all, a way of establishing a framework of study. However, this may also enable a better understanding of a regime's structure and functioning (Lauth 2010: 95). A typological understanding of authoritarian political systems, based on their identifiable core characteristics and empirical findings, may furthermore help to develop hypotheses and draw preliminary conclusions about an expected political behavior of a regime as well as possible *policy outcomes*. Typologies can help shed light on how politics work in democratic and authoritarian contexts. Typologies can also help illuminate the political decision-making in specific subtypes, indicate which legitimacy resources can be mobilized by a regime type and which ruling strategies are employed, or what political outcomes are likely; that is, to what extent a regime tends to use direct repression, co-optation or ideological indoctrination, for example; how susceptible a regime is to civil war; or how likely it is to react to economic sanctions. Finally, typologies also provide indicators with regard to the stability of a political system, the likelihood of a regime's intent to pursue warlike external aggression, the likelihood of internal civil wars, and offer insights into chances for democratization (Frantz 2018: 67 f.). This is particularly helpful in view of the considerable variation among autocratic regimes (ibid: 11). Some of these political systems do not correspond to the common clichés of an authoritarian state. Authoritarian regimes may include, among others, electoral autocracies, military dictatorships, one-party dictatorships, religious-Islamist or otherwise ideologically legitimized dictatorships, and personalist dictatorships based on more or less unrestricted one-person rule.

A regime is defined by the form of its legitimization and the structure of power relations between ruling elites and populations. In other words, a regime is defined by the relationship between those in power and those subjected to power (Merkel 1999).[3] Regime types can be distinguished by identifying a set of basic formal and informal rules that determine who selects the political leaders and how political decisions are made. This includes identifying the group(s) from which leaders can be selected and who determines or influ-

[3] As a *root concept* or basic concept, the regime type is to be distinguished from the 'system of government' in that the latter concept is aimed at "specific institutional patterns within a regime type" and thus at *subtypes* such as presidential or parliamentary forms of democratic rule "which fully fulfil both regime characteristics of democracy" (Lauth 2010: 96).

ences the regime's policy-making process and decisions (Geddes, Wright & Frantz, 2014). Different forms of political rule correspond to different forms of legitimation (Lauth 2010: 96), while all regime types – not just democracies – need some form of legitimacy to stay in power at all. Accordingly, *autocratic regimes* can be understood as political regimes that exercise their rule, policies, and strategies of legitimation undemocratically (Frantz 2018). They operate in the absence of structurally secured, regularized democratic processes, rules, and regulations enabling the general public's representation and participation in the election and selection of political leadership, the process of decision-making, and policy outcomes.[4]

On the one hand, autocratic systems can thus basically be conceptualized as the opposite or counter-pole of a democratic system in which, according to Giovanni Sartori's classical definition of democracy, "no one can choose himself", no one can usurp the power to govern all by himself, and therefore no one can allocate unconditional and unlimited power (Sartori 1992: 210). On the other hand, genealogically speaking, only the emergence of new types of totalitarian regimes in the twentieth century ignited the evolution of more systematic political science research on authoritarian regime types. And in the context of totalitarianism, the conceptual polarity between autocratic and democratic rule appears problematic. For Hannah Arendt (1955), for instance, totalitarian rule represented a completely new type of government: a dictatorship that executes an all-encompassing totalitarian ideology, in the form of superhuman laws, by means of total terror and permanent mass mobilization. Such movement-mobilization is primarily directed against entire groups that are declared to be "objective enemies" – that is: "enemies" to be annihilated as groups independent from any individual convictions, beliefs, or behavior. In so doing, totalitarian government is to be fundamentally distinguished from

---

[4] Less minimally formulated and defined, the authoritarian regime type is overarchingly characterized by a limitation or absence of practically realised civil and/or political liberties and the rule of law, by the suppression of opposition, and by a structural lack of guaranteed and transparent democratic procedures for free and fair elections and participation in political decision-making processes, the absence or structural lack of guaranteed separation of powers (especially an independent judiciary), and real democratic control over political institutions. The latter are largely or fully dominated by authoritarian leaderships that determine policies, decisions, and the selection of government personnel. By contrast, democratic forms of rule and democratic inclusion, which is lacking in autocratic regimes, empirically presuppose not just democratic procedures for representation such as free and fair elections and institutionalized mechanisms of democratic control but also constitutionally protected civil and political freedoms and fundamental rights, freedom of assembly, a free public sphere, and separations of powers, including most importantly an independent judiciary – without any of these conditions a democracy is arguably not sustainable.

autocracies that exercise rule "lawlessly". Despite numerous differences in content, conceptualization and argument, structural approaches to the study of totalitarianism, in particular advanced by Carl Friedrich and Zbigniew Brzezinski (1969), followed Arendt in emphasizing the special role of a total ideology and the comprehensive penetration of society in all its spheres – and thus also stressing the distinctiveness of the totalitarian type.[5]

According to Juan Linz's typology (2000) authoritarian regimes in turn represent an independent form of rule, "which is to be located between totalitarian and democratic regimes" (Lauth 2010: 104). Linz distinguishes between regime types based on three categories and indicators: the degree of pluralism; the degree of state-directed political mobilization; and the character of a government's legitimacy. Accordingly, for Linz authoritarian regimes are political systems which only display limited, unaccountable pluralism; which have no elaborate guiding ideology (unlike totalitarian regimes) and which lack extensive or intensive political mobilization; and in which a leader or sometimes a small group exercises power within formally barely defined, but, in fact, quite predictable, limits (Linz 2000).[6]

Hans-Joachim Lauth's typology (2010: 105), adapted from Linz, differentiates between totalitarian, authoritarian and democratic regime types also based on three decisive dimensions: political freedom, political equality, and political and legal control, whereby all three dimensions partially exist in the case of authoritarian rule systems. They do not exist at all in the case of totalitarian regimes. And they are basically fulfilled in democratic systems. Lauth concedes, however, that there can be difficulties and "grey areas" when we classify political systems, "since they lie on the continuum between the two poles" – totalitarianism and democracy – and can thus be located in border zones between the two regime types (Lauth 2010: 105).

Against the background of such a basic system typology, comparative government studies have developed subtypes. Current research on authoritarianism and authoritarian systems distinguishes between *continuum-based typologies* and *categorical typologies* for classifying subtypes of contemporary authoritarian systems (Ezrow & Frantz 2011). Continuum-based typologies locate systems in a totalitarianism-authoritarianism-democracy-continuum or – more commonly – a democratic-autocratic scale. Following standardized criteria for measurement, e.g. independence of the judiciary and legal practice,

[5] However, a considerable number of comparative regime researchers classify both "totalitarian" and "authoritarian" political systems as non-democratic, autocratic regimes (e.g. Merkel 1999; Linz 2000; Lauth 2010).

[6] Lauth (2010: 105) problematizes the criterion of mobilization, since it is questionable to what extent totalitarian regimes are necessarily characterized by constant mass mobilization.

degree of freedom and fairness in elections, degree of free publicity or media freedom, civil rights norms and practices etc (Lauth 2010), such typologies make use of various instruments and systematic data sets (Freedom House, V-Dem, Polity data set). They enable empirical classifications using a broad but fine-grained set of indicators capturing even small changes from one year to another.[7] In this lens, a large number of *hybrid systems* has emerged, which includes so-called "deficient" or "defective" democracies. They are, however, partly indistinguishable from electoral autocracies[8] and "competitive authoritarianism" (Levitsky & Way 2002).[9] Continuum-based typologies are more sensitive to changes within systems – for example, with regard to autocratization processes in states such as Turkey or Brazil, where democratic rights were successively abolished by elected authoritarian leaders. However, they often do not recognize the structural patterns constituting an autocratic regime and enabling its stability, and thus tend to fail to account for the robustness of authoritarian (and democratic) types and their origins.

Categorical empirical typologies avoid the questionable assumption that authoritarianism is a linear concept (Frantz 2018: 71). In contrast, they refer to essential regime features, such as their ruling strategies and strategies of legitimation (Wintrobe 1998). They emphasize their *makeup*, i.e. their organizational form, and the composition of the ruling elite and its patterns of power allocation. Categorical typologies aim to shed light on systemic structures. In so doing, these typologies also illuminate structural differences among (authoritarian) subtypes, pointing to heterogenous systemic patterns and divergent strategies of rule. Rather than registering minor changes in sub-areas, they highlight what structurally holds the system together at its core and potentially shed light on a system's stability.

According to Erica Frantz (2018), four authoritarian subtypes are relevant in the global system today, reflecting common scholarly categorical typologies

---

[7] Systematic global comparison is made considerably more difficult by the fact that hardly any reliable and transparent demographic data, opinion polls, or social or economic data are available from and for autocratic political systems (Frantz 2018: 15-16).

[8] Juan Linz (2005), however, criticizes the subtyping of "democracies with adjectives", i.e. types such as the 'deficient' or 'defective' democracy. According to Linz, these are conceptual euphemisms. If a democracy is 'defective', it is actually no longer a democracy at all. Probably the most radical example of a euphemistic use of an adjective before the concept of democracy is the term 'managed democracy', originally introduced by Indonesian President Sukarno and later used propagandistically by Putin.

[9] Not to be forgotten are structures of deficient, ineffective or failing statehood in which authoritarianism or forms of unmediated violence prevail. These include civil war zones, weak states or terrorist-dominated zones (for example temporarily ISIS, and arguably Afghanistan under Taliban rule).

(Wahman, Teorell & Hadenius 2013; Geddes, Wright & Frantz 2014). In a *military dictatorship*, the military rules as an institution. The military takes political decisions and selects the government. The supporting elite groups usually also come from the military. In organizational terms, military dictatorships are guided by a clear, hierarchical decision-making structure which corresponds to that of the military. Military dictatorships prove to be particularly susceptible to coups. They are the most short-lived regime types. However, their empirical significance – formerly very strong in Africa and Latin America, including the highly populated countries of Argentina and Brazil – has declined significantly in recent decades (Frantz 2018: 72 f.).

In a *dominant party dictatorship*, a single party dominates the policies and the selection of decision-makers. The ruler or leader usually also leads the party. In numerous empirical manifestations of this regime type, elections are held and presidential or parliamentary democratic systems are imitated (Frantz 2018: 75). We can thus speak of democratic mimicry. Other parties exist and are even represented in parliament. This is a feature, to be sure, which is also typical for several other authoritarian subtypes that are prevalent today (such as personalist dictatorships, see below). However, the other parties have no significant influence on the decision-making processes. This type of dictatorship tends to be less repressive overall than other authoritarian systems (Davenport 2007), even though exceptions confirm this rule. The type generally leads to fewer internal and external military conflicts. Typical historical examples are Angola or Mexico's PRI authoritarianism (*Partido Revolucionario Institucional*) from 1915–2000, lasting almost a century. For a long time, post-Maoist Communist China could also be categorized this way. The Chinese regime, however, is increasingly marked by a high degree of repression and a weakened elite and is currently transitioning from a dominant party dictatorship into personalist dictatorship. If we apply the framework on which categorical typologies are based, the one-party dictatorship model was the dominant authoritarian regime type worldwide. This dominance is now being challenged by personalist dictatorships.

In a *personalist dictatorship*, one leader alone (at least for the most part) exercises and controls governing power. The leader controls the system and the state, allocating power centrally to one individual. With the help of the state apparatus, the leader organizes control over society and makes key political decisions. The personalist system depends on the personal preferences of the leader. It can be adjusted structurally and ideologically in the service of the leader, and while the leader stays in power. Personalist dictatorships are often accompanied by weak institutions. A supporting party may exist, but it does not exercise independent institutional power (examples include, on the one hand, the *Baath Party* under Bashar al-Assad's personalist dictatorship in Syria and, on the other hand, *United Russia* in Russia under Putin). Similar to dominant party dictatorships, here democratic mimicry, which only thinly conceals authoritarian rule, is employed to legitimize the authoritarian system. The most powerful personalist dictatorship of the present – Russia under Putin – can be placed here alongside numerous cases among economically weak states of the so-called “Third World”. Personalist dictatorships also include several political systems that until a few years ago were still considered democratic, even if “deficiently” so (e.g. Nicaragua under Daniel Ortega, and Turkey under Recep Tayyip Erdoğan). Many others (e.g. Hungary under Orbán, the Philippines under Rodrigo Duterte and afterwards) are moving in this direction. The typological categorization of an authoritarian regime type as a personalist dictatorship (PD) allows for particular predictions about the expected political behavior and the stability of the system. For example, among authoritarian regimes, PDs appear most willing to enter into military conflicts with other states (Weeks 2002). The lack of accountability and liability leads to more risk-prone behavior. PDs tend to be more willing to wage wars because they surround themselves with “yes men” and receive “bad intelligence” (Reiter & Stam 2003). Overall, PDs are less interested in cooperative international behavior and multilateral agreements (Mattes & Rodriguez 2014).

Dynastic monarchies hardly exist anymore outside the Middle East (although the North Korean system, for example, has dynastic features), whereas the subtype of *authoritarian theocracy*, which is often neglected in current typologies, remains highly relevant – mostly as Islamist dictatorships. This type is constitutively characterized by a system of religious-clerical rule, which is essentially theologically legitimized and aims at the total enforcement of politically framed religious laws (*Sharia*). The system features a dominant religious ideology, which constitutes the system's main strategy of legitimation. This type tends to be characterized by a high degree of open repression and violence. There are, to be sure, elections in Iran, but these are completely unfree (in addition to the almost total absence of media and press freedom, similar to the dictatorships of North Korea and Eritrea; see Reporters without Borders 2022). The “Islamic Republic of Iran” could therefore be conceived as an authoritarian theocracy and the prototype of an Islamist dictatorship. Some scholars also view Iran as a variant of a “totalitarian” dictatorship (Wahdat-Hagh 2003). They point to particularly high intensity of repression and state-sanctioned violence exercised against actual and imagined regime opponents. This type is also represented by the Taliban in Afghanistan.

Typological classifications can provide relevant indicators for grasping the nature, structure, goals and modes of operation of authoritarian systems, and they may help illuminate empirical patterns of political behavior. However, they also clearly face analytical and empirical limits. For instance, currently several autocracies – in particular Russia and China, which have teamed up – display global power aspirations. In contrast to previous periods, they now self-confidently aim for a "new system competition" and conflict with democracies. This change requires explanatory accounts for which typologies offer little, although we do learn from the lab of history that personalist dictatorships are more likely to engage in aggressive military posturing and war. We will now turn to a brief sketch of four current real types – i.e. typical representatives – of authoritarian rule which actively promote today's global autocratization process: China, Russia, India, and Hungary. In so doing, the section draws on, but also proceeds beyond, the framework of continuum-based and categorical typologies.

3. EXPANSIONIST AUTOCRACIES: CHINA AND RUSSIA IN THE 21ST CENTURY

3.1 The Expansion and Radicalization of an Authoritarian Social Model: The Chinese Dictatorship as a Global Actor

China has long been the most politically significant and largest "consolidated authoritarian regime" in the world. In line with the long-term global trend of authoritarian regimes to engage in *constitutional-democratic mimicry*, China's economically and militarily powerful regime has in recent years increasingly labeled itself a "democracy," or even the "better democracy" in comparison to Western-style democratic-pluralistic systems. To be sure, the Communist constitution of the People's Republic already stipulated that China is a "socialist democracy". But, especially in recent years, an Orwellian use and re-evaluation of the concept of democracy can be observed. The authoritarian state proclaims itself to be a model for the rest of the world. The repressive, technologically enhanced state apparatus, which exercises brute force, is hereby described as the embodiment of "true democracy". This proclamation functions, on the one hand, as a legitimization strategy to "cover up totalitarian tendencies and adorn them with the term democracy" (Wu Qiang, quoted from Eyssel 2021). On the other hand, such proclamation is part of a global ideological battle cry, backed by great economic power, to further expand China's global sphere of influence while suggesting that the Chinese system offers a superior model of political order in the world.

The regime has reclaimed "democracy" and has become globally more aggressive while it simultaneously turned more repressive under Xi Jinping, who has been the General Secretary of the Communist Party of China since 2012 as well as Chairman of the Central Military Commission and State President of the People's Republic since 2013. Xi has transformed China's regime in a Mao-like fashion. The strong personality cult around Xi – a leader cult long discredited by the Chinese Communist Party after Mao – and interlinked concentrations of power, has led China from a one-party dictatorship increasingly into a system that can now be classified as a personalist dictatorship, as it largely was under Mao. The regime largely subordinates the party to Xi's decision-making power. Indeed, it hardly is coincidental that aggressive claims about being a "better democracy" accompany the period since Xi assumed power. His path to a one-person-dictatorship has been supported by a new systematic expansion of the repressive apparatus in the last ten years, exercised even against opponents within the ruling elite of China's Communist Party. In the meantime, freedom of expression largely lost its last vestiges in the digital space and beyond. Using technologically supported mechanisms for near-total surveillance of communication, China became one of the least-free countries in the world. Reporters Without Borders (2022) now ranks China 175th out of 180 countries in terms of press freedom. Hence, China demonstrates that there is potential for accelerated autocratization even in long-consolidated, authoritarian regimes.

The expansion of surveillance and the repression apparatus under Xi's leadership has been enabled by a continuously repressive dictatorial system that has existed since the People's Republic was founded. The system has been responsible for numerous mass crimes with millions of victims, especially under the rule of Mao Zedong. However, there has been a fluctuating level of repression since the end of Mao's rule, from which the Chinese Communist Party (CCP) distanced itself in significant part (especially in relation to the murderous "Cultural Revolution" from 1966 until Mao's death in 1976), and after the Tian'anmen Square massacre in 1989. The massive new wave of repression under Xi is backed by new technology aimed at total surveillance and repressive conformism. "State security" is hereby equated with the protection of the CCP (Hoffman 2022: 79). This has recently included a variety of social experiments, including systematic digital surveillance via facial recognition ("face scan") in public spaces. These scans are used to impose negative sanctions for social behavior. The negative sanctions (and positive ones for "good", conformist behavior in support of the CCP) are based on a points system ("social credit system"). The scans are intended to reinforce repressive social norms and cement support of the CCP and its ideology, especially in "smart cities" (Yang 2019). In so doing, the regime also uses the legacies of an authoritarian-collectivist political culture that is the hallmark of China's political modernity. Shaped by a violent twentieth century and continuously oppressive regimes, China has no social experience with democracy.

The Chinese regime uses new technological strategies for the purpose of social domination and political oppression. China is arguably the global leader of a *new digital authoritarianism*. These digital means serve both China's goal to (i) expand power across the world and (ii) consolidate Xi's power to influence and control public opinion domestically. In many ways, this strategy has already come to fruition. As an economic and digital superpower, the regime manages to export digital technology around the world, including popular software like TikTok, the leading source of information for young generational cohorts around the globe, while Chinese companies that produce such technology are legally and systemically bound to China's government, i.e. completely subjected to the rules of Xi's dictatorship. Moreover, China almost succeeded in taking over critical digital infrastructure (such as the 5G network) in Germany under Angela Merkel's chancellorship. As an authoritarian world power, China has installed new channels to disseminate authoritarian propaganda globally. The regime also participates in cyber wars, in many cases using new media, while media are extremely restricted within China. Xi's regime has also been undermining free speech far beyond national borders. New studies show to what extent emerging technologies are utilized by China's goal to bend the world to its authoritarianism (Hoffman 2022). The regime displays its power to spread regime propaganda in key institutions in liberal democracies – media and universities – which are designed, according to Hannah Arendt, to protect factual truth. Since 2004, so-called Confucius Institutes – propagating the dictatorship's ideology – have flourished globally with Chinese funding, offering lucrative cooperation agreements with Western universities and content-influenced chair foundations (Wojcik 2021). Moreover, the Chinese regime, which is the economic winner of neoliberal globalization, uses its enormous economic influence worldwide, especially through neocolonial relations and investments in Africa, but also in leading liberal democracies (including the USA and Europe and for a long time Australia).

Three *ideological dimensions* are relevant for the analysis of China's expansionist authoritarian dynamics and its active contribution to global democratic disintegration. First, the regime effectively mobilizes an aggressive, in particular anti-Western Chinese *nationalism* using propaganda employed domestically, where it is omnipresent, as well as internationally. Such nationalism seems to find broader resonance in Chinese society, and it nurtures the suppression and violent persecution of minorities such as the Uyghurs. The regime's nationalism also overshadows reinvigorated elements of Communist ideological dogma. "Communism" as an ideology is, to a large extent, only an empty shell that takes a back seat to nationalism (and the cult of personality in relation to Xi). Second, this nationalism nurtures and legitimizes China's new military expansionism in the region as well as the regime's global leadership claims. At the Party Congress in 2017, Xi announced the goal of having "the world's strongest army" (quoted from Büchenbacher 2021). China's annexation of Hong Kong after the violent suppression of the democracy movement there has been only one step towards an expansionist agenda, which is tied to both nationalism and imperial ambitions. Third, there is the socio-psychological appeal of authoritarianism and conformism in China's political culture, which needs to be explored further: the historical and politico-cultural roots of the ideological longing in parts of society for an authoritarian "strong leadership".

The critical political and societal analysis of the regime's use of authoritarian-nationalist ideology appears to be of particular importance if we are to understand why the Chinese regime currently risks the source of its current power – neoliberal economic globalization – by threatening to invade Taiwan and by building a close alliance with Putin's war-mongering, yet increasingly unstable and, in the long run, possibly failing regime in Russia. Understanding the specific relationship between ideology as a driver of the regime and elements of rational power calculations may be critical for grasping the full extent – and limits – of China's authoritarian dynamic and reach. Only by comprehensively analyzing this relationship we may come to understand why China under Xi may be willing to possibly jeopardize its leading world market position in numerous sectors (Büchenbacher 2021) and attached global political weight by considering a war of aggression against the independent island of Taiwan; or if there are sufficient rational forces left, in view of Russia's disastrous war in Ukraine, that make the Xi regime abstain from war, the great destabilizer of nation-states, societies, and political regimes.

3.2 The Putin Regime's Personalist Dictatorship: Authoritarian Rule, Imperialist Nationalism and Disinformation in Russia

The world's second most important consolidated authoritarian regime, Russia under Putin, has been a personalist dictatorship since the 2000s, notwithstanding regular unfree elections and democratic mimicry. As indicated, personalist dictatorships make military aggression more likely than most other types of autocracy. The former also more often tend to show disinterest in international treaties and obligations. In Russia, the mimicry of democracy and the rule of law at home have been steadily rolled back during the more than two decades of Putin's rule. Free media, and press freedom in general, have been gradually dismantled until there was virtually nothing left (Heinemann-Grüder 2017). After 20 years of increasing repression, the start date of the war of aggression against Ukraine in 2022 also marked the end of the last remnants of freedom of the press and freedom of expression in Russia – the end point of a long-term process that always included the targeted persecution and murder of dissidents and declared "enemies", both in Russia and on international soil (e.g. in European democracies like the UK and Germany); a practice that is also designed to stifle future opposition (Shevtsova 2015; Heinemann-Grüder 2017).

In the analysis of the Putin regime's authoritarian and destructive potential, the dictatorships' radical right-wing ideology deserves special attention. For years, the regime has politically mobilized ultra-nationalist, authoritarian and imperialist propaganda as a key element of its legitimation strategy. Indeed, in *The Road to Unfreedom* (2018) Timothy Snyder reconstructs how an aggressively nationalist and imperialist ideology has become the cornerstone of the regime over the last decade. Snyder shows that a Great Russian-"Eurasian" ideology, linked to radical right-wing and fascist theories, forms the very core of Putinism today. The main sources are fascist thinkers of the Russian counter-revolution, in particular the writings of philosopher Ivan Ilyin[10] and contemporary fascist and racist radical right ideologues such as Alexander Dugin, who declare the West, liberalism, and democracy to be hereditary enemies of the Eurasian space led by Russia (Snyder 2018; Shekhovtsov 2018; Binswanger 2022). Putinism's ideological foundations point to the political imaginary of a great, imperial Russia, unified under the rule of Putin as Russia's great, strong leader, and molded together by extreme Russian nationalism. The latter weaves together nostalgic fantasies of Russian superiority and greatness; conspiracy-mythical antisemitism that is charged with orthodox-Russian Christian symbolism; homophobia and misogynist contempt for women; and militarism. Together they compose a radical right-wing ideological narrative and system. This fascist ideology is peculiarly flanked, and thinly rationalized, by a rhetoric of anti-Nazism, as this constitutes a deep-seated political-cultural remnant from Soviet times after the victory in World War II, the "Great Patriotic War". Western "hyper-liberalism" is hereby contrasted with "traditional Russian values," and this binary construction is translated into a friend–foe logic that identifies Putin with the Russian nation defensively yet self-confidently and assertively facing "the Russophobic West" and Russia's enemies. This ideological amalgam, which has evolved over the years, has translated into a widespread, grassroots "foreign policy of the everyday" (Gaufman 2022). However, such ideology is fostered by official propaganda which seeks to create and solidify the cult of an authoritarian leader and to constantly reproduce an everyday nationalist-imperialist, yet also nihilist cultural climate. Its affinity to violent action pushes for ongoing conquests. This culture, which deserves further analysis, originates in the Kremlin. But it benefits from an authoritarian Russian political culture lacking an enduring experience with democracy. Despite the regime's high level of repression, nationalism, imperialism, and authoritarianism also continuously emerge "from below."

Beyond the systematic suppression of opposition that is typical of autocracies, it has been a particular signature of the Putin regime since its early days to distribute targeted disinformation domestically and worldwide. Rather than

---

[10] In early 2014, all members of Russia's ruling party and all public employees received a selection of Ilyin's political writings from the Kremlin (Snyder 2018).

disseminating straightforward propaganda, the regime's global (dis)information policy is to destabilize democracies by instigating conflicts and undermining a shared factual world (Töpfl & Lauer 2022). The regime does so by offering material and ideological support for both left-wing and radical right authoritarian-populist actors and parties in Western democracies who advance such disinformation (Shekhovtsov 2018). This support is now on full display during the war against Ukraine. Assisted by some Western political collaborators and protest movements, the Putin regime calls the military invasion "self-defense" and suggests that the ruthless bombing of Ukrainian cities and civilians is a step towards "denazification" and the prevention of "genocide": pace Orwell, '*war is peace*'. This is the endpoint of a decades-long Orwellian project to destabilize the factual world, until it is turned, via various narratives and camps, into a world where "facts can no longer be distinguished from opinions" (Arendt 1977) at all.

This global destabilization project, advanced by the Putin regime, has been backed by power, money, multiple cyber war resources involving troll factories – and violent force if needed. The Russian government's radical Orwellian campaign during the Ukraine war represents the culmination of 20 years of nationally and globally disseminated systematic disinformation based on significant investment in a global cyber war.[11] On the part of Putin's authoritarian regime, its overarching goal is the destabilization of democracies, with which the Russian government wants to compete on a global scale. Like China, Russia has also been working on creating a separate internet environment and, with an additional massive increase of bans and other restrictions since the Ukraine war, is "sealing off the digital sphere against outside influences and information", sorting out what is critical and persecuting "every individual" seen as a threat (Hanfeld 2022). This digital strategy is flanked by permanent propaganda from the Russia state (television) media, which particularly target the rural population and elderly cohorts. Here, the West is portrayed as weak, degenerate, decadent, and incapable of action (Töpfl & Lauer 2022), although Putin's regime for many years financed itself primarily by exporting energy to Western democracies.

Finally, against the backdrop of the regime's ultra-nationalist propaganda during the last 20 years, the brutality of Putin's system of rule established at home, and the military campaigns and atrocities abroad, the regime's current war of aggression against Ukraine hardly seems surprising. The war crimes,

---

[11] Signs were put up in occupied areas in Ukraine, which post-factually claimed: "Russia does not start wars, Russia ends wars"; "Russia did not invade Ukraine"; "Russia denazifies Ukraine"; "Russia defends itself against NATO aggression"; "Russia is on a peace mission"; "Russia does not target civilians", "The real power lies in justice and truth, which are on our side".

many of which can be classified as crimes against humanity, were preceded by, in terms of human cost, largely unrestricted bombing campaigns against Chechens and Syrians, as well as violations of international law in the war in Georgia and in the case of the annexation of Crimea in 2014. They point to an internal lack of rules and a largely unrestrained logic of violence. Both characterize Putin's personalist dictatorship – at least when push comes to shove. However, the authoritarian, destructive logic of violence and power, over the last decade legitimized and supported by ideologies of radical nationalism, homophobia, misogyny and imperialism, has apparently been inscribed in Putin's regime all along.

Yet, the risk of self-destruction, which the Putin regime took by invading Ukraine and by rendering superfluous hundreds of thousands of its own soldiers alongside Ukrainian lives, has also become evident. Dynamics of potential self-destruction are built into personalist autocratic regimes that lack any checks on dictators, who consequently may believe their own ideologies and delusions about their power. Personalist dictators may pursue ideology-driven aggressions and follow megalomaniac ambitions while overreaching their power. However, typological approaches assuming that authoritarian regimes such as Putin's primarily aim at maintaining power and stability (Frantz 2018) do not grasp this self-delusion but tend to ignore inherent authoritarian dynamics, the megalomania of autocratic leaders in personalist dictatorships, and the power of ideologies as independent driving factors that can lead regimes to pursue a possibly self-destructive course of action. Putin's unprovoked war against Ukraine, ideologically construed as a "special military operation," has produced far more than 100,000 Russian casualties and almost as many Ukrainian civilians and soldiers. It has left an economically, militarily and political severely weakened Russian autocracy, despite all the aggressive, self-confident rhetoric – constantly disseminated and reiterated by government-controlled public media – of a superpower capable of total destruction and possibly willing to annihilate Ukraine and much of the West. The Russian case, thus, illuminates both the potentially expansionist ambitions of consolidated autocracies but also their limitations. It also shows how ideological delusion and self-deception can backfire – all of which tends to be overlooked in rationalist political science analyses of autocratic regimes and their political behavior.

4. HYBRID SYSTEMS, 'DEFECTIVE DEMOCRACIES,' OR NEW ELECTORAL AUTOCRACIES? AUTOCRATIZATION AND DEMOCRATIC DISINTEGRATION IN INDIA AND HUNGARY

4.1 Farewell, Democracy? Populism, Disenfranchisement and Violence in India's Hindu-nationalist Electoral Autocracy

While the ongoing transnational autocratization wave emboldened large-scale autocracies and expanded their authoritarian politics in recent years, fragile and unstable democracies have often also autocratized. Some of them have turned into hybrid systems or even electoral autocracies, as the example of India illustrates. The Bharatiya Janata Party (BJP), led by the authoritarian populist Narendra Modi, won its first election victory in 2014 by mobilizing radical Hindu nationalist propaganda. In addition to the appeal of authoritarian nationalism, which currently resonates around the globe, Modi's government has continuously benefitted from the effects of neoliberal capitalism (Chacko 2018) for which India supplies cheap labor and hereby experienced limited but stable economic growth. Modi was re-elected as prime minister in 2019. For years, the Modi government has been carrying out harsh repression and prosecution of media representatives, regime critics, oppositional parties, and lawyers.

Modi's assumption and consolidation of power has bolstered authoritarianism and nationalism, which the government uses to justify and implement censorship measures and political repression, including restrictions on freedom of the media and freedom of assembly (Gottschlich 2021). This includes, in particular, the method of using anti-terrorism legislation to end or limit democratic freedom and civil rights. These laws are intended to give autocratization the appearance of legal legitimacy. As in Russia and China, arbitrary laws to combat "terrorism" and "sedition" are now used by Modi and the BJP to massively restrict individual rights and liberties.

This also mirrors other "learning processes" from global processes and autocratic practices elsewhere, i.e. the *transnational imitation of autocratic methods*. Following the lead of Russia, China, Turkey, and several other (electoral) autocracies, the Modi government in India also uses funding regulations and requires declarations from NGOs as 'foreign agents' to restrict NGOs or make their work impossible. Another salient feature of the successive transformation of the formerly fragile, precarious or 'deficient' Indian democracy towards an authoritarian system is the largely sanction-free violence against religious minorities and critics. Such violence is de facto state-supported or ideologically driven, and at times overtly instigated by government politicians (Gottschlich 2021; Peltz 2021).

All of this has resulted in self-censorship out of fear of reprisals (Peltz 2021). Today, India can be classified as an electoral autocracy rather than being a 'defective' democracy. At best, the real type of the Indian political system represents a hybrid regime facing continuous democratic backsliding. Out of 180 states, India is ranked 150th by Reporters Without Borders (2022); only five places ahead of Russia. The Freedom House (2022) "Global Freedom Score", however, still classifies India as "partly free." Still, it is no surprise, in light of the authoritarian turn, that the government keeps close ties with Russia even after the invasion of Ukraine. Autocracies tend to sympathize with autocracies – call it *autocratic alliance theory.*

4.2 From Authoritarian Populism in Power to an Autocratic System Within the EU: Hungary's Road to Dictatorship

The process of autocratization and the regression of a formerly unconsolidated, partly functioning and developing "defective democracy" into an authoritarian system can also be illustrated by the example of Hungary since Viktor Orbán entered government as prime minister after the 2010 election. Hungary, an EU member state, is one of the most prominent cases of hybrid transition systems which have gradually transformed into competitive authoritarianism. Hungary, which serves as the government model for Trumpist Republicans in the US and American nationalist-populism represented by formerly conservative think tanks like the Heritage Foundation, today comes closes to an electoral autocracy given the broad destruction of the separation of powers, an independent judiciary, civil liberties, and fair elections. Like India, however, Hungary is still classified as "partly free" according to Freedom House criteria and measures (2022), largely because Orbán has not yet succeeded in controlling *all private media* through actors close to Orbán's *Fidesz party*. He exerts, however, complete control of public, state-funded media. These he has transformed into propaganda channels for his leadership and authoritarian-nationalistic agenda. Moreover, Orbán and his party have extensive control of the private media landscape. There can no longer be any talk of free and fair elections, functioning political pluralism, or democratic equality. For this reason, Samuel Salzborn (2015) has classified Hungary as a "dictatorship" into which the state had "creepingly" transformed already nine years ago. Hungary also moves towards a personalist dictatorship. *Fidesz* only serves Orbán and is not an independent factor of government. Orbán himself openly advocates a system of "illiberal democracy" (see Frankenberg/Heitmeyer in this volume).

The Orbán government uses various political-legal means to autocratize Hungary. They include, first, a new, authoritarian constitution, which the government introduced and which systematically questions the separation of powers and the rule of law itself. Second, individual laws are legislated that directly undermine both liberal and democratic core principles (Salzborn 2015). This corresponds, third, with a broad authoritarian-nationalist ideological mobilization of society. This state-funded political, cultural and social mobilization is intertwined with and supported by a specific authoritarian patronage policy favoring members of the *Fidesz* party in government. Violating core principles of equality before the law, which are required by the EU, members of the party directly receive political, economic and legal favors by public means and by virtue of their membership. They range from economic benefits and exclusive licences for tobacco stores to dual citizenship for ethnic Hungarian voters in neighboring countries.

The Hungarian government actively focuses on Hungary's "past glory". The government's ideology of ethnic nationalism manifests itself, thus, especially in nostalgic nationalism (Rensmann 2021) and ethnopopulism (Vachudova 2020), both of which allude to and glorify Hungary's "imperial greatness" the alleged "superiority" of the Hungarian nation. Such government-sponsored nationalism is also funded in the cultural sphere. Moreover, ethnic nationalism is mobilized by *Fidesz* and the government in political campaigns against minorities, migrants, and presumed "foreign interests". Furthermore, this nationalism culminates in racist and antisemitic laws, including the so-called "Soros Law", This is a *Fidesz* signature law of the last legislative period. It aims at restrictive refugee and migration measures and links migration to Hungary to the Hungarian-American Jewish philanthropist George Soros. Adopting a widespread antisemitic conspiracy fantasy, Orbán's party holds Soros responsible for migration flows to Europe and Hungary. The law itself advances the far right "Great Replacement" conspiracy myth, which suggests that Jews orchestrate Muslim migration to Europe and other predominantly "white" countries to replace the autochthonous populations. In 2017, a *Fidesz* election poster displaying the picture of a large, grinning Soros declared: "99 percent reject illegal migration: Let us not allow Soros to have the last laugh!" (quoted by Thorpe 2019) Creating a direct nexus between illegal migration and Soros, *Fidesz* overtly appeals to and mobilizes the wide-spread antisemitic fantasy that a wealthy Jewish businessman pulls the strings behind "illegal migration" into Hungary, a "threat" which allegedly only Orbán's heroic resistance is capable of preventing.

5. NEW IDEOLOGIES AND TECHNOLOGIES OF AUTHORITARIAN RULE: COMPARATIVE PERSPECTIVES

The analysis of today's dominant authoritarian systems of rule and of autocratization trends in unstable democracies or hybrid systems indicates the limits of typological approaches. In particular, these limits underscore the need for a broader and interdisciplinary understanding of the causes, structures, and interaction dynamics at play in today's global autocratization. They also point beyond institutional and strictly speaking political science perspectives (Rensmann, Hagemann & Funke 2011).[12] In addition to *democratic mimicry*, the return of aggressive *nationalist ideologies*, new technologies advancing *disinformation, digital surveillance and cyberwars* at home and abroad, and an *authoritarian cult of personality* serve as transnationally popular and effective methods driving, legitimizing and exporting authoritarian dynamics today. We can hereby observe *transnational strategic adaptation processes* among autocracies and aspiring autocracies in competition with democratic systems (i.e. the mutual adoption of effective ideological, systemic and technological means). Understanding the appeal and effectiveness of these methods, however, requires the inclusion of research from cultural and new media studies, political psychology, and sociology, among others (Rensmann 2017).

Increasingly turning into personalist dictatorships, the majority of authoritarian regimes today already make use of numerous elements of democratic mimicry. They pretend to represent democratic normative claims suggesting some sort of "rule of the people" and rule of law. Moreover, these regimes incorporate various forms of "powerless pluralism", i.e. the political imaginary of a pluralistic public will-formation process without granting any actual power to plural or dissenting public voices, and interests not in line with the regimes' interests, to interfere in political decision-making. Democratic mimicry evolved as a strategy in response to the large-scale democratization wave during the early 1990s. Today, 94 percent of authoritarian governments operate with a supporting party, and 87 percent even rule with a "pluralistic" party system and legislatures (Frantz 2018). The vast majorities of autocracies, 71 percent, hold elections more or less regularly (Frantz 2018). Most authoritarian regimes have formally legislating parliaments, a supposedly independent judiciary, officially competing parties and (mostly unfree and unfair) elections to secure regime legitimacy.

---

[12] Moreover, critical political economy (e.g. Wintrobe 1998; Acemoglu & Robinson 2006) deserves renewed attention for analyzing the complex relationship between authoritarianism and democracy.

Furthermore, there is a notable global return of social authoritarianism. It is especially manifest in increasingly popular *authoritarian personality cults* in consolidated authoritarian regimes and hybrid systems (here: Xi, Putin, Modi, Orbán), and beyond. There is a strong political-communicative focus on the allegedly special competences of a "strong leader," who supposedly guides society and who is presumably the only one who can save it. Corresponding authoritarian longings continue to exist among electorates across the globe (Adorno 1982; Löwenthal & Guterman 2021; Rensmann 2020). The interplay of propagandistic personality cults and the appeal of authoritarian ideas and ideals partly explains the observable recent rise and global expansion of personalist dictatorships.

The rise of personalist rule is backed by a general re-ideologization within authoritarian governance. This includes, first and foremost, the return of *aggressive nationalism*. The respective leader is propagandistically construed as embodying and expressing the genuine will of the people – just as authoritarian-nationalist populists do in democracies. Specific politico-cultural authoritarian legacies and nationalist cultural nostalgia are often employed to legitimize repression and even overt violence against so-called "enemies of the people". However, such nationalism is not just instrumental, i.e. a means for a leader or regime, but leads an ideological life of its own. It motivates imperial expansionism that ultimately puts an autocratic regime at risk. Without doubt, it is important to identify existing conventional systemic pillars of autocratic rule, such as their adaptivity, continuity and persistence (Gerschweski 2018). And by no means, it should be added, are all authoritarian regimes today expansionist; many, like the GDR once, continue to aim for a quiet domestic rule and stability by means of societal control and surveillance. However, many authoritarian systems today are driven by aggressive nationalism. These ideologies can function as independent factors driving authoritarian, potentially destructive dynamics. Furthermore, authoritarianism and repressive conformism are not just system functions emerging in or serving a regime; they are also phenomena of global society as a whole. Today authoritarian regimes effectively sell authoritarian transitions and "illiberal democracy" as global ideological export models. They often find numerous supporters within Western democracies who are willing to collaborate with a global culture war against "Western decadence" and effeminacy, and for "national sovereignty" and "cultural identity".

A crucial trend within the autocratization process today is the *use of new, especially digital technologies* to disinform citizens and surveil their behavior.[13] Countries such as Russia, China and Iran aim to *destabilize democracies* by technologically and politically fostering polarization and disinformation in the global context. Unwittingly, this happens with the help of the algorithms used by new media corporations and a new media ecology that incentivizes responses and frequency of use.[14] However, the process of global autocratization meets processes of democratic backsliding even within robust, consolidated democracies. The authoritarian challenges and the dangers of autocratization within democratic societies, will now be briefly analyzed and discussed.

6. AUTHORITARIANISM IN CONSOLIDATED DEMOCRACIES: THE PRECARIZATION OF DEMOCRACY AND POPULIST CHALLENGES

In principle, democracies procedurally enable participation through regularized free and fair elections selecting and electing those in political decision-making positions for limited time periods. Democracies also allow for continuous participation in public will-formation, the decision-making process, and in shaping the decision-making content through the public realm. Furthermore, democracies enable control mechanisms vis-à-vis the government, whereby democratic participation "finds its expression in dimensions of political freedom, political equality and political and legal control" (Lauth 2010: 100). Free and fair elections with universal suffrage, freedom of assembly and political association, the rule of law, civil rights and an independent judiciary, as well as freedom of speech and expression and free sources of information are widely regarded as prerequisites for democratic systems to function (Dahl 1998; Lauth 2010; Linz 2009).Ideally defined, in democratic political systems citizens, the people, are both the author and the subject of laws and rules and policies, which are democratically exercised and implemented. This, however, requires a stable framework of constitutionally secured civil liberties, political freedom, legal equality and the rule of law which, as such, cannot be subject to political decisions. Democracies require upholding inalienable rights, which point to modern, pluralistic constitutional democracies' universalistic underpinnings, which transcend both unrestricted democratic majoritarianism and the idea of any absolute 'sovereign will'. Democracies thrive on inclusive and

---

[13] The 2022 Moscow Joint Declaration, signed by China and Russia, aims to ban "extremist content" on the internet (Hanfeld 2022).

[14] This also reveals further transnational learning processes (Peltz 2021), for example, by banning NGOs to prevent "foreign" funding and influence.

pluralistic deliberative decision-making in which those affected by a norm or decision must have a chance to have a say in it (Habermas).

In the case of democratic states, too, the degree and nature of a state's internal constitution can help predict political behavior, policies and stability. Institutionally, democracies guarantee a political process in which the state and the intermediary actors operating within it function as transmission belts for public and political will-formation. Intermediary institutions contribute to the mediation of social and political interests. This stands in contrast to the massive civil restrictions, the structurally organized suppression of free opinion, and the repressive measures against oppositional political participation and pluralism that we find in autocracies. The most decisive difference, however, is the extent to which formal claims to democratic legitimacy, inalienable rights, and private and public freedom are realized in practice. *Consolidated democracies*, then, can be regarded as stable political systems which, over a longer period of time, have consolidated support of democracy for the sake of democracy, i.e. by non-instrumental democratic social values that are widely shared by the population.[15] Secured by the rule of law democracies are, following Jürgen Habermas, procedurally and substantially underpinned by values that are both democratic and profoundly universalistic (deliberative and inclusive). Empirically, they combine the constitutional protection of civil and political liberties with the *practically enforced* rule of law and separation of powers as well as procedurally secured, functioning mechanisms of free and democratic deliberation and participation, which also presuppose pluralistic free media and freedom of opinion.

Beyond these definitions, empirical democracy research shows significant differences with regard to the nature of the political representation of interests, preferences, and social groups, or the trust and support democratic polities are able to generate. There are considerable systemic divergences regarding the practical exercise of legal and political equality, pluralism, and democratic participation opportunities in various sub-areas of the political community (Rensmann, Hagemann & Funke 2011). The quality of institutionalized procedural democratic mechanisms, which help to secure the *input legitimacy* of the system, depends to a considerable extent on conditions of material democracy; the combination of both allows reliable conclusions to be drawn about the stability and survivability of the respective democratic system.

Formal institutional procedures ultimately need to turn into, and require as a prerequisite, certain conditions of political, political-cultural as well as economic substance. The stability of democratic systems depends on the com-

---

[15] In contrast to a purely instrumental relationship to democracy, see Inglehart & Welzel (2005).

bination of the quality of democratic input legitimacy and *output legitimacy* of the political process. In particular, empirical research on democracy points to socio-economic preconditions for stable democratic participation and robust trust in democratic systems, and thus for the stability of democracy at large (Levin-Waldman 2016). Conversely, material insecurity and the structural absence or loss of socio-economic inclusion also destabilize political inclusion and trust in democracy (Boix 2003). Extreme social divisions, which have been exacerbated by neoliberal economic globalization processes, consequently constitute grave dangers for democracy's long-term survival, as they tend to undermine even otherwise robust support of democratic social values.

6.1 Trumpism in Power: Autocratization in the US

Since the rise of the authoritarian populist Donald J. Trump and his presidency from 2017 to 2021, US democracy has been experiencing an attack on its institutional pillars and democratic political culture that was hitherto unthinkable. The attack on the United States Capitol Building and the violent insurgence led by Trump on 6 January 2021 marked the end of Trump's presidency but not the end of Trumpism and the ongoing authoritarian attack on US democracy. Trump had mobilized for this uprising together with some Republican congressmen and continues to deny the certified results of the 2020 election, led an insurgence against the American Republic, and claims, in overt fascist rhetoric, that undocumented immigrants are "poisoning the blood of our country", yet he became once again the Republican Party's presidential nominee in 2024. January 6, then, only constituted a climax in the development of Trumpism as an authoritarian-nationalist populist movement and ideology, which continues to fundamentally question the oldest continuously existing and most powerful democracy on the planet; this challenge includes the dismissal of the principle of free and fair elections, the unconditional protection of independent, free media, and entails the idea that the president stands above the US Constitution and should be immune from criminal prosecution even if he suspends the Constitution (Rensmann 2021). Four years after Trump's electoral defeat by his Democratic competitor Joe Biden, two-thirds of the Republican electorate still believe Trump's fact- and evidence-free belief that the 2020 US democratic elections were rigged and that Trump actually won. These voters thus no longer recognize free elections and the peaceful democratic transfer of power that usually goes along with them. Meanwhile, the former US president continues to dispute any free and fair election he does not win and democratic institutions in the name of a "will of the people" he claims to embody. In turn, Trump advances free-floating conspiracy ideologics and a dynamic process of ideological radicalization in American society from inside and outside the White House, none of which have reduced his political support.

The rebellious authoritarianism which Trumpism represents is directed against intermediary organizations and pluralistic forms of interest mediation that are constitutive for constitutional democracies. Trump dubbed competing political parties "vermin" and free media "enemies of the people". During the Trump administration, such authoritarianism has also been flanked by the systematic ideological dismantling and delegitimization of independent, supposedly "disloyal" democratic institutions and actors as part of an alleged "deep state" run by civil servants. This entailed threats via Twitter; the frequent disparagement of democratic and constitutional procedures and court rulings; the dissemination and support of anti-pluralistic nationalist propaganda that only Trump voters were "real Americans" or "true patriots"; the politicization and hollowing out of the civil service; and the spread of an authoritarian cosmos of "alternative facts" and conspiracy myths as the basis of government policy, including advice to drink disinfectants against Covid-19 and culminating in the *big lie* that the 2020 presidential elections were rigged (cf. Muirhead & Rosenblum 2020: 80 ff.; Rensmann 2021).

Trumpism as an illiberal, authoritarian movement consolidated itself in power with Trump's success in the 2016 presidential election. It has since become the dominant factor in the formerly conservative Republican Party – even after Trump's electoral defeat (cf. Muirhead & Rosenblum 2020). In order to understand the success of Trump and the Trumpist movement as actors of de-democratization and autocratization, a comprehensive analysis needs to include the media environment supporting his rise but also Trump's enablers in the Republican Party, the rank and file, the Republican base, and voters as a whole, as well as the specific political-psychological appeal of Trumpism and the politico-cultural and socio-economic conditions in a fractured US democracy (Abromeit 2018).

These conditions point to a hardened cleavage structure and a high degree of political polarization in US society. Some reconfigured societal and politico-cultural cleavages seem to point to groups which are by now irreconcilably opposed to each other and no longer share common democratic values (Horst 2018). Ronald Inglehart and Pippa Norris note a long-simmering cultural *backlash* against a long-observed "silent" social value revolution, i.e. against the socio-cultural value shift of recent decades towards post-material, democratic and cosmopolitan self-expression values (Norris/Inglehart 2017). The simmering discontent of the supposed "silent majority", which is increasingly losing its status as a majority in demographic terms, has been directed against this socio-cultural democratic norm revolution. Authoritarian populists like Trump have hereby gathered support especially among white, uneducated, old men and rural voters, which form part of the Trumpist base, but also among wealthy supporters of an authoritarian 'cultural revolution' and tax cuts for the affluent. Many Trump voters yearn for a regressive reorientation towards authoritarian values and nostalgic nationalist ideologies – which are now evident and openly politically mobilized in the global context (Norris/ Inglehart 2017). Inglehart and Norris identify politico-economically generated "material insecurity" and socio-economic precarization as important enabling conditions for this cultural *backlash* (Inglehart & Norris 2017). Like elsewhere in the world, the restructuring of the public sphere and the expansive dissemination of disinformation or "fake news" through social networks and powerful broadcasters such as Fox News also have had significant favorable effects for authoritarian populism, and here for Trump and Trumpism (Allcott, Hunt & Matthew Gentzkow 2017). Whether US democracy would survive another Trump presidency, or the election of another authoritarian populist, is therefore by no means a foregone conclusion. Instead, recent years have shown how precarious and unstable the future of US democracy is.

6.2 Precarious Democracy? Authoritarian Challenges in Germany

The long-term trend among a growing minority of *Millenials* in the US to distance themselves from democracy (Foa & Mounk 2016) is also evident in Germany, which today also faces new authoritarian challenges. While intergenerational approval of democracy "as an idea" remains comparatively high in Germany, satisfaction with its implementation is significantly lower, and also much lower than in the past. In eastern Germany, dissatisfaction with democracy has been rising again since 2008; it was even higher in 2018 than in 1991 (Busch 2020: 12). A significant minority of citizens who are profoundly dissatisfied with democracy and who feel existentially threatened by immigration and elites, seek to make their authoritarian opposition heard through protests and by voting for the radical right Alternative for Germany (AfD) in an increasingly polarized and fragmented party system. Their authoritarian rebellion *also* refers to the socio-economic precarization of society and the dismantling of the welfare state over the last two decades. In addition, there are sections of the educated elites who harbor resentment against democratic-liberal norms and procedures. After the Covid-19 crisis and in the wake of Russia's war of aggression against Ukraine, surveys displayed further increased scepticism towards democracy, a widespread belief in conspiracy myths, and sympathy for the Putin regime. Many Germans now believe we live in a "sham democracy", and according to a population-representative survey from April 2022, 12.2 per cent believe completely and another 19.77 per cent "partly" that Putin is "acting against a global elite pulling the strings in the background" in the war (Lamberty et al. 2022). This points to a considerable polarization in the political landscape, which is partly being reshaped by authoritarian ideas and conspiracy myths.

The success of the AfD in recent years, which became the biggest opposition party in the German Bundestag from 2017 to 2021, has brought this relevant minority position into parliament, where the AfD now advances its authoritarian party-political ideas (Rensmann 2018). Resentment-soaked, anti-immigrant and pro-Moscow radical right-wing movements such as "Pegida" bring this opposition to liberally constituted democracy onto the streets (Volk 2022), sometimes using antisemitic rhetoric that denounces free media as the "lying press", while the AfD functions as the parliamentary wing of the radical right. Authoritarian "critics of democracy" can exploit the weaknesses of established actors, unprepared media journalists, eroding political trust in democratic institutions, and the widespread loss of competence to distinguish between facts and fictions. In Germany, like in the US, we can observe how democratic standards in political discourse have come under pressure; how political polarization in the public sphere has increased sharply over the last decade; and in some cases factual relativism favoring autocratic nihilism spreads across social strata – a process that favors authoritarian states. The boundaries of what is considered socially acceptable and legitimate in the political public sphere have been eroding for decades now. Physical and verbal attacks against politicians, journalists, and minorities are no longer an exception. Anti-democratic resentments often resonate in the public mainstream, while authoritarian regimes are presented in a mild light. These trends point to a simmering crisis of democracy even in Germany's robust, and still robustly supported, liberal and pluralistic democratic system.

7. GLOBAL AUTOCRATIZATION AND DEMOCRATIC BACKSLIDING: EXPLANATORY FACTORS

Many democracies previously considered consolidated have become unstable or face democratic backsliding. This includes the erosion of trust in democratic institutions, parties, and norms as well as an intergenerational increase in scepticism about democracy, all of which are indicators of "democratic deconsolidation" (Foa & Mounk 2016). Crises of democracy have become manifest as crises of representation, of established parties and party systems, of trust, and of input as well as output legitimacy. These crises have been both exploited and accelerated by authoritarian actors and, in some cases, even within established and consolidated liberal, pluralistic democracies. They are further challenged by new societal conflicts, in particular economic precarization, as an effect of more than three decades of neo-liberal economic policy regimes affecting democracies and the world at large. These policies have fostered welfare state regress, economic deregulation favoring the wealthy, increasing social inequality, the precarization of living and working conditions, and increased material insecurity among significant parts of society even within Western liberal democracies. In addition, established liberal constitutional democracies face centrifugal trends of polarization and new socio-cultural divisions undermining political communities (Przeworski 2020). Consolidated democracies are not only threatened from the outside by authoritarian powers, but also from within.

Processes of democratic disintegration and the *precarization of democracy*. i.e. democracy's systemic, economic and political-cultural erosion, are particularly driven by *authoritarian-populist actors, parties and movements*, which ultimately aim to radically transform if not abolish liberal democracy altogether. They learn from each other and network transnationally in search of successful strategies (McDonnell & Werner 2019). This is a global phenomenon (Moffitt 2015). Authoritarian populists, especially on the radical right, are now electorally successful in many places (Bernhard & Kriesi 2019), represented in parliaments (Albertazzi & McDonnell 2015), and often also govern or serve as junior partners in government (Bartha, Boda & Szikra 2020). In some cases, they actively undermine the rule of law, constitutional frameworks, divided government, the protection of minorities, and the very principles, practices and conditions enabling pluralistic democracy. In addition to formerly consolidated democracies, this also affects democracies which are relatively young but have previously been robust. In Brazil, Argentina and throughout Latin America, for example, we have witnessed a renaissance of authoritarian populism. Within democratic political systems, we note strengthened authoritarian actors and tendencies. These are neither the product of repression, nor merely of propaganda. Rather, they indicate a broader appeal of authoritarian models and ideologies within democratic societies.

A number of destabilizing factors contribute to these processes. These include *authoritarian legacies* shaping societies throughout political modernity. The precarious conditions of modern global capitalism interact with specific *political cultures* and historical legacies. In addition to politico-institutional systemic differences, i.e. the weakness or strength of democratic institutions and the way they function and are legitimized, this partly explains variations in the degree of democracy crises and authoritarian challenges (Rensmann, Hagemann & Funke 2011). The persistence appeal of *nationalist, racist and antisemitic ideologies* and conspiracy fantasies also stands out. They point to a long simmering nostalgic-nationalist *cultural backlash* in society drawing on idealized images of a golden past (Couperus, Rensmann & Tortola 2023). It is directed against socio-cultural value change, pluralism, diversity, as well as norms and practices of democratic inclusion. The scope of this backlash, which includes a culturally based opposition to climate change policy (Lockwood 2018) and a decidedly masculine nationalism advocating for traditional gender relations (Agius, Bergman Rosamond & Kinnvall 2020), has only recently become apparent (Inglehart & Norris 2017). Ultimately, the backlash is part of a significant reconfiguration of politico-cultural cleavages structuring societal divisions and political conflicts. This backlash has further unleashed and fostered extreme political polarization, in which political opponents appear as "enemies" to be fought with all means, and in which the reference to democracy as a shared political community has, so it seems, partly been lost along the way.

Add to this a significant long-term erosion of trust in democratic-pluralistic parties, intermediary institutions, media, and the political system as a whole, further fueled by insufficient democratic policies vis-à-vis new economic and political crises – from pandemics to climate change, war and migration. In recent years, authoritarian-populist actors, who present themselves as the direct expression of the "will of the people", have often effectively exploited such crises, conflicts, and corresponding grievances (Urbinati 2015; Moffitt 2015). All of these challenges have contributed to delegitimization processes within constitutional democracies.

Authoritarian actors and parties within democracies have also tremendously benefitted from the *digital structural transformation of the public sphere*. The dynamics of many-to-many social network communication, "alternative media" and outright disinformation channels promoting manufactured or manipulated *fake news* content have contributed to the transformation of public communication and advanced an overall post-factual misinformation culture (Bergmann 2020). These developments, enhanced by unchecked corporate algorithms of the new attention economy, have also accelerated the erosion of the boundaries of the speakable, of what can be said (Rensmann 2018; Wodak 2013), especially regarding hate speech and cyber-mobbing. These changes are favorable to advancing authoritarian populism's discontent with pluralistic democracy and thus autocratization. Small wonder that the communicative destabilization in consolidated democracies has also been actively sponsored by authoritarian states such as Russia and China for many years – an issue long neglected.

Finally, the precarization of democracies especially benefits from the effects of neo-liberal globalization (Rensmann, Hagemann & Funke 2011; Heitmeyer 2001; Heitmeyer 2018). Neoliberal welfare state regress, economic deregulations in sync with bureaucratic control and economic pressure on dependent labor, and grand-scale privatizations of public goods and housing have enabled tremendous concentrations of power throughout the world, and they profoundly undermine the very conditions for upholding democratic standards of political equality. The political and legal precarization of social rights and economic conditions, implemented over the last four decades, and the *dismantling of institutional, democratic and socio-economic welfare systems* have undermined democratic control mechanisms and both individual and societal conditions for exercising public autonomy and will-formation. These politico-economic transformations also "emptied democracy" (Heitmeyer 2001: 517 ff.). The neoliberal welfare state regress, which has gone hand in hand with the support of global capital interests (Biebricher 2021), has led to a massive rise and spread of material insecurity, which is empirically linked to a turn away from democratic values (Inglehart & Norris 2017). The negative consequences of neoliberal globalization, which have contributed to democratic legitimacy crises under conditions of globalized capitalism (Ibsen 2019), have at the same time boosted authoritarian systems like Russia and China – the main beneficiaries of a neoliberal global economy which does not grant or care about rights for labor, or citizens at large.

8. TOWARDS AN AUTHORITARIAN AGE? POLITICAL, CULTURAL AND ECONOMIC DYNAMICS IN A GLOBAL CONTEXT

The year 2006 marked the end of the third wave of democratization. This is the first year since Freedom House – representative of similar democracy measurements – has recorded a decline in political and civil rights in the global context. The *Varieties of Democracy Project* has registered autocratization processes in 25 countries in 2020 alone; this contrasts with 16 smaller nations displaying democratization processes (Peltz 2021). The trend has further intensified in recent years, in some cases dramatically. The recent acceleration of autocratization is primarily due to the fact that already existing authoritarian regimes have further expanded systemic repression, while some highly populous societies formerly classified as hybrid political systems, such as Turkey and especially India, have pushed ahead with far-reaching de-democratization. Key drivers of systemic autocratization are no longer coups or other forms of violent systemic change (Frantz 2018; Peltz 2021). Rather, autocratization primarily emerges through creeping transitions after the election of authoritarian politicians, behind rule-of-law facades, and by democratic mimicry. It happens through gradually increased restrictions on freedom of expression and other steps curtailing civil and political rights. Moreover, even long-consolidated democracies are now often exposed to authoritarian challenges and actual autocratization, as the cases of Brazil, Argentina, and the USA demonstrate. In these cases, institutional and political-cultural *firewalls* assumed to be robust turned actually out being surprisingly weak. All too often, democratic forces and institutions have been utterly unprepared to counter the rise of authoritarian actors and movements (Levitsky & Ziblatt 2018). The diagnosis of a "third wave of autocratization," then, is based on robust empirical evidence, and the danger of an "authoritarian age" is just as real.

The analysis presented here has highlighted, from a comparative global perspective, various dimensions of this wave of autocratization. The chapter has shown how certain features, structures and processes play out in different autocratic, hybrid, and democratic political systems. This contribution has also illuminated today's common trends and causes of autocratization across different systems. While political science provides tools for measuring and analyzing de-democratization trends and offers some plausible mid-level theoretical explanations, conventional political science frameworks do not seem sufficient to explain the global autocratization process we currently face in a satisfactory way. The globally improved political-cultural opportunity structures for autocrats and aspiring wanna-be-autocrats need to be placed in the context of, on the one hand, broader societal and politico-cultural developments. On the other hand, these improved politico-cultural opportunity structures are to be understood in the horizon of dynamic, interactive and partly context-dependent processes that cannot be adequately grasped in terms of straightforward causal mechanisms. Understanding these processes requires, at any rate, the integration of interdisciplinary perspectives (Rensmann 2017). These include a renewed focus on socio-psychological studies of authoritarianism and the appeal of authoritarian ideology; new transnational approaches in media and communication studies, focusing especially on social media and the new online politics of disinformation; as well as theory-guided sociological research and global research in critical political economy, which examines the effects of neoliberal global capitalism and its national and international enabling conditions. Interdisciplinary findings on accelerated transformations affecting world society in the current global age – social, political, cultural, economic and last but not least communicative – indicate that a mix of factors fostering societal conflicts have created more favorable conditions for new "attacks by anti-democrats" (Salzborn 2017) and "authoritarian reactions" (Rensmann, Hagemann & Funke 2011).

Social science findings also point, if only implicitly, to some strategies for democratic politics and intervention against democratic deconsolidation. Democratic responses arguably require a profound political change towards authoritarian regimes, especially expansionist-imperialist ones. These regimes include Russia, China and Iran, three of the most repressive regimes on the planet today. For decades, policy approaches were dominated by complacency vis-à-vis human rights violations and even crimes against humanity – often for the sake of a profit-based neo-liberal economic order. The cozying up to these regimes by democracies under the mantra of "change through trade" to advance neoliberal globalization has helped enable, if not bolster, the continuous expansion and consolidation of authoritarian regimes – whereby, alongside global corporations, China's autocratic system has been the biggest profiteer of neoliberalized global capitalism.

The new, increasingly stark system competition between autocracies and democracies, which is openly sought by China and Russia, calls for renewed attention to the origins of processes of democratic precarization and destabilization within democracies. In order to find ways out of democracies' legitimacy crisis, democratic polities need to regain means of democratic inclusion. This implies a profound reversal away from decades of neoliberal policy-making, which is based on welfare state regress and the economic deregulation, privatization and precarization of public affairs and private lives by means of social pressure and control. This policy has strongly affected the very conditions of democratic inclusion, enabling an enormous transfer of wealth from the bottom to the top and, along with it, an equally gigantic political-economic concentration of power. Such a concentration of power, just like extreme social inequality, is presumably incompatible with democracy and its long-term survival. Moreover, it appears to be necessary to strengthen democratic institutions, which have been weakened and undermined by budgetary policy, and engender new forms of inclusive democratic deliberation. Furthermore, the current operating framework of a digitally restructured public sphere, currently dominated by the intransparent and profit-oriented algorithms of a small number of private corporations such as Google, TikTok and Meta, has advanced widespread misinformation. But a post-factual democracy cannot exist or survive as a democracy. It is therefore necessary for democracies' survival to find new answers to the ongoing assault of organized and bottom-up disinformation on new media, often advanced with the help of autocratic regimes. The unchecked spread of disinformation and hate speech has profoundly harmed the very conditions for free speech without fear of violence and intimidation. Against the post-factual erosion of the boundaries of what can legitimately be said, democracies need to enable a responsible culture of *"you cannot possibly say that"*.

No democracy can be taken for granted (Peltz 2021). Today, authoritarian threats flourish both outside and inside democracies. Just as democracies have historically perished or "died" from the inside, dynamics of democratic disintegration are currently also, as in the first half of the twentieth century, transnationally interwoven. Driven by structural transformations and both national and global authoritarian actors and movements, autocratization is a global danger that extends far beyond national political communities. The current corrosive process of democratic deconsolidation that has gripped numerous democratic political systems – albeit to significantly different degrees – appears to be almost as threatening to the global future of democracy and human rights as the powerful expansionism of authoritarian states. Yet, while the new war against democracy is ongoing, the struggle for democracy and human rights continues. And democracy – as an idea, a political system, and a form of life – is still alive.

REFERENCES

Abromeit, John (2018), "Frankfurt School Critical Theory and the Persistence of Authoritarian Populism in the United States", in: Morelock, Jeremiah (Hg.), *Critical Theory and Authoritarian Populism*, London, 3–27.

Acemoglu, Daron & Robinson, James A (2006), *Economic Origins of Dictatorship and Democracy*, Cambridge.

Adorno, Theodor W. (1982), "Freudian Theory and the Patterns of Fascist Propaganda", in: *The Essential Frankfurt School Reader*, hrsg. v. Arato, Andrew & Gebhardt, Eike, New York, 118–137.

Agius, Christine u.a. (2020), "Populism, Ontological Insecurity and Gendered Nationalism: Masculinity, Climate Denial and Covid-19", in: *Politics, Religion & Ideology* 21, 4, 432–450.

Albertazzi, Daniele/McDonnell, Duncan (2015), *Populists in Power*, New York.

Allcott, Hunt/Gentzkow, Matthew (2017), "Social Media and Fake News in the 2016 Election", *Journal of Economic Perspectives* 31, 2, 211–236.

Arendt, Hannah (1955), *Origins of Totalitarianism,* New York.

Arendt, Hannah (1977), "Truth and Politics," in Arendt, *Between Past and Future: Eight Exercises in Political Thought* (New York, 227–264

Bartha, Attila u.a. (2020), "When Populist Leaders Govern: Conceptualising Populism in Policy Making", in: *Politics and Governance*, 8, 3, 71–81.

Bergmann, Eiríkur (2020), "Populism and the Politics of Misinformation", in: *Safundi: The Journal of South African and American Studies*, 21, 3, 251–265.

Bernhard, Laurent/Kriesi, Hanspeter (2019), "Populism in election times: a comparative analysis of 11 countries in Western Europe", in: *West European Politics* 42, 6, 1188–1208.

Biebricher, Thomas (2021), *Die politische Theorie des Neoliberalismus*, Frankfurt a.M.

Boese, Vanessa A. u.a. (2021), "Waves of Autocratization and democratization: a Rejoinder", in: *Democratization* 28, 6, 1202 –1210.

Boix, Carles (2003). *Democracy and Redistribution*, Cambridge and New York.

Büchenbacher, Katrin (2021), "Xi Jinpings größter Trumpf", in: *Neue Zürcher Zeitung*, 28. Juli, https://www.nzz.ch/meinung/china-nationalismus-ist-der-groesste-trumpf-von-xi-jinping-nzz-ld.1634428/.

Busch, Kathrin (2020), "Krise oder Unterstützung der (repräsentativen) Demokratie in Deutschland? Die Entwicklung der letzten zwei Jahrzehnte 1991–2018", in: *Informationsdienst Soziale Indikatoren* 65, 7 –14.

Couperus, Stefan Couperus, Rensmann, Lars, Tortola, & Pier, Domenico (2023), "Historical legacies and the political mobilization of national nostalgia: Understanding populism's relationship to the past", *Journal of Contemporary European Studies* 31, 2, 253–267.

Chacko, Priya (2018), "The Right Turn in India: Authoritarianism, Populism and Neoliberalisation", in: *Journal of Contemporary Asia* 48, 4, 541–565.

Dahl, Robert A. (1998), *On Democracy*, New Haven, CT.

Davenport, Christian (2007), "State Repression and the Tyrannical Peace", in: *Journal of Peace Research* 44, 4, 485–504.

Diamond, Larry (2015), "Facing up to the Democratic Recession", in: *Journal of Democracy* 26, 1, 141–155.

Ezrow, Natasha M. & Frantz, Erica (2011), *Dictators and Dictatorships: Understanding Authoritarian Regimes and Their Leaders*, London.

Foa, Roberto Stefan/Mounk, Yascha (2016), "The Danger of Deconsolidation: The Democratic Disconnect", in: *Journal of Democracy* 27, 3.
Frantz, Erica (2018), *Authoritarianism: What Everyone Needs to Know*, New York.
Freedom House (2022), *Countries 2022,* https://freedomhouse.org/countries/freedom-net/scores.
Friedrich, Carl J. & Brzezinski, Zbigniew (1969), "The General Characteristics of Totalitarian Dictatorship", in: Blondel, J. (ed.), *Comparative Government: A Reader*, London, 187–199.
Fukuyama, Francis (1992), *The End of History and the Last Man*, New York.
Gaufman, Elizaveta (2022), *Everyday Foreign Policy: Performing and Consuming the Russian Nation After Crimea*, Manchester.
Geddes, Barbara, Wright, Joseph & Frantz, Erica (2014), "Autocratic Breakdowns and Regime Transitions: A New Data Set", in: *Perspectives on Politics* 12, 2, 313–331.
Gerschewski, Johannes (2018), "Persistenz – Kontinuität – Adaptivität: Konzeptionen politischer Stabilität in der Vergleichenden Autokratieforschung", in: *Leviathan* 48, SH 36, 21–38.
Gottschlich, Pierre (2021), "Narendra Modi: Ein Populist an der Macht", in: *Populismus an der Macht: Strategien und Folgen populistischen Regierungshandelns*, Wiesbaden, 103–125.
Heinemann-Grüder, Andreas (2017), "Die Resilienz des Putinismus", in: *Zeitschrift für Politik* 64, 2, 214–234.
Heitmeyer, Wilhelm (2001), "Autoritärer Kapitalismus, Demokratieentleerung und Rechtspopulismus. Eine Analyse von Entwicklungstendenzen", in: Loch, Dietmar/ Heitmeyer, Wilhelm (Hg.), *Schattenseiten der Globalisierung. Rechtsradikalismus, Rechtspopulismus und separatistischer Regionalismus in westlichen Gesellschaften*, Frankfurt am Main, 497–534.
Heitmeyer, Wilhelm (2018), *Autoritäre Versuchungen*, Berlin.
Hoffman, Samantha (2022), "China's Tech-Enhanced Authoritarianism", in: *Journal of Democracy* 33, 2, S. 76–89.
Horst, Patrick (2018), "Eine liberale Demokratie in der Krise: Die US-Demokratie im Spiegel der Indizes empirischer Demokratiemessung und der Einstellungen ihrer Bürger", in: Horst, Patrick u.a. (Hg.), *Die USA – eine scheiternde Demokratie?*, Frankfurt am Main, 33–60.
Huntington, Samuel P. (1991), *The Third Wave of Democratization in the Late Twentieth Century*, London.
Ibsen, Malte Frøslee (2019), "The Populist Conjuncture: Legitimation Crisis in the Age of Globalized Capitalism", in: *Political Studies*, 67, 3, 795–811.
Inglehart, Ronald & Norris, Pippa (2017), "Trump and the Populist Authoritarian Parties: The Silent Revolution in Reverse", in: *Perspectives on Politics* 15, 2, 443–454.
Inglehart, Ronald & Welzel, Christian (2005), *Modernization, Cultural Change, and Democracy*, Cambridge.
Kurlantzick, Joshua (2013), *Democracy in Retreat: The Revolt of the Middle Class and the Worldwide Decline of Representative Government*, New Haven, CT.
Lamberty, Pia, Goedeke Tort, Maheba & Heuer , Corinne (2022), "Von der Krise zum Krieg: Verschwörungserzählungen über den Angriffskrieg gegen die Ukraine in der Gesellschaft", *Cemas,* https://cemas.io/publikationen/von-der-krise-zum-krieg-verschwoerungserzaehlungen-ueber-den-angriffskrieg-gegen-die-ukraine-in-der-gesellschaft/2022_05_CeMAS_ResearchPaper_Verschwoerungserzaehlungen_Ukraine.pdf.

Lauth, Hans-Joachim (2010), "Regimetypen: Totalitarismus – Autoritarismus – Demokratie", in: Lauth, Hans-Joachim, ed, *Vergleichende Regierungslehre*, Wiesbaden, 95–116.
Levin-Waldman, Oren M. (2016), "How Inequality Undermines Democracy", *E-International Relations*, 10 December, https://www.e-ir.info/2016/12/10/how-inequality-undermines-democracy/.
Levitsky, Steven and Way, Lucan A. (2002), "The Rise of Competitive Authoritarianism", in: *Journal of Democracy* 13, 2, 21–35.
Levitsky, Steven and Ziblatt, Daniel (2018), *How Democracies Die: What History Reveals About Our Future*, New York.
Linz, Juan (2003), *Totalitarian and Autocratic Regimes*, Boulder, CO.
Linz, Juan (2005), "S chritte zu einer Definition autoritärer Regime", in: Raimund Krämer (Hg.), Autoritäre Systeme im Vergleich, Potsdam, 5–17.
Lockwood, Matthew (2018), "Right-wing Populism and the Climate Change Agenda: Exploring the Linkages", in: *Environmental Politics* 27, 4, 712–732.
Löwenthal, Leo and Norbert Guterman (2021), *Prophets of Deceit: A Study of the Techniques of the American Agitator*, London.
Luce, Edward (2017), *The Retreat of Western Liberalism*, London.
Lührmann, Anna and Lindberg, Staffan (2019), "A Third Wave of Autocratization is Here: What is New About it?", in: *Democratization* 26,7, 1095–1113.
Mattes, Michaela and Rodriguez, Mariana (2014), "Autocracies and International Cooperation", in: *International Studies Quarterly* 58, 3, 527–538.
McDonnell, Duncan and Werner, Annika (2019), *International Populism. The Radical Right in the European Parliament*, Oxford.
Mechkova, Valeriya u.a. (2017), "How Much Democratic Backsliding?", in: *Journal of Democracy* 28, 4, 162–169.
Merkel, Wolfgang (1999), *Systemtransformation: Eine Einführung in die Theorie und Empirie der Transformationsforschung*, Opladen.
Moffitt, Benjamin (2015), "How to Perform Crisis: A Model for Understanding the Key Role of Crisis in Contemporary Populism", in: *Government and Opposition* 50, 2, 189–217.
Muirhead, Russell and Rosenblum, Nancy L. (2020), *"A Lot of People Are Saying": The New Conspiracism and the Assault on Democracy*, Princeton.
O'Donnell, Guillermo (1993), "On the State, Democratization and Some Conceptual Problems", in: *World Development* 21, 8, 1355–1370.
Peltz, Patrick (2021), "Wie Demokratien erodieren", in: *Jungle World* 14, https://jungle.world/artikel/2021/14/wie-demokratien-erodieren/.
Przeworski, Adam (2020), *Krisen der Demokratie*, Berlin.
Reiter, Dan and Stam, Allan C. (2003), "Identifying the Culprit: Democracy, Dictatorship, and Dispute Initiation", in: *American Political Science Review* 97, 3, 333–337.
Rensmann, Lars (2017), "The Noisy Counter-Revolution: Understanding the Cultural Conditions and Dynamics of Populist Politics in Europe in the Digital Age", in: *Politics and Governance* 5, 4, 123–135.
Rensmann, Lars (2018), "Radical Right-Wing Populists in Parliament: Examining the *Alternative for Germany* in European Context", in: *German Politics and Society* 36, 3, 43–71.
Rensmann, Lars (2020), "Die Rückkehr der falschen Propheten: Leo Löwenthals Beitrag zu einer kritischen Sozialforschung des autoritären Populismus in der Gegenwart," in: Henkelmann, Kathrin, Stahl, Andreas, Zopes, Benedikt, Jäckel,

Christian, & Wünsch, Niklas (eds.): *Konformistische Rebellen: Zur Aktualität des autoritären Charakters* Berlin, 21–52.
Rensmann, Lars (2021), "Im Schatten des Trumpismus: Autoritärer Populismus in der Regierung und die Neuformierung der radikalen Rechten in den USA", in: *ZRex – Zeitschrift für Rechtsextremismusforschung* 1,1, 5–25.
Rensmann, Lars, Hagemann, Steffen and Funke, Hajo (2011), *Autoritarismus und Demokratie: Politische Theorie und Kultur in der globalen Moderne*, Schwalbach.
Reporter ohne Grenzen (2022), *Rangliste der Pressefreiheit 2022*, https://www.reporter-ohne-grenzen.de/.
Salzborn, Samuel (2015), "Schleichende Transformation zur Diktatur. Ungarns Abschied von der Demokratie", in: *Kritische Justiz* 48, 1, 71–82.
Salzborn, Samuel (2017), *Angriff der Antidemokraten: Die völkische Rebellion der Neuen Rechten*, Weinheim.
Sartori, Giovanni (1992), *Demokratietheorie*, Darmstadt.
Shekhovtsov, Anton (2018), *Russia and the Western Far Right: Tango Noir*, New York.
Shevtsova, Lilia (2015), "The Authoritarian Resurgence: Forward to the Past in Russia", in: *Journal of Democracy* 26, 2, 22–36.
Snyder, Timothy (2018), *The Road to Unfreedom*, New York.
Thorpe, Nick (2017), "Hungary vilifies financier Soros with crude poster campaign", *BBC News*, 10. Juli, https://www.bbc.com/news/world-europe-40554844.
Töpfl, Florian & Lauer, Stefan (2022), "Russische Propaganda ist wie ein Gemälde, das in die Köpfe der Menschen gemalt wird", in: *Belltower News*, 9 March, https://www.belltower.news/interview-russische-propaganda-ist-ein-gemaelde-das-in-die-koepfe-der-menschen-gemalt-wird-128719/.
Tomini, Luca (2021), "Don't think of a wave! A research note about the current autocratization debate", in: *Democratization* 28,6, 1191–1201.
Urbinati, Nadia (2015), "A Revolt against Intermediary Bodies", in: *Constellations*, 22, 4, 477–486.
Vachudova, Milada Anna (2020), "Ethnopopulism and democratic backsliding in Central Europe", in: *East European Politics* 36, 3, 318–334.
Volk, Sabine (2022). "Explaining PEGIDA's 'Strange Survival': An Ethnographic Approach to Far-right Protest Rituals, *Political Research Exchange*, 4, 1: https://www.tandfonline.com/doi/full/10.1080/2474736X.2022.2136036.
Wahdat-Hagh, Wahid (2003), *Die islamische Republik Iran: Die Herrschaft des politischen Islam als eine Spielart des Totalitarismus*, Münster.
Wahman, Michael, Teorell, Jan and Hadenius, Axel (2013), "Authoritarian Regime Types Revisited: Updated Data in Comparative Perspective", in: *Contemporary Politics* 19, 1, 19–34.
Weeks, Jessica (2002), "Strongmen and Strawmen: Authoritarian Regimes and the Initiation of International Conflict", in: *American Political Science Review* 106, 2, 326–347.
Wintrobe, Ronald (1998), *The Political Economy of Dictatorship*, Cambridge.
Wodak, Ruth (2013), "'Anything Goes!' – The Haiderization of Europe", in: Wodak, Ruth, Khosravinik, Majid & Mral, Brigitte (eds.), in *Right-Wing Populism in Europe: Politics and Discourse*, London, 23–38.
Wojcik, Nadine (2021), "Konfuzius-Institute in der Kritik", *Deutsche Welle*, 28 October, https://www.dw.com/de/konfuzius-institute-kritik-stefan-aust-adrian-geiges-xi-jinping/a-59636041.

Yang, Xifan (2019), "China: Wir sehen Dich!", *Die Zeit*, 10 January, https://www.zeit.de/2019/03/china-regime-ueberwachungsstaat-buerger-kontrolle-polizei?utm_referrer=https%3A%2F%2Fwww.google.com%2F.

4. Self-assertion without self-determination

The new ideological appeal of old authoritarian concepts

Klaus Günther

All world-historical facts and personages occur twice, according to Karl Marx's famous dictum (borrowed from Hegel) in his treatise on the 18th Brumaire of Louis Napoléon – the first time, he adds, as tragedy, the second time as farce. Perhaps this also applies to ideologies, in any case to those which currently advocate the (re)establishment of authoritarian government. One may doubt whether there have ever been great tragedies among these heterogeneous movements, even if a common feature of these movements is a fixation on tragedy. In particular, they generally lament the French Revolution of 1789 and its associated values, which they consider a tragedy of world-historical dimensions. But the growing gap between early authors such as Edmund Burke, Louis de Bonald, Joseph de Maistre, and Donoso Cortés, through later ones such as Charles Maurras, Julius Evola, and Carl Schmitt, to their present-day epigones such as Steve Bannon or Alexander Dugin is so considerable that it is difficult to dismiss the impression that today we are dealing with a farce. Of course, this does not change the fact that even a farce, if it is not seen through or does not want to be seen through (as was once the case with Victor Hugo's "Napoléon le Petit", with few exceptions), can develop the same power of fascination and effect on political consciousness and action as a great tragedy of fate. In the process, old patterns of argumentation are repeated, with appropriate modifications in the face of changed circumstances, whether consciously or unconsciously.

1. THE DELETION OF THE IDEAS OF 1789

One of the central and salient patterns of argumentation is the opposition to the ideas of 1789, which used to be explicit but is now implicit – possibly also due to fading historical knowledge. Goebbels had formulated it succinctly in a radio speech at the beginning of April 1933, shortly before the start date of the book burnings: the Nazis would "erase the year 1789 from German history". Admittedly, hardly anyone today makes reference to this historical event, which occurred more than 200 years ago, and (with a few rather bizarre exceptions) there is hardly anyone left who advocates the re-establishment of a monarchy like the proponents of the Restoration after 1815.[1] This was no longer the case for the Nazis, who used the Hohenzollerns only as a vehicle for the establishment of their authoritarian and totalitarian state (Malinowski 2021). In France, too, the *Action française*, founded in reaction to the outcome of the Dreyfus crisis, was only interested in the restoration of the Bourbon monarchy for instrumental reasons, despite its inspiration from the work of de Maistre (Eisfeld 1986: 114); its present-day offshoots have abandoned this desire altogether and even renounced anti-Semitism. Nevertheless, the opposition to 1789 remains decisive. It has meanwhile transformed into a fundamental opposition to a supposedly decadent, hyper-individualistic, consumerist modernity that contradicts human nature. In the following, it will be shown that there is still a constant pattern of argumentation that feeds on this original opposition and is directed today against the complex arrangement of a liberal constitutional state based on human rights, democracy, and the separation of powers.

This can be seen above all in a pattern of argumentation that *Action française* had brought to the pair of opposites "*pays réel*" and "*pays légal*" (Günther 2021). More recently, the pays réel, the "true people", has been revived in opposition to the institutional structure of a representative democracy with a separation of powers, constitutional executive, constitution with fundamental rights, constitutional court control, and the corresponding civil society pluralism. Marine le Pen already made use of this in her 2017 presidential election campaign. The invocations of a true people orchestrated the successful campaigns for *Brexit* in the UK, the protests of the *gilets jaunes* in France, Donald Trump's election campaign and presidency in the US, Bolsonaro's in Brazil and Chavez's in Venezuela, but also the creeping transformation of that institutional structure in Poland and Hungary and, last but not least, the propaganda of the AfD as well as the Pegida, *Querdenker*, and other right-wing sympathising protests in Germany. The radical democratic undertone that often accompanies those invocations should not obscure the fact that the imagined true *Volk* cannot be asserted without an aggressive exclusion of foreigners and other minorities (for example, against the "global elites", foreigners and citizens with a migration history, selected religious

---

[1] This was the case with Karl Ludwig von Haller, who gave this epoch its name with the title of his main work: "Restauration der Staatswissenschaft" (Haller 1817).

minorities, minorities with a non-heterosexual orientation) and that it mostly cannot do without strong, preferably charismatic leaders who give the "true *Volk*" a voice that wins public attention. This was already recognised by Louis Napoléon, later Emperor Napoleon III, the protagonist of that real-life spectacle apostrophised by Marx at the beginning as a farce. Before he staged a successful coup in 1851 with broad popular support, he had repeatedly positioned the "true people" against the constitutional government. Using a distinction only possible in French, he claimed in 1848 that he wanted to return with the people to *law* against a government that could only claim *legality*: "*de sortir de la légalite, pour rentrer dans le droit*" (Schmitt 1950/1973: 445). For his later interpreter Carl Schmitt, this slogan was particularly attractive because he could draw a direct line from it to his distinction between legality and legitimacy. Admittedly, in an essay serving his own defence in Nuremberg in 1947, he camouflaged this origin with a seemingly merely observational statement about the history of political opposition in France, which he equated one-sidedly with the reactionary *Action française*: "Since about 1900, the opposition in France has spoken of a '*pays légal*', against which it represents a '*pays réel*'" (Schmitt 1950/1973: 445; on this Günther 2021).

These examples already prove that the talk of a "true people" is associated with extensive conceptual registers which receive their meaning primarily through the conceptual contrast to the institutions of a modern constitutional democracy and thus to the ideas of 1789 that originally justified them. Here is a compilation that is not intended to be exhaustive (see Table 4.1):

Admittedly, these oppositions are not to be understood absolutely and the respective terms overlap in some respects; moreover, not every authoritarian movement uses all terms from the respective register equally. They are used regardless of whether they correspond to any reality – whether an ethnically homogeneous people actually exists, whether its members are actually honest, and whether the economic as well as political elites are corrupt. Moreover, the fact that the terms in the left-hand column tend to fit together into a coherent cluster, a kind of catalogue of topoi, does not mean that this is also true for the terms in the right-hand column, which are predominantly projections from the register of terms in the left-hand column (for example, *gender* can easily be raised to "gender delusion"). What is crucial is the manoeuvre of dichotomisation, which serves to devalue the topoi of the right column (see the analogous account in Heitmeyer 2018: 248, who analyses the same structural manoeuvre, as well as Frankenberg & Heitmeyer in this volume). More generally, dichotomisation is itself one of the practices of authoritarian movements, since dichotomies can be used to make supposedly clear friend-enemy distinctions, in-group and out-group markings, and to generate loyalties. A complex "both/and" characteristic of modern constitutional democracies – for example in the

Table 4.1 *Conceptual political dichotomies of the authoritarian*

Pays réel	*Pays légal*
Natural, simple	Artificial, complex
Given	Made
Tradition/history	Invention/modernity
Collective identity/solidarity	Individualism/egoism
Home/origin/descent	Multi-culturalism/cosmopolitanism
Community	Society
Homogeneous	Heterogeneous, pluralistic, diverse
People, ethnic	Citizens, legal association
"Normal" people (local/regional/national)	Cultural, economic elites (global)
"Cleanliness"/honesty	Corruption, hypocrisy, decadence
Personal, bounded trust	Generalised system trust
"Natural" genders, man/woman	Dissolution of gender roles, "gender"
Traditional/patriarchal family	Diverse forms of life and relationships among equals
Habits/mores	Abstracts (legal rules), administration, bureaucracy
(Substantive) legitimacy	(Positivist) legality
Substance	Function
Body and soul	Machine
Organism	Mechanism
Emotion	Mind

relationship between legality and legitimacy – is to be avoided in favour of simple and unambiguous attributions.

Against this backdrop, the following section examines how the phantasm of the true people has left its mark as a pattern of argumentation against a modernising constitutional democracy and which factors can explain its persistence since 1789. In essence, the question is why and under what circumstances the simple authoritarian appears more attractive than the complex system of a constitutional democracy.

2. THE IDEA OF LAW FROM 1789 TO TODAY: POLITICAL AUTONOMY AND HUMAN RIGHTS

In his *Lectures on the History of Philosophy*, delivered between 1820 and 1830, Hegel depicts the French Revolution in dramatic words, apparently borne of his own youthful euphoria during his time at the Tübingen Stift: "Never since the sun had stood in the firmament and the planets revolved around him had it been perceived that man's existence centres in his head, i.e., in Thought, inspired by which he builds up the world of reality" (Hegel 1840/2001: 466 seq.). This oft-quoted eulogy was presumably one of the occasions for Marx's critical remark that dialectics was "upside down" in Hegel and therefore had to be "turned inside out", while Engels later spoke directly of it being turned "from its head onto its feet" only through its connection with materialism (on this Wolf 2019). Engels thus established a reading of the metaphor that relativises the belief in the transformative power of the spirit in social relations in favour of the analysis of material social power relations and their determining effect on the spirit. This is the basis for the well-known opposition between theory and practice or philosophical insight and revolutionary action, which gives priority to changing the world over interpreting it. This reading is certainly not wrong, but perhaps there is another element in Hegel's dictum: the monstrous thing about the French Revolution was that it founded the state based solely on law. For the idea that Hegel invokes is the conception of Right: "The conception, the idea of Right asserted its authority *all at once*, and the old framework of injustice could offer no resistance to its onslaught. A constitution, therefore, was established in harmony with the conception of Right, and on this foundation all future legislation was to be based" (Hegel 1840/2001: 466, emphasis in the original). What is new, then, is that constitution and state are produced and legitimised by the thought, the concept of law, by the citizens themselves through their own actions, while tradition, dynastic genealogy, religion, or nature lose their justifying significance. With the act of declaring human and civil rights, as with the making of a constitution, the people performatively accomplish their political autonomy.[2]

Hegel's emphatic explanation hits at the heart of what the supporters of the Restoration later denigrated as the "*pays légal*". For its part, it stands in a tradition that stretches from Roman law, Cicero, and the modern theorists of the social contract to Abbé Sieyès and Kant (Günther 2016, 2020 and 2021). Sieyès brought this idea to a point in his influential writing on the *Third Estate of 1789*, which also marks the central starting point for the opposing narrative. To the self-posed question of what a nation is, he answers: "A body of associates living under a common law and represented by the same legislative assembly" ("*Qu'est-ce qu'une nation? Un corps d'associés vivant sous une loi commune, et représentés par la même législature*") (Sieyès 1789/1991: 124). The nation, then, is a legal construction, a corporation or association that one can enter and leave like a club, whose members therefore unite by virtue of individual, free choice to live under common laws given by a legislature that

[2] Admittedly, Hegel only succeeds in this by metaphysically enriching the concept of freedom with his Philosophy of Mind, cf. on this, among others, Ritter (1977: 186).

represents them. The nation may have different origins and characteristics, its members may belong to different ethnic groups and share different cultural traditions or even speak different languages, the only decisive factor is the voluntary union of its members in a legal association. Only through the common, human rights-based constitution does the nation become what it is. This alone, and nothing else, is the homogeneity of an otherwise heterogeneous nation. The opposing narrative of the "*pays réel*" will reverse this relationship: pre-constitutional characteristics are claimed to determine the homogeneous being of a people; these are what make a nation what it is. First the nation, then the constitution as its manifestation.

This union is legitimised by human rights. Therefore, a *Declaration of Human and Civil Rights* precedes the nation-state constitution on 26 August 1789. Article 2 explicitly states: "The purpose of every political association is the preservation of the natural and inviolable rights of man." Citizens united in a nation as a corporate body thus do not pursue the purpose of embodying or politically realising an ethnic, cultural or otherwise determined being, but solely the purpose of preserving human rights through a constitution and representative legislation. Even if human rights are initially interpreted and justified in terms of natural law as if they were immutably bound to democratic legislation, they also crystallise an essential moment of political autonomy at the same time: the purpose of the political association to preserve human rights is directed namely at people, who are already holders of subjective human rights and therefore also have individual autonomy. Only insofar as they also have individual autonomy can they exercise their political autonomy, and only insofar as they have political autonomy can they pass laws that make their individual autonomy possible.

To the extent that this succeeds, the unsaturated nature of human rights is also discovered, namely the rights to equality and freedom, which are now being put to use to confront changing social conflict situations, especially in the constantly expanding protection against discrimination. It is these conflicts and struggles for the realisation of human and fundamental rights on which a collective identity is formed step by step – conflicts fought out in democratic opinion-forming and will-forming processes, between civil society publics with political organisations and subjective rights of freedom of expression, information, and assembly on the one hand and democratically elected representative legislatures on the other, often with constitutional court supervision in the case of fundamental conflicts. If they succeed, these conflicts and struggles produce a common experience of overcoming dissent and conflict, which invites identification with the respective state of realisation of human and fundamental rights – and in terms of which each nation of equal citizens differs from the other.

3. AFTER 1789: FOUR CRITIQUES

Of course, the Revolution, at the latest with the *Terreur* from 1793 on, also became the subject of widespread public criticism inside and outside France. The restoration that was enforced politically in Europe after 1815 by the monarchs of the Holy Alliance and advocated by many was still nourished by counter-revolutionary efforts. However, the first, still-tentative criticism of the one-sided reading of human rights as rights to which only adult men were entitled – not in the wording of the Declaration but in legal and political practice, which began early, in 1791 – was silenced by the guillotining of its protagonist Olympe de Gouges in 1793 and then quickly and for a long time forgotten. Only a few months later, with the slave uprising in Haiti, criticism of the racist and colonialist aspects of the human rights actually practised began – also only for a short time, whereas racist practices persisted even after hard-won abolition and the end of colonialism. It took a few more decades for Marx to make the purpose of every political community, handed down in the Declaration of Human Rights of 1789 and in subsequent revolutionary constitutions, the pivot of his critique. The human rights would be galvanised by this purpose and thus depoliticised, withdrawn from democratic political self-determination, with the consequence that the contradiction between formal equality of human rights and simultaneous extreme inequality of social, namely economic, conditions would be sanctioned and politically immunised. What these three critiques of the patriarchal, white, and class-oriented readings of human rights have in common is their justification by reference to human rights principles which, though valid in themselves, have remained unfulfilled by the one-sided readings. This tradition of critique is not the negation of the ideas of 1789, but the initiation – laboriously achieved in bloody struggles against massive opposition – of the unfinishable process of critiquing the partisan interpretation and inappropriate application of these ideas and realising the untapped potential of their content. (Even though Marx explicitly opposes human rights in the form of subjective rights, he primarily means the immunisation of their unfulfilled content from political exploitation.) What all three movements are fighting for – until today – is the transition from the *preservation of* human rights still apostrophised in Article 2 of the *Declaration* and sanctioning of existing conditions to their continuous *exhaustion of their potential, which is* activated in the constant confrontation of the democratic political process with conflicting social conditions.

In contrast, the supporters of the Restoration in particular question the ideas of 1789 as a whole. They oppose political autonomy, which Hegel had emphatically emphasised as a central feature of the revolution, and they cultivate a general suspicion against human rights that is still harboured today in different variants. The figure of argumentation mobilised against the idea of political autonomy is that which, according to Hegel, served to justify the injustice of absolutism: "such as the social impulse, the desire of security for property, etc., (…) the religious sentiment, as does that of the Divine appointment of the governing power" (Hegel 1840/2001: 465). Karl Ludwig von Haller explicitly opposed the "theory of the natural-social state" to the "*chimera of the artificial-bourgeois*" in the subtitle of his main work (Haller 1817; emphasis K.G.). It is always a matter of reducing the constitution to the subsequent manifestation and affirmation of a divine order or natural properties withdrawn from the will. But the constitution only asserts these naturally given properties, puts them into the linguistic form of mostly declaratively formulated but normatively intended sentences; it is not the medium and execution of political self-determination. Human rights are overrun with the suspicion that they only give free rein to particular, idiosyncratic, individual passions detrimental to the moral community; that by granting a licence to enjoy these unbridled passions and perversions, they ultimately degrade man and make him a slave to his nature.

Today, this pattern of argumentation returns in the claim that human rights privilege minorities, namely sexual and non-Christian religious ones, at the expense of the rights of the majority. This criticism by no means excludes the fact that the majority has a libertarian understanding of freedom and protests loudly against any restriction of fundamental rights to freedom. However, it is usually only a matter of defending the claimed normality of white people's ways of life (not only the economically privileged, but also and above all those threatened by a reduction in social status), in many cases combined with the restoration of a patriarchal conception of marriage and family and a return to the traditional role of women. This is expressed above all in the often successful efforts to prohibit the public presentation of non-binary gender roles in the name of the rights of (binary-gender) parents, insofar as children and adolescents might get exposed to them; or to more heavily restrict or altogether abolish women's right to determine their own pregnancies. The libertarian understanding of freedom therefore has no trouble massively restricting women's rights of freedom, especially over their own bodies, and denying equal rights to those who represent forms of life that deviate from heteronormative whiteness. Brazilian President Jair Bolsonaro put it in a nutshell: "Human rights only for righteous people" (Cardoso 2019). It is also this self-perceived righteous, homogeneous majority which sometimes invokes political autonomy via radically democratic channels – an autonomy to be expressed as far as possible in plebiscites. However, this is not an autonomy based on equal human rights, but the normativisation of those essential features constituting the homogeneity of the majority (for example, the way of life of whites). And because they are claimed as given, as natural, the majority does not and cannot behave autonomously on the basis of these characteristics. If at all, political autonomy is reduced to the act of subsequently affirming and reinforcing those natural characteristics, which is then articulated and defended not in the mode of self-determination, but only of self-assertion vis-à-vis minorities as an expression of an apparently democratic majority will.

This can be exemplified by a borderline case such as Edmund Burke's early critique of the French Revolution published in 1790. Unlike the supporters of restoring the monarchist state, Burke was concerned with defending the complex English constitutional structure with its constantly reset equilibrium between monarchy and parliament, which he understood as a mixed constitution and thus as an ideal type of rule in the general interest, drawing on Aristotle's typology of forms of government. Because it stored the experiential knowledge accumulated from past conflicts and – above all through unequally distributed property – ensured a careful selection of suitable (male) people for political offices below the monarch, Burke polemically opposes revolution as an autonomous new beginning, with abstract human rights derived from philosophy and not from experience. But he bases his polemic on an argumentation that will become paradigmatic for the ensuing generations and will recur in authoritarian patterns of argumentation.

Without explicitly naming it, Burke also takes up Article 2 of the Declaration and its rationale. But he opposes the concept of political association by equating it with a private law contract: "The state ought not to be considered as nothing better than a partnership agreement in a trade of pepper and coffee, calico or tobacco, or some other such low concern, to be taken up for little temporary interest, and to be dissolved by fancy of the parties" (Burke 1790/2014: 100).[3] It is true that society is also a contract according to Burke, but of a completely different kind than a private law contract, namely only "a clause in a great primaeval contract of eternal society" (Burke 1790/2014: 101). Burke thus subtracts the moment of the participants' autonomous decision from the foundation of a political association, such that it appears only as the necessary implementation of a predetermined and historically concretised order, "according to a fixed compact sanctioned by the inviolable oath which holds all physical and all moral natures, each in their appointed place" (Burke 1790/2014: 101). This law is not at the disposition of an individual human will and demands compliance out of necessity. Beyond individual private autonomy there is no political autonomy, only the virtue of state wisdom,

[3] Hegel argues similarly to Burke when he states in his *Elements of the Philosophy of Right* from 1820/21 in § 258 that membership in a state is not something arbitrary, and in §§ 273 and 274 that no one can *make* a constitution because it is always already given for a people. Unlike Burke, however, the constitution embodies the spirit of freedom.

which is enriched by historically accumulated and handed-down experiential knowledge and which is found only in carefully selected men, especially among the wealthy.

Burke also consistently denies any pre-contractual validity to the rights of liberty, whose conception as inviolable and inalienable human rights he considers an aberration. They can only emerge from the convention that realises the primordial original contract, and only as liberties that are always already limited and protected by the state. Their limits can only be drawn by that state wisdom, based on experiential knowledge of human nature and its needs. The assertion of universal human rights that apply prior to any convention, on the other hand, would place each individual in a state of nature in which each is a "judge in his own cause" and can make his individual, undisciplined passions the law (Burke 1790/2014: 60). It is the argument that human rights are only established by legislation that Thomas Paine opposed in his equally famous reply to Burke: "It is a perversion of terms to say that a charter gives rights." What becomes clear in both of Burke's polemics, against political autonomy and against human rights, is the fear of a social order based on the idea of law as the execution of political autonomy, which Habermas (reflecting on Carl Schmitt's polemic, which was identical in this respect) characterised as the "horror of autonomy" (Habermas 1987: 113).

With the figure of the primordial contract, Burke takes aim at the moment of political autonomy invoked by the revolution. The precondition of an existence that is not at the disposal of citizens who voluntarily unite under common legislation, but which is given to them and can only be manifested and asserted by them. This primordial existence is subsequently imagined, interpreted, and shaped in various ways, but its function of making the political autonomy first claimed in 1789 a mere derivative of itself always remains the same. If for Burke it is a supra-individual, physical-moral order represented in the primordial contract and concretised through experience and history, for the supporters of the Restoration on the continent (for example de Maistre, de Bonald, Julius Stahl) it is primarily the sacral monarchy with a corporative state.[4] In the

---

[4] In de Maistre, similar to Burke, it is said: "An essential error consists in imagining the state of society as a state of choice, founded on the agreement of men, on a decision and an original contract which cannot exist" (de Maistre 1794/2021: 8). However, in contrast to Burke, sovereign rule can only be created by God. De Bonald denies man's ability to create a constitution at all, because the (correct) constitution is always already given by the nature of human society: "Man is no more able to give a constitution to religious or political society than he is able to give gravity to bodies or volume to matter" (*Théorie du pouvoir politique et religieux*, 1796, here quoted from the translation in Eisfeld 1986: 112). Stahl, on the other hand, developed a Protestant conception of constitutional monarchy in the Vormärz period based on the "principle of legitimacy", according to which "the lawful (legitimate) authorities and order are sanctified

course of the nineteenth century, this political-theological concept of legitimacy became increasingly questionable as a result of increasing secularisation and the emergence of industrial capitalism. Starting with the wars against the French occupation under Napoleon and a little later under the influence of naturalism and historicism, the nation in the sense of a people determined culturally and by a common history takes the place of the primordial existence which could and should never become a subject of political autonomy. This is already attended by anti-Semitic affects. The *Volk* is then increasingly imagined ethnically in the age of imperialism and nationalism, and conceived according to racist categories as an exclusive *Volksgemeinschaft* (community of "the people") which must prove itself in the mode of struggle against external and internal enemies (Wildt 2019: 25). Although the nation understood in this way is also a constructed, artificially produced entity – as a brief look at the mostly conflict-ridden and bloody historical processes of nation-building shows – it is precisely this contingent, artificially produced character of the people constituting a nation that is supposed to be compensated for or neutralised by those naturalising descriptions and mythicising historical narratives. The self of the people is not performatively called into being through politically autonomous constitution-making, but is considered predetermined by natural features (so-called race, origin, culture, etc.). As such, it can only be asserted through the constitution – self-assertion without self-determination. But this self-asserting "true people" did not and does not exist; it was and is always a phantasm.

4. INSECURITY AND UNCERTAINTY: THE PERSISTENCE OF THE ARGUMENTATION PATTERN

These observations are not new. However, the persistence with which the argumentative pattern of the "true people" has renewed itself in modified forms is still in need of explanation, even if its original thrust against the ideas of 1789 is no longer present in the collective memory. The *ad hoc* explanations that point to acute or protracted experiences of crisis, such as in recent times the financial and migration crises or earlier, in the incubation phase of fascist movements, severe economic crises and national humiliation as a result of military defeat, are certainly not false, but they leave open why this pattern of argumentation can be mobilised again and again with relative success in such

by God and the people are bound to them, subject to them" (Stahl 1833/1856/1963: 536), with a corporative state oriented less to feudal distinctions than to corporations of different professions (ibid. 369.). On Stahl see Puhle (1986: 271–275).

situations. To answer this question, we would have to look at possible cognitive structures that are represented and exemplified by those patterns of argumentation, which allow such crisis experiences to be processed in a particular way. Perhaps these structures embedded themselves in mentalities during the restorative movements around 1789 and have since remained latent as constant companions of the modern democratic constitutional state, ready to become manifest in the face of profound crises. Presumably, the French Revolution itself is the original experience of crisis which has determined all subsequent manifestations as an archetype and paradigm. If one understands "crisis" with Schleiermacher's definition, also formulated under the impression of 1789, as a "time which is so obviously the boundary between two different orders of things" (Schleiermacher 1799/2012: 250), then the insecurity of the existing order and the uncertainty of the future order could be the reason for resorting to these patterns of argumentation, because they promise a way out of the crisis – albeit one that, when viewed objectively, is deceptive. According to this theory, the crisis experience of 1789 would be updated with every new crisis like a trauma that continues to shape mentalities over generations.

Possibly the pattern of argumentation based on the opposition of *pays réel* and *pays légal* articulates a distrust of the more complex relations of modern democratic rule of law. Especially under the impression of crises, this distrust structures the experience, interpretation, and available options for response in such a way that this order appears as if it were incapable of overcoming the crisis altogether or as if it would only exacerbate the crisis. The horror of political autonomy sublimates itself, as it were, into the horror of the complexity of a constitutional democracy in a modern, functionally differentiated society. To the extent that political autonomy creates such conditions – in permanent tension with a capitalism that is more or less tamed – and realises itself in them in a way that remains unfinished and deficient, therefore open to critique and ongoing change with reference to its fundamental justifying principles, the suggestive iconography of historically effective and popular images and narratives loses meaning. It is no longer the mass movement, no longer the ballroom oath of the revolutionary National Assembly handed down by Jacques Louis David in sketches and a monumental painting fragment that convey the image of political autonomy, but rather a complex machinery that (apart from rare moments of profound political upheavals and constitutional reforms) is banalised in everyday operations, which does not seem to function properly under crisis conditions and spreads feelings of insecurity. It is no coincidence that those suggestive historical images of revolutionary mass movements are appropriated by authoritarian movements today when they want to attack the complex institutions of constitutional democracies with protest marches or violent actions against parliamentary buildings.

A democratic order based on the rule of law inevitably goes hand-in-hand with a high degree of openness to results and revisability of decisions. In a social system with a functional differentiation of various social subsystems, plural civil society public spheres, and individualism based on individual rights along with a simultaneous pluralism of identities and voluntary membership of communities, normative orders remain in a process of permanent revision whose rules and procedures they must simultaneously stabilise and reproduce in every conflict. A certain degree of insecurity and uncertainty is therefore built into such orders *a priori*, so to speak; they are the condition of openness to the future and freedom. *Therefore*, there is not only a contingent but also an *internal connection* between the high degree of complexity of democratic rule of law in functionally differentiated societies and a larger scope of the system of equal individual liberty rights. Such a system of liberty rights is highly dependent on corresponding institutional and societal preconditions – the legal design of which in turn guarantees freedom in the form of democratic rule of law, i.e. through legally institutionalised political autonomy. It is this connection between the degree of complexity and freedom that is denied or disputed under the impression of the authoritarian temptation – one sees only chaos, arbitrariness, corruption, and state prohibitions everywhere, which seem to unconstitutionally restrict a supposedly limitless individual freedom. Only simpler and authoritarian structures can bring order to this supposed chaos. Armin Nassehi got to the heart of the internal connection between complexity and freedom in an essay written under the impression of Putin's recently begun war against Ukraine – because it is this connection that is feared by authoritarian regimes:

> Such a society presupposes openness to results, is thus prone to error, allows for changes of government, needs competing offers, and has to prove itself before an audience. However, not everything in a society is decided by democratic-political means. But experiences of openness to results also prevail in other areas as complexity increases: it is not for nothing that the political form of democracy always goes hand in hand with free-market economies, positive law, creative art, a strong understanding of education, and self-critical science. These different logics come into conflict with each other and are difficult to control. But what emerges is a society whose dynamics are characterised above all by the fact that it must renounce complete determination of its possibilities – and must therefore build freedom into its self-understanding. (Nassehi 2022)

The insecurity built into the existing democratic constitutional order and the structural uncertainty about the future of this order can now, under experiences of crisis, assume a magnitude that leads to authoritarian temptation.

5. TRUST

Such an order not only places high demands on the ability to differentiate between multiple roles (between private person and public official, between consumer, patient, recipient of academic achievements, voter, etc.), but also on the ability to develop sufficient trust despite repeated experiences of conflict, dissent, openness to results, and the resulting insecurity and uncertainty. This includes a sufficient degree of *self-confidence* to experience such an order not as an existential threat, but as an opportunity to lead one's life independently, both as a member who belongs to differnet communities as well as an individual among other individuals with equal rights to private autonomy – that is, to live in freedom. Only in this way is a "trust in the control of one's own life planning" possible (Heitmeyer 2018: 50). Finally, a *generalised political* or *systemic trust* in the functional and self-correcting abilities of the institutional arrangement of the democratic rule of law is required, as well as a *personal trust* in the actors of this system to orient their actions not only to their own interests but also to the – for their part trustworthy – norms and procedural rules of the system (see on this Herzog 2013). As Mark E. Warren has shown, a functioning democratic constitutional state is characterised by two types of institutional trust. First of all, individuals must trust that the state (above all its executive agencies) will treat them fairly and impartially, because administrative action is subject to public norms and a violation of these norms by public officials is sanctioned; because administrative action is transparent to individuals even from a distance; and because there is publicly accountable control, especially where administrative action requires special expertise (*first-order institutional trust*) (Warren 2018: 89). This trust must be complemented by a trust in the functioning of the democratic process itself, so that the political interests of particular groups in society cannot assert themselves through coercion, manipulation, or direct influence on members of parliament or officeholders in the executive functions of the state, but only by bringing them "into the institutions that channel conflict into democratic media of talking and voting" (ibid., 90). It is above all this *second-order institutional trust* on which the openness of the democratic political process and the revisability of decisions depend. Their experience must show that engaging in politics and raising their voice makes a difference and that political decisions are taken in the general interest; only then do citizens have the chance to confirm their institutional trust. In short, trust in the functioning of democracy is a trust that the inevitable uncertainties and insecurities of the democratic process – uncertainties which at the same time guarantee freedom – "pay off" in the end.

The ability to develop these different types of trust is, of course, not naturally given and the willingness to take risks is unequally distributed. The ability must first be generated and then protected, the willingness can only be fostered – and neither of them can be intentionally produced by administrative means. They require accommodating, favourable conditions, above all a corresponding socio-economic framework. Whether and to what extent such basic conditions exist and are sufficient for sustainable trust-building is itself a topic of public dispute.

If the moments of insecurity and uncertainty are intensified by large-scale crises, some people's confidence in these abilities weakens, causing not only their self-confidence to erode, but also, above all, their combined personal and systemic confidence in the ability of the constitutional-democratic system and its actors to cope with crises (Heitmeyer 2018: 51). If these losses of trust are not countered by self-correcting forces of the constitutional-democratic arrangement, the alternative can be an attitude in which the complexity of the democratic-legal order in a pluralistic civil society is seen as the central exacerbating factor in the crisis. This motivates the search for less complex structures of social and political organisation such as the homogeneous community of the *Volk*, whose leader not only knows the needs of the "true people" or allows them to be articulated with the help of plebiscites but is also assertive enough, with the assistance of a loyal executive and judiciary branch, to satisfy these needs against dissenting – from the majority's point of view "disruptive" – minorities or the global elites.

To avoid misunderstandings: this hypothesis does not, of course, exclude the possibility that criticism of the deficits of a more complex democratic rule of law – and even more so of its everyday practice – can be justified in itself (for examples see Zürn's contribution in this volume and Heitmeyer 2018, especially 118 and 177). Nor, of course, can it be denied that institutional trust of the first and second order is repeatedly disappointed – whether by public officials who fail to fulfil their obligations or are prone to corruption, or by well-organised and influential interest groups that hijack the democratic process to advance their particular interests (on this, see also the examples in Warren 2018: 90). But it makes a difference whether this criticism, based on fundamental rights such as freedom of expression, information, press, and assembly, can be raised publicly at all and whether it refers to the principles of democratic rule of law, relying on their inherent capacity for self-correction; or whether it only uses these principles as a pretext to gradually transform the institutions that realise them into simpler, authoritarian structures.

One example is the conflict between a constitutional jurisdiction empowered to review norms and the democratic representative legislature, which is unavoidable for a highly complex structure and productive for a politics based on human rights and democracy. This conflict can undercut a government majority if the court declares one of its laws unconstitutional or obliges the legislature to amend the law in parts or even to pass a new law that runs counter to the majority's interests. Criticism of such decisions can be used by the government and its majority to gain additional legitimacy through plebiscites, which can be used to mobilise the supposed will of the true people against the court or, in the medium term, to control or restructure the procedure for appointing judges to the court in such a way that constitutional judges are only selected on the basis of their loyalty to the policies of the government majority. The critique is then no longer about re-balancing the productive tension between constitutional jurisdiction and the legislature, between human and fundamental rights on the one hand and the democratic majority on the other, in the mode of a divisible conflict,[5] but about the transformation of the court into a judicial instrument to legitimise the executive and the majority supporting it, which claims to embody the will of the true people. As a result, the *framing* and the perception of the institutional structure of the democratic rule of law change: increasingly, it "merely" appears as a highly complex and non-transparent façade behind which, "in reality", a simple interplay of special interests is taking place – for example, if the judges of the constitutional court are considered to only serve the interests of influential but covertly operating groups ("global elites", minorities whose way of life deviates from the majority's, etc.) at the expense of the "true people", the popular will must take them in hand. In this perception, the productive, divisible conflict changes into a destructive, indivisible conflict in which only one side may prevail, the court or the will of the people.

6. LEVELS OF HIERARCHICAL COMPLEXITY OF POLITICAL RULE

As soon as the manifold demands of maintaining a functioning democratic rule of law, of faithfully handling its inherent uncertainties and insecurities, and of productively managing conflicts and dissent become overwhelming as a result of intensified experiences of crisis, the authoritarian temptation arises to sidestep the path of immanent critique and self-correction and instead to seek alternatives that seem to make fewer demands and have a lower degree of complexity. Above all, it is a question of replacing the combination of institutional and personal trust with personal trust in an authoritarian leader and replacing the universalism of human rights with the phantasm of personal closeness and social trust between the members of the *Volksgemeinschaft*, of the "true people".

---

[5] On the distinction between divisible and indivisible conflicts, see Hirschman (1994).

To this end, we can refer to studies that attempt to explain why the transfer of differentiated systems of democratic rule of law to countries with other forms and traditions of governance, social cooperation, and political identities often fails; why former authoritarian state techniques and notorious corruption continue to persist even after an attempted transfer; or why terrorist organisations are formed that fight democracy and human rights under the rule of law. Especially in the studies by Ross, Commons, and Chilton, it is assumed that the causes lie less in a lack of insight or willingness on the part of those affected, but rather in cognitive differences (Ross/Commons 2008; Chilton 1991). The rejection would be based primarily on a (socio-)cognitive structure that influences the perception of the social world, social interactions, and the accompanying practices of producing social meaning, as well as the hierarchical organisation of political rule. Drawing on studies of moral development by Jean Piaget and Lawrence Kohlberg, a model has been developed that distinguishes between different stages of logical-mathematical operations, moral judgement, and the formation of hierarchical complexity for the organisation of political rule.[6] One of the central features of this model is that the path from lower to higher levels follows a developmental logic determined by specific tasks and challenges, which is why a society can only develop from one level to the next in its problem-solving behaviour and cannot skip any. The hypothesis of a developmental logic also includes that the (socio-)cognitive structure prevailing at one level differs from the respective structure at a higher one, such that the respective actors on two different levels do not understand each other. What is an accepted and functioning form of social interaction at one level appears as corruption at the higher level.

The assumption to be substantiated in the following is that authoritarian movements structurally persist on a lower level of hierarchical complexity and defend against the higher levels. However, where authoritarian movements develop within democratic constitutional states or transform them insidiously or openly, the question then arises whether a *regression* from a higher to a lower level is possible.

The stage model can only be sketched roughly and with the features relevant for this chapter. The decisive factor is the ability to generalise and abstract, which not only makes it possible to carry out more complex logical operations, to form different conceptual systems and to relate them to each other, but also to move in the socio-cognitive dimension from an egocentric perspective to an inclusively expanding social perspective. Accordingly, different levels of

---

6 For the stage model of moral development, see the overview by Nunner-Winkler 2004; for the stage model of hierarchical complexity, see the overview by Fein 2012: 61–74.

hierarchical complexity of political organisation and social cooperation can be distinguished, characterised above all by the increasing ability to distinguish between people, roles, and offices, as well as by the ability to follow rules not rigidly but in a principle-oriented way, to balance a complex structure of tensions both between the three classical state powers and between other sovereign actors, to respect the inherent logic of different social functional systems, and to admit democratic pluralism. The stages begin with the *concretism* of personal relationships and dependencies, in which social interactions and political domination are organised through friendships, exchange relationships, or the raw exercise of power. Therefore, there is no distinction between offices/roles and persons. At the next level, more abstract formations emerge in which, beyond personal proximity, more general group- and community-related features shape the structure of social interaction and political rule. Such groups are based on the strict loyalty of their members and are characterised by specific features shared equally by all of them, who, in addition, depend on the group's values and ideals for the formation of their individual identity. They favour the rise of paternalistic and charismatic leaders who ensure fairness and harmony among group members (who are treated like children), and propagate an ideology with rigid ingroup/outgroup distinctions. A further step of abstraction is achieved on the following level of the formal, when no longer only group-related, particular values and norms are formed, but more general formal rules on the basis of which politics and economy can differentiate themselves as formally regulated social subsystems. This makes possible a general and equal private law and an administrative law for the regulation of bureaucracy, admittedly with a rigidly practised formalism that follows rules to the letter. The processes of democratisation that begin at the formal level can be successfully completed at the ensuing system level. At this level, different social spheres, each with its own logic, can be integrated into a social system (e.g. a nation-state) so that different goals can be pursued and realised simultaneously. Democratically enacted law plays a central role in this process, but is no longer simply interpreted and applied in such a formalistic manner, but rather in a principle-oriented manner. However, these principles still remain bound to the system in its particularity and are therefore also compatible with nationalistic attitudes; only at the following stages of the meta-systematic and the paradigmatic is a universalistic horizon reached in which problem-solving behaviour is oriented towards human rights, universal principles, and criteria of international justice beyond the respective particular system.

7. THREE REDUCTIONS: *VOLKSGEMEINSCHAFT*, PERSONAL TRUST, PATRON-CLIENT RELATIONSHIP

In the following, the aim is not to transfer this stage model schematically to the argumentative patterns of restorative and authoritarian movements. But it proves helpful insofar as it can be used to identify three decisive dimensions in which a reduction or shift from the more complex to the simple takes place, whereby the "true people" are positioned against constitutional democracy and its institutions and actors: (a) in the social-cognitive dimension, the reduction of the paradigmatic universalism of human rights to the concretism and formalism of a *Volkgemeinschaft* (community of "the people"); (b) in the dimension of trust, the reduction of the combined institutional and personal trust to an exclusively personal trust; and (c) in the dimension of the organisation of political power, the reduction of the hierarchical complexity of democratic rule of law to a patron-client relationship.

7.1 The Social-cognitive Dimension: *Volksgemeinschaft* Instead of Human Rights

To the extent that the complexity level of a democratic rule of law based on universal human rights of the pays reel is countered by a pays reel (i.e. the narrative of the true people of a *Volksgemeinschaft*), the scope of social perspective-taking or the willingness to adopt the perspective of others, especially strangers, is reduced to the radius drawn by membership in a *Volksgemeinschaft*. The *Volksgemeinschaft* itself is constituted *concretistically* through an imagined, personal closeness among those with whom one shares the same way of life, or more abstractly through membership in a single group with the same, predominantly ethnically determined characteristics. Even at the levels of the *formal* and the *system*, which already have a higher degree of differentiation and generalisation that transcends group affiliations, the common features that characterise a supposed homogeneity remain characteristic. These can then be attributed to the nation itself, thereby simultaneously recategorising the citizen-nation based on mere legal status into a homogeneous people. It is this perceived closeness – mostly only imagined, but also brought to mind by suggestive conceptions of homogeneity – to those who one is convinced are similar to oneself, which ensures a higher degree of social trust (Lenard/Miller 2018: 62 and 65). Admittedly, the influence of national identity and national identifications on social and political trust is not clear-cut and varies between different states, but a strong identification with one's own nation is associated with a higher likelihood of an ethnic conception of the nation (Lenard/Miller 2018: 70). Therefore, strategies of ethnicisation and homogenisation are designed to strengthen social and political trust by asserting ostensibly natural ethnic similarities – but in the mode of particularised, pseudo-personalised, not generalised trust.

The constitution is then regarded as a manifestation of the homogeneous national community, i.e., the setting and application of all formal rules and procedures must be substantively oriented to the nation's identity. It forms the boundary of the social horizon. The social and political conflicts, dissent, and the open-endedness of the political process in particular, which increase with growing complexity, are internally reduced or stopped altogether, especially under the impression of experiences of crisis. Fairness and harmony are supposed to prevail within the national community; the obligations of the individual towards the community take precedence over individual rights. Conflicts can then be framed internally in such a way that minorities appear to have instigated them – minorities who either have not yet been sufficiently homogenised in the national community or whose foreignness excludes them from it entirely. Those who nevertheless insist on a deviating position and do not adapt are either criminals or show a lack of "patriotism" (or both, if "unpatriotic behaviour" is criminalised), and easily fall under a vague suspicion of terrorism. At the same time, the national community is constituted by a more or less aggressive demarcation from the outside. Internal conflicts can then also be externalised to alleged external enemies who only seek to weaken or completely destroy the cohesion of the national community by secretly and continuously fomenting internal conflicts. The strengthening of bounded trust within the national community is to be achieved by increasing mistrust against external enemies. In the struggle against these, the national community is at the same time constituted as a community of fate, which imagines itself in permanent constellations of danger or self-defence and is dependent on a constant activation and reaffirmation of the distinction between friend and foe. In such constellations, there is then also an increased use of medical and biological metaphors: the national community, imagined as a living body, must cleanse itself of foreign and heterogeneous elements, eliminate them and dispose of them in places as far away as possible, spit them out like vermin, or fight them like dangerous germs.[7] Thus, in a speech on the twenty-first day of the war against Ukraine, Russian President Putin, faced with internal enemies and traitors, expressed his conviction "that such a natural and necessary self-purification of society will only strengthen our country, our solidarity, our

---

[7] On the role and function of purity and cleansing commandments for the order systems of societies and their threats, see Mary Douglas (1966/1988).

cohesion, and our readiness to respond to all challenges".[8] The struggle for national self-assertion is always also a purifying struggle for internal cohesion.

Beyond concrete and beneficial bilateral agreements with other states, the community of fate also opposes an international political order based on international law and human rights. Inter- and, above all, supranational institutions and organisations only count when they serve one's own national interests; otherwise, as in the populist criticisms of the EU, they are demonised as undemocratic bureaucratic monsters that would only serve the interests of foreign powers at the expense of one's own people. In place of such an order – that created and maintained by the people and the states representing them through the joint production of law and binding state sovereignty – there is a multipolar world order dominated by great powers, which watch over their respective spheres of influence in *Großraumordnungen* (orders predicated on large spaces) of a Schmittian type with dependent states. Their relationship to each other ultimately remains in a state of nature that is hardly tamed by international law. This is determined by the variations of the respective power and (above all military) strength, above which only fate rules, determining the weal and woe of the people in battle and war between the great powers. It can be imagined as a world-historical gigantomachy that continuously produces tragic conflicts, such as those found in the Iliad, the Hildebrandslied or the Saga of the Nibelungs, which populate the collective memory in infinitely diverse variations that are no longer conscious of their origins, right up to film series such as Star Wars. What could be a matter of political autonomy, of deliberation and argumentation, justification and application of norms of justice, is substituted by justificatory narratives of loyalty and betrayal, honour and defiance, heroism and cowardice, sacrifice and retribution. Such a belief in fate has always been draped in archaising kitsch, which also serves to project the genesis of the *Volksgemeinschaft* itself back to time immemorial, with mythical heroes who either fought victoriously against sinister foreign powers at great cost or who lost tragically (cf. exemplarily Naumann 1934).

7.2 The Dimension of Trust: Personal Trust Instead of Trust in Institutions

Just as the *Volksgemeinschaft* is constituted by something that creates homogeneity and similarities among its members while at the same time remaining beyond their control, it also needs a strong guardian, a charismatic, fatherly, caring, but also strict patron who must protect the dependent, child-like members of this national community and lead them through the crises, con-

---

8 *Der Tagesspiegel* 19 March 2022.

flicts, and struggles caused by internal and external enemies. Since the people can only articulate themselves through plebiscites with a "yes" or "no", the leader must also recognise their will, bring it to expression and decision, and realise it. This applies above all to the level of group-related abstractions: "Strong, paternal-type leaders, often charismatic, tend to be preferred, on the assumption they will take care of their children/followers and keep the group or society harmonious and fair" (Ross/Commons 2008: 485).

Weber defines charisma as a "a certain quality of an individual by virtue of which he is considered extraordinary and treated as endowed with supernatural, superhuman, or at least exceptional powers or qualities. These are such as are not accessible to the ordinary person, but are as of divine origin or as exemplary, and on the basis of them the individual concerned is treated as a leader" (Weber 1921/1968: 241). This definition already names one of the most important differences to the complexity of a constitutional democracy. Whereas the latter presupposes trust in the (political) system, the lower level of complexity relies primarily on personal trust in the leader's extra-ordinary qualities. To the extent that the uncertainty and insecurity associated with experiences of crisis are attributed to the complexity of democratic rule of law, it is precisely extra-ordinary qualities and abilities, however much their public display and proof may be staged, that appear as the only possible way out. Devout, personal devotion to the leader is born, as Weber aptly puts it, out of enthusiasm, despair, and hope (ibid: 242).

The difference between the levels of complexity is also expressed in the fact that the rule of law and bureaucracy are increasingly deformalised. There are no officials appointed according to formal rules in a hierarchy subject to general laws, but only "trusted men" appointed by the leader on the basis of his supposedly infallible intuition. Here, too, only personal trust counts. In legal conflicts, there is "no system of formal rules, of abstract legal principles, and hence no process of rational judicial decision oriented to them [...], there is no legal wisdom oriented to judicial precedent. Formally concrete judgments are newly created from case to case"(Weber 1921/1968: 243). Of course, a charismatic rule that relies on extra-ordinary qualities must also become "routinized" (ibid.: 246) in order to make social cooperation possible in the long term and to restore to the individual that (above all material) security in everyday life whose endangerment motivated the search for the exceptionally gifted authoritarian leader in the first place. This, in turn, requires the training of an administrative staff which, due to its bureaucratic structure, however, often comes into conflict with the charismatic claim of the leader and his trusted men, who rely on the spontaneity of the "movement".

This is particularly evident in the transition to the *complexity level* of the *formal*. While formal norms increasingly regulate administration and the economy and thus enable predictability, the informal sphere orientated towards the leader, relying on personal trust rather than normative trust, operates in parallel with ad hoc measures and spontaneous interventions. Formal norms and organisations can then also serve as a façade to hide the informal practice of political rule, orientated towards charisma and personal trust, and exploit it for one's own network of particular interests: "[T]he new forms of government or business procedure provide new façades to which conventional behaviours of patronage adapt and persist, usually more effectively because access to new resources is available" (Ross/Commons 2008: 486).

In this way, the parallel structure of formal legality and informal hierarchy characteristic of authoritarian states emerges, with the latter forming the actual political centre of action, while the former, especially the constitution, predominantly serves only (self-)representative purposes and the strategic pursuit of interests (Frankenberg 2020: 305). This applies not least to those states in which a constitutional-democratic order has already existed, but which is now being transformed step by step into an authoritarian one. Using the example of the Nazi state, Ernst Fraenkel has characterised this simultaneity as a "double state", which is at the same time a state of norms and a state of measures – alongside the formal legal norms (for example of civil and administrative law) come the individual case-related measures by the movement's confidants, who are not bound by any rules (Fraenkel 1974/2019; cf. also Frankenberg 2020: 143). Another variant can be found wherever formal law and the judiciary are instrumentalised for the prosecution of political opposition, of dissidence in general, as well as of minorities, not only with an explicitly political criminal law, but above all through the politically manipulated prosecution of politically neutral offences – for suspected terrorism, tax evasion, corruption, child pornography, and so on.

7.3 The Dimension of the Organisation of Power: Clientelisms Instead of Political Autonomy

The two aforementioned processes of reduction – *social-cognitive* and *trust-related* – find their adequate form of expression in patronage-client relationships, a paradigm in human history that has been largely underestimated in social, political, and legal studies up to the present (see the overview in Combes/Vommaro 2015, as well as Fein 2012). They were constitutive (and therefore also concept-forming) for the cohesion of the ancient Roman Republic up to the time of the Principate (Ganter 2015); they belonged to the characteristic features of feudalism; and they can be found in modern times in many societies that were not able to form a modern state or whose statehood is in a process of disintegration. In different variants, they also occur under conditions of halfway functioning statehood, as in the case of party clientelism in many Latin American states or in some Mediterranean littoral states. The

Soviet-Russian history and present are also characterised by it (Fein 2012). Finally, corresponding characteristics can also be found in larger criminal organisations such as the Mafia (Hess 1986).

Systematically, the patron-client relationship is determined by an asymmetry between the patron (usually with his family circle), who alternatively or cumulatively has a higher social rank, more extensive resources of power and means of violence, social influence/prestige, or wealth/capital, and the client, who permanently lacks such resources to a greater or lesser extent. If there is no authority superior to the patron or if this is divided among several patrons, as in the Roman Republic, the future clients have no other option than to seek protection, care, and the defense or representation of their interests by a patron vis-à-vis more powerful third parties. Conversely, it is not infrequent for the future patron to impose such goods and services on the future client (the notorious "offer that cannot be refused") under the latent or manifest threat of putting the person concerned in a situation that either drastically demonstrates his and his family's need for protection or cautions him against disloyalty. The dependency relationship is characterised by reciprocity. For the services rendered to his clients, the patron receives their loyalty, goodwill, favours, as well as the willingness to render services and the execution of orders. It is a relationship of collusive "direct protective trust" (Warren 2018: 83) based on the personal relationship between the two parties. As a fiduciary relationship (fides), it can only be marginally formalised in law at best; any reference to explicit formal rules would weaken the personal trust that prevails between patron and client. Usually, this also includes the obligation to keep silent about internal matters vis-à-vis external third parties; intransparency to the outside world is essential for the functioning of patronage systems. There are only rudimentary differentiated roles beyond the patron and the client, especially the role of the intermediary or broker, who acts between the patron and his clients and is important for a large number of clients.

Authoritarian regimes, of course, cannot simply be equated with patronage systems. As in the ancient Roman Republic and in states with party clientelism, this usually involves competition between several patrons for many clients. However, it can also be said for the Roman Principate that the later Caesar Augustus, as one patron among many, seized a dominant position and brought the people of Rome as a whole into a generalised clientele relationship with him. Essential features of clientelism remain even if in the end there is only one patron instead of many, so that the patron who emerges victorious from the battles can claim to have eliminated the opposing patrons along with their corrupt patronage relations and to have restored justice.

For the transformations described here, it is crucial in any case that the ruler successfully adopts the narrative of a protective patron and that the population understands, describes, and expresses itself through a patronage-based narrative at each step. Indeed, the temptation of authoritarianism is also to give up one's political autonomy by clientelising oneself in a final act of autonomy. Analogous to the prima facie self-contradictory acts of voluntary servitude or free consent to one's own enslavement, the people can also deprive themselves of their political autonomy by transforming themselves into a community of clients. In negative-protective terms, driving factors are above all the staging of emergency-like situations in order to emphasise the need for protection of one's own clientele against internal and external threats, which are marked above all by personalising attributions as possible attacks by internal and external enemies. In addition to dissenting minorities and foreigners, internal enemies can also be competing patrons and oligarchs who allegedly only exploit the institutions of the democratic rule of law for their particular interests. Those who want to make themselves the sole patron of a patronised *Volksgemeinschaft* would do well to denounce and later also prosecute their opponents as corrupt patrons who only serve their respective clientele behind the façade of democratic rule of law. At the same time, the patron must camouflage his role as one patron among others as if he had been appointed by the people to a higher mission, which gives him a particularly exalted position vis-à-vis his competitors.[9] This mission is, in turn, the militant assertion and defence of that national essence which supposedly constitutes the homogeneity of the patronage community of the people against its "decomposition" by internal and external enemies.

Above all, however, the pays légal itself functions as the internal enemy, against whose complex institutional structure – with its open-ended procedures, conflicts, dissent, and constantly revised decisions – a strong and charismatic patron is needed to protect the particularly vulnerable groups of society, disappointed in their generalised institutional trust and exploited by elitist and corrupt actors. Accordingly, one of the central messages of all Republican presidential candidates in the US since George W. Bush has been: "Trust me, not the government!" (Warren 2018: 87 and 90). In terms of positive privileges, they offer welfare-state-draped financial benefits (especially popular: special benefits for children and large families) to create the impression of being close to the people and turning a sympathetic ear to (traditional) families with children and their financial burdens, while the "corrupt elites" only care about their own welfare and that of their own clientele. Special privileges are also awarded to particularly loyal groups of voters (provision of "posts") as well as to businessmen with close ties (preferential treatment in the awarding of public contracts).

---

9 This is how Bertolt Brecht parabolically portrayed Hitler's rise in his 1941 play *The Unstoppable Rise of Arturo Ui*.

To the extent that this (self-)clientelisation succeeds, the phantasm of a homogenous national community is consolidated, in which *social trust* among clients and *personal trust* in a protective, charismatic, and caring patron can prevail on the basis of common characteristics. Those who have established themselves in this regard have a profoundly different relationship to the complex institutional structure of the democratic rule of law. In contrast to the patronage-based *Volksgemeinschaft* and its patron, a more complex institutional structure depends above all on *institutional trust*, which allows one to experience the structure's inherent openness to results and the associated uncertainty and insecurity not as existentially threatening, but as guaranteeing freedom. Personal trust in the actors of the democratic rule of law – horizontally in politically engaged citizens and vertically in public officials – is based above all on the assumption, which is counterfactual but not constantly refuted, that the rules of the democratic rule of law will be adhered to and that freedom will in turn be guaranteed through the complex, uncertainty-inducing interplay of these rules. By contrast, every client who imagines himself in a national community with supposedly high social trust and in a personal relationship of trust with a protective, charismatic leader-patron can only perceive the alternative of democratic rule of law as threatening to his existence. This is why clients are usually prepared to accept the disadvantages inherent in the relationship of loyalty to the patron saint. The leader-patron may have whims that have to be endured, demand reluctant expressions of loyalty, demand services that are perceived as unpleasant, and even expect people to refrain from critical statements, but in return he promises to take care of the worries and needs of the "little people" in particular, suggesting personal closeness and security.

Especially with the help of modern media technologies, this phantasm can also be successfully and permanently staged for the population of an entire nation. This includes, among other things, the parasocial interaction (already for film and television: Horton/Wohl 1956) between patron and client, which can be organised in social networks in such a way that the client is convinced that he is communicating directly with the patron. This can be used particularly effectively to discredit as untrustworthy the complex structure of pluralistic-democratic rule of law, which by its very nature is only capable of parasocial interaction to a limited extent, and can at best convey the dual message of simultaneous trust in the system and in people through its actors. Parasocial interaction in social networks therefore contributes significantly to the patronisation of the population because and to the extent that it inspires a *parapersonal trust* that is positioned against a supposedly repeatedly disappointed institutional trust, thus convincing people that only a patron can "really listen" and compensate for this loss of trust. Mark Warren has characterised this as a mediatised clientelism:

> A mediated clientelism, in which a strong public figure promises personal protection against an untrustworthy and exploitive government as well as numerous special interests and foreign powers that have 'betrayed' and 'suckered' the people. Information about policy, ideology, and conflicts of interest tend to be submerged by claims for personal protection. This kind of trust, and the distrust with which it is paired, is directly corrosive of democracy. (Warren 2018: 87)

8. CONCLUSION

Three characteristic elements of the ideology of the "true people" are laid out above: the narrowing of the social-cognitive dimension to the concretism of a *Volksgemeinschaft* (community of "the people"), which appeals to an imagined closeness based on the similarity of given characteristics; the reduction of the combined institutional and personal trust to the exclusively personal trust in a charismatic leader; and the (self)transformation of the citizen-nation into a *Volksgemeinschaft* of clients. The conceptual register of the left-hand column from the table presented at the beginning can be connected to this without any problems. This is accompanied by the renunciation of political autonomy: the self-determining citizen-nation of a democratic constitutional state is transformed into a *Volksgemeinschaft* that defends itself in the mode of self-assertion against internal and external enemies. The horror of autonomy is diverted into the constant fear of terrible enemies. One of the many prices to be paid for this is the shrinking of the dynamic complexity that produces uncertainty, insecurity, and at the same time freedom. Whether the reduction in complexity that accompanies the return of the authoritarian is a regression, as suggested by the stage theory of hierarchical complexity, seems an idle question: it is a pattern of argumentation that has been virulent since 1789 – sometimes stronger, sometimes weaker, depending on the experience of crisis – and that has always absolutised the ambivalences of modernity (Heitmeyer 2018: 79) in a one-sided and negative way.

9. CODA

During the pandemic, "*Putin hilf!*" was a frequently displayed banner by Pegida supporters, COVID-19 deniers, and others who wished for an authoritarian state and at the same time, in an incredibly performative self-contradiction, protested against an alleged (Corona) dictatorship of the complex "system" of a constitutional democracy. Since the Russian president started his war of aggression against Ukraine on 24 February 2022, he has been supported by parts of these movements.[10] It is well known that Putin and his supporters actively promote authoritarian movements worldwide, be it through covert interventions in election campaigns, through financial contributions to right-wing nationalist parties, or through disinformation campaigns by media actors financed by the Russian state. In his war speech, Putin uses many topoi from the dichotomous conceptual register of the *pays* réel, which he contrasts with a West that he presents as the virtual epitome of the pays légal, because it supposedly defends values (i.e. human rights) that contradict the nature of human beings and even degrade and "degenerate" them, corroding the natural substance of the true *Volk* from within like a disease:

> Yes, in fact, until recently, attempts have not stopped to use us in their own interests, destroy our traditional values and impose on us their pseudo-values that would corrode us, our people from the inside, those attitudes that they are already aggressively planting in their countries and which directly lead to degradation and degeneration, because they contradict the very nature of man. It won't happen, no one has ever done it. It won't work now either.[11]

REFERENCES

Burke, Edmund (1790/2014), Revolutionary Writings, Cambridge 2014.

Cardoso, Rafaele (2019), "Schule, nicht schießen", in: Frankfurter Allgemeine Zeitung, 23.07.2019.

Chilton, Stephen (1991), Grounding Political Development, Boulder.

Combes, Hélène and Vommaro, Gabriel (2015), Sociologie du clientélisme, Paris.

Douglas, Mary (1966/1988), Reinheit und Gefährdung. Eine Studie zu Vorstellungen von Verunreinigung und Tabu, transl. Brigitte Luchesi, Frankfurt/Main.

Eisfeld, Rainer (1986), "Joseph de Maistre und L.-G.-A. de Bonald", in: Fetscher, Iring/ Münkler, Herfried (eds), Pipers Handbuch der politischen Ideen, vol. 4, München, 103–114.

Fein, Elke (2012), "Kognition und politische Kultur. Sozialpsychologische Perspektiven in der Diskursforschung am Beispiel von Patronage, Klientelismus und Korruption in Russland", in: Oberthür, Jörg/Rosa, Hartmut (eds), Kultureller und sprachlicher Wandel von Normen- und Wertbegriffen in Europa, Frankfurt/M., 61–100.

Fraenkel, Ernst (1974/2017), Der Doppelstaat, Hamburg.

Frankenberg, Günter (2020), Autoritarismus. Verfassungstheoretische Perspektiven, Berlin.

Ganter, Angela (2015), Was die römische Welt zusammenhält. Patron-Klient-Verhältnisse zwischen Cicero und Cyprian (Klio/Beihefte. Neue Folge 26), Berlin.

Günther, Klaus (2016), "Geteilte Souveränität, Nation und Rechtsgemeinschaft", in: Kritische Justiz, 49, 321–337.

---

[10] See the report in the *tageszeitung* of 15 March 2022: https://taz.de/Querdenker-unterstuetzen-Putin/!5838247/.

[11] From Putin's speech of 24 February 2022, translated into English: https://www.spectator.co.uk/article/full-text-putin-s-declaration-of-war-on-ukraine/.

Günther, Klaus (2020), "Pays réel, pays légal, patria naturae, patria iuris. Vom Sinn und Unsinn einer begriffspolitischen Unterscheidung", in: Bung, Jochen & Kuhli, Milan (eds), Volk als Konzept in Recht und Politik, Berlin/Boston, 63–72.
Günther, Klaus (2021), "Legalität als Waffe? Kommentar zur Dialektik von Entlegitimierung und Relegitimierung der Legalität bei Schmitt und Kervégan", in: Rechtsphilosophie – Zeitschrift für die Grundlagen des Rechts, 7, 141–157.
Habermas, Jürgen (1987), "Die Schrecken der Autonomie. Carl Schmitt auf Englisch", in: ders., Eine Art Schadensabwicklung, Frankfurt/M., 103–114.
von Haller, Karl Ludwig (1817–1834), Restauration der Staats-Wissenschaft oder Theorie des natürlich-geselligen Zustands der Chimäre des künstlich-bürgerlichen entgegengesetzt, 6 vols (in zwei Auflagen), Winterthur.
Hegel, Georg W. F. (1840/2001), *The* Philosoph*y of History*, with Prefaces by Charles Hegel and the Translator, J. Sibree, Kitchener/Ontario: Batoche Books
Heitmeyer, Wilhelm (2018), Autoritäre Versuchungen. Signaturen der Bedrohung I, Berlin.
Herzog, Lisa (2013), "Persönliches Vertrauen, Rechtsvertrauen, Systemvertrauen", in: Deutsche Zeitschrift für Philosophie, 61, 529–548.
Hess, Henner (1986), Mafia. Zentrale Herrschaft und lokale Gegenmacht, Tübingen.
Hirschman, Albert O. (1994), "Wie viel Gemeinsinn braucht die liberale Gesellschaft?", in: Leviathan, 16, 293–304.
Horton, Donald & Wohl, R. Richard (1956), "Mass Communication and Para-Social Interaction. Observations On Intimacy at a Distance", in: Psychiatry 19, 215–229.
Lenard, Patti Tamara & Miller, David (2018), "Trust and National Identitiy", in: Uslaner, Eric M. (ed.), The Oxford Handbook on Social and Political Trust, Oxford, 57–74.
de Maistre, Joseph (1794/2021), Von der Souveränität, transl. Claudia Oestmann, Berlin.
Malinowski, Stephan (2021), Die Hohenzollern und die Nazis, München.
Nassehi, Armin (2022), "Die Rückkehr des Feindes", in: DIE ZEIT online, 25 February 2022, Zugriff: 22 April 2022, https:// www .zeit .de/ kultur/ 2022 -02/ demokratie -bedrohung -russland -ukraine -krieg -wladimir -putin ?utm_referrer=https %3A %2F %2Fwww.google.com%2F/.
Naumann, Hans (1934), Germanischer Schicksalsglaube, Jena.
Nunner-Winkler, Gertrud (2004), "Sozialisation und Lernprozesse am Beispiel der moralischen Entwicklung", in: Geulen, Dieter & Veith, Hermann (Hg.), Sozialisationstheorie interdisziplinär, Stuttgart, 131–154.
Puhle, Hans-Jürgen (1986), "Von der Romantik zum konservativen Konstitutionalismus", in: Fetscher, Iring & Münkler, Herfried (eds), Pipers Handbuch der politischen Ideen, München, 268–276.
Ritter, Joachim (1977), "Hegel und die französische Revolution", in: ders., Metaphysik und Politik, Frankfurt/M., 183–255.
Ross, Sara Nora and Commons, Michael Lamport (2008), "Applying Hierarchical Complexity to Political Development", in: World Futures, 64, 480–497.
Schleiermacher, Friedrich (1799/2012), Über die Religion. Rede an die Gebildeten unter ihren Verächtern, eds Peter, Niklas et al., Zürich.
Schmitt, Carl (1950/1973), "Das Problem der Legalität", in: ders., Verfassungsrechtliche Aufsätze, 2. ed., Berlin, 440–451.
Sieyés, Emmanuel Joseph (Abbé) (1789/1991), "Was ist der Dritte Stand?", in: ders., Politische Schriften 1788–1790, transl. E. Schmitt & R. Reichardt, 2. Aufl. München/Wien.

Stahl, Friedrich Julius (1833/1856/1963), Die Philosophie des Rechts, Bd. 2: Rechts- und Staatslehre auf der Grundlage christlicher Weltanschauung, Reprint of the 3rd edn, Darmstadt.
Warren, Mark E. (2018), "Trust and Democracy", in: Uslaner, Eric M. (ed.), The Oxford Handbook on Social and Political Trust, Oxford, 75–94.
Weber, Max (1921/1968), *Economy and Society: An Outline of Interpretative Sociology* (transl. and ed. G. Roth and C. Wittich), New York: Bedminster Press
Wildt, Michael (2019), Die Ambivalenz des Volkes, Berlin.
Wolf, Dieter (2019), "Zur metaphorischen Umschreibung, Hegels idealistische Dialektik ›vom Kopf auf die Füße zu stellen‘ oder 'umzustülpen'", in: Beiträge zur Marx-Engels-Forschung. Neue Folge 2018/19, Hamburg 2019, 21–71.

5. The authoritarian direction of radicalised conservatism

Natascha Strobl

1. INTRODUCTION

The extreme right[1] is becoming increasingly crowded. In addition to the well-known actors of the traditional extreme right, new phenomena are emerging. These include diffuse new forms of organisation that are being generated online and are accompanied by new forms of radicalisation of conservative, nationalist currents (Strobl 2021) and identity politics agendas. But there are also shifts in the traditional party spectrum. Among them are conservative mainstream parties that adopt the language and strategy of the traditional far right as well as right-wing populist elements. New logics and dynamics are emerging that accelerate existing processes of political erosion. The "*authoritarian temptations*" (Heitmeyer 2018: 10) have long since reached conservatism. In its most extreme form, it is evident in the USA, where President Trump has helped a proto-fascist milieu to flourish. In Europe, for example in the Kurz regime in Austria, there are and have been attacks on the foundations of the rule of law and democratic coexistence. They are an expression of a "crude bourgeoisie" (Heitmeyer 2018: 310–314) that is taking shape, which simply denounces a (precarious) consensus of solidarity. In this text, I explore the question of how this newly forming, party-political, conservative milieu can be conceptualised. Is it a form of right-wing extremism, right-wing pop-

---

[1] I do not use the term "extreme right" or "right-wing extremist" in the sense of the definition used by the *Verfassungsschutz* (Germany's domestic intelligence agency) but instead follow Willibald Holzer's definition. He defines right-wing extremism as an ideology centred on the idea of a "natural inequality" of people and the "people" or the "national community". In addition, there is the element of a "nationalising view of history", which, with regard to the Holocaust, for example, can also lead to historical revisionism. The relationship to violence in the party form of right-wing extremism consists of the acceptance of violence or latency to violence, which is expressed primarily verbally, while militant right-wing extremism also considers violence to be a legitimate part of political practice (Holzer 1993).

ulism, or fascism? Or are we dealing with an intermediate spectrum? What are the characteristics of radicalised conservatism? How can radicalised conservatism be understood as an actor of contemporary authoritarianism?

2. CONCEPTUAL FRAMEWORK

This text is based on my book *Radicalised Conservatism: An Analysis*, published in 2021 (Suhrkamp). The term has so far only been used for the historical phenomenon of the so-called "Conservative Revolution", i.e. the right-wing intellectual network in the Weimar Republic, as well as for a European phenomenon stemming from it, by the historian Bernhard Dietz (n.d.).[2] In the recent past, the political scientist Thomas Biebricher has again taken up the crisis of (German) conservatism, for example in 2018 in *Geistig-moralische Wende. Die Erschöpfung des deutschen Konservatismus.* As the title suggests, Biebricher analysis the "intellectual-moral turn" invoked by Helmut Kohl in 1983 to reverse the cultural revolution of 1968. However, this text asks how the current phenomenon of radicalised conservatism, as I have defined it, can be distinguished from categories of right-wing ideology such as right-wing populism, right-wing extremism, and fascism. Here I refer to the definition of (right-wing) populism given by the historian and political scientist Karin Priester in *Rechter und linker Populismus. Annäherung an ein Chamäleon* (2012). To complement this, I use the schema of the populist quadrilateral that Sebastian Reinfeldt developed in his book *Wir für euch. Die Wirksamkeit des Rechtspopulismus in Zeiten der Krise* (2013). The basis for my concept of right-wing extremism is the definition by the historian Willibald Holzer, which appeared in 1993 under the title "Rechtsextremismus – Konturen, Definitionsmerkmale und Erklärungsansätze" ("Right-wing Extremism – Contours, Defining Characteristics and Explanatory Approaches") in the anthology *Handbuch des österreichischen Rechtsextremismus*. Still authoritative for research on fascism is the approach of Roger Griffin who, since the start of the 1990s, with what he calls the *new consensus*, has been arguing that fascism is a palingenetic[3] ultranationalism which strives for a complete reversal of the ruling system (Griffin 2004: 5).

3. WHAT IS "RADICALISED CONSERVATISM"?

Similar to social democracy, conservatism has also experienced unprecedented crises in recent years. While globalisation led to the emergence of phenomena

---

2 For the University Archives of Conservatism, see Henderson (2018).
3 According to Griffin, this is the utopia of a national rebirth (2004: 5).

such as Clinton's "progressive neoliberalism" on the left, the last few decades also saw the rise of right-wing populist parties (Heitmeyer 2018: 72). The latter took advantage of the conservatives' loss of hegemony, caused by the economisation propagated by their own icons such as Reagan and Thatcher and by major crises such as 9/11 and the 2008 financial crisis. Within conservative parties, the new competition and loss of hegemony raised the question of their own identity. As mentioned above, Biebricher sees the start date of the crisis in the "spiritual-moral" turnaround announced by Helmut Kohl in 1982, which then largely failed to materialise. The question has also been discussed time and again in the media, resulting in titles such as "Die Zwillingskrise" ("The Twin Crisis") (Heitmann 2018), "Was ist heute konservativ?" ("What is Conversative Today?") (Deutschlandfunk 2021), or "Anger and Gloom: The Right in Crisis" (Fawcett 2022). Radicalised conservatism is a reaction to this crisis and describes a faction within conservative parties that abandons a statist consensus and becomes increasingly radical. In doing so, it acts from a position of power and with the resources of an established popular or even governing party.

The reign of Western party-based post-war conservatism was characterised by an extensive political consensus between a conservative party on the one side and a social democratic or progressive party on the other (Strobl 2021: 31). In Austria and Germany, this manifested itself in the concepts of social partnership and the social market economy, respectively (ibid.). In the USA, this corresponds to the idea of *bi-partisanship* (Fallows 2020), i.e. the idea of dealing with important laws and crises across party lines. In the UK, there was *post-war consensus*, for which a balance of employers' and employees' interests was also central, although the British party system does not require formal consent even from the non-ruling party, as is more often necessary in the US (Blackburn 2018: 211–212). All these similar ideals are informed by the notion of consensus for the sake of social and economic stability and the balancing of interests. However, this consensus has always been precarious and has facilitated both inclusion and exclusion. There have been historical moments when this consensus was attacked and even revoked, for example under Prime Minister Margret Thatcher in Great Britain. However, the constitutional democratic system as such was not fundamentally questioned. This post-war consensus ensured extensive internal stability. However, it is subject to a process of erosion. On the one hand, the hegemonic, national post-war system is being limited in its power to shape policy by international and European political integration processes. On the other hand, economic globalisation is generally causing a weakening of political agency. In *Post-Democracy after the Crises*, Colin Crouch describes the tendency for Western democracies to still be formally fully existent, but in fact to have hardly any decision-making power (Crouch 2020: 66). In a similar vein, former German Chancellor Angela

Merkel spoke of finding ways "to shape parliamentary co-determination in such a way that it nevertheless also conforms to the market" (Baum 2011). The causes of these erosion processes are manifold. Bader et al. describe the resulting situation as a "multiple crisis" (2011: 8), i.e. a crisis dynamic that goes beyond the economic sphere and leads to crises of democracy, but also ecological crises and crises of reproduction. At this specific moment, the bloc in power is threatened with a loss of hegemony. Radicalised conservatism is a symptom of the crises. It is an attempt to counter the loss of hegemony of the post-war consensus with a new, authoritarian offer of hegemony. To this end, it uses right-wing populist elements and discourses of the extreme right. The question now is how it can be distinguished from other right-wing ideologies and political styles.

4. A RIGHT-WING POPULISM OF THE CONSERVATIVES?

Karin Priester defines European right-wing populism decidedly not as a pure variety of organised right-wing extremism, but as an "amalgam" (2012: 92) of bourgeois-conservative and right-wing extremist politics inside and outside parliaments. It distinguishes itself from right-wing extremism insofar as it does not adopt the latter's hard ideological convictions and abandons them in favour of a broad impact within social majorities (Priester 2012: 92). Sebastian Reinfeldt outlines this right-wing populist style on the basis of the populist quadrilateral. In this schema, the implicitly good "we" are contrasted with two negatively valued groups, "those up there" and "not us". In addition, there are "not them", which can be used as a diffuse group positioned against the devalued groups (for example, as "concerned citizens") and who are implicitly right in their rejection of "those up there" (Reinfeldt 2012: 50). These forms of populist action do not exclude extreme right-wing or even fascist sentiments, but they conceal or negate them in favour of populist effectiveness. At the same time, they allow actors with flexible ideological convictions to use this style.

The right-wing populist elements of radicalised conservatism include, above all, the double role of martyr and victim. The leaders of radicalised conservatism always depict themselves as oppressed by dark forces, i.e. an unspecific "them up there" group. This is paradoxical, since the person him or herself is already acting from a position of power. Despite the office of chancellor, prime minister, or president, there are supposedly external forces at work who want to prevent this person from implementing their policies. The leader becomes the personified "we" who has to defend us against "them up there" – either the *swamp*,[4] as with Donald Trump, or "red networks",[5] as with Sebastian Kurz. This also includes the demonstrative and performative turning away from "normal politics". A staged break and a deliberately induced caesura with what happened before one came to power (be it in the party or in government office) or was common as political practice. Unlike the application of the right-wing populist style among classically extreme right-wing parties such as the FPÖ or the *Front National*, now the *Rassemblement National*, radicalised conservatism operates from a (greater) position of power. It is not a matter of younger, newly founded parties competing against the "old parties", but rather of the radical transformation, both externally and internally, of a party that has held governmental responsibility for decades.

This does not mean that "right-wing populism" is a conclusive description of the transformation of former conservative parties. The sole attribution of right-wing populism obscures the differences that exist due to the particular constellations of a governing or popular party on the one hand and an opposition or small party on the other. Especially since right-wing populism is not the cause but the symptom of the transformation of the parties. Not every action of radicalised conservatism is based on right-wing populist logic. Rather, there is a permanent role reversal between the right-wing populist "we" and the bourgeois logic of a person who doesn't need to be active in politics and whose mere existence in the political arena supposedly deserves gratitude. Billionaire Trump entered the political arena because he felt a calling to do so, because he felt an obligation to "make America great again" – according to the narrative of his 2015/16 election campaign and afterwards. He was running against Hillary Clinton and other professional politicians who, in his opinion, were part of the problem, the *swamp* that Trump promised to drain. Kurz also made a point of being perceived as a "wunderkind" (Horaczek/Toth 2017), a "rock star" (Tomlinson 2018), or a "political talent" (Klatzer 2017).

So right-wing populist action involves a mix of elitist and meritocratic logics. Depending on the situation, one or the other narrative is called upon. The apparent arbitrariness is a characteristic of radicalised conservatism. However, it is only a pseudo-form of arbitrariness; a PR strategy that goes well beyond right-wing populism. The contradictions that are united in one candidate do not need to be resolved, because the constant and calculated overtaxing of democratic discourse leaves no space and no time to problematise these contradictions sufficiently and to give them the necessary weight. The front

---

4 A general negative term for the established political-media establishment in Washington and the USA as a whole.

5 Kurz is alluding to alleged social democratic networks within the Austrian judiciary that would investigate or act against him and his entourage for political reasons.

figure thus presents himself as the people's advocate, expert, martyr, humble servant, victim, and genius all in one. The common feature of all these stagings is that the figure is never presented at eye level – neither with the population nor with the political competitor or the media. The person is withdrawn from the political sphere and thus implicitly from the control of the political system. The figurehead becomes a super-figure who serves as the projection surface for solutions to all the real, perceived, concrete, and diffuse societal rifts of the crisis period.

5. RADICALISED CONSERVATISM AND RIGHT-WING EXTREMISM

If radicalised conservatism has right-wing populist characteristics, the question still arises as to whether its ideological content can (still) be assigned to conservative ideology or whether one must already speak of right-wing extremism due to its radicalisation. Willibald Holzer defines right-wing ideologies primarily by "the assumption of natural inequality, for the justification of which essentially supra-rational references are brought to the fore" (1993: 21; cf. also Frankenberg/Heitmeyer in this volume). Right-wing extremism and conservatism thus have an obvious common denominator in their recourse to a supposed "natural order" between people and within societies. Where are the possible differences? For Karin Priester, the "homogeneous national community" (2010: 34) is at the centre of right-wing extremist thinking. This results in the demand for the exclusion of "people categorised as 'foreign', anti-Marxism, anti-liberalism, anti-pluralism as well as the rejection of democracy as an organisational form of human coexistence with formally egalitarian opportunities for participation" (Bruns et al. 2017: 26). Instead of aggressive *völkisch*-nationalist rhetoric, as found in right-wing extremist parties in slogans such as "Germany to the Germans", "Love your neighbours – For me, these are our Austrians" (ORF 2013), or "Stop the invasion, migration kills!" (NPD Saxony 2019), radicalised conservatism is joined by a culture war adopted from the New Right. Through signal terms and codes such as "identity" or "culture", *völkisch* nationalists can feel addressed without appearing objectionable to bourgeois sensibilities. For example, then-Chancellor Kurz said in September 2019: "I also say one thing quite deliberately, which many do not want to hear and which many also do not dare to say: Yes, we want to maintain our cultural identity" (Kurz 2019). In contrast to right-wing extremists, the "specific crudeness of the bourgeois milieu (because of the façade of civilised manners) is often expressed covertly" (Heitmeyer 2018: 311).

Holzer sees a further distinction between right-wing extremism and conservatism in the relationship to violence. A right-wing extremist is "always open to violent and demagogic-manipulative styles of assertion" (1993: 28).

While radicalised conservatives such as Sebastian Kurz or Boris Johnson could be said to have distanced themselves from violence, the situation is different with Donald Trump. During his presidency and even after his election, his relationship with paramilitary groups like the Proud Boys was more than ambivalent. In a televised debate with his rival Joe Biden, Trump addressed the group directly after the moderator's call to stop white supremacists, saying: "Proud Boys, stand back and stand by" (Associated Press 2020). Trump's speech on 6 January 2021, after which his supporters stormed the Capitol, also contained passages that his supporters interpreted as legitimising and calling for violence. The most explicit passage is: "If you don't fight like hell you're not going to have a country anymore" (BBC 2021). In a further step, Holzer examines the validity of the gradation of right-wing ideology into a radical and an extremist form. He explains the difference (for both left and right ideology) as follows:

> While the radical, by virtue of his rationality, retains an eye for what is possible without giving up reflection on what is currently still impossible, the extremist, in his thinking and acting, lives deeply severed not only from the scope for action of his time, but also from the experiences of the past, whose potential significance for orientation in the present and the perspective of the future is claimed in a biographically understandable but historically inadmissible way". (Holzer 1993: 28)

With regard to right-wing ideology, Holzer concludes that "in the absence of central preconditions of true radicality, it can probably only be described as tending towards extremism" (1993: 29), while political action on the left can be considered both radical and extremist. However, if one relates the longer quotation above to the actions of radicalised conservatives such as Trump and Kurz, it becomes clear that their actions, which are always orientated towards popularity and thus initially appear limited, create precisely the space for the "currently still impossible" by constantly contributing to a shift in reality. The speed with which the Kurz regime and Trumpism have broken rules and destroyed old certainties would probably have been difficult to imagine almost thirty years ago, especially since the dynamics of social media and their effect as drivers of radicalisation and agents of an unprecedented immediacy of politics (on this, Frankenberg 2020: 255–304) could not have been foreseen. A US president who makes policy in real time on Twitter and breaks with every custom of the political establishment before the eyes of the world means a massive acceleration of political practice. Radicalised conservatism is both a mirror and a driver of a crude bourgeoisie that expands the boundaries of what can be said (and what is politically feasible) on the political as well as the cultural level in the person of "intellectual 'transmission actors'" (Heitmeyer et al. 2020: 268) and spreads them throughout society. Radicalised conservatives show a much greater ideological flexibility in certain fields of social discourse than the actors of extreme right-wing parties such as the FPÖ. For example, they do not take part in the fight against "marriage for all", which is so important for the extreme right, because it meets with broad social approval. Instead, the Austrian People's Party under Kurz concentrated on the complex of issues of asylum seekers, migration, Islam, and identity, where it could again fall back on the support of large parts of the population for its authoritarian laws. Radicalised conservatism thus differs from right-wing extremism in terms of its (open) *völkisch* nationalism. The relationship to violence is ambivalent, at least with Donald Trump. Radicalised conservatism contains right-wing populist elements but goes beyond them.

6. RADICALISED CONSERVATISM: COMPLETE FASCISM OR PROCESS OF FASCISATION?

We have seen that radicalised conservatism is not merely a right-wing form of conservatism such as national conservatism. With its attacks on the rule of law, its aggressive rhetoric against minorities, its destructive treatment of parliamentarism as well as political opponents, and its dismantling of democracy internally and externally, it represents a real danger to liberal democracy. The question now is how it relates to fascism.

With regard to Donald Trump, this question was discussed not only in the US media but also in research even before his election victory in autumn 2016. In 2015, for example, Roger Griffin was of the opinion that Trump did not fulfil the criterion of palingenesis, which is a central component of Griffin's well-known one-sentence definition of fascism: "Fascism is a genus of political ideology whose mythic core in its various permutations is a palingenetic form of populist ultranationalism" (Griffin 1991: 26; ibid., 2004: 5 and 2020). Dylan Matthews agrees: "As long as Trump does not advocate the abolition of America's democratic institutions, and their replacement by some sort of post-liberal new order, he's not technically a fascist" (Matthews 2021). Griffin stuck to his assessment even after the storming of the Capitol in January 2021. He referred to Trump's incoherence and lack of intellectual capacity and culture that men like Hitler and Mussolini possessed (ibid.). In the summer of 2021, the debate was finally continued in a condensed form in the journal *Fascism*. Previously, Robert O. Paxton, a renowned fascism expert, had already revised his assessment that Trump was not a fascist after 6 January. In a *Newsweek* commentary, Paxton concludes: "Trump's incitement of the invasion of the Capitol on January 6, 2020 removes my objection to the fascist label. His open encouragement of civic violence to overturn an election crosses a red line. The label now seems not just acceptable but necessary" (Paxton 2021). Before the attempted coup, Paxton had argued against it, pointing to the difference between the socio-political situation of today's USA and that of

Germany at the start of the 1930s and Italy at the start of the 1920s. The institutions of American democracy were neither at a dead end like the last cabinets before Hitler, nor was there unemployment comparable to that time or such a heated mood as in Italy after the First World War and its *vittoria mutilata*.[6] Nor did Trump use anti-capitalist rhetoric, as Hitler and Mussolini had, at least initially (Paxton 2021).

The researchers in *Fascism*'s debate article largely agree that Trump's (outwardly portrayed) personality makes it difficult to speak of him as a fascist. Paxton's and Griffin's objections can be found in more or less similar form in Ruth Wodak (2021: 4) or Mattias Gardell (2021: 3), for example. But both also point out that Trumpism does not exist solely in and with the person of Donald Trump. For Gardell, for example, one of the fascist core elements, namely palingenesis, was at the centre of Trump's presidential campaign with the demand and utopia "Make America Great Again" (MAGA) (Gardell 2021: 2). Wodak, in turn, recommends "a focus on the range of discursive and material practices realising and implementing the ideological positions of the Trump administration" (2021: 4). She explicitly refers to the influence of ideologues such as Steve Bannon on Trump's policies. But she also sees Trump's historical and socio-political context as relevant. Extremist politicians such as Barry Goldwater and fundamentalist movements such as the Tea Party, which received support from the GOP, media moguls, and business, are the roots of Trumpism. These movements, in turn, could be called "fascist" (Wodak 2021: 4). Finally, she sees in Trump's rhetoric "salient discursive practices of fascism" (ibid.: 5).

This brief overview shows that research on Donald Trump and Trumpism does see fascist elements, although there is no consensus on categorising Trump or Trumpism as a phenomenon as fascist. On Sebastian Kurz, on the other hand, there has not yet been any discussion in relation to this question, either academically or in the media. However, this is not necessarily due to the characteristics of the politician or the person Sebastian Kurz, or to his regime. Research as well as social discussion in Austria is a blank space as far as the *topos* of bourgeois fascism is concerned. The most authoritative work on bourgeois fascism in Austria between the wars was published by the American historian Janek Wasserman in 2014: *Black Vienna: The Radical Right in the Red City, 1918–1938*. In its attacks against the rule of law, the judiciary, and

[6] Although Italy had sided with the Entente and thus the victorious powers in the First World War, the country did not receive the promised territories in the eastern Adriatic, Turkey, and Africa. The nationalists saw the members of the government as *rinnunciatari* ("renunciants") and described the result as *vittoria mutilata*, i.e. a "mutilated victory" (Payne 2006: 121).

the executive, however, radicalised conservatism shows signs of a fascist process, as will be shown by means of examples.

6.1 The Leader

In radicalised conservatism, there is a concentration of power with the leader and the circle surrounding him or her. For the disempowerment of internal party structures, the path to power is irrelevant. When the leader is in power, he or she secures it through the concentration of power. The cabinet around the leader degenerates into extras. The government and the decision-making bodies are only a façade. The real decisions are made beforehand in small (and not democratically legitimised) circles.

6.2 Deliberate Rule-breaking

In radicalised conservatism, there is a twofold breaking of the rules. The first is the breaking of formal rules, i.e. norms laid down by law. This shows the elimination of democratic control and the self-evident pushing or overstepping of legal boundaries. But there is also the breaking of informal rules shown by the transgression of boundaries of decency, morality, or etiquette. Breaking the rules is part of staging oneself as new and different and is celebrated as crossing boundaries.

6.3 Polarisation

Polarisation in radicalised conservatism takes place along populist lines. The "not us" is constructed based on religious and ethnic affiliations and contrasted with an "us" or a "not them". The threat situation is thereby presented between a diffuse "them up there" and a "not us". "Those up there" refers to a political system of which one defines oneself as a non-member, although one is at its top.

6.4 The Permanent Election Campaign

Radicalised conservatism operates in permanent campaign mode. PR no longer functions solely to popularise certain *policy agendas* but becomes an end in itself. Categories such as truth and lies no longer play a relevant role. What is important is the frequency of PR and thus its dominance in public discourse.

6.5 The Creation of New Realities: Conspiracy Narratives

In its rhetoric, radicalised conservatism makes use of topoi from conspiracy narratives. This includes the suggestion of constant danger to the leader. The leader must be protected by a network of followers and insiders. These technologies mean that the source of truth and reality is no longer plural but lies solely with the leader. Criticism and justifications, even from established media, are simply no longer recognised by these faithful.

6.6 The Authoritarian Restructuring of the State

Radicalised conservatism uses its position in the executive branch to act against the judiciary and the legislature. The welfare state is being undermined in line with neoliberal logics. The judiciary is one of the most sensitive areas of a state. Its political independence is therefore central to democracy. The attacks against it by the actors of radicalised conservatism are not only of a selective or occasion-related nature, but systematic.

7. CONCLUSION

The phenomenon behind radicalised conservatism is difficult to grasp with purely ideological categories or stylistic ascriptions. It is not (yet) fascism, not classic right-wing extremism, and not only right-wing populism. What is special is the transformation of state-supporting mainstream parties into authoritarian and populist parties. They act from a position of power. This phenomenon presents itself in very different ways and these differences must be appreciated. The bookends of radicalised conservatism are the former Austrian Chancellor Sebastian Kurz and the Kurz regime behind him, and Trumpism under US President Donald Trump. Both, for all their differences, have created similar regimes that have an impact beyond their time in office. It is no longer a matter of working out a comprehensive, substantial programme and advocating it as convincingly as possible. It is about providing a new sense of security. In times of "authoritarian capitalism" (Heitmeyer 2018: 23) of social and economic dislocation, this is not a defensive and static feeling, but one which is aggressive and dynamic. This promise is the ideological core of radicalised conservatism.

Radicalised conservatism cannot therefore be understood as a coherent ideological innovation. Rather, it combines neoliberal devaluations and crude bourgeoisie with a right-wing populist style. It also represents different factions of capital than classically far-right parties such as the AfD or (in their rhetoric) the FPÖ. In radicalised conservatism, the authoritarian interests of parts of big business are combined with the authoritarian destruction of democratic negotiation at the political level. Radicalised conservatism thus combines post-democracy, right-wing populism, culture war, authoritarian counter-hegemony, and crude bourgeoisie under the umbrella of a formerly state-supporting and stability-orientated conservative party.

REFERENCES

General Sources

Blackburn, Dean (2018), "Reassessing Britain's 'Post-war consensus', the politics of reason 1945–1979", in: *BrPolit*, H.13, S. 195–214.
Bruns, Julianm Glösel, Kathrin & Strobl, Natascha (2017), *Die Identitären. Handbuch zur Jugendbewegung der Neuen Rechten in Europa*, Münster.
Crouch, Colin (2020), *Post-Democracy After the Crises*, London.
Demirovic, Alex, Dück, Julia, Becker, Florian & Bader, Pauline (2011), *VielfachKrise im finanzmarktdominierten Kapitalismus*, Hamburg.
Frankenberg, Günter (2020), *Autoritarismus. Verfassungstheoretische Perspektiven*, Berlin.
Gardell, Mattias (2021), "Debate: Donald Trump and Fascism Studies", in: Paul Jackson (Hg.), *Fascism*, H. 10, S. 2–3.
Griffin, Roger (1991), *The Nature of Fascism*, New York.
Griffin, Roger (2004), "General introduction", in: Roger Griffin (Hg.). *Fascism*, London/New York, S. 1–16.
Griffin, Roger (2020), Faschismus. Eine Einführung in die Faschismusforschung, Stuttgart.
Heitmeyer, Wilhelm (2018), *Autoritäre Versuchungen. Signaturen der Bedrohung I*, Berlin.
Heitmeyer, Wilhelm, Freiheit, Manuela & Sitzer, Peter (2020), *Rechte Bedrohungsallianzen. Signaturen der Bedrohung II*, Berlin.
Henderson, Archie (2018), *Conservatism, the Right Wing, and the Far Right: A Guide to Archives*, 4 Bde., Stuttgart.
Holzer, Willibald (1993), "Rechtsextremismus – Konturen, Definitionsmerkmale und Erklärungsansätze", in: Dokumentationsarchiv des österreichischen Widerstandes (Hg.), *Handbuch des österreichischen Rechtsetremismus*, Wien.
Horaczek, Nina and Toth, Barbara (2017), *Sebastian Kurz. Österreichs neues Wunderkind?,* Wien.
Jackson, Paul Nicholas (2021), "Debate, Donald Trump and Fascism Studies", in: *Fascism*, H. 10, S. 1–15.
Payne, Stanley (2006), *Geschichte des Faschismus. Aufstieg und Fall einer europäischen Bewegung*, Dresden.
Priester, Karin (2010), "Fließende Grenzen zwischen Rechtsextremismus und Rechtsextremismus in Europa?", in: *Aus Politik und Zeitgeschichte*, H. 44, S. 33–39.
Priester, Karin (2012), *Rechter und linker Populismus. Annäherung an ein Chamäleon*, Frankfurt am Main.
Reinfeldt, Sebastian (2013), "*Wir für Euch". Die Wirksamkeit des Rechtspopulismus in Zeiten der Krise*, Münster.
Strobl, Natascha (2021), *Radikalisierter Konservatismus. Eine Analyse*, Berlin.

Wasserman, Janek (2014), *Black Vienna. The Radical Right in the Red City, 1918–1938*, New York.
Wodak, Ruth (2021), "Debate: Donald Trump and Fascism Studies", in: Paul Jackson (Hg.), *Fascism*, H. 10, S. 3–5.

Online Sources

Associated Press (2020), "Trump tells Proud Boys, 'Stand back and stand by'", in: *youtube.com*, letzter Zugriff, 27 March 2022, https//www.youtube.com/watch?v=qIHhB1ZMV_o/.
Baum, Andreas (2011), "Eurodebatte", Informationen am Abend, in: *Deutschlandfunk*, 01 September 2011, letzter Zugriff: 24 April 2022.
BBC News (2021), "Capitol riots, Did Trump's words at rally incite violence?", in: *bbc.com*, letzter Zugriff, 27 March 2022, https//www.bbc.com/news/world-us-canada-55640437.
Deutschlandfunk (2021), "Was ist heute konservativ?", in: *deutschlandfunk.de,* letzter Zugriff, 01 April 2022, https//www.deutschlandfunkkultur.de/krise-der-union-krise-des-buergerlichen-lagers-was-ist-100.html.
Dietz, Bernhard (o. J.), "Radikalisierter Konservatismus in Europa. Radikaler Konservatismus im Europa der Zwischenkriegszeit", in: *neuestegeschichte.uni-mainz.de*, letzter Zugriff, 25 March 2022, https//neuestegeschichte.uni-mainz.de/europaeische-geschichte-in-der-zwischenkriegszeit/radikalisierter-konservatismus-in-europa/.
Fallows, James (2010), "Why bipartisanship can't work, the expert view", in: *theatlantic.com*, letzter Zugriff, 25 March 2022, https//www.theatlantic.com/technology/archive/2010/02/why-bipartisanship-cant-work-the-expert-view/35101/.
Fawcett, Edmund (2022), "Wut und Schwermut: Die Rechte in der Krise", in: *internationalepolitik.de*, letzter Zugriff, 25 March 2022, https//internationalepolitik.de/de/wut-und-schwermut-die-rechte-der-krise.
Heitmann, Matthias (2018), "Die Zwillingskrise", in: *cicero.de*, letzter Zugriff, 03 April 2022, https//www.cicero.de/innenpolitik/angela-merkel-cdu-konservative-parteienkrise.
Klatzer, Jürgen (2017), "Ist Sebastian Kurz ein 'politisches Talent'?", in: *kurier.at*, letzter Zugriff, 25 March 2022, https//kurier.at/politik/inland/essay-ueber-das-politische-talent-hat-sebastian-kurz-das-zeug-dazu/268.322.937.
Kurz, Sebastian (2019), "Unsere Identität bewahren", in: *facebook.com*, letzter Zugriff, 27 March 2022, https//www.facebook.com/sebastiankurz.at/videos/493886014726056/.
Matthews, Dylan (2021), "The F Word. The debate over whether to call Donald Trump a fascist, and why it matters". In, vox.com, letzter Zugriff, 27 March 2022, https//www.vox.com/22225472/fascism-definition-trump-fascist-examples/.
NPD Sachsen (2019), "'Hände weg von unseren Plakaten!' NPD Sachsen klagt gegen Anordnungsverfügung der Stadt Görlitz zum Abhängen ihrer Wahlplakate 'Stoppt die Invasion – Migration tötet! '" in: *npd.de*, letzter Zugriff, 25 March 2022, https//npd.de/2019/05/haende-weg-von-unseren-plakaten-npd-sachsen-klagt-gegen-anordnungsverfuegung-der-stadt-goerlitz-zum-abhaengen-ihrer-wahlplakate-stoppt-die-invasion-migration-toet/.
ORF.at (2013), "Plakate präsentiert", in: *orf.at*, letzter Zugriff, 27 March 2022, https//orf.at/v2/stories/2194528/2194456/.

Paxton, Robert O. (2021), “I’ve Hesitated to Call Donald Trump a Fascist. Until Now”, in: newsweek.com, letzter Zugriff, 27 March 2022, https//www .newsweek .com/ robert-paxton-trump-fascist-1560652/.

Tomlinson, Chris (2018), “Trump’s Right-hand Man in Europe Rick Grenell Wants to ‘Empower’ European Conservatives”, in: breitbart.com, letzter Zugriff, 25 March 2022, https//www.breitbart.com/europe/2018/06/03/trumps-right-hand-man -in-europe-wants-to-empower-european-anti-establishment-conservatives/.

PART III

Capitalist economies and social crises

6. Loss of control, authoritarianism and exterminism in the Great Transformation

Klaus Dörre[1]

1. BABI YAR: WAR DRIVES AUTHORITARIANISM, AUTHORITARIANISM FACILITATES WAR

Babi Yar is the name of a valley in the Greater Kyiv area in Ukraine. In September 1941, a few weeks after the German invasion during World War II, more than 33,000 Jewish men, women and children were murdered within 48 hours. Famous Russian composer Dmitri Shostakovich dedicated his 13th Symphony to the victims of the Babi Yar massacre. Ever since the Russian attack on Ukraine, a new chapter should be added to Shostakovich's music: the "secret history of Russia". Not long after the invasion, in February 2022, Russian rockets hit the very museum that was supposed to commemorate the horrors of Babi Yar. The missiles were fired in a war that allegedly seeks the "de-militarisation" and "de-Nazification" of Ukraine.

The rockets on Babi Yar symbolise, almost grotesquely forcefully, what may become a key driver of authoritarianism in the twenty-first century. In Putin's war against Ukraine – yet also, subtly and unintentionally, in some of the West's responses – a destructive tendency is coming to the fore that can be termed, in reference to the British historian E.P. Thompson, *exterminism*. Exterminism – a neologism from the Cold War era, a time of escalating bloc confrontations and a mutual arms build-up that included middle-range nuclear missiles – denotes those mechanisms of national economies, political orders and ideologies which "act as impulsion in a direction that necessarily implies the annihilation of large groups of people" (Albrecht 1997: 1190; for a more basic treatment, see Thompson 1980).

1 Greatest thanks for important hints and the precise, knowledgeable translation of the text go to Jan-Peter Herrmann and David Broder.

2. HYPOTHESES

My first hypothesis holds that, against the backdrop of an epochal, pincer-like economic-ecological crisis,[2] exterminism and authoritarianism are entering a dangerous elective affinity. This is occurring in authoritarian states, such as Russia under Putin's regime, that are prepared to fight for their spheres of influence by means of wars of annihilation. The outward aggressiveness, I assert in my second hypothesis, is legitimised internally in modern societies through ethnic nationalisms that are also gaining influence in Western democracies: incapable of self-organisation, subaltern classes or class factions tend to delegate their interests to the twenty-first-century Bonapartes, the Putins, Trumps, Le Pens or other leading figures of the far right.[3] Authoritarian regimes and movements prompt responses by their adversaries that can equally entail a hollowing out and weakening of democracy. Therefore, in my third hypothesis I assert that democratic communities need to take care not to degenerate into a form of "catastrophic society" (Beck 1992: 79) in which the state of emergency has become the norm.

To substantiate this view, I first outline the meta-crisis that has prepared and continues to prepare the ground for twenty-first-century authoritarianism (Section II). Next, I present an analysis of imperial rivalries "between" nation-states, which engender – in the case of Putinism, highly aggressive – elective affinities of exterminism and authoritarianism (Section III). These elective affinities feed on the transformation conflicts "internal" to increasingly unequal societies – conflicts that accelerate the loss of control and heighten the potential for aggression (Section IV). The alternative espoused here is a sustainability revolution, enabled by the infrastructure socialism[4] of transformative democracies (see sections V, VI).

---

[2] A pincer crisis implies that the most important method of overcoming economic stagnation and pacifying internal conflicts within capitalism, namely the generation of economic growth, has increasingly, under the conditions of the status quo, become a primary driving force of ecological destruction and thus of social corrosion. Here, status quo refers to the coupling of economic growth with high carbon emissions, resource-intensive modes of production and lifestyles as well as a constant increase in the use of fossil-based energy.

[3] I speak of the radical far-right in reference to Wilhelm Heitmeyer's (2018a) "authoritarian national radicalism". This term suggests that the classification of many organisations and movements as right-wing-populist amounts to downplaying their true nature. If right-wing populism initially acted as a "hinge" between right-wing conservatism and right-wing extremism, its radicalised form has now advanced to the point where it is blurring the boundaries with the violent far right.

[4] "Infrastructure socialism" denotes policies which seek to fulfil modern societies' promises of security – protection from social uncertainty, threats to public safety and threats from natural disasters and war – by strengthening the public sector.

3. PINCER CRISIS, EXTERMINISM AND AUTHORITARIANISM

Let us begin with the crisis whose peculiarities provide the "raw material for fear" (Duhm 1972: 108) that stands behind twenty-first-century authoritarianisms. According to its general definition, a crisis is a state of affairs that can potentially be overcome. Modern societies proceed in (constant) crisis mode: there is always some social sub-area or functional mechanism that is in crisis, meaning temporarily disrupted. In our time, crises are mounting at a scale that makes it plausible to regard the "uncertainty of the future, experienced and managed as crisis" as "the next society's mode of integration" (Baecker 2018: 94).

3.1 Capitalist Landnahme, Pincer Crisis and Social Transformation

The epochal economic-ecological pincer crisis of our times is the outcome of "successful" capitalist expansion, as it arises from the elementary form of movement of capitalist socialisation. This form of movement can be conceived as a *Landnahme* (literally: 'land grab'), which means the systemic compulsion to engage in the continuous conquest, incorporation and gradual destruction of a non-capitalist Other. The term *Landnahme* implies that capitalism must expand in order to exist. In all of its variants, capitalism relies on the continuous conquest of 'new land' (or new 'ground'). In this context, 'land' does not denote actual territories or physical land, but rather serves as a metaphor for population groups, modes of production, lifestyles and bodies of knowledge which are not or not yet fully subject to capitalist commodity exchange. In terms of control theory, *Landnahme* commonly implies a gain in control for the capital side, accompanied by a loss of control on the part of the subaltern classes (see Heitmeyer 2018b).

At the same time, *Landnahmen* never occur as linear processes, because the capitalist mode of production, over the course of its successful expansion, gradually destroys that which it needs for its own extended reproduction. The more successful the accumulation and growth machine, the more strongly it undermines the capacity for the self-reproduction of social and natural resources, without which modern capitalist societies cannot survive. However, the crisis-ridden expansion entails no automatic collapse of capitalism, nor can the loss of control continue indefinitely. Ideally, such loss of control will cause the emergence and evolution of systemic mechanisms of self-stabilisation, which may well achieve certain temporary gains in control even for subaltern classes and populations. In this sense, we are dealing with a double movement. On the one hand, the systemic compulsion towards market expansion and an expanded reproduction of capital engender the global generalisation of capitalist market imperatives (i.e., the drive towards accumulation, the exploitation of wage labour and the compulsion for economic growth). On the other hand, this is only possible because societies ensure the social and institutional embedding of markets, in the sense of a fundamental precondition for their functioning. The more successful the capitalist expansion, the more elaborate and complex the self-stabilising mechanisms it requires for a functioning market socialisation. Essential stabilisation mechanisms include the credit system and innovation, welfare-state social security, organised industrial relations, institutions of social reproduction as well as the institutional regulation of society-nature relations. The social infrastructure ensures the smooth interplay of these self-stabilising mechanisms. It is an indispensable precondition for functioning markets, as it provides the education, professional training and qualification, research institutions, communication structures and transport routes without which society as we know it would not be conceivable.

Investments in social infrastructure not only shape the capitalist geography but are also helpful in mitigating, at least temporarily, a structural problematic that David Harvey has termed the "capital surplus absorption problem" (Harvey 2010: 94). To put this in simple terms: a capitalist economy that grows during a period of production must create markets capable of absorbing the additional surplus value during the subsequent economic cycle – a task only possible through market-expanding investments (ibid.: 94–6). The higher a given society's level of wealth and the greater its economic growth, the more difficult it becomes to acquire and develop new markets. This capital surplus absorption problem represents a central socio-economic driving force of capitalist *Landnahmen*. Capitalism is a "unique system of market dependence" that "must constantly expand in ways and degrees unlike any other social form" (Wood 1999: 97).

Currently, the blowback effects of market-driven globalisation have reached such a scale as to undermine important self-stabilising mechanisms of market socialisation. The economic-ecological pincer crisis surely denotes a historical turning point, for it will most likely entail the transition to a new era: the Anthropocene.[5] This term signifies that humans have become the most important factor in the reproduction of non-human nature. Humanity can destroy its own basis of existence, while humans themselves can choose to overcome their instrumental relation with natural resources and non-human living things. But since humanity exists only as a collective that is differentiated by nations,

---

[5] In earth sciences, the term is controversial and it may still be "rejected [...] outright". Ellis, Erle C. (2018): *Anthropocene. A Very Short Introduction*, Oxford, p. xv. I nevertheless use it in order to highlight the particularity of the pincer crisis.

classes, genders, and regions, social scientists like Jason Moore consider the term *capitalocene* to be more appropriate. According to Moore, we are witnessing "the breakdown of the strategies and relations that have sustained capital accumulation over the past five centuries" (2015: 1) – an assessment with which I fully agree. The pincer crisis is more severe than the *modus operandi* of major accumulation crises. It signals that the expansive movement of capitalist market socialisation eventually encounters, on a planet with finite resources, insurmountable boundaries. Man-made global warming or rising resource and energy consumption can entail dramatic impacts on the planet and its ecosystems and make vast regions across the world uninhabitable for human beings. To call this a crisis only makes sense because there is now a *politically established* end of the pincer crisis. The world's most important economies are planning to fully decarbonise by 2050. This forces societies to implement a transformation which is comparable in significance and extent to the first Industrial Revolution. It encompasses all sectors and areas of the economy. Ultimately, there are only two options for limiting man-made climate change and for controlling, at least to some extent, the related major ecological threats. Either economic growth is successfully decoupled from its ecologically destructive consequences, or else a transformation will be needed to liberate societies from the economic compulsion to pursue endless *Landnahmen*, a profit-driven market expansion and permanent, rapid economic growth.

3.2 Uncertainty and Loss of Control as the Consequence and Driver of Exterminism

Regardless of which path is ultimately chosen, uncertainty is mounting. Even more than economic crises, major ecological threats harbour multiple unknown variables. The specific impacts, interactions and most likely consequences represent highly controversial issues in the scientific community. Take, for example, climate change. Although the overwhelming majority of scientists have no doubt about the reality of human-caused climate change, there remain "endless predictive uncertainties" (Foster et al. 2010: 425). Standard values and climate tipping points depend upon shared knowledge and definitions and thus are also sites of struggle over interpretation, political negotiations and social conflicts. Man-made climate change is causing the increased occurrence of extreme weather phenomena such as heat waves, flooding, droughts and severe storms. Furthermore, it leads to glacier melting, water shortages, famine, wars and rising levels of forced migration – all phenomena which can impact societies and their development (IPCC 2022). Yet ultimately, a single event like the disastrous flooding in what was once the idyllic Ahr valley in western Germany cannot be unequivocally proven to be the result of man-made climate change.

The radically new element of the economic–ecological pincer crisis is thus rooted in its complexity and potential finality, in the opaqueness of its causes and in its far-reaching consequences, including for individual lifestyles. Such a scenario can prompt a societal search for certainty, security, predictability and accountability, as a reaction to the loss of control. This kind of search may – by no means necessarily, but with some likelihood – potentially engender the aforementioned dangerous blend of exterminism and authoritarianism. Exterminism denotes a society-engulfing urge for extermination. According to E.P. Thompson, exterminism is synonymous with the final stage of human civilisation which began with the use of the atomic bomb in 1945. The structural roots of exterminism lie in the constant growth of the military sectors of capitalist and – formerly – state-socialist countries. It takes shape through a form of (arms) technology that can cause the extinction of the human species. It ultimately culminates in war, though it simultaneously produces major ecological dangers. In the final analysis, however, it cannot be attributed monocausally to the intentional, planned action of powerful elites, even though divergent strategic actions by social actors surely do influence each of its specific variants. Exterminism takes shape through isomorphy, via path dependencies which commonly arise in both military apparatuses and political decision-making centres. That is why the concept of exterminism resists interpretations based on conspiracy theories.

E.P. Thompson considered it likely that exterminism would ultimately lead to nuclear war. This proved to be mistaken, as a reading of the bipolar world of the Cold War era. Following the implosion of state socialism, the exterminism diagnosis thus seemed to have fallen flat, with many instead convinced that the triumphal march of liberal democracy and the VCR had simultaneously brought the history of social evolution to an end. Today, we know that this prediction was wrong not only when considering now-outdated video recorders. The bloc confrontation has returned – this time between empires with ill-defined external boundaries, each headed by the respective superpowers America and China, and certainly no less dangerous. It therefore appears appropriate to revive the analytical concept of exterminism and fill it with new substance. In the process, we must keep in mind that the fight for a new world order is taking place against the backdrop of the pincer crisis and the conflicts it causes over socio-ecological transformation. The important aspect about the exterminism hypothesis is that it locates the driving forces of a systemic expansionism not exclusively in the profit motive underlying capitalist societies. Military apparatuses and security authorities develop their own, often aggressive logic independently of the economic profit motive. But how do the contemporary elective affinities between exterminism and authoritarianism emerge?

4. CLIMATE CHANGE, INTER-STATE CONFLICTS, AGGRESSIVE NATIONALISM

To find answers to this question, it seems conducive to focus our analytical gaze on the specific conflict dynamics that arise from the economic–ecological pincer crisis. The example of climate justice illustrates what I mean by this. Evidently, the level of climate-damaging greenhouse-gas emissions varies in accordance with both a country's rank within the social geography of nation-states and class positions within national societies. While in 2015 the richest 10 per cent of the world's adult population caused a staggering 49 per cent of these damaging-emissions through their lifestyles and consumption patterns, the bottom half accounted for a mere 10 per cent (see Gallagher & Kozul-Wright 2019: 5). From this asymmetry emerge two closely intercoupled justice issues that generate distinct types of conflict. The first problem is rooted in countries' unequal contribution to climate-relevant emissions and the resulting "inter-state" conflicts; the second justice problematic can be found within national societies and often manifests itself in Polanyian-type movements.

4.1 Climate Justice, Exterminism and Authoritarianism

Let us begin with transformation conflicts *between* countries. The historical national shares of greenhouse-gas emissions illustrate this problematic: by 2015, 26.3 per cent of all emissions ever recorded had been caused by the United States, 23.4 per cent by the EU, whereas China (11.8 per cent) and Russia (7.4 per cent) lagged far behind. With a view to *current* national shares in global emissions, however, China tops the list, emitting the greatest amount of greenhouse gases worldwide, while India ranks third, right after the US, and the Russian Federation fourth (4.65 per cent). In the per-capita calculation, again, a different picture emerges: in the US, per-capita greenhouse emissions are twice as high as in China. Germany's per-capita share exceeds that of India many times over. Furthermore, absolute per-capita emissions vary considerably. The greenhouse gas emissions of a member of the richest top *1 per cent* in the US, Luxembourg, Qatar, or Saudi Arabia are around two thousand times higher than those of a poor person in countries like Chad, Malawi, Honduras, Rwanda or Tajikistan (see World Resources Institute 2021).

The justice issue that these unequal relations engender is being fought out globally by and between nation-states or alliances of states. On the one hand, a swift reduction in climate-damaging emissions is only possible if the large countries of the Global South, above all China and India, implement a radical, immediate course correction.

On the other hand, developing countries may justifiably insist that the early industrialised countries should take the lead in combating climate change and shoulder the brunt of the costs. This divergence of interests places a heavy burden on any attempt at a systematic decarbonisation of the world economy. Climate change and emissions have thus become a matter of imperial rivalries and inter-state disputes and conflicts. If the EU's economies seek to reach zero carbon by 2050 but the Chinese economy only by 2060, this represents an undue competitive advantage from the EU's perspective, while China may regard it as a fair compensation for the former's colonial legacy.

Given the unequal distribution of the emissions share between countries, it is hardly surprising that thus far there has been relatively limited progress in terms of climate policies at a global and international level. With a view to the causes of the Ukraine war, another complex problem emerges, as attempts to get into Putin's head usually overlook one central cause of the escalation. *The Russian Federation is among the greatest losers of globalisation.*

The Russian Federation is a state structure with an economic status that can only be described as semi-peripheral today, yet with elites who continue to lay claim to superpower status. The "fortress socialism" (Derluguian 2013: 105) of the former Soviet Union was followed – after Stalinism, post-Stalinist superpower, the latter's decline and a transitional period that was, in fact, marked by an openness for various paths forward – by an oligarchic "fortress capitalism". This variant of capitalism is characterised, just like most other post-Soviet countries, by a deeply divided society. "Largely impoverished populations face small elites of oligarchs, and in Russia, the so-called 'new Russians' [...]", as the historian Philipp Ther notes (2018: 151). Ther also clearly calls out the cause of this development: "Under the influence of Western advisors, Russia began privatization before an institutional and constitutional framework was in place. As a result, the state was plundered, and a small class of oligarchs formed. Deindustrialization, wiping out countless workplaces, also had disastrous effects. Due to the lack of legal security and opportunity for export to the EU market, there was hardly any inflow of foreign capital other than the oligarchs' laundered money" (Ther 2018: 152).

While only a small middle class formed in the cities, creating a market for informal, often low-paid services (Gürth 2021; Morris 2020), the situation in rural areas was often marked by outright destitution. The relative economic stabilisation following the turn of the millennium has changed very little about this situation to this day. Although the Russian Federation did manage, prior to the Ukraine war, to diversify its economy to some extent, the country's economic performance continues to rest primarily on exports of fossil energy sources. Indeed, Russia earns up to 43 per cent of its revenue through oil and gas exports, some 52 per cent of which are made up of mineral fuels, oil and downstream products based on these materials (Destatis 2022). Its dependence on natural resources implies that the Russian Federation will inevitably be on the losing side of a sustainability transition should it fail to enact radical economic restructuring. The more rapid the phaseout of fossil energies in buyer markets, the quicker the decline in value of Russian oil and gas reserves. At the same time, a swift phaseout of resource extractivism would severely aggravate internal social tensions in the Russian Federation.

All of this may well contribute to a grim future outlook for the circles of power surrounding the autocrat Putin. In fact, it appears to constitute one of the main reasons for the particular aggressiveness of this regime, seeing as the window of opportunity for rectifying Russia's semi-peripheral status is likewise closing. The military and a readiness for a brutal war of aggression constitute the remaining power resources which, however, can be brought to bear in the international state system more or less successfully only as long as the enemy depends on Russian gas and oil.

4.2 Putinism and the "Choke Chain Effect"

By launching its aggression against Ukraine, the Putin regime is thus accelerating a crisis mechanism that economist James Galbraith has termed a "choke chain effect" (2015). During uncertain times, high fixed costs for gas and oil expose the particular vulnerability of an economic system that is built on cheap natural resources and high levels of resource consumption. Just like a dog's chain, economic and political instability may not prevent economic growth entirely, but energy prices – and thus the prices for many other goods, too – rise quickly before then decreasing again temporarily, as influenced by the actions of speculators. The ups and downs impact the profitability of the affected companies, while their readiness to invest decreases sharply, and distributional struggles intensify not only between classes (or class factions), but also within the state apparatus.

Although it may not always seem clear whether its actions are reckless or strategically planned, the Putin regime is undoubtedly pursuing an aggressive high-risk strategy to take advantage of this effect, even though it will likely harm itself in the long run. After all, before the war, the EU was one of Russia's most important foreign-trade partners. Accelerated through international sanctions, the military confrontation and rising prices will have negative rebound effects on the Russian economy. This could gradually erode the mass loyalty for Putin's expansionism, yet the West will likely suffer consequences too. China's nominal Communists, who act as brokers between their own population and foreign capital interests while pursuing their own power ambitions, hope to emerge as the main beneficiary. Those who will lose out are the poor countries of the Southern periphery. Rising prices for wheat and maize, because of this war between two of these goods' main exporters, will lead to soaring food prices, leaving the poorest unable to afford even flour or bread.

The prospect of such an economically destructive expansionism raises the question as to how the Putin regime should be classified analytically. To put it more succinctly: the reasons for the ongoing war of aggression can neither be reduced to economic motives nor be found exclusively in the – doubtless, highly problematic – eastward expansion of NATO (Wood 2022). The expansionist nature of Putinism rests on a will to accumulate political power which, as it currently stands, can continue without having to fear any kind of restrictions from a democratic civil society or the political system. This distinguishes the Putin administration from Trumpism which – for the time being, at least – was defeated in a democratic election. Putinism, which is supported by a social bloc[6] that is by no means limited exclusively to the tiny groups of influential oligarchs but also integrates segments of the subaltern classes, evolves entirely free of any possibility for a democratic self-correction of the political system. The imperial ambition to expand its own domain has developed a life of its own, independently of economic interests. In this sense, it resembles classic imperialism, as Hannah Arendt notes: the "limitless process of capital accumulation needs the political structure of so 'unlimited a power' that it can protect growing property by constantly growing more powerful" (Arendt 1958: 143).

Putinism, too, utilises its state and military power resources to extend its influence beyond the national territory. However, it is neither classic imperialism nor a renaissance of Soviet Communism. Putin embodies an exterministic authoritarianism that constitutes a reaction to the decline of the former Soviet superpower under the conditions of the pincer crisis. The Putin regime's variant of exterminism blends elements of the Tsarist claim to great-power status with Pan-Slavic ethnic nationalism, Russian Orthodox religious fundamentalism, Soviet nostalgia and a world view that corresponds to the friend-or-foe reasoning of figures like Carl Schmitt. This fabricated ideology, which, in the multinational Russian Federation only became dominant as ethnic Russian nationalism from 2012 (Wood 2022: 9), is designed to legitimise expansive ambitions, but it has very few (if any) appealing elements and contains no vision of a future society or utopian elements that could induce a lasting positive impact. Its mass compatibility rests on repression, combined with a leader cult, the evocation of traditional values, loyalty through igno-

---

6 The category of the social bloc underscores that far-right radicalism constitutes a multi-level phenomenon. A distinction must be made between (a) conceptual ideas, (b) organisations and movements and (c) the everyday consciousness of sympathising groups.

rance and the Russian population's profound capacity for suffering. What remains as the bare core of Putinism is its drive to expand spheres of influence in combination with the desire to absolutise political power. It is this latter aspiration that Madeleine Albright identified as the key feature of a new fascism (Albright 2018).

One could argue whether or not this assessment is accurate as, before the war, there were at least some rudimentary forms of a democratic civil society in the Russian Federation, albeit constantly threatened with repression. Putin himself goes to great lengths to make his politics appear strictly legally sound. And yet, despite all its particularities, Putinism is marked by several characteristics that Albright has rightly pointed out as the reality of a new fascist threat. With no claim to completeness, at least three features stand out that Putinism shares with other far-right mobilisations.

Firstly, these kinds of formations present themselves as the protagonists of a "counter-*Landnahme*" that is justified in terms of power politics. "Take back control!", "We want our country back!", are their battle cries. Such slogans can only take hold because they perform a reinterpretation of the structural causes of capitalist *Landnahmen* and the loss of control they entail. According to Carl Schmitt, an intellectual stooge of the far right, processes of *Landnahme* are legitimate when the supposedly culturally and civilisationally superior nations and peoples assert themselves. In Schmitt's view, *Landnahme* "thus is the archetype of a constitutive legal process externally (vis-à-vis other peoples) and internally (for the ordering of land and property within a country)." (Schmitt 2003 [1950]: 47). Furthermore, *Landnahmen* are legitimate if the occupied territory has been robbed from previous owners and populations in the name of a higher stage of civilisation (Schmitt 2003 [1950]: 137 ff.). The appropriation of the land of others is thus not seen as a problem, in normative terms; each and every original *Landnahme* is a law-establishing, amoral act. In the concept of the *nomos*, i.e., *Landnahme* as a constitutive legal act, the allegedly higher civilisation stage asserts a relation of culturally bound superiority and subordination.

The ideology of Putinism adds another idiosyncrasy to this legitimation of *Landnahme*. By denying Ukraine's state sovereignty and declaring the country's existence to be itself a land grab, it simultaneously underscores a Russian claim to domination, which, however, can only be enforced through violent means in a country that is increasingly oriented towards the West both economically and politically. From the perspective of Schmitt's concept of *Landnahme*, the world can be understood as a battlefield in which each country seeks to assert itself vis-à-vis other countries. A multipolar world order, based on the willingness to agree on universal, globally applicable sustainability goals, appears as an expression of a naïve One World ideology to which all negative consequences of globalisation are attributed. The enemy is stereotyped in terms of Western, liberal elites who allegedly disown national interests and make large parts of the population strangers in their own country, through economic liberalism, mass immigration, support for minorities and the "betrayal" of ordinary people.

Secondly, this self-positioning within the international hierarchy corresponds to the discontent of men and women who feel humiliated. Such emotions may have various causes. They may arise from defeat in war and the decline of major powers just as much as from a persistent position in the (semi-)periphery of the global geography. Authoritarian regimes exploit such affects. They consolidate their power by exercising control over the information system and tend to use a language which, as George Orwell anticipated, declares that war is peace and that tyranny is freedom. In this way, this new authoritarianism destroys democratic public spheres and, along with them, the basis for scientific reason.

This can only succeed, thirdly, if rationality and scientificity are replaced by (mis)beliefs and conspiracy myths, which seek to respond to extreme insecurity and uncertainty with ostensible imputability and promises of order. The most important glue of any historic bloc of the far right are the fears that unite the poor and the rich, the rulers and the subaltern. "Fear", Madeleine Albright notes (2018: 9), "is why Fascism's emotional reach can extend to all levels of society. No political movement can flourish without popular support, but Fascism is as dependent on the wealthy and powerful as it is on the man or woman in the street – on those who have much to lose and those who have nothing at all." This fascism, as the most extreme form of the new authoritarianism, is not so much a coherent ideology, but rather "a means for seizing and holding power" (ibid.).

In the case of the Putin regime, this drive for power may engender a distinct isomorphy. Putin may be neither insane nor suicidal – and yet, his military's internal dynamic could nevertheless lead him to put his threatening remarks about World War III into action. It is precisely this exterministic consequence that ultimately derails all attempts at an explanation proceeding from the interpretative cosmos of political science and international relations, which, despite all the latter's scientific validity, remain caught in their respective rationales. In an age of nuclear, chemical and biological weapons of mass destruction, the logic of deterrence implies an exterministic tendency, and no government in the world can guarantee the permanent containment of the drive for extermination which this logic entails.

5. INTERNAL TRANSFORMATION CONFLICTS AND NATIONALIST MOBILISATION

To explain why an ethnic nationalism resonates with a considerable proportion of the Russian population, however, another explanatory factor must be added which pertains to internal social tensions and transformation conflicts.

5.1 "Imitation Democracy" and Suppressed Class Conflict

The political system of the Russian Federation corresponds to that of an "imitation democracy" (Wood 2022: 11). In this system, tensions resulting from class-specific inequalities cannot be resolved in appropriate democratic institutions. A society in which 89 per cent of total wealth is concentrated among the richest 3 per cent of the population, whereas one-third of the population die before reaching retirement age, has no system of organised industrial relations that could act as a corrective. The official trade union federation FPNR maintains a pro-government stance, while the (independent) KTR association is threatened with repression. Protests such as in the automotive industry and the health sector find no corresponding echo within the political system. "Class politics in Russia", Jeremy Morris notes (2020: 2), hardly ever features "in the mainstream media"; workers' protests and social unrest are publicly ignored. At the same time, scepticism about whether Russian workers "will see any kind of real improvements in terms of living or work standards" (ibid.: 5) may well have contributed to the considerable loss of support which the Putin administration has suffered. Nationalist mobilisations thus also serve internal social pacification, as the escalatory rhetoric of war attracts followers. The approval of the war among the Russian population currently lies between 60 and 70 per cent (Ishchenko 2022: 38).

We can establish that anger and disappointment arise in large parts of the population because Russia has failed to install mechanisms through which conflicting interests that emerge from structural inequalities can be reconciled in democratic institutions and through democratic processes. As a result, protest can be channelled into ethnic nationalisms that proclaim an ideal that supposedly transcends all class antagonisms. The war thus helps Putin to pursue an important objective on the domestic front. This entails transforming a weak "post-Soviet Caesarism", whose inability to lead subaltern classes and nations became more than evident in the recent uprisings in Belarus and Kazakhstan, into a supposedly more stable imperial project (ibid.: 35). The repressive approach to dealing with class tensions, and their being channelled into ethnic nationalisms, which we encounter in almost all post-Soviet societies,[7] point to a problematic that E.P. Thompson did not anticipate. The notion of classes and class conflicts has largely disappeared from public discourse not only in post-Soviet societies but also in Western democracies. This is a key reason why the radical far-right is able to exploit social suffering, experiences of inequality and also the dimension of fairness and justice in the context of the ecological social conflict to advance its own agenda.

5.2 Climate Justice and Radical Right-wing Orientations Among Wage Earners

Let us take the example of climate change once again, this time with a view to EU member states. Currently, the compliance of EU households with the stated climate goals is at only 5 per cent, while the inequality within national societies remains highly conflict laden. The highest-income decile of households in 26 European countries are responsible for 27 per cent of emissions, while the bottom half produce about 26 per cent of climate-damaging gases. Admittedly, emissions across the EU were cut by around 25 per cent from 1990 to 2015, showing that decoupling economic growth and emissions is certainly possible, at least regionally and for a limited period of time. But on a global scale, emissions are falling far too slowly for this to lead to sustainable climate protection. Moreover, such emissions reductions as have taken place are primarily to be chalked up to lower-income households. While emissions from the richest 1 per cent of households increased by 5 per cent and those from the highest-income decile by 3 per cent between 1990 and 2015, they decreased by 34 per cent for the poorer half of the population over the same period (see Oxfam 2020: 1, 3). In Germany, the richest 10 per cent of households accounted for 26 per cent of the emissions burden, while the bottom half was responsible for 29 per cent. Whereas the richest 1 per cent saved nothing, the bottom half reduced their emissions by one-third.

Bluntly put, this means that the West, too, displays a structural injustice which has simply appeared in a far more dramatic form in post-Soviet societies. Evidently, the production of luxury goods for the upper classes and their consumption by wealthy households have become the main drivers of climate change – the consequences of which, both nationally and globally, primarily affect the poorer, most socially vulnerable population groups. The lower classes' oft-involuntary renunciation of consumption causes the growing share

---

[7] Nationalism and restrictions of basic social rights are also common in Ukraine. However: "Whatever the problems post-Euromaidan Ukraine had – and there were many [...] – these were all Ukrainian problems that Ukrainians should and could solve themselves in a political process, without Russian tanks and bombs" (Ishchenko 2022: 35).

of emissions by the highest-income upper decile of the European population to disappear from the statistics. Only because people with 'thin wallets' are having to tighten their belts due to falling incomes and rising prices are the lavish lifestyles of the upper classes still possible in the first place.

In the West, too, this problematic affects societies that have long suppressed their class character. It acquires additional explosive force in the socio-ecological transformation conflicts that arise when climate change is combatted with market-oriented measures. Transformation conflicts in which the social axis of conflict and the ecological one are increasingly diverging and drifting apart, are a characteristic feature of demobilised, self-abnegating class societies, including in the West. As Didier Eribon (2015) has impressively demonstrated, however, class relations also take effect in the absence of an emancipatory class politics from below. After all, if you "simply remove 'classes' and class relations as categories [...] from political discourse, there is certainly no guarantee that those denoted by those terms will not feel collectively abandoned" (Eribon, 2015: 122). In this case, class relations take effect via cultural symbolism, which controls social behaviour primarily through the class-*un*conscious – namely via distinction, demarcation and self-elevation through the social debasement of others.

The most recent French presidential elections illustrate this: the manifestation of a "new class struggle" (Brändle 2022) was already noticeable in the first round of voting. While Emmanuel Macron secured above all the urban middle-class vote, the less well-off in the suburbs (*banlieues*) voted for left-wing candidate Jean-Luc Mélenchon, but in rural areas they backed far-right Marine Le Pen. She managed to present herself as somewhat moderate only because of the candidacy of her even more extreme far-right competitor Éric Zemmour. Le Pen promotes a value system that is based on contempt for Western liberalism and marked by an anti-European attitude. Her corresponding agenda won her more than 40 per cent support in the run-off election, with a staggering 67 per cent of workers voting for the far-right candidate – despite the war in Ukraine and her public expressions of sympathy for Russian president Vladimir Putin (Wiegel & Záboji 2022). Le Pen very purposefully seized on the question of the "choke-chain-effect" of expensive resources and made rising energy, heating, food and mobility prices her number one campaigning issue. She was able to do so because in France – just like in many other Western European societies – class-specific inequalities are increasing while the regulative power of organised industrial relations has long been in decline.

5.3 A Right-wing Deep History: The Example of Lusatia

Generally speaking, right-wing orientations among wage earners are no new phenomenon. They have been observed in Germany's former West and East alike for decades. Over 30 years of research into right-wing worker milieus, we have been able to reconstruct a certain deep history, which, subjectively, feels true without necessarily corresponding to reality in every aspect. The workers we interviewed see themselves as if standing in line for the mountain of justice, patiently waiting their turn to climb it. However, new barriers constantly appear, endlessly prolonging their ascent – economic crises, globalisation and competition among production sites, the costs of German reunification etc. Suddenly, strangers, whom nobody invited, are cutting in front of those who waited in line. Refugees and others who have contributed "nothing to national wealth" are now being given "everything", many respondents believe, while they must continue to wait. They have witnessed the gradual erosion of public infrastructure, a lack of funding to employ more teachers, the slow death of their towns – with the supermarket closing down first, followed by the bus stop and doctors' practices. At the same time – at least as the respondents perceive things – millions of euros are being allocated to fund the integration of people from other "cultural environments" that are allegedly incompatible with the German national culture. This is being perceived as profoundly unfair – an emotionally charged code which the radical far-right has learned to exploit for its political purposes.

The deep history we have here briefly outlined pertains in particular to male industrial workers in relatively secure positions, indeed with somewhat decent incomes, who fear for their social status. Such orientations are especially widespread in the eastern German periphery, often arising from a perceived three-fold social devaluation. Those in question feel devalued not only as a worker, but also as an "*Ossi*" (person from former East Germany) and as a man – a subjective stance which the *Alternative für Deutschland* (AfD) responds to with a fictitious political revaluation in the sense of "Ordinary German workers first!" (for a summary, see Dörre 2020). Our research findings contradict explanations that mechanically interpret the motives for workers' support for the far-right in terms of social protest versus culture war. Respondents' statements commonly contain both: the deployment of resentment in the struggle for improving or maintaining one's social status on one side, and the desire for recognition and preservation of one's own way of life on the other. This helps explain why male workers tend towards the radical far right far more strongly than women from the same milieu. In the case of the men, the ineluctable constraints of their social position correlate with preferences for a conformist lifestyle based on clear-cut gender-specific roles in which the shift in the balance of power towards a more egalitarian gender order constitutes a male experience of loss.

The decarbonisation of the economy, a process which is already underway, produces a new "raw material for fear" that the far right is able to exploit. As the example of the phaseout of lignite mining in the Lusatia region illustrates, there is a real danger of social security and ecological sustainability being pitted against one another (Köster et al. 2022). Workers for whom lignite mining continues to provide a decently paid job and an opportunity for a good life perceive plans for an accelerated phaseout of coal mining and electrification as an attack on their hard-earned social status. The group works council of the affected company LEAG announced, just like management, that it would stage fierce resistance should the plans be implemented. For some of the interviewed opponents of lignite and opencast mining, then, the accelerated phaseout represents a "declaration of bankruptcy of German sustainability policies", seeing as the government's coalition agreement stipulates no reduction of total energy demand (Dörre et al. 2022).

Conflicting interests and objectives have engendered opposing camps among the population in the eastern German Lusatia region, with members of either side no longer even mingling or communicating with one another. Yet they are united by one common trait: those who live in Lusatia, love this region. Leaving it just for a secure job is inconceivable for many, regardless of their stance in the conflict over coal. Just like in similar conflicts elsewhere, however, shared local ties are not enough for people to collectively define the common good regionally, let alone nationally. Those benefiting from the transformation conflicts and correspondingly arising (or anticipated) losses of control include far-right political forces who deny man-made climate change and regard the sustainability agenda as proof of a conspiracy by global elites, who are allegedly plotting to systematically destroy national and regional identities through their "one-world ideology". In the regional elections of 2019, the radical far-right party AfD managed to garner 32.8 per cent of the vote, emerging as the strongest party by far. As in the state of Brandenburg as a whole, the party enjoys above-average support among workers. It has established itself as the only political force that opposes the energy transition and promises a bright future for lignite mining.

Certainly, transformation conflicts can just as easily take a very different course than in Lusatia, where the ecological and the social axes of conflict have each developed a life of their own. At the same time, the configuration of the conflict which we have described is not a case apart either. The public controversy over a buyer's premium for cars with a traditional combustion engine suggests that a similar conflict dynamic has engulfed the automotive sector, which is far more significant economically. The example of Lusatia also shows that the first-hand experience of wage earners often lacks what Erik Olin Wright (2015) deems the indispensable precondition for a conscious mobilisation of subaltern classes: that is, a reference to the adversary that allows for accurately pinpointing the causes and effects of the actions of ruling classes, as this clarifies that the well-being of privileged classes is the root cause of the unprivileged classes' social hardships. If, in contrast, the adversary – not the enemy! – is an abstract market force whose origins and effects cannot be clearly attributed, this may drive a search for scapegoats and thus the tendency towards the personalisation and mystification of the causes of crisis.

5.4 The Radical Far Right as a Polanyi-type Movement

In their "movement" stage, we may summarise, the political formations of the radical far right benefit from mobilisations of the Polanyian type. This latter implies that members of demobilised, subaltern classes without representative political actors of their own have little choice but to delegate their – unvaryingly contradictory and therefore possible-to-interpret – interests to supposedly cross-class "higher powers". Class positions thus never entail any specific political orientation per se. Regardless of such complex relations between socioeconomic class positions and the political space, the dynamic of capitalist societies arises from a fundamental conflict which continues to have a structure-forming effect to this day, beyond historical-philosophical attributions. As Ralf Dahrendorf (1958) writes in a study that is certainly worth reading again today, class theories reflect social structures which "are capable of producing within themselves the elements of their supersession and change". Hence, classes constitute "interest groupings emerging from certain structural conditions which operate as such in social conflicts and effect social structure changes" (Dahrendorf 1959: viii–ix).

In capitalism, class movements from below commonly emerge in the struggle against exploitation and for a greater share of the socially produced value-added. They are directed against a clearly identifiable opposing class, aim primarily at equality and rely on the utilisation of various sources of wage earners' power.

Polanyi-type movements are marked by different characteristics: according to Polanyi, class interests only provide "a limited explanation of long-term social developments" (Polanyi 2001: 159), since "sectional interests" must ultimately always be related to "a total situation" (ibid.). Moreover, class interests "most directly refer to standing and rank, to status and security" and are therefore "primarily not economic but social" (ibid.: 160). An all-too-narrowly defined concept of interest must therefore lead to a "warped vision of social and political history" (ibid.: 213), because it ignores the fact that purely economic facts are far less relevant for class behaviour "than questions of social recognition" (ibid.: 160).

Movements of a Polanyian type are commonly directed against an expansive market power that appears diffuse and abstract to the members of the subaltern classes. This power can seldom be clearly identified, and criticism of it can be politicised in different directions. It is possible for market-critical movements to take on reactive-nationalist or even fascist traits. In contrast to the implications of Marxian class universalism, which assumed that the "exploitation of the world market" would give "a cosmopolitan character to production and consumption in every country" (Marx and Engels 1976: 488), Polanyi considers it just as likely that the exact opposite will occur, arguing that a levelling market power could reinforce an "endemic tendency" among wage-earners to "draw nonclass borders and boundaries as a basis for claims for protection from the maelstrom (of the market, K.D.)" (Silver 2003: 22). Movements of a Polanyian type arise primarily out of alienation, social contempt and collective devaluation. They claim the right to protection not only from social insecurity, but also from threats to public security. Their effectiveness rests mainly on their ability to polarise society and to exercise blocking power in political decision-making processes. Their resources include the willingness to use force against state institutions, but also against competitors and dissenters. Their frame of reference is the nation state, whose protective function is frequently and emphatically invoked.

With this in mind, we may add three further structural features of an exterministic authoritarianism. Firstly: in the wage-dependent classes, and particularly among the shrinking industrial workforce, this authoritarianism feeds on suppressed class conflicts that have been made politically invisible. This explains the overrepresentation of workers among the voters of countless radical far-right parties. This overrepresentation is an international phenomenon (see Evans & Tilley 2017; Williams 2017), which reveals a tendency towards an exclusive solidarity. Although those parts of the working class who fall prey to the lure of authoritarianism can by all means display solidarity, they do so only within the boundaries of their company, workplace and core workforce. This tendency towards exclusive solidarity seeks the dissociation not only from capital, management or superiors, but also from precarious workers, migrants, the poor and the unemployed. These kind of world views lend themselves to radicalisation by a right-wing authoritarianism which reframes class-specific conflicts between the top and the bottom as exclusionary inside-outside conflicts. All this occurs in the name of a higher national ideal that allegedly stands above and beyond all class relations. In a scenario in which national unity takes priority, a rhetoric critical of capitalism can easily be transposed into an ethnic-nationalist (or *völkisch*) discourse. National communities – incidentally, a construct that is also conceivable in pan-European terms – are thus destined to reconcile class antagonisms. Correspondingly, the "social question today" does "not primarily" pertain to the "distribution of national wealth from the top to the bottom, or from the bottom to the top, or from young to old" (Höcke 2017: 25–29). The image of the enemy is rather that of the "politicians from the old parties" who "have opened up our social security systems to millions of people who have never paid into our systems" and are thereby "intentionally [destroying] the foundations of our evolved community of solidarity" (ibid.).

Exclusive solidarity and the reinterpretation of the social question, secondly, allows for a conserving or even exclusionary orientation to be attached to class action that aims at an improvement or at least preservation of social status. Such dispositions are by no means exclusive to low-income workers. The perception of social devaluation engulfs the entire life context – the economically underdeveloped region; the part of town you avoid; high (and rising) rents in the cities; an eroding social infrastructure and mobility barriers in rural areas. That is why, especially in peripheral regions, the perception of social devaluation is particularly widespread even among high-skilled workers with above-average income. This high-income engineer from eastern Germany personally knows "people who earn a lot less, or perhaps even more, simply depending on where you are" (Engineer, opto-electronic industry). As a workplace representative, moreover, he is aware of the growing inequalities of wealth and income in the country as a whole. That is why, subjectively, there is no contradiction in being "satisfied" with his own income while at the same time noting that "[t]hose who have something to say are those with power or money", and they can "simply impose their [decisions] on others."

The perception of one's own powerlessness unites wage earners, low-wage workers and the unemployed. Indeed, subjectively it can weigh even more heavily when the mode of devaluation operates not only via social status but also geographically. Those who become the target of negative classifications time and again tend to become more impatient with those situated below them in the social hierarchy. Although self-revaluation through the devaluation of others may not be the only possible reaction, it is one that is at least seemingly self-evident subjectively.

All this, thirdly, points to a fateful political dynamic, which may be best described as follows: the less likely that the prospect of successful, solidarity-based, transformative class action appears subjectively, the more likely workers are to adopt an attitude that Ralf Dahrendorf once characterised – with remarkable foresight – as follows:

> Marx thought that bourgeois society was unique in that for the first time the suppressed class [...] would [...] topple the ruling minority. In one sense, the opposite has happened. [...] In any case, they [the people] have discovered life chances which their parents and grandparents barely dreamed of. But they are not sure that the good times will last. They begin to draw boundaries that leave some out in the cold. Like earlier dominant classes they have all kinds of reasons for drawing such lines, and they are prepared to let those in who accept and adopt their values. Also, they argue with conviction, if [albeit] not very convincingly, that boundaries of class should not exist. They want them removed; but they are not prepared to do what it takes to remove them. Lack of imagination on the part of a class that lives in the

> provisions world and therefore does not recognize the entitlement claims of others is coupled with vested interest in preserving one's own position. Things are not quite as bad yet, but the signs of persistent unemployment and hard poverty could be ominous. (Dahrendorf 2008 [1994]: 149)

Today we know that things are, indeed, getting as bad. Decreasing unemployment aside, a rise in inequality and uncertainty, particularly in rich countries, has led some sections of the working class to set their hopes on a politics of conservation that seeks to exclude those deemed unwanted guests. These workers are opposed to rapid socio-ecological transformation, especially if they see their jobs at risk in the process. The reason for this reaction is that they fear that the times of plenty are over, or that the anticipated changes will not offer them any opportunities. Seeing as they still have something to lose, these groups of workers – particularly in the declining carbon industries – tend to align themselves with management and other representatives of capital. In the case of the regional lignite mining company and electricity provider LEAG in eastern Germany's Lusatia region, this collaboration between management, trade union, works council and the workforce is so close that it virtually binds them together as a team. In the car industry and its supply industries, too, cross-class workplace alliances channel the pressure coming from decarbonisation targets and transformation plans. Here, the main conflict lines run through the camps of capital and labour.

However, even with this variant of social-bloc formation, all matters pertaining to wages, working hours and working conditions continue to entail negotiating opposing interests. These conflicts are at the very heart of organised industrial relations; yet they are superimposed by the struggle for the preservation of social status and employment, which may not mute class antagonisms entirely, but nevertheless facilitates cross-class alliances. However, these spaces of democratic class struggle based on collective regulations, negotiations and the readiness for compromise on all sides are getting smaller. Less than one-third of wage earners in the EU still have some form of collective workplace representation. The unionisation rate is declining and the adherence to systems of collective bargaining agreements and contractual norms has been eroding since the 1990s. In Germany, barely 16 per cent of wage earners are unionised today. Electoral and political abstentionism are widespread among workers. In part, this makes them susceptible to the appeal of the radical far right. In the sense that this fosters structural conservatism, resulting in the postponement of the transition towards ecological sustainability goals, this social barrier, too, implies a latent exterministic consequence.

6. GAINS IN CONTROL THROUGH INFRASTRUCTURE SOCIALISM IN TRANSFORMATIVE DEMOCRACIES?

Let us summarise: the control over one's own life represents a basic need which, in modern capitalist societies, is articulated in the form of demands for social and public security. Under the conditions of an epochal economic-ecological pincer crisis, these demands are complemented by those for protection from natural disasters, epidemics and military conflicts as an overarching syndrome of threat. The twenty-first-century radical far right reacts to this scenario by tying the promise of security to the fate of the nation itself, whereby nation is understood as a largely homogeneous, ehtnic-cultural community that transcends all conflicts of interest. In the midst of a seemingly chaotic world, right-wing radicalism presents itself as the force of order and strength, which knows how to assert itself – if need be by breaching the rules, oppressing the weak and using violence, up to all-out war. Its influence relies on the systematic assault on scientific reason. Civil standards are replaced by – partly religiously cloaked – beliefs and conspiracy myths that serve as constructed causal mechanisms for making sense of the world. We may speak of "authoritarianism" because the agenda of these currents, even though they emerge in democracies and at times may even demand an expansion of direct democracy, ultimately implies the elimination of their opponents. These said currents can be described to be "radical right-wing", not merely right-wing populist, if they are based on ideologies of inequality whose propagation implies the option of violent system change (Heitmeyer 2018a, 2018b). During the stage of opposition movements, these formations feed on the "homeless anticapitalism" of self-abnegating class societies. They react to the powerlessness of subaltern class factions, which are increasingly incapable of self-organising and conducting an organised interest-based politics, with a fictitious self-elevation through the social devaluation of others. Furthermore, given that the new social blocs forming, which support the new authoritarianism, combine structural drivers with the personality traits of unifying leader figures, they embody the articulation of a twenty-first-century "Bonapartism". The Trumps, Bolsonaros, Melonis, Le Pens or Putins are the bonapartists of our time (Beck/Stützle 2018), responding to the yearning for control through strength and assertiveness. These formations acquire a novel "fascist" quality if they pursue, once in office and ready to use force, the totalisation of their power. Indeed, it remains to be seen how the recently elected Italian prime minister Giorgia Meloni from the (post-)fascist "Brothers of Italy" (*Fratelli d'Italia*) party develops in office. The readiness to wage large-scale war, then, is not the only proof of "exterminism"; their urge for extermination can equally find expression in the denial of man-made climate change, the coronavirus pandemic, the overconsumption of resources or the eradication of indigenous communities.

Bearing in mind the catastrophic potential of the economic-ecological pincer crisis, there is the danger that exterministic authoritarianism could gain the upper hand in the struggle for a new world order. Liberal democracies, which are creepingly turning into states in which the state of exception becomes the norm, could unwittingly accelerate this process (on the state of exception, see Frankenberg 2017). But what kind of "antidote" might be appropriate to successfully combatting exterminism and authoritarianism in the twenty-first century? The answer is anything but simple and can be, at best, preliminary, tentative and incomplete. The following three considerations regarding the great promises of social (and societal) security can perhaps help point a way forward.

6.1 Protection From Exterminism

The tools that democratic societies can draw on to defend themselves against the aggression of authoritarian-exterministic regimes are limited. That said, the greatest mistake would be to turn the state of exception – as it formed over the course of the coronavirus pandemic within constitutional norms (see also Frankenberg 2022) – into a permanent state, on account of wars or natural disasters. Unfortunately, in the political reactions to the attack on Ukraine, which have included declaring major armaments programmes to be without alternative and attempting to give them constitutional status without any public debate, we can see just that happening. It is one thing to grant Ukraine the right to armed self-defence; making arming Ukraine a constitutional obligation is something very different. After all, despite the Russian aggression, there is no need for gigantic armaments programmes. As of today, the total military budget of NATO's member countries is multiple times that of Russia (SIPRI 2022). And yet, the NATO summit in Oslo in May–June 2023 resolved that the 2 per cent of GDP that member countries are to earmark for for military spending should henceforth no longer be a "target" but the bare minimum. Armed forces with a strictly defensive mission, yet strong enough to stand up to exterministic regimes, could be easily funded at an EU level even with reduced defence spending. This is urgently needed, because the funds that are being channelled into the growing military budgets will be sorely missed when it comes to meaningfully combatting climate change and mitigating the ecological conflict in society. Increasing spending to more than 2 per cent of GDP effectively amounts to a declaration of war on ecological and social sustainability. Military spending can never be sustainable, let alone under the conditions of the pincer crisis. Aggressors can be confronted in different ways:

through the toughest economic sanctions and, in the case of the Putin regime, with an immediate import ban on Russian oil and gas which may have been officially implemented but is being undermined by various important economies as well as some EU countries. The price of a European recession would certainly be lower than that of a long war of attrition, especially given the ever-increasing danger of escalation as well as food shortages and an outright ecocide in the Global South.

6.2 Social Security

As Thomas Piketty (2014: 59) illustrates with disturbing lucidity, rising social inequality in the absence of corrective measures ultimately leads to war. This is another reason why ecological sustainability is inconceivable without social sustainability. Given that the inflationary development likewise driven by the war will likely continue for some time despite falling prices, at least in some areas, the residual income – the money left after substracting taxes, social security contributions and fixed costs for rent, heating, etc. – will decrease considerably. Preventing the bottom half of income earners from being driven into the camp of the new Bonapartes and their far-right formations requires a willingness to engage in the democratic contest. Dispute and argument connect people (Simmel 1908/1922); they are the lifeblood of functioning democracies. That is why the all-pervasive appeal to preserve social cohesion is disastrous if it is merely used to conceal conflicts and impose a false social harmony. A democratic class struggle, as cited by the liberal sociologist Ralf Dahrendorf in the sense of a driver of social change, may contradict capital's utopia of unlimited market coordination; in fact, in the welfare-state capitalisms, it was an important mechanism to ensure both system and social integration for several decades.

Erik Olin Wright illustrated this insight in a model of class compromise in capitalist societies which corresponds to a J-curve. The model is based on the premise that class conflicts can be curbed through real concessions to subaltern classes. The stability of such compromises depends on the power resources the conflicting parties can mobilise. If the organised power of working classes contributes positively to resolving or mitigating social problems, such compromise will likely be relatively stable (Wright 2015: 230). However, one fundamental problem in demobilised class societies is precisely that capital's drive towards gaining ever-more control has invalidated this insight. In the absence of democratic mobilisations from below that seriously challenge capitalist elites, this inequality will be impossible to rectify.

Given that industrial class conflicts are increasingly turning into socio-ecological transformation conflicts, another aspect also has to be considered: namely, the tension between social and ecological sustainability targets is real. Whether or not this tension can be processed and negotiated in political systems and civil societies that follow democratic rules and establish an efficient management of the pincer crisis within a democratic framework will shape the trajectory and outcome of transformation conflicts. In this context, it is a promising sign when climate movements and trade unions forge new, unconventional alliances (Liebig & Lucht 2022) – as has been the case, for example, in the fight for sustainable mobility and affordable high-quality public transport.

6.3 Public Security

Pincer crises and war call for a new state interventionism. Even apart from rebuilding the economy after the coronavirus pandemic, this is needed to guarantee public security. This state interventionism marks a field that democratic counterforces must engage, as the new authoritarianism will undoubtedly make it a battlefield. Consequently, the mere affirmation of the state is just as useless as a fundamental critique of the state. It appears far more conducive to seek out starting points for a sustainable infrastructure socialism that could take shape in practice immediately through investments in the everyday economy (Foundational Economy Collective 2018) and public (social) services. Infrastructure socialism means guaranteeing the particular protection of modes of production, institutions, forms of work and living that maintain people's everyday lives in the first place. The aim is to decouple these areas as far as possible from private profit interests. At the same time, it is about more than simply securing additional public funds for roads, hospitals, childcare facilities and broadband internet. It aims to strengthen the democratic power of civil socity – a power that mobilises people for cooperative, volunteer collective actions of all sorts.

Generally, the national economies of advanced capitalisms are divided into sectors of largely unpaid care work, areas of (semi-)commercial public social services (e.g., healthcare, energy), basic (e.g., food supply) and expanded (e.g., restaurants) local amenities, the partly export-oriented market economy (e.g., car and supplier industry) and the rent economy (e.g., stock markets, housing markets). The greatest use-value ought to be attached to public social services or activities related to basic and expanded local amenities (Plank & Prausmüller 2020).

The foremost economic sector that would require comprehensive downsizing is the rentier economy; the export economy needs to be restructured. Conversely, the areas of public services and local amenities have to grow. As Wolfgang Streeck emphasises, such a recognition of the everyday ecenomy of public goods is highly compatible with sustainable socialist agendas, not least as it moves beyond the primarily redistributive focus (Streeck 2019).

The transition to sustainable high-quality production may represent a viable alternative to capitalist expansionism, but also to postulates of "degrowth" that at best serve as an orientation for minoritarian subcultures. This would entail producing and consuming less in terms of overall physical material, but higher-quality goods, available to all. Setting the course towards long-lasting goods is impossible without abandoning production processes conceptualised primarily with a view to markets and consumers. The transition to sustainable high-quality production can only succeed if the goods resulting from such a type of production can be consumed by the lowest-income groups as well, despite the higher prices. This, in turn, is impossible without a redistribution of social wealth in favour of low-income groups and from the economic centres to the (semi-)peripheries. An infrastructure socialism based on cooperatives and municipal ownership, funded through a fairer, redistributive taxation policy, as well as greatly expanded public social services would mark a significant step towards enabling a more carefree life for all. Infrastructure socialism marks a break with an economy of cheap goods and the devaluation of reproductive tasks. It is thus a contribution to the urgently needed search for an emergency exit from the pincer crisis.

With a view to deminishing time budgets left to implement fundamental political course corrections, infrastructure socialism proposes a gradual concept. It entrusts the allocation of resources, the control over production and the distribution of goods to civil-society actors, whose task it is to strengthen all areas serving the actual production and maintenance of life. It treats the revaluation and re-appropriation of public goods in the production of essential goods – from vaccines to advanced professional training and on to mobility – as absolutely indispensable. This is what distinguishes it from primarily market-, technology-, or (nation-)state-centred strategies for managing the pincer crisis which move within the capitalist expansion paradox. Infrastructure socialism ultimately means abolishing an expansive ownership principle that requires endlessly repeated *Landnahmen*. To achieve this, it relies on collective forms of ownership that strengthen people's confidence. Its aim is a transformative democracy that includes the economic domain, too. Its objectives include a solidarity-based redistribution of collectively produced wealth, participatory planning and the transition to sustainable forms of production and lifestyles. Today, such alternatives are indeed being discussed in earnest, albeit under different labels, within the climate movements, but also in trade unions, environmental organisations, political parties and the scientific community. This reflects the use value of concrete utopias (Dörre 2021) that point beyond existing reality and thereby deliver a blow to exterminism – which has no appealing development project in store (Ishchenko 2022: 35) – in its perhaps weakest spot.

7. CONCLUSION

Let us return once again to the hypotheses which we posited at the beginning. Regarding the first, exterministic authoritarianism cannot be effectively combatted within the logic of arms races. Simply because the money spent on the military is therefore unavailable to effectively combat a potential ecocide as the result of accelerated climate change and resource depletion. Incidentally, the military craze dominating the media since the outbreak of the Ukraine war is paralleled by the alarming news that the $100 bn annually stipulated by the resolutions of Copenhagen of 2009 and 2020 to combat climate change have not been mobilised thus far. As hinted at in the second hypothesis, if we really want to overcome exterministic path dependencies, we have to begin in our own societies: we need a readiness to curb glaring social inequalities; mitigate the ongoing transformation conflicts through security guarantees for directly or indirectly affected workforces; and invest the accumulated peace and security dividend in a protective social infrastructure. Doing so necessarily requires greater public awareness of and political support for a democratic class struggle. Organised industrial relations, intact trade unions and a functioning system of codetermination represent minimum requirements for sustainability and, at the same time, represent a quality standard of any democracy. It is in recognition of just this that economist Thomas Piketty has explicitly turned from being a liberal to a socialist (Piketty 2021). Regardless of whether one wishes to follow suit or not, in the absence of fundamental changes in society, as my third hypothesis predicts, there will be no effective "antidote" for exterminism and authoritarianism. Rockets on Babi Yar, that is the message of the apocalypse. "Better quality, instead of always more", indeed, "for all, not just for the few" (Glättli & Meyer 2021: 148), is a counter-message that points the way towards a sustainability revolution. And here again, Shostakovich wrote the matching piece of music – namely his Symphony No 11, composed in memory of the anti-Tsarist, bourgeois revolution of 1905.

REFERENCES

Albrecht, Ulrich (1997), "Exterminismus", in *Historisch-Kritisches Wörterbuch des Marxismus* (Historical-Critical Dictionary of Marxism), Vol. 3, Columns 1188–1192.

Albright, Madeleine (2018), *Fascism: A Warning*, New York: Harper Collins.

Arendt, Hannah (1958), *The Origins of Totalitarianism*, Cleveland/New York: Meridian Books.

Baecker, Dirk (2018), *4.0 oder: Die Lücke, die der Rechner lässt,* Leipzig: Merve.

Beck, Martin & Stützle, Ingo (eds.) (2018), *Die neuen Bonapartisten. Mit Marx den Aufstieg von Trump und Co. verstehen*, Berlin: Dietz.

Beck, Ulrich (1992), *Risk Society. Towards a New* Mondernity, London: Sage.

Brändle, Stefan (2022), "Neuer Klassenkampf", in *Frankfurter Rundschau* (12 April 2022).
Crutzen, Paul J. (2019), *Das Anthropozän*, Munich: oekom.
Dahrendorf (1959 [1957]), *Class and Class Conflict in Industrial Society*, Stanford, CA: Stanford University Press.
Dahrendorf (2008 [1994]), *The Modern Social Conflict: The Politics of Liberty*, New Brunswick/London: Transaction Publishers.
Derluguian, Georgi (2013), "What Communism Was", in Wallerstein, Immanuel, Collins, Randall Collins, Mann, Michael, Derluguian, Georgi & Calhoun, Craig (eds.), *Does Capitalism Have A Future?*, Oxford: Oxford University Press, 99–130.
Dörre, Klaus (2018a), *A Right-Wing Workers' Movement? Impressions from Germany*, in *Global Labour Journal* 9 (3), 339–347.
Dörre, Klaus (2018b), "Europe, Capitalist Landnahme and the Economic-Ecological Double Crisis: Prospects for a Non-Capitalist Post-Growth Society", in Rosa, Hartmut/Henning, Christoph (eds.) (2018), *The Good Life Beyond Growth. New Perspectives*, Abingdon: Routledge, 241–249.
Dörre, Klaus et al. (2020), *In der Warteschlange. Arbeiter*innen und die radikale Rechte*, Münster: Westfälisches Dampfboot.
Dörre, Klaus et al. (2021), *Die Utopie des Sozialismus. Kompass für eine Nachhaltigkeitsrevolution*, Berlin: Matthes & Seitz.
Dörre, Klaus et al. (2022), "Abschied vom Abschied? Transformation, Nachhaltigkeit, Krieg. Nachwort zur zweiten Auflage", in Dörre, Klaus et al. (eds.), *Abschied von Kohle und Auto? Sozial-ökologische Transformationskonflikte um Energie und Mobilität*, Frankfurt am Main: Campus, 2nd revised edn, 309–324.
Duhm, Dieter (1972), *Angst im Kapitalismus*, Lampertheim: Verlag Kübler.
Ellis, Erle C. (2018), *Anthropocene: A Very Short Introduction*, Oxford: Oxford University Press.
Eribon, Didier (2013), *Returning to Reims*, Cambridge, MA/London: MIT Press.
Evans, Geoffrey & Tilley, James (2017), *The New Politics of Class. The Political Exclusion of the British Working Class*, Oxford: Oxford University Press.
Foster, John B., Clark, Brett & York, Richard (2010), *The Ecological Rift: Capitalism's War on the Earth*, New York: Monthly Review Press.
Foundational Economy Collective (2018), *The Infrastructure of Everyday Life*, Manchester: Manchester University Press.
Frankenberg, Günter (2017), "Im Ausnahmezustand", in *Kritische Justiz* 50, Issue 1, 3–18.
Frankenberg, Günter (2022), "Leviathan mit Schnabelmaske: Zum Autoritarismus von Gefahrenabwehr- und Infektionsschutzrecht", in: Frankenberg, Günter & Heitmeyer, W. (eds.) (2022), *Treiber des Autoritären. Pfade von Entwicklungen zu Beginn des 21. Jahrhunderts*, Frankfurt/New York: Campus, 439–468.
Frankenberg, Günter & Heitmeyer, Wilhelm (eds.) (2022), *Treiber des Autoritären. Pfade von Entwicklungen zu Beginn des 21. Jahrhunderts*, Frankfurt/New York: Campus.
Galbraith, James K. (2014), *The End of Normal. The Great Crisis and the Future of Growth*, New York: Simon & Schuster.
Gallagher, Kevin P. & KozulWright, Richard (2019), *A New Multilateralism for Shared Prosperity. Geneva Principles for a Global Green New Deal*, Geneva: UNCTAD. Available at: https://www.bu.edu/gdp/2019/04/10/a-new-multilateralism-for-shared-prosperity-geneva-principles-for-a-global-green-new-deal/ (last accessed: 20 April 2022).

Glättli, Balthasar & Meyer, Mattea (2021), "'Besser statt mehr' und zwar 'Für alle statt für wenige'", in Franzini, Luzian et al. (2022), *Postwachstum? Aktuelle Auseinandersetzungen um einen grundlegenden gesellschaftlichen Wandel*, Denknetz-Jahrbuch 2021, Zurich: Edition 8, 147–158.
Gürth, Lisa (2021), *Russland. Gewerkschaftsmonitor*, Berlin: Friedrich-Ebert-Stiftung.
Harvey, David (2010), *The Enigma of Capital. And the Crises of Capitalism*, London: Profile Books.
Heitmeyer, Wilhelm (2018a), "Autoritärer Nationalradikalismus", in: Becker, Karina, Dörre, Klaus & Reif-Spirek, Peter (eds), *Arbeiterbewegung von rechts? Ungleichheit – Verteilungskämpfe – populistische Revolte*. Hamburg: Campus, 117–134.
Heitmeyer, Wilhelm (2018b), *Autoritäre Versuchungen. Signaturen der Bedrohung I*, Berlin: Suhrkamp.
Heitmeyer, Wilhelm, Freiheit, Manuela & Sitzer, Peter (2020), *Rechte Bedrohungsallianzen*, Berlin: Suhrkamp.
Höcke, Björn (2017), "Widerstand gegen den Raubtierkapitalismus. Die AfD muss auch den sozialen Auftrag übernehmen, den die Linke verraten hat", in Höcke, Björn (2019), *Höcke. Interviews, Reden, Tabubrüche,* Compact Edition, 25–29.
International Panel on Climate Change (IPCC) (2022), *Climate Change 2022. Impacts, Adaption and Vulnerability*. Available at: https:// www .ipcc .ch/ report/ ar6/wg2/downloads/report/IPCC_AR6_WGII_SummaryForPolicymakers.pdf/ (last accessed: 20 April 2022).
Ishchenko, Volodymyr (2022), "Towards the Abyss. Interview", in: *New Left Review* 133/134, pp. 17–39. Available at: https:// newleftreview .org/ issues/ ii133/ articles/ volodymyr-ishchenko-towards-the-abyss/ (last accessed: 20 April 2022).
Ivanova, Diana & Wood, Richard (2020), "The unequal distribution of household carbon footprints in Europe and its link to sustainability", in: *Global Sustainability* 3, e18, 1–12. https://doi.org/10.1017/sus.2020.12/ (last accessed: 20 April 2022).
Köster, Jakob et al. (2022), "Nach der Braunkohle. Konflikte um Energie und regionale Entwicklung in der Lausitz", in: Dörre, Klaus et al. (eds.), *Abschied von Kohle und Auto? Sozial-ökologische Transformationskonflikte um Energie und Mobilität*, Frankfurt am Main: Campus, 2nd revised edn, 71–127.
Liebig Steffen & Lucht, Kim (2022), *Fahren wir zusammen?*, Hamburg: VSA.
Luxemburg, Rosa (2015 [1913]), "The Accumulation of Capital", in *The Complete Works of Rosa Luxemburg, Volume II, Economic Writings 2,* London: Verso, 7–344.
Marx, Karl & Friedrich Engels (1976 [1848]), "Manifesto of the Communist Party", *in Marx and Engels Collected Works (MECW),* Volume 6, New York: International Publishers, 477–519.
Moore, Jason W. (2015), *Capitalism in the Web of Life. Ecology and the Accumulation of Capital*, London/New York: Verso.
Morris, Jeremy (2020), "Arbeiterprotest, Organisation und Klassenpolitik in Russland", in: *russland-analysen* No. 389 (20 July 2020), 2–5.
Oxfam (2020), *Confronting Carbon Inequality in the European Union. Why the European Green Deal must tackle inequality while cutting emissions.* Available at: https://www.oxfam.org/en/research/confronting-carbon-inequality-european-union/ (last accessed: 20 April 2022).
Pantel, Nadia (2022), "Macron sind wir egal, aber Le Pen greift uns an", in: *Süddeutsche Zeitung* (16/17/18 April).
Piketty, Thomas (2014), "Das Ende des Kapitalismus im 21. Jahrhundert?", in *Blätter für deutsche und internationale Politik* 12/2014, 41–52.

Piketty, Thomas (2021), *Time for Socialism: Dispatches from a World on Fire, 2016–2021*, New Haven/London: Yale University Press.

Plank, Leonhard & Prausmüller, Oliver (2020), "Ist die Zukunft öffentlich?", in: *Makroskop. Magazin für Wirtschaftspolitik*, pp. 1–8. Available at: https:// www .researchgate .net/ publication/ 348369826 _Ist _die _Zukunft _offentlich/ (last accessed: 20 April 2022).

Polanyi, Karl (2001 [1944]), *The Great Transformation. The Political and Economic Origins of Our Time*, Boston: Beacon Press.

Röthig, Marcel & Yarmolyuk-Kröck, Kateryna (2021), *Ukraine Gewerkschaftsmonitor*, Berlin: Friedrich-Ebert-Stiftung.

Schmitt, Carl (1950), "Das Recht als Einheit von Ordnung und Ortung", in Dünne, Jörg & Günzel, Stephan (eds) (2006), *Raumtheorie. Grundlagentexte aus Philosophie und Kulturwissenschaften,* Frankfurt am Main: Suhrkamp, 409–419.

Schmitt, Carl (2003 [1950]), *The Nomos of the Earth in the International Law of the Jus Publicum Europaeum*, transl. by G.L. Ulmen, Candor: Telos Press.

Silver, Beverly J. (2003), *Forces of Labor. Workers' Movements And Globalization Since 1870*, New York: Cambridge University Press.

Simmel, Georg (1908/1922), "Der Streit", in Simmel, Georg, *Soziologie. Untersuchungen über die Formen der Vergesellschaftung*, Berlin: Duncker & Humblot, 186–255.

SIPRI (2022), *Database*, available at: https:// www .sipri .org/ databases/ milex/ (last accessed: 20 April 2022).

Statistisches Bundesamt (Destatis) (2022), *Russische Föderation. Statistisches Länderprofil*, Issue 02/2022, Wiesbaden.

Streeck, Wolfgang (2019), "Vorwort", in: Foundational Economy Collective (ed.), *Die Ökonomie des Alltagslebens. Für eine neue Infrastrukturpolitik*, Berlin: Surhkamp, pp. 7–32. [Foreword to the German edition of: *The Infrastructure of Everyday Life*, Manchester: Manchester University Press (2018)].

Ther, Philipp (2016), *Europe after 1989. A History*, Princeton, NJ/Woodstock: Princeton University Press.

Thompson, Edward P. (1980), "Notes on Exterminism, the Last Stage of Civilization", in: *New Left Review*, I/121, pp. 3–31. Available at: https://newleftreview.org/issues/i121/articles/edward-thompson-notes-on-exterminism-the-last-stage-of-civilization/ (last accessed: 20 April 2022).

Wallerstein, Immanuel, Collins, Randall, Mann, Michael, Derluguian, Georgi & Calhoun, Craig (2013), *Does Capitalism Have A Future?*, New York/Oxford: Oxford University Press.

Williams, Joan C. (2017), *White Working Class. Overcoming Class Cluelessness in America*, Boston: Harvard Business Review Press.

Wood, Ellen Meiksins (1999), *The Origin of Capitalism*, London/New York: Verso.

Wood, Tony (2022), "Matrix of War", in: *New Left Review* 133/134, pp. 41–64. Available at: https:// newleftreview .org/ issues/ ii133/ articles/ tony -wood -matrix -of -war/ (last accessed: 20 April 2022).

World Resources Institute (2021), *CAIT Climate Data Explorer 2021*, Washington, D. C. Available at: https://cait.wri.org/(last accessed: 20 April 2022).

Wiegel, Michaela & Záboji, Nilklas (2022), "Die 'strahlende' Verliererin", in: *Frankfurter Allgemeine Zeitung* (24 April 2022). Available at: https://www.faz.net/aktuell/ politik/ ausland/ wahlen -in -frankreich -die -strahlende -verliererin -marine -le -pen-17980910.html (last accessed: 20 April 2022).

Wright, Erik Olin (2015), *Understanding Class*, London/New York: Verso.

7. Crises and loss of control: opportunity structures for the drivers of authoritarian social developments

Wilhelm Heitmeyer

1. INTRODUCTION

Crises are among the special drivers of authoritarian developments and right-wing extremist activities. This thesis, which forms part of the conceptual framework of this book, will be pursued here in two ways: firstly by connecting it to longer-term developments, and secondly by focusing on the COVID-19 crisis.

If developments are to be analysed, then the dimension of time is always of particular relevance. Therefore, it is useful to build upon previous analyses.

This chapter is an update of my own analyses from 2001, 2018, and 2020 on authoritarian developments. This means that it does not push something entirely new onto the scientific agenda, but rather traces how the temporally condensed crises of the past years have increasingly driven social and political conditions in an authoritarian direction.

2. THE PROBLEM OF AUTHORITARIANISM FOR THE OPEN SOCIETY AND LIBERAL DEMOCRACY

Fukuyama's large-frame assessments of economic, political, and social developments towards the end of the twentieth century, in particular his formula of the "end of history" (1992), which found expression in the "universalisation of Western liberal democracy as the final form of human government", were – despite later relativisation – wrong, as was recognisable early on (cf. Heitmeyer 2001: 501–534). They had an unmistakable ideological imprint of Western–American attitudes of hegemony. These assessments were made without a detailed assessment of the interaction of global financial capitalism, social processes such as disintegration and inequality, and changes in the perception of the political system by parts of the population.

2.1 What Were and What Are the Implications of this Interaction for Paths of Development in Western Societies?

One of these paths leads in an authoritarian direction, as shown by evidence on the development of democracy in this book's conceptual framework and contributions. The basic narratives of the authoritarian – they are listed there – include the struggle against the alleged threat to social order, the claimed destruction of hierarchies and dominance, the feared dissolution of identities, and the demise of German culture and the German people.

The extent to which such basic narratives meet with positive resonance in parts of the population and political, media, and economic elites when faced with conditions of crisis and loss of control will be investigated in this analysis (see section 4).

3. THE CONCEPT OF ANALYSIS

The sociological analytical concept for this specific question has already been used several times as the basis for research, in particular in the books *Autoritäre Versuchungen* [*Authoritarian Temptations*] (2018) and *Rechte Bedrohungsallianzen* [*Right-Wing Threat Alliances*] (2020). This concept is now being adapted and focuses on the question of the drivers of authoritarian development.

This analytical concept encompasses economic, social, and political dimensions. These dimensions are qualified with regard to structural developments, their individual processing, and the political consequences of action. This was the previous scheme in the analyses listed, which was laid out with theoretical approaches and filled in with empirical data. Figure 7.1 now makes it clear that various crises with different effects have had an impact on the structural developments of the three dimensions mentioned and have influenced the individual psychological and social processing of current events. Depending on how the crises affected people, this process was at times associated with a loss of control. In the sense of the general need for control over reality, this gave rise to options for action that varied in several ways and even extended to authoritarian temptations. The analysis scheme of 2018 and 2020 has now been expanded to include the two central escalatory factors of crises and losses of control (see Figure 7.1).

On the one hand, crises represent escalations of events in economic, social, and political areas; on the other hand, they have an impact on individual processing, which consequently expresses itself in parts of the population as perceptions or experiences of loss of control (see section 4).

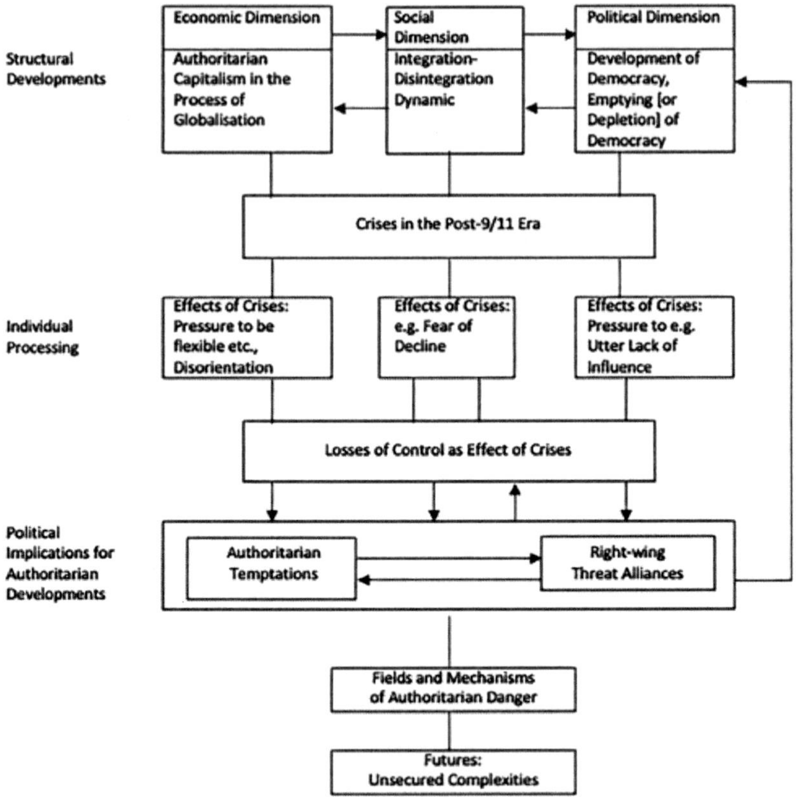

Source: Extended and adapted version from Heitmeyer 2018: 21.

Figure 7.1 Analysis scheme

This analytical scheme is to be filled out with a complementary network of theories, whose individual facets start at different levels as well as in the differentiated areas. These include the theory of social disintegration (Anhut & Heitmeyer 2005), conflict theory (Hirschman 1994), the theory of capitalist land grabbing (Dörre 2009 and in this volume), anomie theory (Thome 2016), and the control theory approach from social psychology (Frey & Jonas 2002).

These theoretical approaches are each called upon with reference to the central thematic question of this chapter.

4. CRISIS TYPES IN THE UNSECURED DECADES AND VARIANTS OF LOSS OF CONTROL

The basis of the analysis are crisis events in the post-9/11 era (as described by Frankenberg/Heitmeyer in this volume), i.e. after the start of the twenty-first century, which have given us "unsecured decades" (Heitmeyer 2018: 89–117).

In order to classify events, it is first necessary to be more specific about what characterises a crisis. Here, the two criteria that Oevermann (2016) emphasises are taken as a basis: first, that the previous political and social routines for coping with events no longer work; secondly, that the conditions before the event cannot be restored; and thirdly, that in crisis situations, different ways of coping compete with each other, creating anomic behavioural insecurities, among other things. It is this combination that suggests linking crises to the problem of loss of control.

What does the survey show after the start date of the twenty-first century?

- In 2001, we had a crisis as a result of 9/11, when Islamist terrorism entered the world stage. It was a political crisis sparked by religious motives.
- In 2005 we had the introduction of Hartz IV laws in Germany. It was experienced as a social crisis by the affected parts of the population.
- In 2008/2009 came the banking and financial crisis with an imminent collapse of a central social system.
- In 2015 the refugee movement in Europe became significant as a political-cultural crisis for parts of the political system and various population groups.

These crises had four other characteristics. First, they each affected different social groups or subsystems of society and the political system. Secondly, the crises occurred one after the other over time. Thirdly, German society had different instruments at its disposal to deal with them. Fourthly, there were justified assumptions about the time structure, i.e. when these crises could be dealt with, resolved, ended, or at least contained.

From a theoretical perspective, these crises can be grouped into what can be classified as a sectoral crisis type, which is associated with corresponding sectoral losses of control for affected people and institutions.

The routines for political and social processing have been largely suspended by the COVID-19 crisis, resulting in social shutdowns and unknown time horizons for the migrating and mutating virus variants. A new, systemic type of crisis has thus emerged. This gives the losses of control a new dimension. They range from individual losses of control to the German Chancellor's confession: "The thing has slipped away from us."[1]

So the question now arises whether this is the basis for authoritarian temptations and structures. In this way, the analysis ties in with Ralf Dahrendorf's now much-cited forecast from 1997, in which he argued that there was much to suggest that an authoritarian century would develop (see, in detail in the introductory chapter of this book). Dahrendorf did not have the crises listed – certainly not the COVID-19 pandemic – in mind, but the dangers of disastrous interaction between the economy, social integration or disintegration, and political participation.

He linked this to the image of "squaring the circle". In his diction, this meant that considerable tensions existed between the tasks of maintaining competitiveness in rabidly competitive capitalism; ensuring social cohesion, i.e. social integration; and being able to exercise political participation in institutions of free societies (see Dahrendorf 1997). The question was thus in the world to whose detriment these tensions would go. Even then, it was an open question how the individual, collective, and institutional losses of control would play out under the pressure of capitalist gains in control.

In crises, loss of control is expressed in different ways. One of these is that the behavioural options for controlling reality, i.e. for solving problems, are massively narrowed. This is especially true in systemic crises. These crises generate fears through the impairment or loss of security-guaranteeing everyday structures, low possibilities of influencing external circumstances, feelings of being at the mercy of others, feelings of powerlessness, and loneliness. Such feelings and the associated "tunnel vision" that comes with a lack of escape routes can in turn contribute to extreme behaviours, including depression, violence against oneself, increased aggressiveness and indiscriminate aggression targets and objects of violence, loss of orientation coordinates ("Where is my social and political location?"), norm diffusion ("What is valid, what is not?"), and blocked future perspectives.

Set against this are search movements to satisfy the fundamental need for control over reality. This includes political search movements for authoritarian actors who promise to restore control by reducing the complexity of the crisis.

5. THE CENTRAL THESIS

The fact that crises and losses of control function as drivers of authoritarian political and social development is explained by the fact that the central need

---

1 Quoted from *Neue Westfälische*, 26 January 2021 and *Berliner Zeitung*, 26 January 2021.

for control of reality can no longer be realised to the extent to which people were previously accustomed. The lived-in and functional normality has been damaged or even destroyed. This applies, to varying degrees, to those in power in the three structural areas mentioned (the macro-level), to actors in central political and social institutions (the meso-level), and to individuals in different life situations and histories (on the micro-level).

This raises the question of what losses of control mean in terms of individual social and political behaviour and in terms of mutual interaction with authoritarian offers in the form of movements and parties (see analytical scheme, Figure 7.1).

With regard to the authoritarian offers, these often appear with the claim of decreasing problem-solving and coping capacities provided by liberal democracies with their complex voting procedures and instead put forward their central slogan of the restoration of control. However, this restoration – in the sense of the definition of crisis used here – is not a restoration of the state that preceded the crisis, but an authoritarian change of control and thus also a change of economic, social, cultural, and political conditions.

6. THE BASIC FRAMEWORK: PARADIGMS OF MODERNITY AS CATALYSTS OF THE AUTHORITARIAN

In order to defend the thesis on which this chapter is based, it is necessary to refer back to the fundamental paradigms of modernity, which Zygmunt Bauman in particular has characterised as the "ambivalence of modernity" (2005).

Two mechanisms stand out in particular. The first is ambivalence, i.e. the countless contradictions that permeate economic, social, and political life. Certainties dissolve, but the search for them remains and is reactivated under conditions of crisis and loss of control. This is when conspiracy theories come into play. They provide (see Butter 2018; 2021: 4–11) new, surrogate certainties in the COVID-19 crisis. They are unquestionable "explanations", quasi-compasses of faith. They are not mere "narratives" but, at their core, ideological strategies of power that come to light. The authoritarian character of conspiracy theories consists in the assertion of the possession of absolute truth. The reason for the spread of conspiracy theories "is not the expression of a lack of enlightenment, but the result of late-modern individualisation", according to Amlinger & Nachtwey (2021: 18). This would mean that the potential for the spread of conspiracy theories is inherent in modernity and is then "activated" by crises and losses of control, because explanations for losses of control and the overall misery are needed and guilty parties are to be identified and held accountable.

The second important mechanism is ambiguity. With the increasing complexity of modern societies, ambiguous situations and futures also increase. Analyses (e.g. Bauer 2018) show that the ability to deal with ambivalences and to endure ambiguities about future economic, social, and political paths of development seems to be declining among the population. Bauer registers an urge to "unify the world" in various social spheres (ibid.). "Truth obsession, denial of history and striving for purity are [...] three traits or basic concepts of ambiguity intolerance" (ibid.: 29). This can be understood both as the basis of religious fundamentalism and of the politically authoritarian, especially in the extreme right-wing field. Bauer's thesis is "that our time is a time of low tolerance of ambiguity. In many areas of life [...] offers that promise redemption from the inescapable ambiguity of the world therefore appear attractive. [...] In contrast, diversity, complexity and plurality are often no longer perceived as enrichment" (ibid.: 30).

This goes hand in hand with the blurring of social coordinates (political: left/right; socio-economic: top/bottom; ethnic-cultural: open/closed; socio-cultural: homogeneous/heterogeneous; informational: true/false). Such coordinates are assurances of one's own positions in social space. This blurring activates the search movements for those political actors who pretend to resolve such contradictions, transform ambiguities into apparent clarities, and promise the restoration of control (see Heitmeyer 2018: 109–112).

Here, additional elements of conflict theory come into play for the analysis (see Frankenberg & Heitmeyer, in this volume). Albert Hirschman (1994) has distinguished between two types of conflict: "more or less" conflicts and "either-or" conflicts. The first type follows a logic of negotiation, the second a logic of decision-making that has a power-emphasising authoritarian undertone.

Ambivalences and ambiguities as a basic paradigm of modernity acquire a new force under the pressure of crises and the associated loss of control, which pushes society in an authoritarian direction. For example, a preference for a decision-making logic in "either-or" conflicts is designed to eliminate ambivalences and ambiguities and is thus conducive to authoritarian paths.

The authoritarian then serves as a strategy to reduce economic, social, and political complexity – and at the same time spheres of freedom.

Overall, there is no opposition of modernity and the authoritarian. The authoritarian is not pre-modernity. Modernity contains the authoritarian. This is shown, among other things, by the analyses of *Modernity and Barbarism* (Miller & Soeffner, 1996).

7. FIELDS AND MECHANISMS OF AUTHORITARIAN DANGER

In order to shed light on the fields and mechanisms of authoritarian danger, the starting point in 2001 should be recalled here for the purpose of the aforementioned update on my own work:

> The guiding thesis assumes that an authoritarian capitalism is emerging that generates manifold losses of control, which also contribute to an emptying of democracy, so that new authoritarian temptations are promoted by state policies of control and repression as well as thuggish right-wing populism. (Heitmeyer 2001: 500)

This thesis stood at the start of the "unsecured decades" and at the start of the series of various crises already mentioned, which have brought with them various forms of loss of control for parts of the population as well as for institutions – as well as authoritarian temptations and their consequences for the political system.

The task is now to elucidate the general topic of drivers and paths of authoritarian development by applying the underlying analytical concept to the connection between crises and loss of control. This will be done in two steps. First, the interaction of structural developments (crises), individual processing (loss of control), and political consequences (authoritarian temptations) will be described. Second, we will focus on the description of intensified radicalisation processes during the COVID-19 pandemic.

7.1 Economics: Authoritarian Capitalism in the Globalisation Process

Neoliberal policies around the turn of the century have produced the ductus of an "authoritarian capitalism" (Heitmeyer 2001) that has secured far-reaching economic control over location decisions where what shall be produced, social standards of wages, and social security, which has been accompanied by extensive "land grabbing" (Dörre 2009) in the social spheres of life: "The expansion of capitalism takes place in the medium of time, outside as well as inside national societies, sectoral as well as field-specific, and it encompasses modes of production, social groups, ways of life and even personality structures" (Dörre 2012: 106). The housing market, health care, and even the quantifying measurement of education (cf. Mau 2017) are just some of the central areas in which people's lives come under capital-driven pressure. As Lessenich (2016: 41) puts it: "Capitalism cannot sustain itself on its own. It lives from the existence of an 'outside' that it can assimilate, it feeds on all possible – material as well as immaterial – forms of 'fuel' to be supplied to it."

It is thus about encroaching processes in societal life, so that economic dominance proves to be a source of anomie and lack of control. Thome (2016) shows this following the classical anomie theory of Durkheim and the Institutional Anomie Theory of Messner & Rosenfeld (1994). He assumes that the anomic potential, i.e. of normlessness, will continue to intensify and displays some of the negative consequences for social coexistence. Thome still made these fundamental statements without reference to the issue of crisis, in a sense in the "normal state" of capitalist society.

In a further concept, Neckel (2021) focuses on the "decay of orders", which he associates with a "refeudalisation of modern capitalism" (Neckel 2013: 39–56), from which "new counter-orders" (Neckel 2021: 640) to open society and liberal democracy emerge, i.e. authoritarian counter-orders.

The drivers of authoritarian development also include those processes in digital media "which have transformed utopias of unlimited exchange into dystopias of the digital". Zuboff (2018) has used the terms "surveillance capitalism" and "digital violence" (Zuboff 2021: 14): "Surveillance capitalism leaves a trail of social devastation in privacy, the exacerbation of social inequality, the destruction of social norms and the weakening of democratic institutions." In the context of crises, Zuboff (ibid: 15) states: "The surrender of our information and communication spaces to surveillance capitalism has become the metacrisis of every republic because it impedes the resolution of all other crises." The authoritarianism of this economic sector has become structure-forming, generating opportunity structures for rampant authoritarian forms of expression and presentation that can be condensed into directed mobilisation flows.

One can choose any of the above-mentioned analytical perspectives; each of them reveals the authoritarian potential of political developments.

These far-reaching gains in control by capital were already contrasted at the beginning of the new century with equally far-reaching losses of political control by nation-state politics (see Heitmeyer 2001: 497–536), which for parts of the population led to social disintegration processes associated with biographical losses of control, and the erosion of trust in a functioning democratic system, i.e. the "emptying of democracy". Political consequences with the opening to authoritarian temptations then became relevant when a political offer – particularly evident in the course of the political-cultural crisis in 2015 in the context of the refugee movement – came on the scene through the authoritarian national radicalism of the political party AfD (Alternative for Germany).

7.2 Social Conditions: Social Disintegration Dynamics as an Approach to Instrumentalisation for Authoritarian Offers

The correlations between crises and loss of control that support the general thesis of this chapter will now be shown on the basis of the consequences for group-focused enmity (Heitmeyer 2002). The basis is formed by empirical analyses with representative population surveys using the financial and banking crisis in 2008/2009 as an example. The focus is not primarily on the spread of attitudes, but on the connections and mechanisms which, it is assumed, also come into play in other crises. These include the facets of fears, repudiations of the equal value of people, and attributions of causes to certain groups.

Mansel & Spaiser (2010) show the connections between control problems as a result of perceived crises with regard to lifestyle, everyday life, and life planning, on the one hand, and devaluation processes of socially marked groups, especially in the form of established privileges and racist, xenophobic, and Islamophobic resentments, on the other hand. This is especially true for those in lower social positions, who, in times of crisis, are confronted with social disintegration processes that stop them from participating in material and cultural goods and opportunity structures in the usual way.

If one mirrors these correlations to the different crises cited, then it can be assumed that losses of control become relevant above all when an entire way of life, the organisation of everyday life, and life planning are affected, as they have been in the various waves of the corona pandemic since 2019.

Since this combination of loss of control and devaluation processes correlates so strongly with authoritarian attitude patterns (Heitmeyer & Heyder 2002), the successful instrumentalisation of other crises by right-wing authoritarian or right-wing extremist groups cannot be coincidental.

Zick, Lobitz & Groß (2010) add to these connections another perspective: the repudiation of the equality of groups by those who see themselves as the losers of a crisis. In times of crisis, inequality is then a particularly expandable field of manoeuvre and mobilisation for right-wing authoritarian and right-wing extremist groups. This is especially true when collective fears can be established that produce different enemy images depending on the type of crisis. In the corona pandemic, for example, state actors were demonised for measures taken against the spread of COVID-19 and its variants.

Becker, Wagner & Christ (2010) add another facet. They explicitly suggest that perceived threats from crises do not, per se, lead to more group-focused enmity. Rather, they emphasise that this depends on which groups are seen as causing the crisis. It is thus a matter of attributing causes in order to find subjective explanations for social, political, and economic distress. In particular, blame is attributed to groups for which certain collective stereotypes already exist. These always include "the Jews" as "financial speculators", "world conquerors", et cetera. This context can then be used to explain the current attributions of causes in the COVID-19 crisis. They take place within the framework of various conspiracy theories, which in many variations build upon existing anti-Semitic stereotypes in parts of the population and are thus relevant for mobilisations by authoritarian and right-wing extremist groups.

The control-theoretical approaches from social psychology (among others Frey & Jonas 2002: 42) also point to the importance of loss of control in connection with political and economic crises for devaluation, discrimination, and also violence against weak groups. Moreover, Frey and Rez (2002) have also used this approach for the partial explanation of National Socialism, i.e. that instabilities generated by crises were linked to the need to restore control, which then promoted the fatal authoritarian paths that led to the victimisation of certain groups of people and the dismantling of the democratic system.

7.3 Development of Democracy: Authoritarian Reactions in Politics and the State

The view of authoritarian temptations in political and state institutions can also be noted independently of crises and losses of control. This applies above all to the various police laws at federal and state level, which are not explicitly dealt with here. Nevertheless, it must be pointed out that the "encroaching powers" must also be re-evaluated in connection with the right-wing extremist incidents in various state and federal German police forces. Though every democratic society has a right to know what is going on in its institutions, which it provides with weapons and the monopoly on the use of violence, the Minister of the Constitution and the State Ministers of the Interior have tended to shield and immunise the police after such incidents become public. In this way, the police have shown themselves to be an "unreceptive institution" in a double sense of the word (Heitmeyer 2022).

In the context of crises and losses of control, the COVID-19 crisis since 2020 has been one of the most far-reaching political and social losses of control in decades, resulting in expansions of authoritarian temptations and entrenchments. Frankenberg has accurately recorded this from a constitutional perspective: "The powers penetrating out of the corset of the rule of law register as a kind of *emergency law* in the police-legal regulatory system" (Frankenberg, in this volume). It is a "normalisation of the state of emergency" (ibid.).

In the political sphere, this line of authoritarianism can be traced through the political-cultural crisis of the refugee movement from 2015 on, which considerable parts of the population (especially in eastern Germany) associated with a loss of control over their own social space. This loss of control increasingly gave a boost to "right-wing threat alliances" (Heitmeyer et al. 2020). An assertion of the AfD's authoritarian national radicalism played a central role in this. Their political goal is the restoration of control: "We will take back our country and our people" (Gauland 2017).

The paths of authoritarian social development include different variants of identity politics that have developed powerful dynamics. Authoritarian motifs can always be found in them. These include the classic forms of conservative identity politics, which appear as the "German *Leitkultur*" and have produced the "us" and "them" groups. This extends to the call for a "conservative revolution" – a historically loaded formula – by CSU politician Dobrindt in 2018.

In addition to the right-wing extremist identity politics, which traditionally relies on the homogenisation of the ethnically and culturally diverse population by way of corresponding exclusions and discriminations, a left-wing identity politics has also been on the scene for some time, which is increasingly finding expression in a special language policy, i.e. who is allowed to say what on which topic and in which style. This, too, has an unmistakably authoritarian underlying melody, which also drowns out calls for the necessary reduction of social inequality and generates psychological reactance. Thus, Feddersen/Gessler (2021) plead for a return to leftist ideals in the struggle of identities.

As different as the motivations are, the mechanisms are the same: groups are established and group boundaries are sharpened, i.e. "them" and "us", and thus the inequality of groups is further entrenched. This then leads to the "either-or" conflicts already mentioned. There is no such thing as a bit of identity. It is always about the big picture. Thus, left identity politics also falls into the trap of the authoritarian and also has a socially destructive effect.

This can be assumed when the positive goals to reduce group-focused enmity and ensure structure-based social equality are carried out with a negative political strategy of group delimitations and new group superiorities.

8. AUTHORITARIAN TEMPTATIONS AND THREAT ALLIANCES: RADICALISATION PROCESSES IN TIMES OF CRISIS

The quality changes in the right-wing spectrum represent an important driving force of the authoritarian. These include the differentiation of manifestations and legitimising points of contact for violence, the brutalisation of language in parliamentary and public space coupled with threats to political office holders and committed citizens, the dynamisation of the ability to mobilise, the intellectualisation of ideological production with points of connection for broader groups of the population, the normalisation of attitudes of group-focused enmity in parts of the population, the stabilisation of voter strata, and the offensive use of structural changes in the public sphere (Heitmeyer, Freiheit & Sitzer 2020: 266–280).

These quality changes have developed above all after the crisis surrounding the refugee movement that began in 2015. This became publicly visible above all through the party-political and parliamentary development of the authoritarian national radicalism of the AfD, within which right-wing extremist actors gained ever-widening influence. These opportunity structures for mobilisation against refugees and state and social integration policies have narrowed and no longer have a spreading effect. At that time, a central mechanism was the "struggle for victimhood" to advance mobilisation and propagation. The corresponding fighting terms such as repopulation (*Umvolkung*) and the downfall (*Untergang*) of German culture and the German people were central. The victim role is the key category, because those who can credibly present themselves to the public as victims thus create a central "morality-soaked" category to legitimise resistance as a right of self-defence, including violence.

The basic narrative of authoritarianism (see in more detail Frankenberg & Heitmeyer, this volume), to which correspondingly oriented movements and parties refer, consists of control through the confinement of liberal lifestyles, control of cultural freedoms, control through the exclusion of marked population groups such as refugees, et cetera. They act as "control perpetrators" who make others victims of their authoritarian control paradigm. Against the open society, the closed society is brought into play (Loch 2001); against liberal democracy – depending on the political location in the right-wing authoritarian or right-wing extremist spectrum – the authoritarian variant is brought into play.

In the course of the pandemic, the relations have been reversed in the public debate, in the digital media, and at the radicalised demonstrations. This is also due to the fact that the mechanism of a changed "perpetrator-victim" construction is now being put in place.

Now, new structures of opportunity and mobilisation activities – quite contrary to the basic control paradigm of the authoritarian – are being expanded and radicalised in the figures of "freedom fighters", as actors of "anti-repression" and "anti-control".

While during the refugee movement it was mainly the male refugees who were presented as threatening perpetrators (in connection with rapes and killings), whom politics and state institutions let "have their way" in the sense of "repopulation", in the COVID-19 crisis the state appears as the perpetrator, driving the population into lockdown and subjecting them to massive restrictions on freedom as well as trying to bring the vaccination doubters and opponents to their knees through a "corona dictatorship". Here, too, in the sense of the "concentric escalation continuum" (see Section 8.3), further escalation-orientated modes of action are then spurred on from positions of parliamentary influence via conceptually "self-defence-relevant" bridges of legitimacy.

These "new" figures – "freedom fighters" against the state's coercive measures – by no means represent a departure from the control paradigm of the right-wing authoritarian or right-wing extremist spectrum already mentioned, because the current, egoistic understanding of freedom is likely to change back to an ethnically homogeneous ("*völkisch*") control paradigm with increased promotion of group-focused enmity after a possible abatement of the pandemic.

This leads to a far-reaching structural change of the public sphere. It places unmanageable elements of authoritarian potential in the acoustic space. They show themselves in the change from an inclusive public sphere (in the singular) to exclusionary public spheres (in the plural). The ubiquitous formats of communication in the digital networks with their capitalist business models sustain the kind of constellations that do not necessitate argumentative disputes about political solutions, but rather primarily a rejection-oriented, often hateful, anonymous "build-up mechanism" for the confirmation and solidification of positions. Habermas (2020: 27) describes his helplessness to restore an inclusive public sphere. Especially since an "increasing infiltration of the political public sphere [...] into a 'post-truth-democracy' [...] has become a frightening normality" (2021: 491).

An ideological conception is threaded perfectly into this structural change, which both latches onto crises and benefits from losses of control: the above-mentioned authoritarian-charged conspiracy theories. On the one hand, they form substitute solutions for the certainties lost in the course of modernity, and on the other hand they mark out enemy groups for authoritarian political "solutions", above all with anti-Semitic objectives. Conspiracy ideologies present themselves as quasi-religious, faith-based instruments of struggle.

American research by Whitson & Galinsky (2008) shows that those who believe in conspiracy theories tend to fear losing control over their lives (see also Nocum & Lamberty 2020). This is where a "politics of fear" (Wodak 2021) can be very effective.

9. FROM ANGRY APATHY TO VIOLENT RAGE ATTACKS: THE CONFLUENCE OF MECHANISMS TO RADICALISE AGAINST COVID-19 MEASURES

As discussed in the introduction, this chapter focuses on the COVID-19 crisis. The various mechanisms of authoritarianism listed above are related to the systemic type of crisis and linked to radicalisation processes. In so doing, we accept repetitions from previous chapters because the topics are now placed in a specific crisis context.

Descriptions of COVID-19 protests in autumn/winter 2021/2022 were manifold in both East and West Germany and were updated daily in their similarities and differences, especially journalistically. They included multiple hateful slogans, the documentation of death threats, and violent attacks, culminating in the killing of a petrol station worker in the small town of Idar-Oberstein.

It is also known that changed mobilisation strategies have emerged, which show different contours. As of this writing, large demonstrations in metropolises like Berlin, Stuttgart, Frankfurt, Hamburg, etc. have become rather rare. In contrast, small-scale "walks" in small towns have increased in number and in aggressive radicalisation, especially in southern East Germany. It is also known that the protests in West Germany have a different, partly esoteric social composition as compared to East Germany with its increasingly violent right-wing extremist influence. By now, the mobilisation concept is also widely known through the extensive use of the Telegram "channel" as an organising tool. Finally, increasing violent activities have been reported by the various security agencies. These descriptions will be supplemented below.

The following section will focus on mechanisms that contribute to radicalisation. Mechanisms are understood as couplings and interactions of different elements in social processes, among other things in the sense of mutual reinforcement or consolidation of radicalisation processes.

These mechanisms are divided into three areas: (1) basic social conditions, (2) radicalisation constellations, and (3) escalation activities. Attention must always be paid to the interaction of the different mechanisms. However, we still face considerable empirical problems. For example, not all people who are affected by structural problems of integration and violation of recognition are at the same time supporters of conspiracy theories. Nor are all those who live in rural opportunity structures for radicalisation susceptible to escalating dichotomous worldviews, et cetera.

There remain the open questions for future research to be empirically clarified, in which combinations these mechanisms occur and represent the greatest possible dangers of radicalisation.

9.1 Basic Social Conditions of Protest and Radicalisation

9.1.1 Integration-disintegration dynamics of social recognition and political representation problems as motivations for radicalisation

What processes have taken place behind this publicly visible surface and what social and political mechanisms are having such a dramatic effect today in terms of radicalisation against open society and liberal democracy?

To this end, a look should be taken at East Germany in particular, with its low vaccination rate in combination with higher aggressiveness and propensity to violence, as well as greater willingness to vote for the authoritarian national radicalism of the AfD in comparison to West Germany. Since these processes are always developments with "previous histories", as emphasised above, it is also necessary to look further back in time.

A central starting point for the analysis of mechanisms of radicalisation is the integration-disintegration dynamic (Heitmeyer 2018: 149) in Germany after the integration of the East German into the West German system. If one considers "social integration" as the solution of various tasks that every society has to perform, then it is firstly about the opportunity structures for one's own economic reproduction via work, which is needed in order to be able to participate in the exchange of material and cultural goods. This then gives rise to "positional recognition" via status, residential address, opportunities for advancement, etc. Secondly, it is about political participation, i.e. the chances to participate in public affairs and in the discussion about basic values of society, i.e. fairness, justice, and solidarity, among others. This then results in "moral recognition" as a citizen whose positions are perceived and recognised as legitimate by political actors in parties, governments, et cetera. Thirdly, it is about support for the development of individual and social identity. This gives rise to "emotional recognition" to ensure psychological and social stability.

From the perspective of such a concept of individual and collective recognition, there have been enormous violations and deficits in all three dimensions, especially in East Germany after the so-called German turn ("*Wende*"). Since no one can live without recognition, there were and are different forms of reaction. They range from individual depression to withdrawal to anger-soaked apathy to political resistance – if, among other things, there is an appropriate political movement and party. An early political alienation from the Western-style democratic system was clear, coupled with a feeling of relative deprivation, i.e. a sense of injustice in comparison with the West German population.

Thus, the mechanism of the "struggle for the victim role" always plays a driving force. Normally, a "struggle for the victor role" dominates. Against the background of damage to recognition, political alienation, and social deprivation, it is rather a "diversion struggle", i.e. a diversion from the victim role to the victor role. Moralisation and emotionalisation are used as instruments to legitimise, among other things, measures of self-defence or the right to self-defence – by all means.

9.1.2 Crises and loss of control as drivers of radicalisation

An important mechanism for radicalisation arises from the interaction of social, economic, and political crises with losses of control (see Section 3).

In the COVID-19 pandemic, the loss of control has had a particular impact because it concerns one's own physical integrity and mental health or the biographical future of oneself and one's children. In this respect, the pandemic crisis has had a broader significance than, for example, the so-called refugee crisis of 2015/2016, which was a sectoral social-cultural crisis that did not affect individual integrity. Furthermore, in the case of this systemic crisis, the emotionalisation practices of political movements and parties, i.e. their instrumentalision of narratives about loss of control, have had a much stronger effect. Here, the next element of this mechanism can be connected. The conspiracy theories have a special effect in this context.

9.1.3 Radicalisation in socio-spatial opportunity structures

Another effective mechanism of radicalisation, especially in East Germany, is related to a socio-geographical structure dominated by villages and small towns. This structure accommodates the new strategies of increasing number of walks in smaller groups, in which a considerable proportion are likely to know each other personally. Our research with representative population surveys on group-focused enmity showed that, firstly, the results of devaluation and discrimination were significantly stronger in rural than in urban areas. One reason for this is that social homogeneity is significantly greater in such socio-spatial contexts than in urban areas. This homogeneity is also accompanied by a significantly higher pressure to conform. The mechanism does not stop at police officers in these areas when it comes to controlling those who can also be encountered in everyday life. This connection between social homogeneity and an ingrained culture of conformity were also at work in the aggressive protests against the "corona dictatorship" and plans dor compulsory vaccinations that were never put into effect. This is especially the case when political parties – the AfD in particular – provide targeted bridges of legitimacy for escalations, enabling this (increasingly extremist) authoritarian national radicalism to present itself as a collection of "freedom fighters".

In such socio-spatial contexts, it is extremely difficult to break the "spiral of silence" in one's close social reference groups – on which one is also dependent to a certain extent. This can entail high social costs, such as exclusion.

In the public debate on the introduction of compulsory vaccination, the argument was often introduced that vaccination sceptics or opponents of vaccination would then have an argument in their respective close social reference groups – i.e. among relatives, in circles of friends, sports clubs, fire brigades, church congregations, workplaces – to get vaccinated without "losing face". This may be plausible, but there is no empirical evidence that vaccination mandates would function in this manner. And even if they did increase vaccination numbers, this still would not invalidate the mechanism of radicalisation, because the factors of social homogeneity and conformity would remain effective. It is known from other contexts of extremisation that "deviants" have to prove in a correspondingly radical way that they are still "in line". Thus, in order to regain trust in their close social reference groups, these "deviants" face particular pressure to defend the argument that compulsory vaccination is proof of submission to the "corona dictatorship". The mechanism will also continue to work because in villages and small towns one cannot simply change social reference groups – there are usually no alternatives at all. It is possible that in this process the vaccination rate increases, but radicalisation does not decrease.

Overall, there has long been a dangerous underestimation of the social-geographical periphery as a context of cause, mobilisation, and, above all, normalisation for authoritarian temptations and right-wing threat alliances.

9.2 Radicalisation Constellations

9.2.1 Differentiations of the right-wing authoritarian and right-wing extremist spectrum with new possibilities of connection

Two other interrelated mechanisms increase the widening and the force of protests and radicalisation. These are the often overlooked qualitative changes in the right-wing authoritarian and right-wing extremist spectrum (see Section 7). These changes give rise to two new mechanisms that could not have arisen earlier in times of the right-wing extremist party NPD (Nationaldemokratische Partei Deutschlands) as the main party representing right-wing extremist politics. While people naturally distanced themselves from extreme Nazi groups, new possibilities for connection arise for the "raw bourgeoisie".

By "raw bourgeoisie" I do not mean social class membership, but that underneath a thin layer of civilised external manners, hidden authoritarian attitudes are becoming increasingly public, usually appearing in increasingly thuggish rhetoric. This jargon of contempt refers both to weak groups and to principles of justice, fairness, and solidarity (see Heitmeyer 2018: 310–314).

Secondly, it is the mechanism of the "blurring" of group and even party boundaries within the conservative spectrum; they have been documented many times at the corona demonstrations. The composition of demonstrations is important for escalation. In most cases it is a social and motivational mix. It combines individuals with different motives and also an interest in avoiding any "blemish" on their normal bourgeois biography. Then – and this is the decisive driver – there are people who are linked by an explicit group consciousness with socially destructive political aims and a self-defined understanding of the elite, who also have a corresponding "stock of legitimacy" for violence.

9.2.2 Publics: digital networks as drivers of radicalisation and escalation

From here, the path leads to a mechanism of radicalisation that functions through political communication on digital networks (see Sections 6.1 and 7 above). The Telegram channel as a preferred instrument has already been mentioned. Two important mechanisms are at work in the mechanisms of radicalisation: firstly, sealed-off "echo chambers", which are not a place of public debate but of self-affirming build-up; secondly, a new independence, for example from public broadcasting or the established private broadcasters. So there is a multiplicity of duplication machines in which broadcasting takes place according to its own criteria of success. Ruling politics lacks the power, will, and ideas to intervene here, once again proving the thesis that the digital networks as capital-driven instruments have become "political battlegrounds" that can barely be controlled. This mechanism is one of the most serious ways in which the combination of crises and loss of control can contribute to the destruction of open society and liberal democracy. Here, the very foundation of modern democracy is at stake, for every dispute in this system "has as its precondition that one lives in the same world" (Bogner 2021: 54). Moreover, attention must be drawn to a widespread "error of perception and evaluation". For that audience that is informed by the traditional television images of the demonstrations, what is being concealed is the poisoning of the social climate that is developing across a far greater area and with a more intensive, aggressive quality – above all due to anonymity.

9.2.3 Escalations of radicalisation through expansions or disintegrations of movements

This leads to another mechanism. Usually, the dangerousness of such movements is linked to numerical growth. But growth is usually accompanied by the heterogenisation of the movements, which can have a moderating effect. Until recently, this was the source of the all-clear after big "maverick" demonstrations became smaller or stopped altogether. This reassurance formula overlooks the fact – as evidenced by current mobilisation strategies – that the disintegration of a large "unified" movement can lead to even more extreme radicalisation, right down to small, homogeneous terrorist cells. There are already examples of this, such as the "National Socialist Underground" (NSU).

Those "heads" who have developed a sense of themselves as an elite because they succeed in "driving" both governing and controlling institutions in their intended directions with ever new tactics and provocations or violence will not resign themselves to a loss of significance and, on the other hand, are counting on an increase in power and significance through increased radicalisation and violence, up to and including terrorist forms in homogeneous small groups.

9.3 Escalation Activities

9.3.1 Political mobilisation through emotionalisation, enemy images, dichotomous worldviews, and either-or conflicts

Until the rise of the authoritarian national radicalism of the AfD in 2014, there was no political movement to engage a certain segment of the East German population. Anger-soaked apathy dominated. The refugee movement came as a "gift" for the AfD and the social movement PEGIDA to galvanise people, particularly those who suffered from a lack of social and political recognition, via the emotionalisation of social-cultural problems and with dichotomous worldviews (people versus elite; closed versus open society; us versus them; homogeneity versus heterogeneity; inside versus outside; being German versus being international; inequality of people versus equivalence; truth versus untruth; et cetera). The method that had lasting success was to address recognition problems and to produce experiences of self-efficacy: People finally felt seen, heard and recognised and thus became ready to act. This developed authoritarian orientations entirely in the sense of the mobilisation actors, which could then be reactivated again and again depending on the topic. After the refugee debate died down, the same effective mechanism was used in the COVID-19 debate and demonstrations against vaccination and possible compulsory vaccination. This mechanism is associated with a type of conflict that is prone to escalation.

In the history of the demonstrations against the COVID-19 measures, the above-mentioned type of either-or conflicts (see section 6) has emerged as the dominant form, a development largely driven by emotionalisation and dichotomous worldviews. It is a dangerous mechanism because it is about "everything" – about collective identity, about the "system", about the "people", et cetera. The connections of the above-mentioned systemic type of crisis with an either/or conflict structure favour a social development that is not adequately described as a "split" in society, but as an asymmetric polarisation between the majority of the vaccinated population and the minority of opponents of vaccination. In this constellation, the interaction of the mechanisms listed above is extremely prone to violence – a propensity which accumulates over time.

9.3.2 Escalation continuum: legitimation bridges between the population, political parties, right-wing extremist violent actors, and right-wing terrorist small groups

The mechanisms listed so far as components of radicalisation processes also form the basis for the emergence of physical violence, ranging from bodily harm to right-wing terrorist acts of destruction. To illustrate this mechanism, the concept of the "concentric escalation continuum" (Heitmeyer, Freiheit &

Sitzer 2020: 58–90) can be used. It can be imagined as an "onion pattern" with five different "shells". In the "shells", the escalating groups of actors become smaller, but the orientation towards violence becomes larger. The different bridges of legitimacy comprise the core mechanism.

The largest "shell" is formed by hostile authoritarian attitudes towards democratic politics and "the state" in parts of the population, which provide legitimacy for the AfD's authoritarian national radicalism.

At the start of the pandemic, the AfD stuck to its style of emotionalising social and political problems in line with the authoritarian control paradigm and initially called for particularly harsh measures against the spread of the virus. It soon became apparent that this would not achieve an increase in approval among its potential electorate, so the party took a radical change of direction – virtually the opposite. This makes it clear that the party is not concerned with objective principles but with opportunistic calculations of benefit for the expansion of approval or the consolidation of the electorate – and visibility in the streets.

Therefore, slogans had to be coined such as "corona dictatorship" (Gauland, AfD honorary chairman). In addition, conspiracy ideologies of the "Great Reset" are propagated, according to which governments, media, the pharmaceutical industry, etc., aim to establish authoritarian regimes (see *FAZ.net*, 1 December 2021). In addition to this calculative turn and its self-staging as "freedom fighters", the AfD has been as a major driver of the COVID-19 protests in autumn and winter 2021/2022.

At the same time, the party is using these slogans – as it did in the refugee crisis – to build bridges of legitimacy for right-wing extremist groups that already use violence. They can then use these slogans to legitimise the right to self-defence against a "dictatorship" and combine it with "coup fantasies". These groups still move publicly in demonstrations and at the same time supply clandestine right-wing terrorist small groups, which then draw legitimation for attempts to overthrow the system. This mechanism is so serious because parts of the population are among the suppliers of legitimacy, so that the violent actors can refer to "the people".

Overall, the mechanisms briefly outlined point to threats to open society and liberal democracy. This is also connected to the fact that a politics built on appeals to the "defence of democracy" as well as on state control apparatuses – can no longer "get a grip" on several of these mechanisms in terms of their effects. Civil society is needed more than ever. But it must be noted that anomic behaviour can be seen in parts of the population, i.e. normlessness coupled with aggressive self-empowerment, a kind of vigilante justice that also makes communication in everyday social life dangerous.

The mechanisms that have been pointed out – some of which were already effective during the crisis surrounding the refugee movement and have now achieved further success because, among other things, they have taken hold of further circles of the population such as the aforementioned "raw bourgeoisie" – will continue to have an effect beyond the COVID-19 pandemic. The triad of crises, conflict structure, and loss of control as an effective context for authoritarian developments has been established. The themes of the crisis will change, but the socially and democratically destructive mechanisms will remain.

10. FUTURE PERSPECTIVES: EXHAUSTION OF VISIONARY IDEAS OF SOCIETY AND DEMOCRACY AS AN OPPORTUNITY FOR AUTHORITARIAN TEMPTATIONS?

In the face of unsecured decades with regard to different paths of development for an open society and a liberal democracy, "the future" must be pluralised. What futures are conceivable when, among other things, the conviction seems to be fading in considerable parts of the population that the democratic form of government holds sufficient problem-solving capacities for systemic crises?

Authoritarian conditions can then become attractive as resources that provide control and security, in order to at least contain the unsecured confusion that has arisen as a result of crises. In parts of the population and politics, authoritarian orders are not seen as threats, but rather as a liberation from the impositions of rapid social change in times of crisis in an open society and liberal democracy.

All of this comes up against the exhaustion of utopian energies diagnosed by Habermas as early as 1985, which finds confirmation especially in times of crisis, especially in the subsystems of society paralysed by the corona pandemic. The fewer visionary and future-proof ideas of society and politics as well as available forms of participation are perceived by citizens, the greater the chances for a "politics of fear" (Wodak 2020) as a permanent state with ambitions of normalisation, which would run through numerous fields of society and politics.

Does the authoritarian then contain a new utopian energy that would mean a reversal of previous narratives of social progress?

From the Indian-American economist and winner of the 2020 Peace Prize, Amartya Sen, comes the assessment (2020): "The world today is confronted with a pandemic of authoritarianism that is affecting human life in different but interrelated ways. [...] There is little more urgent social need today than global resistance to the rise of authoritarianism around the world."

REFERENCES

Amlinger, Carolin & Nachtwey, Oliver (2021), "Sozialer Wandel, Sozialcharakter und Verschwörungsdenken in der Spätmoderne", in: *Aus Politik und Zeitgeschichte*, 71, 35–36, 13–19.

Anhut, Reimund & Heitmeyer, Wilhelm (2005), "Desintegration, Anerkennungsbilanzen und die Rolle sozialer Vergleichsprozesse", in: Heitmeyer, Wilhelm & Imbusch, Peter (eds.), *Integrationspotenziale einer modernen Gesellschaft*, Wiesbaden, 75–100.

Bauer, Thomas (2018), *Die Vereindeutigung der Welt. Über den Verlust an Mehrdeutigkeit und Vielfalt*, Ditzingen.

Bauman, Zygmunt (2003), *Moderne und Ambivalenz. Das Ende der Eindeutigkeit*, Hamburg.

Becker, Julia, Wagner, Ulrich & Christ, Oliver (2010), "Ursachenzuschreibung in Krisenzeiten: Auswirkungen auf Antisemitismus und Fremdenfeindlichkeit", in: Heitmeyer, Wilhelm (ed.), *Deutsche Zustände*, Folge 8, Berlin, 128–143.

Bogner, Alexander (2021), *Die Epistemisierung des Politischen. Wie die Macht des Wissens die Demokratie gefährdet*, Ditzingen.

Butter, Michael (2018), *Nichts ist wie es scheint. Über Verschwörungstheorien*. Berlin.

Butter, Michael (2021), " Verschwörungstheorien: eine Einführung", in: *Aus Politik und Zeitgeschichte*, 71, 35–36, 4–11.

Dahrendorf, Ralf (1997), "An der Schwelle zum autoritären Jahrhundert. Die Globalisierung und ihre sozialen Folgen werden zur nächsten Herausforderung einer Politik der Freiheit", in: *DIE ZEIT*, 14. November, 14–15.

Dörre, Klaus (2009), "Die neue Landnahme. Dynamiken und Grenzen des Finanzmarktkapitalismus", in: ibid., *Soziologie-Kapitalismus-Kritik*, Frankfurt am Main, 21–86.

Feddersen, Jan & Gessler, Philipp (2021), *Kampf der Identitäten. Für eine Rückbesinnung auf linke Ideale*, Berlin.

Frankenberg, Günter (2020), *Autoritarismus. Verfassungstheoretische Perspektiven*, Berlin.

Frey, Dieter & Jonas, Eva (2002), "Theorie der kognizierten Kontrolle", in: Frey, Dieter & Irle, Martin (eds.), *Theorien der Sozialpsychologie*, vol. 3, Bern, 13–50.

Frey, Dieter & Rez, Helmut (2002), "Population and perpetrators: Preconditions for the Holocaust from a control-theoretical perspective", in: Newman, Leonard S./Erber, Ralph (eds.), *The Social Psychology of the Holocaust*, Oxford, 188–221.

Fukuyama, Francis (1992), *Das Ende der Geschichte. Wo wir stehen*, München.

Habermas, Jürgen (2020), "Moralischer Universalismus in Zeiten politischer Regression", in: *Leviathan*, 48, 1, 7–28.

Habermas, Jürgen (2021), "Überlegungen und Hypothesen zu einem erneuten Strukturwandel der politischen Öffentlichkeit", in: *Leviathan*, 49, Sonderband 37, 470–500.

Heitmeyer, Wilhelm (2001), "Autoritärer Kapitalismus, Demokratieentleerung und Rechtspopulismus", in: Loch, Dietmar & Heitmeyer, Wilhelm (eds.), *Schattenseiten der Globalisierung*, Frankfurt am Main, 497–534.

Heitmeyer, Wilhelm (2002), Gruppenbezogene Menschenfeindlichkeit. Die theoretische Konzeption und erste empirische Ergebnissse, in: id. (ed.): Deutsche Zustände, vol. 1, Frankfurt am Main, 15–36.

Heitmeyer, Wilhelm (2018), *Autoritäre Versuchungen. Signaturen der Bedrohung I*, Berlin.
Heitmeyer, Wilhelm (2022), "Polizei als uneinsichtige Institution", in: Hunold, Daniela & Singelnstein, Tobias (eds.), *Rassismus in der Polizei. Eine wissenschaftliche Bestandsaufnahme*, Wiesbaden, 561–577.
Heitmeyer, Wilhelm, Freiheit, Manuela & Sitzer, Peter (2020), *Rechte Bedrohungsallianzen. Signaturen der Bedrohung II*, Berlin.
Hirschman, Albert O. (1994), "Wieviel Gemeinsinn braucht die liberale Gesellschaft?", in: *Leviathan* 22, 293–304.
Lessenich, Stephan (2016), *Neben uns die Sintflut. Die Externalisierungspolitik und ihr Preis*, Berlin.
Mansel, Jürgen & Spaiser, Viktoria (2010), "Ängste und Kontrollverluste. Zusammenhänge mit Gruppenbezogener Menschenfeindlichkeit", in: Heitmeyer, Wilhelm (ed.), *Deutsche Zustände*, Folge 8, Berlin, 49–71.
Miller, Max & Soeffner, Hans-Georg (eds.) (1996), *Modernität und Barbarei. Soziologische Zeitdiagnosen am Ende des 20. Jahrhunderts*, Frankfurt am Main.
Neckel, Sighard (2013), "'Refeudalisierung' – Systematik und Aktualität eines Begriffs der Habermasschen Gesellschaftsanalyse", in: *Leviathan*, 41(1), 39–56.
Neckel, Sighard (2021), "Der Zerfall von Ordnungen", in: Forst, Rainer & Günther, Klaus (eds.), Normative Ordnungen, Berlin, 632–647.
Nocum, Katharina & Lamberty, Pia (2020), *Fake Facts. Wie Verschwörungstheorien unser Denken bestimmen*, Berlin.
Oevermann, Ulrich (2016), "'Krise und Routine' als analytisches Paradigma in den Sozialwissenschaften", in: Becker-Lenz, Roland et al. (eds.), *Die Methodenschule der Objektiven Hermeneutik*, Wiesbaden, 43–114.
Sen, Amartya (2020), *Bücher und Freiheit. Dankesrede anlässlich der Verleihung des Friedenspreises des Deutschen Buchhandelns*, Frankfurt am Main.
Thome, Helmut (2016), "Zur Normalität von Anomie in funktional differenzierten Gesellschaften", in: *Zeitschrift für Soziologie*, 4, 261–280.
Whitson, Jennifer & Galinsky, Adam (2008), "Lacking Control Increases Illusory Pattern Perception", in: *Science*, 3. October, 115–117.
Zick, Andreas et al. (2010), "Krisenbedingte Kündigung der Gleichwertigkeit", in: Heitmeyer, Wilhelm (ed.), *Deutsche Zustände*, Folge 8, Berlin, 72–86.
Zuboff, Shoshana (2018), *Das Zeitalter des Überwachungskapitalismus*, Frankfurt am Main/New York.
Zuboff, Shoshana (2021), "Überwachungskapitalismus ist die Mutter aller Krisen", in: *Die Welt*, 1. December, 14–15.

8. Of 'bulwarks' and 'sacred borders': authoritarian refugee policies in Europe

Maximilian Pichl

1. POP FOR 'PUSHBACKS'[1]

The Polish Ministry of Defence and the *TVP* television channel organised a concert for Polish border guards at a military base in December 2021. At that time, the situation on the Polish-Belarusian border had already been in the public eye in Europe for weeks: refugees were trying to cross Belarus into Poland and thus into the European Union. The EU and the Polish government accused the Belarusian dictator Lukashenko of using the refugees as 'weapons in a hybrid war' against the EU by issuing visa papers and allowing them to enter via Minsk airport. Poland denied the refugees approval to enter the territory and systematically enforced pushbacks (Pichl 2022). The concert in early December featured an international line-up: pop singers such as Lou Bega, Captain Jack, Loona and Las Ketchup, who had success in the 1990s and early 2000s. Former Polish Defence Minister Mariusz Błaszczak said: 'We are grateful to the soldiers and officers who protect our border.'[2] Lou Bega also thanked the military forces directly during his performance with the words: 'Dziękuję za obronę naszej granicy' ('I thank you for defending our border').[3] Parallel to the concert, newspapers published that a 38-year-old Kurdish

[1] The term "pushback", the "Unword of the Year 2021", refers to the illegal rejection of refugees at the borders (to Europe).

[2] Mariusz Błaszczak, @mblaszczak, 2021, December 5 (Twitter) *Jesteśmy wdzięczni żołnierzom i funkcjonariuszom, którzy chronią naszą granicę. To dzięki Wam Polska i UE jest wciąż bezpieczna. Dzisiejszy koncert #MuremZaPolskimMundurem jest wyrazem tej wdzięczności. Słowa uznania dla TVP za organizację tego przedsięwzięcia!* Twitter. https://twitter.com/mblaszczak/status/1467585328294862852.

[3] Kapturak, @kapturak, 2021, 5 December (Twitter) *Lou Bega hat den Spruch "Dziękuję za obronę naszej granicy" ("Ich danke für die Verteidigung unserer Grenze") auswendig gelernt* Twitter. https://twitter.com/kapturak/status/1467554814003453957.

woman, Avin Ifran Zahir, who had tried to cross the border in November and had suffered a miscarriage, had died in hospital. This simultaneity, on one hand the pop-cultural staging and symbolic legitimisation of a rigorous border regime, and on the other hand the real deadly consequences of this European closure, impressively show how authoritarianism is increasingly normalised in refugee policies.

2. THE ROLE OF REFUGEES IN AUTHORITARIAN AGITATION

In the public debate, the rise of actors such as the German right-wing party *Alternative für Deutschland* (*AfD*), the Polish *Law and Justice Party* (*PiS*) and other movements and parties that stand for such authoritarian isolationism, is often associated with the large refugee movements from 2015 onwards. In their agitation, the Hungarian *Fidesz party* and *PiS* label refugees as a danger to European integration and thus mobilise broad sections of the electorate. However, Wilhelm Heitmeyer's long-term studies in Germany argue against this thesis, 'because the attitudinal potential on which the success of the [*AfD*] is based already existed long before the summer of 2015' (Heitmeyer 2018: 344). The situation is similar in the *Fidesz party*, under Viktor Orbán, whose upsurge and authoritarian transformation in Hungary began long before the summer of 2015, when migration was barely addressed in the political discourses in Eastern Europe (Kallius 2017). The issue of migration may be an 'accelerating factor' for authoritarian movements (Heitmeyer 2018: 344), but its actual causes are located in a deeper socio-structural upheaval, an accompanying insecurity (ibid.: 146 ff.) and racist relations of domination. Specifically linked to this last factor, migrant and refugees are the enemy images of authoritarian agitation, as Leo Löwenthal and Norbert Guterman noted in their groundbreaking study *Falsche Propheten* (*False Prophets*) at the end of the 1940s:

> In the agitational image of the enemy, the foreigner tends to be transformed from a specific dangerous but tangible power into an uncanny, irreconcilable extra- or sub- human being. This role of the foreigner in the agitator's total image of the enemy is explicitly seen in his reference to the refugee. (Löwenthal & Gutermann 1949: 50)

The authoritarian right appropriates the field of refugee policy to replace social questions with racist narratives and thus expand its scope for political action. It has successfully managed to undermine the specific protective status of refugees, who are entitled to indispensable rights under the Geneva Refugee Convention, in the public sphere, for example by replacing the word 'refugees' in many public debates with the much more unspecific term 'migrants' or 'irregular migrants'. For all the conflicts that also pervade authoritarian movements and parties, they are usually often in agreement on the question of asylum and border policy: a rigorous sealing-off of borders, the undermining of subjective rights of those affected and an authoritarian inward policy towards those seeking protection.

The fact that authoritarian movements have a central interest in constructing images of the enemy in migration policy is no surprise, however, and does not need to be reconstructed in detail in this article. Instead, I will focus on the different strategies that authoritarian actors pursue outside and inside parliament and government policy. First, I will cursorily describe the significance of borders and migration in right-wing thought and action (see Section 8.3). Then, using paradigmatic examples, I will discuss which concrete strategies can be derived from this and how they are implemented in the various spheres of authoritarian refugee and border policy (Section 8.4). To this end, I look at the activities of the authoritarian right outside of parliaments (Section 8.1), the authoritarian right in government using the example of Hungary (Section 8.2) and the authoritarian moments in European migration control policy (Section 8.3). Finally, I discuss political possibilities to challenge authoritarianism in the context of the refugee question (see Section 8.5).

3. THE IMPORTANCE OF BOUNDARIES IN THE AGENDA AND ACTION OF THE AUTHORITARIAN-RIGHT

Borders fulfil the function of establishing and distinguishing imagined political communities (Anderson 1991), they mark an 'outside' and 'inside'. The territorial demarcations are the result of an incrementally intertwined process of nationalist, capitalist, colonialist and racist relations of power and domination. In the Global North, this historical–social, precisely non-natural process of the formation of modern borders is hardly questioned, 'there is rather a deeply anchored hegemony of the border' (Buckel et al. 2014: 34).

Authoritarian actors can use this hegemony to their advantage. They do not have to go through a lengthy process of convincing people why borders should exist; rather, this assumption is deeply anchored in the everyday minds of members of society. In this respect, the securitisation of refugee policy and the everyday reproduction of the border offers them a much easier connectivity for their strategies to the hegemonic consensus than it is possible for actors who fundamentally question borders and their controls. However, it would be a mistake to deduce from this an automatic dominance of authoritarian discourses in refugee policy. Rather, European refugee and migration policy is hegemonically contested.[4] According to Fabian Georgi, the current dynamics of racist border policies in Europe is not an expression of an authoritarian offensive, but rather a defensive strategy that can be traced back to protests by migrants, refugees and transatlantically organised pro-migrant actors (Georgi 2019: 102 ff.). Successful struggles by self-organised refugee groups, human rights organisations and lawyers had progressively changed the political balance of power before the summer of 2015 (ibid.: 102; Jakob 2016). This was reflected in reformed asylum laws, an erosion of detention pending deportation, a greater positive public perception of refugees, as well as the emergence of new transnational networks of solidarity. For the authoritarian, national-radical right, which until then had seen its interests in a rigorous sealing-off of borders at least partially suspended in a fragile compromise with national-conservative actors. In Germany, the asylum compromise of the 1990s is exemplary for this convergence of authoritarian and conservative strategies (Demirovic 1996; Kannankulam 2014). These shifts in discourse, judgements and changes in the law meant a threat to their social basis. Stuart Hall argues that migration erodes the symbolic boundaries between the cultural 'inside' and its constitutive 'outside' (Hall 2018: 163) and questions homogenous identities. Thus, migration movements are a danger for the social basis of authoritarianism.

This defensive position is clearly evident in important writings of the so-called *New Right.* Renaud Camus is considered as an important ideologue for the New Right due to his book *The Revolt Against the Great Exchange* (2016). Camus calls in his book for the gathering of forces against the so called 'Great Replacement' (2016: 66), an important conspiracy chiffre in the discourse of the New Right, which suggest that white European populations are being replaced with people from Muslim countries. Camus speaks of an urgency to act together now to stop and push back the consequences of a supposedly liberal migration policy. In the sense of the New Right, Camus does not understand this as a purely national task; rather he advocates for an ethnopluralist and authoritarian European policy, behind which political forces from different member states should unite. The strategy of the authoritarian right is therefore to build a genuinely European gated community, but this must, at the same time, go hand-in-hand with a change in the social power relations in Europe itself. For Camus the real problem is 'mass migration', which he connects with a struggle and conquest about resources and living space (ibid: 105).

Authoritarian movements and parties translate such identitarian notions of democracy, historical revisionist narratives and fetishisations of the border

---

[4] Research Unit "Staatsprojekt Europa" 2014; Buckel et al. 2021; Hess et al. 2016; Hänsel et al. 2022.

into practical politics to legitimise rigorous border closures. Viktor Orbán recalls that Hungary has always been the 'bulwark of Europe' against the expansion of the Ottoman Empire, a cipher for today's migration movements, which he describes as 'Muslim invaders': 'I have to say that when it comes to living together with Muslim communities, we are the only ones who have experience because we had the possibility to go through that experience for 150 years.'[5] In Austria, the myth about the 'Battle of Kahlenberg' near Vienna in 1683 provides the basis for the extreme right-wing *Freiheitliche Partei Österreichs* (*FPÖ*) to conduct election campaigns in the once-plundered rural regions and to stage itself as a freedom fighter against the 'Ottoman besiegers' or today's migrants (Frankenberg 2020: 141). In other political-cultural contexts, the reference to history is complemented by a sacralisation of the border, exemplified by the public strategy of the clerical-conservative *PiS* party in Poland. Former Prime Minister Mateusz Morawiecki, a member of the PiS party, declared on Facebook on the occasion of the humanitarian escalation on the Polish-Belarusian border in November 2021 that the Polish border is not just a line on a map, but is sacred because Polish blood was spilled for it.[6] Actually, behind the Polish border protection infrastructure real blood was and continues to be spilled. Grupa Granica, an NGO network monitoring the situation of refugees at the border, reported, that at least 37 humans have died on the border since August 2021.

Such discourses about the border and implemented border spectacles (De Genova 2013) illustrate how successful the authoritarian right has become in normalising its framings and narratives in the broader public. As I already explained, the refugees at the Polish-Belarusian border have been described almost exclusively by commentaries in the media and by politicians from conservative and social democratic parties as 'weapons' that Belarusian dictator Lukashenko is using in a 'hybrid war' against Europe. In such a discourse on security and order, there is no talk about the rights of refugees at the border, to which they are entitled according to European law and the Geneva Refugee Convention. Political justification is only needed for the *means of* securing borders, not *whether* there are political alternatives. The effects of the authoritarian counter-offensive can be seen in the large number of deportations, violent *pushbacks* at various borders and the deployment of the military, a border police repertoire that has been used on a daily basis at the Greek,

---

5 Viktor Orbán, quoted by the *New York Times*, 3 September 2015.

6 Williams, M., & Plucinska, J. Poland warns of further large migrant clashes on Belarus border (Reuters, 9 November 2021). https://www.reuters.com/world/europe/poland-fears-major-incident-migrants-belarus-head-border-2021-11-08/ accessed 10 October 2023.

Spanish, Italian, Croatian, Hungarian and Polish borders since the summer of 2015.

4. POLITICAL AND LEGAL SPHERES OF AUTHORITARIAN MIGRATION CONTROL POLICIES

Actors from the authoritarian right increasingly translate their ideas of border, refugee and migration policy, into an offensive political practice that is simultaneously reflected in law and legal practice. In doing so, they pursue their strategies both outside and inside parliaments. They can also benefit from the fact that authoritarian moments are structurally inherent in European migration control policy.

4.1 Militias at the Border: The Strategy of the Far Right

At the end of October 2021, many German media headlined that the police had stopped a large group of neo-Nazis at the German-Polish border in Brandenburg.[7] The group followed a call by the extreme right-wing micro party 'Der III. Weg' (*The Third Way*) to carry out a so-called 'border walk'. Against the background of the new escape route from Belarus via Poland to Germany, the neo-Nazis wanted to demonstrate through their presence that they acted as the real defenders of the border.

The extreme right in Germany organising itself as vigilantes is not a new phenomenon. As early as the 1950s, there were anti-communist vigilantes who wanted to prevent a presumed invasion by the Soviet Union because they did not trust the state to put up the necessary resistance. In the 1980s, so-called Wehrsportgruppen (paramilitary groups, such as the 'German Action Groups' or the 'Wehrsportgruppe Hoffmann') carried out various attacks (Virchow 2016). However, these vigilante groups usually did not aim to establish a self-organised border guard. However, the 'border walk' of 'The Third Way' is part of a strategy that the extreme and authoritarian right is now pursuing all over Europe. Wherever 'border spectacles' (de Genova 2013) have taken place in recent years, right-wing groups have mobilised their supporters to display a presence at the borders. They feed militaristic discourses of a 'war on migration' into the political mainstream, but also reinforce pre-existing narratives of governments using historical-revisionist and sacred myths (see Section 3).

When the EU–Turkey deal collapsed in February/March 2020, right-wing radicals of the so-called *Identitarian Movement* travelled to the Greek island

[7] See for example *ZEIT* Online from 24 October 2021.

of Lesbos, organised hunts for people seeking protection and threatened activists and journalists who campaigned for the rights of refugees (*Süddeutsche Zeitung*, 6 March 2020). They also networked with Greek fascists on the ground. In February 2021, when more and more refugees fled to the Canary Islands, self-appointed vigilantes organised themselves and called for a 'hunt for Arabs' (*Süddeutsche Zeitung*, 1 February 2021). In Eastern Europe, 'private sheriffs and vigilantes carry out border control measures on a daily basis (Verseck 2016). At the Croatian border, the transitions between private vigilantes and the state border police are sometimes fluid; journalists were able to show how presumably members of the Croatian intervention police without official insignia brutally mistreated refugees in the border region and pushed them back to Bosnia-Herzegovina (*WDR Monitor*, 7 October 2021). These self-proclaimed vigilantes see themselves as the executors of the actual 'will of the people' and stage themselves as the upright fighters in defence of the nation, whereby they can tie in with revisionist historical narratives (in the case of Eastern Europe, the war against the Ottoman Empire). Lithuania even legalised push backs and vigilante practices in the *Law on the State Border and Protection*. So called 'sponsors' are allowed to patrol the border and support official border guards in searching for refugees and then help to arrest them. (Nielsen 2023).

Sociologist Matthias Quent divides vigilante groups into three categories (2016a): First-order vigilantism is primarily directed against supposedly weak groups, such as refugees, the homeless or other groups marked as enemies by the authoritarian right. Second-order vigilantism is primarily directed against political opponents who are seen as a threat to the implementation of vigilantist goals, for example anti-fascist groups, human rights organisations, lawyers or investigative journalists. Third-order vigilantism attacks the state and its representatives. Vigilantees justify such procedures by claiming that the state has fallen into the 'hands of the enemy'. During the arrival of many asylum seekers in the summer of 2015, this form of vigilantism gained momentum, also promoted by conspiracy ideologies such as the talk of 'The Great Replacement'. Attacks such as the assassination of the conservative German politician Walter Lübcke in 2019 (Steinhagen 2021) fall into this category. 'Vigilantism is thus a vote of no confidence in the efficiency of the state, not in the concept of the state itself' (Quent 2016b: 139). Authoritarian and extreme right strategies do not aim to overcome the state, but rather to restore the state and use violence against the enemy groups and political opponents constructed by authoritarian agitation (see Löwenthal/Guterman, section 2).

Vigilantist strategies sometimes have a direct influence on the direction of nation-state migration control policies. In this respect, Hungary is a paradigmatic example. The mayor of the border town of Ásotthalom, László Toroczkai, published a video in 2015 in which he called for the construction of a border fence. The mayor used the symbolism and phraseology of right-wing vigilantes. In another video, which received over 1 million views and resonated in international media, paramilitary troops were shown patrolling the border and hunting down refugees, as if in an action film (*ntv*, 19 September 2015). The fact that the Hungarian government under Viktor Orbán actually built a border fence and secured it militarily in 2015 followed the *Fidesz government*'s interest in rigorous border closure. The fence symbolism can also be traced back to pressure from the extreme right. The influences of the far right therefore aim to change social relations in a way that gives authoritarian policies greater room to manoeuvre. 'The politics of mutual closure', writes Zygmunt Bauman, 'which builds walls instead of bridges [...] leads nowhere but to the wasteland of mutual mistrust, alienation and aggravation' (2016: 23).

4.2 The Authoritarian Right in Government

The strategy of the vigilantes demonstrates how the extreme right can take up and reinforce anti-migration narratives outside of parliaments and influence the concrete tightening of border policies. To use the example of Hungary again, the aim is to illustrate how the strategies of the authoritarian and extreme right are condensed into government policy and can function as a blueprint for authoritarian actors in Europe.

4.2.1 The Hungarian laboratory of authoritarianism

Viktor Orbán's *Fidesz party* pursues a line of radical exclusion of refugees; with the exception with refugees of Ukraine, who fled the country after the invasion of Russia in 2022. Yet migration did not play a significant role in Hungarian politics even before the summer of 2015. However, Orbán used existing racist narratives in Hungarian society (Marsovsky 2013) and reinforced them, combined with security dispositives (Thorleiffson 2017), to build his policy on the demonisation and exclusion of refugees.

In addition to the construction of the border fence with Serbia and Croatia, the government tightened asylum and migration law (Nagy 2017) by setting up a transit zone where refugees were to be de facto detained and in part deterred by inhumane treatment (such as deprivation of food, etc.). Serbia was treated as a safe third country by the authorities to avoid having to substantively examine the asylum applications of asylum seekers. Although the European Court of Justice clearly identified Hungary's asylum policy as contrary to European law in several cases,[8] the Orbán government circumvented such rulings by, for example, completely outsourcing the asylum procedures

[8] See for example ECJ, judgment FMS and others, C-924/19PPU and C-925/19PPU.

to Hungarian embassies. The government also made use of the toolbox of authoritarian constitutionalism (Frankenberg 2020) by making a constitutional amendment according to which no 'foreign population' may be settled in Hungary (Article 5). With this amendment, Hungary not only positioned itself against the quota-based distribution plans of the European Union, but also continued its racist constitutional policy, which it had already started with the new Basic Law of 2011 (Uitz 2015; Pichl 2019).

In addition to the stricter legislation, the Hungarian government also pursued an authoritarian, radical nationalist agitation and criminalisation campaign against refugees and political opponents, as already typologically described by Löwenthal and Guterman (see Section 8.2). However, the authoritarian agitation not only serves the purpose of self-dramatisation, it also functions as part of a strategy to criminalise civil society actors. As early as 2014, during a speech in Baile Tusnad, in which he presented the contours of his illiberal concept of democracy, Orbán marked foreign-funded NGOs as opponents of his government project (Orbán 2014). In the context of migration movements, the government massively intensified this course. The youth organisation of *Fidesz* carried out 'house visits' to NGOs such as Amnesty International, the migration NGO Menedek or the Hungarian Helsinki Committee and put signs on their office doors that read, for example: 'Organisation that supports migration.' The pro-government magazine *Figelyö* published an article targeting so-called Soros mercenaries. Jewish entrepreneur George Soros has been supporting civil society networks and organisations in Eastern Europe for many years with his Open Society Foundation. Orbán, who ironically had himself received a scholarship from Soros in his student days, uses him as a conspiracy ideological cipher in countless speeches, suggesting that Soros is supporting an alleged invasion of Europe by Muslim migrants.

The government implemented its authoritarian agitation and criminalisation strategy using legislative procedures. *Fidesz* built the 2018 election campaign on the 'Stop Soros' package, which Orbán won with an absolute majority. The 'Stop Soros'-laws, implemented only a few months after election day, makes the promotion of migration a punishable offence (with 'migration' subsuming all forms of immigration and asylum applications), threatens those who monitor the external border or produce or disseminate information material on the topics of asylum with prison sentences, and also provides for special taxation of NGOs who work on behalf of refugees and migrants. The law impressively shows how the dismantling of the rule of law and democracy at the border also has an internal effect on the 'others' and how 'enemies' of the government are constructed to legitimise the dismantling of citizens' rights.

The European Court of Justice found this law to be contrary to European law,[9] in that it restricts the rights guaranteed by EU law of people seeking international protection. While the government initially agreed to recognise the EU ruling, it stressed that it would stick to its position on 'migration'.

Extreme right-wing and authoritarian actors across the EU refer positively to Hungary's migration control policies. The *AfD* has on several occasions defended measures such as those at the Hungarian border and joined campaigns by the Hungarian government, such as in its rejection of the Global Compact for Migration. Martin Sellner, a leading Austrian member of the Identitarian Movement, wrote approvingly: '[Orbán's] path was a metapolitical one, his goal was to build a narrative and myth that polarised society in such a way that people as a whole defected to the patriotic fraction' (Sellner 2016).

4.2.2 Adoption of authoritarian state techniques in liberal constellations

The criminalisation of civil society is a strategy that is not only pursued by clearly authoritarian governments such as in Hungary. In 2019 alone, 99 people were charged with or convicted of so-called solidarity crimes in Europe, as documented in the report *When witnesses won't be silenced* by the London *Institute for Race Relations* (Fekete et al. 2019), including, for example, the Stanstead 15 group who blocked an aircraft from taking of the London airport to prevent deportation and faced criminal charges for interfering with aviation security as an alleged terrorist group.

After the summer of 2015, political actors in Germany also copied strategies, promoted discourses of criminalisation against refugees and pro-migrant actors and transferred them into the political mainstream. This can be illustrated with an example from the deportation discourse in Germany. At the beginning of May 2018, the Baden-Wurttemberg police wanted to arrest a young Togolese man in his refugee accommodation and transfer him to Italy. The man entered the EU via Italy before coming to Germany. Numerous residents in the accommodation protested against the transfer with civil disobedience. Allegedly to avoid further escalation, the police released the man and ended the operation. The vice-president of the federal police department in charge said: 'It is also quite clear that the rule of law cannot be deterred by an aggressive crowd in the enforcement of the rule of law. The law will be enforced, that is what we stand for' (Police press conference, 3 August 2018). Many media and politicians unquestioningly adopted the police account, even though journalistic research from the scene proved that the account was incorrect (Jakob 2018).

---

[9] Case C-821/19 *European Commission v Hungary*, Judgment (Grand Chamber), 16 November 2021.

In the nationwide deportation debate, a picture was drawn of violent refugees who do not accept the law on the one hand and supposedly defenceless police officers who are at the mercy of the 'mob' on the other. Armin Schuster, one of the leading figures of interior policies in the Conservative party, declared: 'In our constitutional state, there are clear red lines that are now deliberately crossed almost daily by asylum seekers' (*Süddeutsche Zeitung*, 3 May 2018). However, it was not just national-conservative actors who took a stand against the refugees. Even among the liberal Greens, who otherwise publicly advocate a humanitarian refugee policy, Cem Özdemir, a member of the Bundestag from Stuttgart, pointed out that 'lawless spaces must not be tolerated anywhere in Germany', while former party leader Robert Habeck issued a warning in the direction of the refugees that law and order would apply to everyone 'in our constitutional state'.[10] The head of the Bavarian conservative party's parliamentary group (*CSU*) Alexander Dobrindt intensified the debate and declared in an interview with *BILD-Zeitung*, that he saw an 'anti-deportation industry' at work,

> an unspeakable alliance of coercive ideologues and special interests that tries to prevent deportations and sabotage the enforcement of the rule of law through waves of lawsuits. This alliance is not working for the right to asylum, but against social peace.[11]

Dobrindt used narratives of extreme right-wing actors in his agitation. As early as the mid-2000s, the Austrian *FPÖ* politician Heinz-Christian Strache used the term to defame the work of welfare organisations in the Austrian debate on the right to stay at the time, and in Hungary, as explained, the struggle against the supposed 'asylum industry' has been condensed into state doctrine. In an interview with the Funke-Mediengruppe, Dobrindt said shortly after the Hungarian election that Orbán was a close partner and friend of the *CSU* and that he saw no problem in orienting his own 'bourgeois-conservative policy' towards Hungary (*WAZ*, 11 April 2018). One year after the deportation attempt in Ellwangen, the Ministry of the Interior, led by Horst Seehofer (*CSU*), introduced a bill which initially still provided for a tightening of penalties in the Residence Act, according to which all staff, without limitation, who made deportation dates public would be punished. This paragraph could have potentially hit refugee organisations, lawyers and journalists, as in Hungary. After a public outcry, this aggravation of punishment was withdrawn in the further legislative project. Overall, the deportation discourse shows how authoritarian strategies have become normalised in dealing with refugees and their support-

---

[10] Both quotes from: *Welt*, 3 May 2018.
[11] Sources: *BILD am Sonntag,* 12 May 2018; *FAZ.net,* 6 May 2018.

ers. There are fluid transitions between the authoritarian right and the supposed political 'centre', which rely on 'law and order' to solve social problems.

4.3 Authoritarianism in European Migration Control Policy

Authoritarianism is usually contrasted with liberal systems of government and strategies as antagonistic. However, this undercuts the illiberal valences in liberalism (Frankenberg 2014) and does not explain how strategies of authoritarian actors can become normalised in the political mainstream. Particularly in refugee and migration policy, it is striking that authoritarian measures have clearly gained attraction since 2015, such as the systematic disenfranchisement of refugees in camps at the EU's external borders or the now-normalised brutal push backs.

Before 2015, European migration policy was even more ambivalent (Buckel et al. 2014). Although there were already numerous closure mechanisms, such as the border agency Frontex, the Dublin regime with its lack of solidarity, and policies to externalise border controls (Pichl 2021: 5 ff.), at the same time the EU Commission also pursued a strategy of inclusion by granting subjective rights to those seeking protection under European law. European migration control policy since 2015 has been conducted in a way that primarily makes concessions to the demands of the authoritarian right, while pro-migrant positions are increasingly marginalised. This approach is based on two assumptions: the erosion of migration control at the external borders could lead to a threat to the Schengen internal free movement of persons and thus the existence of the European Union would be threatened. This fear was expressed by representatives of the EU Commission and also by France's President Macron when he took over the European Council Presidency in order to justify a tightening of asylum and migration policy (EU-COM 2021). Finally, it is believed that a pro-migrant policy that prioritises the rights of refugees to protection and reception could overstretch the receptiveness of European societies, bring about tensions and polarisation, which in turn would gain support for the extreme right and thus, in the long run, jeopardise the project of European refugee protection. More order and control at the EU's external borders would contribute to the defence of the Geneva Refugee Convention.

This leads to the conclusion that migration and flight are treated primarily as a danger by the EU and the European public (Qualmann et al. 2021) and that migration policy is therefore oriented towards regulatory policy and adjusted to averting danger. This is initially displayed by the fact that the EU Commission's draft migration laws of 2016 (Dublin IV Regulation) as well as the *New Pact on Migration and Asylum* introduced in 2020 adhere to an outsourcing of migration control to the external border states by establishing new border procedures, take back subjective rights of asylum seekers in the legal protection system and, in addition, more third countries are to be treated as allegedly safe in order to externalise responsibility for refugee protection. Charles Heller and Bernd Kasparek therefore state:

> Thus, the EU Commission's attempt to square the circle of member states' conflicting interests has resulted in a European pact against migration, which perpetuates the promises of the EU's (anti-)migration policy over the last three decades: externalisation, enhanced borders, accelerated asylum procedures, detention and deportations to prevent and deter migrants from the global South (Heller & Kasparek 2021).

The draft was adopted in the European trilogue in December 2023, the harshest asylum restrictions for the last 30 years, which will have the *de facto* effect of more pushbacks at the borders and more externalization of refugee responsibility. This conclusion is also a victory for authoritarian actors in the EU, who were able to dismantle the rights of refugees in many provisions.

The disenfranchisement and dehumanisation of refugees at the EU's external borders is tacitly or openly accepted. Violent pushbacks in violation of international and European law take place in the Greek-Turkish Aegean, at the Croatian-Bosnian, Hungarian-Serbian, Polish-Belarusian and Spanish-Moroccan borders. While there are still institutions such as the European Court of Human Rights or the European Court of Justice that find such practices unlawful, the EU Commission seems less and less able to act as the 'guardian of the treaties'. Despite these repressive migration control policies, the EU's attempt to counter authoritarianism through partial concessions has so far not worked. Viktor Orbán's power is still untouched, and now that hardly any refugees can enter Hungary, domestic political actors such as journalists and lawyers have been declared enemies. If one looks at the social reality, it becomes clear that an authoritarian migration control policy of the EU has the opposite effect: it does not lead to a pacification of the authoritarian forces, but rather strengthens their positions, normalises them in the discourse and thus also provides legitimacy to more radical policies of disenfranchisement.

5. COUNTER-HEGEMONY TO AUTHORITARIANISM

Since the summer of 2015, authoritarianism has manoeuvred itself from a defensive position to the offensive and has had a lasting impact on Europe's current policy how to treat refugees at its borders. The European Union has all the instruments at its disposal to counter this strategy with a rights-based policy. The European treaties and secondary law guarantee the right to asylum (Article 18 of the Charter of Fundamental Rights), contain the principle of *non-refoulement*, and grant refugees access to legal assistance, legal protection and decent material care (EU Reception Directive). However, simply insisting on compliance with European refugee law is obviously not enough; not only because European member states' ministers of the interior try to circumvent the validity of the law at the borders anyway, but also because refugee law has increasingly lost even symbolic legitimacy in the public debate. A pushback against authoritarian strategies, in combination with a defence of rule-of-law principles, would additionally require a comprehensive change in European migration control policy that would have to start at various levels.

The European Union is currently not in enough shape to credibly stand up for the rights of refugees. The concessions the EU has made to far-right and national-radical authoritarian organisations since 2015 has thoroughly compromised its basic approach to refugee policy. A progressive transformation of European refugee policy would therefore require new political institutions and spaces for action – with the power to re-define how to receive (welcome) those seeking protection. The discussion about 'cities of refuge' ('solidarity cities') can be linked to this. Cities in Europe, such as Barcelona, Palermo, Potsdam, Krakow, and others, have joined together in transnational networks to demonstrate their willingness to accept refugees and to take a path of solidarity in refugee policy. It is interesting to note that cities from nation states are also proactively declaring their willingness to take in refugees where the national governments are pursuing a rigorous course of sealing themselves off. In contrast to the nation state, as Mario Neumann describes, 'a politics of cities has both a local and a transnational dimension. Cities are local sites of globalisation and thus sites of a social and political common that both subvert and transcend the nation-state' (Neumann 2019). For such a policy of the transnational 'common', however, a different political framework would be needed: in many EU member states, cities and municipalities do not have the competence to take in refugees on their own (Scherr & Hoffmann 2016: 86–97). A 'Europe of solidary reception from below' would therefore have to fight for this right. This would also require the conception of a post-sovereign membership policy, which would have to be able to undermine ethnic narratives through a different composition of the *demos* and thus at the same time a democratisation of the border (on this fundamentally: Alhaus 2020).

Finally, the real causes of flight and migration would have to be systematically addressed. Migration control policy is, after all, a form of regulating unequal North–South relations (Castles 2005). It is precisely a characteristic feature of authoritarian movements not to want to structurally change the real social causes of social problems and experiences of dissonance:

> The agitator does not try to diagnose the relationship of this symptom to the underlying social situation. Instead he tricks his audience into accepting the very situation that produced its malaise (Löwenthal & Guterman 1949: 15).

A progressive refugee policy, on the other hand, should neither reproduce the status quo of European migration controls nor persuade the European public to accept the current social situation. Instead, it should deal with the actual causes that force people to flee. However, this requires an understanding that the causes of why people flee are by no means only to be found solely in the countries of origin of the refugees, but that the Global North had and continues to have numerous negative effects on living conditions in the Global South, notably through unjust trade and economic policies, arms deliveries, climate-damaging emissions and the exploitation of natural resources. Combating the causes of flight would then mean 'that the change does not have to start in the Global South, but that European states have to fundamentally change their own societies to a sustainable one, so that they no longer live at the expense of others' (Buckel & Kopp 2021: 91).

Such a social-ecological and, as it were, internationalist political programme is not without precedent in history. At the International Socialist Congress of 1907, the Second International opposed the isolation of migration in the industrialised nations and advocated solidarity with migrating people:

> The immigration and emigration of workers are as inseparable from the essence of capitalism as unemployment, overproduction and underconsumption of the workers. [...] The Congress cannot see any means of remedying the possible consequences of emigration and immigration for the working class in any exceptional economic or political measures, since these are fruitless and reactionary in their nature, i.e., in particular, not in a restriction of freedom of movement and in an exclusion of foreign nationalities or races. [...] However, it does not see in the exclusion of certain nations or races from immigration, which, incidentally, is also reprehensible from the point of view of proletarian solidarity, an adequate means of combating it. (International Socialist Congress 1907)

Specifically, the Congress called for the introduction of a minimum wage, the abolition of all restrictions that exclude certain nationalities from residing in a country and from the social, political and economic rights of the natives, easier naturalisation and the call for trade unions to grant immigrant workers unrestricted approval of their organisations and to actively sponsor trade unions in the immigrants' home countries (ibid.). Why should such a comprehensive understanding of solidarity from 1907 not be transferred and justified in the twenty-first century to address the global refugee question and deprive authoritarian forces of their social basis?

REFERENCES

Alhaus, Svenja (2020), *Die Grenzen des Demos. Mitgliedschaftspolitik aus postsouveräner Perspektive*, Frankfurt am Main/New York.

Anderson, Benedict (1991), *Imagined Communities: Reflections on the Origin and Spread of Nationalism,* London.

Bauman, Zygmunt (2016), *Die Angst vor den Anderen*, Berlin.

de Benoist, Alain (2017), *Kulturrevolution von rechts*, Dresden.

Błaszczak, M. (2021) [Twitter] 5 December. Available at: https:// twitter .com/ mblaszczak/status/1467585328294862852 (Accessed 10 October 2023).

Brown, Wendy (2018), *Mauern. Die neue Abschottung und der Niedergang der Souveränität*, Berlin.

Buckel, Sonja & Kopp, Judith (2021), *Das Recht, nicht gehen zu müssen. Europäische Politik und Fluchtursachen*, Studie im Auftrag der Kammer für Arbeiter und Angestellte für Wien, Wien.

Buckel, Sonja, Georgi, Fabian, Kannankulam, John & Wissel, Jens (2014), 'Theorie, Methoden und Analysen kritischer Europaforschung', in: Forschungsgruppe 'Staatsprojekt Europa' (ed.), *Kämpfe um Migrationspolitik*, Bielefeld, 15–84.

Büsser, Martin (2018), *Music is my boyfriend*, Mainz.

Camus, Renaud (2016), *Revolte gegen den großen Austausch*, Schnellroda.

Castles, Stephen (2005), 'Warum Migrationspolitiken scheitern', in: *Peripherie*, Nr 97/98, 10–34.

De Genova, Nicholas (2013), 'Spectacles of 'Migration Illegality': The Scene of Exclusion, the Obscene of Inclusion', in: *Ethnic & Racial Studies*, 1180–1198.

Demirovic, Alex (1994), 'Rechtsextremismus in der Bundesrepublik', in: Institut für Sozialforschung (ed.), *Rechtsextremismus und Fremdenfeindlichkeit: Studien zur aktuellen Entwicklung*, Frankfurt am Main/New York, S. 29–57.

Edwards, Maxim (2016), Rethinking 'Eastern European Racism', in: *OpenDemocracy.net*, 2 March 2016 (last accessed 25 November 2021) https://www.opendemocracy.net/en/can-europe-make-it/rethinking-eastern-european-racism/.

EU-Kommission (2021), 'Hin zu einem stärkeren und widerstandsfähigeren Schengen-Raum', (last accessed 25 November 2021), https:// ec .europa .eu/ commission/presscorner/detail/de/QANDA_21_2707.

Fekete, Liz, Webber, Frances & Edmond-Pettitt, Anya (2019), 'When Witnesses Won't be Silenced: Citizens' Solidarity and Criminalization', *Briefing Paper No 13*, Institute for Race Relations, London.

Forschungsgruppe 'Staatsprojekt Europa' (ed.) (2014), *Kämpfe um Migrationspolitik*, Bielefeld.

Frankenberg, Günter (2014), *Political Technology and the Erosion of the Rule of Law. Normalizing the State of Exception*, Cheltenham.

Frankenberg, Günter (2020), *Authoritarianism. Constitutional Perspectives*, Cheltenham.

Georgi, Fabian (2019), 'The Role of Racism in the European 'Migration Crisis': A Historical Materialist Perspective', in: Satgar, Vishwas (ed.), *Racism After Apartheid: Challenges for Marxism and Anti-Racism*, Johannesburg, 96–117.

Hall, Stuart (2018), *Das verhängnisvolle Dreieck. Rasse, Ethnie, Nation*, Berlin.

Hänsel, Valeria, Heyer, Karl, Schmidt-Sembdner, Matthias & Violetta Schwarz, Nina (eds.) (2022), *Von Moria bis Hanau: Brutalisierung und Widerstand. Grenzregime IV*, Berlin.
Heitmeyer, Wilhelm (2018), *Autoritäre Versuchungen. Signaturen der Bedrohung I*, Berlin.
Heller, Charles & Kasparek, Bernd (2021), 'Der Europäische Pakt gegen Migration', in: *Movements. Journal for Critical Migration and Border Regime Studies*, 6(1) (last accessed 25 November 2021), https://movements-journal.org/issues/09.open-call/07.heller,kasparek--der-europaische-pakt-gegen-migration.html.
Hess, Sabine, Kasparek, Bernd, Kron, Stefanie, Rodatz, Mathias, Schwertl, Maria & Sontowski, Simon (eds) (2016), *Der lange Sommer der Migration. Grenzregime III*, Berlin.
International Socialist Congress (1907), *Internationaler Sozialistenkongress zu Stuttgart, 18–24 August 1907*, V.I. Lenin, *Collected Works XIII*, 1972, Moscow.
Jakob, Christian (2016), *Die Bleibenden. Wie Flüchtlinge Deutschland seit 20 Jahren verändern*, Berlin.
Jakob, Christian (2018), 'Was geschah in Ellwangen?', in: *taz*, 3 May 2018 (last accessed 25 November 2021), https://taz.de/Neuer-Blick-auf-Vorfall-in-Unterkunft/!5500584/.
Kallius, Annastiina (2017), 'The East-South Axis: Legitimizing the 'Hungarian Solution to Migration', in: *Revue Européenne des Migratons Internationales*, Vol. 33, 133–155.
Kannankulam, John (2014), 'Kräfteverhältnisse in der bundesdeutschen Migrationspolitik. Die Asyldebatte als Schlüsselereignis des schwerfälligen Wandels vom Gastarbeiterregime hin zu Managed Migration in der Bundesrepublik Deutschland', in: Forschungsgruppe 'Staatsprojekt Europa' (ed.), *Kämpfe um Migrationspolitik*, Bielefeld, 93–112.
Kapturak. (2021) [Twitter] 5 December. Available at: https://twitter.com/kapturak/status/1467554814003453957 (last accessed 10 October 2023).
Löwenthal, Leo & Guterman, Norbert (1949), 'Prophets of Deceit. A Study of the Techniques of the American Agitator', New York.
Marsovszky, Magdalena (2013), 'Geschlossene Gesellschaft. Zu den ideologischen Hintergründen der völkischen Entwicklung in Ungarn', in: Andreas Koob et al. (eds), *Mit Pfeil, Kreuz und Krone*, Münster, 13–62.
Mayblin, Lucy (2017), *Asylum after Empire: Colonial Legacies in the Politics of Asylum Seeking*, London/New York.
Nagy, Boldiszár (2017), 'Renegade in the Club – Hungarys's Resistance to EU efforts in the Asylum Field', in: *Osteuropa Recht*, 4/2017, 413–427.
Neumann, Mario (2019), 'Die Solidarität der Städte', in: *Online-Schwerpunkt 'Migration und Metropolen'* der Rosa-Luxemburg-Stiftung, 25 November 2021, https://www.rosalux.de/publikation/id/39792.
Nielsen, Nikolaj (2023), 'Lithuania law to allow 'volunteer' border guards to use violence, in: EU-Observer (last accessed, 20 June 2023), https://euobserver.com/migration/156944.
Orbán, Viktor (2014), 'Prime Minister Viktor Orbáns Speech at the 25th Bálványos Summer Free University and Student Camp' (last accessed 25 November 2021), https://2015-2019.kormany.hu/en/the-prime-minister/the-prime-minister-s-speeches/prime-minister-viktor-orban-s-speech-at-the-25th-balvanyos-summer-free-university-and-student-camp.

Pichl, Maximilian (2021), 'Der ‚Moria-Komplex'. Verantwortungslosigkeit, Unzuständigkeit und Entrechtung fünf Jahre nach dem EU-Türkei-Abkommen und der Einführung des Hotspot-Systems', Studie für medico international, Frankfurt am Main.
Pichl, Maximilian (2021), 'Der ‚Moria-Komplex'. Verantwortungslosigkeit, Unzuständigkeit und Entrechtung fünf Jahre nach dem EU-Türkei-Abkommen und der Einführung des Hotspot-Systems', Studie für medico international, Frankfurt am Main.
Pichl, Maximilian (2022), 'Europas Abschied vom Asylrecht: Das Drama an Polens Grenze', in: *Blätter für deutsche und internationale Politik*, 1/22, S. 17–22.

Qualmann, Felicias u.a. (2021), 'Von Bedrohungsszenarien und Grenzregimen. Die Verschränkung von Flucht- und Terrordiskursen', in: *movements*, 6(1), (last accessed 25 November 2021), http://movements-journal.org/issues/09.open-call/04.qualmann,bicer,brink,nieves-camacho--von-bedrohungsszenarien-und-grenzregimen.html.

Quent, Matthias (2016a), 'Vigilantistischer Terrorismus', in: *Aus Politik und Zeitgeschichte*, 24–25/2016, S. 20–26.

Quent, Matthias (2016b), *Rassismus, Radikalisierung, Rechtsterrorismus. Wie der NSU entstand und was er über die Gesellschaft verrät*, Weinheim/Basel.

Scherr, Albert & Hofmann, Rebecca (2016), 'Sanctuary Cities: Eine Perspektive für deutsche Kommunalpolitik?', in: *Kritische Justiz*, S. 86–97.

Sellner, Martin (2016), 'Von Ungarn lernen', in: *Sezession* vom 1 February 2016 (last accessed 25 November 2021), https://sezession.de/57178/von-ungarn-lernen.

Steinhagen, Martin (2021), *Rechter Terror. Der Mord an Walter Lübcke und die Strategie der Gewalt*, Hamburg.

Thorleifsson Cathrine (2017), 'Disposable Strangers: Far-right Securitisation of Forced Migration in Hungary', in: *Social Anthropology*, 25, 3, S. 318–334.

Verseck, Keno (2016), 'Privatsheriffs machen Jagd auf Migranten', in: *Spiegel Online* vom 17 April 2016. Abrufbar unter: https://www.spiegel.de/politik/ausland/fluechtlinge -in -osteuropa -regierungen -dulden -selbstjustiz -der -buergerwehren -a -1087388.html.

Virchow, Fabian (2016), *Nicht nur der NSU. Eine kleine Geschichte des Rechtsterrorismus in Deutschland*, Erfurt.

Williams, M., & Plucinska, J. (2021, November 9). Poland warns of further large migrant clashes on Belarus border. Reuters. https://www.reuters.com/world/europe/poland-fears-major-incident-migrants-belarus-head-border-2021–11–08/.

PART IV

Authoritarian mentalities and identity politics

9. Dynamics of authoritarianism: an essay[1]

Oliver Decker

When Herbert Marcuse, looking at psychoanalysis in the 1960s, described it as obsolescent, he did not so much mean that it had become obsolete for social research and especially for social criticism (Marcuse 1963). On the contrary, his title was already a dialectical trick, which consisted of emphasising the still-great importance that psychoanalysis had through its reconstruction of subjectivation as part of a critical theory of society – precisely because the conditions of socialisation in society had changed so radically. Psychoanalysis should depict the traces of violence that the individual experiences in growing into society. Human needs are worked on in socialisation, and thus made available for domination. The strength of psychoanalysis for Marcuse is its ability to show this time and time again. Freud described growing up in the patriarchal nuclear family and the resulting subjectivity as scar tissue. However, it could no longer be as it was for the nineteenth century, when Freud came upon the archetype of his Oedipus Rex. But not much else yet either, since it was clear to the historical-materialist Marcuse that the contradictions of society persisted and found their way into the subject structure of the individual. Society was too dominated by the same mechanisms that had already been in place in the 19th century. Psychoanalysis was intended to trace the change in socialisation from the *Seelenende der Gesellschaft* ("soul end of society"; Freud 1962, 194), while at the same time working out what was identical in the change.

The paradoxical formulation chosen by Marcuse to denote the validity of psychoanalysis is in principle true for the theory of authoritarianism. However, the concept of authoritarianism can no longer apply today as it applied at the time of its origin – but neither can it have become completely obsolete. And the changes in authoritarianism can also be used to describe the persistence of social conditions that seem to have been overcome long ago. To apply Marcuse's idea of the obsolescence of psychoanalysis to the idea of authoritarianism is as consistent as it is compelling in the logic of this social theory: the

1 Translated by David West.

historical process brings forth something new, with the old never disappearing completely, but being suspended in the new.

This chapter will outline what this means for research on authoritarianism in social psychology today, and what this tells us about society. As a co-founder of Critical Theory, Marcuse was also involved in the first studies on the authoritarian character, these going back to a research plan from the end of the 1920s (Horkheimer, Fromm & Marcuse 1936). Authoritarianism had as its object the "rancor of the dominated subjects of the domination of nature", thereby including the relation to nature in the analysis of domination (Horkheimer & Adorno 1944, 172).

My initial thesis is that the theory of authoritarianism is applicable precisely because it is obsolete. But it is also as obsolete as the society in which we live, despite all its caprices of innovation (Türcke 1998). One claim linked to this initial thesis is that contemporary society is still permeated by an authoritarian dynamic. Authoritarianism has an individual and a social side. The latter will be referred to here as the authoritarian dynamic, that historically specific form that domination takes, and the entities that mediate domination and anchor it in the individual. The former was defined in the early studies on authoritarianism as "character", and we will discuss this shortly. What was meant was the deposit that the authoritarian dynamic leaves in the individual. This deposit takes on different forms over time and from one person to another. Because the notion of character has a number of implications (Ebrecht 2010), our series of studies have instead referred to this individual side as the authoritarian syndrome, but this chapter does not consider syndromes in depth (Decker, Schuler & Brähler 2018; Decker et al. 2020).

If we return to the thesis of authoritarian dynamics today, it is important that the phenomena in question are not authoritarian movements or Führer. These are only that extremity that allows the authoritarian dynamic itself to appear. Drawing on psychoanalytic social psychology, I would like to cast a spotlight on contemporary society and thereby take up the concept of authoritarianism in Critical Theory. This can help us understand not only resentment in its current form, but also perhaps something of the incomplete that underlies this resentment.

Not only Critical Theory is concerned with (not only authoritarian) domination, but also the social sciences as a whole. In designing their studies, the authors around Max Horkheimer, Herbert Marcuse and Erich Fromm also drew extensively on the analyses provided by the nascent discipline. It is no coincidence that Horkheimer's historical reconstruction of ever more refined and internalised domination itself ended with Calvinism and Protestantism (Horkheimer 1936, 371). Marx had already discerned Protestantism's ambivalent internalisation of domination when he wrote: "Luther certainly conquered servitude based on *devotion*, but only by replacing it with servitude based on *conviction* ... He transformed the priests into laymen, but only by transforming the laymen into priests. He freed mankind from external religiosity, but only by making religiosity the inner man" (Marx 1844, 251). Horkheimer, however, does not so much draw on Marx's polemic, since he no longer recognised religion as a relevant counterpart at the same point. In contrast, perhaps less to Marx than to many of those who read him, Horkheimer already pointed in the preparatory work of the authoritarianism studies to their broader goal. His starting point was that "the way people act at a given point in time cannot be explained by economic processes alone" (Horkheimer 1936, 343). The authority relationship certainly strengthens the "economic relationship" and this, in turn, "interacts with it", i.e. the authority relationship. But the authority relationship is not exhausted in a merely economic relationship (Horkheimer 1936, 380). Horkheimer had obviously read Max Weber carefully and understood the great inner need that chained the Protestant more than ever to an authority after being emancipated from authoritarian priestly domination (Weber 1920). There is definitely something to be found in Weber that illuminates the relationship between economy and authority. What is more, something that illuminates the currency of religious expectations of salvation precisely in the apparent rationality of economic action.

Marx only wanted to analyse the economy with the value-form – and that was already more than he wanted to do. He constantly uses religious analogies, these overflowing in the famous passage on the fetish character of the commodity (Marx 1867, 87ff; see in more detail Decker 2011). But he never took them seriously enough and the religious metaphors emanated from the object itself. Weber, on the other hand, was not only concerned with how capitalist accumulation and Protestant religion were connected; he also asked the burning question of what conditions lead a person to follow an instruction in the first place. Weber was not at all interested in the command executed under coercion. What concerned him was what motivated the recipient of the command to carry it out. Tyranny needs no explanation. But legitimate domination, be it even authoritarian, is not self-explanatory (Weber 1922). Its characteristic is that the action of the authority-bearer "proceeds essentially as if he had made the content of the command his conduct for its own sake" (Weber 1922, 159).

Horkheimer's co-author, Erich Fromm, defined the task of their studies on authority and family in a way that resembled Weber's analysis of domination: why people not only act as they ought, but also equate this "ought" with their own will (Fromm 1936, 179). Fromm's formulation was not only influenced by his reading of Weber; he probably had another author in mind, too. Georg Simmel had already stated in 1908 that an authoritarian dynamic always requires the "freedom of the person subjected to authority" (Simmel 1908, 102). This entanglement of submission and submissiveness, of external coercion and internal drive, was the main challenge of psychoanalytical studies on the authority relationship. Fromm's initial suspicion was that authority offers a "'prosthetic' security" (ibid.), which already suggests the high price of this security. On the one hand, prostheses are necessary additions to the human body, but on the other they are a constant reminder of the deficiency that they are designed to remedy. Prostheses are preceded by an injury, they remind us of it, yet they can never completely remedy the deficiency and they always remain insufficient (Decker 2004). As an attentive reader of Freud's *Civilisation and Its Discontents* (Freud 1930, 451), Erich Fromm was certainly familiar with the fact that this double logic of the prosthesis, of being expansive and damaging, by no means only happens to a few, for example after a traumatic amputation. Freud already recognised that all institutions of culture have this ambivalent character. Culture may have transformed the human being into "a kind of prosthetic God" (280) but, as a constant reminder of the absence removed, the prostheses evoke the fantasy of an undamaged prehistory. The authority relationship is also not without ambivalence towards authority – and the authors who write about it cannot avoid religious motifs.

It is only the ambivalent relationship to authority that is initially significant for empirical research, however. The preliminary work of Max Horkheimer, Herbert Marcuse and Erich Fromm led to a large-scale questionnaire survey in Germany in the early 1930s. Using standardised questionnaires, they surveyed the political attitudes of Germans at the end of the Weimar Republic and found how widespread an anti-democratic attitude was among the population. Only 15% of those surveyed could be expected to defend democracy at all "in critical times" (Fromm 1937/38, 188). These findings (published when the authors were already in exile) partly helped to cement their decision to leave Germany in 1932. This series of studies on authority and family was followed by the Berkeley group's study "The Authoritarian Personality", which was published in the US in the 1940s.

As already mentioned, the intention in each case was to use "modern depth psychology", as Max Horkheimer put it, to learn more about society (Horkheimer 1936, 398). Horkheimer was thinking of Freud's psychoanalysis, still in its infancy at the time, which he wanted to use to gain insight into the effect of society on the individuals living in it. This was not meant as an academic exercise, as the time of its creation reveals immediately: the mass phenomenon of fascism needed to be understood and the authors hoped that Freudian mass psychology would shed light on the psychic bond between the masses and their Führer. The Freudian figure of socialisation was to be used to reconstruct the subject form of bourgeois society – and thus the ambivalent relationship to authority, since the child's needs are worked on through "the violence emanating from the father" and the social norms "internalised" through violence, as Fromm called it (Fromm 1936, 147).

This provided a relevant insight for the study of what threatens society from within. Something about socialisation, growing into society and its demands, produced a fundamental ambivalence towards that society. The father was still the primary image of violence in patriarchal society at the beginning of the twentieth century. He could demand submission and in return promise (the sons) a share in his power. But this submission created an ambivalence towards authority. The sons identified with him – the father became the "ideal self-object", as psychoanalysis calls it. While the person identified with the father's goals and norms and made him the deeply anchored point of orientation for her own actions, the person's aggression resulting from the experience of violence and the loss of her own desires had to remain elsewhere. The weak and the seemingly deviant offered themselves as an outlet for aggression. This was the "authoritarian character" that gave the studies their name. It is the succinct name for this subject form, which was driven by the desire for submission to an authority, and at the same time sought victims for the rage resulting from the person's own submission. This stimulated a mass psychology, the longing for a Führer who constitutes the mass from which the weak and deviant can be persecuted. He also allows the group members to identify with him and his power, and thereby to compensate themselves for their own subjugation.

But all this is in the past, and why should we find here of all places answers to questions of the present? It was long ago that the father lost the prominent position that he still held in the patriarchal family of Freud's time. Despite Trump, there also seems to be no Führer who actually constitutes the authoritarian masses in the first place. As early as 1919, Paul Federn (Federn 1919) spoke of a "fatherless society", an analysis that Alexander Mitscherlich then took up after the war (Mitscherlich 1963). This cannot lack repercussions for the concept of the authoritarian character.

This scepticism is certainly justified. Much more evidence is available. Today, parents and children act as partners in the latter's education, and lessons in school are not conducted as socialisation in an authoritarian-bureaucratic society with a time regime and heteronomy (Jackson 1975), but rather in a flexible and participatory manner (Forneck 2009). And when the child who has been educated in this way enters the workplace as an adult, a joint performance agreement determines the work goals to be achieved. A 360-degree feedback, which also includes the supervisor, rounds off this picture of democratic everyday culture (Bröckling 2000).

But what is a cause for concern is the constant influence of authoritarianism on anti-democratic attitudes and resentment,[2] which many sociological and

---

[2] See Altemeyer 1981; Cohrs & Ibler 2009; Duckitt et al. 2002; Fuchs 2003; Heitmeyer 1987; Lederer 2000; Oesterreich 1996; Stellmacher 2004.

socio-psychological studies still confirm strongly today. This is perhaps no wonder: is the phenomenon of group-based misanthropy not almost identical to authoritarian aggression (Heitmeyer 2002; 2018)? In fact, it seems that this misanthropy is mainly found among those who still exactly fit the type of authoritarian today. Also, people still grow up with experiences of violence, and childhood needs are dealt with in a way that benefits general requirements. And the unconscious in its dynamics and desire is still produced socially. The authoritarian father is the historical special case. Authority is a social position that is attributed to a person, or even an institution, and that leads to other people acting in accordance with it. Freud already described not only the "primary" mass with a concrete Führer, but also mentioned the growing influence of "secondary masses" (Freud 1921) at the end of his *Group Psychology and the Analysis of the Ego* (1921). These are bound together by identification no longer with a person, but with an abstract object. This is exactly what Herbert Marcuse expected from the future: identification with the Führer would be replaced by something more abstract, which he explicitly named "capitalism" (Marcuse 1963, 69). This suspicion is worth considering. For, just as Marcuse's formulation of the "obsolescence of psychoanalysis" was intended to emphasise precisely the strength of this psychology (namely, its ability to discern the traces of social violence in the individual, and how the changed traces also reveal something about society), so the "obsolescence of authoritarianism" would also mean exposing the persisting forms of socialisation alongside the new social conditions. Horkheimer had already identified a strong driving force behind the desire for authority in precisely this economic basis of society: "In deciding the fate of people ... it is not freedom that has taken the place of arbitrariness, but the blind economic mechanism, an anonymous god" (Horkheimer 1936, 372). And this economic basis continues to have an effect.

When as part of the Leipzig Authoritarianism Studies we found in the group discussions across the generations not only the centrality of the strong economy, but also the historical background, we chose to formulate this in terms of "economic prosperity as narcissistic filling" (Decker et al. 2013). This was designed to name the connection between the defence against narcissistic disparagement and the economic miracle in post-war Germany. We drew on the analysis of the "inability to mourn", as Margarete and Alexander Mitscherlich called the psychological condition of post-war society (Mitscherlich & Mitscherlich 1967). What applies to the loss of a loved one also applies when many lose a revered object. This reaction of mourning is work, the work of mourning. And this is precisely what was not done in post-war Germany which, along with the "Führer", should also have abandoned the collective greatness of self. Instead, the "collective narcissism ... that had been severely damaged by the collapse of the Hitler regime was replaced by economic recovery, the awareness of how capable we are" (Adorno 1959, 563–564). But we also drew on the theory of perversion outlined by the ethnopsychoanalyst Fritz Morgenthaler, who used the concept of the "filling" to describe the means of choice to counter an imposition in reality. This reality is simultaneously recognised consciously – and denied in its significance. A fetishised object takes the place of reality and conceals the loss. According to Morgenthaler, this is much more often a socio-cultural practice than an individual fate (Morgenthaler 1974).

Can we pursue this observation further? Is the economy, as Marcuse suspected, bound up in an authoritarian dynamic? A filling, prosthesis or fetishised object – in short, an ideal self-object constituting an authoritarian mass? Some things point to this. The influence that the collective fear of economic deprivation has on right-wing extremist attitudes, especially in Germany, is well documented. Let us take the thesis of the special position of the economy seriously and look for further evidence. Using the "economic miracle" and the strong economy as a substitute for the "Führer" and to stabilise self-esteem probably worked so well because this connection already existed. A "German economic miracle" did not take place only in post-war Germany, the term having already been used in 1936 by the economist Hans Priester to describe economic development after the NSDAP's seizure of power (Priester 1936). Even if the material benefits of the miracle did not reach the population, this first German economic miracle nevertheless integrated people, and this by means of "immaterial collective goods" such as a sense of community and national pride. And it was the Führer who was seen as the source of this success (Spoerer 2005).

That is probably why it was so easy after the war for people themselves to join in the cause: in the economy as a "secondary Führer", to echo Freud. But this also means that the authoritarian character is not obsolete. Contemporary society is a secondary mass that has its authoritarian institution in the economy. And there is much to be said for such secondary authoritarianism, including the fixation on steady growth, since authority must not be weak if it is to offer the prosthetic security that Fromm attributed to authority. And, like any authority, an economy committed to growth can demand that its followers align their own actions with its primacy and subordinate their own lives to its rules, no matter how high the costs to individuals.

Evidence supporting my thesis of secondary authoritarianism can be seen in the pejorative reactions to certain groups, even in times of economic prosperity, that the Bielefeld study series "Group-related misanthropy" and the Leipzig Authoritarianism Studies have been uncovering since the beginning of the 2000s. Those who neither comply with the demands of authority nor seem to identify with the group ideal are disparaged. The aggression is not directed against migrants *per se*, as long as they seem to strengthen the person's own authority, to secure growth. A shortage of skilled workers and demographic change are the relevant keywords. Those, however, who are imagined as posing a threat to the strength of the ideal self-object are faced with disparagement, such as is currently the case with asylum seekers. Also provoking rage are those who evoke the fantasy of having a good life without subjugation, without being subject to a king. And secondary authoritarianism also leads to hatred against migrants from cultural circles that are fantasised as "foreign" and "backward" because they belong to a different religion, one "archaic" and unenlightened, the antipode of modernity.

Xenophobia and anti-Semitism rose to alarming levels in Germany not during the movement of refugees in 2015, but in 2012, at the height of the global economic crisis (Decker, Kiess & Brähler 2016). Authoritarian resentment is at its strongest when the idealised object is threatened. But this also means that authority depends much more on the receiver than on the sender. Authoritarian dynamics can only be understood in the first place by adopting the needs approach. Needs can be manipulated, exploited, and used for social conflicts. But we must always pose anew the question of the social genesis of these authoritarian needs and reframe the question as one about the needs and how they come about.

There are, therefore, two reasons why the notion of a secondary authoritarianism is not only relevant for understanding authoritarian dynamics in Germany. First, we must increasingly reckon with an authoritarian dynamic even if no personal authority is immediately apparent. In general, the function of authority seems to have changed insofar as this ideal follows less of a father identification (as it was still described for the beginning of the twentieth century), and increasingly resembles a fusion with an all-powerful (mother) figure. This change is also of great relevance for the social structure. While father authority in the wake of an ambivalent father relationship, as described by Erich Fromm, offers power and prosthetic security, this authority equally demands recognition both of its demands and thus also to a certain extent of a reality that is outside the individual.

And if we establish that the conspiracy mindset and superstition are essential components of authoritarian syndromes today, then this change of motifs may also cause authoritarian dynamics in society to take a new shape. Even in groups where a Führer is to be found, such as is the case with Trump, for example, it is no longer the leader but the group itself that serves as wish fulfilment and prosthetic security: authority represents no longer a paternal power in which the group participates, but only the group itself. Leo Löwenthal showed in his analysis of fascist propagandists that it is not so much that they seduce the audience as that they read the wishes from the audience's eyes and deliver what the audience wants to hear (Löwenthal 1949). This presupposes something other than an authoritarian father proclaiming his own law. And today's agitators are even more receptive to the moods of their audience and are, perhaps, even more dependent on the group than any other member. They become part of the group and the group illusion of healing the narcissistic wound, of denying it through a prosthesis so that the offending reality need not be acknowledged (Chasseguet-Smirgel 1975). This raises the suspicion that it is not about the father but about an earlier, first-lost-love object whose power is to be re-enthroned. In this respect, the significance of the person Donald J Trump (or even other right-wing authoritarian politicians such as Boris Johnson, Vladimir Putin and Jair Bolsonaro) is clearly overestimated. But the authoritarian dynamics within the US, Russia, Britain and other societies are underestimated to at least the same extent. Identifying with an authority as a maternal bond serves the power of thought and the denial of reality (Chassguet-Smirgel 1975). This aspect is particularly important for understanding the conspiracy mindset and superstition as components of the authoritarian syndrome. The prosthetic security that emanates from an authority is either too insufficient or the fantasy of its antecedents too alluring – or both.

Second, and relatedly, the idealisation of economic strength in Germany illuminates the significance of capitalist modes of production in democratic societies in general. After all, the economy could only acquire such an important function as a secondary authority in post-war Germany because it was already significant in several respects. Weber (Weber 1904/1905) saw this clearly when he exposed the motif behind capitalist accumulation already cited above. The communal cultivation of nature by human beings always had the aim of satisfying sensual bodily needs with food. But the ever-further refinement of this activity, the working of nature, also had another drive that pointed beyond the factor of mere satisfaction of needs in the here and now: no longer merely to satisfy lack, but to eliminate it in the long run. Hence the threat of stagnant growth, which endangers not only the status quo, but also capitalism's specific promise of salvation. If this thesis is correct, then it will not only apply in Germany, but will also help to determine the legitimacy of the political system in other societies.

It is here that the points mentioned separately come together. The authority of the capitalist economy derives its power from a promise of salvation. In this respect, we can also describe the shift in the authoritarian dynamic in terms of psychodynamics: instead of recognising the reality of the paternal law, it is the reality of the group representing the ego ideal that becomes the reality: the regression to a mystical-political belief (Chasseguet-Smirgel 1975, 90).

REFERENCES

Adorno, Theodor W. (1959). Was bedeutet: Aufarbeitung der Vergangenheit? In: Tiedemann, R. (eds) *Theodor W. Adorno – Gesammelte Schriften Vol. 10.2, 555-572.* Frankfurt/M.: Suhrkamp.

Altemeyer, Bob. (1981). *Right-Wing Authoritarianism.* Winnipeg: University of Manitoba Press.

Bröckling, Ulrich. (2000). Totale Mobilmachung. Menschenführung im Qualitäts- und Selbstmanagement in Bröckling, Ulrich, Krasmann, Susanne & Lemke, Thomas (eds.) *Gouvernementalität der Gegenwart,* 131–167. Frankfurt/M.: Suhrkamp.

Chasseguet-Smirgel, Jeanette. (1975). *Das Ichideal. Psychoanalytischer Essay über die "Krankheit der Idealität".* Frankfurt/M.: Suhrkamp (1987).

Cohrs, J. Christopher & Ibler, Sina (2009). Authoritarianism, threat, and prejudice: An analysis of mediation and moderation. *Basic and Applied Social Psychology* 31, 81–94.

Decker, Oliver (2004). *Der Prothesengott. Subjektivität und Transplantationsmedizin.* Giessen: Psychosozial.

Decker, Oliver (2011). *Der Warenkörper. Zur Sozialpsychologie der Medizin.* Springe: Zu Klampen.

Decker, Oliver, Kiess, Johannes, & Brähler, Elamr (eds.) (2016). *Die enthemmte Mitte. Rechtsextreme und autoritäre Einstellungen in Deutschland.* Gießen: Psychosozial.

Decker, Oliver, Rothe, Katharina, Weißmann, Marliese, Kiess, Johannes & Brähler, Elmar (2013). Economic Prosperity as "Narcissistic Filling": A Missing Link Between Political Attitudes and Right-Wing Authoritarianism. *Journal of Conflict and Violence* 7, 135–149.

Decker, Oliver, Schuler, Julia & Brähler, Elmar (2018). Das autoritäre Syndrom heute, in Decker, Oliver & Brähler, Elmar (eds). *Flucht ins Autoritäre. Rechtsextreme Dynamiken in der Mitte der Gesellschaft,* 117–156. Gießen: Psychosozial.

Decker, Oliver, Schuler, Julia, Yendell, Alexander, Schließler, Clara & Brähler, Elmar (2020). Das Autoritäre Syndrom., in: Decker, Oliver & Brähler, Elmar (eds). *Autoritäre Dynamiken. Alte Ressentimens - neue Radikalität,* 179–210. Gießen: Psychosozial.

Duckitt, John, Wagner, Claire, du Plessis, Ingrid, & Birum, Ingrid (2002). The psychological bases of ideology and prejudice: Testing a dual process model. *Journal of Personality and Social Psychology* 83, 75–93.

Ebrecht, Angelika (2010). Charakter, Persönlichkeit und soziale Beziehungen, in Bahrke, Ulrich (ed.). *"Denk' ich an Deutschland..." Sozialpsychologische Reflexionen,* 54–77. Franfurt/M.: Brandes & Apsel.

Federn, Paul (1919). *Zur Theorie der Revolution: Die vaterlose Gesellschaft.* Leipzig: Anzengruber Verlag.

Forneck, Hermann, J. (2009). Zur Gouvernementalität schulischer Zeitregimes, in: Schönbächler, Marie-Theres, Becker, Rolf, Hollenstein, Armin & Osterwalder, Fritz (eds). *Die Zeit der Pädagogik. Zeitperspektiven im erziehungswissenschaftlichen Diskurs,* 87–101. Bern.

Freud, Sigmund (1921). Massenpsychologie und Ich-Analyse, in Freud, Sigmund. (ed.). *Sigmund Freud - Gesammelte Werke Vol. XIII,* 71–161. Frankfurt/M.: Fischer.

Freud, Sigmund (1930). Das Unbehagen in der Kultur. In: Freud, A. (ed.). *Sigmund Freud – Gesammelte Werke Vol. XIV,* 419–506. Frankfurt/M.: Fischer.

Freud, Sigmund (1962). *Aus den Anfängen der Psychoanalyse 1887–1902. Briefe an Wilhelm Fließ.* Frankfurt/M.: Fischer.
Fromm, Erich. (1936). Studien über Autorität und Familie. Sozialpsychologischer Teil, in Fromm, Erich (ed.). *Gesamtausgabe* Vol. 1, 139–187. Stuttgart: Deutsche Verlagsanstalt.
Fromm, Erich (1937/1938). Arbeiter und Angestellte am Vorabend des Dritten Reiches. Eine sozialpsychologische Untersuchung, in Fromm, Erich (ed.). *Gesamtausgabe* Vol. 3, 1–224. Stuttgart: Deutsche Verlags-Anstalt (1980).
Fuchs, Marek (2003). Rechtsextremismus von Jugendlichen. *Kölner Zeitschrift für Soziologie und Sozialpsychologie* 55, 654–678.
Heitmeyer, Wilhelm (1987). *Rechtsextremistische Orientierungen bei Jugendlichen. Empirische Ergebnisse und Erklärungsmuster einer Untersuchung zur politischen Sozialisation.* Weinheim: Juventa.
Heitmeyer, Wilhelm (ed.) (2002). *Deutsche Zustände – Vol. 1.* Frankfurt/M.: Suhrkamp.
Heitmeyer, Wilhelm (2018). *Autoritäre Versuchungen.* Berlin: Suhrkamp.
Horkheimer, Max (1936). Autorität und Familie. In: Schmid Noerr, G. (ed.). *Max Horkheimer – Gesammelte Schriften* Vol. 3 - Schriften 1931–1936, 336–417. Frankfurt/M.: Fischer.
Horkheimer, Max. & Adorno, Theodor. W. (1944). Die Dialektik der Aufklärung, in Schmid Noerr, Gunzelin (ed.) *Max Horkheimer – Gesammelte Schriften* Vol. 5, Frankfurt/M.: Fischer.
Horkheimer, M., Fromm, E. & Marcuse, H. (1936). *Studien über Autorität und Familie.* Springe: zu Klampen (Reprint, 1987).
Jackson, Philip W. (1975). Einübung in eine bürokratische Gesellschaft: Zu Funktion der sozialen Verkehrsform im Klassenzimmer, in Zinnecker, Jurgen (ed.). *Der heimliche Lehrplan,* 19–34. Weinheim: Beltz.
Lederer, Gerda (2000). Autoritarismus und Fremdenfeindlichkeit im deutsch-deutschen Vergleich. Ein Land mit zwei Sozialisationskulturen, in Rippl, Susanne, Seipel, Christian & Kindervater, Angela (eds). *Autoritarismus. Kontroversen und Ansätze der aktuellen Autoritarismusforschung,* 199–214. Opladen: Leske + Buderich.
Löwenthal, Leo (1949). Falsche Propheten, in Dubiel, Helmut (ed.). *Leo Löwenthal – Schriften 3 – Zur politischen Psychologie des Autoritarismus,* 11–160. Frankfurt/M.: Suhrkamp (1982).
Marcuse, Herbert (1963). Das Veralten der Psychoanalyse. In: Marcuse, Herbert (ed.). *Kultur und Gesellschaft 2,* 85–106. Suhrkamp: Frankfurt/M. (1970).
Marx, Karl (1844). Zur Kritik der Hegelschen Rechtsphilosophie. Einleitung. *Karl-Marx/Friedrich-Engels-Werke* Vol. 1, 378–391. Berlin: Dietz.
Marx, Karl (1867). Das Kapital. Kritik der politischen Ökonomie. Erster Band. *Karl-Marx/Friedrich-Engels-Werke* Vol. 23, Berlin: Dietz.
Mitscherlich, Alexander (1963). *Auf dem Weg zur vaterlosen Gesellschaft.* München: Piper (1989).
Mitscherlich, Alexander & Mitscherlich, Margarete (1967). *Die Unfähigkeit zu Trauern. Grundlagen kollektiven Verhaltens.* Munich: Pieper.
Morgenthaler, Fritz (1974). Die Stellung der Perversionen in Metapsychologie und Technik. *Psyche - Zeitschrift für Psychoanalyse und ihre Anwendungen* 28, 1077–1088.
Oesterreich, Detief (1996). *Flucht in die Sicherheit: zur Theorie des Autoritarismus und der autoritären Reaktion.* Opladen: Leske + Budrich.
Priester, Harry E. (1936). *Das Deutsche Wirtschaftswunder.* Amsterdam: Querido Verlag.

Simmel, Georg (1908). *Soziologie. Über die Formen der Vergesellschaftung.* Frankfurt/M.: Suhrkamp.
Spoerer, Mark (2005). Demontage eines Mythos? Zu der Kontroverse über das nationalsozialistische 'Wirtschaftswunder'. *Geschichte und Gesellschaft* 31, 415–438.
Stellmacher, Jost (2004). *Autoritarismus als Gruppenphänomen.* Marburg: Tectum.
Türcke, Christoph (1998). Das Altern der Kritik. *Pädagogische Korrespondenz* 22, 5–13.
Weber, Max (1904/1905). *Die Protestantische Ethik und der ‚Geist' des Kapitalismus.* Weinheim: Beltz.
Weber, Max (1920). Die protestantische Ethik und der Geist des Kapitalismus, in Weber, Max (ed.). *Gesammelte Aufsätze zur Religionssoziologie I,* Tübingen: Mohr.
Weber, Max (1922). *Wirtschaft und Gesellschaft. Grundzüge der verstehenden Soziologie.* Tübingen: Mohr.

10. Authoritarian cultural identities: understanding the new right in the tradition of Oswald Spengler

Volker Weiß

As part of the meta-political strategy of an emerging modern right in Germany and Europe, building a campaign around the term 'identity' was a successful move. First, a New Right youth organisation promoted itself in a media-effective way as the '*Identitäre Bewegung*' (IB) ('Identitarian Movement'); soon after, a large part of the New Right around the world claimed the label 'identitarian' for itself. The aim of this 'identity' offensive was to provoke a cultural struggle from the right and to take it to the centre of society. As the Austrian IB founder Martin Sellner put it, the aim was to 'rebel' against the concept of ''world citizens' of a borderless globalisation' and to find 'a new reference to identity, origin, culture, and tradition' that left the ideological distortions of modernity behind (Sellner 2017: 12). By sharpening identity consciousness, distinguishing the 'own' from the 'foreign' in the globalised world, was supposed to become easier.

What sounded like contemplative self-examination, however, was conceptual window dressing by a leading cadre of the far right. In fact, the IB and the New Right pursued an offensive concept of the 'modernisation of historical ideologies' (Heitmeyer et al. 2020: 266). After failed attempts to play a major role in the Austrian neo-Nazi scene, Sellner and his comrades-in-arms had studied the concepts of the grassroots movements and communication guerrillas of the New Left and set out to make them usable for the right (Sellner 2017: 102).[1] 'Culture' became a keyword in this identity politics campaign; after all, the decades-old demand of the French right-wing intellectual Alain de Benoist (1985) for a 'cultural revolution from the right' had long since become common knowledge on the German right as well. At the same time, *culture wars* adapted from US society became a major topic in intellectual debates. Last but not least, the new right-wing positions rose up to meet the

[1] On the IB: Bruhns et al. (eds) 2016, Goetz et al. (eds) 2017; on the IB and the New Right as a whole: Weiß 2017 and Speit 2016.

challenges of a society that was becoming more diverse, in which immigrants sometimes claimed similarly determined religious and cultural identity models for themselves and, like their xenophobic opponents, regarded these identities as 'non-negotiable'.[2] The far right also profited from this trend and shifted its interventions to cultural identity in order to better mobilise against foreign cultural influences. In this chapter, we will show which ideas of 'culture' as an indissoluble bond predominate in the milieu of a New Right, which historical sources are used for these ideas, and what form a society would take if they were implemented.

1. SPENGLER'S GUIDELINES

The founding of the German Empire in 1871 was already marked by intense debates about the relationship of the German 'cultural nation' to the new state. Even if the traditional ideas of a culture far removed from power eventually changed to an offensive cultural patriotism, the core of both was 'a romantically tinged revolt against modernity and the devaluation of "civilisation" versus "culture"' (Lepenies 2006: 66, see also Pähler 2021: 59–96 and Albrecht 1993: 11–29). The understanding of the First World War as a struggle of the German 'idea of 1914' against the French 'idea of 1789', led to notions of national culture as an inevitable fate with correspondingly binding validity. The quintessence of such authoritarian conceptions of culture can already be found in the first volume of Oswald Spengler's *The Decline of the West* (*Der Untergang des Abendlandes*, Vol. 1 1918, Vol. 2 1922; English translation 1926/1928), which presents cultures as separate entities, 'each springing with primitive strength from the soil of a mother-region to which it remains firmly bound throughout its whole life-cycle; each stamping its material, its mankind,

---

[2] As an example, the Cologne speech of the Turkish President Erdoğan on 10 February 2008 can be mentioned here, in which he called on migrants living in Germany and their children and grandchildren to preserve their traditions: 'No one can expect you to submit to assimilation. Because assimilation is a crime against humanity.' 'This is what Prime Minister Erdoğan said in Cologne', in: *Die Welt* v. 11 February 2008, last accessed: 13 March 2022, https://www.welt.de/debatte/article1660510/Das-sagte-Ministerpraesident-Erdogan-in-Koeln.html.

Another example is an advertisement on the German public video on demand service FUNK for the international 'Hijab Day' on 1 February 2022, which was intended to support traditional Muslim women in Europe. The attributes 'faith, discipline, protection, worship' mentioned in the advertisement would have been rightly identified as an expression of extremely conservative practice of faith in a Christian context but served as evidence of authenticity here. On this complex as a whole, see Fourest 2020. Pascal Bruckner (2020: 28) also writes of an 'ambivalence of anti-racism' that, despite all universalist rhetoric, sees 'special areas worthy of protection in cultural differences'.

in its own image; each having its own idea, its own passions, its own life, will and feeling, its own death' (Spengler 1926: 21). Spengler emphasised the adjective *eigne* ('own') in each case to underline the unchanging bond between 'substance' and 'form' in cultural development. According to this conception, the cultural products of a society are determined and created exclusively from within it. The possibilities of expression and action of the members of a culture are thus limited to this *own*.

Spengler distinguishes between 'possible' and 'actual' culture, i.e. 'culture as an idea in the (general or individual) existence and culture as the body of that idea' (1926: 55). Accordingly, what is completed in world history is, in a sense, the 'soul' of a culture; the people, in turn, are considered 'a unit of the soul' (1928: 165). In concrete 'humanity', a higher spirit materialises physically, as it were, through culture. This idea goes hand in hand with Spengler's organic idea of the 'ages of culture', according to which all cultures go through the same cycles before blossoming and stagnating and finally dying off in the state of civilisation. However, according to Spengler's ideas, each individual culture goes through this process in a monad-like manner, isolated from other cultures and without interaction with them. This idea of *separate*, i.e. closed, cultural cycles that always follow the same pattern across peoples and times is at the centre of his 'Morphology of World History' as a historical theory of forms.

This concept was criticised early on by experts. The philosopher Manfred Schröter remarked critically on the constructions of the philosophical autodidact Spengler that the model was 'fixed, paralysed by its overpowering one-sidedness'. In Spengler's case, 'the whole of one half of cultural-historical observation and research is omitted: the side of cultural interconnections, disseminations and transmissions, of the independent further growth of systematic cultural connections and factual cultural superimpositions'. His view of 'the cultural-historical absurdity of individual cultures, selectively separated, standing side by side and one after the other' constructed 'a permanent scheme of the organic course of culture (from becoming to maturing, ageing, withering and solidifying)', which does not cover the 'objective reality of life' (Schröter 1949: 207). Contrary to Spengler's ideal of cultural self-generation, however, 'one's own' could only develop in interaction, differentiation, and unification with 'the other'.

2. SPENGLER'S POLITICAL HEIRS

Notwithstanding this obvious objection, Spengler's thinking has taken root among his admirers and continues to have an effect along with other super-historical conceptions of 'culture'. The reception is not limited to philological debates; rather, such determinism, which excludes foreign influences on and exchange among cultures, strongly appeals to isolationists. In a political context, this model of order is especially attractive to nationalist perspectives. Indeed, in the recent past there have been various attempts by the far right to revitalise Spengler's work and thinking politically.

In January 2018, the 'Oswald Spengler Society for the Study of Humanity and World History', an organisation dedicated to cultivating Spengler's ideas, was founded around the economist Max Otte and the ancient historians Alexander Demandt and David Engels.[3] In November 2019, an 'Oswald Spengler Foundation e.V.' appeared in the sphere of the far-right party *Alternative für Deutschland* (AfD) in Dresden and invited the public to an event where, among others, the far-right-wing publisher Götz Kubitschek would discuss the question 'What is conservative?' Kubitschek is also co-founder of the private Institut für Staatspolitik, which places itself in the tradition of the New Nationalism of the interwar period. Because of this orientation alone, Spengler is part of the ideological canon there. In 2005, the Institute's journal *Sezession* published a thematic issue on Oswald Spengler that confirmed Spengler's fundamental finding: 'No matter how much two cultures may converge, a final, insurmountable barrier always remains' (Hubert 2005: 18). The seventy-fifth anniversary of Spengler's death in 2011 also showed how closely such circles feel connected to his cultural theory. At that time, a delegation held a memorial service at his grave in Munich. Activists of the Institute laid a wreath there, and among the guests who listened to the speech of the Institute's co-founder and Kubitschek's political mentor Karlheinz Weißmann was Max Otte.[4]

Otte once again underlines the political place of these binding cultural ideas of Spengler today.[5] Having been a long-time member of the German conservative party CDU, he became a member of the board of trustees of the AfD-affiliated Desiderius Erasmus Foundation from 2018 to 2021. Later he became federal chairman of the 'WerteUnion', a CDU-affiliated conservative pressure group. In 2022, Otte was chosen by the AfD as their candidate for the office of Federal President and resigned from the board of the 'WerteUnion'; the CDU also initiated party expulsion proceedings. The structures around Kubitschek's publishing house, in turn, had played a central role in radicalising the AfD.[6] These activities testify to the fact that the ideas of Spengler and

---

[3] See https://www.oswaldspenglersociety.com/ accessed: 25 March 2022.

[4] See Andreasch 2011 and Weiß 2015: 108–109, Otte gave the commemovative address and published an essay on Spengler before the event (Otte 2011).

[5] The Oswald-Spengler-Stiftung e.V. was formerly the AfD-affiliated Stresemann Foundation, which changed its name after legal difficulties with the heirs of Gustav Stresemann (Semsrott & Jakubowski 2021: 17).

[6] The influences of the meta-political cartel around the Antaios Publishing House and the Institut für Staatspolitik of the AfD can be seen, among other things, in the

similar authors are being brought back into German politics, from which they had disappeared after the defeat in the Second World War.

This is by no means an exclusively German phenomenon; the French Nouvelle Droite also reads Spengler. The journal *Nouvelle École*, edited by Alain de Benoist and one of its leading journalistic publications, also presented a thematic issue on the successful German author of the Weimar years in 2011. For Benoist, Spengler's work was already a source of inspiration for a New-Right concept of culture decades ago. With Spengler (and Norbert Elias), Benoist assumed an 'eternal primordial ground' and in doing so took up the traditionally German distinction between 'culture' and 'civilisation'. While 'civilisation' is characterised by the process of constant development, 'culture' points back to the origin. 'The concept of culture contemporises an eternal past. The man of "culture" is not fundamentally different from the "original": he merely updates it' (Benoist 1983: 186). This model maintains prehistory as a fixed point and limits the possibilities of cultural development to the trajectories set by this past.

In this eternal self-procreation lies the interest that the political right shows in the binding properties of culture. It ultimately serves them as a constant self-affirmation of *their own*, of identity and determined tradition, instead of, for example, a concept of culture that allows for openness, questioning, and development. 'Culture', writes a relevant handbook of the scene, has a 'core identity' that leads to 'extraordinary readiness to fight in case of real or imagined threat' (Lehnert & Weißmann 2009: 92). This brings the community-building factor of culture to the fore, which makes it attractive for authoritarian worldviews.

In this context, the rediscovery of the German counter-revolutionary tradition around Oswald Spengler also plays an important role in Russian nationalism. Alexandr Dugin, the protagonist of Russian ultra-nationalism and advocate of the 'neo-Eurasian' idea, which has also been adopted by the western New Right, professes his belief in Spengler's conception of culture (Dugin 2013: 111). Dugin's body of thought offers representatives of the far-right a high recognition factor, because the 'Conservative Revolution' represents overall one of his 'most important sources of reference'. Contemporaries of Spengler such as Carl Schmitt, Moeller van den Bruck, and Julius Evola provide Dugin with the keywords for an anti-Western ultranationalism with the goal of a rebirth of the Russian world (Höllwerth 2012: 329; see also Laruelle 2006:

visits of numerous top party officials to Schnellroda and the close contact with the Thuringian AfD politician Björn Höcke. The circle around Kubitschek has supported the *völkisch*-national forces in the party since its foundation (see Speit 2016; Amann 2017: 146–151 and Bender 2017: 87–103).

7 and Umland 2019). Sometimes the recognition even functions the other way round; in the neo-right's own literature, Dugin is named as the 'godfather' of the IB's rediscovery of Martin Heidegger (Möller 2017: 109).

Dugin offers inspiration for all those who see in the alliance with a 'Third Rome' awakening in the East the antidote to US-American influences in Europe, as these are getting in the way of the development of the 'own'. The turn away from the West as a return to true 'identity' should lead to spiritual renewal, but also takes on very concrete forms. In his 2015 work 'Gold Ground Eurasia', the author Dimitrios Kisoudis applauded how under Russian President Putin 'the Third Rome has turned from esoteric to exoteric state doctrine' (Kisoudis 2015: 49). Like Dugin, he wants Germany to be on Russia's side in the future and writes that the latter sees 'a geopolitical confrontation between Eurasians and Atlanticists [...]. Projected onto the ideological level, this is supposed to be a confrontation between traditionalists and liberals' (ibid.: 66). In addition to the idea of Russia as a conservative protective power, Kisoudis is also particularly motivated by Dugin's recourse to 'German masterminds' of the 1920s (ibid.: 62). Kisoudis is the author of various publications of the New Right and a long-time collaborator of the AfD, so his preference for this classical canon is no trifling matter. In March 2022, shortly after Russia's invasion of Ukraine, he became AfD leader Tino Chrupalla's policy advisor, which can be seen as a clear commitment by the party to a Eurasian orientation with all its historical references. During the Ukraine war, other senior AfD politicians such as Björn Höcke and Hans-Thomas Tillschneider have further affirmed this worldview. They want Germany's place to be by Russia's side in the fight against 'decadent liberalism' and the 'rainbow empire' of the US-led 'West'.[7]

Even the US 'Alt-Right' deals with this canon. An example of this ideology transfer is the distribution of an English edition of Armin Mohler's bibliography on the 'Conservative Revolution', the foundational work of the New Right, with an afterword by Alain de Benoist. Nina Kourprianova, who has also served as Dugin's translator, was involved in the edition (Mohler & Weißmann 2018). Thus, the counter-revolutionary cultural ideas of the 'own' adapted from the 1920s are inspiring New-Right currents worldwide today.[8]

---

[7] See the speech of AfD politician Björn Höcke at a 'peace demonstration' on 3 October 2022 in Gera (https://www.youtube.com/watch?v=mgAB46ny5_g/) and the report on the founding of the AFD-affiliated German-Russian friendship association 'Ostwind' at Elsässer 2023.

[8] An overview of the Alt-Right's ideological transfer and text translations is provided by Vandiver 2018.

3. THE SUBSTANCE OF THE 'OWN'

However, the establishment of a binding cultural destiny does not definitively solve the problem of belonging. To this day, the internal debates of the New Right have not created any final clarity as to whether 'identity' is primarily culturally or ethnically produced, or to what extent these are themselves already interlocked. There is, however, a consensus that nationality alone can no longer be a criterion in the age of citizen nations.

Fabrice Robert, a founding figure of the French 'identitarians', stressed to the New Right weekly *Junge Freiheit* why his movement fights for more than a 'national identity' based on citizenship. Rather, they 'stand up for the bodily-generative identity (i.e. the regional), the historical (the French) and the civilisational (the European) identity' (Schwarz & Brilla 2013). Therefore, in his eyes, even a law-abiding, perfectly French-speaking French citizen of North African origin could never become French. German 'identitarians', who distance themselves from the concept of the nation because they are bothered by its potential for integration, argue similarly. Immigrants can assimilate into a nation, whereas this remains impossible within a 'community based on ethno-cultural preconditions' because it is built 'on invariable affiliation'.[9] This brings descent into play in the sense of a 'bodily-generative identity', without this having to be traced back conceptually too clearly to a bloodline.

In view of the multi-ethnic realities in Western societies, the question of affiliation is now usually answered with a mixture of different identity models. This poses a particular challenge to the definition of the 'European identity' that has been strongly invoked for several years. Johannes Poensgen (2017), author of the New-Right magazine *Sezession*, which is closely linked to the IB, first reviews this problem by invoking the race-theoretical jargon of past times: 'The example of the Algerian Muslim with a French passport' shows the 'theoretical weaknesses' of a classification based 'either only on culture or only on race.' 'From a racial point of view', an 'Algerian is white'. 'Arabs, Jews, Afghans, Pakistanis, Turks, etc.' are also 'not Mongolians and certainly not Negrids, but Europids'. But this category does not help to form a group out of the Europeans. The aforementioned are 'further away from a German [...] than [...] a Swede', but a Sicilian is 'genetically closer to an Algerian than to a Finn'. Because of these complications, genetic material alone is of limited use in assigning and forming group identities. The text continues: 'Race is real,

---

[9] See https://www.identitaere-bewegung.de/blog/warum-wir-identitaerenicht-nationalist -are/ ; see also https://generation732.wordpress.com/2013/07/21/ethnokulturelle-identitat -bewahren-fur-die-vielfalt-der-volker/ [Accessed: 25 March 2022].

and relative racial homogeneity is necessary for most political groups. But one cannot derive a person's proper group from the result of a genetic test' (ibid.).

For the right, the problem now arises that there must nevertheless be a material bond somewhere, otherwise identity could be changed at will. Anyone who assumes human viability beyond what is determined already shares the premises of the political opponent, writes Poensgen: 'The logical consequence of every anti-racism is the unlimited modifiability of every bipedal mammal' (ibid.). An orientation that disregards all bonds is ruled out. As an act of free will by autonomous subjects who can defy ethnically and culturally determined paths, such an orientation stands for the universalist counter-model. However, a concrete answer is not offered in the debate. Thus, the *Sezession* article goes on to state: '[E]ven if biology and culture together may be sufficient to understand who we are, though this puzzle can never be definitively solved, this only half answers the question of who "we", the political self-group, are' (ibid.).

The examples show that today the representatives of the far right are usually clever enough not to make a clear choice between 'spirit' and 'blood' in determining what is *one's own*. Instead of the unembellished terminology of classical racial theory, people today prefer to resort to modern-looking terms such as 'ethnocultural', in which the synthesis between the two is sought. Mostly, the terms are used according to expediency, which is facilitated by the different meanings in the change of the times. Thus, Martin Lichtmesz can write in his remarks on 'ethnopluralism' that 'the terms race, people, and culture' are 'semantically ambiguous and interchangeable depending on the context, although they do not, in themselves, denote the same things' (2020: 28).[10]

This manoeuvering between cultural and biological determination reproduces Spengler's own ambivalence on the 'race' issue (Rosenberger 2020: 137–138). For the New Right, this relative indeterminacy has the advantage of not being able to be associated with a conception of race that is linked in public memory primarily to National Socialism. However, the periodic flaring up of the debate on the 'position on race' (Spencer 2014), even in the US *Alt-Right* with recourse to Spengler and Dugin, testifies to the insecurity of one's own identity, which is not least the result of international networking.

4. EXCURSUS ON SOUL AND BLOOD

However, this problem is by no means new, as the discussion about the degree of biological influence has accompanied racist doctrines from the very beginning. The conceptual ambiguities and scope for interpretation in the con-

---

[10] In an abridged version of the text, Lichtmesz adds the remark that 'race' is a 'scorched', but 'indispensable' term (2021: 22).

struction of 'races', which serve as mimicry for today's far right, have always been present. However, as Peter Walkenhorst (2007: 102) notes regarding the German Empire, the adoption of racial categories was not affected by these ambiguities. On the contrary, although it was one of the 'most ambiguous terms of radical nationalist semantics' and had a 'broad spectrum' of 'meanings', the concept of race, during its popularisation in the late nineteenth century, was able to contribute significantly to the 'biologisation of the nation' (Walkenhorst 2007: 102).

The contradictions concerned the question what would be the ultimately dominant factor of the manifestation of 'race': Was it the spirit or the blood that prevailed? The first pre-modern considerations of 'race' were still based on the physique as a mirror of the soul. In the course of scientific progress, however, the focus was to shift increasingly to aspects of skin and blood. The mythological narrative was now replaced by one which was quasi-scientific, and an 'anthropolgical concept of race' emerged (Hund 2007: 14). Léon Poliakov (1974: 224–225) describes how, as a result of this development, 'race' was declared a determining factor and 'moving power' of history. Both emphases preserved the irresolvable link between a core essence, the external appearance, and the spectrum of creative abilities, which entailed an 'elementary connection between racism and culture' (Hund 2007: 12). The main interest of categorisation always remained the creation and preservation of a grading order, first internally and, with colonialism, also externally.

In particular, Arthur Graf Gobineau's systematisation of the concept of race as a 'historical-philosophical construction' exerted 'a considerable influence' on the German right (Breuer 2001: 49). His crucial role is attributed to the fact that he 'merged the older meanings of the concept of race with the idea of a constant development and change of 'races'' and thus softened 'the boundary between biology and history' (Walkenhorst 2007: 203). This was to have consequences. As Uwe Puschner argues, the worldview of the *völkisch* movement in the German empire (*Kaiserreich*) rested on 'two iron foundations' informed by Gobineau: the 'principle of inequality and [...] of racial predestination' (2001: 77).

Gobineau's 'Essay on the Inequality of the Human Races' offered nothing substantially new, but 'bundled anthropological, linguistic, and historical approaches into a comprehensive theory, at the centre of which was the all-explanatory concept of race' (Spitta 2013: 177). Gobineau assumed an alleged connection between the inner and outer constitution of human beings, which included culture. For example, to the description of 'Slavs', he added that their 'mental dispositions' were 'in perfect accord' with the 'external features' and had 'never ceased to sustain themselves therein'. This had limited their creative power, which is why all 'their main inclinations' had always amounted to the 'mediocre', to 'the cultivation of an undemanding, almost entirely material well-being' (Gobineau 1940: 4). According to Gobineau, the consequences could be seen even in the field of social organisation. Due to their lack of talents, the Slavs did not even manage to expand or form a nation with corresponding administrative complexes; as a consequence, they have always remained subservient to 'a power alien to their race'. The reason for this 'eternally passive position' was their 'immoderate connection with the Yellows', i.e. their Asian neighbours (Gobineau 1940: 10). According to this reasoning, inner predispositions, which cannot be escaped, determine the entire external life, right down to the sphere of social order.

Such explicitly racist conceptions of culture, of which even Spengler remained sceptical because he considered them materialistic, saw the blood-related preconditions of human beings as the basic material of culture.[11] To the field of culture they consistently transferred the belief that 'the entire physical appearance of a human being points towards his race' (Mosse 1991: 100). In their view, culture is an expression of the blood and spirit of the collective subject 'people', connected with the landscape ('blood and soil'). According to this interpretation, however, if this culture were to reach maturity in its highest form, its organic bearers would have to keep to themselves. 'Mixtures', Gobineau wrote, led to 'inevitable devaluations' (1940: 44). He interprets the blossoming and decadence of cultures as the results of 'miscegenation'.

This assumption had far-reaching consequences, for the concept of decay through 'chemical' contamination 'was to become, thanks to Gobineau, a dogma of modern racism' (1974: 229). Whereas for Spengler cultures had to remain among themselves, for Gobineau it had previously been the bloodlines. But even Spengler was not entirely free of such interpretations, since for him the death of culture in civilisation also occurs biologically. His 'ideal of the racial man is [...] the tradition-conscious peasant, firmly rooted in his soil, who leads a simple life close to nature, untroubled by history' (Rosenberger 2020: 131). With the transition to urban civilisation, decay begins, as Spengler

---

[11] On Spengler's use of the term 'race' in the contemporary context see Pöhl 2018. In general, Spengler was inconsistent on this issue, to be sure he classified peoples and nations according to 'races' to which he ascribed or denied 'youth', 'soul', and 'qualities', but he strictly emphasised: 'Race that one has, not a race to which one belongs. The one is ethos, the other – zoology' (1934: 225) ('*Rasse, die man hat, nicht eine Rasse, zu der man gehört. Das eine ist ein Ethos, das andere – Zoologie*' 1933: 161). This led to confrontations with other authors: 'Like Chamberlain, Rosenberg also criticises [in Spengler's work – VW] the lack of a biologistic theory of race, which leads to a deficiency of personality, intrinsic value, and culture-promoting impulse. Just as Chamberlain's utopia of the culture-creating Aryan was diametrically opposed to Spengler's prophecy of doom, so too was it of no use to Rosenberg's National Socialist ideology of the master race' (Rosenberger 2020: 136).

demonstrated with reference to the history of the 'city' as a place of disastrous commingling: '[G]rowing from primitive barter-centre to Culture-city and at last to world-city, it sacrifices first the blood and soul of its creators to the needs of its majestic evolution, and then the last flower of that growth to the spirit of Civilization – and so, doomed, moves on to final self-destruction' (1928: 107). Spengler thus takes up a classic motif of the *völkisch* movement: the city as a 'racial grave'.[12]

Just as Spengler insists on the *own* characteristics of cultures, Gobineau also attributes essentially different cultural characteristics to peoples and races. As an extreme example, his idea of creative Aryanism should set a precedent. According to Gobineau, the term 'Aryan' as a self-designation of prehistoric white peoples derives from 'honour'. It denotes the 'superior' and 'most beautiful of all human races' (Gobineau 1939: 187–188).

The belief in the unity of inner and outer purity, which had already driven the early physiognomic teachings, is further formulated in Gobineau's 'Aryans' in connection with cultural creative power: 'The species of man thus richly endowed with the highest physical beauty was no less superior in spirit. It had an inexhaustible sum of life and strength to expend, and the form of government which it gave itself corresponds perfectly to the needs of such an energetic nature' (Gobineau 1939: 191). In the readings that prevailed as a result of Gobineau, this myth of creative Aryanism was contrasted with the counterpart of an allegedly destructive Judaism. The 'Essay on the Inequality of the Human Races' became significant above all through its popular reception, which reached as far as the Wagner circle around H.S. Chamberlain and ultimately also flowed into the worldview of National Socialism.[13] The image was to shape the whole of anti-Semitism and finally came to a head with Hitler and Rosenberg.

What is remarkable about these conceptions of a 'racially' conditioned creative power is that they again abolish the classical categorical separation between 'culture' and 'nature'. If its conditions of development are tied to blood, culture itself becomes nature again, from which it actually had to emancipate itself in the thinking of the Enlightenment. This deprives it of any impulse to overcome and liberate itself. Modification is not possible; in culture, only what is materially determined takes place. Political systems that

---

12 See Puschner 2001: 115–119, on the connection between the city and 'racial' decay in Gobineau and Spengler, see Biddiss 1997: 92–93. For a list of the semantics that Spengler offers in the context of the separation of 'culture' and 'civilisation', see Rosenberger 2020: 132.

13 See Poliakov 1974: 255–263 and Breuer 2001: 70–71. On the on the role of the Gobineau associations and the popularisation of Gobineau by the Bayreuth Circle see also Puschner 2001: 66–82.

are oriented towards this order therefore restrict leeway and allow coercion to take its place, so as not to endanger the completion of that which is determined qua plants. 'Race', wrote Max Horkheimer and Theodor W. Adorno, 'is not, as the racial nationalists claim, an immediate, natural peculiarity. Rather, it is a regression to nature as mere violence' (2002: 138).

5. THE STRUGGLE FOR A CENSUS SUFFRAGE

More recent theories assume that 'race' is not an objective basis of racism but is first socially constructed by racism itself. Wulf D. Hund notes that racism alone is 'inadequately conceived as an interested disparagement of race'. The 'discriminatory potential' of the construct is also endowed with a 'cultural core' and has 'never been content with the blueprint of a racial hierarchy, but also related the element of deficiency and imperfection to the relations of genders, classes, and nations'. Racism, he argues, should therefore be understood as a 'social process' that 'not only has structural and ideological dimensions, but has to be produced again and again through social action' (Hund 2007: 9). So, whereas the physical reality of 'race' must always remain in the realm of the speculative, the social and cultural practice by which the order of 'one's own' is confirmed, promotes conditions whose results are then taken as evidence of racial traits.

Gobineau's 'Essay on the Inequality of the Human Races' already created a close connection between the purity of the blood and a strictly graduated social order. In the nobility he saw 'the more or less similar image of the victorious race', followed by a 'bourgeoisie formed from mongrels close to the main race' and, finally, at the end of the hierarchy, the 'people, enslaved or at least in a strongly inferior position as members of a lower human species – in the South the Negroes, in the North the Finns' (Gobineau 1940: 156–157).

This pessimistic narrative of the decline of peoples as the decline of nobility is informed by the experience of the French Revolution. Poliakov (1974: 233) quotes Gobineau's confession that he developed his worldview only to satisfy his 'hatred of democracy and of the Revolution'. Warning that 'egalitarianism threatens our identity', authors of a modernised post-war right invoked Gobineau decades ago to defend their demand for collective inequality (Krebs 1981: 22). Michel Biddiss also sees the approaches of Spengler, Chamberlain, and Gobineau as linked by the concept of a 'negative classism' (1997: 93), which sees a levelling mass society as a clear symptom of doom.

In view of this basic attitude, it does not come as a surprise that Gobineau's followers were always guided by the idea of being able to bring about an improvement in society by improving the 'races'. A new nobility was to emerge to reassemble the order disturbed by the idea of equality; 'racial' and social divisions were to correspond with each other again. For racial breeding fantasies, as they flourished up to National Socialism, Gobineau therefore served as the 'key witness' and 'progenitor of virtually all concepts of a new racial nobility' (Gies 2019: 225).

In the justification for a world order structured by the superiority and inferiority of cultures, Spengler ultimately merges his concept of the 'cultural soul' with an ethnocentric approach. For all his scepticism about modern racial doctrines, he sees the concrete danger of a 'coloured world revolution' overtaking the 'white' world, which, at the zenith of its 'Faustian' creative power, threatens to grow weak and infertile. In both *Man and Technics* (*Der Mensch und die Technik*, 1931; Engl. translation 1932) and his later work *The Hour of Decision* (*Jahre der Entscheidung*, 1933; Engl. translation 1934), he identifies the greatest threat as the uprising of the global subalterns, whom he identifies based on class and skin colour: 'The Western Civilization of this century is threatened, not by one, but by two world revolutions of major dimensions. [...] The one comes from below, the other from without: class war and race war' (1934: 204). Only a clear demarcation downwards and outwards could help against this.

Such positions are the basis for a Spengler reception by the New Right with regard to global migration and the alleged 'weakness' of Europe (Demandt 2017). In the internal right-wing literature, Spengler's *The Hour of Decision* is received as a 'manifesto of pragmatic aristocratism' and is said to be astonishingly topical. In the *Staatspolitisches Handbuch*, the authors see their own contemporary critique confirmed: 'Many of the cultural-political symptoms that Spengler addresses have only fully matured today' (Weißmann & Lehnert 2010: 128–129). Lichtmesz also emphasises the topicality of Spengler's interpretation in times when migration by the 'West' is hardly opposed any more and Europeans are talked into having a bad conscience because of colonial crimes. He approvingly quotes Spengler's lament of the white decline: 'The white master nations have descended from their former rank. They negotiate today where they commanded yesterday, and tomorrow they will have to flatter in order to be allowed to negotiate. They have lost the consciousness of the self-evidence of their power and do not even notice it' (Lichtmesz 2020: 209).

In its original version, this Spengler quote used by Lichtmesz goes even further. It emphasises the role of 'Moscow' in this attack on 'white' supremacy, since in 'Russia in 1917 both revolutions, the white and the coloured, broke out together' (Spengler 1934: 211). With this reference, Spengler wants to stress once again the connection between the cultural and political fate of the world. For him, the uprising of the proletariat goes hand in hand with the decline of Europe.

Spengler's requiem for white culture can be seamlessly integrated into the current main narratives of the New Right, the 'Great Exchange', and the 'Great Reset'.[14] These campaigns to displace 'indigenous' Europeans through migration, allegedly carried out by 'globalist elites', reveal the true identity-destroying nature of 'globalism' and liberal democracy. It is not a peace order, but rather leads to the final dissolution of the Western world. Lichtmesz drastically describes this scenario 'as a slow, decades-long ethnic cleansing, a "molecular civil war", a "death of a thousand cuts"' (2020: 295). The 'identitarian' policy is therefore the last chance to concretely preserve the European peoples with their culture. This expectation of an escalation has been widespread in the neo-right milieu for decades; as early as the beginning of the 1980s, Pierre Krebs wrote: 'The year 2000, as the pivotal point of two millennia, will undoubtedly also be the crossroads of two worldviews: universalism or ethnopluralism, the doctrine of equality or the doctrine of differentiation, resignation to the levelling process or the right to diversity' (1981: 17).

The next step in identitarian thinking is to declare universalism itself to be ethnic particularism since its emergence will also have to be traced back to a certain basis. Thus Lichtmesz (2021: 23–24) writes that the advocates of universalism 'do not realise that their conceptions of values stem from a historically as well as genetically determined particularity and thus cannot have an absolutely universal validity'. This would already limit the possibility of the Enlightenment itself to members of the European peoples.

This leads to the further question of how this worldview affects the concrete social and political ideas of the New Right. Benoist's remarks on Spengler, quoted at the beginning of this chapter, make the points of contact clear for a New Right diagnostics of time: 'Civilisations merely represent their last, degenerate and solidified forms. While cultures as natural, organic forms are characterised in particular by the persistence of "original landscapes", the "world city" is predominant in civilisations. Size and scale work against the quality of life there. The cultural soul disappears. Massification produces powerlessness. Society exists, but it no longer lives' (Benoist 1983: 190).

In the eyes of today's Spengler epigones, this stage has long since been reached; that is why the heroic task of maintaining the lost position falls to them, as guardians of identity. For them, both cultural decay and immigration are closely linked to the modern claim to equality, which has permanently damaged the culture's defences against pernicious influences. It is therefore only logical that they want to counteract 'massification' and establish a model of society based on opposing premises. Here, too, they do not deviate from

---

[14] The formula of the 'great exchange' comes from the French author Renaud Camus, whose tract *Revolt against the Great Exchange* was published in German translation by Antaios Verlag in 2016. At the same time, the motif served the 'identitarians' as a campaign theme (see Sellner 2017). An integration of the various theorems into a comprehensive worldview is attempted by Dugin 2021; see Weiß 2021.

their historical models, since ethnic and political threats already merge in Spengler's diagnosis.

How Spengler's New-Right epigones today are inspired by his rejection of all kinds of egalitarianism and universalism is clearly evident from Martin Lichmesz's presentation of 'ethnopluralism'. He summarises Spengler's cultural theory for New-Right readers: 'The upper culture-creating classes are the bearers of national consciousness and constitute the actual people. A Culture-people [*Kulturvolk*] which is coincident with "all" does not exist. The nation exists in the will of its elites. When this destiny is exhausted, peoples continue to exist at best as dehumanized fellahs' (Lichtmesz 2020: 206). In this worldview, the existence of culture can only be guaranteed if everyone remains in their places determined by fate and descent. Every self-proclaimed elite can identify with this finding, regardless of whether they derive their sense of status from cultural, ethnic, or economic superiority.

Ultimately, this leads to questions of social organisation and division. In times when the 'healthy' stratification of society is disturbed, the reintroduction of income-based electoral rights for the higher estates is considered a tried and tested remedy in the circles of the New Right, for example along the lines of the three-class Prussian census-based electoral system that was in force until 1918. In addition to the traditionalist touch, such a restriction of electoral rights would both take into account the meritocratic ideology popular in the milieu and, at the same time, benefit state authority. In a 2015 discussion volume, Torsten Hinz, author of the weekly *Junge Freiheit*, stressed that 'we would need the three-class franchise [*Dreiklassenwahlrecht*] right now'. The income-based re-assessing of electoral votes is considered quite soberly, since '[i]n Berlin, where welfare recipients outvote taxpayers, [...] no sensible financial policy, nothing sensible at all can be made any more' (Kositza & Kubitschek 2015: 110). For the discussants, there is no question that modernity is characterised by a 'rule of the inferior' (Kositza/Kubitschek 2015: 22). With this reference, it once again becomes clear which sources the New Right milieu draws upon for its diagnosis of the times. In 1927, the German jurist and Mussolini admirer Edgar Julius Jung described Weimar democracy as a 'rule of the inferior'.[15]

---

[15] In the *Staatspolitisches Handbuch* published by the Institut für Staatspolitik, Jung's writing is listed as a 'key work' of his own thinking. Accordingly, it is to be considered 'alongside Arthur Moeller van den Bruck's *Das dritte Reich* (1923) and Othmar Spann's *Der wahre Staat* (1921)' as 'one of the most influential books of the Conservative Revolution' (Lehnert & Weißmann 2010: 117). Jung and Spengler were definitely close; Jung, like Spengler, was an author for the *Deutsche Rundschau* and invited the latter to lecture at his young conservative club in Munich (see Magub 2017:

Oswald Spengler also saw 'that the Estates have a natural build which in its evolution and action forms the basic structure of every Culture's life-course' (1928: 347). Their existence only guaranteed nobility, bond, race, and rank; with modern civilization's democracy, this order had come under threat.

'The change sets in as soon as, with the great city, the Non-Estate, the bourgeoisie, takes over the leading role. [. . .] The powers of intellect and money set themselves up against blood and tradition' (1928: 448–449). These 'powers', however, were unquestionably superior to the masses and would immediately endanger the sovereignty that had only just been achieved: 'The more nearly universal a franchise is, the less becomes the power of the electorate. [...] The more radical the political elimination of the matured old order of Estates and callings, the more formless and feckless the electoral mass' (1928: 455–457). In order to form an actual political power, the gradation of the electorate was the best means of counteracting its degeneration into an amorphous and ultimately powerless mass.

Measures to undermine the still juvenile system of universal suffrage were widespread in Spengler's time. Friedrich August von Hayek, for example, an author who his reader Max Otte feels indebted to, also flirted with such models.[16] He advocated to withhold the franchise from groups of the population directly dependent on state payments – that is, recipients of social benefits, but also civil servants (see Hayek 2005: 135–137). Even today, similar plans for the political disenfranchisement of the precariat are championed, for instance, by the gold trader Markus Krall, who repeatedly appears alongside Max Otte. In his treatise for a 'bourgeois revolution', Krall demands:

> Every voter should be allowed to choose between exercising his right to vote and the right to receive state transfers. [...] Anyone who receives money from the state, and thus from his fellow citizens and fellow voters, whether as a citizen or in the form of social transfers or as an entrepreneur in the form of subsidies, does not go to the polls. If he decides to vote and against transfers, he cannot receive state transfers for the duration of the legislative period. (2020: 233)[17]

84 and 97). There were also influences on Jung from Gobineau's worldview (see ibid.: 250).

[16] In recent years, the Friedrich A. von Hayek Society has repeatedly been rocked by controversies surrounding some prominent AfD members in its ranks, which led to the resignation of a significant number of members (see http://www.erklaerung-leipzig.de). Otte was a keynote speaker at the award ceremony for the Hayek Prize in Münster (2018) and a speaker at the Hayek Club Berlin. See https://hayekclubmuenster.wordpress.com/2018/06/21/hayek-preis-zu-muenster-2018/ and https://hayek.de/2018/12/prof-dr-max-otte-beim-hayek-club-berlin/, in the same year (accessed: 20 March 2022).

[17] Krall had already been invited by Max Otte to speak at the 'New Hambach Festival', where a 'bourgeois revolution' has been promoted since 2018, in appropriating the historical German democracy movement.

The systematic reproduction of this elite discourse, directed against modern mass society, leads the New Right to the anti-democratic demand for restricting franchise to the higher estates. If this approach that whoever is alimented or salaried by the state must give up their democratic rights of co-determination is taken to its final consequence, all trade union work could also be rendered impossible. By the same token, in a basically agonally structured understanding of society as an order in which the best must prevail, another element would be the abolition of women's suffrage. The New-Right author Caroline Sommerfeld, who, like Lichtmesz, is mainly present in the *Secession*, formulated this idea unequivocally. She wrote that it is in line with her 'female nature to let men decide for me'. After all, from her point of view, women's suffrage produces undesirable results: 'If men – as all electoral analyses teach [...] – vote more reasonably than women, everything is conducive to changing suffrage' (Sommerfeld 2017). In order to preserve the threatened 'cultural soul', the New Right is not only prepared to make fundamental cuts in democratic social structures but also considers such cuts to be inevitable.

6. CONCLUSION

For this understanding of culture, including the considerations of protecting one's 'own' people, it is ultimately less relevant whether 'culture' is derived from the 'spirit', the 'blood', the 'soil', or all these together. What is important are the resulting premises and their immediate implications for political demands. Accordingly, culture is the expression of a firmly shaped, supra-historical, and supra-societal identity that is not determined by its bearers but is used instead to express itself in the course of time. It goes hand in hand with a concrete form constraint that determines what belongs to 'one's own' and what does not. Culture thus becomes a fate from which both the individual and entire peoples can only escape on pain of degeneracy ('*Entartung*'). Negatively linked to this organic concept of culture is the complaint about culture-destroying 'decadence' and 'loss of identity' due to foreign influences, which is shown by the dissolution of form. Incidentally, this does not always have to follow a nationalist logic. As is currently the case with all right-wing populisms, larger entities can also be invoked: 'the white peoples', 'Europe', 'the Occident', etc. Depending on preference, the role of biological characteristics such as blood, skin colour, body shapes, etc. can be more or less linked to that of the 'spirit' or the 'soul' of peoples, races, and cultures, especially since the historical precursors to the New Right offer a great deal of latitude with regard to this question. Michael Biddiss notes, in a comparison with Gobineau and Spengler, that as late as H.S. Chamberlain, the concept of the racial figure was 'a heady cocktail of external physical qualities and inner spiritual ones' (Biddiss 1997: 84).

More important than a consistent scheme of categories is the order-creating function that lies in the determination of the comparative value of different groups and thus the safeguarding of a social hierarchy. In view of the two 'iron foundations' of *völkisch* thinking according to Puschner (2001: 77) – inequality and predestination qua 'race' – the social order is also predetermined. As a result, the 'ethnocultural' identity of Germans can only be preserved in the struggle against equality and democracy. The aim of the New Right is to build a society in which the foundations of a culture, considered essential on the basis of these premises, remain sealed from outside influence. Ultimately, the connection between 'blood', 'spirit', and 'culture' assumed in the Gobineau tradition is reactivated under the label of 'identity' and 'own'. The struggle for the 'own' as a predetermined expression of cultural identity has thus hardly changed since Spengler's time.

REFERENCES

Albrecht, Clemens (1993), 'Kultur und Zivilisation. Eine typisch deutsche Dichotomie?', in König, Wolfgang & Landsch Marlene (eds), Kultur und Technik. Zu ihrer Theorie und Praxis in der modernen Lebenswelt, Frankfurt am Main, 11–29.

Amann, Melanie (2017), Angst für Deutschland. Die Wahrheit über die AfD: wo sie herkommt, wer sie führt, wohin sie steuert, München.

Andreasch, Robert (2011), 'Geheimes Treffen auf dem Münchner Waldfriedhof', in Aida Archiv, accessed: 25 March 2022, https://www.aida-archiv.de/2011/05/20/geheimes-treffen-auf-dem-muenchner-nordfriedhof/.

Bender, Justus (2017), *Was will die AfD? Eine Partei verändert Deutschland*, München.

de Benoist, Alain (1983), *Aus rechter Sicht. Eine kritische Anthologie zeitgenössischer Ideen*, Tübingen et al.

de Benoist, Alain (1985), *Kulturrevolution von rechts*, Krefeld.

de Benoist, Alain (ed.) (2011), 'Oswald Spengler', *Nouvelle École* N° 59–60, März 2011.

Biddiss, Michael (1997), 'History as Destiny: Gobineau, H. S. Chamberlain and Spengler', in *Transactions of the Royal Historical Society*, Vol. 7, 73–100.

Breuer, Stefan (2001), *Ordnungen der Ungleichheit – die deutsche Rechte im Widerstreit ihrer Ideen 1971–1945*, Darmstadt.

Bruckner, Pascal (2020), *Der eingebildete Rassismus. Islamophobie und Schuld*, Berlin.

Bruhns, Julian, Glösel, Kathrin & Strobl, Natascha (eds) (2016), *Die Identitären. Handbuch zur Jugendbewegung der Neuen Rechten in Europa*, Münster.

Camus, Renaud (2016), *Revolte gegen den Großen Austausch*, Schnellroda.

Chamberlain, Houston Stewart (1899), *Die Grundlagen des neunzehnten Jahrhunderts*. Bruckmann, München.

Demandt, Alexander (2017), *Untergänge des Abendlandes. Studien zu Oswald Spengler*, Köln.

Dugin, Alexander (2012), *The Fourth Political Theory*, London.

Dugin, Alexander (2021), *The Great Awakening versus the Great Reset*, London.

Elsässer, Jürgen (2023), Vereinsgründung: Der Ostwind besiegt den Westwind, in: Compact online v. 31. Januar 2023, https:// www .compact -online .de/ vereinsgruendung-der-ostwind-besiegt-den-westwind/.

Fourest, Caroline (2020), *Generation Beleidigt. Von der Sprachpolizei zur Gedankenpolizei. Über den wachsenden Einfluss linker Identitärer. Eine Kritik,* Berlin.

Gies, Horst (2019), *Richard Walther Darré. Der 'Reichsbauernführer', die nationalsozialistische 'Blut und Boden'-Ideologie und Hitlers Machteroberung*, Köln.

Gobineau, Arthur Graf (1939), *Versuch über die Ungleichheit der Menschenrassen.* Zweiter Band [1853], deutsche Ausgabe von Ludwig Schemann, Stuttgart.

Gobineau, Arthur Graf (1940), *Versuch über die Ungleichheit der Menschenrassen, Vierter Band* [1855], Stuttgart.

Goetz, Judith, Sedlacek, Joseph M. & Winkler, Alexander (ed.) (2017), *Untergangster des Abendlandes. Ideologie und Rezeption der rechtsextremen 'Identitären'*, Hamburg.

von Hayek, Friedrich August (2005), 'Die Verfassung der Freiheit', in ders., *Gesammelte Schriften in deutscher Sprache, Abt. B, Bücher 3*, Tübingen, 135–137.

Heitmeyer, Wilhelm, Freiheit, Manuela & Sitzer, Peter (2020), *Rechte Bedrohungsallianzen. Signaturen der Bedrohung II*, Berlin.

Höllwerth, Alexander (2012), *Das sakrale eurasische Imperium des Aleksandr Dugin: Eine Diskursanalyse zum postsowjetischen russischen Rechtsextremismus*, Stuttgart.

Horkheimer, Max & Adorno, Theodor W. (2002*), Dialectic of Enlightenment Philosophical Fragments*. Edited by Gunzelin Schmid Noerr, translated by Edmund Jephcott, Stanford [1944].

Hubert, Peter R. (2005), 'Kulturtheorie und Kulturkonflikt', in: *Sezession, Sonderheft Oswald Spengler (Mai),* 13–18.

Hund, Wulf D. (2007), *Rassismus,* Bielefeld.

Jung, Edgar J. (1927), *Die Herrschaft der Minderwertigen. Ihr Zerfall und ihre Ablösung*, Berlin.

Kisoudis, Dimitrios (2015), *Goldgrund Eurasien. Der neue Kalte Krieg und das Dritte Rom,* Leipzig.

Kositza, Ellen & Kubitschek, Götz (eds.) (2015), *Tristesse Droite. Die Abende von Schnellroda*, Schnellroda.

Krall, Markus (2020), *Die Bürgerliche Revolution. Wie wir unsere Freiheit und unsere Werte erhalten*, Stuttgart.

Krebs, Pierre (1981), 'Weltanschauung, Gedanken zu einer kulturellen Wiedergeburt', in ders. (ed.), *Das unvergängliche Erbe. Alternativen zum Prinzip der Gleichheit,* Tübingen, 13–31.

Laruelle, Marlene (2006), 'Aleksandr Dugin: A Russian Version of the European Radical Right?', in *Kennan Institute Occasional Papers*, No. 294, 7.

Lehnert, Erik & Weißmann, Karlheinz (ed.) (2009), *Staatspolitisches Handbuch, Band 1: Leitbegriffe*, Schnellroda.

Lehnert, Erik & Weißmann, Karlheinz (ed.) (2010), *Staatspoltisches Handbuch, Bd. 2: Schlüsselwerke*, Schnellroda.

Lepenies, Wolf (2006), *Kultur und Politik. Deutsche Geschichten*, München/Wien.

Lichtmesz, Martin (2020), *Ethnopluralismus. Kritik und Verteidigung,* Schnellroda.

Lichtmesz, Martin (2021), 'Klarstellung über den Ethnopluralismus', in *Tumult, Vierteljahresschrift für Konsensstörung* (Sommer 21), 21–24.

Magub, Roshan (2017), *Edgar Julius Jung, Right-wing Enemy of the Nazis. A Political Biography,* London.

Mohler, Armin & Weißmann, Karlheinz (2018), *The Conservative Revolution in Germany*, Whitefish MT.
Mosse, Georg L. (1991), *Die völkische Revolution. Über die geistigen Wurzeln des Nationalsozialismus,* Frankfurt am Main.
Müller, Mario Alexander (2017), *Kontrakultur*, Schnellroda.
Otte, Max (2011), 'Das Zeitalter der Cäsaren. Weltbeamte, Freihändler, Milliardäre: Oswald Spenglers Schicksalsfragen und düstere Prophezeiungen sind von bestechender Aktualität', in *Junge Freiheit* vom 6. Mai 2011, 16.
Pähler, Alexander (2021), Kulturpolitik für eine pluralistische Gesellschaft. Überlegungen zu kulturellen Grenzen und Zwischenräumen, Bielefeld.
Pöhl, Friedrich (2018), 'Oswald Spenglers Rassebegriff im Kontext seiner Zeit: Boas, Chamberlain, Lenz, Rosenberg, Sombart', in Fink, Sebastian & Rollinger, Robert (eds.), *Oswald Spenglers Kulturmorphologie. Eine multiperspektivische Annäherung*, Wiesbaden, 643–674.
Poensgen, Johannes (2017), 'Wer sind wir? Wer sind 'Wir'?' (3), in: Sezession im Netz v. 16. März, accessed 25. März 2022, https://sezession.de/57029/wer-sind-wirij-wer-sind-wirij-3.
Poliakov, Léon (1974), *The Aryan Myth. A History of Racist and Nationalist Ideas in Europe*, New York.
Puschner, Uwe (2001), *Die völkische Bewegung im wilhelminischen Kaiserreich. Sprache, Rasse, Religion*, Darmstadt.
Rosenberger, Sebastian (2020), 'Oswald Spenglers 'Der Untergang des Abendlandes'. Eine völkische Geschichtsphilosophie?', in Fahlbusch, Michael, Haar, Ingo, Lobenstein-Reichmann, Anja and Reitzenstein, Julien (eds.), *Völkische Wissenschaften: Ursprünge, Ideologien und Nachwirkungen*, Berlin, 118–139.
Schröter, Manfred (1949), *Metaphysik des Untergangs. Eine kulturkritische Studie über Oswald Spengler*, Munich.
Schwarz, Moritz & Brilla, Luise (2013), 'Das Beste kommt noch', Gespräch mit Fabrice Robert, in *Junge Freiheit* 10 v. 1. März, 3.
Sellner, Martin (2017), *Identitär! Geschichte eines Aufbruchs*, Schnellroda.
Semsrott, Arne & Jakubowski, Matthias (2021), *Desiderius-Erasmus-Stiftung. Politische Bildung von Rechtsaußen.* OBS Arbeitspapier 51, Frankfurt am Main.
Sommerfeld, Caroline (2017), 'Zivilisationsrettung - Phylomasochismus', in: *Sezession im Netz* v. 17. July, accessed: 25. March 2022, https:// sezession .de/ 57327/ zivilisationsrettungij-phylomasochismusij.
Speit, Andreas (2016), *Bürgerliche Scharfmacher. Deutschlands neue rechte Mitte – von AfD bis Pegida,* Zürich.
Spencer, Richard B. (ed.) (2014), 'The real Dugin', *Radix Journal* v. 30 August 2014, accessed 25 March 2022, https:// radixjournal .com/ 2014/ 08/ 2014 -8 -30 -the-real-dugin/.
Spengler, Oswald (1926), *The Decline of the West, Volume 1: Form and Actualuty.* Authorized Translation with Notes by Charles Francis Atkinson, New York [1918].
Spengler, Oswald (1928), *The Decline of the West, Volume 2: Perspectives of World-History.* Authorized Translation with Notes by Charles Francis Atkinson, New York [1922].
Spengler, Oswald (1932) *Man and Technics. A Contribution to a Philosophy of Life.* Translated by Charles Francis Atkinson, New York and London [1931].
Spengler, Oswald (1934) *The Hour of Decision, Part One: Germany and World-historical Evolution.* Translated by Charles Francis Atkinson, London [1933].

Spitta, Juliane (2013), *Gemeinschaft jenseits von Identität? Über die paradoxe Renaissance einer politischen Idee*, Bielefeld.

Umland, Andreas (2019), 'Alexandr Dugin. Kreuzzug gegen den Liberalismus und Verbindungen nach Deutschland', in Zentrum liberale Moderne (ed.), *Das alte Denken der Neuen Rechten. Die langen Linien der antiliberalen Revolte*. Berlin, 109–119.

Vandiver, Josh (2018), 'The Radical Roots of the Alt-Right.' *Political Extremism and Radicalism in the Twentieth Century,* Cengage Learning (EMEA) Ltd, https://www.gale.com/intl/essays/josh-vandiver-radical-roots-alt-right.

Walkenhorst, Peter (2007), *Nation – Volk – Rasse. Radikaler Nationalismus im Deutschen Kaiserreich 1890–1914,* Göttingen.

Weiß, Volker (2015), 'Die ‚Konservative Revolution. Geistiger Erinnerungsort der Neuen Rechten', in Langebach, Martin & Sturm, Michael (eds), *Erinnerungsorte der extremen Rechten.* Wiesbaden, 101–120.

Weiß, Volker (2017) *Die Autoritäre Revolte. Die Neue Rechte und der Untergang des Abendlandes*, Stuttgart.

Weiß, Volker (2021) 'Gemeinsam gegen den 'Great Reset' Synergien zwischen Neuer Rechter und Corona-Protesten' in Benz, Wolfgang (ed.), *Querdenken. Protestbewegung zwischen Demokratieverachtung, Hass und Aufruhr*, Berlin, 214–229.

11. Left-wing identity politics as a driver of authoritarian developments

Bernd Stegemann

1. ON THE DIFFERENCE BETWEEN RIGHT-WING AND LEFT-WING IDENTITY POLITICS[1]

As different as the motives and worldviews of right-wing and left-wing identity politics are, they have fundamental parallels in their political methods. In order to make political capital out of the fault lines in society, both use the resentment of those who do not feel sufficiently recognised. The answer of right-wing identity politics consists in the old recipes of the *Volksgemeinschaft* and the nation. The responses of left-wing identity politics are more contradictory, combining the assertion of a recognisable identity with the theories of deconstruction. Right-wing identity politics assumes an intrinsic, natural identity. Left-wing identity politics combines the deconstruction of all identities with the assertion that certain constructions have a quality of their own. The quality is supposed to consist in the fact that these identities are constructed but nevertheless have an 'actual' core. The political claim of a contingent and at the same time essentialist identity makes the method of left-wing identity politics more analytically demanding than that of the right. But it is not only more complex in the way it constructs identities; it is also incomparably more compatible to a neoliberal public sphere.

Since left-wing identity politics harmonises well with the zeitgeist of a capitalist society, its authoritarian tendencies are much harder to discern. The contingency of identity is not only woven into the fabric of the general atomisation of social bonds, but its promise of progress also seems to correspond to the life plans of singularised subjects. An ideological tendency is all the more difficult to recognise the more closely it is interwoven with the dominant currents of the time. This explains why the authoritarian features of left-wing identity politics

[1] This text is based on numerous publications that the author has written on the subject in recent years, above all *Identitätspolitik*, published in 2023 by Matthes & Seitz, Berlin.

are analysed far less critically than the historically better-known aggressions of right-wing identity politics. Left-wing identity politics, because it seems to correspond to the prevailing values, gives less of an impression of authoritarian politics and therefore experiences less critical opposition.

The thesis to be elaborated in the following is that there is a difference between the political-moral goals of left-wing identity politics and the methods it uses. The methods have a tendency towards authoritarian constrictions that show more affinity with right-wing identity politics than the actors seem to be aware of and is helpful for their moral intentions.

2. THE PARADOX OF LEFT-WING IDENTITY POLITICS

A momentous guide to the construction of identities has been provided by Gayatri Spivak in her globally acclaimed essay 'Can the Subaltern Speak?' (Spivak 2008). The title poses a provocative question, which is answered with an equally provocative 'no' in the text. Her study takes as its starting point the case of an Indian widow who, after the death of her husband, is supposed to agree to her own cremation in order to comply with Indian tradition. The dilemma now is that saying no to her own cremation would not only be a protest against Indian tradition, but would also be in line with the logic of the colonial power, England, which rejects the inhuman tradition of widow cremation. The widow is thus faced with the dilemma that in order to save her own life, she must submit to the logic of the colonial power. This leads Spivak to realise that multiply oppressed groups of people have no language of their own. They can only choose between different forms of oppression, from which it follows that they have no possibility to speak for themselves.

The way out that Spivak then develops has been a serious predicament for left-wing identity politics ever since. She recommends a sophisticated combination of factual and counterfactual thinking, which she calls 'strategic essentialism'. By this she means that the oppressed group must first strengthen its own identity in order to even achieve its own ability to speak. For example, the black civil rights movement in the USA in the 1950s, in order to become capable of protest, had to strengthen its 'black' identity. In order to achieve equality – so the thinking goes – inequality must be promoted. Thus, through Spivak's proposal, a fundamental paradox enters identity politics.

In her essay, Spivak describes the dangers that can follow from this. She emphasises that empowerment of the oppressed identity group can only be an intermediate step towards equality. In order for the difference between the oppressors and the oppressed to be overcome, it must be magnified one last time. She warns that it cannot be in the interest of the oppressed minority to assert a permanent and essential difference between groups of people. For it is precisely this assertion of 'natural' differences that is the cause of racism, which was used in the history of the USA and Europe by the white majorities to legitimise their colonial power.

Whenever strategic essentialism is used, it is therefore important to emphasise that it is a deliberate use of a dangerous method. The justification for this strategy is that, against the tradition of inequality, a new inequality is first needed in order for the weaker side to be able to assert itself at all. The danger of this method, however, is that the self-aware and convinced assertion of a special identity is not only understood as an intermediate step, but that the new self-confidence thus gained declares itself the goal of all efforts. However, if strategic essentialism becomes actual essentialism, the new group identity repeats the mistake that right-wing identity politics made in the past. The latter derived legitimacy from the conviction of its essentialist identity in order to claim different rules for itself than for everyone else.

Strategic essentialism marks the worldwide start date of left-wing identity politics. And at the same time, the developments of right-wing and left-wing identity politics diverge here. The right-wing identity politics of nations and religions claims as its origin an actual and therefore essentialist truth. It denies the fact that identity came into being at some point as well as the share of human choice in this process. The essence of right-wing identity is identical with itself. Left-wing identity politics, on the other hand, shapes the essence of its identity as a paradoxical construction. On the one hand, all actual identities are to be deconstructed (one is born as a human being and made into a woman/man). On the other hand, deconstruction runs up against limits that it does not want to cross. One is made a woman/man, but not everyone is allowed to make themselves a woman/man.

The paradoxical relationship between deconstruction and essence leads to insoluble contradictions in the debate about the concepts of 'black' and 'white'. For if 'black' means a concept of identity and does not denote the tint of skin colour, then anyone of any skin colour can call themselves 'black'. But precisely this designation is surrounded by multiple taboos in left-wing identity politics, one of which is the prohibition that a person with white skin may never call himself or herself black. Anyone who nevertheless attempts to do so is accused of the offence of 'cultural appropriation'. Here, the paradox of an identity that sometimes takes skin colour as its basis and sometimes vehemently rejects this very basis unfolds in such a way that white skin is always disadvantaged by the assessment.

While right-wing identity politics asserts an actual foundation that resists any political influence, left-wing identity politics asserts an essentialism that is sometimes actual and sometimes can be deconstructed in an act of political decision-making. The development of left-wing identity politics shows that consequential problems arise from this paradox. On the one hand, in deciding when the essentialist and when the strategic part counts, room for arbitrariness is opened. On the other hand, it becomes apparent that the essentialist part becomes more and more decisive the more often it is successful as a political argument. Thus, left-wing identity politics successively approaches the unconditionality of right-wing identity politics through the success of the share of actual identity assertions. The first burden of left-wing identity politics is thus the paradox of strategic essentialism, which leads to the problematic power of arbitrary decisions and strengthens the side of essentialism in political practice.

The second burden is a phenomenon that Nancy Fraser has called 'progressive neoliberalism' (Fraser 2013 and 2017; Lilla 2017). What is meant by this is that the questions of recognition, which are posed with particular insistence by left-wing identity politics, displace the underlying social questions. Not only do recognition politics consume more attention; they also help rent-seeking interests in their effort to replace competition in the distribution of produced surplus value with questions of equal recognition. Capitalism's positive attitude towards identity politics is explained by the simple fact that class struggle reduces returns, while a more equitable distribution of recognition costs comparatively little money. Moreover, the moralistic appearance of left-wing identity politics promises an image boost behind which capital interests can be hidden. The demonstrative display of recognition-political signals has become so profitable in the marketing of consumer goods that capital in particular has an interest in a society governed by identity politics. Progressive neoliberalism unites the various consequences of left-wing identity politics and turns them into a successful business model under the artificial slogan 'woke capitalism'.

3. THE COMMUNICATIVE MEANS OF ENFORCING LEFT-WING IDENTITY POLITICS

The identity of the victim is defined by the fact that he or she does not act, but that he or she suffers the actions of others. He or she can report this suffering with unquestionable legitimacy, which results in the special credibility of intimate communication (Luhmann 1984). The relationship between the experience of one person, which becomes a call to action for another, characterises this type of communication. The experience does not have to be a particularly threatening event, but it is enough that an everyday experience becomes the subject of communication. In the concrete situation, it is meant that one person communicates their experience and the communication leads to an empathic reaction in another person. If one person is shivering, the other can ask whether he should close the window. What is special about this communication is that the experiencer does not perform any action. The shivering is not an action, but an experience. In the communicative situation, however, this experience can become an action if the other person reacts to it as if it were an act of communication. If the shivering leads to a concerned enquiry, the experience becomes a request to enquire about one's well-being.

Intimate communication can give rise to a variety of conflicts. Both the experiencer and the responder may value their actions differently. The shivering may have been just an involuntary twitching of the body and the shiverer may then feel misunderstood if the other person understood the twitching as a request for a concerned query. Conversely, the shivering may have been meant as a sign and the shiverer would be offended if the other did not respond. The special thing about this kind of communication is that it is ignited by an event that is ambivalent. The experience of the one can be an unintentional physical behaviour, but it can also be meant as a sign waiting for a response. And on the other hand, an involuntary shiver can be understood as a demonstrative sign awaiting an obedient action, and conversely, a demonstrative shiver can be overlooked because it is only understood as an unintentional twitch. Since both possibilities are always present on both sides, communication can fail in different ways. One particular type of failure is that the other person reacts to the intimate communication with resistance: Why can't the person who is cold just ask to close the window?

The peculiarity of intimate communication is that it establishes a power structure without appearing like power communication. Recognisable power communication always exists when one side wants to limit the understanding and response possibilities of the other side. In court, for example, only statements within the rules of jurisprudence are allowed. Anyone who does not comply and, for example, disrupts the proceedings or lies as a witness, must expect penalties. The simplest form of power communication is the red light. It reduces the choice to exactly one possibility.

The power of intimate communication is incomparably more complicated. Because the experience of one person lies undecidably between action and non-action for the other, the experiencer is in the more powerful position. He alone can decide whether the other has reacted correctly or not. The essential aspect, then, is that the experiencer takes no responsibility for how the communication goes, but retains the power to evaluate it at any time. He can freely choose to present the initial shudder as an involuntary reflex that 'doesn't mean anything', or he can express his disappointment that the other did not react sensitively enough. In both cases, the experiencer is innocent because he has only experienced and therefore not acted. And in both cases, the responsibility for the correct reaction lies with the other person, who, however, cannot decide whether he or she has acted correctly or incorrectly.

The identity-political demand that the victim must always be believed is a narrowing of the rule of intimate communication to only one possible response. The ambivalence of how to interpret the experience is reduced to an act of faith. Thus, the open situation of intimate communication becomes the closed form of a communication of power. The victim identity formed by identity politics combines the quality of the inactive experiencer with the power position of the identity politics victim – a position grounded in the assumption that his or her experience is the truth for everyone else. For this new communication of victimhood to work beyond the private sphere, public communication must be transformed into intimate communication.

The powerful means by which public communication is transformed into intimate communication consists in the enforcement of double standards. For this purpose, arguments are switched from the factual dimension to the social dimension. No longer are the rules of rational discourse to apply, in which arguments are judged on their intersubjective credibility, but the speaker's position becomes the standard for the truth of what is said. In the identity-political application of the social dimension, this means that some identities are accorded a special truth, while others are fundamentally excluded from having a say. In concrete terms, these double standards mean that all victim identities enjoy a special credibility, while an identity such as that of the 'angry white man' only has a limited right to speak.

The special authority of the victim position is based on a double argumentation. On the one hand, it rightly states that victims need to be given a voice and that there are many victim groups that have not been heard for too long. The second argument is more systematic in that it uses the particular mode of speech of intimate communication as a political tool. Used in this way, the experience becomes an authority that shields itself from objections. By claiming that one's experience cannot be understood by anyone who has not experienced the same thing, the conversation becomes a monologue that allows no contradiction. The claim to power is that only the one truth is to be heard and only the one truth is to be believed.

The political intention is to gain an advantage in the hierarchy of speaker positions. If the victim's experiences are incomparable, his claims are absolutely valid. It is above all this narrowing to the one truth of the victim that leads to authoritarian radicalisation in left-wing movements. Under the acronym 'Defma' (*Definitionsmacht*), which means 'power of definition', is hidden the concrete power of double standards. Any accusation made by a woman or a member of a discriminated minority against a member of the 'powerful majority society' is considered an absolute truth (Balcerowiak 2022). The consequences of this double standard are drastic. The accused is excluded without a hearing. At the same time, he or she is required not to speak out or even defend himself to anyone. The combination of automatic conviction on the basis of an indictment, the refusal of a hearing, and the prohibition of defence contradicts all the rules that should apply in a constitutional state. Instead of the presumption of innocence, Defma applies the certainty of guilt instead of the expectation of proof of the accusation; obedience to the accuser is demanded. The argument used to reject an obligation for the prosecution to provide evidence is that the 'compulsion to prove' is always a distrust of the victim, who would be 're-traumatised' by it. This authoritarian procedure, which leads to denunciation and unjust conviction, is summarised with the slogan 'We do not act according to the rule of law, but morally' (Balcerowiak 2022).

Once a majority is convinced of the double standards, as in the cases described by Balcerowiak, a defence is no longer possible. This radical form of left-wing identity politics, in gaining such incontestable power, it negates not only the equality that the rule of law is supposed to guarantee, but also the basic human characteristic of empathy. The ability to empathise with the other is rejected and replaced by the demand that everyone submit to the experience of the victim.

But what is this submission based on if the ability to empathise has been ruled out in advance? Those who cannot put themselves in another person's shoes will not empathise with the victim's monologue. In this respect, identity politics abuses the willingness to recognise the suffering of others by denying the recognisers their ability to empathise and at the same time demanding submission to the experience of others. It disenfranchises people by refusing to experience others' feelings vicariously and instead forces them into a position where they are only allowed to listen silently. In this way, the identity-political application of intimate communication turns fellow human beings into subordinates and empathisers into recipients of orders.

The more the power of authoritatively formed intimate communication asserts itself and the more unchallenged the speaker position may decide on the legitimacy and truth content of statements, the more irreconcilably the contradictions are fought out. The principle that the progress of a debate should be determined by the unconstrained compulsion of the better argument – which represents a civilisational achievement – is replaced by the new hierarchy of speaker positions. It is no longer the argument that is decisive, but the position of the person who says something that determines whether he or she is believed or even heard.

As power shifts from the argument to the speaker position, the nature of argumentation also changes. The focus is no longer on the counter-argument or the refutation of the factual statements, but on the defamation of the other speaker's position. Whoever succeeds in portraying the other as morally evil has an unassailable advantage. This shift from argument to defamation explains the aggressive tone in social networks, where the destruction of the other and the cultivation of one's own good image consume the overwhelming majority of attention. The unleashing of the 'shitstorm' finds its breeding ground in the archaic willingness to come together as a mob. Its frequent use, however, is explained by the fact that the speaker position has taken the position of the better argument.

The term 'cancel culture' is used to describe the structure that results from this shift. What is meant by cancel culture is the conversion of communication from argumentation to defamation. It is no longer a matter of publicly contrasting the pros and cons, but of determining who may be heard publicly at all. The preferred means of the cancel culture is therefore defamation, which leads to the public image being so damaged that the person is no longer allowed to be heard. The more often cancel culture is successful, the more it changes public communication. Because with every act of cancelling, the fear of being publicly humiliated and defamed spreads; the more people become afraid of this, the more they withdraw from the public space and leave it to those who share the same opinion. This is how homogeneous sub-areas of the public sphere are created, in which it is no longer the argument and the relevance of the issues but the image of those involved that decides what can be publicly negotiated.

4. IDENTITY-POLITICAL ATTACKS ON UNIVERSALISM

Left-wing identity politics not only reconstructs the mode of communication; it also attacks universalism on an ideological level. To do this, it draws a connection from its historical genesis to the validity of its regulative idea. If one looks at the historical development of universalist ideas, it is obvious that, in addition to their progressive agenda, they have also been used to justify inequalities. For example, bourgeois liberal societies have not only tolerated but promoted the inequalities of capitalism. And the white societies of Europe and the USA have long limited universalism to the colour of their own skin, from which they have derived a legitimacy to enslave and colonise other people. Criticism of universalism is therefore necessary and belongs to the development of an enlightened society.

The identity-political critique of universalism, however, starts at the foundation by failing to recognise that historical misuse is not a sufficient objection to the regulative idea of universalism. That a regulative idea is misused does not disprove the value of that idea. Nevertheless, identity politics uses historical mistakes to turn the universal idea into a partisan doctrine of white people.

The consequences of such an attack seem to be underestimated by the representatives of identity politics. For on what basis should the claims of minorities be formulated if there is no agreement that the same rights should apply to all? If each interest group wants to impose its own standards for a good society, a conflict arises that takes place on two levels at the same time. For then there is not only a negotiation about the respective clash of interests, but also a dispute about which interests are entitled to become the subject of negotiation in the first place. This meta-debate determines communicative behaviour in social networks. Here, the right of other opinions to be heard is questioned just as often as it is pointed out which group has not been heard enough.

The dangerous consequence of the attack on universalism is thus that its validity is already destroyed the moment it is challenged. By rejecting the possibility of empathic understanding, an unbridgeable chasm opens up between people. When no one is allowed to understand the other because they have a different identity, every identity becomes an island. And by evaluating universalism as a partisan opinion, every defence of universalism is devalued into a partisan argument.

The regulative idea of universalism is a fragile invention. It demands a high degree of humility: everyone must refrain from the attempt to make his or her own needs the standard for all others. And it presupposes that everyone practices hermeneutic benevolence. This means that everyone tries to understand what the other person might have meant. Both empathy and benevolence are rare commodities in a public inflamed by identity politics. Instead, suspicion and condemnation prevail. As in a class society, the identity of the speaker decides what value a statement has. And the degree of indignation becomes a weapon with which particular demands are enforced. If the public climate is poisoned by aggressive defamation, it becomes increasingly difficult for the representatives of universalism to uphold the civilisational achievements of empathy and the informal compulsion of the better argument.

The identity-political attack on universalism is momentous because it works in two directions at once. On the one hand, the validity of universalism is already weakened by the claim that it is only a particularism of 'angry white men'. And secondly, the foundation of equality is destroyed when mutual understanding is restricted. How can equality between different claims be established at all if the assertion that no one can understand the situation of the other prevails?

The strategies of anti-universalism lead to quick successes in terms of identity politics, because they quickly facilitate an erosion of the belief in universalism, which allows every vocal interest group to impose its new rules. But in doing so, particularism saws away at the branch that its demands for recognition are sitting on. For which authority will they turn to when there is no longer any universal authority, but society consists only of groups pursuing their own interests?[2]

---

[2] This is the question posed by Jürgen Habermas, who therefore rejects the method of identity politics, as it leads to a battle of all against all with no referee. See Stegemann (2021: 39).

5. CONSEQUENCES FOR THE FREEDOM OF COMMUNICATION

The new particularism and the escalation of contradictions into enmities in which morally charged parties confront each other is also reflected in a regressive understanding of language. One could call this regression the return of a magical understanding of language, because it is characterised by the fact that a word is supposed to have an immediate effect regardless of its context. A magical understanding of language ascribes an ineluctable performative effect to certain words. Just as curses, blasphemies, or magic spells once did, words are now supposed to have an immediate power of action. This language magic ignores not only the context-dependency of performative speech acts but also the insights of twentieth-century sign theories.

The concrete consequence of the new language magic is that no distinction is to be made any more between the actual use of a word and the many varieties of inauthentic speech such as irony, quotation, or the language of dramatic role-playing. In enlightened societies, this indiscriminate taboo is only known in the case of political signs such as the swastika or in certain areas of religion where believers are not allowed to pronounce the name of their god.

That words should have a magical effect is a characteristic of pre-modern thinking. Turkish President Recep Tayyip Erdoğan openly admitted this in an interview. His revealing answer to the question why so many journalists were imprisoned sums up the authoritarian character of language-magical thinking: 'In my opinion, he [the journalist who interviews a terrorist] is someone who supports the terrorist because he knows that this person is a terrorist. If you print the thoughts of a terrorist in your publication, what is that? That is the publication of terrorism itself' (di Lorenzo 2017).

Using the same logic, a *New York Times* editor was fired for using the 'N-word' within a quote during a study tour (Pfister 2021). For language-magical thinking, the fact that the bad word was framed in a quotation does not change the fact that it was uttered. In this understanding of language, a word always has the same value regardless of its context, so it is not a sign whose context decides its designation and performativity, but rather a magical object.

This regressive understanding of language has far-reaching consequences for communication. It was language-magical thinking that caused the longest period of censorship of the theatrical arts in their 2,500-year history. Only in the twentieth century and, in Germany, only after 1945, can the performing arts be called free. Unfortunately, this recently won freedom seems to have less and less meaning for the theatre-makers themselves, who are proving themselves to be attentive students of identity-political methods. In large parts of the theatre scene, language-magical thinking and double standards are now part of the firm canon of faith. Thus, in the small section of society called 'theatre', the concrete consequences of cultural regression can be observed vividly.

The furore of artists moved by identity politics is rapidly unwinding the hard-won freedoms of theatre and film. The achievements of making a distinction between role and actor seem superfluous, and it seems to have been forgotten that, not long ago, female actresses were put in the same category as prostitutes. Even at the end of the nineteenth century, it was difficult to find an actress who wanted to play the role of Nora in Ibsen's drama of the same name, because every actress feared for her reputation if she played such an 'emancipated' woman.

The identity-political theatre makers want to roll back this freedom. Their dogma is that the speaker's position determines the truthfulness of the statement. If this dogma is transferred to the performing arts, it follows that there should again be a direct link between the actor's private identity and his role. This calls into question the fundamental freedoms of theatre: the actor no longer plays but 'is' the character, and the quality of representation is no longer an artistic achievement but results from the relationship of the role to the actor's private identity. From these revenants of an archaic ideology of embodiment follow practical instructions for casting roles. From now on, the identity of the actor is to decide whether a character may be played or not. The freedoms of art that have only just been achieved seem tiresome to the identity-political theatre makers, and that is why they are issuing more and more rules to determine the casting of roles based on the identity of the actors.[3]

The driving forces of this regressive development not only deny that they are restricting the freedom of art; they feel driven by the tailwind of progress. Their argument, in the spirit of left-wing identity politics, is that the freedom of art was only a particularised freedom for a minority, and that this reorganisation is needed to establish equality. Even if one acknowledges that an intermediate step of inequality may be needed to achieve equality, the concrete consequences for artistic freedom are striking. This is because the central distinctions that characterise art in the modern era are reversed: work of art and author, as well as content and form, are once again made one. The distinction between the performer (author) and his representation (work of art) is negated. And no distinction is made any more between what a work of art says (content) and how it is shown there (form).

For the concrete theatre performance, this means that a character who utters the N-word because he is a Nazi is no longer allowed to utter this word. Since the distinction between role language and everyday language is ignored and

---

[3] A prominent and far-reaching example is the new canon of rules enacted by Amazon Studios in 2021 (accessed 12 February 2022), https://dei.amazonstudios.com.

the bad word may not be reproduced under any circumstances, it is also banned on stage. The consequence is that even the character of a Nazi on stage is no longer allowed to speak like a Nazi. The justification is that evil must not be given a stage, based on Erdoğan's premise that the representation of evil itself should be considered evil (Stegemann 2018). Following this logic, there are more and more cases where works of art may no longer be shown, characters may no longer be played, and books may no longer be published because their authors have the 'wrong' identity or the 'wrong' content is reproduced.

6. TIPPING POINTS OF IDENTITY POLITICS

By reducing universalism to the interest of white people, the accusation is made that this universalism has always been white identity politics. This accusation not only lacks historical knowledge but also inverts the regulative idea of universal equality with the logic of double standards. From this perspective, all social action collapses into a struggle. The power paradox of the identity politics method is that it justifies its struggle against universalism by claiming to address a current inequality. However, inequality can only be criticised on the basis of the normative rule of universalism. The new ideology thus wants to destroy the very standard it needs in order to be able to reject inequality.

The blind spot of the identity politics paradox thus lies in claiming that each identity should have its own truths while simultaneously basing its critique of inequality on the universal rule of equality. The more vehemently this blind spot is denied, the more the double standards tip over to the side of an identity politics activism. Here, the rules of battle apply, which only knows friends and enemies. One's own position is granted every right, while the enemy is no longer granted any rights. The struggle for equality negates the equality of people.

At the centre of the struggle is the question of which authority legitimises the new powerful victim status. Since the circular assertion that belonging to a victim group determines victim status does not establish anything, the dispute between victim discourses is insoluble. And since these discourses are subject to fluctuations of fashion, which sometimes privilege one group and sometimes another, the struggle in the pre-political space over the respective victim hierarchies is decisive (Kohlenberg 2021). Here, the group that manages to generate the most outrage has the advantage. Only those who turn the smallest occasion into a 'moral panic' can assert their victim identity. This explains the phenomenon that in societies that experience less and less discrimination, complaints about discrimination increase more and more.

The more the integration and sensitivity paradox increases, the more the defenders of universalism find themselves in a hopeless situation, because they cannot support the struggles for equality without also having to defend the idea of universalism against the activists. This double argumentation entangles them in an insoluble dilemma. For while left-wing identity politics takes the unilateral standpoint that different identity groups must be treated differently and they claim to decide the inequality conflicts 'correctly', the defenders of universalist equality must support the struggles for the particular rights of minorities and at the same time reject the consequences of undermining universalism.

As left-wing identity politics exploits this predicament to its advantage, the defence of universalism is increasingly impossible. Their method drives a wedge between the arguments for minority rights and the arguments for universalism. The aim is to discredit the arguments for universalism as evidence of the evil thinking of white societies, thus separating them from the arguments for minority rights that are beneficial to them. One side of universalism (equality) is thus assigned to the camp of evil, while the other side (the protection of minorities) is incorporated into particularism (Kendi 2020).

7. THE AUTHORITARIAN GESTURE OF LEFT-WING IDENTITY POLITICS

The authoritarian gesture of left-wing identity politics has worrying consequences for the political climate. By turning contradictions into questions of recognition and by declaring factual differences to be a proxy conflict between higher values, political debates become intractable conflicts. The civilising achievement of politics was to loosen the polemogenic tendency of morality and the reframing of factual issues to ideologies. Only when factual questions could be dealt with factually and not as a question of honour or worldview could politics reach collectively binding decisions without violence. In the present, this standard of civilisation is being abandoned more and more frequently and the old patterns of friend/foe distinctions are returning.

This regressive development of asserting one's own opinion as an absolute demand can be found in more and more policy areas. In a gesture of power, climate policy claims to represent the interests of nature, against which no human voice is allowed to object any more. Language changes are put forward with the attitude that anyone who does not go along with them automatically falls on the side of the reactionary. And particular claims for special rights are presented with a furore that no longer wants to allow any questioning. All these developments feed from the same source: the rejection of universalism. And all these developments have the same tendency: the escalation of contradictions into conflicts in which there can only be winners and losers.

The authoritarian gesture of left-wing identity politics is rooted in its method. By simultaneously justifying the political power of identity with deconstruction and uncriticisable victimhood, its method inevitably leads to double standards. And the more successful it is in asserting its special rights, the more universalism is destroyed by these double standards.

The method of paradoxical identity assertion and double standards leads to self-radicalisation through self-victimisation, which was previously considered a negative consequence of right-wing victim narratives. The authoritarian appearance of left-wing identity politics approaches the aggressive irreconcilability of historically past political styles. The willingness to compromise is judged as a betrayal of one's own mission and the possibility that the counter-argument could also be right is rejected as an insult to one's own truth.

Because left-wing identity politics seems to represent the values of liberal milieus, its methods are penetrating more and more areas of the democratic spectrum. The authoritarian tendencies that go hand in hand with this have so far been insufficiently recognised and accordingly rarely criticised. But we should know from history that politics made in the mode of identity politics loses the pacifying quality of democratic processes and gets caught up in the maelstrom of primal struggle. Thus, there is a threat of repeating a historically dangerous development, which is criticised in many ways as right-wing identity politics, but whose authoritarian work meets little resistance when it appears in the new guise of left-wing identity politics.

REFERENCES

Balcerowiak, Rainer (2022) 'Cancel Culture. Wir handeln nicht rechtsstaatlich, sondern moralisch', in *Cicero*, H.1 (28. 2.2022), https://www.cicero.de/innenpolitik/cancel-culture-wir-handeln-nicht-rechtsstaatlich-sondern-moralisch-linke-deutsche-wohnen.

Fraser, Nancy (2017) 'Eine neue Linke oder: Das Ende des progressiven Neoliberalismus', in *Blätter für deutsche und internationale Politik*, H. 2, S. 71–76. Engl. 'The End of Progressive Neoliberalism' In Dissent, 2. 1. 2017

Fraser, Nancy (2013) 'Neoliberalismus und Feminismus: Eine gefährliche Liaison', in *Blätter für deutsche und internationale Politik*, H. 12, S. 29–31.

Kendi, Ibram X. (2020) *How to be an Antiracist*, München.

Kohlenberg, Kerstin (2021) 'Bye-bye USA', in *Die Zeit* v. 18.08.2021.

Lilla, Mark (2017) 'Das Scheitern der Identitätspolitik', in *Blätter für deutsche und internationale Politik*, Jg. 62, H.1, S. 48–51. Engl. 'The End of Identity Liberalism' in *New York Times*, 18 November 2016.

di Lorenzo, Giovanni (2017) 'Sie sollten erstmal nachschlagen, was das ist, ein Diktator', in *Zeit online* v. 05. 07., Nr. 28, (Zugriff: 12.12.2021), https://www.zeit.de/2017/28/recep-tayyip-erdogan-g20-gipfel-interview?utm_referrer=https%3A%2F%2Fwww.google.com%2F/.

Luhmann, Niklas (1984) Liebe als Passion. Frankfurt am Main.

Pfister, René (2021) 'Wie die berühmteste Zeitung der Welt zu einem Haus der Angst wurde', in *Der Spiegel* Nr. 8, Zugriff: 23.03.2022, https://www.spiegel.de/ausland/new-york-times-wird-die-beruehmteste-zeitung-der-welt-zu-einem-haus-der-angst-a-00000000-0002-0001-0000-000175447385/.

Spivak, Gayatri Chakravorty (2008 [1988]) *Can the Subaltern speak? Postkolonialität und subalterne Artikulation*, Wien. Engl. in Nelson, Cary & Grossberg, Lawrence (eds), *Marxism and the Interpretation of Culture*, University of Illinois Press, Chicago 1988.

Stegemann, Bernd (2018) 'Wie frei ist das Theater noch?', in *Frankfurter Allgemeine Zeitung* v. 04. Mai, S. 11.

Stegemann, Bernd (2021) *Die Öffentlichkeit und ihre Feinde*, Stuttgart.

PART V

New role assignments, affective narratives, and media concepts of politics

12. Women, gender and right-wing authoritarian populism

Birgit Sauer

1. RIGHT-WING AUTHORITARIAN AMBIVALENCES: INTRODUCTION AND RESEARCH QUESTIONS

Although migration, integration, and Islam are central to the mobilization of the authoritarian right, over the past fifteen years, these actors have also become noticeably fixated with gender issues via their development of a new gender ideology and associated populist propaganda. Therefore, this chapter asks about which gender images the authoritarian right has mobilized from the turn of the twenty-first century and what significance "gender" has for the right-wing authoritarian political project. I answer these questions by analyzing the discursive strategies employed in programs, publications, and websites by authoritarian right-wing parties and organizations in Germany and Austria.

The emergence of authoritarian right-wing gender strategies can be contextualized within the joint mobilizations of authoritarian-right and conservative, religious, and fundamentalist actors against what they call "genderism," i.e., against the deconstructivist gender concept, gender studies, gender mainstreaming as an equality strategy, and against sexual diversity (for a critical discussion: Hark & Villa 2015; Kuhar & Paternotte 2017). This new authoritarian right-wing gender ideology differs – though not fundamentally – from the binary imageries of women and men that have traditionally dominated the extreme right; it fits into a new right-wing struggle for cultural hegemony and political power. Above all, as I will demonstrate, these new gender ideas also refer to the authoritarian tendencies of the new – often populist and antagonist – right-wing mobilization. However, this perspective complicates my initial research question, since it requires determining the authoritarian character of the parties and organizations that are commonly characterized as populist. This authoritarian character is arguably grounded in its ability to evoke the crisis, threat, and insecurity of masculinity, and the promise of overcoming it through control and sovereignty from right-wing leadership.

Gender relations and women's equality serve as starting points to highlight how the authoritarian right moderates a new conjuncture of bourgeois–patriarchal societies in Europe, an authoritarian–masculinist conjuncture. I use Stuart Hall (1987) and Lawrence Grossberg's (2019) concept of conjuncture to emphasize the *connection* between economic transformations, social and political power relations, and changes in the gender and sexuality order. Thus, I am not primarily concerned with identifying causes (e.g., economic changes and insecurities) and consequences (e.g., the strengthening of the authoritarian right), but rather with stressing the contradictions in thoroughly intertwined contemporary developments – even within the discourses and programmes of the authoritarian right. In other words: I will demonstrate how the authoritarian right wing in Germany and Austria redefine economic and social questions – especially the "women's question" – and gender equality as anti-gender and anti-migration problems. Furthermore, I will engage with how the anti-gender discourse is transformed into an argumentative "driver" of authoritarian developments (see Frankenberg & Heitmeyer in this volume).

The authoritarian masculinist conjuncture cannot be simply derived from economic or social changes and therefore needs a perspective on actors. The authoritarian right clearly translates changes in the relationship between market and state, as well as the globalization and financialization of capitalism, into anti-migration resentments and policies. However, redefining such neoliberal changes within the right-wing gender struggle, i.e., the new gender ideology, also fits into the right's struggle for the cultural hegemony and political power needed to advance its authoritarian solutions to the social and economic transformations that it perceives and (re-)interpret as crises of masculinity. Its depictions of an authoritarian masculinist conjuncture, i.e., disciplinary, hierarchical, and leader-centered "solutions" create "authoritarian temptations" (Heitmeyer 2018) and, hence, not only offer links to people's authoritarian desires but create such desires. What are the anti-democratic consequences of this reformulated gender ideology when contextualized within a new conjuncture – of gender relations and migration, as well as transformations to the economy and (paid) labor, ideas of individuality and subjectivity – but also of social cohesion and solidarity?

Furthermore, I argue that the anti-gender discourse employed by the authoritarian right in Germany and Austria is generally not anti-modern, but rather seeks to preserve the anti- or pre-modernity of gender relations as maintained in an "unfinished modernity" (Beck/Beck-Gernsheim 1995) in a thoroughly contradictory way. This contradiction in the ideas of the authoritarian right underpins how the conjuncture is established, i.e., a discursive assemblage of disparate transformations that propose and legitimize their solutions. Thus, the right not only takes anti-modern or anti-liberal approaches to gender relations and roles, but also incorporates "arch-liberal" and neoliberal views.

The authoritarian right simultaneously promotes anti- or illiberal arguments regarding certain rights, e.g., gender equality, female self-determination or recognizing of sexual diversity and LGBTIQ people. Making this picture more paradoxical, the authoritarian right of today, in its specific historical moment, seizes on the contradictions of liberal modernity, including liberal democracy, to advance its hegemonic anti-democratic and authoritarian (power) project. These actors aspire to preserve gender inequality, the separation of public and private, and sovereign white bourgeois masculinity – in other words, the liberal ideas of the eighteenth and nineteenth centuries. At the same time, the authoritarian right is also neoliberal: It simultaneously mobilizes against the sole neoliberal interpellation of women as workers by focusing on motherhood, yet also links motherhood to the neoliberal value of individual responsibility and life choices.

Next, I will use the following steps to highlight the ambivalences of the right-wing authoritarian gender project and its significance for proposed authoritarian solutions to current crises, i.e., the right-wing masculinist conjuncture. First, I outline: (a) How women and care work are situated as a problem or design flaw within capitalist modernity; and (b) the thematization of gender (in)equality by the women's movements as a critique of liberal–capitalist bourgeois modernity. This will help conceptualize the contradictory mobilization of gender by the authoritarian right in this article. Second, I will summarize the current anti-gender arguments made by the German and Austrian authoritarian right, i.e., their new gender ideology. Third, I will show liberal continuity on the one hand, and the discontinuities and the authoritarian character of the new right-wing masculinist conjuncture under neoliberal conditions on the other hand. I will conclude by briefly and critically examining the associated anti-democratic, authoritarian project.

2. THE POSITION OF WOMEN AS A BOURGEOIS–CAPITALIST CONSTRUCTIONAL FLAW: LIBERAL CONCEPTIONS OF GENDER

The alleged "women's question" has been repeatedly invoked in political modernity in line with changing economic and social constellations as well as social power relations. The gender order has always maintained certain constants to the gender order and women's positioning in the gender relations in western capitalist and patriarchal societies; for example, women's precarious involvement in gainful employment relationships, i.e., as auxiliary workers for a male wage. This is enabled through the social reproduction of society, i.e., care work, which is not integrated into the process of capitalization, value circulation, and wage labor. Hence, this work is primarily unpaid or poorly paid – and is often not even considered "work." This externalization of care work remains a constructional flaw of capitalist economy by making both social reproduction and the capitalist mode of production crisis-prone through the threat of (care) resource scarcity. Historically, this form of organizing social reproduction was successful in the Global North by feminizing such "non-work" considering it as women's work, and by separating a public from a private sphere to where care work occurs and to which staff – people identified as women – are relegated. The male breadwinner model, the housewife marriage, and the heterosexual nuclear family, which were codified and secured by law in Germany and Austria after the Second World War, institutionalize this form of the bourgeois–capitalist division of labor.

At the same time, women were to remain excluded from the public sphere to ensure their availability in managing the supposed private sphere, thereby becoming dependent on the family breadwinner (Bock & Duden 1977; Hausen 1976). Political citizenship in the Global North was restricted to men well into the twentieth century: Only men received citizenship rights such as voting, whereas women were even denied the fundamental right of self-determination over their bodies, i.e., reproductive rights. This "dispositive of separation" (Sauer 2001: 184) was legitimized through the argument of naturalness. Karin Hausen (1976) describes the invention of polar "gender characters" in the nineteenth century, namely a hierarchical gender binary that was thought to be natural.

While the ideal bourgeois woman was intended to become a stay-at-home mother and subsist on the income of the male head of the household, proletarian women were forced into gainful employment outside of the home. However, this constellation that characterizes gender relations and the position of women in patriarchal capitalism has changed quite a bit since the nineteenth century along class positions: The contemporary situation of a working class woman in Germany or Austria with a double burden of family and work is fundamentally different from that of a female university professor – who can hire a migrant woman from Eastern Europe for her two children, thus partially buying herself off from care work and devoting herself to her job. Gender relations, therefore, are always linked to class and to ethnic and national structures. Nevertheless, women, members of lower socioeconomic classes, and people identified as ethnic Others all continue to be systematically denied the same rights as white bourgeois men.

Gender relations and the regulation of social reproduction have always remained flexible and have been transformed according to capitalist necessities and economic, political, and civil society power relations. Therefore, the transformation of capitalist accumulation and the struggles and interventions of women's movements have changed the situation for women of very different class positions throughout history in the states of the Global North.[1] Bourgeois–capitalist modernity has always been characterized by women's struggles for civic rights; for citizenship; for full citizen status. Women have never wanted to be dependent on male citizens, fathers, brothers, or husbands – or only have rights derived from them. Women have been fighting for the right to education, gainful employment, and political participation – as well as for bodily self-determination – since the French Revolution. Despite this multifaceted discrimination, liberal political modernity opened up opportunities for women to claim rights, and thus for the democratization of democracy. However, women's movements have traditionally gone beyond the struggle for integration into the male world by criticizing the liberal and male notion of the citizen; the autonomous individual, who was imagined as detached from all relationality; dependency and care for other people. While it may sound unusual today, the slogan of the first bourgeois women's movement in Germany (at the turn of the nineteenth and twentieth centuries) was "spiritual motherhood," which criticized the male-centered design of society, state, and democracy (Jacobi 1990). Like today, a masculinist, anti-feminist, and authoritarian conjuncture was emerging in response to social changes and demands made by women's movements (Theweleit 2019).

Since the second half of the twentieth century, there have certainly been advances made in women's integration into gainful employment, education, and welfare state security as well as political decision-making in the Global North – although belatedly in Germany and Austria. However, "unfinished modernity" began to be partially gender-modernized from the middle of the twentieth century and liberal modernity enabled women to at least somewhat realize their claims to political, social, and cultural participation.

Starting in the 1970s with the second wave of the women's movement – and especially since the 1990s – the "women's question" has transformed into a gender question, i.e., a problem of the relationship between men and women and the problematization of the supposedly natural gender binary. This was followed by the strengthening of LGBTIQ movements and their successes in the legal recognition of homosexuality and transgender. It is precisely these transformations that have become the focus of right-wing authoritarian organizations and parties in the last decade – which, as I will show, want to re-establish the "liberal conditions" that existed before the successes of the second women's movement. Hence, their fight against what they call "genderism" often refers to "liberal" arguments about equality rights.

[1] These capitalist transformations certainly also changed the situation of women in the Global South, but my remarks are limited to transformations in the Global North.

In the following section, I will first outline the core elements or the central patterns of this right-wing authoritarian anti-gender discourse. Next, I will include reflections on the significance played by anti-gender mobilization in the authoritarian right's struggle for cultural hegemony and political power as well as for its authoritarian project.

3. THE NEW GENDER IDEOLOGY OF THE AUTHORITARIAN RIGHT IN GERMANY AND AUSTRIA

The "women's question" has always been central to the extreme right's nativist or "völkisch" project: Women, mothers, hierarchical gender binary, and the heterosexual nuclear family have remained at the ideological center of the extreme right. As mothers, women were expected to be responsible for the reproduction of the people; always linked to racist concepts of the purity of the people and the exclusion of those identified as Others (Birsl 1994; Bitzan 1997; Rommelspacher 2011). However, the "new" right has shifted its focus not only, but primarily, for strategic reasons within the framework of "metapolitics" (de Benoist 1985). They replaced explicit anti-feminist ideology with an anti-gender discourse and a new kind of gender ideology. Metapolitics, a strategic re-orientation towards the cultural dimensions of social order and people's everyday lives, is not completely new to the radical right. However, the strategic emphasis on the need to achieve political and state power through cultural hegemony implies a new orientation that is more clearly rooted in people's everyday understanding or existing everyday practices than merely enforcing norms – such as the ideal of motherhood and (aggressive) masculinity.

In order to outline this new right-wing authoritarian gender ideology, I will next discuss ten central patterns of argumentation made by the authoritarian right in their fight against the deconstructive "gender" concept (see also Mayer & Sauer 2017).

First, the pattern of argumentation emphasizes the naturalness of the gender binary. The Freedom Party of Austria (FPÖ) publishes a weekly magazine, *Zur Zeit*,[2] which by the late 1990s (i.e., before the FPÖ officially joined the anti-gender movement) was already lamenting the "lack of recognition of the biological foundation of gender difference" (ZZ 29, quoted in Geden 2004: 75, transl. BS) and praised men's public engagement as a "species-appropriate

[2] *Zur Zeit* is a weekly magazine oriented towards German nationalism that was founded in 1997; it has been edited by the FPÖ politician and former EU parliamentarian Andreas Mölzer, among others.

division of roles" (ZZ 71, quoted in Geden 2004: 76, transl. BS). The former FPÖ politician and presidential candidate Barbara Rosenkranz was one of the first right-wing politicians in Europe who, in her fight against so-called "genderism," invoked a danger wherein gender studies aspired to abolish both the naturalness of the two sexes and the unambiguous distinctness of exactly two sexes. In her book *MenschenInnen. Gender Mainstreaming. Auf dem Weg zum geschlechtslosen Menschen*[3] (Rosenkranz 2008), she emphasizes her opposition to the deconstructive notion of "gender," the supremacy of gender binarity and gender hierarchy as well as their naturalness (ibid.: 39–40). For example, she writes: "Gender theory goes far beyond the ostensibly claimed equality. It is nothing less than the attempted abolition of biologically determined genders; the end of man and woman" (ibid.: 40, trans. BS).

Second, gender studies allegedly provide destructive knowledge. The Alternative for Germany (AfD) therefore explicitly opposes gender studies in its programme (AfD 2016: 11). In recent years, the AfD overwhelmed the German Bundestag and several provincial parliaments with "parliamentary questions" about funding for gender studies at universities in hopes of proving that taxpayers' money was being wasted on unscientific projects and university programs (Mauer 2021). Likewise, in April 2015, then-FPÖ leader Heinz-Christian Strache also threatened to eliminate funding for gender studies at Austrian universities if the FPÖ were in government (Strache 2015). However, after forming a government coalition with the Christian-conservative Austrian People's Party (ÖVP) in 2017, these threats failed to materialize – not least because of the "Ibiza scandal" causing an abrupt end to the FPÖ's government participation.[4]

Third, the FPÖ and AfD, as well as other right-wing parties in Europe, align themselves with a traditional, gender-specific division of labor and its associated gender roles of the male family breadwinner and the woman serving as a mother and housewife – again, imagined as natural (Sauer et al. 2016: 113; Mayer, Sori & Sauer 2016). In this sense, the authoritarian right in Austria invokes an anti-capitalist or anti-neoliberal topos to criticize mothers' coercion into gainful employment, which prevents them from caring for their

---

3 The word "MenschInnen" is used to disparage German gender-sensitive language that uses an "I" to indicate both genders for a male word. "Mensch," which means human being/man, is a male noun; however, using the feminine gender "MenschIn" would seem absurd in German. The book title reads further: "Gender Mainstreaming. Towards a genderless man."

4 After the release of a secretly recorded video in which the then FPÖ party leader and Vice-Chancellor Strache spoke with an alleged Russian oligarch's niece about selling off Austria's largest daily newspaper, Strache had to resign and the government coalition broke up.

children and exposes them to the capitalist market, i.e., exploitative work situations without protection (Sauer et al. 2016: 112). Thus, women are no longer reduced to their purpose of biological motherhood alone in the contemporary legitimization of the gender-specific division of labor. Rather, the FPÖ stands for the "free choice" between waged work and motherhood that allows women (and clearly only women) to consciously choose to take up the role of a mother (Sauer et al. 2016: 112). In FPÖ parlance, women's freedom of choice means that they can "stay with their child themselves without financial worries" (Neue Freie Zeitung 26,[5] cited in Geden 2004: 73, transl. BS). This appeal for freely chosen motherhood has a clear nationalist slant: Women must be protected, not least because of the importance of motherhood for the nation (Mudde 2007: 92–94).

Fourth, however, Helga Amesberger and Brigitte Halbmayr (2002: 308) suggest that today the Austrian FPÖ along with other European right-wing parties follow "modernized traditional gender roles." This is similar to statements by Sarah de Lange and Lisa Mügge (2015: 63) for Belgium and the Netherlands, respectively. This model no longer confines women to motherhood and family within right-wing gender ideologies, but instead gives them permission to take up public positions in the labor market. This modernization is evident through women's notably increasing participation in right-wing parties and their claims to representation and take on leadership positions (Meret 2015). Not all of these right-wing women – such as Marine Le Pen from the *Rassemblement National* in France, Pia Kjærsgaard from the Danish People's Party, Frauke Petry, and Alice Weidel from the AfD or Giorgia Meloni from *Fratelli d'Italia* – correspond to a right-wing mother image. On the contrary, they embody a modern female lifestyle, but an ultimately masculinist type of politician (Geva 2020): They stand "their ground" in the political sphere. Whereas right-wing women have long provided support for the group or organization's social cohesion with an inward orientation, they now show an outward orientation. Hence, despite the vehement rejection of quotas by right-wing parties, these female leaders must and can assert themselves in an entirely male environment.

Fifth, this strategy of "gender modernization" thus relativizes the image of right-wing authoritarian parties as "men's parties," which can therefore be used strategically to "de-demonise" them (Mayer 2013: 161) to win over young women as supporters, voters, and functionaries (Lang 2015). Furthermore, gender modernization provides right-wing authoritarian parties with an argument for delegitimizing gender equality policies (Mudde/Kaltwasser 2012: 22). In the fight against "genderism," the FPÖ, AfD, and other right-wing

[5] The *Neue Freie Zeitung* is the weekly official party organ of the FPÖ.

organizations particularly focus their criticism on the supposedly excessive equality policy of gender mainstreaming, which they argue – unlike women's policy of the 1970s – goes too far. To them, earlier measures intended to promote women had already achieved professional equality between women and men, so there was no need for further efforts towards equality (e.g., Unterberger 2015: 148–149).[6] PEGIDA's December 2014 position paper[7] also specifically attacked gender mainstreaming, which it described as "insane" and a "compulsive, politically correct gender neutralization of our language."[8]

Similarly, the AfD programme (AfD 2016: 11) and the FPÖ's handbook for party officials (FPÖ Bildungsinstitut 2013) pursue this anti-equality policy desire. Equality is only praised if it implies an alignment of female and male lifestyles, but it denigrates and rejects any challenge towards the male systems of gainful employment or language. In April 2021, the FPÖ caucus of the Austrian parliament (*Nationalrat*) directed a "Parliamentary Question" to the Federal Minister of Education, Science and Research about the guidelines for gender-sensitive language at "schools, universities and in the field of scientific work." Like the PEGIDA position paper, the Parliamentary Question reduced gender mainstreaming to language regulations that allegedly confuse pupils and cost too much money.[9] Additionally, right-wing discourse disparages gender equality politicians, feminist academics, and successful women. By contrast, right-wing authoritarian parties in Nordic countries are more open to gender equality policies, seeing them as part of the national culture (Mayer, Sori & Sauer 2016).

Sixth, invoking equality has another strategic function: The right-wing authoritarian gender discourse in Germany and Austria is linked to anti-migration policies and a racist–exclusionary project. This discourse is intensely critical of Muslim gender inequality, unlike gender inequality within their "own" communities. Despite its emphasis on traditional notions of family and gender and their vehement criticism of gender equality policies, right-wing authoritarian discourse positions the supposed gender equality in European societies against migrants – especially against Muslim men. This pattern of interpretation is not new; the authoritarian right previously spread such nar-

---

6 Andreas Unterberger, former editor-in-chief of the liberal-conservative Austrian daily *Die Presse*, wrote this in a book released through the publishing house of Austria's short-lived, right-wing populist party *Team Stronach*.

7 The abbreviation PEGIDA (Patrioten gegen die Islamisierung des Abendlands) means "Patriots against the Islamization of the Occident."

8 See https://www.menschen-in-dresden.de/wp-content/uploads/2014/12/pegida-positionspapier.pdf (accessed 30 August 2021, trans. BS).

9 See https://www.parlament.gv.at/PAKT/VHG/XXVII/AB/AB_06294/index.shtml#/ (accessed 3 September 2021, trans. BS).

ratives as part of the "headscarf controversy" at the start of the twenty-first century. For example, during the FPÖ's 2004 election campaigns, the party put up posters stating, "Free women instead of forced headscarves" to simultaneously scandalize the oppression of Muslim women and characterize Austrian women as "free" (Sauer 2012). In the summer of 2016, this narrative was again taken up in the "burqa debates," which portrayed Muslim women as victims of "their" men and led to a ban on full-body coverings.[10]

Even if the parties differ, as Sarah de Lange and Liza Mügge (2015: 62) show using the example of Flemish and Dutch right-wing parties, evaluating one's own "culture" as equality-oriented, pro-women, and liberal is used to specifically stigmatize, devalue, and exclude Muslim migrants as patriarchal, pre-modern, and ultimately misogynistic and violent. Sara R. Farris (2017) refers to this discursive phenomenon as "femonationalism," which upgrades one's own nation to being feminist and equality-oriented. Gabriele Dietze (2016b) describes "ethnosexism," i.e., the construction of devalued ethnic groups through the argument of sexism. This strategy of "exclusionary intersectionality" (Mokre & Siim 2013: 34–36) provides new ways to present and legitimize anti-immigration policies, i.e., via discursively linking gender, religion, ethnicity, nationality, and migration. The right-wing authoritarian gender discourse thus fits into a politics of *Othering* – into a "politics of fear" of the Others (Wodak 2021) – especially Muslims, migrants, refugees, and Roma people.

Seventh, the topos of dangerous masculinities is directly linked to this strategy of stigmatizing migrants. This narrative of the threat posed by young migrant men has also long been part of the right-wing authoritarian repertoire (Mayer, Sori & Sauer 2016: 94–99). For example, the political right used reports of sexual assaults that took place in some German cities on New Year's Eve 2015/2016 to stir up resentment against Muslim migrants and refugees. One example of how the right has incorporated the visual language of the feminist anti-violence movement into its own strategies is in a video produced by members of *129 Decibels*, who are a women's group within the Identitarian movement called *Frauen wehrt Euch.*[11] The young women featured in the video use personal-sounding statements to accuse the federal German government of not protecting them against violence imported by migrant men. In response to the 2015 "Summer of Migration" (Hess et al. 2016), right-wing parties in Germany and Austria, also used this gendered argument to advocate

[10] For example, the discussions in the Constitutional Committee of the Austrian Parliament: https://www.parlament.gv.at/PAKT/PR/JAHR_2016/PK1316/ (accessed 14 March 2022).

[11] "Women fight back." See www.youtube.com/watch?v=FSXphiFknyQ/ (accessed 30 September 2021).

for stricter asylum and deportation policies (Dietze 2016a). However, criticizing structural patriarchal violence against women in European countries does not belong to the policy repertoire of right-wing authoritarian parties and organizations.

Eight, the threat scenario that uses gender as an example for the extreme right-wing trope of "feminization" (Reichel 2015: 109), i.e., a general threat to the order of Western societies through women's visibility and their increased decision-making power (see the manifesto by the extreme right-wing murderer, Anders Breivik 2011). This narrative connects to other threat and conspiracy narratives; for example, the overbearing influence that the "homo lobby" has on children and young people (Mayer & Sauer 2017: 32–33). This eighth argumentation also highlights the supposed threat of an Other sexuality, whether homosexuality (Unterberger 2015: 151) or the sexuality of male migrants. Hence, the authoritarian right uses the gender question to dramatically demonstrate a comprehensive loss of order, control, and security.

Ninth, the strand of argumentation portrays men as victims of both women and equality policies. Boys, according to the right-wing authoritarian debate, are victims of female teachers and gender equality policies in schools because they must adapt to girls' behavior, which prevents them from learning masculine values like "bravery" and "risk" (Reichel 2015: 109). Another example characterizes how fathers are victims of unjust divorce laws, which favor mothers and rob men of their children. At the same time, all men would be incapacitated as perpetrators by defamatory violence protection laws (Unterberger 2015: 152–156). The first government coalition between the ÖVP and the FPÖ in 2000 introduced immediate measures to protect men, including the Ministry of Social Affairs' establishment of a *Basic Department for Men* in 2001 and the dissolution of the Ministry for Women's Affairs. Oliver Geden calls this a "symbolic masculinisation of equality policy" (2004: 99, transl. BS). In any case, these measures were intended to devalue women's and gender equality policies.[12]

Ten, the authoritarian right uses these victimization arguments to propagate a "crisis of masculinity" with a discourse that constructs a group of masculinities as being subjugated and marginalized by equality policies and social developments (on the concept of masculinity, see Connell/Messerschmidt 2005). For example, the AfD's Björn Höcke wishes to counter this supposed crisis with a new heroic – even militaristic – masculinity. At a 2015 AfD party rally, he declared to his audience: "We must rediscover our masculinity. Because only when we rediscover our masculinity will we become manly. And

[12] The department was closed in 2020 by Social Minister Anschober (The Green party).

only when we become manly do we become defensible, and we must become defensible, dear friends!"[13]

This militaristic male bonding and reference to masculinity emerged earlier in Austria than in Germany, presumably because of the FPÖ's firm roots in fraternities and the *Cartellverband*, which is an association of Catholic reactionary fraternities. For example, the weekly magazine *Zur Zeit* appealed that "The country needs new men" (ZZ 87, quoted in Geden 2004: 76, transl. BS), which also appropriated feminist song lyrics from 1982 by the Ina Deter Band (Neue Männer braucht das Land). These "new men" should be distinguished by their "commitment to [...] homeland, people and fatherland;" they are "comrades in uniform, the nation's dress of honor, (who) take up arms and lay down their lives" (ZZ 96, quoted in Geden 2004: 78, transl. BS).

This scaremongering of a crisis of masculinity, along with Höcke's appeal to rediscover masculinity, and the FPÖ's militaristic comradeship, serve as a resovereignization of masculinity (on the term: Forster 2006), i.e., the restoration of the idea of an autonomous – but also aggressive and militaristic – male subject. In the discursive gesture about the general threat to order and the loss of control (Heitmeyer 2018: 125–128), the authoritarian right offers a proposal of self-affirmation; the self-affirmation of masculinity.

The authoritarian right actively engages in what I call "masculinist identity politics." What do I mean by this? In the neoliberal context of insecurity – in light of the threat of losing wealth or one's job – right-wing authoritarian anti-gender appeals offer starting points for re-establishing old certainties, namely traditional gender constellations and hierarchies. This is essentially a discursive offer and a remedy against masculinity that is perceived as degraded and marginalized (on the terminology: Connell & Messerschmidt 2005). Admittedly, it is also attractive to certain women: those who feel overwhelmed by neoliberal inequality, their activation to gainful employment, and lack of care infrastructure. The "reassertion" of masculinity that Björn Höcke demands and implicitly promises contains a consolidation of the hierarchical gender binary, male supremacy, and aggression. This implies the re-evaluation of masculinely coded characteristics: Höcke references "fortitude" (*Wehrhaftigkeit*), while Werner Reichel mentions the "bravery" and "risk" that men should relearn in the above-mentioned *Team Stronach* (2015: 109). At the right-wing think tank *Institut für Staatspolitik*, Marc Jongen (2017), the AfD's chief ideologue, advocates for "thymos training" in the age

---

[13] Björn Höcke at the November 2015 AfD party conference in Erfurt. See https://www.youtube.com/watch?v=dvFJiPv93gc (accessed 30 August 2021, trans. BS).

of migration, i.e., the rightful emphasis on white men's bravery, anger and aggression.[14]

Right-wing political communication simultaneously contains the promise that a charismatic–masculinized leader (who can also be a woman) can elevate these groups of male victims and provide them with new (self-)security. Moreover, femonationalist argumentations enable men in Western dominant societies to designate themselves as liberal, enlightened, and modern – distinguishing them from Muslim men (de Lange & Mügge 2015: 62). Finally, this argumentation figure is also suitable for elevating men as protectors of the women from the majority society against migrant men.

The "masculinist identity politics" of the authoritarian right is linked to its nationalist identity politics. The intended return to traditional gender relations, to a hierarchical gender binary, and to the heterosexual nuclear family; the rejection of gender equality policy and gender mainstreaming – as well as the curbing to women's reproductive rights – are all linked in right-wing authoritarian discourse to the new formation of "the people." This biopolitical reformulation of the population into an ethnically conceived people – to which those identified as Others cannot belong – requires a traditional, hierarchical gender binary. This ensures, as the FPÖ articulated, a successful reversal of the negative Austrian demographic development and against "gender madness" (FPÖ Wahlprogramm Wienwahl 2015).

4. THE STRUGGLE FOR CULTURAL HEGEMONY OF THE AUTHORITARIAN RIGHT: GENDER AS A MODE AND MOVENS OF THE AUTHORITARIAN

In order for the authoritarian right to simultaneously re-establish liberal gender inequality and reverse the "modernization" that has influenced gender relations since the second half of the twentieth century, this project – like the liberal gender project of the nineteenth and early twentieth centuries – has integrated these into the struggle for cultural hegemony and political power. Therefore, it would be politically reductive and incorrect to only accuse the authoritarian right of a women's political backlash. The far right not only aims to push women "back to the hearth" and justifies sovereign masculinity; today's right-wing responses to the gender question are also embedded in a more comprehensive cultural–hegemonic strategy of illiberalization, de-democratization, and authoritarianism. It is a modernized, anti-feminist strategy.

---

[14] Jongen refers to Aristotle, but primarily to his teacher Peter Sloterdijk (2008) and his book *Zorn und Zeit*.

In the current conjuncture, the authoritarian right has been reviving the cultural struggles of the 1960s, i.e., when questions about social equality and gender justice were given new answers and integrated into a new hegemonic compromise through Keynesian welfare state expansion – a compromise symbolized by the slogan "Dare more democracy!" As a result, gender equality experienced an enormous boost; for example, reforms to marriage and family laws that leaned more towards partnership between women and men, opening up universities and higher labor market positions for women, equality laws and quota regulations within political parties to expand political decision-making bodies for women, and the liberalization of abortion laws. In later years, these were followed by protection laws concerning violence against women and the recognition of child-rearing in old-age provision, to name just a few measures.

These equality policies have been partially withdrawn in the context of neoliberal restructuring that has taken place since the 1980s; for example, the dismantling of a redistributive welfare state; the increase in individualization and partial re-familialization of care activities for children, sick, and elderly people. However, some equality policy measures were further advanced in the neoliberal project, such as the integration of women into gainful employment while lowering or freezing family wages. However, this integration of women into the labor market was neither accompanied by a relief from care work nor the supply of public childcare and care facilities for elderly people. This remains a challenge today, especially for women who cannot hire a care worker and who are often concurrently worried about their (typically precarious) gainful employment.

The above neoliberal transformations were also accompanied by an affective mobilization against the supposedly unproductive and those who do allegedly not deserve certain (welfare) state measures – an important element of the neoliberal competition and risk repertoire. Thus, a constellation of individualization, insecurity, and desolidarization emerged. People could not emotionally cushion the consequences of how this social and economic precarization affected their everyday lives, and therefore experienced fears about jobs and income, social positions, and rights (Candeias 2016: 19); these were nevertheless still accompanied by hopes of overcoming precarization through one's own achievement. The neoliberal justification of social inequality; the subjectification as a competitive, "entrepreneurial self" (Bröckling 2016) and the establishment of law-and-order measures to enforce this subjectification – for example, through "workfare programs" – led Stuart Hall (1985: 116) to describe this constellation as "authoritarian populism" as early as the 1980s in Great Britain. The discourse of insecurity that accompanies the right-wing masculinist conjuncture like a general bass inevitably leads to policy proposals of securitization, control, and discipline. The authoritarian character of the populist right is characterized by this discursive combination of threat, loss of control, as well as insecurity and the promise of security through leadership, discipline, hierarchy, subordination, and exclusion as well as the right to (male) aggressiveness.

The moral panic around "gender" that the authoritarian right has been successfully fueling should be located in a context of the failure by mainstream parties to address social inequality. Right-wing parties have been able to seize on male disappointments and feelings of powerlessness and turn them into hatred for women, equality policies, and migrants. The authoritarian right thus capitalizes upon the ambivalent, contradictory situation created by neoliberalism (Brown 2019) and pushes contradictoriness forward. They do so, not least, through their exclusive offers of belonging based on nationality or gender in order to simultaneously establish a short-term – authoritarian – solution and stability; for example, in hierarchical gender relations. Today, the right-wing authoritarian parties discursively intensify these neoliberal processes of insecurity and overload; they reinterpret the causes of social inequality in the context of the increasing numbers of refugees from a class issue into a migration, refugee, and also gender issue. The authoritarian-right gender project proves to be ambivalent, and it fits into an equally contradictory national-social project (Balibar 2010) of exclusion and marginalization. Authoritarian right-wing parties and movements in Europe are not only aiming for a more restrictive immigration policy to win votes. Rather, they are pursuing a redefinition of the nation state; namely on the basis of an ethnically defined people and through excluding people defined as Others. This is linked to new ideas of social cohesion, or a "care racism" (Mulinari & Neergaard 2017: 92), as a new form of solidarity exclusively within the national community.

Since the last decade, gender and sexuality relations have played a prominent role in this struggle for cultural hegemony as well as for a new state project of a neoliberal–authoritarian and nationalist state – albeit at different speeds and with different manifestations in European countries. The exclusion of migrants and blaming the "gender ideology" are part of a strategy to create consensus for this reconstruction of the state, i.e., to make authoritarian and exclusionary discourses and practices common sense. The threat to gender certainties, as explained above, becomes the focal point for justifying authoritarian social order in order to re-establish security and control.

The authoritarian right thus partially takes up neoliberal strategies, but also wants to stop certain key neoliberal changes – both economic and social globalization – especially migration, as well as women's employment, and the erosion of the male family breadwinner model. Furthermore, the authoritarian right, which is completely in line with neoliberal ideologies, delegitimizes notions of social equality. In other words, the right is concerned with restoring a "liberal state" of gender relations and the social relations of the nineteenth century, including authoritarian features that are already inherent to neoliberalism. The strategy of the authoritarian right can therefore be understood as a new kind of intensification of the already-existing gender inequality and sexism within capitalist societies and liberal democracy, but in completely new, neoliberal contexts.

5. CONCLUSION: DEMOCRATIC PERSPECTIVES?

Within its gender-political, project the authoritarian right can draw on neoliberal contradictions and a long tradition of inequalities that have been tolerated, even preferred, by liberal ideology. This right-wing project is directed against new forms of relations between men and women as partners, measures for achieving women's legal equality in the world of gainful employment, the media and politics, women's reproductive rights, and LGBTIQ people. These complexes of rejection are core components of the right-wing authoritarian "solution" to the current gender question, as they offer starting points for hierarchical and authoritarian policy proposals through their threat potential.

In the authoritarian-right struggle for cultural hegemony and political power, the gender question serves to combine growing social inequality, as well as the changes experienced by men to their way of life, such as the precarization of work and their changed role within the family, into an interpretative pattern. This pattern can be positioned against the social democratic reforms and against the liberalization of ways of life from the 1970s, but also against migration as a central outcome of neoliberal globalization. The authoritarian right can thus refer to "old" liberal traditions, values, and norms, as well as to neoliberal ideas and their illiberal components. These contradictions enable the authoritarian right to succeed in depicting a new conception of society, politics, and the state as well as modulating new hegemonic relations and conjoining a national–populist, authoritarian project; a new masculinist conjuncture of heroism and the right to aggression and exclusion.

Gender ideology can be used to transport numerous ideas about the "we" – the "people," which discursively produce a fundamentally new concept of democracy. The gender discourse reveals that the authoritarian right is particularly concerned with destroying an idea of the "demos" and replacing it with an ethnic and nativist idea of the "people." This encompasses the natural view of families and the patriarchal idea of the people and follows an anti-democratic gesture against self-determination and popular sovereignty: The people as constructed through the right-wing gender discourse is a weak, passive, and incapable unit; a deceived victim who must be saved from the seduction of corrupt political elites or the media. Authoritarian right-wing leaders imagine themselves as saviors, which allows their loud appeal to the people as sovereign, as well as their demand and promise of direct democratic procedures, to suggest a need for leadership rather than an opportunity for participation.

Representative democratic procedures, norms, and rules are instrumentalized in the authoritarian right's political struggle for power, but they are not only diametrically opposed to their political project – they stand in the way.

The anti-democratic and authoritarian project of the right was established during neoliberalism. Angela Merkel's talk of a "market-conforming democracy"[15] was already an indication of the strategic erosion of liberal democratic basic values. The authoritarian right thus also picks up on the anti-democratic tendencies inherent to liberal party democracy and pushes them further.

REFERENCES

AfD (2016) *Grundsätze für Deutschland. Programm der Alternative für Deutschland.* Kurzfassung, https://www.afd.de/wp-content/uploads/sites/111/2021/02/2016-06-20_afd-kurzfassung_grundsatzprogramm_webversion_k.pdf (accessed: 21 March 2022).

Amesberger, Helga & Halbmayr, Brigitte (2002) (eds) *Rechtsextreme Parteien – eine mögliche Heimat für Frauen?*, Opladen.

Balibar, Etienne (2010) "Kommunismus und (Staats)Bürgerschaft. Überlegungen zur emanzipatorischen Politik", in Demirovic, Alex, Adolphs, Stephan & Karakayali, Serhat eds, *Das Staatsverständnis von Nicos Poulantzas. Der Staat als gesellschaftliches Verhältnis*, Baden-Baden, 19–33.

Beck, Ulrich & Beck-Gernsheim, Elisabeth (1995) *The Normal Chaos of Love*, Cambridge.

de Benoist, Alain (1985) *Kulturrevolution von rechts. Gramsci und die Nouvelle Droite*, Krefeld.

Birsl, Ursula (1994) *Rechtsextremismus: weiblich – männlich? Eine Fallstudie zu geschlechtsspezifischen Lebensverläufen, Handlungsspielräumen und Orientierungsweisen*, Opladen.

Bitzan, Renate (1997) ed., *Rechte Frauen. Skingirls, Walküren und feine Damen*, Berlin.

Bock, Gisela & Duden, Barbara (1977) "Arbeit aus Liebe – Liebe als Arbeit: zur Entstehung der Hausarbeit im Kapitalismus", in Gruppe Berliner Dozentinnen (eds.), *Frauen und Wissenschaft: Beiträge zur Berliner Sommeruniversität für Frauen, Juli 1976*, Berlin, 118–199.

Breivik, Anders Bering (2011), *2083: A European Declaration of Independence*, London.

Bröckling, Ulrich (2016) *The Entrepreneurial Self. Fabricating a New Type of Subject*, London.

Brown, Wendy (2019) *In the Ruins of Neoliberalism. The Rise of Antidemocratic Politics in the West*, New York.

Candeias, Mario (2016) "Gegenmittel. Autoritärer Neoliberalismus und Rechtspopulismus. Perspektiven einer verbindenden linken Partei", in Demirovic, Alex (ed.), *Transformation der Demokratie – demokratische Transformation*, Münster, 9–34.

[15] Speech by Angela Merkel at a press conference in 2011; https://www.youtube.com/watch?v=y4CIiBL-EKg (accessed 1 September 2019).

Connell, Raewyn & Messerschmidt, James W. (2005) "Hegemonic masculinity. Rethinking the concept", in 6 *Gender & Society*, 829–859.
Dietze, Gabriele (2016a) "Das 'Ereignis Köln'", in 1 *femina politica*, 93–102.
Dietze, Gabriele (2016b) "Ethnosexismus. Sex-Mob-Narrative um die Kölner Sylvesternacht", in 1 *Movements. Journal for Critical Migration and Border Regime Studies*, https://movements-journal.org/issues/03.rassismus/10.dietze--ethnosexismus.html (accessed: 30 August 2021).
Farris, Sara R. (2017) *In the Name of Women's Rights. The Rise of Femonationalism*, Durham/London.
Forster, Edgar (2006) "Männliche Resouveränisierungen", in 2 *Feministische Studien*, 193–207.
FPÖ (2015) *Wahlprogramm Wienwahl 2015*. https:// web .archive .org/ web/ 20150929033151/ http:// www .fpoe -wien .at/ themen/ wahlprogramm -2015/ ja -zu -familien-statt-gender-wahnsinn/ (accessed 8 March 2022).
FPÖ Bildungsinstitut (2013) *Handbuch freiheitlicher Politik. Ein Leitfaden für Führungsfunktionäre und Mandatsträger der Freiheitlichen Partei Österreichs*. https:// www .fpoe .at/ fileadmin/ user _upload/ www .fpoe .at/ dokumente/ 2015/ Handbuch_freiheitlicher_Politik_WEB.pdf (accessed: 16 November 2018).
Geden, Oliver (2004) *Männlichkeitskonstruktionen in der Freiheitlichen Partei Österreichs. Eine qualitativ-empirische Untersuchung*, Opladen.
Geva, Dorit (2020) "Daughter, mother, captain Marine Le Pen, gender, and populism in the French National Front", in 1 *Social Politics*, 1–26.
Grossberg, Lawrence (2019) "Cultural studies in search of a method, or looking for conjunctural analysis", in 96–97 *New Formations. A Journal of Culture, Theory, Politics*, 38–68.
Hall, Stuart (1985), "Authoritarian populism: A reply to Jessop et al.", in I *New Left Review*, 115–124.
Hall, Stuart (1987) "Gramsci and us", in June *Marxism Today*, 16–21.
Hark, Sabine & Villa, Paula-Irene (eds.) (2015), *Anti-Genderismus. Sexualität und Geschlecht als Schauplätze aktueller politischer Auseinandersetzungen*, Bielefeld.
Hausen, Karin (1976) "Die Polarisierung der 'Geschlechtscharaktere'. Eine Spiegelung der Dissoziation von Erwerbs- und Familienleben", in Conze, Werner (ed.), *Sozialgeschichte der Familie in der Neuzeit Europas*, Stuttgart, 363–393.
Heitmeyer, Wilhelm (2018) *Autoritäre Versuchungen. Signaturen der Bedrohung 1*, Berlin.
Hess, Sabine et al. (2016) *Der lange Sommer der Migration. Grenzregime III*, Berlin & Hamburg.
Jacobi, Juliane (1990), "'Geistige Mütterlichkeit': Bildungstheorie oder strategischer Kampfbegriff gegen Männerdominanz im Mädchenschulwesen?", in *Zeitschrift für Erziehungswissenschaft, Bildungspolitik und pädagogische Praxis*, 209–224.
Jongen, Marc (2017) *Migration und Thymos-Training*. Vortrag auf der Winterakademie des Instituts für Staatspolitik, https://www.youtube.com/watch?v=cg_KuESI7rY (accessed 5 July 2019).
Kuhar, Roman & Paternotte, David (eds.) (2017), *Anti-Gender Campaigns in Europe. Mobilizing Against Equality*, London.
Lang, Juliane (eds.) (2015) "Mehr als die 'emotionale Kompetenz' der Partei", in Wenzel, Uwe, Beate Rosenzweig & Ulrich Eith, *Mädchen und Frauen in der extremen Rechten*, Schwalbach, 53–74.

de Lange, Sarah & Mügge, Liza M. (2015) "Gender and right-wing populism in the Low Countries: ideological variations across parties and time", in 1 *Patterns of Prejudice*, 61–80.
Mauer, Heike (2021) "Nichts als Wahn und Ideologie? Rechtspopulistische Angriffe auf die Geschlechterforschung und die Politisierung von Geschlechterverhältnissen", in Kim, Seongcheol & Selk, Veith (eds.), *Wie weiter mit der Populismusforschung?*, Baden-Baden, 271–292.
Mayer, Nonna (2013) "From Jean-Marie to Marine Le Pen: Electoral change on the Far Right", in 1 *Parliamentary Affairs*, 160–178.
Mayer, Stefanie & Sauer, Birgit (2017) "'Gender ideology' in Austria: Coalitions around an empty signifier", in Kuhar, Roman & Paternotte, David (eds.), *Anti-Gender Campaigns in Europe. Mobilizing against Equality*, London & New York, 23–40.
Mayer, Stefanie, Sori, Iztok & Sauer, Birgit (2016) "'Gendering 'the people': heteronormativity and 'ethno-masochism' in populist imaginery", in Ranieri, Maria (ed.), *Populism, Media and Education. Challenging discrimination in contemporary digital societies*, London & New York, 84–104.
Meret, Susi (2015) "Charismatic female leadership and gender: Pia Kjaesgaard and the Danish People's Party", in 1–2 *Patterns of Prejudice*, 81–102.
Mokre, Monika & Siim, Birte (2013) "European public spheres and intersectionality", in Siim, Birte & Mokre, Monik (eds.), *Negotiating Gender and Diversity in an Emergent European Public Sphere*, London, 22–42.
Mudde, Cas (2007) *Populist Radical Right Parties in Europe*, Cambridge.
Mudde, Cas & Kaltwasser, Cristobal Rovira (eds.) (2012), *Populism in Europe and the Americas. Threat or Corrective for Democracy?*, Cambridge.
Mulinari, Diana & Neergaard, Anders (2017) "Theorizing racism. Exploring the Swedish racial regime", in 2 *Nordic Journal of Migration Research*, 88–96.
Reichel, Werner (2015) "Der Genderismus und seine Opfer", in Günther, Christian & Reichel, Werner (eds.), *Genderismus(s). Der Masterplan für die geschlechtslose Gesellschaft*, Wien, 99–128.
Rommelspacher, Birgit (2011) "Frauen und Männer im Rechtsextremismus – Motive, Konzepte und Rollenverständnisse", in Birsl, Ursula (ed.), *Rechtsextremismus und Gender*, Opladen & Farmington Hills, 43–68.
Rosenkranz, Barbara (2008) *MenschInnen. Gender Mainstreaming. Auf dem Weg zum geschlechtslosen Menschen*, Graz.
Sauer, Birgit (2001) *Die Asche des Souveräns. Staat und Demokratie in der Geschlechterdebatte*, Frankfurt am Main & New York.
Sauer, Birgit (2012) "Politiken der (Nicht-)Zugehörigkeit. Verhandlungen von *citizenship* und Geschlecht in Diskussionen um das muslimische Kopftuch in Deutschland und Österreich", in Bereswill, Mechthild, Rieker, Peter & Schnitzer, Anna (eds.), *Migration und Geschlecht. Theoretische Annäherungen und empirische Befunde*, Weinheim & Basel, 192–212.
Sauer, Birgit et al. (2016) "Exclusive intersections: constructions of gender and sexuality", in Lazaridis, Gabriella & Campani, Giovanna (eds.), *Understanding the Populist Shift. Othering in a Europe in Crisis*, London & New York, 104–121.
Sloterdijk, Peter (2008) *Zorn und Zeit. Politisch-psychologischer Versuch*, Berlin.
Strache, Heinz-Christian (2015) "Thema Kinder und Jugend". http:// www .meinparlament.at/frage/9050/ (accessed 2 March 2015; Site no longer accessible).
Theweleit, Klaus (2019 [1977]) *Männerphantasien*, Berlin.

Unterberger, Andreas (2015) "Die Männer: verunsichert, feige und perspektivenarm", in Günther, Christian & Reichel, Werner (eds.), *Genderismus(s). Der Masterplan für die geschlechtslose Gesellschaft*, Wien, 145–160.

Wodak, Ruth (2021) *The Politics of Fear. The Shameless Normalizaiton of Far-Right Discourse*, London.

13. Promises of sovereignty in authoritarian populism: a feminist critique

Brigitte Bargetz and Nina Elena Eggers

1. INTRODUCTION

The current rise of authoritarian populism is a symptom of political, social, and economic change. The limits of what is sayable are constantly being reexamined, and previously marginalised far-right ideologies are – once again – made speakable. Through shameless and attention-seeking breaches of taboo and provocations, authoritarian populists provide offers of identification and by doing so promote the "normalisation" (Wodak 2020) of right-wing extremist content. This process is also largely embedded in the contemporary crisis of democracy (e.g. Finchelstein & Urbinati 2018; Diehl 2019). Invoking the will of "the people", authoritarian populists tell a story of democracy and popular sovereign agency. In their view it is a pre-political will of an already given collective subject. At the same time, this will is supposedly embodied in the sovereign leader, which makes the distinction between the popular will and the leader seem obsolete (Diehl 2019: 131).[1]

We interpret this way of addressing "the people" as a populist mode in view of "authoritarian temptations" (Heitmeyer 2018) and a "longing for a lost sovereignty" (Bargetz 2021). We argue that authoritarian politics make an attractive offer in times of insecurity and uncertainty by calling upon authority and sovereignty. Moreover, they do so by way of what we call affective narratives (Bargetz & Eggers 2023). In speaking of affective narratives, we emphasise that narratives and affects are mutually entangled in the realm of

[1] The chapter is a slightly modified and updated translation of Brigitte Bargetz and Nina Elena Eggers, "Versprechen auf Souveränität im autoritären Populismus. Eine feministische Kritik", published in "Treiber des Autoritären. Pfade von Entwicklungen zu Beginn des 21. Jahrhunderts", 2022 (eds Günter Frankenberg & Wilhelm Heitmeyer).

the political, where they constitute a crucial mode of political mediation. By employing such affective narratives, authoritarian populism manages to link up with people's feelings of insecurity and by this means can win approval for far-right ideologies. In this way, elements of authoritarian politics are insidiously normalised.

In our chapter, we interrogate the affective and narrative practices of authoritarian populism and show how authoritarian populism mediates between moods of anxiety and far-right offers by appealing to narratives of political sovereignty. Thus, we claim that authoritarian temptations also draw on atmospheres and feelings. Moreover, we argue that this populist mode of authoritarian politics is a form of normalisation of right-wing extremism. It is a complex process of affective-narrative mediation that addresses "the people" by orienting their feelings, organising their sense of belonging, and providing enticing offers. At the same time, the promise of sovereignty in authoritarian populism is mediated in gendered ways.

In order to make this argument, we will start by discussing our theorisation of authoritarian seductions in times of uncertainty and insecurity. We will continue by elaborating on authoritarian populism's promises of sovereignty on the basis of our understanding of affective narratives. Referring to this concept, we will then show that these promises unfold as gendered and racialised narratives and thereby develop their affective appeal. We conclude that the promises of sovereignty are part of authoritarian seductions and in this way form a corridor through which extreme right-wing ideologemes can pass into the political centre.

2. ATMOSPHERES OF INSECURITY AND AUTHORITARIAN SEDUCTIONS

Already in the early 1990s, Zygmunt Bauman (1991: 6) identified an "obsession" with order in Western modern societies and proposed to understand this obsession as a reaction to feelings of "ambivalence", chaos, and the loss of control and certainty. In the same year, in the face of contemporary debates about a so-called risk society, Anthony Giddens (1991) introduced the concept of "ontological security", which he considered an essential basis for human action. Since then, neither the loss of certainty nor questions of security have lost any relevance as crucial "structures of feeling" (Williams 1977 [1961]). On the contrary, they have further intensified in the ongoing "multiple crisis" (Demirović et al. 2011: 8). Consequently, the concepts of "ontological security" (Krahmann 2018), resilience (Graefe 2019), and certainty (Edkins 2019) have been widely discussed until today. Likewise, under the auspices of increasing insecurity, a politics of securitisation has been set in motion. This securitisation draws upon real insecurities and governs through moral panics and repressive legislation, also by making use of narrative techniques (The Institute for Precarious Consciousness 2014).

As the editors of this volume claim, the threat to the state order, the destruction of hierarchies and masculinist relations of dominance, as well as the loss of identities combined with concerns about the demise of "one's own people" are crucial narratives that encourage the development of authoritarianism. One could argue here that these narratives encounter a passive "mass" who, due to a lack of knowledge and education, could be easily instrumentalised and driven into the hands of right-wing populists and the New Right alike. Such a picture was painted by Gustave Le Bon's (1947 [1895]) mass-psychological approach, which portrays the "masses" as irrational, emotionally driven, and easily controllable by authoritarian leaders. Individuals are supposedly unable to act because they are guided and influenced in their thoughts and feelings by political leaders. This image of the "masses" is thus in contrast with the ideal of the citizen as an individual capable of making judgements (Eggers 2015: 275). Le Bon assumes that the affective dimension of the political is diametrically opposed to its rational dimension and consequently prone to endanger democracy. However, such a one-sided understanding of instrumentalising the supposedly duped "masses" proves to be highly problematic when looking at the political and media debates on populism: when populists suggest that people's worries be taken seriously, they do so in a moralising and paternalistic tone while neglecting to discuss the post-democratic and neoliberal structures of conditions (Bargetz 2021: 21) underlying the public's fears and insecurities.[2]

Here we follow Stuart Hall and understand authoritarian populism as part of neoliberalism and as a strategy in the field of struggles for democracy. Referring to the Thatcher government since the end of the 1970s and its predecessors, Hall and others were able to show that the political right has been successful precisely when linking to "real problems" (Hall 1979: 20) and related insecurities and anxieties: that is, when they "harness to its support some popular discontents, neutralize the opposing forces, disaggregate the opposition and really incorporate some strategic elements of popular opinion into its own hegemonic project" (Hall 1988b: 152; see also Hall et al. 1979). For Hall (1988a [1980]: 143), the right succeeded in doing what the left had failed to do "in its one-sided rationalism": to consistently "educate the commonsense of the common people" in line with their hegemonic project (Hall 1988a [1980]: 143). This means to take up the experiences of the working class and give them a clear orientation. Hall (1988b: 151) thus describes authoritarian populism as an authoritarian "shift from above" which was simultaneously bolstered, har-

---

2 On moralisation in populism research, see for instance Manow 2018; Jörke & Selk 2017.

nessed and, to a certain extent legitimised, by a "populist groundswell below". Consequently, the success of authoritarian populism is not based on "its capacity to dupe unsuspecting folk" (Hall 1979: 20) but rather on the way it "addresses real problems, real and lived experiences, real contradictions – and yet is able to [...] [pull] them systematically into line with policies and class strategies of the Right". Authoritarian populism is not a "rhetorical devise or trick" but has a "rational and material core" (Hall 1979: 20). In this sense, it is also an explicitly "contradictory strategy" when it presents itself ideologically "as anti-state, for the purposes of populist mobilization", but at the same time does not refuse to "operate through the state" (Hall 1988b: 152).

Against this background, we suggest that the current normalisation of authoritarian populist politics should be understood not as an "authoritarian mass deception", but rather in terms of "authoritarian temptations" (Heitmeyer 2018), "the seductive lure of authoritarianism" (Applebaum 2020), or as "affective enticements" (Bargetz & Ludwig 2017: 118) via promises of sovereignty. Authoritarian populism can connect to people's experiences of insecurity precisely by offering security, belonging, and happiness (Bargetz, 2023) and by thus winning them over to right-wing conservative and right-wing extremist ideologies. While right-wing extremism has always been openly anti-democratic due to its ideology of natural inequality (Birsl 2016), authoritarian populism explicitly operates on a democratic terrain. Authoritarian populist forces make use of representational crises by pursuing a "politics of populist democracy", which takes democracy as the field of contestation but is characterised by a "creeping authoritarianism", as Alex Demirović (2018: 29, our translation) argues following Stuart Hall. This "plebiscitary strategy" (Demirović 2018: 34) of authoritarian populism does not serve to strengthen the free will of the *demos*, but mobilises the people through moral panics along racist and nationalist lines.

In this light, we consider the contemporary economic, political, reproductive, and ecological crises a fertile ground for authoritarian politics. Therefore, it is necessary to take a closer look at how moral panics are used to introduce extreme right-wing ideologemes into the political mainstream. Our concern is to discuss how authoritarian populism succeeds in bringing the commonsense of the people – to use Hall's term, following Gramsci – in line with their ideological goals. Wilhelm Heitmeyer has shown that authoritarian temptations especially flourish when they manage to hitch onto threatening situations:

> "Perceived or actual threats can be interpreted as a loss of control – whether by a single person who believes they are losing control over their biography, or by a society which is allegedly or actually losing its grasp on the social order. In such situations, people can fall into temptation". (Heitmeyer 2018: 20, our translation)

It is the "longing for security" (Heitmeyer 2018: 10) that also makes people susceptible to "authoritarian temptations". While fears and insecurities are not necessarily associated with authoritarian governing they can still provide the "very conditions of possibility" (Bargetz 2021: 21) for developing an "authoritarian mood" (Hall et al. 1988: 27).

Authoritarian populist politics are attractive in times of crises, and especially in times of capitalist and representational crises (e.g. Hall et al. 1979, Hall 1988c; Demirović 2018; Finchelstein & Urbinati 2018; Diehl 2019; Sauer 2020; Frankenberg & Heitmeyer in this volume). In this sense, Helmut Dubiel (1986a: 90), following Lawrence Goodwyn, speaks of "populist moments"[3] as social-historical moments: these populist moments are characterised "by the fact that emotional ties to the traditional social order of affected population groups are abruptly undermined. Traditional orientations suddenly lose not only their economic basis but their cultural place within societal rationality as well". However, current crises do not only show up in the increasing loss of social ties. They also become visible in rising economic inequalities and the successive dismantling of the welfare state. They give rise to diffuse anxieties and insecurities, which political movements and especially authoritarian populist forces know how to exploit. Still, some claim that the argument of uncertainty is "only conditionally durable" since the "voters and supporters of right-wing populist parties are not only recruited from social groups that are obviously threatened by social decline" (Sauer 2017: 7, our translation). In our approach, we consider uncertainty and insecurity a wide-ranging affective basis of neoliberal rationality and governing, while also acknowledging that different social positions are affected in different ways by intersectional systems of oppression (Bargetz 2021: 30). Yet we do not consider the population as "deceived masses" who can easily and arbitrarily be seduced and harnessed. Instead, we argue that authoritarian populism establishes a potential for affective identification and an anchor in the political field by addressing people's fears and insecurities while offering orientation to help overcome them.

3. AFFECTIVE NARRATIVES OF AUTHORITARIAN POPULISM AND THEIR PROMISES OF SOVEREIGNTY

Authoritarian populists appeal to "the people" with promises of sovereignty and political agency (Bargetz 2021, 2023). More explicitly, they offer affectively and narratively promoted promises of sovereignty which are conveyed

---

[3] On contemporary "populist moments", see also Mouffe 2018; Gebhardt 2019.

through leadership figures. These leaders in turn are emotionally bound to the supposedly "true people".

Our concept of affective narratives (Bargetz & Eggers 2023) assumes that narratives and affects are neither separate nor separable entities. Rather, affects are narratively mediated while narratives are affectively powerful. Political narratives can seize upon moods and atmospheres and orient them towards new goals. Equally, narratives work through affects: they sort feelings, make one's own emotional reactions intelligible, and evoke affects. More precisely, narratives are narrative practices (Eggers 2020: 182–184) that give voice to people's experiences and feelings and relate them to collectively shared worlds and imaginations. In this understanding, narrative practices are acts of storytelling that form an affective space of resonance (Bargetz & Eggers 2023). Narrating as an act and activity mediates between the narrator, the story told, and the audience. In line with Paul Ricœur (1984), this understanding of narrative does not take narratives in terms of a single *story*. Rather, it allows a complex set of practices of affective narrative mediation to come to the fore. The narrative itself is constituted by a plot with a beginning and an end, where real and fictional events are placed in a (new) context of meaning. This mode of emplotting, then, does more than tell a convincing story. It also operates through "affective attachments" (Bargetz 2020) between the narrator, the narration, and the audience.

By taking affective narrative practices in authoritarian populism as a starting point, we do not primarily engage with the very concrete stories used by politicians and political movements in order to politically mobilise people through emotions. These issues might be addressed by analysing the political content, as for instance the German Amadeu Antonio Foundation, an organisation against right-wing extremism, racism, and anti-semitism, which identifies "toxic narratives" (Baldauf et al. 2017) in the context of action-oriented political education work. Rather, we aim to go beyond a one-dimensional understanding of narratives and affects here: to do so, we consider the way affective narratives are told and how certain narratives are narratively structured but also performed in such a way that allows them to affect narrators and audiences alike. We thus emphasise the levels of the story told, the audience, and the narrators, as well as how these different levels are affectively connected.

Based on this understanding of affective narratives, we can identify current authoritarian populist promises of sovereignty as complex affective and narrative modes of mediation between the leader and the people. As Helmut Dubiel (1986b: 7) already noted long ago, populism is characterised above all by a particular way politicians bond with the people. To speak of affective narratives here shows how their manner of addressing "the people" through a democratic promise of sovereignty goes beyond an instrumental understanding of affective mobilisation and a cooptation of the supposedly deluded masses.

The opposition of the people and the elite is a crucial question in populism research (Mudde 2004; Mouffe 2018; Rucht in this volume). The populist interpretation, as Dirk Jörke and Veith Selk argue (2017: 67), selectively narrows discussions about the democratic representational gap to one single explanation: they accuse the corrupt elite of not pursuing politics in the interest of the people. Populists counter this gap by presenting an "authentic people" as the "true and good community". As Paula Diehl (2019) has demonstrated, populists invoke an antagonism by telling "a story of the betrayed people" who have been duped by the elites. Two things are telling here: first, a democratic loss of agency, which is presented as a loss of sovereignty; and second, the invocation of "the people" as a collective subject that is supposed to resist this abuse and loss of power. When populists imagine a harmonious relationship between "the people" and the leader, the populist leader takes on a double and ambivalent role (Diehl 2019: 127): on the one hand, he appears as "a man of the people". This means that he is like the common people and joins them against the political establishment. On the other hand, he is also their leader and consequently to a certain extent above "the people". This is why Paula Diehl (2019: 121) identifies a "populist twist" between a horizontal claim to equality and a vertical claim to leadership. It is a successful twist because the relation between "the people" and the leader translates into the leader's embodiment of the people, thereby levelling the distinction between the "will of the people" and the will of the leader himself.

Following these considerations, we propose to analyse the specific relationship between the leader and "the people" as an authoritarian populist promise of sovereignty. Here, popular sovereignty is proclaimed and at the same time successfully undermined by the leader figure. Björn Höcke (2018),[4] politician of the Alternative for Germany (AfD, *Alternative für Deutschland*), performs such a paradoxical authoritarian populist fusion of the leader and "the people" in his autobiographical interview volume *Nie zweimal in denselben Fluss (Never in the Same River Twice)*. Taking into account the affective interplay of narrator, narrated story, and addressed audience in accordance with our approach, we can show how Höcke's promise of regaining agency builds a multi-layered affective narrative bridge between the leader and "the people". This is the case when he describes the concern about his own children as a concern about "Germany". Likewise, Höcke presents his personal marginalisation – not only as a right-wing politician but also as a white heterosexual

---

4 It is true that Höcke and his former comrades of the far-right parts of the AfD ("*Der Flügel*") are usually assigned to the extreme right. Here, however, we draw on Alexander Häusler (2021: 62), who speaks of a "völkisch-authoritarian populism" for the AfD.

man – as a collective experience shared with those addressed (Höcke 2018: 108, 106; cf. also Bargetz & Eggers 2021). He links fears and insecurities with feelings of exclusion and, in this vein, narratively reworks them into anger and resentment towards the political elite. The story's turning point lies in Höcke's imagination of the future of Germany. In this future, so the story goes, Höcke himself becomes the saviour of the "betrayed people" (Diehl 2019). He promises sovereign agency by recasting those who consider themselves marginalised as the "true people". This affective narrative makes him appear as a selfless man who sacrifices himself for the wealth of the nation. In a similar way, Höcke casts his personal story of entering politics in a heroic light. He describes the political landscape in Germany at the time as a "feminised" liberal terrain hostile to right-wing politicians like him (Höcke 2018: 106). His personal challenge was then to heroically rise against this threat and, by doing so, to stand up for "his people". Here, Höcke equally embodies empathy and strength as well as a sense of responsibility and decisiveness. He not only seizes on on existing moods and sentiments among the population but also offers an affective narrative that the reader can identify with. His offer suggests that the proclaimed political sovereignty, in the sense of popular sovereignty, is accessible to everybody. It can thus connect to feelings of powerlessness that have emerged with the erosion of various social structures: with socio-economic threats in the course of ongoing neoliberalism, the crisis of democratic representation, the crisis of social reproduction, the dismantling of the welfare state, or the climate crisis. Through a narrative that can both absorb and mobilise affects, Höcke aims to transform perceived threats into approval for right-wing extremist ideologies. The political sovereignty is here embodied in the charismatic leader, ergo in himself.

Authoritarian populist forces make use of the current constellation of crises by narratively addressing everyday experiences of insecurity and uncertainty and by trying to counteract them with a performative promise of sovereignty. They do so by taking up the democratic promise of popular sovereignty via affective narratives. This means to offer narratives which ultimately help people navigate through contemporary atmospheres of insecurity and uncertainty while steering them towards the promise of recovering sovereign agency. We thus assume that authoritarian populists reinforce the previously described situations of threat while also offering instruments for orientation through affective narrative promises of sovereignty. However, while authoritarian populists' affective narratives promise political agency and the restoration of the autonomous self, this agency ultimately remains directly linked to the leader.

4. THE GENDERED AND RACIALISED PROMISE OF SOVEREIGNTY

Interestingly, authoritarian populists' promise to bring back (popular) democratic sovereignty is gendered in many ways.[5] This is the case when the narrated story of lost sovereignty and feelings of powerlessness is affectively linked to a "crisis of masculinity" (Forster 2006: 199; see also Sauer 2017: 6–10). In speaking about a "crisis of masculinity", authoritarian populists invoke the powerful topos that white heterosexual masculinity is in crisis and that women and feminism are primarily to blame. Feminism, then, is not only supposedly responsible for the loss of masculine virtues and uncertain masculinity but also, more generally, for what has been framed as society's "moral decline". As Gabriele Dietze (2019: 59 ff.) has shown, various "white" masculinities subscribe to this picture of masculinity in crisis: not only bourgeois masculinities, which sometimes consider themselves liberal, but also right-wing populist and right-wing extremist masculinities.

The French far-right politician Éric Zemmour, for instance, not only denounces Simone de Beauvoir but also blames all feminist struggles and equality policies when he claims in his book *Le Premier sexe* (*The First Sex*):

> "This subtle balance between men and women, between dominant masculinity and influential femininity, was shattered by the abdication of white men in the twentieth century as they put down their patriarchal sceptre. Since nature abhors a vacuum, feminism, whether French or American in inspiration, has attempted to fill this power vacuum". (Zemmour 2006: 202, our translation)

Here, Zemmour seeks to stage an endangered masculinity. He tries to affect his audience by playing the victim card: the white heterosexual man's role has turned from performing superiority to suffering oppression. This example shows how linking the leader to "the people" is mediated through gender. The authoritarian promise of sovereignty addresses "the 'little man of the streets'" as "part of a masculinist identity politics" (Sauer 2020: 30). Especially for (some) "subordinate masculinities", as Birgit Sauer (2020: 30) emphasises,

---

[5] For the gendered right-wing extremist and right-wing populist dynamics, see among others Ajanovic, Mayer & Sauer 2014; Lang 2015; Kuhar & Paternotte 2017; Femina Politica 2018; feministische studien 2018; Dietze & Roth 2020. For different narratives about a "crisis of masculinity" from a historical perspective, see Hämmerle & Opitz-Belakhal 2008. For discussions about crisis and (hegemonic) masculinity, see Casale & Forster 2006; Bereswill & Neuber 2011; Sauer & Penz 2023. For the gendered and racialised aspects of (promises of) (nation-state and subjective) sovereignty as promises of agency, see Bargetz 2021, Bargetz 2023.

this also includes the "promise" to increase their self-confidence through a "charismatic leader".

However, these interpellations and promises of integration are still highly exclusive, since they rely on the devaluation of gays, lesbians, bisexual, trans*, and inter* persons. Sometimes, these new images of the enemy even seem to replace the "arch enemy of communism". In this vein, Polish president and former PiS (Prawo i Sprawiedliwość) politician Andrzej Duda claimed in an election campaign speech:

> "The LGBT movement is more destructive than communism. My parents' generation fought against communist doctrine for 40 years and they did not fight for the emergence of a new, even more destructive ideology. LGBT has become a form of neo-Bolshevism that has a negative impact on children". (The Reporter 2020)

This speech, made shortly before the 2020 presidential elections, has often been associated with Duda's success. In an equally pejorative manner, Brazil's far-right former president Jair Bolsonaro declared in the context of the Corona crisis:

> "I regret the deaths. I really do. But we're all going to die someday. There's no use fleeing reality. We have to stop being a country of ~~fags~~[6] ... We have to face up to it and fight. I hate this ~~faggot stuff~~". (Pink News, 2020)

Evoking the old topos of a supposedly weak (because feminised) gay masculinity, Bolsonaro appeals to a combative masculinity that must be placed in the service of national defence.[7] He presents himself as a strong man and aims to seduce his audience by drawing a line from his personal hatred of gays to the collective identity of "the people" as a national identity. He emphasises a transformation from a country that, as he claims, has been feminised by gays to a country for which men are prepared to die in battles. Likewise, Bolsonaro speaks of "my army" and maintains that the loyalty of the military should be primarily directed towards his government and not to the constitution (Franzen 2021). In doing so, he rhetorically ties the future of the Brazilian population

---

[6] We adopt Gayatri Chakravorty Spivak's (1997: xiv) method of "under erasure", where she follows Jacques Derrida and states: "This is to write a word, cross it out, and then print both word and deletion. (Since the word is inaccurate, it is crossed out. Since it is necessary, it remains legible.)"

[7] Using the example of the French National Front, now National Rally (*Front National,* now *Rassemblement National),* Gudrun Hentges (2020) shows that authoritarian populism sometimes addresses and "includes" homosexual masculinities, yet at the same time links them as an aspect of "hegemonic masculinity" to the "marginalization" (Connell 2005: 80) of "foreign" masculinities, in the case of the FN/RN for instance "Muslim masculinities".

to himself as the leader of the people; Bolsonaro's middle name, "Messias", seems almost treacherous in this light.

The narrative of the "crisis of masculinity" thus attempts to affect parts of the population by touching upon their everyday experiences and feelings and by helping them make sense of their "affective states" (Chmilewski & Hayek 2018: 172). However, authoritarian populists do not just "provide a language for these affective states and make them socially intelligible", as Katja Chmilewski and Katharina Hajek claim in regard to the New Right and the German actional alliance, *Demo für Alle* (Demonstration for All).[8] Even more, they promise to compensate for men's individual loss of control and restore social order and agency. They unfold an affective space of resonance for insecure subjects insofar as they offer affective narratives of identification. Authoritarian populists' way of evoking hegemonic masculinity (Connell 2005 [1995]) and making it accessible through narratives is profoundly emotionally driven: it relies on pride and strength, aggressiveness and heroism. "'Real guys'", Gabriele Michalitsch (2017: 273, our translation) aptly notes, referring to Trump and Putin, "are running the show again", and she continues:

> "On the trail of one of the last remaining tigers, one gallops through the vastness of Siberia, proudly presenting his naked upper body to the cameras. While the other, at his desk, issues an entry ban for 'dangerous Muslims', he may think he is riding on horseback in the prairies of the Wild West, hunting 'bloodthirsty ~~Indians~~'[9]". (Michalitsch 2017: 273)

Authoritarian promises of sovereignty succeed precisely by staging a male narrator who also narrates his own rise from victim to hero. Where authoritarian leaders see an increasing loss of power and prestigiousness as right-wing politicians and white heterosexual men, they tend to liberate themselves through a "narrative re-sovereignisation" (Eggers 2024). Höcke's (2015) Erfurt speech has become paradigmatic in this sense. The speech ties together the so-called problem of the loss of masculinity in Germany, and consequently also Europe,[10]

---

[8] *Demo für Alle* was founded in Germany in 2014 by right-wing conservative activist Hedwig von Beverfoerde and her organisation *Initiative Familienschutz* (Initiative for Family Protection) in the style of the French "*Manif pour tous*". The movement gathers conservative, right-wing populist, and extreme right forces and is led by anti-feminist as well as racialised heteronormative narratives (Hark & Villa 2015; Chmilewski & Hajek 2018).

[9] For the method of "under erasure" see fn 6.

[10] The full quote of Höcke's prominent speech (2015, our translation) is as follows: "I love my *Volk*! Dear friends, do you know what the big problem is? The big problem is that Germany, that Europe have lost their manhood. I say: We need to rediscover our masculinity, because only if we rediscover our masculinity will we become manly, and

with a promise to rediscover masculinity and therefore to fortify the nation militarily. In his narrative he takes on the role of the proud heroic man and empathetic sovereign leader. In this sense, his act of self-narration becomes a masculine re-sovereignisation (Forster 2006; Sauer 2020: 32; Eggers 2024),[11] which not only promises the recovery of masculine political sovereignty but is also affectively embodied in the person of the political narrator.

However, the call for hegemonic masculinity as a promise of re-stabilisation is ambivalent. On the one hand it is directed against women, since rising gender equality has made the labour market more competitive and consequently contributed to the supposed threat to men's position in general; on the other hand, the call for re-masculinisation is also addressing women themselves (Sauer 2020: 30): in particular, affective narratives speak to those women who are exhausted by emancipation in neoliberal times – where gender equality has only partially been successful and patriarchal gender relations continue to exist, for instance in the form of reproductive labour or sexualised violence – and who therefore tend to "long for a 'male hero or saviour'" (Sauer 2020: 30). This trend has also become important for the New Right in its attempt to build a bridge between traditional conservative gender images and right-wing extremist gender ideologies. In this vein, the anti-feminist blog *Neokonservativ*, which emerged within the context of the Identitarian movement in Germany, proclaims a return to traditional gender roles by blaming feminism for "misogyny" in an oblique move. Feminism, the blog maintains, "is ultimately mysogenistic. It tells women that everything feminine is bad. It tells them that only masculine qualities are good and that women should therefore work hard to become like men" (*Neokonservativ* 2017, our translation). Affective narratives of the crisis of masculinity thus also operate as a masculinist response to everyday insecurities of both men and women – and, based on the sexual difference, of only men and women. They promise stability and security by suggesting a return to a heteronormative gender order.

However, authoritarian populists not only turn insecurities into resentment against (certain) women, feminists, or gay, lesbian, bisexual, trans*, and inter* persons; they also use promises of sovereignty for racist mobilisation. In narratively staging the crisis of masculinity, authoritarian populists direct the negative feelings towards concrete enemies and here above all towards migrantised and racialised "Others". With these "official enemy images" (Frankenberg

---

only if we become manly will we able to defend ourselves. And we need to become able to defend ourselves, dear friends."

[11] While Edgar Forster (2006, our translation) uses the term "male re-sovereignisation" primarily in order to grasp a new discourse of men and masculinity *within* feminism, the term is used more broadly here and also more generally for male reclamations of affective narrative sovereignty.

1977: 361, our translation), "interpretative models for social conflicts are provided" and "an increased need for appeasement and harmonising authoritative symbols is produced". Authoritarian populists create (gendered, sexualised, classed, and racialised) embodied "objects" of fear in order to reduce complexity. Migrantised and racialised "Others" serve as specific "objects" of distinction and as affective reassurance in times of neurotic anxiety (Bargetz 2021: 31). They become part of a "narrative of self-assurance" (Eggers 2020: 195) for the Western "dominance culture" (Rommelspacher 1995), whose protagonists imagine themselves as superior. This "narrative of superiority in migration defence", as Gabriele Dietze (2019, our translation) aptly calls it, conveys the promise of restoring political agency by multiple processes of Othering. For instance, narratives of "foreign masculinity" (Eggers 2020, our translation) or "*othered* masculinities" (Scheibelhofer 2017: 96) can offer a framework and an orientation for certain feelings. They paint a picture of violent delinquent Muslim men who threaten "their own women" and restrict their freedom and rights (Dietze 2019). Authoritarian populism takes the sexualised violence of certain men and the related fears as a starting point for outlining a menace in their storylines about fear, powerlessness, and resentment. Talking constantly about (mass) sexual assaults by men from North Africa and of mainly Arab origin helps them to mobilise against migrating people and refugees. At the same time, authoritarian populists offer a counter-narrative against this outlined menace: they present a story of a reawakening, proud "masculinity" as a promise of security. Diffuse anxieties are thus invoked as legitimate feelings of the supposedly threatened "people". However, these feelings are not only addressed, but they are also reworked and directed into distinct channels by elaborating on the need for security in a way that convinces people of an exclusionary racist politics.

These authoritarian populist narratives are affective because they melancholically invoke the picture of a former state of security and national sovereignty (Bargetz 2021) in which strong men were supposed to protect the nation's "own women". Conceiving of women in need of protection updates the myth of the nation under threat – the nation itself imagined as a woman which must be defended against men marked as "foreign" (Eggers 2020: 193). Historically, the masculinist image of a "strong" nation-state as a saviour has always corresponded with a racist colonial state (Bargetz 2021). The promise of nation-state sovereignty is therefore also a promise of re-installing a (neo-) colonial nation-state and, consequently, a form of "postcolonial melancholia" (Gilroy 2005). This narrative of threatened national femininity operates affectively too, since it describes, as Gabriele Dietze (2017: 230, our translation) notes, a "lustful suffering" charged with "erotic pleasure". This is on display, for instance, when the Freedom Party of Austria (FPÖ, *Freiheitliche Partei Österreichs*) uses the picture of a "busty girl in a skimpy white bikini top" to visualise how Austria as a nation is being threatened by refugees (Dietze 2017: 230). The image reveals a "strong affective ethno-masochism" that "lustfully" turns the "majority … into the victim of minorities" (Dietze 2017: 230) in a double sense: as a pleasurable indulgence in (supposed) victimhood and as a (hetero-)sexualised way of addressing the seeming threat against femininity. The lust for fascism as a political force has already been identified as a guiding motif for National Socialism. For Klaus Theweleit (2019 [1977, 1978]), it is directly linked to the lustful exercise of violence by "soldierly men". In authoritarian populism this desire is twisted once again when authoritarian populists brazenly exploit the victim role for the purpose of mobilising against multiple "Others".

In telling a story of lost masculinity that is equally threatened by liberal (gender) policies and migrant "Others", authoritarian populism addresses people's diffuse fears and insecurities and offers to orient these affective states. This re-sovereignisation aims to restore a strong masculinity and is narratively linked to a state that Eva Kreisky (1997) has called "*Männerbund*". This state of "male association" is a state characterised, among other things, by the dominance of privileged men, "male" interests, and generally a male-bonding structure as well as by the fact that it establishes and aims to reproduce the sexual difference in multiple ways. Authoritarian populism is thus about male re-sovereignisation through narratives but also about the longing for masculinist statehood. It promises (popular) sovereignty and agency by creating images of the enemy onto which one's own insecurities can be projected. At the same time, identification figures are created that are embodied by strong leadership figures and therefore promise agency to those who identify with them. In this sense, Gabriele Michalitsch (2017: 275, our translation) notes:

> "For the bottled-up destructive affects of powerlessness the euphemistically called 'right-wing populist' leaders and their daughters offer outlets: the weaker ones, 'the others'. The community of the 'nation' is their alternative to the global competition of human capital. Supposedly exposed to the rigours of globalisation, they want to save what remains of their 'own' by invoking an imaginary 'homeland' that offers protection and security, to hold on to its remnants at all costs before they slip away completely."

The nation and "the people" merge here based on a "fictive ethnicity" (Balibar 1991: 96) positioned against "the Others". As a place of (be)longing, both lost and to be regained, the nation is invoked through a strong patriotism and a proud "people", thus counteracting the feeling of powerlessness with a promise of political agency.

5. CONCLUSION: PROMISES OF SOVEREIGNTY AS AUTHORITARIAN SEDUCTIONS AND AS A CORRIDOR FOR RIGHT-WING EXTREMIST IDEOLOGEMES

Recently, Ruth Wodak (2020) has shown how parties of the political centre in Europe and the United States tend to adapt strategies of the extreme right and by doing so contribute to their normalisation. This mode of normalisation is based on an ambivalent promise of political agency (Bargetz 2023) and reveals that an analysis of authoritarian populism fails when it reduces populism to the seduction of the presumably irrational "masses". Because fear is not (only) stirred up "from above". Authoritarian populist strategies can establish themselves because they provide specific affective narratives that facilitate orientation and navigation in the current moment of uncertainty and confusion. Meanwhile, they present themselves as offering a democratic promise of sovereignty. This is why authoritarian populism's promise of sovereignty is always ambivalent. As we have argued in line with Stuart Hall, right-wing authoritarian forces operate in the field of democracy by latching on to people's threat situations and weaving them into their own strategies. In this way, authoritarian populists set their sights on the centre of society, as Marc Jongen from the AfD emphasises:

> "[T]he resistance has started. The bourgeois centre is today – paradoxically enough – the real revolutionary class. The ultimate purpose of this revolution is admittedly not a classless society, but the restoration of the social market economy and the sovereignty of the people vis-à-vis lobbyism". (Jongen, quoted from Heitmeyer 2018: 240, our translation)

Referring to the concept of affective narratives (Bargetz & Eggers 2023), we have argued that the normalisation of right-wing extremist ideologies is also a matter of narratives and feelings. Affective narratives contribute to the creeping legitimisation of authoritarian politics. Their promise of sovereign agency widely resonates in times of uncertainty by reorienting feelings of powerlessness through narratives of strength, autonomy, and authority. As our examples illustrate, authoritarian populists campaign against the elites' abuse of power by narratively promising "the people" to restore their lost agency and by staging themselves as saviours who bring redemption (Diehl 2019). This strategic move affectively suggests not only people's agency but also the tendency to transfer decision-making power to a strong leader figure.

As we have also shown, these affective narratives of authoritarian populism are often mediated in gendered ways. The people are interpellated by a narrative of a crisis of masculinity, which allows them to consider themselves as victims. Authoritarian populists promise both the recovery of masculinity and the restoration of a heroic, masculine nation-state sovereignty. As such, authoritarian populism often takes on the function of a "hinge" (Decker 2015: 113, our translation) which mediates between different ideologemes. As research on right-wing populism and right-wing extremism has revealed, shared anti-feminism and "anti-genderism" (Hark & Villa 2015)[12] are often a unifying moment between right-wing authoritarian, conservative, and liberal positions as well as between men's rights movements and right-wing extremism (e.g. Kemper 2011; Ajanovic, Mayer & Sauer 2014; Lang 2015; Dietze 2019; Beck 2021). Moreover, both usually come in a racist guise and in the mode of femonationalism (Farris 2011).[13] White superiority narratives about emancipated women and protective white men are mobilised against "Black" or "Muslim masculinities" and in this way are harnessed into an otherwise anti-feminist and homophobic movement.

By affectively telling a story of the crisis, the nation, "the people", and masculinity, right-wing extremist political interpretations are made accessible and speakable. This is how they succeed in resonating beyond right-wing extremist contexts. Authoritarian populists promise not only a traditional but above all a "soldierly masculinity" (Virchow 2010; Beck 2021), just as it is known from right-wing extremism and National Socialism. As the example of Bolsonaro demonstrates, this narrative implies heterosexuality but also of "serving the people and the nation, a soldierly attitude, uncompromisingness, toughness, and the performance as a leader and creator" (Virchow 2010: 42, our translation).[14] Thus, this mode of masculinity can affect and unfold power precisely through its embodiments and stagings (Diehl 2010).

Antifeminism and racialised masculinism are, on the one hand, a promise of order, certainty, and sovereignty. On the other hand, they become a corridor

---

[12] According to Sabine Hark and Paula-Irene Villa (2015: 18, our translation), anti-genderism refers to representatives of an "anti-gender alliance against a supposedly totalitarian 'gender ideology'", who claim that this "gender ideology" imposes gender roles on people and intends to alienate society from its nature. We use the term anti-genderism here in an analytical sense, in order to grasp a specific form of anti-feminist mobilisation that insists on a naturalistic and essentialist understanding of sex and thereby also discredits gender studies as a scientific discipline.

[13] Sara Farris (2011) uses the term femonationalism to describe a rhetorical strategy and political practice where women's rights and gender equality are instrumentalised for anti-Muslim racism and nationalism.

[14] Referring to Russian President Putin's war of aggression on Ukraine, Isabell Lorey (2022) illustrates how trans- and homophobic motifs and the "cult of the strong, heterosexual man" merge in a recurring "heroic martial masculinity" in his justification of war. At the same time, she highlights that the Ukrainian president Zelensky is also celebrated as a counter-hero in his warlike masculinity.

through which right-wing extremist ideologemes can connect with positions of the social centre because they mediate in a specific way between an authoritarian populist strategy from above and the population itself. Authoritarian populist promises of sovereignty thus inscribe themselves in affective atmospheres of insecurity. By means of affective narratives, they offer a nationalist masculinist politics of re-sovereignisation which applies both to men and the state in order to contribute to a sense of security and consequently to the reclaiming of democratic agency.

REFERENCES

Ajanovic, Edma, Mayer, Stefanie & Sauer, Birgit (2020) "Man, Woman, Family. Gender and the Limited Modernization of Right-Wing Extremism in Austria", in Dietze, Gabriele & Roth, Julia (eds.), *Right-Wing Populism and Gender: European Perspectives and Beyond*, Bielefeld, 101–115.

Applebaum, Anne (2020) *Twilight of Democracy: The Failure of Politics and the Parting of Friends*, London.

Baldauf, Johannes, Dittrich, Miro, Hermann, Melanie, Kollberg, Britta, Lüdecke, Robert & Rathje, Jan (2017): *Toxische Narrative. Monitoring rechts-alternativer Akteure*, Amadeu Antonio Stiftung (ed.), Berlin, retrieved 19 March 2022, from https://www.amadeu-antonio-stiftung.de/wp-content/uploads/2018/08/monitoring-2017-1.pdf.

Balibar, Etienne (1991) "The Nation Form: History and Ideology", in Balibar, Etienne & Wallerstein, Immanuel, eds, *Race, Nation, Class. Ambiguous Identities*, translated by Chris Turner, London & New York, 86–106.

Bargetz, Brigitte (2019) "Affective Attachments. Women's Suffrage in Austria and the Social Democratic Struggle for Women's Votes in *Die Unzufriedene*", in 4 *Frontiers in Sociology. Sociological Theory.*

Bargetz, Brigitte (2021) "Haunting Sovereignty and the Neurotic Subject: Contemporary Constellations of Fear, Anxiety and Uncertainty", in 25 *Citizenship Studies*, 20–35.

Bargetz, Brigitte (2023) "Affect, Populism, Politics: Paradoxical Promises of Agency", in Diehl, Paula & Bargetz, Brigitte (eds.), *The Complexity of Populism: New Approaches and Methods*, New York, 73–89.

Bargetz, Brigitte & Eggers, Nina Elena (2021) "Affektive Narrative des Rechtspopulismus: zur Mobilisierung von Männlichkeit", in Kim, Seongcheol & Veith, Selk (eds.), *Wie weiter mit der Populismusforschung?*, Baden-Baden, 247–269.

Bargetz, Brigitte & Eggers, Nina Elena (2023) "Affektive Narrative: Theorie und Kritik politischer Vermittlungsweisen", in 64 *Politische Vierteljahresschrift (PVS)*, 221–246.

Bargetz, Brigitte & Ludwig, Gundula (2017) "Affektive (Ver-)Führungen. Machttheoretische Überlegungen zu Heteronormativität", in 26 *Femina Politica. Zeitschrift für feministische Politikwissenschaft*, 118–130.

Bauman, Zygmunt (1991) *Modernity and Ambivalence*, Cambridge.

Beck, Dorothee (2021) "Diskursive Brückenschläge: Medien, Maskulinismus, Rechtsextremismus", in 1 *Zeitschrift für Rechtsextremismusforschung (ZRex)*, 90–107.

Bereswill, Mechthild & Neuber, Anke (2011) *In der Krise? Männlichkeiten im 21. Jahrhundert*, Münster.

Birsl, Ursula (2016) "Rechtsextremismusforschung reloaded – neue Erkenntnisse, neue Forschungsfelder und alte Forschungsdesiderate", in 61 *Neue Politische Literatur*, 251–276.

Brown, Wendy (1992) "Finding the Man in the State", in 18 *Feminist Studies*, 7–34.

Casale, Rita & Forster, Edgar (2006) "Einleitung: Der neue Mann oder die Wiederkehr der Natur im Sozialen", in 24 *Feministische Studien*, 185–192.

Chmilewski, Katja & Hajek, Katharina (2018) "Mobilizing Affects About Intimate Relationships – Emotional Pedagogy Among the New Right in Germany", in Juvonen, Tuula & Kolehmainen, Marjo, eds, *Affective Inequalities in Intimate Relationships*, New York & London, 171–185.

Connell, Raewyn (1995) *Masculinities,* Cambridge.

Decker, Frank (2015) "Die Veränderungen der Parteienlandschaft durch das Aufkommen der AfD – ein dauerhaftes Phänomen", in Zick, Andreas & Küpper, Beate (eds.), *Wut, Verachtung, Abwertung. Rechtspopulismus in Deutschland*, Bonn, 109–123.

Demirović, Alex (2018) "Autoritärer Populismus als neoliberale Krisenbewältigungsstrategie", in 48 *PROKLA*, 27–42.

Demirović, Alex, Dück, Julia, Becker, Florian & Bader, Pauline (eds.) (2011), *VielfachKrise. Im finanzmarktdominierten Kapitalismus*, Hamburg.

Diehl, Paula (2010) "Körperkodierungen der SS-Männer und symbolische Wirkung ihrer Uniformen", in Claus, Robert, Lehnert, Esther & Müller, Yves (eds.), *"Was ein rechter Mann ist...". Männlichkeiten im Rechtsextremismus*, Berlin, 100–108.

Diehl, Paula (2019) "The Populist Twist. The Relationship Between the Leader and the People in Populism", in Pollak, Johannes & Castiglione, Dario (eds.), *Making Present. Theorizing the New Politics of Representation*, Chicago, 110–137.

Dietze, Gabriele (2017) "Zwischen Ethnomasochismus und Androsadismus – Bausteine zu einer geschlechtersensiblen Affekttheorie von Rassismus", in Bargetz, Brigitte, Kreisky, Eva & Ludwig, Gundula (eds.), *Dauerkämpfe. Feministische Zeitdiagnosen und Strategien*, Frankfurt am Main & New York, 229–238.

Dietze, Gabriele (2019) *Sexueller Exzeptionalismus. Überlegenheitsnarrative in Migrationsabwehr und Rechtspopulismus*, Bielefeld.

Dietze, Gabriele & Roth, Julia (eds.) (2020), *Right-Wing Populism and Gender, European Perspectives and Beyond*, Bielefeld.

Dubiel, Helmut (1986a) "The Specter of Populism", in 31 *Berkeley Journal of Sociology*, 79–91.

Dubiel, Helmut (1986b), "Vorwort", in Dubiel, Helmut (ed.), *Populismus und Aufklärung*, Frankfurt am Main, 7–11.

Edkins, Jenny (2019) *Change and the Politics of Certainty*, Manchester.

Eggers, Nina Elena (2015) "Mehr Leidenschaft für Europa? Zur Bedeutung von Emotionen und Identitäten im Kontext des Europawahlkampfes 2014", in Korte, Karl-Rudolf (eds.), *Emotionen und Politik. Begründungen, Konzeptionen und Praxisfelder einer politikwissenschaftlichen Emotionsforschung*, Baden-Baden, 271–296.

Eggers, Nina Elena (2020) "Narrative Identität und kulturelle Differenz – Eine erzähltheoretische Perspektive auf Konstruktionen des Anderen", in Bizeul, Yves & Rudolf, Dennis Bastian (eds.), *Gibt es eine kulturelle Identität?*, Baden-Baden, 177–196.

Eggers, Nina Elena (2024) *Narrative Identitäten: Zum Verständnis (neu)rechter Selbsterzählungen von Nation und Männlichkeit*, Dissertationsschrift, Universität Bremen (forthcoming).

Farris, Sara R (2017) *In the Name of Women's Rights: The Rise of Femonationalism*, Durham, NC.

Femina Politica. Zeitschrift für feministische Politikwissenschaft 27 (2018), *Angriff auf die Demokratie*, Wilde, Gabriele & Meyer, Birgit (eds.).

feministische studien. Zeitschrift für Frauen- und Geschlechterstudien. 36 (2018), Normalisierung neoreaktionärer Politiken, Hark, Sabine & Oloff, Aline (eds.)

Finchelstein, Federico & Urbinati, Nadia (2018) "On Populism and Democracy", in 1 *Populism*, 15–37.

Forster, Edgar J. (2006) "Männliche Resouveränisierungen", in 24 *Feministische Studien. Zeitschrift für Frauen- und Geschlechterstudien*, 193–207.

Frankenberg, Günter (1977) "Angst im Rechtsstaat", in 10 *Kritische Justiz (KJ)*, 353–374.

Franzen, Niklas (2012) *Bolsonaro im Panikmodus*, taz, 31.3., retrieved 31 March 2023, from https://taz.de/Druck-auf-Brasiliens-Praesidenten/!5763748/.

Giddens, Anthony (1991) *Modernity and Self-Identity*, Stanford.

Gebhardt, Mareike (2019) "The Populist Moment: Affective Orders, Protest, and Politics of Belonging", in 22 *Distinktion. Journal of Social Theory*, 129–151.

Graefe, Stefanie (2019) *Resilienz im Krisenkapitalismus. Wider das Lob der Anpassungsfähigkeit*, Bielefeld.

Hall, Stuart (1979) "The Great Moving Right Show", in 1 *Marxism Today*, 14–20.

Hall, Stuart (1988a) [1980] "Popular-Democratic vs Authoritarian Populism: Two Ways of 'Taking Democracy Seriously'", in Hall, Stuart, *The Hard Road to Renewal. Thatcherism and the Crisis of the Left*, London, 123–149.

Hall, Stuart (1988b) "Authoritarian Populism: A Reply to Jessop et al", in Hall, Stuart, *The Hard Road to Renewal. Thatcherism and the Crisis of the Left*, London, 150–160.

Hall, Stuart (1988c) *The Hard Road to Renewal. Thatcherism and the Crisis of the Left*, London.

Hall, Stuart, Critcher, Charles, Jefferson, Tony, Clarke, John & Roberts, Brian (1979) *Policing the Crisis: Mugging, the State, and Law and Order*, London & Basingstoke.

Hall, Stuart, Critcher, Charles, Jefferson, Tony, Clarke, John, & Roberts, Brian (1988) "Living with the Crisis", in Stuart Hall, *The Hard Road to Renewal. Thatcherism and the Crisis of the Left*, London, 19–37.

Hämmerle, Christa & Opitz-Belakhal, Claudia (eds.) (2008), Krise(n) der Männlichkeit, Köln, Weimar & Vienna.

Hark, Sabine & Villa, Paula-Irene (2015) "'Eine Frage an und für unsere Zeit'. Verstörende Gender Studies und symptomatische Missverständnisse", in Hark, Sabine & Villa, Paula-Irene (eds.), *Anti-Genderismus. Sexualität und Geschlecht als Schauplätze aktueller politischer Auseinandersetzung*, Bielefeld, 15–40.

Häusler, Alexander (2021) "Von Rechtsaußen in die Mitte? Politische Gelegenheitsstrukturen des völkisch-autoritären Populismus in Deutschland", in Schütz, Johannes, Kollmorgen, Raj & Schäller, Steven (eds.), *Die neue Mitte? Ideologie und Praxis der populistischen und extremen Rechten*, Göttingen, 61–77.

Heitmeyer, Wilhelm (2018) *Autoritäre Versuchungen. Signaturen der Bedrohung I*, Frankfurt am Main.

Höcke, Björn (2015) Speech at the 8th Demonstration of the AfD on 18 November 2015, retrieved 31 March 2023, Youtube, https:// www .youtube .com/ watch ?v = 8BstFeshPNY.

Höcke, Björn (2018) *Nie zweimal in denselben Fluss. Björn Höcke im Gespräch mit Sebastian Hennig*. With a preface by Frank Böckelmann, Lüdinghausen.

The Institute for Precarious Consciousness (2014) "Anxiety, Affective Struggle, and Precarity Consciousness-raising", in 2 *Interface. A Journal for and about Social Movements*, 271–300.

Jörke, Dirk & Selk, Veith (2017) *Theorien des Populismus. Zur Einführung*, Hamburg.

Kemper, Andreas (2011) [r]echte Kerle: zur Kumpanei der MännerRECHTSbewegung, Münster.

Krahmann, Elke (2018) "The Market for Ontological Security", in 27 *European Security*, 356–373.

Kreisky, Eva (1997) "Diskreter Maskulinismus. Über geschlechtsneutralen Schein politischer Idole, politischer Ideale und politischer Institutionen", in Kreisky, Eva & Sauer, Birgit (eds.), *Das geheime Glossar der Politikwissenschaft. Geschlechtskritische Inspektion der Kategorien einer Disziplin*, Frankfurt am Main & New York, 161–213.

Kuhar, Roman & Patternotte, David (2017) *Anti-Gender Campaigns in Europe. Mobilizing against Equality*, London.

Lang, Juliane (2015) "Familie und Vaterland in der Krise. Der extrem rechte Diskurs um Gender", in Hark, Sabine & Villa, Paula-Irene (eds.), *Anti-Genderismus. Sexualität und Geschlecht als Schauplätze aktueller politischer Auseinandersetzung*, Bielefeld, 167–181.

Le Bon, Gustave (1947 [1895]) *The Crowd: A Study of the Popular Mind*, Stuttgart.

Lorey, Isabell (2022) "Martial Masculinity and Authoritarian Populism", translated by Kelly Mulvaney, retrieved 31 March 2023, from https://transversal.at/transversal/0422/lorey/en.

Manow, Philip (2018) *Die Politische Ökonomie des Populismus*, Berlin.

Michalitsch, Gabriele (2017) "Die Herrschaft der weißen Männer: Feministische Überlebenskämpfe im Kapitalismus der Gegenwart", in Bargetz, Brigitte, Kreisky, Eva & Ludwig, Gundula (eds.), *Dauerkämpfe: Feministische Zeitdiagnosen und Strategien*, Frankfurt am Main & New York, 273–281.

Milbrecht, Leander (2020): Bolsonaro: "Wir müssen aufhören, ein Land von Schwuchteln zu sein!", in männer*, retrieved 31 March 2023, from https://www.maenner.media/gesellschaft/ausland/bolsonaro-muessen-aufhoeren-land-von-schwuchteln-zu-sein/.

Mouffe, Chantal (2018) *For a Left Populism*, Verso.

Mudde, Cas (2004) "The Populist Zeitgeist", in 39 *Government and Opposition*, 541–563.

Neokonservativ. Blog für konservative Erneuerung (2017) "Radikal feminin", 30 September 2017, retrieved 31 March 2023, from https://neokonservativ.wordpress.com/2017/09/30/radikal-feminin/.

PinkNews (2020) "Raging Homophobe Jair Bolsonaro Tells Brazil to Stop Dealing with Coronavirus Like 'a Country of F*gs'", retrieved 31 March 2023, from https://www.thepinknews.com/2020/11/11/jair-bolsonaro-brazil-president-coronavirus-homophobia-pandemic-death-toll/.

Reisigl, Martin (2020) "Mit zweierlei Maß gemessen – Kalkulierte Ambivalenz in rechtspopulistischen Repräsentationen von Geschlechterverhältnissen", in 50 *Zeitschrift für Literaturwissenschaft und Linguistik*, 203–229.

Der Reporter (2020) "Der polnische Präsident vergleicht die LGBT-Bewegung mit dem Kommunismus und zeigt, was gefährlicher ist", retrieved 31 March 2023, from https://de.topcor.ru/15176-prezident-polshi-sravnil-lgbt-dvizhenie-s-kommunizmom-i-nazval-chto-opasnee.html?__cf_chl_tk=yZjCqWlZT77a0zc3L2fg4yQDfiiP8lVveEHdIos4bRU-1647482873-0-gaNycGzNCD0.

Ricœur, Paul (1984) *Time and Narrative. Vol. 1,* Chicago.
Rommelspacher, Birgit (1995) *Dominanzkultur. Texte zu Fremdheit und Macht*, Berlin.
Sauer, Birgit (2017) "Gesellschaftstheoretische Überlegungen zum europäischen Rechtspopulismus. Zum Erklärungspotenzial der Kategorie Geschlecht", in 58 *Politische Vierteljahresschrift (PVS)*, 1–20.
Sauer, Birgit (2020) "Authoritarian Right-Wing Populism as Masculinist Identity Politics. The Role of Affects", in Dietze, Gabriele & Roth, Julia (eds.), *Right-Wing Populism and Gender. European Perspectives and Beyond*, Bielefeld, 23–39.
Sauer, Birgit & Penz, Otto (2023) *Konjunktur der Männlichkeit. Affektive Strategien der autoritären Rechten*, Frankfurt am Main.
Scheibelhofer, Paul (2017) "'It Won't Work Without Ugly Pictures': Images of Othered Masculinities and the Legitimisation of Restrictive Refugee-Politics in Austria", in 12 *International Journal for Masculinity Studies*, 96–111.
Spivak, Gayatri Chakravorty (1997) "Translator's Preface", in Derrida, Jacques, On Grammatology, Baltimore & London, ix–lxxxvii.
The Institute for Precarious Consciousness (2014) "Anxiety, Affective Struggle, and Precarity Consciousness-Raising", in 2 Interface. *A Journal for and about Social Movements*, 271–300.
Theweleit, Klaus (2019 [1977/78]) *Männerphantasien,* Complete Edition with Extended Epilogue, Berlin.
Virchow, Fabian (2010) "Tapfer, stolz, opferbereit – Überlegungen zum extrem rechten Verständnis 'idealer Männlichkeit'", in Claus, Robert, Lehnert, Esther & Müller, Yves (eds.), *"Was ein rechter Mann ist...". Männlichkeiten im Rechtsextremismus*, Berlin, 100–108.
Williams, Raymond (1977 [1961]) "Structures of Feeling", in id., *Marxism and Literature*, Oxford, 128–135.
Wodak, Ruth (2020) *The Politics of Fear: The Shameless Normalization of Far-Right Discourse*, London.
Zemmour, Éric (2006) *Le Premier Sexe*, Denoël.

14. Media entertainment and right-wing authoritarian political ideas, an example: the storming of the Capitol

Paula Diehl

1. INTRODUCTION

On 6 January 2021, a crowd of Trump supporters, QAnon believers, evangelical Christians, right-wing extremists, neo-Nazis, members of the White Power Movement, and various paramilitary groups such as the Proud Boys or the Oath Keepers stormed the Capitol. Their goal was to prevent Joe Biden from winning the election and to restore Donald Trump's supposedly stolen victory. The slogans chanted ranged from populist statements like 'That building belongs to 'the people', to 'Stop the steal', to the murderous demand 'Hang Mike Pence'. The outcome of the event was a shock to US democracy: three police officers and one civilian were killed that day, and another civilian was trampled by the crowd.[1] In the months that followed, four police officers who were present took their own lives. What was left behind was a society in which state order and democracy could not be guaranteed without further ado. The scenes that unfolded in the Capitol and at its entrance were dramatic and circulated via media outlets all over the world. One could say it was an old-style right-wing extremist revolt. But the way it was communicated and staged showed new components. On the one hand, the storm to the capitol was not centrally organised, rather it relied on independent networks, linking the protests with different ideological contents: QAnon, Proud Boys and Evangelicals give only a glimpse of this diversity. On the other hand, the event marked a new element of political communication: blurred borders between reality and fiction and between entertainment and politics that is characteristic of mass-media hyperreality (Eco 1986). The iconic image of Jacob Chansley,

[1] These Are the People Who Died in Connection with the Capitol Riot, *The New York Times*, 2 January 2022. https://www.nytimes.com/2022/01/05/us/politics/jan-6-capitol-deaths.html/ (Accessed 10 October 2023).

the man with the buffalo horn fur hat and the painted torso who cried like a wolf, became the symbol of the event.[2] What is new about the so-called QAnon Shaman is above all the ironic distancing and the playful approach to the own political performance. Many of the participants seemed to switch their approach between entertainment and serious political act, between the real and simulation. The distinction between reality on the one hand and fiction on the other can no longer be made. Despite the ironic and playful approach, the assaulters of the Capitol were willing to use physical violence.

Facing mass-media transformations in the last decades, political performances of right-wing populists and extremists take on hyperreal features and thus generate situations in which seriousness and play as well as reality and fiction are difficult to be distinguished. These situations differ from traditional right-wing extremist or fascist propaganda. In the new configuration, right-wing extremist participants play with the deconstruction of their own staging and link it to the hyperreal logic of mass-media entertainment. This chapter reflects on the significance of mass media and their hyperreal effects on the discursive articulation, communication, and staging of right-wing populist and extremist actors and movements. It seems to me that a fundamentally new component can be found in the communication and performance of right-wing extremist groups and movements: the blending of fiction with reality. Taking this component into consideration is indispensable for the understanding of right-wing populism and extremism in the twenty-first century. My suspicion is that right-wing extremist and populist actors' perception of truth and reality has become more fragile. Trump and his supporters are a paradigmatic illustration of this new tendency. Surely, political actors from the far-right use populism, but the concept of right-wing populism alone cannot capture the complexity of this new phenomenon. For this purpose, the consideration of mass-media hyperreality and entertainment is crucial. They help to better understand the new configurations of right-wing extremism and corresponding authoritarian ideas in the 21st century.

Right-wing extremist narratives, movements, and groupings play a leading role in the storming of the Capitol, but their articulation in the political discourse and their staging differed greatly from historical totalitarian-fascist and later right-wing extremist movements in the twentieth century exactly because they incorporated mass-media entertainment and hyperreality in populism and totalitarian ideology.[3] If one wants to understand the new formation of

---

[2] See Sonja Thomaser, 'Symbol des Kapitolsturms: Was aus dem QAnon-Schamanen wurde', *Frankfurter Allgemeine Zeitung* v. 6 January 2022.

[3] However, the scholars involved in the DFG Villa Vigoni project 'Populism between Fascism and Democracy' found out that historical fascism and national socialism adopted populism at least in the movement phase. Once in power, they tended to

the extreme right and right-wing populism and especially its normalisation today,[4] it is crucial to consider populism on the one hand and entertainment and hyperreality on the other. The key point of this new development is that new right-wing authoritarian formations[5] play with the ambiguity of hyperreality, at least in addressing sympathisers and broader audiences. This allows them to operate with irony and deconstruction, which facilitates the reproduction of their anti-democratic ideologemes in the public sphere and drives their normalisation.

2. POPULISM AND RIGHT-WING POPULISM

In the immediate commentaries on the events of 6 January 2021, the term populism was often used. And indeed, since the late 1980s, right-wing extremist movements have increasingly taken on populism. After right-wing ideologemes have become more and more normalised in the new millennium, right-wing populist parties and movements are now radicalising their agenda and political communication.[6] Against this background, the boundary between right-wing populism and right-wing extremism is blurred. Not just journalists, but also scholars working on populism increasingly use the word populism for any questioning of representative democracy. Lane Crothers and Grace Burgener rightly ask: 'If populism is all of this, then what isn't populism?' (2021: 131).

Surely the movement that led to the storming of the Capitol could not have happened without populism. Without Trump's appeal to popular sovereignty and his claim that the elites stole the election from the US people, the frustra-

---

decrease populism and to become more totalitarian. Interestingly, while in national socialism populism was reduced to a minimum, in Italian fascism, Mussolini continued to use populist communication techniques, although less intensively. See Diehl & Cavazza (2012).

[4] At this point, it should be pointed out that with the increasing normalisation of far right ideologemes, the boundaries between right-wing populism and right-wing extremism have become blurred. In this context, normalisation and radicalisation must be examined as mechanisms of a connected process. The conference 'Normalizing the Extreme Right' in 2019 and the following project 'Normalizing the Far Right' (2022–23), at the Center for Interdisciplinary Research in Bielefeld, focus on these mechanisms.

[5] This text does not distinguish between authoritarianism, right-wing extremism and fascism (see Frankenberg & Heitmeyer and Zürn in this volume). Rather it privileges right-wing authoritarian formations, ideas and ideologies.

[6] The FPÖ (Freedom Party of Austria) was one of the first right-wing extremist parties to use populism in order to penetrate the democratic public sphere. A similar strategy can be observed in the case of Le Front National under Marine Le Pen. See the pioneering work of Hans-Georg Betz (2002) and Rydgren (2008).

tion of his supporters would not have been channelled politically. In his rallies before the 6 January, Trump repeated the populist narrative of the betrayed people and promised the populist happy ending with the restoration of popular power. Populism, however, is not the magic word to describe the complex context in the case of Trump and his supporters. Rather, it is one – albeit central – component of it. Populism enables the articulation of right-wing authoritarian ideas with the democratic claim of popular power.

Populism is a controversial term. For some it is a political style (Moffitt 2016), for others it is a political strategy (Weyland 2001), a political ideology (Mudde 2004) or a mode of political communication form (de Vreese et al. 2018). One can certainly argue that the numerous definitions of the term take different aspects of the phenomenon into account (see Rucht and Frankenberg & Heitmeyer in this volume). Elsewhere, I have proposed a multidimensional concept that takes these different facets of populism into consideration (Diehl 2022). Populism is a way of doing politics that centers on popular sovereignty and the dichotomy between the people and the elite. Accordingly, politics is supposed to be an expression of the will of the people. In doing so, populism idealises the people and builds an enmity with the elite. Here, the populist leader functions as the 'voice of the people' and promises to state the will of the people. Populism tells the story of the betrayed people: through the leader – usually a man – the people realise that they are being oppressed by the corrupt elite. Together the leader and the people fight for popular power. This narrative promises a happy ending when power is returned to the people. Donald Trump's 'Inauguration Speech'[7] is an example of this: 'Today we are not merely transferring power from one administration to another, or from one party to another, but we are transferring power from Washington, D.C., and giving it back to you, the people.' Those who adopt populism defend the people and rely on the idea that the people are morally pure whereas the elite is portrayed as corrupt (Diehl 2022). This creates a vertical axis of opposition between 'those up there' (elite) and 'the people down there'.

However, despite this strong narrative, the question of who belongs to the people is still open. Cas Mudde has brought an important characteristic of populism into focus: ideologically, populism is underdetermined, it cannot offer a complete political orientation and is dependent on a strong ideology to take over this task (Mudde 2004). Only in combination with a more robust ideology can populism provide a definition of the people. This explains why populism appears in different ideological forms: as right-wing, left-wing or neoliberal populism. In the case of right-wing populism, 'the people' is primarily imagined as a homogeneous body. It is culturally, ethnically, religiously,

[7] *Politico*, 20 January 2017.

and often racially constructed as a unit. Only those who share the same cultural and 'innate' identity belong to the people. Yet, these are ideologemes of the far right. By incorporating the definition of the people from right-wing extremism, right-wing populism builds a second axis of opposition – this time horizontally: inside versus outside. Right-wing populism thus works with two fundamental oppositions: the populist vertical opposition between the elite and the people, and the right-wing extremist opposition between the homogenous and 'superior' people on the one hand and the 'inferior' others on the other hand. The problem for democracy is clear: right-wing populist movements do not recognise the democratic principle of equality, laying on the idea of the 'organic body of the people' and excluding minorities. The stronger the populist component, the more discrete the exclusion; as the right-wing extremist ideology increases, xenophobia, racism, anti-Semitism, anti-Muslim resentment, homophobia, sexism, etc. become prominent.

3. POPULISM AS A BRIDGE

In some respects, right-wing populist parties accept the democratic framework for political debate, even if they try to re-define and change this framework by introducing anti-democratic ideologemes. Right-wing populists must compromise with democracy in order to place their anti-democratic messages in the democratic public sphere. Populism functions as a bridge to the democratic public sphere facilitating the infiltration of right-wing extremist ideologemes into the public sphere. Once they succeed, right-wing extremist ideologies can be normalised. The process of transformation begins the moment they are reproduced in the public sphere. As Ruth Wodak observed, right-wing populism has led to a normalisation of right-wing extremist and authoritarian ideas (Wodak 2021). It seems to me that in many cases this normalisation is followed by a phase of radicalisation. This can be observed in the USA, Brazil, India and in many European countries such as Germany, Hungary or France – in the latter case, Marine Le Pen was even outdone on the right by her competitor Éric Zemmour, which led her to radicalise many of her own (already) right-wing extremist and authoritarian positions.[8] Normalisation paves the way for right-wing and authoritarian ideas becoming more extreme. Since populism is privileged in the public eye because of its affinity with the mass media, the use of populism in the case of right-wing populism is an attractive way to normalise right-wing extremist ideologies.

---

[8] Marine Le Pen durcit son discours dans son duel avec Eric Zemmour (Marine Le Pen toughens up in her duel with Eric Zemmour), *Le Monde* 11 February 2022.

Populism allows citizens to articulate their experience of not being adequately represented in democracy. Therefore, populism can bind different emotional states such as disappointment, resentment or anger but can also generate solidarity, hope, and empowerment. Populism thus functions like a catalyst and can become politically very effective. In the case of right-wing populism, right-wing extremist ideologies are combined with populism. In this combination, anti-democratic ideas and notions, such as the belief in a presumably superior culture or 'biology,' can navigate through the democratic public sphere more easily because they are embedded in a narrative that refers to popular sovereignty and democracy. In this context, populism serves as a bridge between anti-democratic ideologies and the democratic public sphere. Therefore, populism must be taken into account when observing the normalisation of right-wing extremist ideologies and practices. However, there is a second component that is neglected by the social sciences. In the case of Trump and his supporters, it becomes clear: right-wing populist actors can combine populism and right-wing extremism with performative elements of mass-media entertainment and thus integrate the hyperreal logic into their political communication, performances, and political actions. This topic will be explored later in this chapter.

4. THE AFFINITY BETWEEN POPULISM AND MASS MEDIA

The bridging function of populism is closely connected to the mass-media logic. Populist communication and mass media share structural affinities. Indeed, populist communication matches mass-media's selection and presentation criteria. This systemic affinity to the mass media is fundamental to the success of right-wing populism worldwide (Diehl 2017). Both populism and mass media simplify their statements. Their common goal is to reach a mass audience and ensure their attention for as long as possible. Moreover, populism and mass media try to surprise their audience by creating and promoting new events and presenting unexpected occurrences or scandals. Breaking taboos is part of this. A systematic comparison between the mass-media logic and populist communication shows a strong correspondence between both: the main criteria that confirm this affinity are the reduction of complexity, breaking taboos and scandals or privileging of extraordinary statements and events, emotionalisation, dramatisation, Manichaeism or conflict structure, immediacy and, finally, the focus on the leader or personalisation (see Table 14.1). The more dependent the media are on commercial success and on the audience's attention, the more likely they will privilege populist actors. From Beppe Grillo to Jörg Haider, Hugo Chávez to Donald Trump, politicians who adopt populist communication receive more mass-media attention than their political rivals (Diehl 2017).

Table 14.1 Systemic affinity between populism and mass media

Populist communication	Attention logic of the mass media
Charismatic leader	Personalisation
Reduction of complexity	Reduction of complexity
Taboo breaking and scandal	Privileging the extraordinary
Emotionalisation	Emotionalisation
Narrative of the betrayed people	Archetypal narrative structure
Manichaeism/Friend and foe scheme	Privileging conflict
Immediacy of popular opinion	Creating a sense of immediacy for the audience

Source: Author

5. MASS-MEDIA ENTERTAINMENT AND HYPERREALITY

If right-wing populism fosters authoritarian ideas and contributes to the dissemination of right-wing extremist ideologemes, two questions remain unanswered: How can these ideologemes and ideas circulate and be appropriated given the hyperreal character of mass media communication? How does this appropriation affect right-wing authoritarian ideas? Hyperreality is coined by the uncertainty in distinguishing between reality and fiction, between privacy and the public sphere, and between seriousness and play. Hyperreal performances are self-referential and use deconstruction. They do not primarily refer to reality but to the circulating images and simulations within the mass media. In addition, hyperreality is a source of entertainment and promises a detached attitude to the produced media events. As early as the 1990s, hyperreal performances established themselves as an effective instrument of political communication, contributing to attracting the audience's attention. The problem for politics is that they blur the boundary between politics and entertainment.

The German Media scholar Andreas Dörner noticed that mass-media entertainment made greater use of political content, while more and more politicians regarded their communication as entertainment. He used the term 'politainment' to describe this mix of politics and entertainment. Politainment 'refers to a particular form of public and mass-mediated communication in which political issues, actors, processes, patterns of interpretation, identities and concepts are assembled into a new reality of the political in the mode of entertainment' (Dörner 2001: 31). It builds an intersection between politics and entertainment, where political messages are themselves conveyed as entertainment. Politicians like Silvio Berlusconi in Italy, Gerhard Schröder in Germany, and George W. Bush in the USA not infrequently resorted to hyper-real entertainment. When the social-democrat candidate Gerhard Schröder appeared as the private person Gerhard Schröder and as a candidate for chancellor (1996) in the fictional series 'Gute Zeiten, schlechte Zeiten' (Good Times, Bad Times) and on top of that made a comment on his then current divorce, the confusion was complete: Was this a political performance? Was it the staging of a fictional role or the role of a politician? Where does public messaging begin, where does private representation of the self end?

A few years later, Barack Obama made politainment one of his effective communication tools by purposefully playing with audience's knowledge of mass-media entertainment production. His appearances on talk shows, in which he jumped back and forth between the roles of the president and of a celebrity, are legendary. On 'The Ellen DeGeneres Show' in March 2014, he was addressed as 'my friend's husband' and 'Mr. President' and introduced by Ellen as 'Michelle's husband'.[9] In his last speech at the 'Correspondent's Dinner' in 2015, Obama made in fact use of a typical staging element of mass-media music entertainment, simply dropping his microphone – like many music and movie stars – and receiving applause for it.

Obama's appearance at the White House Correspondents' Dinner demonstrated how deconstructive performances, self-referential quotations from the mass-media entertainment, and playing with the audience's knowledge of mass-media production can be used in political communication. Dropping the microphone was a quote from a highly performative entertainment tool: '[T]he mic drop signals the end of a statement so definitive that it cannot possibly be followed. It's an act of destruction.'[10] Deconstruction as a staging method is aimed at an audience that already knows the staging techniques and can decode them accordingly. In Bertolt Brecht's theatre, it serves as a distancing technique to make the audience aware of the staging situation. This is intended to stimulate the audience's (self-)criticism. In the commercial mass media, however, this point has already been overcome. Deconstruction of the staging, frame, role, scenario or content are today the playful component of entertainment. Steven Spielberg's earlier comedies provide good examples of this. The actors look into the camera and comment on the action of other protagonists. They speak directly to the audience and reveal in a Brechtian manner that the entire performance is just staging. Harrison Ford's ironic smile during *Indiana*

---

[9] See https://www.youtube.com/watch?v=2RN1A9rpArs (accessed: 10 March 2022).

[10] Stuart Heritage: 'Obama out': a brief history of mic drops; in *The Guardian*, 2 May 2016.

Jones' dangerous situations demonstrates the distance not only of the protagonist to the story, but also of the audience to the content.

In general, deconstruction breaks with the principle of authenticity and offers the audience a way to distance themselves from the action. The audience is simultaneously inside the fictional reality of the game, while being outside of it. Even among celebrity fans, empirical studies have been able to identify this hybrid attitude of the audience. Already in the 1990s, a large part of the 'celebrity-watching audience' showed that 'textual authenticity and celebrities' claim to fame are unproblematic simply because they are moot. Rather than dwelling on either the inauthentic or the real, audiences simply go about the business of gossip without an overall concern for questions of authenticity' (Gamson 1994: 173). For this audience, the question of authenticity is hardly relevant since they are more concerned with enjoying the production (Gamson 1994: 49).

What appeared in the 1990s as a playful tendency in mass-media consumption became part of the perception of reality and is reinforced by digital media and digital communication in the new millennium. Those who present themselves on Instagram or TikTok accounts and maintain their friendships on Facebook or communicate via other social media, navigate between played and experienced identity without clear boundaries between the two. This creates a tension between trying to stage oneself professionally and expressing oneself authentically. It is a 'tension between the laboratory of self-presentation and the felt demand for "authentic" self-expression. Many users [...] feel compelled to conceal their laboratory in order to maintain an "authentic front"' (Pooley 2014: 242). It is no longer about being authentic in the sense of being truthful, but about staging authenticity; this requires professional techniques and means that make the produced 'authenticity' compatible with the attention rules of the mass media – including social media. Politicians and their advisors in the new millennium know this.

No politician went as far as Donald Trump. 'Trump mastered the idiom of mediated authenticity on reality TV's *The Apprentice*' (Turner 2018: 147). He was not only a product of reality TV, but also transferred the logic of reality shows, games, and wrestling to his political communication as president. In Trump's case, politainment is more than a mere tool to gain attention, it becomes the goal of his communication. This fundamentally changes the way politics is made. Right-wing populism and the authoritarian ideas generated by Trump are closely interwoven with politainment. If one wants to understand the functioning and effects of his politics and analyse the events of 6 January in their complexity, one needs to take into account the ways in which politainment is used by right-wing extremist populist actors.

6. WRESTLING: THE LOGIC OF PERSIFLAGE AND THE AMBIGUITY OF AUTHORITARIAN DISCOURSE

One particular genre of mass-media entertainment is significant in this context: wrestling. Trump was a producer of wrestling shows and actively played in such events before his presidency. The famous meme 'Trump vs. CNN' from 2017, in which Trump knocks down a man in a suit and tie whose head is covered with the CNN logo, originated from the wrestling context (Diehl 2017).[11] The original scene was manipulated by a user and posted on Reddit. Shortly afterwards, Trump shared it via Twitter, first from his private account and then from the POTUS account. Both posts have since been deleted.

The wrestling video that provided the basis for the 2017 tweet was broadcast on television in 2007. There, Donald Trump appears as a celebrity and as a 'millionaire'. At the same time, he was the main protagonist of 'The Apprentice', a reality show in which Trump played himself and was ostensibly looking for a manager for his own companies. Highlights of the show were always the phrases 'You are a loser' and 'You are fired'. Humiliation, shame, and victory poses were among the most important elements of this dramaturgy. The 'Winner against Loser' scheme is quite clear. The sequence seen in the 2017 tweet and the correspondingly aggressive performances that also characterise Trump's rallies are just a sample of this scheme. His rallies have incorporated wrestling staging techniques, encouraging participants to insult, intimidate, and sometimes even attack potential opponents. Such an invective was observed shortly before 6 January. Understanding how wrestling entertainment works is crucial to make sense of this component in right-wing extremist movements and performances.

Wrestling is a mixture of sport, carnival, and reality show that was established as a TV entertainment genre in the USA in the 1990s. In a boxing ring, two fighters compete against each other, usually in costumes reminiscent of the 'super-heroes' from the comic TV series of the 1960s. There are only a few rules for the fight. Everything that harms the enemy and confirms the clear position of the winner is allowed. The fights are acted out. They take place with an audience and are broadcast live on television. The appeal of the format is summed up by a manager of the production company WrestleMania: 'The world has no meaning for a few hours. You can forget about it. That's all that matters at the moment: Good versus evil, conflicts are resolved with

[11] Video available at: https://www.independent.co.uk/news/world/americas/donald-trump-cnn-video-tweet-reddit-islamophobic-violence-antimuslim-stabbing-a7820151.html.

violence, there is a simple drama.' Anthropologist Annette Hill describes it as an 'overwhelmingly chaotic event' (Hill 2015: 180) in which emotions can be experienced uncontrollably (Diehl 2017: 26). For theatre scholar Sharon Mazer, the affinity between Trump's communication and wrestling is evident:

> Wrestling is about heat, not truth. It's never a fair fight. The guy with the money decides who wins, who loses, and on what terms. The audience knows this and plays along regardless. These are the people who voted for Trump. This is their, and his, ethos. This is how, having converted his fans into voters, he is running the presidential show: the unreal violence of the game now the all too real brutality of the current regime. (Mazer 2018: 175)

Wrestling shows blur the lines between reality and fiction and work with self-deconstruction, irony, role inversion, and satire. 'When you go to a live wrestling match, it is easy to see why professional wrestling has a reputation; there are wrestlers in bright costumes, caps and masks, performing heroes and villains to a crowd who cheer and boo for these stars of the wrestling ring' (Hill 2015: 175). In addition, wrestling shows are highly self-referential and build on allusions to other matches. Today, a fan needs the knowledge of at least 20 years of wrestling history to decipher what is actually happening (Franz 2016: 46). Persiflage of violence and violent persiflage refer to these stories, which are themselves a fictional product of mass-media entertainment. Yet, knowledge of staging techniques is equally important in wrestling interactions. The fans and anti-fans are not naïve, just as the QAnon Shaman at the Capitol was not an ignorant actor in the events, even if his lawyer claimed otherwise during his defence in court. 'A smart fan is someone who thinks they know how professional wrestling works, gathering knowledge on the various schools of wrestling, acrobatics, and mixed martial arts and knowing the back stories to professional wrestling characters' (Hill 2015: 175).

Wrestling fights differ from other forms of sport or theatre in the space of interaction they offer. In such a space, symbolic and physical violence can be played and effectively exercised at the same time. For political actions, like the storming of the Capitol or the the Planalto (the Parliament building in Brasilia), this playfulness is latently precarious, as the exercise can potentially tip over into 'serious' violence. In addition, wrestling shows divide the audience into fans and anti-fans. Fans can physically attack the opposing fan group or even the opposing player in the ring at any time and the boundaries between stage and audience are also fluid. Violence and enmity are emotionally experienced at the same time as they are objects of satire. In Trump's rallies, the precariousness of the boundaries between acted and actual violence has been observed time and again. The episode in March 2016 became famous when Trump fans attacked a democratic 'anti-fan' to use the wrestling vocabulary. Trump cheered on his fans and, as one of them was escorted outside the arena by the security after attacking an opponent, Trump supportively promised 'I will pay the legal fees'.[12] In wrestling, as in Trump's rally, violence against the 'enemy' is a source of amusement. Many of the rioters outside and inside the Capitol on 6 January seemed to be enjoying themselves. They filmed the action and themselves, sent selfies from the parliamentary offices and took 'commemorative objects' as trophies. To what extent the chanted slogan 'Hang Mike Pence' could have actually ended in murder is difficult to say. What is certain is that armed extreme right-wing paramilitary groups were in the crowd. There was indeed the death of a police officer who was involved in a physical struggle against the stormy crowd.

The wrestling logic activated by Trump and his supporters can certainly contribute to brutalisation. According to this logic, the world is divided into top and bottom. Losers 'deserve' humiliation and opponents must be fought with violence. But beyond that, such staging creates a special way of dealing with reality that can be described as postmodern and can also be found in reality shows. For the sociologist Elena Esposito (2007: 75), this way of dealing with reality is paradoxical because it both emphasises and negates reality. The persiflage, exaggeration, and self-deconstruction observable in wrestling shows, Trump's enactments and the QAnon Shaman on 6 January create an ambiguous approach to reality. The socially shared construction of reality, which allows the distinction between reality and fiction, as well as between entertainment and politics, loses its contours. The relevance and presentation of facts become arbitrary.

Politically, this creates an explosive situation because frustration towards political institutions and those in power is articulated without any need for justification and any willingness to engage in dialogue with other positions. Since a generally accepted reality is no longer necessary for this articulation, the common ground for political dialogue is also lost. Therefore, the combination of brutalisation and loss of reality that was observable on 6 January poses a dangerous threat for democratic culture.

7. FROM THE PASSIVE AUDIENCE TO THE ACTIVE USER AND THE LOGIC OF THE NETWORK

However, there is another factor that must be taken into account in order to examine the articulation of right-wing populist, extremist and authoritarian ideas today. One of the main changes in mass-media communication in the

---

12 See https://www.dailymail.co.uk/video/news/video-1248837/Donald-Trump-hitting-protesters-pay-legal-fees.html/ (accessed 21 March 2022).

twenty-first century is the elimination of the distinction between sender and receiver in online media. For political communication, this means an additional complex dynamic in which mass-media users leave their passive status and become producers and disseminators of political content. If offline media send from 'one to many' and their audience can only receive the messages but not produce them, online communication creates a network in which messages can be sent from many users to many receivers. Recipients can become senders and producers at the same time. Social media provides the main sites of this network communication.

Communication scholars Lance Bennett and Alexandra Segerberg have found that a new logic of political communication and organisation has emerged with digital internet communication. They call it 'connective logic' (2012). This political communication logic is personalised and based on sharing content in digital networks. It removes the distinction between senders and receivers of political communication and is susceptible to viral communication as in the case of memes. The example of Trump's tweeted video against CNN inscribes itself in the connective logic. The manipulated video from 2017 was not made and posted by Trump, but by a Trump supporter. Thanks to digital technology, the user manipulated the original video and made his own product (now with CNN's logo on the attacked man's face) that became available to everyone, including the president. The visual manipulation gave the video a completely new message and emerged in a context where, for the first time, a US President was accusing the media and journalists of spreading 'fake news' on a daily basis. This, in turn, encouraged Trump to tweet the video, first from his private account and then from the presidential account under the #Fraud-CNN. As a result of the intra-media circulation, other users, mostly from the conservative camp, were motivated to use the motif. 'Trump vs CNN' became a meme and was shared on various networks. On YouTube, minutes-long compilations mount various film scenes, cartoon motifs and game situations by using Trump's face against a CNN logo as their major motive. The meme 'Trump vs. CNN' not only circulated on websites and social media, but was also picked up, commented on and disseminated by offline media, including CNN.

A meme, Bennet and Segerberg write, is 'a symbolic packet that travels easily across large and diverse populations because it is easy to imitate, adapt personally, and share broadly with others' (Bennett/Segeberg 2012: 745). Memes circulate through appropriation and manipulation and are subject to personal use. They do not necessarily have to be understood as political messages by users but can be shared and appropriated for their wit alone. Meme production allows users to demonstrate their mass-media production skills and get creative. In the digital age, audiences accumulate a specific knowledge of mass-media constructions that can be applied to produce and distribute by themselves thanks to digital technical tools. This ludic and creative aspect of digital manipulation makes it easier for anti-democratic messages to penetrate the public sphere and the semi-publics of the networks. In addition to users who employ memes as a political tool, there may also be people who ideologically sympathise with this political position while not being politically active themselves. Furthermore, this playfulness also attracts those who consume, produce, and disseminate such memes because of the entertainment value, regardless of the political content. This explains why memes play a strategic role for far-right groups (Donavan et al. 2019; Tuter 2019; Fielietz & Ahmed 2021). With memes, 'even the most taboo symbols can be disconnected from their fixed historical meaning and made to function as floating signifiers for those who understand the rules of memes'' (Tuter 2019: 42). Drawing on Ernesto Laclau's concept of the 'floating signifier', Marc Tuter attempts to describe how symbols can be emptied to such an extent that they can be received in different milieus and contexts and function as a projection surface for different ideas. The problem, however, is that 'floating signifiers' always carry a residue of the original meaning. Thus, their appropriation can be affirming, ambivalent or subversive, but it is never neutral.

A European study on the role of humour and internet interaction in the spread of right-wing extremism concludes that the internet has become a 'game changer in terms of organising, communicating and mainstreaming' (Fielitz/Ahmed 2021). Memes play a key role in this.

> At a time in which memes have become a universal means of communication, far-right groups have recognised [sic!] this popular potential for politicisation. They put a lot of time and energy into meme production, spread their ideology – sometimes more, sometimes less openly – and act according to the motto: if the meme is good, the content cannot be bad. As inane as these pictures may seem, they are important as they offer a low threshold to interact with extremist ideas. (Fielitz & Ahmed 2021: 7)

On the one hand, by using memes, right-wing extremist symbols can circulate more easily. On the other hand, image motifs, logos and symbols from mass-media entertainment can be reappropriated by right-wing extremist discourses, as the famous case of 'Pepe the Frog' as a symbol of the extreme right in the USA and later worldwide shows (Miller-Idris 2019: 126).

A second aspect concerns the organisation form of the movement., Decentralisation of content production is also linked to decentralisation of the organisation of right-wing extremist groups: 'As a new generation of violent extremists emerges from digital subcultures without a clear organisational centre, prevention strategies need to renew focus and cope with the intangible nature of online cultures' (Fielietz & Ahmed 2021: 4). The study by Fielietz and Ahmed focuses on more or less clear right-wing extremist groups and examines the targeted use of social media for their political purposes. The role of users who do not focus on sharing and changing right-wing extremist content is rarely examined. However, for the mechanism of normalisation of right-wing authoritarian ideas, these groups should be the focus of attention in further research.

8. WHEN TRUTH AND LIE ARE NO LONGER GUIDING CATEGORIES

When the boundaries between politics and entertainment, between reality and fiction become blurred and enjoyment becomes the motor of political communication as in the case of meme production, the status of facts, truth and reality becomes precarious. Certainly, it would be a misunderstanding to presuppose an absolute truth since truth is socially constructed (Berger & Luckmann 2001). Both right-wing extremists and democrats in the twenty-first century know this. But something seems to have changed in view of the development outlined here. The editors of this book address the problem indirectly when they ask whether there is a modernisation of the authoritarian and place this question in the context of new communication media. In doing so, they speak of 'entirely new, mass-effective possibilities of manipulation and mobilisation' (Frankenberg & Heitmeyer in this volume). The question here is: What changes with regard to authoritarian right-wing extremist attitudes when irony, deconstruction and hyperreality are taken into account? Comparing the communication and staging of right-wing extremist actors today with those of the German national-socialists and Italian fascists can help to elucidate this question.

In 1943, Alexandre Koyré published a critique of fascism and national socialism. He claimed that totalitarianism – meaning only right-wing totalitarianism – was based on lies. The 'Modern man – *genus totalitarian* – bathes in the lie, breathes the lie, is in thrall to the lie every moment of his existence' (Koyré 19453: 291).[13] At the same time, he was aware that the concept of lie presupposes truth (véracité), just as the concept of 'falsehood' presupposes the concept of the 'real'. For totalitarian regimes, therefore, the distinction between truth and lies would remain essential, but its significance had been reversed: Totalitarian regimes are founded on the primacy of the lie (Koyré 1993: 181), more than that, the lie becomes a virtue (Koyré 1993: 183). As Hannah Arendt later developed in *The Origins of Totalitarianism*, totalitarian

[13] Original: 'L'homme totalitaire baigne dans le mensonge, respire le mensonge, est soumis au mensonge à tous les instants de sa vie.'

societies and groups rely on lies, the more their cohesion is threatened by confrontation with the outside world. This was already anticipated by Koyré:

> Within and for this group, the ability to lie will become all the more necessary, the virtue of the lie all the more praiseworthy, the greater the external pressure, the greater the tension between it and the others, the more the hostility of the 'others' toward 'us' intensifies and increases. (1945: 294)[14]

This is where the main inversion of totalitarianism takes place: The lie is declared to be the truth. When Arendt writes a few years later that totalitarianism is forced to end its dependence on truth (Arendt 2003: 820), she means that the lie and the invented world of totalitarianism take the place of truth. Totalitarian propaganda is about the domination and transformation of reality.

> They do not believe in anything visible, in the reality of their own experience; they do not trust their eyes and ears but only their imaginations, which may be caught by anything that is at once universal and consistent in itself. What convinces masses are not facts, and not even invented facts, but only the consistency of the system of which they are presumably part. Repetition, somewhat overrated in importance because of the common belief in the masses' inferior capacity to grasp and remember, is important only because it convinces them of consistency in time. (Arendt 1962: 351)

Such systems must appear coherent to the outside world, even if they are based on lies. Deconstruction and irony as self-distancing techniques are counter-productive in such cases.

Looking at the communication and staging of Donald Trump and his supporters, the consistency and coherence that Arendt identifies as the work of totalitarian propaganda seems to be missing. Certainly, there are coherent narratives for some groups calling themselves 'Trump supporters' but the approval of this seems somewhat fractured and deconstructionist. No one else has summed up this approval of reality as precisely as former Donald Trump advisor Kellyanne Conway. On 22 January 2017, she was confronted with a question from a CNN journalist about why the President had sent his Press Officer out to tell falsehoods.[15] To this, Conway replied that they were not falsehoods, but 'alternative facts'. In this way, Conway abrogated the

---

[14] Original: 'Il est clair que, dans et pour le groupement en question, la faculté de mentir sera d'autant plus nécessaire, et la vertu du mensonge d'autant plus appréciée, que la pression extérieure, que la tension entre 'nous' et les 'autre', que l'intimité des 'autres' pour 'nous', que la menace que ces 'autres' font peser sur 'nous', grandira et augmentera d'intensité.'

[15] Kellyanne Conway, 'Press Secretary Sean Spicer Gave "Alternative Facts"' (https://www.youtube.com/watch?v=VSrEEDQgFc8).

social pact that makes possible a common construction of reality. In the place of a universally binding reality, everyone can produce their own alternative facts. This is more than the subversion of truth, as some philosophers suggest (McIntyre 2018: 7). If we take the research of media sociologist Joshua Gamson seriously, modern societies in the twenty-first century may just be facing a new and much more playful approval of social reality than the sociologists of knowledge Peter Berger and Thomas Luckmann (2001) could have imagined. Certainly, I am not arguing that society as a whole has abandoned concepts such as truth and reality; however, I think that an additional and new social perception of truth and reality is already emerging, in which the boundaries between reality and fiction and between politics and entertainment have become more fluid as in hyperreality.

When entertainment, persiflage, deconstruction and 'alternative facts' are combined with violence and right-wing extremist attitudes, as the storming of the Capitol shows, the ways in which right-wing extremist ideas are articulated and generated need to be re-evaluated. It is not enough to investigate milieus, socialisation, psychological mechanisms, movement organisations, ideologies and authoritarian attitudes; rather this investigation needs to include mass-media construction of reality(ies) and the way right-wing extremist and populist movements dealt with them. In order to understand the current heterogeneous and complex right-wing extremist phenomena and their normalisation, researchers from sociology, psychology and political science urgently need to include the results of media and cultural studies. The production and dissemination of right-wing extremist ideas must be examined in terms of staging, mass-media production, interaction in the social media and the access to reality produced by them.

REFERENCES

Arendt, Hannah (1962). *The Origins of Totalitarianism* Cleveland and New York. Meridian Books.

Arendt, Hannah (2003), *Elemente und Ursprünge totaler Herrschaft. Antisemitismus, Imperialismus, totale Herrschaft*, München.

Berger, Peter & Luckmann, Thomas (2001), *Die gesellschaftliche Konstruktion der Wirklichkeit,* Frankfurt am Main.

Bennett, W. Lance & Segerberg, Alexandra (2012), 'The Logic of Connective Action: The Personalization of Contentious Politics, Information', in *Communication & Society*, 15 (5), 739–768.

Betz, Hans-Georg (2002), 'Rechtspopulismus in Westeuropa: Aktuelle Entwicklungen und politische Bedeutung', in *ÖZP*, 31 (3), 251–264.

Bogerts, Lisa & Fielitz, Maik (2019), ''Do You Want Meme War?'. Understanding the Visual Memes of the German Far Right', in Fielitz, Maik & Thurston, Nick (eds), *Post-Digital Cultures of the Far Right. Online Actions and Offline Consequences in Europe and the US*, Bielefeld, 137–154.

Cameron, Chris (2022, 13 October). These Are the People Who Died in Connection with the Capitol Riot. *The New York Times*. https://www.nytimes.com/2022/01/05/us/politics/jan-6-capitol-deaths.html/.

Crothers, Lane & Burgener, Grace (2021), 'Insurrectionary Populism? Assessing the January 6 Attack on the U.S. Capitol', in *Populism*, 4, 129–145.

Diehl, Paula (2010), 'Zwischen dem Privaten und dem Politischen – die neue Körperinszenierung der Politiker', in Seubert, Sandra & Niesen, Peter (eds.), *Die Grenzen des Privaten*, Baden-Baden, S. 251–265.

Diehl, Paula (2016), 'Einfach, emotional, dramatisch. Warum Rechtspopulisten so viel Anklang in den Massenmedien finden', in *Die Politische Meinung*, Nr. 539, Juli/August, 61. Jg., 78–83.

Diehl, Paula (2017), 'Antipolitik und Postmoderne Ringkampf-Unterhaltung', in *APuZ, Wandel des Politischen*, 44–45, S. 25–30.

Diehl, Paula (2017), 'Massenmedien, Populismus, Rechtspopulismus', in *Polar – Halbjahresmagazin für Politik, Theorie, Alltag*, 23, 35–42.

Diehl, Paula (2022), 'For a Complex Concept of Populism', in *Polity*, Vol. 3 (forthcoming).

Diehl, Paula & Cavazza, Stefano (ed.) (2012), 'Populismus und Faschismus', in *Totalitarismus und Demokratie*, 9, 203–210.

Donavan, Joan, Lewis, Becca Lewis & Friedberg, Brian (2019), 'Parallel Ports. Socialtechnical Change from the Alt-Right to the Alt-Tech', in Fielitz, Maik & Thurston, Nick (eds), *Post-Digital Cultures of the Far Right. Online Actions and Offline Consequences in Europe and the US*, Bielefeld, 49–65.

Dörner, Andreas (2001), *Politainment. Politik in der medialen Erlebnisgesellschaft*, Frankfurt am Main.

Eco, Umberto (1986), *Travels in Hyperreality. Essays*, New York.

Esposito, Elena (2007), *Die Fiktion der wahrscheinlichen Realität*, Frankfurt am Main.

Fielitz, Maik & Ahmed, Reem (2021), *It's Not Funny Anymore. Far-right Extremists' Use of Humour*, Luxemburg.

Franz, Franz-Xaver (2016), 'Wrestling und Donald Trump', in *POP. Kultur und Kritik*, H. 9, 45–49.

Gamson, Joshua (1994), *Claims to Fame: Celebrity in Contemporary America*, Berkeley/Los Angeles/London.

Koyré, Alexandre (1945), 'The Political Function of the Modern Lie', in *Contemporary Jewish Record* Volume VIII, The American Jewish Committee New York.

Mazer, Sharon (2018), 'Donald Trump Shoots the Match', in *The Drama Review*, 62, No. 2, 175–200.

McIntyre, Lee (2018), *Post-Truth*. Cambridge, MA/London.

Miller-Idriss, Cynthia (2019), 'What Makes a Symbol Far Right? Co-opted and Missed Meanings in Far-Right Iconography', in Fielitz, Maik & Thurston; Nick (Hg.), *Post-Digital Cultures of the Far Right. Online Actions and Offline Consequences in Europe and the US*. Bielefeld, S. 123–135.

Moffitt, Benjamin (2016), *The Global Rise of Populism. Performance, Political Style and Representation*, Stanford.

Mudde, Cas (2004), 'The Populist Zeitgeist', in *Government & Opposition*, 39, 541–563.

Pooley, Jeff (2014), 'Sociology and the Socially Mediated Self', in Waisbord, Silvio (Hg.): *Media Sociology: A Reappraisal*, Cambridge, UK, 224–247.

Rydgren, Jens (2008), 'France: The Front National, Ethnonationalism and Populism', in Albertazzi, Daniele/McDonnell, Duncan (Hg.), *Twenty-First Century Populism. The Spectre of Western European Democracy*, Basingstoke/New York, 166–180.

Sorensen, Lane (2017), 'Populism in Communication Perspective. Concepts, Issues, Evidences', in Heinisch, Reinhard C. u.a. (Hg.), *Political Populism. A Handbook*, Baden-Baden, 137–151.

Thomaser, Sonja (2022), 'Symbol des Sturms: Was aus dem QAnon-Schamanen wurde', in *Frankfurter Allgemeine Zeitung* v. 06 January 2022.

Turner, Fred (2018), 'Trump on Twitter: How a Medium Designed for Democracy Became an Authoritarian's Mouthpiece', in Boczkowski, Pablo J. & Papacharissi, Zizi (Hg.), *Trump and the Media*, Cambridge MA/London, 143–151.

Tuters, Marc (2019), 'LARPing & Liberal Tears. Irony, Belief and Idiocy in the Deep Vernacular Web', in Fielitz, Maik & Thurston, Nick (eds.), *Post-Digital Cultures of the Far Right. Online Actions and Offline Consequences in Europe and the US*, Bielefeld, 37–48.

de Vreese, Claes H. et al. (2018), 'Populism as an Expression of Political Communication Content and Style: A New Perspective', in *The International Journal of Press/Politics*, 23(4), S. 423–438.

Weyland K. (2001), 'Clarifying a contested concept: populism in the study of Latin American politics', in *Comparative Politics* 24(1), 1–22.

Wodak, Ruth (2020), *Politik mit der Angst*, Wien.

PART VI

Repressive instruments and authoritarian movements and the state

15. Leviathan with a beaked mask

Günter Frankenberg

During the COVID-19 crisis, people around the world were forced – by the threat of sanctions – to drastically restrict their freedom of movement and social contacts, professional activities, schooling, and other rights and freedoms in the name of public health and protection against infection. Whereas security is interlocked with freedom even in normal situations, the fight against the pandemic gave safety concerns an almost absolute priority, as is commonly experienced in catastrophes and other situations of extraordinary danger. I reconstruct this tectonic shift from freedom to security, which opens the door to the state of emergency, in three steps: after examining how the authority of law generally relates to its authoritarian forms, I discuss authoritarian impulses in the development of the law of danger prevention and infection control law during the pandemic.

1. AUTHORITY AND AUTHORITARIANISM OF LAW

Law expresses its claim to validity and compliance in statutes, ordinances, and judgments, thereby signalling its authority at the same time. This authority arises in the reciprocal relationship between, on the one hand, the institutions and actors who are legitimised to set norms or make decisions by way of law – and who in turn expect compliance with their orders – and, on the other hand, those who communicate this legitimisation to them without constraint and are recognised in return as *subjects* of law in a double sense, as addressees and authors of law. In normal situations, the authority of law is founded on and develops in this interrelation between voluntariness and coercion.

This symmetry of normalcy and normal law is distorted by (authoritarian) legal acts that break out of the structure of consensual reciprocity, that is, legal acts that relegate the subjects of law to the status of objects of state regulation and thus extinguish voluntary consent (see Frankenberg & Heitmeyer in this volume). This happens through measures that (a) register the subjects only as passing items (and, like traffic signs, perceive the participants in road traffic as abstract-general ordinances), (b) dissolve the fundamental rights that maintain the interrelation between the safeguarding of freedom and interference with freedom, or (c) completely suspend the legal authorship of the subjects in the state of emergency.

That pandemics trigger authoritarian political reflexes and drive law towards authoritarianism is anything but a bold assumption. Whoever is tasked with preventing widespread transborder infections, and is expected by the public (Munich Security Index 2022) to prevent serious or critical damage to its health, will hardly be selective in the choice of (legal) means. Laws intended to avert hazards (or dangers) already have an inherently authoritarian tendency because of their preventive orientation, the prognostic structure of decisions, and the resulting uncertainty as to which state measures would be appropriate and reasonable. Hence, it is in the nature of pandemics to reinforce autocratic security values and strategies (rather than solidarity or care) in infection protection law – values which settle like mildew over both virological-epidemiological and medical knowledge as well as the routines of a rule-of-law regulatory system.

While this last statement may be rather controversial in view of the relationship between the apology and critique of danger prevention and, more generally, security,[1] it is unclear how and where the driving forces of authoritarianism might be anchored in the legal structures, with what and by what means they are normatively charged, and how they can be defused. The following considerations attempt to shed some light on this ambiguity. After a cursory discussion of the points of entry for authoritarian developments in hazard prevention law (or police law), I will concentrate on the set of regulations formerly known as epidemic law, now known as infection control law, and the control strategies in which it is rooted in a number of countries.

2. UNLEASHING THE LEVIATHAN IN SECURITY LAW

2.1 Taming the Danger: Preventing Leviathan

The basic ideal-typical model of averting danger[2] under the rule of law is to keep police action on a safe course between the necessity of interfering with

---

[1] For the breadth of the discussion and the oscillation between apology and critique, see, for example, the contributions to the *Journal of Conflict and Security Law*; the interrelated package of national security, cyberspace, and law enforcement legislation drafted under Xi Jinping in China; or Victor Ramray et al. (2005) *Global Anti-Terrorism Law and Policy*, Cambridge.

[2] According to the standard definition, a danger (in national police or security law) presupposes a situation or behaviour which, if unhindered, will with sufficient probability damage a legal asset (*Schutzgut*) in an individual case (concrete danger) or in general, with statistical probability (abstract danger). The International Law of Security

Source: Author.

Figure 15.1 *Frontispiece to Thomas Hobbes, Leviathan, 1651, designed and printed by Abraham Bosse.*[1]

[1] Bredekamp, Horst (1999), *Thomas Hobbes – Visuelle Strategien*, Berlin, 12.

freedom and the preservation of principles and rights that safeguard freedom, as stipulated in the constitution (Rachor 2021). Again, in ideal-typical terms, this means that only a (concrete or at least abstract) danger rather than a mere statistical risk (Denninger 2021) can trigger the measures necessary to defend against it and preserve or establish the state of security. *Ex post facto*, the legality, exercise of discretion, and proportionality of a police intervention can then be reviewed by the courts. In this way, excessiveness can be, if not prevented, at least corrected in retrospect and, if necessary, compensated.[3] Executive measures that break out of this framework (meaning interventions that go beyond the limits of the constitution and cannot be contained by it) can thus, if all goes well, be prevented *lege artis* (in the best case structurally) or 'retrieved' judicially. As a result, the danger-preventing Leviathan – as Erhard Denninger, one of the few advocates of democratic police law, put it – would be 'tamed' by the rule of law (1990a).

Necessary conditions for successful taming in police law are, in particular, a system of competences that ensures the division of labour and powers between security authorities in a predictable and resilient manner, a sufficient reservoir of knowledge available for preventive police action, clearly outlined standard powers that determine the application, and, finally, effective judicial control of the measures taken. These conditions concretise the preconditions of reciprocity of legal authority discussed above and balance the relationship between voluntariness and coercion.

2.2 How the 'Special Police Law' Unleashes the Leviathan

The conditions of reciprocity are put to the test in hazard prevention law (and, as will be shown, even more so in infection control law), particularly through

---

and Protection is based on a broader definition of dangers: 'the threats to peace and security in the twenty-first century include not just international war and conflict, but civil violence, organized crime, terrorism and weapons of mass destruction. They also include poverty, deadly infectious disease, and environmental degradation since these can have equally catastrophic consequences. All of these threats can cause death or lessen life chances on a large scale. All of them can undermine States as the basic unit of the international system' (Simma, Bruno et al. (2012) The Charter of the United Nations: A Commentary vol. I., 3rd edn, Oxford, 111).

[3] As a rule, national law provides for compensation in the case of vaccination damage (see, for Germany, §§ 56 ff. and 60 of the Infection Protection Act and Bundesversorgungsgesetz). In the case of encroachments on fundamental rights, the path to compensation leads to the international and supranational level, i.e. the International Convention for Civil and Political Rights and in the International Convention against Torture and Other Cruel, Inhuman or Degrading Treatment or Punishment and the European Convention on Human Rights (Art. 41 ECHR).

the crisis phenomena and problem situations outlined below, and are undermined in the case of increased prevention.

(a) On the side of hazard or danger prognosis, increased uncertainty gives rise to an authoritarian tendency. It is triggered by the lack of precise action-guiding information, which unsettles the prognostic assessment and hazard research underlying all preventive decisions, which also applies to the assessment of dangerous technologies or infection control.
(b) On the side of the norms authorising police measures, their porosity exceeds the everyday level of indeterminacy, and their lack of structure opens up the space for executive measures to break out of the rule-of-law frame. They are consequently liable to favour authoritarian developments.
(c) On the side of the principles securing freedom, in particular proportionality and legal certainty, the partial failure of dogmatic specification and/or losses of certainty incline towards the development of a casuistry that follows an insufficiently controlled methodology and a science that has come to perceive itself as providing assistance to the executive instead of critically commenting on the evolution of security law and police action.
(d) On the level of danger prevention as a whole, the Leviathan is released from ties along a broad front when the loss of control dictates a shift in this task – more precisely a shift forward from danger itself to the anticipation of danger and an expansion from preventive to hyper-preventive interventions, from danger prevention to risk management.

2.3 From Danger Prevention to Risk Management

The ruptures, lane changes, and authoritarian impulses – which are explained in detail elsewhere (Denninger 1990b; Frankenberg 2014: Chapters V and VI) but can only be hinted at here – have been caused and partly propelled by state anti-terrorism measures and the prosecution of 'organised crime' as well as the regulation of risky technologies (Damm & Hart 1987). As a result, the factual indeterminacy of police law under the rule of law, the loss of certainty in police law doctrine, and the transition from danger prevention to risk management has found expression in national security laws and, in the case of Germany, in the police laws of the *Länder*: with the blessing of the 'prevailing opinion' in doctrine and case law (Barczak 2020), they assign the police the task of danger and risk prevention (Preuß 1996).[4] Notably, they deconstruct the constitutional

---

[4] E.g. Decisions of the Federal Constitutional Court (BVerfGE), vol. 113, 348/369; and 150, 244.

model of action with a provision that allows the police to take 'precautions for the prosecution of future crimes'.[5] This rule disembogues into a delta of provisions (in reality: dummies) that constitute a 'special police law' of informational measures, such as eavesdropping, dragnet searches, and online searches, extending their far-reaching interventions into the zone preceding danger (*Gefahrenvorfeld*). They upgrade the police assessments of situations and 'findings' to a 'right to invent danger' and thus undermine the ends-means scheme necessary for the subsequent proportionality control. Herold, the former president of the Federal Criminal Police Office (the German equivalent to the FBI), put this advance shift or hyper-prevention in legendary terms: 'The police must be at the scene of the crime before the perpetrator' (Albers 2001: 116).

The extent to which the Leviathan has been unleashed in security law can be demonstrated with regard to telecommunication interception systems.[6] It was recently illustrated by the somewhat unwieldy 'source telecommunication surveillance', i.e. the police authorities' handling of security gaps or vulnerabilities in programmes or other information technology systems that are not known to the system manufacturers (so-called zero-day vulnerabilities).[7] The German Constitutional Court had just ruled that the state's general duty to protect becomes a *concrete* duty to protect under fundamental rights if the state authorities become aware of any such security vulnerabilities. According to the court, this concrete duty to protect is based on the high risk and damage potential of security vulnerabilities, on the lack of possibility for those affected to protect themselves, and precisely on the fact that the authorities have knowledge of the security vulnerability. In the meantime, it has become known that the much sought-after software 'Pegasus', produced by the company NSO Group, which enables the exploitation of zero-days, i.e. the surreptitious intrusion into information technology systems ('hacking'), was acquired and used by the Federal Criminal Office in autumn 2020 (see Biermann in this volume).[8]

---

[5] See, for example, § 2 IV HSOG (Police Law in Hessen); § 1 I 2 PolG-NRW (Police Law in North-Rhine Westfalia).

[6] Telecommunication interception systems enable law enforcement personnel to gather data for investigative purposes. They can be used to track calls to or from a particular number, record audio and data messages, determine the location from which cell phone calls were placed, and help determine the scope of an investigation by establishing relationships between callers.

[7] The term 'zero-day' is used when security teams are unaware of their hardware or software vulnerability, and they have had zero days to work on a security patch or an update to fix the issue. As to the window of vulnerability: Johansen et al. 2007.

[8] 'Pegasus' can be surreptitiously installed on smartphones in order to monitor them. It provides access to almost all user activity, even encrypted communications (see Biermann in this volume). A sorry comfort: the Federal Criminal Office assured

Parliamentary questions on the use of 'state Trojans' went unanswered by the federal government – on the grounds of protecting the 'welfare of the state'.

2.4 Normalising the State of Exception

One can take these deficits in the rule of law into account – both in police practice and in legal thought – or even consider them necessary to enhance security. If so, the consequences should be included in the balance: within the corset of the rule of law, powers and interventions find their legal justification and popular acceptance, despite their inevitable authoritarian tendency, in the promise of security and the corresponding expectations of the citizenry. As hyper-preventive measures, however, they break out of the normal rule-of-law framework and infiltrate the body of police regulations as a kind of emergency law. This applies above all to the data networks of intelligence services as well as to informational interventions in the absence of concrete danger, especially in places without 'criminogenic valence' (such as the dragnet, which has become a favoured surveillance instrument in a number of countries worldwide). They are instructive insofar as they operate on the basis of a general presumption of dishonesty and are designed, for example through video surveillance, dragnets, or veil searches, to invent danger and suspicion without cause and to legalise everyday practices contrary to the rule of law. Such practices include racial profiling, for example in the identification of 'persons in international transport facilities ... on the basis of situational knowledge or police experience', if 'it can be assumed that they are of considerable importance for cross-border crime'. Another problematic measure is the use of 'state Trojans', an apparently harmless but in fact malicious programme that is downloaded and installed on a computer for the clandestine exploration of information and decryption of private communications.

Targeting dangerless zones, especially with the ensemble of informational powers, can be reconstructed as a gradual proliferation or *normalisation* of the state of emergency (Frankenberg 2014: 25–29; Volkmann 2008; Barczak 2020). In this context, normalisation refers to the legalisation of instruments that deviate from standard powers and draw on powers of emergency law, legitimated by emergency law's argumentative figures. With their registration in the context of normal law, special authoritarian competences and the legal measures they authorise are called upon on a case-by-case basis and, as needed, wrapped in the cloak of normative normality, made permanent and thus commonplace.

the public that it did not use the standard version, but a variant that is largely compatible with data protection.

As a rule, normalisation is triggered by crises such as terrorism, 'organised crime', or, as will be shown below, a pandemic or epidemic threat. It appears, first of all, in a semantics of *trivialisation* that covers up the extraordinary character of a measure. Particularly striking examples are the banalisation of taboo-breaking as 'rescue torture', the targeted fatal shot in police law as a 'rescue shot' or, most recently, the 'federal emergency brake' for severe nationwide encroachments on basic rights, in particular the night-time curfew.

Second, normalisation is reflected in *topographical breaks* in normal law, which security law is designed to conceal. Since the mid-1990s, this has been known at the European level and with regard to NATO as the 'new security architecture', which corrects the structures of the 'Cold War' (Berndt 2007). This architecture was adopted for police and security authorities under the influence of the 'War on Terror'. In danger prevention law (or security law), distortions can be seen in the lowering of intervention thresholds (primarily the loosening of the doctrinal concept of danger and disturbance) and in the rededication of danger prevention law to a 'danger invention law'. In addition, the unleashing of extraordinary powers loosens the internal link between encroachments on freedom and the fundamental rights that are to guarantee freedom.

Third, normalisation means that subsequent controls and corrections are made more difficult, or even set up largely for failure, due to the reduced density of judicial review, a process which gives way to executive authoritarianism insofar as rogue legal acts cannot be contained or corrected retrospectively. Symptomatic of this are the porous elements of legal provisions (dummies) and the extent to which the balancing test of the proportionality of state measures in the light of their legitimate purpose is prejudiced by a security priority or fails altogether. (We will come back to this in a moment.)

3. LEVIATHAN WITH A BEAKED MASK

Probably the best-known version of Hobbes' *Leviathan* frontispiece reveals two plague doctors in beaked masks at the bottom of the world landscape in a deserted city. Inspired by Francesca Falk's discovery (2011) and by Thomas Poole's essay 'Leviathan in Lockdown' (2020), I use the figure of the Leviathan with a beaked mask to embody the thesis that infectious disease law and the unleashed Leviathan necessarily express authoritarian impulses. At the same time, the beaked mask is meant to point to aspects of *ultra vires* or 'galloping' infection control measures.

Source: Author

Figure 15.2 *Paul Fürst, engraving, c. 1656, of a plague doctor of Marseilles (introduced as 'Dr. Beak of Rome').*

3.1 Epidemic Law as Danger Prevention

Protection against infections and the spread of infections is a separate area of public health law that, despite its specific features, fits systematically into the respective national security laws, more exactly the laws of hazard (or danger) prevention. Traditional epidemic law can be traced back to the medieval plague ordinances. After the abdication of religious interpretations – the plague as God's punishment, to be met with expiatory sacrifices – and the fading of magical ideas – the disease as the embodiment of evil (Attali 1979) – the plague ordinances were for a long time characterised by the paradigm dispute between miasmatology and contagionism. Adherents of the miasma theory[9] held evil fumes and putrefactive processes in the air, water, or soil responsible for the disease (Mead 1720; Last 2007). Contagionists, propagating the germ theory, assumed that pathogens were transmitted by contagion (Wegner 2005: 985; Benedictow 2020; Crawford 2018). Both interpretative variants produced phantasms and conspiracy theories (Ruffié & Sournia 1984); at the same time, they legitimised drastic, authoritarian measures that were demanded by the panic-stricken population (MacNeill 1976; Vasold 2003), such as walling plague sufferers in their homes, housing them in isolation wards, forcibly administering emetics and bloodletting, and burning down city districts.

In contrast, today's national infection protection laws are generally informed by the scientific knowledge provided by virology, epidemiology, medicine and, more recently, aerosol research, and base their preventive interventions on considerable advances in scientific knowledge (Grossmann 2021). Many of the measures – not only the German Infection Protection Act (IfSG) – operate within the categories and structures of a modified police and regulatory law tailored to the prevention of infections with recourse to information technology. Standard measures are surveillance, the reporting and registration of infected persons, social distancing, and quarantine.[10]

---

[9] The miasma theory, today an abandoned medical theory, held that diseases – such as cholera or the plague – were caused by a *miasma*, a 'pollution' or noxious form of 'bad air' emanating from rotting organic matter (Last 2007). Eventually disproved by the understanding of bacteria and the discovery of viruses, the miasma theory helped establish the connection between poor sanitation and disease and legitimised sanitation laws already in the nineteenth century, e.g. Sanitary Legislation. No. VII. Nuisances Removal and Diseases Prevention Acts Consolidation and Amendment Bill (1855), in 3 Association Medical Journal, 619–621 (Cipolla 1992).

[10] Quarantine was arguably first practiced in Venice in the twelfth century, when the plague was threatening trade relations, Drews 2013. See also US Centers for Disease Control and Prevention: https://www.cdc.gov/quarantine/index.html. A survey of infection protection acts is provided by Grogan & Donald 2022; Hondius, et al. 2021; Huster & Kingreen 2021.

This regulatory scheme of social isolation and surveillance can be illustrated by the development in Germany: as successor to the Imperial Epidemic Act of 1900 and the Federal Epidemic Act of 1961, the IfSG has, since 2001, granted the public health authorities whatever powers are deemed necessary to complete the general tasks (surveillance, prevention, control) as well as the special tasks of infection protection in institutions, with regard to water as well as to the handling of food and pathogens. In the catalogue of measures, the preventive and 'therapeutic' role (Attali 1979: 79–82) of what used to be called the health 'police', today the 'health office', is evident. The more traditional approach of epidemic law concentrated on the isolation of those suspected of being infected and measures to contain the incidence of infection through surveillance. Later, the accent shifted from isolation to observation, in particular to reporting obligations, data collection, tracing chains of infection (WarnApp), and the prohibition of activities.[11] Before the emergency legislation set in, national infection protection laws remained basically within the framework of the rule of law, even if they already interfered rather intensely with fundamental rights. As in the police laws of hazard/danger prevention, broadly framed general clauses complete the more determinate standard powers.[12]

4. AUTHORITARIAN ELEMENTS IN INFECTION PROTECTION LAW

During the COVID-19 pandemic, national governments were challenged to part with the structures and provision of 'normal' infection protection law (Grogan & Donald 2022; Hondius et al. 2021). While some laws already established the authority of a centralised public health agency, other were included in a federal system of division of labour and fragmented competences.[13] Especially after the WHO had declared an international public health emergency on 30 January 2020, many countries rushed to (a) declare the state of exception, (b) pass emergency laws, and (c) 'normalise' extraordinary/emergency infection protection powers.

---

[11] See the national legislation in Grogan & Donald 2022; Hondius, et al. 2021.

[12] Compare the rather indeterminate powers, granted, for instance, by §§ 16 and 28, 28a IfSG, with the so-called standard measures, such as social distancing, hand hygiene, wearing masks, also for special locations and situations, like schools, public transportation etc. (Kießling 2022). See also https://www.cdc.gov/oralhealth/infectioncontrol/summary-infection-prevention-practices/standard-precautions.html/.

[13] In many countries a central, public health institution is authorised as, for instance, in Germany the national prevention authority of the Robert Koch Institute (RKI); the Centers for Disease Control and Prevention, the national public health agency of the United States; the Centre for Disease Control in the United Kingdom; or the European Health Emergency Preparedness and Response Authority (HERA).

4.1 Germany's Search Movements and a Fake State of Emergency

The German Infection Protection Act and its series of amendments testify to the feverish, if erratic, activity within and without the rule-of-law model, which testifies to the normalisation strategy. The catalogue of intensely interventionist pandemic powers signals that, in the assessment of the government (led by the Minister of Health) and the federal institute of public health (RKI) COVID-19 could be read as an implicit critique of the traditional health federalism and of certain scientific experts. The message: the pandemic was not to be contained with the usual, constitutionally legal means and measures.

The many legal interventions evince a considerable loss of control on the part of law and regulation makers (Barczak 2020) in their nervous and desperate attempts to cope with the spread of COVID-19 and its variants and also to the normalisation of emergency measures (Frankenberg 2014). The introduction of four laws to safeguard the 'protection of the population in the event of an epidemic situation of national significance' (as stipulated by § 5 I IfSG) between March 2020 and April 2021, as well as the numerous further adjustments and modifications thereafter, illustrates a considerable lack of reliable, action-guiding information for controlling the 'infection event' and, understandably, a deficit of routine and expertise. The underlying operational uncertainty of this hectic legislative process since the spring of 2020 has forced legislators and governments at the federal and state levels not only to repeatedly amend the infection protection law, but also to alter the leading indicators for protective measures (herd immunity, mortality, seven-day incidence, infection rate, hospitalisation incidence, number of intensive care beds, ventilators, etc.), to modify the prioritisation of vaccination groups, and to change the official classification of measures from a mere recommendation to mandatory rules (masks, testing) and finally to a 'federal emergency brake' (*Bundesnotbremse*). From a distance, through slightly rose-tinted glasses, this might appear as the practice of a learning rule-maker, but in the cold light of day it reveals fractures in the constitutional approach to infection control – fractures that are dictated by intra-governmental competition, the logic of election campaigns, and the groping 'search movements' and trigger authoritarian developments.

In the background of all this (primarily executive) legal activism, the German Bundestag empowered itself to declare a (somewhat phony) state of emergency, that is, 'an epidemic situation of national significance'.[14] While some commentators and, above all, the jurisprudence were unable to extract

[14] Pursuant to § 5 I 1 IfSG, which has been amended several times and has since expired.

anything of relevance for a critique of this provision, other authors are reminded of the vocabulary and grammar of the state of exception (Frankenberg 2017; Barczak: 2020; Volkmann 2020). According to the rules of a (constitutionalised) state of exception, which were included in the Basic Law in 1968 as the enumeration of emergency situations, the epidemic has to be formally declared and expires automatically unless prolonged; if the conditions cease to exist, it must be lifted in advance. Materially, it requires a threatening exceptional situation: 'a serious danger to public health in the entire Federal Republic of Germany' or the 'dynamic spread of a threatening communicable disease over several states in the Federal Republic of Germany'. Such a state of exception or emergency is not provided for by the Basic Law, regardless of the COVID-19 emergency. Yet the governmental interventions demonstrated features of emergency law that can neither be overlooked nor justified as a set of 'diffuse interventions' in response to a 'diffuse infection event' (Barczak 2021). The state-of-emergency character of this response is confirmed by the limited participation of the Bundestag: it corresponds to the 'genuine', that is constitutional, states of emergency certified by the Basic Law (such as legislative emergency, Art. 91 GG; political-military situation of tension, Art. 80a GG; or defence emergency, Art. 115a GG). It is crucial to note that parliamentary involvement was exhausted in the mere determination of the epidemic emergency. After that, the power to issue ordinances and orders was transferred to the executive or, more precisely, to the Federal Minister of Health or his ministry (BGM), who had already been given plenty of powers. Not even the federal cabinet benefited from the self-disempowerment of parliament under the sign of the pandemic state of emergency.

In the manner of a state of emergency, the declared 'epidemic situation of national significance' was therefore not only of declaratory significance, but opened the hatch to emergency-like ordinance authorisations: a considerable number of them (not only applying to infection protection law, but also to health law in the broader sense) were shifted into the regulatory and competence area of the Ministry of Health. An 'emergency ordinance power for health protection' in COVID-19 times may be 'understandable', but this does not change the fact that it propels an authoritarian shift in infection protection law. With the change of track from law-executing to law-replacing ordinances, a large part of the German infection protection law was thus placed under broadly defined executive discretion. Voices in the literature rightly pointed out that the constitutional basis for the authorisation to issue statutory ordinances that replace laws (Art. 80 Basic Law) could not 'bear this burden of necessity' for its lack of determinate content, purpose, and in particular scope.[15] During the pandemic, the legislature repeatedly (and contrary to the constitution) delegated 'programme responsibility' to the ministry.

The decision of the coalition government to let the declaration of 'an epidemic situation of national significance' end in autumn 2021 may have been politically unfortunate because of the timing – the dramatic escalation of the COVID-19 pandemic during the 'fourth wave'. However, on the merits, the decision was difficult to oppose as a matter of legality, for while it did not deny the epidemic emergency, it finally refuted the need to counter it with a largely 'fake state of emergency' and a self-deprived parliament.

4.2 Italy's State of Exception

On 31 January 2020, the Italian Parliament passed a Legislative Decree, based on the Civil Protection Code (and arguably the rather indeterminate Art. 77 of the Italian Constitution), which recognised, very much like § 5 of the German IfSG, that COVID-19 had to be considered as an

> emergency of national importance connected with natural origin or man-made disasters which, by reason of their intensity or extension, must, with immediate intervention, be faced with extraordinary means and powers to be employed during limited and predefined periods of time pursuant to Art. 24.[16]

In consequence, again like Germany, Italy shifted public health powers to the executive – to the detriment of judicial authority and parliamentary oversight. The loss of effective judicial or parliamentary mechanisms of supervision of that executive power and, in particular, the replacement of the judicial role with police operations, represented a typical symptom of how prolonged emergencies are prone to lead to the 'eclipse of legal certainty and may cause the rapid and irreversible degradation of the rule of law' (Canestrini 2020).

As the pandemic developed into a catastrophe, Italy's population – asked to submit to the mantra 'I'm staying at home' – had to pay a high price for the

---

[15] Poscher 2021; Heinig et al. 2020; Wissenschaftliche Dienste des Bundestages 2020.

[16] See http://www.protezionecivile.gov.it/en/transparent-administration/legal-measures/detail/-/asset_publisher/default/content/decreto-legislativo-n-1-del-2-gennaio-2018-codice-della-protezione-civi-1/. Philosopher Giorgio Agamben criticised the Italian government for prescribing quarantining and social distancing without sufficient evidence that COVID-19 was any different from the usual influenza virus. He went overboard in calling it 'the Invention of an Epidemic' and labelled the measure 'frenetic, irrational and entirely unfounded': https://www.quodlibet.it/giorgio-agamben-l-invenzione-di-un-epidemia. Even after the horrendous corona death toll Italy had to pay, he did not change his mind.

previous privatisation and dismantling of the public health service, especially in Lombardy and, albeit to a lesser degree, in Veneto. After a while, when the national government-ordered severe restrictions and draconian measures originally prescribed only for the 'red areas' were extended to the national territory – against the protests of right-wing politicians – Italy was already well on its way to a national disaster (Alviar & Frankenberg 2021; Simoni 2020).

In a first phase, absent a veritable state-of-exception clause in the constitution, the government issued a line of decrees based on a statutory state of emergency that was declared at the end of January 2020. In a series of further steps, the government introduced the prohibition of movement between different municipalities and of any travel abroad, and the interruption of all 'productive, industrial and commercial' activities, except those specifically foreseen in a governmental list as 'essential' activities. Strong protests were directed against the provision that individuals could leave their homes only for certain purposes enumerated by the government. A milder regime, presented as the start of 'Phase 2', came into force in May 2020, but the government already clarified that this still would not include the permission to leave home for purposes beyond those listed in the new decree, with the impossibility, e.g., to visit friends or simply stroll around (Simoni 2020).

The authoritarian turn in Italy passed the stress test (Simoni 2020) but could not completely undo the austerity and privatisation programmes that had damaged the public health service and undermined the first line of defence against a pandemic, especially the community health centres and the practices of general practitioners.

4.3 The State of Exception in China

China's response to COVID-19 was neither significantly hampered by privatised structures nor troubled by the rule of law as a perimeter for legitimacy. It does not come as a surprise that China's handling of the COVID-19 pandemic reflected long-standing features of Chinese law and governance (de Lisle & Kui 2022). The initial troubled response was consistent with the initial misjudgement of COVID-19 as an influenza virus or pneumonia; much later, the central decision-makers seemed to have come to the conclusion that the coronavirus was set free by zoonosis.[17]

A week before the WHO's declaration, on 23 January 2020, China's central government imposed a lockdown in Wuhan and other cities in the region of Hubei in an effort to quarantine the centre of an outbreak of COVID-19 (Alviar

[17] That is why China banned the 'Illegal Wild-Life Trade' and prohibited the 'Bad Habit of Excessive Eating of Wild Animals' (Alviar & Frankenberg 2021: 40).

& Frankenberg 2021). The WHO commended the Wuhan lockdown, calling it 'unprecedented in public health history' (similarly Mattei et al. 2020). Later measures to control the pandemic showed the system's formidable capacity to mobilise vast resources and shape citizens' behaviour. The absence of legal constraints on regime choices facilitated the installation of an (undeclared) state of exception, that is a nation-wide lockdown, accompanied by draconian measures. China fought a centrally monitored 'people's war of disease prevention', closing the borders, banning assemblies in public places, keeping schools closed, and submitting businesses to a strict lockdown. It is hard to tell whether the authoritarian turn of an already authoritarian government 'worked' in terms of contagion prevention and which side-effects it may have had (Zhen et al. 2020) because the Chinese government kept all information under tight control.

The state of exception had to be declared again when the pandemic resurged with a vengeance. In the fall of 2022, a dozen large cities had to go into lockdown again, and about 200 further lockdowns were registered across the country.[18]

4.4 Summing Up

Far from fantasies of a viral state of siege, it is worth recalling that these various forms of social isolation and control of public space have always been the signature of strategies that, in combating pandemic or epidemic emergencies, give no consideration to reciprocity. Since the recurring plague since 1348, the cholera pandemic after 1817, leprosy (limited in their spread, with over 200,000 new cases recorded worldwide as recently as 2019), and the influenza pandemics in the wake of the devastating Spanish flu, the authoritarian thrust of measures of spatial and social isolation to contain epidemics and pandemics has repeatedly come to full fruition. In leprosy wards for lepers, plague houses, typhus hospitals, and similar total institutions (Foucault 1991), one does not find subjects of law but objects of sovereign epidemic discipline. These isolation wards cannot be compared to domestic quarantines and night-time curfews because, on the one hand, not even 'valid reasons' (as provided for by the Italian and German regulations) permitted temporary departure from the ward or the home and, on the other hand, legal protection, in particular recourse to the courts, was not available. Admittedly, one would not want to be guided by medieval legal systems or those of the nineteenth century when

---

[18] 'China Covid: millions back in lockdown as Beijing doubles down on zero covid', BBC News, 22 October 2022 – https://www.bbc.com/news/world-asia-china-63410341/.

identifying authoritarian breaking points and tendencies in infection protection law. Therefore, after the repeated attempts (especially in the spring and autumn of 2021) to adapt infection protection law to the development of the pandemic, it must be assessed whether the measures in many countries, notably those in Germany from November and December 2021 – first and foremost the exit regulations, bans on gatherings, the closure of accommodation establishments, establishments of commerce, and the offer of 'body-related services' as well as indoor sports facilities – fit easily into the rule-of-law system or whether, without exaggeration and alarmism, an authoritarian tendency should be attested to them which, under certain circumstances and where unavoidable, would have to be hemmed in by emergency law.

5. ANTI-AUTHORITARIAN CROSS-EXAMINATION

The identification of authoritarian impulses and developments in infection control law (as well as in the law of hazard prevention) is unlikely to meet with widely shared approval among scholars of public law. In fact, a number of arguments can be put forward which, if valid, would invalidate the thesis of authoritarianism outlined here.

5.1 There Is No Alternative: So It's Not Authoritarian?

Comments on the state's anti-corona measures, which aim to ward off excessive criticism and prevent disruptions of ongoing operations, follow, among other things, the TINA principle: *there is no alternative.*[19] Such arguments suggest, for example, that a diffuse infection event justifies diffuse infection control measures, or that the state acted as it had to act. In other words, no quarantine of fundamental rights, no state of emergency, no partial suspension of the constitution, no virocracy (Barczak 2021) – nothing authoritarian in the infection protection laws.

Apart from the fact that the search movements of the various states' corona policies during the different phases can hardly be shown to have been without alternatives, especially when the strategies of other countries come into view (Alviar & Frankenberg 2021), the thesis of the (alleged) lack of alternatives would in itself be an indication of the authoritarianism of technocratic or autocratic logic, which wants to cut off discussion of state measures and of political omissions and misguided planning (on technocratic authoritarianism: Zürn in this volume). To take the example of compulsory vaccination or strongly

---

[19] For the history and the political context of the slogan: Astrid Séville (2017) *There Is No Alternative*, Frankfurt/München.

recommended vaccination: As an alternative to the practice in many countries, the Spanish government took the path of personally inviting citizens to be vaccinated, sending them the dates and registering those who refused to be vaccinated. This approach was quite successful: Spain had a high (voluntary) vaccination rate. In Portugal, the population was also committed to the 'fight against corona'. In both countries, the vaccination campaigns were planned in detail. In Israel, booster vaccinations were started early and on a broad front, while in Germany it was still being discussed whether only the risk groups should be vaccinated a third time. Despite widespread protests, vaccination became compulsory for the medical and nursing professions in Italy starting in May 2021.

Another example are the lockdowns: that there are alternatives to a comprehensive lockdown is shown by the corona policy in South Korea, where the pandemic was quickly taken much more seriously than in most European countries but no lockdown was commanded (Yoshimura 2021).

5.2 Possibility of a 'Reset'?

An assessment of the corona measures as authoritarian would be difficult to defend, despite the evidence and considerations discussed here, if one could easily assume that, thanks to its resilience, the rule of law would ultimately triumph over the pandemic state once the work to control the disease was done and the infection protection laws of the pandemic could be submitted to a vigorous revision. In view of the history of influenza pandemics,[20] the risks and dynamics of zoonosis (Scott 2017; Crawford 2018; Grange 2021), and the course of corona/COVID-19, one can only reluctantly speak of 'work done' or put stock in the likelihood that after lockdown policies and vaccination campaigns, a continuation of the pandemic (or a new edition) is no longer to be expected.

On the other hand, the time limit on the determination of an epidemic situation of national scope and its expiry as well as the temporary nature of legal ordinances can be cited as indications of the envisaged defusing of the Infection Protection Act. Of course, one should not overlook the 'misery' of exceptions and 'bridging norms' that extend the period of validity of these problematic provisions.

The governments' reactions to critical objections to their plans and measures (see above) also do not speak for a timely constitutional reset. Moreover,

---

[20] From the numerous publications see Vasold 2015; Vögele et al. 2016; Crawford 2018; Kilbourne, Edwin (2006) 'Influenza pandemics of the 20th century', in 12 *Emerg Infect Dis*, 9–14.

there is no strong motive for such a reset if public criticism of the Leviathan with the beaked mask withers away, or if the sciences called upon to supervise the politics of the pandemic exercise restraint so as not to endanger their reputation and funding or stab the state in the back in difficult times.

5.3 Are the Infection Protection Acts of the Pandemic a Democratic Community Project?

The argument of infection protection laws' authoritarian turn would collapse completely if the corona/COVID-19 measures taken – notably the Portuguese, Israeli, or South Korean model (Alviar & Frankenberg 2021) – could be understood as a democratic community project. In other words: a deliberate decision to accept 'unfreedom' or voluntary 'self-empowerment of the citizens of the state for the commonality of politically autonomous action' (Habermas 2021). Indeed, the broad popular approval of most of the corona measures in Germany (apparently unlike Italy) could be used to support this. Although not free of fluctuations, support was consistently relatively high (Brandt 2021; BFR 2021; ifo/forsa 2021). Overall, however, the acceptance of governmental infection control tended to follow the ripples of the pandemic and was quite variable with regard to the individual measures (COSMO COVID-19 2021). In particular, curfews and shutting down schools did not receive the same approval ratings as hygiene rules, mandatory masks, and distancing requirements (which tend to be less restrictive to basic rights). Moreover, the results of the surveys do not exclude the possibility that they were due to the fear of contagion, i.e. that the measures were endured more like a blind, unchangeable fate than as a democratic project (Frankenberg 2023; Munich Security Conference 2022).

The way in which the corona measures came about speaks for 'compulsory solidarity' instead of voluntary participation and an emphatic democratic spirit: alternatives to the curfew or lockdown policy adopted in many countries were never seriously proposed publicly by the governments. The quite successful data-based strategy of tracking, tracing, and testing in South Korea as well as in Singapore and Taiwan (Di Moia 2020) was noted and considered in confidential government papers, but not brought into the public discussion. Elsewhere, in the public space, data protection concerns remained paramount. In addition to coercion, only very limited emphasis was placed on voluntariness and citizen responsibility (Frankenberg 2020). The heads of government at the federal and state levels discussed their lockdown policy informally and *in camera*. Decisions were presented at press conferences without elaborate justification. What was discussed behind closed doors remained the subject of speculation. Legislative procedures were generally downstream of executive government decisions. MPs complained of a glaring lack of participation.

Indeed, this informalism and executivist, partly clandestine procedure, the 'special powers', and the spirit of no alternative need not be dramatised as an 'authoritarian seizure of power'. Much less, of course, is it appropriate to celebrate these aspects and the infection protection laws – with their broad authorisations to close public forums for assembly and public debate – as a democratic community project that succeeded under difficult conditions.

Instead of relying on corona politics and legal norms with annoyance (in the scientific community) or hurt feelings (on the part of the parliamentarians who were passed over), and instead of warning against exaggerated criticism, it would be quite appropriate to make the polity aware of the elements of an authoritarian state technique (Frankenberg 2014 and 2023) and to remove the beaked mask from the Leviathan while still appreciating the difficulty of the situation and the undeniable successes of the decision-makers. The pandemic may be 'the hour of the executive'. However, informed by a democratic constitution, the Leviathan should not be the one setting the pace.

REFERENCES

Albers, Marion (2001) *Die Determination polizeilicher Tätigkeit in den Bereichen der Straftatenverhütung und der Verfolgungsvorsorge,* Berlin.

Alviar, Helena & Frankenberg, Günter (2021), 'Paying for the Consequences. How Privatization and Austerity Disabled Infections Protection Law', in 54 *VRÜ/World Comparative Law*, 27–54.

Attali, Jacques (1979) *L'ordre cannibale. Vie et mort de la médicine,* Paris.

Barczak, Tristan (2020), *Der nervöse Staat: Ausnahmezustand und Resilienz des Rechts der Sicherheitsgesellschaft,* Tübingen.

Barczak, Tristan (2021), *Der nervöse Staat: Ausnahmezustand und Resilienz des Rechts der Sicherheitsgesellschaft*, Tübingen.

Benedictow, Ole J. (2020) *The Complete History of the Black Death,* Woodbridge.

Berlinski, Claire (2010) *There Is No Alternative: Why Margaret Thatcher Matters,* New York.

Berndt, Michael (2007) *Die 'Neue Europäische Sicherheitsarchitektur',* Wiesbaden.

Blankenagel, Alexander (2021), 'Did Constitution Matter?', in *Juristenzeitung*, 702–710.

Bundesinstitut für Risikobewertung (2020) 'Corona Monitor 7–8 July 2020'.

Cipolla, Carlo M. (1992) *Miasmas and Disease: Public health and Environment in the Pre-industrial Age,* New Haven.

COSMO COVID-19 Monitoring (April 2021) – https:// projekte .uni -erfurt .de/ cosmo2020/web/topic/politik/20-akzeptanz/.

Crawford, Dorothy H. (2018) *Deadly Companions. How Microbes Shaped Our History*, 2nd edn, Oxford.

Damm, Reinhard & Hart, Dieter (1987) 'Rechtliche Regulierung riskanter Technologien', in *Kritische Vierteljahresschrift für Gesetzgebung und Rechtsprechung*, 183–216.

Denninger, Erhard (2021) 'D. Polizeiaufgaben', in Lisken, Hans & Denninger, Erhard, eds, *Handbuch des Polizeirechts*, München, Ch. D I.

Denninger, Erhard (1990a) *Der gebändigte Leviathan,* Baden-Baden.

Denninger, Erhard (1990b) 'Der Präventionsstaat', in ders., *Der gebändigte Leviathan*, Baden-Baden, 33–49.

DiMoia, John P. (2020) 'Contact-Tracing and COVID-19: The South Korean Context for Public Health Enforcement', in 14 *East Asian Science, Technology and Society – An International Journal*, 657–665.

Falk, Francesca (2011) 'Hobbes' Leviathan und die aus dem Blick gefallenen Schnabelmasken', in 39 *Leviathan*, 247–266.

Foucault, Michel (1991 [1975]) *Discipline and Punish. The Birth of the Prison*, New York.

Frankenberg, Günter (2014) *Political Technology and the Erosion of the Rule of Law. Normalizing the State of Exception*, Cheltenham.

Frankenberg, Günter (2017) 'Im Ausnahmezustand', in *Kritische Justiz*, 3–18.

Frankenberg, Günter (2020) 'COVID-19 und der juristische Umgang mit Ungewissheit', in Verfassungsblog, 2020/4/25.

Frankenberg, Günter (2023) 'Constituting the negative globality of fear', in 21 *Int'l Journal of Constitutional Law*, 1–9.

Gärditz, Klaus F. & Abdulsalam, Maryam (2020) 'Rechtsverordnungen als Instrument der Pandemiebekämpfung', in 25 *GSZ – Zeitschrift für das gesamte Sicherheitsrecht*, 108.

Gärditz, Klaus F. & Meinel, Florian (2020) 'Unbegrenzte Ermächtigung?', in *Frankfurter Allgemeine Zeitung*, 26 March, 6.

Gibson, Edmund (1721) *The causes of the discontents in relation to the plague, and the provisions against it, fairly stated and consider'd*, London.

Grange, Zoe L. et al. (2021), 'Ranking the risk of animal-to-human spillover for newly discovered viruses', in 118 Proceedings of the National Academy of Sciences, 20 April.

Grogan, Joelle & Donald, Alice, eds (2021), *Routledge Handbook of Law and the COVID-19 Pandemic*, London.

Grossmann, Stefanie (2021), 'Pest bis Corona: Wie die Menschheit gegen Seuchen kämpft', *NDR*, 30. December.

Habermas, Jürgen (2021), 'Corona und der Schutz des Lebens', in 66 *Blätter für deutsche und internationale Politik*, 65–78.

Heinig, Hans Michael, Kingreen, Thorsten, Lepsius, Oliver, Möllers, Christoph, Volkmann, Uwe, Wißmann, Hinnerk (2020), 'Why Constitution Matters. Verfassungsrechtswissenschaft' in Zeiten der Corona-Krise, in 75 *JuristenZeitung*, 861–872.

Hondius, Ewoud, Santos Silva, Marta, Nicolussi, Andrea, Salvador Coderch, Pablo, Wendehorst, Christiane & Zoll Fryderyk (eds.) (2022), *Coronavirus and the Law in Europe*, Brussels.

Huster, Stefan & Kingreen, Thorsten (2021), *Handbuch zum Infektionsschutzrecht*, München.

ifo-Institut/forsa (2020), 'Die Deutschen und Corona, BMG-'Corona-Studie'', 10 July, München/Berlin.

Jestaedt, Matthias & Kaiser, Anna-Bettina (2021) *'Das staatliche Pandemiemanagement im Lichte des Verfassungsrechts'*, *Verfassungsblog*, https://verfassungsblog.de/kritik-ja-verfassungskrise-nein/.

Johansen, Håvard et al. (eds.) (2007) *New Approaches for Security, Privacy and Trust in Complex Environments*. IFIP International Federation for Information Processing, New York.

Kersten, Jens & Rixen, Stefan (2020), *Der Verfassungsstaat in der Corona-Krise*, München.

Kießling, Andrea (ed.) (2022) *IfSG. Infektionsschutzgesetz – Kommentar,* München.

Klafki, Anika (2017), *Risiko und Recht,* Tübingen.

Klemm, Sabine (2021) 'Corona-Diktatur? Zum Umgang mit Verschwörungslegenden und Geschichtsrevisionismus unter 'Corona-Kritikern', in *H-Soz-Kult,* 21 May 2021.

Krings, Günter (2021) 'Kritik ist kein Selbstzweck', in Verfassungsblog- https://verfassungsblog.de/kritik-ist-kein-selbstzweck/.

Last, John M. (2007) 'Miasma Theory', in Porta, Miquel & Last, John, eds, *A Dictionary of Public Health*, Oxford.

Lepsius, Oliver (2020) 'Vom Niedergang grundrechtlicher Denkkategorien in der Corona-Pandemie', in Verfassungsblog, https://verfassungsblog.de/vom-niedergang-grundrechtlicher-denkkategorien-in-der-corona-pandemie/.

de Lisle, Jacques & Kui, Shen (eds.) (2022) 'China and COVID-19', in Hondius, Ewould et al. ,eds, *Coronavirus and the Law in Europe*, Brussels.

Luhmann, Niklas (1964) 'Lob der Routine', in 55 *Verwaltungsarchiv*, 1–33.

MacNeill, William H. (1976) *Plagues and Peoples*, Garden City NY.

Mangoldt, Anna Katharina (2021) 'Grundrechtliche Bewertung einer Ausgangssperre zur Pandemiebekämpfung', Gesellschaft für Freiheitsrechte (ed.), Flensburg, 1–29.

Mead, Richard (1720) *A short discourse concerning pestilential contagion, and the methods to be used to prevent it,* London.

Möllers, Christoph (2020) 'Parlamentarische Selbstentmächtigung im Zeichen des Virus', in Verfassungsblog, 26 March 2020, https:// verfassungsblog .de/ parlamentarische-selbstentmaechtigung-im-zeichen-des-virus/.

Munich Security Conference (2022), *Turning the Tide – Unlearning Helplessness. Munich Security Report 2022*, Munich.

Pieroth et al. (2016), *Polizei- und Ordnungsrecht*, 9th edn, München.

Poole, Thomas (2020), 'Leviathan in Lockdown', in *London Review of Books* , 1 May.

Poscher, Ralf (2021) 'Das Infektionsschutzrecht als Gefahrenabwehrrecht', in Huster, Stefan & Kingreen, Thorsten, eds, *Handbuch des Infektionsschutzrechts*, München, 117–169.

Preuß, Ulrich K. (1996) 'Risikovorsorge als Staatsaufgabe', in Grimm, Dieter, ed., *Staatsaufgaben,* Baden-Baden, 523–551.

Priebe, Manon & Lockhart, Ina (2021) 'Wir müssen zuhause bleiben – wie halten Sie durch? ', in *FAZ.net* vom 21 January 2021.

Rachor, Frederik (2021) 'E. Das Polizeihandeln', in Lisken, Hans & Denninger, Erhard, eds, *Handbuch des Polizeirechts*, 7th edn, München, Kap E.

Statista (2023) 'Dossier: Statistiken und Zahlen zur Corona-Pandemie 2019–2023', in statista - https://de.statista.com/themen/6018/corona/#topicOverview.

Riha, Ortrun (2003) 'Aussatz als Metapher. Aus der Geschichte einer sozialen Krankheit', in Groß, Dominik & Reiniger, Monika, eds, *Medizin in Geschichte, Philologie und Ethnologie. Festschrift für Gundolf Keil,* Würzburg, 89–105.

Ruffié, Jacques & Sournia, Jean-Charles (1984) *Les Èpidémies dans l'histoire de l'homme*, Paris.

Schwarzer, Anke (2014) 'Racial Profiling: Kontrollen jenseits des Rechts' in *Blätter für deutsche und internationale Politik,* 17–21.

Simoni, Alessandro (2020), 'Limiting Freedom During COVID-19 Emergency in Italy. Short Notes on the New 'Populist Rule of Law'', *Global Jurist*, 9 June, 1–10.

Trute, Hans-Heinrich (2020) 'Ungewissheit in der Pandemie als Herausforderung', in 25 *GSZ - Zeitschrift für das gesamte Sicherheitsrecht*, 93–101.

Vasold, Manfred (2015) *Grippe, Pest und Cholera – Eine Geschichte der Seuchen in Europa*, 2nd edn, Stuttgart.
Vögele, Jörg, Stefanie Knöll, Thorsten Noack (2016) *Epidemien und Pandemien in historischer Perspektive,* Wiesbaden.
Volkmann, Uwe (2008) 'Der alltägliche Ausnahmezustand oder: Not kennt viele Gebote', in 798 *Merkur*, 369–379.
Volkmann, Uwe (2020) 'Der Ausnahmezustand', in Verfassungsblog, https://verfassungsblog.de/der-ausnahmezustand/.
Volkmann, Uwe (2021) 'Herbeireden einer Verfassungskrise oder 'Es läuft doch alles prima?': Eine Erwiderung auf Matthias Jestaedt, Anna-Bettina Kaiser, Günter Krings und einige andere' 3 April 2021, Verfassungsblog, https://verfassungsblog.de/herbeireden-einer-verfassungskrise-oder-es-lauft-doch-alles-prima/.
Wegner, Wolfgang (2005) 'Miasma', in Gerabek, Werner E., Haage, Bernhard D., Keil, Gundolf, and Wegner, Wolfgang (eds.), *Enzyklopädie der Medizingeschichte,* Berlin.
Weiß, Volker (2021) 'Gemeinsam gegen den 'Great Reset'. Synergien zwischen Neuer Rechter und Corona-Protesten' (unpubl. ms.)
Wissenschaftliche Dienste – Deutscher Bundestag (2020), 'Ausarbeitung: Staatsorganisation und § 5 Infektionsschutzgesetz', WD 3 - 3000 - 080/20 - .
Yoshimura, Thomas (2021) 'Daten als Schlüssel im Kampf gegen das Virus', in Konrad-Adenauer-Stiftung, (ed.), *COVID-19 und Digitalisierung*, Bonn.
Zheng, Lei et al. (2020) 'Is Lockdown Bad for Social Anxiety in COVID-19 Regions?: A National Study in the SOR Perspective', in 17 *Int. J. Environ. Res. Public Health* 4561.

16. Pegasus: the unbounded surveillance industry in the service of the authoritarian

Kai Biermann

1. A CASE IN HUNGARY

Szabolcs Panyi is a journalist who was born in Budapest. For years he has been writing about the policies of Viktor Orbán's Hungarian government and has published reports about corrupt practices of corruption, arms deals, and the training hand-to-hand combat with Russian intelligence officers. Panyi, an investigative researcher, works for a small news magazine that only appears online and counts as one of the few independent media left in Hungary daring to criticize the government and expose its machinations. Panyi was vilified in the pro-Orbán media and called an agent of the CIA or of George Soros (Panyi 2021). He also suspected that the Hungarian state could intercept his communications. However, he did not know how far this surveillance would go and what dramatic effects it could have on his life and that of other people. By the time he realised this, it was already too late for some of his sources and political contacts.

The NSO Group is an Israeli company and today one of the leading providers of software for government cellphone surveillance. When it was founded more than ten years ago, it was one of many small start-ups in the country dealing with security and surveillance technology. Shalev Hulio and Omri Lavie, two of the three founders, had previously developed a remote access system to help mobile phone companies improve services for their customers. The system worked so smoothly that Hulio and Lavie came up with the idea to transform it into an espionage tool and sell it to secret services and police authorities.

2. MOBILE PHONES: INSTRUMENTS AND TARGETS OF SURVEILLANCE

Mobile phones have become indispensable tools in our everyday life. To use them effectively, their owners must entrust innumerable data to the devices. Every word that a person utters near a mobile phone, every step the owner takes, each contact the user stores in it – all this information is saved indefinitely. Not to mention all the pictures, the surfing history, every location data, countless notes, passwords for bank accounts, online services, cloud storage, etc. Whoever has access to mobile phones can turn them into a bug, into an all-knowing spy who accompanies us all the time. *Pegasus* siphons off all this data and, with its access, uses the information against us like a weapon.

NSO doesn't just provide a solution for secretly copying all this information. The authorities also get software to evaluate and process the data afterwards. For example, they can display on a map, where the monitored person has been walking and driving around. They can register his or her connections by the frequency of contact and carry out a variety of other analyses. All this makes it possible to reconstruct the entire life of the victim. In addition, authorities can look for patterns to predict future actions. For several years now, manufacturers of mobile devices and software vendors have recognised the privacy threats involved and have been offering services that use what is known as end-to-end encryption. So, communication is encrypted and can only be read by the respective sender and recipient. The *asymmetric encryption methods* are mathematically sinewy and can hardly be decoded with reasonable effort. In the operating systems of the devices, new methods are also constantly being installed to make external access to the content as difficult as possible for unauthorised parties.

For investigative authorities, however, mobile phones have long since become the most important target for unravelling criminal structures and investigating offences. About ten years ago, police authorities and intelligence services were mainly interested in computers on desks, whereas now mobile devices are the main target of their surveillance attempts. However, *going dark*, that is, increasing encryption and operating systems and apps to change in rapid cycles, makes it difficult for authorities to access this data. They are more and more in the dark and many potential data sources remain closed to them (Schulze 2017). Not only encryption, but also the rapid technical evolution of systems and apps requires us to always look for new ways to infiltrate the corresponding services. Even large agencies such as the German Federal Intelligence Service or the Federal Criminal Police Office cope with these problems.

There is a global market where security loopholes are traded, sometimes for very high sums, for instance, to circumvent the encryption of an app. Also, companies have emerged who specialise in surveillance software by exploiting security gaps, then selling it to state investigators. Even the largest state administrations worldwide serve themselves to this market and buy individual technical vulnerabilities or even entire surveillance systems – a concept called 'outsourcing'. Outsourcing has been a long-term military strategy, which has now been opened up to private operators – from maintenance, catering and logistics to complete armies. The same development is currently taking place in the area of government investigations and surveillance. *Meta*, the company behind Facebook, calls these providers the 'surveillance-for-hire industry' describing companies operating in it as 'surveillance mercenaries' (Dvilyanski et al. 2021).

3. PEGASUS: THE INSTRUMENT OF THE SURVEILLANCE MERCENARIES

Over the past few years, the NSO Group has grown in this market into a company that earns many millions of dollars annually with governments all over the world as customers. In 2021, the NSO Group was arguably the world's largest producer of surveillance software for mobile devices, thanks to their most important product *Pegasus*. Shalev Hulio and Omri Lavie, the founders, are typical representatives of the Israeli start-up culture, former officers in the Israeli army, they are not shy of contacts with security authorities and grew up in a world where it was important to keep enemies at bay. Accordingly, they used their knowledge and connections to build a company. Lacking contacts with the secret service, they looked for a third partner and found Niv Karmi. He, too, had served as an officer, but he also had experience in the digital fight against terrorists with the Israeli foreign intelligence service Mossad (Biermann 2021). The three founded the new company, NSO being the initials of their first names. *Pegasus* received its name, like the winged horse, from Greek mythology.

Only government agencies are allowed to buy *Pegasus* and by no means all requests are accepted. Numerous countries such as Iran are on an exclusion list, as NSO repeatedly explains. They have strict controls and ethical guidelines to prevent abuse. They are also subject to the so-called Wassenaar Arrangement intended to prevent surveillance software, which could potentially be used as a technological weapon, from falling into the wrong hands. Any sale to the authorities of a foreign country needs the prior approval of the Israeli Ministry of Defense. NSO has repeatedly emphasised that its products were developed solely to fight the most serious crimes and terrorism. In internal events, the company celebrates its programmers as 'superheroes' who have saved 'hundreds of thousands of lives' in the fight against evil (Biermann et al. 2021). According to Hulio, many terrorist attacks have been prevented and human traffickers and drug lords have been caught thanks to the spy software. Over and over again Hulio mentions the hunt for Joaquín Guzmán, known as El Chapo, then head of the notorious Sinaloa drug cartel in Mexico. And yes, Pegasus helped Mexican investigators find his hideout and arrest him. At the same time, Mexico, just like Hungary, is an example of how all the control mechanisms cannot prevent Pegasus from being abused.

4. ABOUT INITIATIVES TO CONTROL *PEGASUS*

An international research consortium provided hundreds of pieces of evidence in 2021. The starting point was a list of 50,000 mobile phone numbers from all over the world which a whistleblower had handed over to *Amnesty International*. Based on the list, an international consortium of editorial offices, coordinated by the French NGO *Forbidden Stories*, started its research into *Pegasus* targets. For years, *Citizen Lab*, an interdisciplinary laboratory at the Munk School of Global Affairs at the University of Toronto in Canada, has been investigating which countries buy and use *Pegasus* because they can see when such servers come online in a country.[1] The researchers were able to prove, for example, that several Saudi Arabian dissidents were spied on using the tool and trace several attacks with *Pegasus* on Mexican journalists. *Citizen Lab* primarily monitors the infrastructure of the internet. Their researchers have developed ways to identify servers from where *Pegasus* is spread around the world. They discover the infrastructure NSO creates which is then used by government agencies for espionage. This is part of the outsourcing of surveillance: the data siphoned off on mobile phones runs through servers NSO rents, sets up and controls. Citizen Lab researchers have succeeded in creating a kind of fingerprint from the specific requirements for Pegasus servers so they can identify them by scanning the network. *Citizen Lab*'s work alone is a significant gain for the public debate on the new surveillance techniques: neither NSO nor the governments involved, and certainly not the secret services, disclose that they own and use the software. Everything related to Pegasus is strictly secret (Stark 2021).

5. SEARCH FOR THE VICTIMS

The whistleblower's list, drawn up by *Amnesty* and *Citizen Lab*, helped identify not only the buyers of *Pegasus*, but also its victims: the 50,000 mobile

---

1 *Citizen Lab* reports on *Pegasus:*

phone numbers that had been selected by customers of the Israeli company as potential targets of mobile phone surveillance between 2016 and 2020. Army units, police forces, and intelligence agencies in dozens of countries had entered these numbers into their systems because they were interested in the people behind them and wanted to monitor them. Capturing a number on this list does not automatically mean that a smartphone will actually be attacked by *Pegasus* afterwards. The list functions a kind of pre-selection. If a number has been included, it means that an NSO customer, i.e. an intelligence service or police authority, wanted to determine the whereabouts of the respective device and whether it could be bugged. Only in a subsequent second step do *Pegasus* customers decide whether to attack the phone. This can take place minutes after the pre-selection, but sometimes days later. Thus, a reliable identification of an attack is only possible through a forensic analysis of the mobile device concerned. Therefore, research teams of *Die* Zeit, *Süddeutsche Zeitung*, *Washington Post*, and *Le Monde* began analysing these numbers in February 2020, coordinated by the non-profit newsroom *Forbidden Stories*. A few months later, other media such as *The Guardian* and *Direct 36* joined in, so that ultimately teams from fifteen editorial offices spent weeks checking these numbers and searching through public and non-public telephone directories. The first step was to identify the owners of the connections and to contact them, in case it could be proved that the corresponding surveillance attempts might have been illegal.

The whole project was technically supported by the *Security Lab* of *Amnesty International*. The lab also carried out the forensic analyses of the mobile phones, provided the owners agreed to have them examined for traces of *Pegasus*. Only an analysis of the operating systems could prove whether a mobile phone had really been spied on. The methods and results were then confirmed in a peer review by an independent second opinion from *Citizen Lab*. The research was carried out under extreme security precautions, not least because some of the research consortium's media partners had been personally spied on with *Pegasus*, as had happened in Hungary or India. The normal service mobile phones and laptops would have provided an attack surface for the research. The teams therefore researched, communicated and wrote via a specially set up, specially protected infrastructure on separate devices and with separate software. For the research, the teams travelled to numerous countries, including Israel, Hungary, France, and Turkey. There they met journalists and human rights activists who had been spied on. They also contacted former and current NSO employees to learn more about the inner workings of the company. The results, published worldwide in the summer of 2021 by the participating media under the name *Pegasus Project*,[2] not only proved the abuse of the spy tool in many countries, such as India, Morocco, and Hungary. They also showed how difficult it is to prevent abuse and described the sometimes-life-threatening effects this form of surveillance can have.

Such effects were experienced by Szabolcs Panyi. Reporters from the *Süddeutsche Zeitung* had warned him that his phone was being spied on with *Pegasus*. In spring 2021, they visited him to check with him more numbers from Hungary. The Hungarian government would not admit that it had bought Pegasus until many months after the projects' reports. On that day in Budapest, hardly anyone in the country knew about it. The investigators found other colleagues of Panyi on the whistleblower's list. One of them, András Szabó, shared Panyi's Budapest office; together they worked for the independent online medium *Direkt 36*. Among the Hungarian numbers listed were suspected criminals whose surveillance may have been legitimate, but there were also journalists, high-ranking media managers, lawyers, and opposition members. They were and are targets of Prime Minister Viktor Orbán's surveillance efforts. He is obviously misusing a tool sold solely for fighting terrorism to collect information on political opponents. On paper, Hungary is a constitutional state and surveillance must be approved by judges. However, the Ministry of Justice can also grant such permission if there is a threat to national security. Human rights organisations have made the point that there is no independent control, especially of the activities of the secret service, that accordingly journalists cannot protect their sources and sensitive information (Kahlweit et al. 2021). At least two people who had been interviewed by Panyi and a colleague subsequently lost their jobs. One of them, until then a government employee, was forced to emigrate to the USA.

Szabolcs Panyi is not the only journalist who has been personally targeted by surveillance. The Azerbaijani investigative journalist Khadija Ismayilova realised her whole house had been targeted. In the autocratically ruled Azerbaijan, it is increasingly dangerous to have and make public one's own opinion if critical of the regime. Undaunted by these practices, Ismayilova has been researching the corrupt machinations of the ruling family for years. She knew that she had been monitored by the government long before *Pegasus* came to light. Her house in Baku had been secretly bugged by the authorities. They had hidden cameras in every room, even in the bathroom and bedroom, had filmed her in every situation, including having sex with her boyfriend, and then tried to blackmail her with the images to keep her quiet. Ismayilova wrote an open letter about the surveillance and the blackmail. She was arrested and

---

2 See, for example, the corresponding collection of publications by various project partners at 'Forbidden Stories', https://forbiddenstories.org/Pegasus-project-articles/.

accused of driving a colleague to suicide; she was also charged with alleged tax evasion and sentenced to seven years in prison. After international protests and a complaint to the European Court of Human Rights, she was released after one-and-a-half years but was not allowed to leave the country until May 2021, after the end of her seven-year ban, when she met investigative journalists from the *Pegasus* project in Turkey.

After Khadija Ismayilova's release from prison, she continued to work and tried to somehow live with the surveillance. For example, she bought a tent, which she put up in her house (Ludwig/Munzinger 2021). She warned friends and family and used encryption methods for her work to protect her sources – a futile undertaking, because her mobile phone number was also on the list of the 50,000, as was confirmed by the forensic analysis of the *Amnesty International* laboratory. For more than three years, her mobile phone had been infected with *Pegasus* and was monitored around the clock by the authorities (Rueckert 2021). Not only Khadija Ismayilova but also her family members and her sources were targets of this surveillance – people who worked with her and shared with her their private secrets (ibid.).

6. WHAT CAN *PEGASUS* DO?

Pegasus is a weapon with unlimited range. Like an intercontinental missile, the programme can attack people on the other side of the world without them noticing. For dissidents and critics of a regime, this means that there is no more protection through distance. This is what the Saudi Arabian dissident Omar Abdulaziz experienced. Having been granted political asylum in Canada in 2014, he studied in Quebec, felt safe there and published his critical comments of the Saudi Government on YouTube. In the summer of 2018, he ordered sports nutrition from Amazon. A few hours later, he received a text message on his mobile phone, announcing the shipment via DHL, which included a link (Marczak et al. 2018). As *Citizen Lab* later discovered, it led to a website set up by NSO. When Abdulaziz clicked on it, believing he could track his shipment, he infected his phone with *Pegasus* and was subsequently tracked himself. The Saudi regime was now monitoring his every move and contact.

Of course, not every use of surveillance software is unjustified. In 2011, the first customer of the NSO Group company was the Mexican government. The country suffered under the power of the billionaire drug cartels who terrorised the population with violence and poisoned every area of public life with bribery. The criminal gangs had so much money that they built their own mobile phone networks for their illegal business (Beaubien 2011) and thus evaded any control. With *Pegasus*, the government promised itself an effective weapon against this. Five different Mexican agencies have been buying licences for it as of 2011, including the intelligence service *Cisen*, the

Ministry of Defence and the Office of the Attorney General. The software certainly helped investigators achieve spectacular successes against the cartels. The most famous is the arrest of Joaquín Guzmán, known only as 'El Chapo', the short one, because of his small size. Guzmán led the cartel named after the Mexican state of Sinaloa and made it one of the most powerful and cruel criminal organisations in the world. Anyone who bothered the cartel was tortured, beheaded, hung from bridges or dissolved in acid. 'El Chapo'[3] had already been arrested twice, and had twice escaped from a maximum-security prison owing to money and helpers. With the help of *Pegasus*, investigators were able to find him in hiding, in 2016.

A success story? Undoubtedly. But in a constitutional state, communication between suspects and their lawyers, which was spied on in El Chapo's case, is protected for good reason. Their phones may not be tapped in a few countries when they communicate with clients. Hulio, however, has no problem with this; he has publicly stated that spying is necessary to catch criminals like 'El Chapo'.

7. THE RESPONSIBILITY OF MANUFACTURERS

The responsibility of a private company like NSO for state surveillance is currently the subject of a lawsuit in the USA. Meta, the owner of Facebook and WhatsApp, brought it against NSO, claiming that it has abused WhatsApp's infrastructure to upload its surveillance Trojan to other people's mobile phones.[4] The lawsuit listed 1,400 customers monitored in this way. In court NSO defended itself arguing that it was not directly responsible for the surveillance but acting merely as a service provider for foreign state authorities. NSO did not select the targets of surveillance and was therefore immune from civil prosecution. The US court rejected this argument which relied on a private company's immunity that applies to foreign sovereign actors under US law (Stempel & Culliford 2021). So, the court opened the way to the main trial and also a discussion about the share and responsibility for (unauthorised) monitoring that falls on these companies of this surveillance-for-hire industry. After all, anyone who buys software like *Pegasus* does not own it, strictly speaking. They rent an off-the-shelf product that many others can also rent. NSO builds and operates the necessary infrastructure. Only the targets are still selected by an administrative agency. However, NSO owns and controls all the technology

3 Ranked # 67 in the Forbes' list of 'The World's Most Powerful People' (2013).

4 *WhatsApp and Facebook v. NSO Group*, filed with the Northern District of California on 29 October 2019 – Case 3:19-cv-07123. Document 1 Filed 29 October 2019.

for attacking and spying on the victims and extracting the data. This goes so far that, for example, NSO formulates the infected SMS and short messages with which victims are enticed to click on a link and thus invite *Pegasus* into their device.

Until 2018, the NSO had relied at least partly on the victims' cooperation in an attack. Due to the security architecture of mobile devices, it only worked if the victims activated the link contained in such a message. Only then could *Pegasus* establish a connection to its home servers and begin spying. In its marketing brochures, NSO advertises (Guarneri 2021) that a separate group within the company trains state authorities to write such SMS that sound as innocuous as possible. In NSO's language, this service is called 'Enhanced Social Engineering Message (ESEM)'. *Pegasus* advertises many tools to 'craft messages that are as innocuous as possible and tailored to victims' (Guarneri 2021: 12–13). Only since 2018 have attacks been observed in which mobile devices are infiltrated without the owner's involvement (Amnesty International 2021). However, such attacks, called zero-click, which exploit previously unknown gaps in individual software and apps, are very complex to develop and therefore very expensive. NSO markets them as the highest stage and most expensive expansion of its spy software but continues to offer the older variant for government clients at lower price.

A consequence of this privatisation is that the monitor(s) and their motivations are concealed and, as in the case of zero-click attacks, even remain completely invisible in case of doubt. The victims can neither recognise that they are being monitored, nor assess how far this intervention extends. For instance, the message infecting the device arrives in the middle of the night. Once the Trojan has crept in, it is deleted immediately, so the owner of the device cannot discover any trace of it. Even if they suspect that their phone is being attacked, they could never find out which authority from which country is interested in them. 'On the Internet, Nobody knows you're a dog' was the caption of a famous cartoon by Peter Steiner, published by *The New Yorker*.[5] It alluded to the fact that anyone could move anonymously on the net. This also applies to digital attacks and surveillance.

NSO refuses to give any information about its customers, invoking company secrets and state secrecy and does not even reveal to which countries *Pegasus* was sold, let alone to which government authorities. And, as long as possible, the responsible governments completely deny using *Pegasus*. They can do so because the attack leaves no traces and bears no seals. In consequence, victims have no possibility to defend themselves, neither legally nor technically.

---

5 The New Yorker, 5 July 1993.

Pitching a tent (Ismayilova) or encrypting communication (Panyi) does not help against *Pegasus*.

In the eighteenth century, when Jeremy Bentham devised the Panopticon, a model prison in which every inmate could be observed at all times by a single supervisor, permanent monitoring was considered desirable. Bentham could not have foreseen how deeply surveillance would once penetrate people's privacy and minds. As research by Melissa Bateson and her colleagues at Newcastle University showed in 2006, the image of a large pair of eyes on a wall suffices to make people in that particular room feel watched and display behaviour they consider more socially desirable. In this case: putting the full asking price for a cup of coffee into a trust fund (Bateson et al. 2006: 412–414). How much more overwhelming and terrifying must it be to feel that one's every move, utterance and human contact is being monitored?

Months of research by the *Pegasus* project testified that Panyi and Ismayilova were and are not alone with this problem. The network revealed systematic abuses of *Pegasus* in many countries. Potential victims include politicians, human rights activists, lawyers, journalists like French reporters from *Le Monde* and *Le Canard enchaîné*, a correspondent from CNN, journalists from 'The Wire' in India, an AFP correspondent in Morocco. French President Emmanuel Macron was among the potential targets with one of his telephone numbers, as were several French ministers and high-ranking diplomats, as well as other current or former heads of state and government. This way, *Pegasus* is not only used for investigation, but also for blackmail, repression and espionage. NSO offers an off-the-shelf product the services only have to apply.

The NSO offer comes at a price that is affordable for many interested state parties. The licences cost between one and two-digit millions, depending on whether only people in their own country or also people in other countries are to be monitored. This makes even countries like Togo or Uganda, which otherwise play no role in international espionage, a threat. Owing to *Pegasus,* they can hack at the highest technical level and eavesdrop on diplomats of even large nations and thus learn about government secrets.

The company justifies itself, claiming it has no responsibility, because its clients are state actors regulated by law, who decide alone who they monitor. One of their lawyers claimed the listed numbers could have 'many legitimate and completely clean uses that have nothing to do with surveillance or NSO', and as surveillance is not the only purpose, it can hardly be said that an operation 'was successful' as an 'attempt at surveillance'(Biermann et al. 2021). This argumentation could be refuted by the forensic analyses of the devices.

8. GLOBAL INFRASTRUCTURE OF UNBOUNDED SURVEILLANCE

Privatisation lends itself to creating a global surveillance infrastructure that can no longer be controlled by national laws. NSO repeatedly claims in public statements that they do not know who the state services are spying on with *Pegasus*, which is not true. At the same time, the company admits in interviews that it has a control system to investigate possible misuse of its products. In an interview with the author, company boss Shalev Hulio said that *Pegasus* is only sold to authorities if they contractually agree that NSO can track what customers do with the system. Hence, every step is logged on a special server and NSO can review these logs in case of doubt (Biermann 2020a). The company attaches great importance to the statement that they do not permanently check the currently active monitoring targets, but only when there is a formal reason for an official investigation, for example a suspicion of abuse. Moreover, NSO does not track who is monitoring whom. This only happens with the approval of the customers – the intelligence services and police authorities. However, these statements have never been independently verified. Outside the company, no one – not even state authorities – knows what exactly NSO can and cannot 'see'.

Even in countries like Germany, with a well-functioning rule of law system, this creates considerable legal uncertainties. The lawyers at the Federal Criminal Police Office (BKA) also had reservations, at least at the beginning of the contact with NSO. In 2017, representatives of the NSO Group presented their spy software to the BKA for the first time. At the time, the officials were enthusiastic about the technical possibilities, participants of the event later reported. But the service's lawyers were concerned because *Pegasus* can see and extract much more data than German laws concerning the surveillance of source telecommunication (Quellen-TKÜ) allow. Two years later, however, the vice-president of the BKA, Martina Link, decided to purchase *Pegasus* anyway, on the condition that NSO revise its Trojan and develop a stand-alone version. The *Pegasus* version developed especially for the BKA was accepted in autumn 2020 (Biermann 2021a). Whereas the software had been adapted to German law, to this day the question has never been answered as to which servers the intercepted data runs through after it has been copied from the mobile phone. Because these servers, wherever they are located, are controlled by NSO and it has not been clarified what exactly the company can perceive and control in the process. *Pegasus* does encrypt the siphoned data before they are exported for security reasons, but the key for this is also constructed and supplied by NSO. It is thus entirely possible that NSO can decrypt and view the data without the authorities even noticing. Even as regards the German version of *Pegasus* and its technical limitations, control is not likely to lie completely in the hands of the authorities who use the surveillance tool: NSO can influence a spy Trojan from afar and if a customer does not honour the contractual agreements, NSO can switch off *Pegasus*. With a 'kill switch' they can send a command to make the software stop working so it can no longer install itself on new mobile phones (Biermann 2020a).

Pegasus also creates a fundamental ethical problem: 'The entire industry of commercial intrusion software vendors is based on a lie. They claim to protect lives and prevent crime, but in many countries this software is used every day to spy on people who are not legitimate targets' (Edward Snowden, quoted by Lewis 2021). Snowden continued:

> Companies could make bugs, hidden microphones, and sell them. But the state gets them or the local police get them ... But if they can do the same thing [enter a person's house – K.B.] remotely, the cost is low and there is no risk at all, then they start doing it all the time, against anyone who is even remotely of interest. And that shows a list of 50,000 staff, people affected. You don't bug 50,000 houses. There are simply not enough bugging experts in all these countries to do anything like that. But if it's possible for them to just get access to what you carry around in your pocket, they can do it and they will do it. (Lewis 2021)

Companies like NSO have few qualms about selling their products to autocratic states. John Scott-Railton of *Citizen Lab* Toronto called NSO an 'insanely problematic industry' and demanded that 'democracies need to stop buying this stuff' (unpublished conversation with the author).

All these technical, legal and ethical problems were already evident in Mexico, NSO's first and for a long time most important customer. To this day, there is sufficient evidence that state organs in Mexico spy on opposition members, journalists and organisations that are critical of the government. The Canadian *Citizen Lab* or the Mexican civil rights group *R3D* have documented dozens of cases[6] in which Mexican journalists and human rights activists were attacked and spied on by spyware. One of them is the case of Mario Patrón, the director of the Centro Prodh Human Rights Centre, one of Mexico's most important human rights organisations. On 20 April 2016, Patrón received a text message. It announced an investigation report by an international commission of experts on the case of the 43 disappeared students from Ayotzinapa. Patrón did not know who sent the SMS, but the content of the message aroused his interest, so he clicked on the link it contained. However, instead of the expected investigation report, a blank page opened. At that moment it was

[6] 'Gobernio Espia', report by the Mexican civil rights organisation R3D, 19 June 2017. See https://r3d.mx/wp-content/uploads/GOBIERNO-ESPIA-2017.pdf.

already too late, Patrón had let the surveillance Trojan *Pegasus* onto his mobile phone and activated it. Several employees of civil society institutions suffered the same fate, as R3D was able to prove in the report 'Gobernio Espia'. The activists found a total of 76 messages with such a *Pegasus* link. All of them were embedded in messages that were designed to get their victims to click and pretend to have important information on the topic they were working on. Clearly, the attackers had spied on their victims beforehand and tailored the messages to them – just as the NSO product manual for the 'Enhanced Social Engineering Message (ESEM)' describes. The messages were sent to journalists, human rights activists and civil society groups whose work the government criticised. For example, to an organisation that advocates for a tax on sugary drinks to combat obesity and diabetes.

9. SPYING ON GOVERNMENTS

It is not just the extra-parliamentary opposition that has been the target of Pegasus attacks in Mexico, but also political opponents. One such case, for example, was about influencing the 2018 presidential election campaign. The former mayor of Mexico City, Andrés Manuel López Obrador, ran against two candidates from established parties. López Obrador, a feisty social democrat, made pervasive corruption the core of his campaign during which his entire environment was monitored by *Pegasus*. The spy software was later found on the mobile phones of his wife Beatriz, those of three of his brothers and three of his children. In addition, his advisors, his driver and even his cardiologist were spied on in this way. He became the president of Mexico in the summer of 2018. To this day, it is unclear who commissioned the surveillance. Mexico's authorities promised to investigate the possible abuse after these surveillance operations became known. This never happened.

The Kingdom of Morocco was also a good customer of the company and used *Pegasus* both against the opposition at home and against political opponents abroad. To the outside world, the country likes to present itself as democratic. Inside, however, anyone who dares to criticise the royal house is persecuted. A first report on spying attacks was published by the human rights organisation Amnesty International in autumn 2019 (*Amnesty International* 2019). It describes the case of Maati Monjib. The journalist is co-founder of the NGO *Freedom Now*, which campaigns for freedom of expression and the rights of journalists in the country. Monjib had long been suspected of being monitored by Moroccan authorities. In 2015, he was charged with allegedly endangering the country's internal security through his 'propaganda'. He approached Amnesty with a request to review his devices. The Amnesty Security Lab found traces that confirmed his fears. To give an example: Monjib had received a text message on 2 November 2017 in which the messaging and phone app *Truecaller*, popular in many Arab countries, announced a new feature: 'See which people searched for your phone number in the past week.' Attached was a link to a website – where *Pegasus* was lurking. There were various such veiled attack messages, repeatedly trying to get him to click on one of the poisoned links. The government wanted to track his every word, his every contact and his every move. This also happened to other journalists, notably Omar Radi (Biermann 2020b), who denounced Morocco as a police state. He had been monitored with *Pegasus* for a long time (*Amnesty International* 2020). Shortly after Amnesty and many international media outlets made the case public, Radi was accused of various offences, including espionage, and sent to prison, where he has remained until today.

In official statements Morocco denies that it owned *Pegasus*. The royal family has filed a lawsuit against the media involved in the *Pegasus project* and wants to stop it being reported. The government also uses the tool abroad to pursue its political interests. In the summer of 2021, investigations revealed that various officials and politicians in the French government were being spied on. Among the potential targets was a mobile phone number of French President Emmanuel Macron (von Randow 2021). The French information security agency *Agence nationale de la sécurité des systèmes d'information* (ANSSI) then examined various mobile devices of civil servants and journalists and confirmed the infection and monitoring by *Pegasus* on several devices. It is likely that the Moroccan authorities' aim was to learn more about France's political intentions in the sub-Saharan region.

10. THE KHASHOGGI CASE

The best known and also the most horrific case of abuse of *Pegasus* is without doubt the case of Jamal Khashoggi. The buyer of the software here is the autocratically ruled Saudi Arabia. That alone is an astonishing fact. Israel and Saudi Arabia were officially enemies at the time of the negotiations, so Israeli citizens are not allowed to visit the kingdom. Israeli companies need a special permission to do business there, because *Pegasus* is classified as a military export. Cyber weapons have been considered armaments since an update of the international Wassenaar Agreement in 2013; Israel has not ratified the agreement but follows its guidelines. Despite all these hurdles, NSO eventually received such a special permit, because the government was obviously also interested in the deal. The Saudis, the calculation goes, will use it to seek out Islamist terrorists and thus benefit Israel as well. Which also shows why fighting and controlling this form of surveillance is so difficult – there are always overriding political considerations. In autumn 2017, the contract was signed. At NSO's headquarters in Herzliya, the Saudi client will in future run under the internal code name 'Subaru' (Biermann et al. 2021).

Saudi journalist Jamal Khashoggi, initially a close friend of the royal family and a champion of conservative Muslim beliefs, had become, over the years, a critic of Saudi politics – especially the policies of the Crown Prince and de facto head of government, Mohammed bin Salman al-Saud (MBS). Khashoggi eventually left his homeland and fled to the US, from where he wrote against MBS in the *Washington Post*. MBS was disturbed by this voice, which attracted a lot of international attention. He sent out an assassination squad to have Khashoggi killed. Unaware of this, Khashoggi visited the Saudi consulate in Istanbul, Turkey. He wanted to marry his fiancée Hatice Cengiz, who lived in Turkey, and had the necessary papers issued by the consulate. The Saudis knew when he would be back and were waiting for him. On 2 October 2018, he was tied up, drugged and suffocated on the second floor of the building. The perpetrators then sawed up his body and destroyed the individual parts. Meanwhile, his unsuspecting fiancée was waiting outside the building for him to return. She waited for hours in vain and finally called friends and acquaintances in Turkish politics because she feared for Khashoggi's life.

Shortly after the murder, there were rumours that Khashoggi had been monitored by *Pegasus*. In various public statements, NSO still claims that an internal investigation was initiated at the time and that no evidence was found that Khashoggi had been infected by and spied on with *Pegasus*. Even though he himself may not have been monitored, his personal environment was, and this has been proven. Forensic analyses carried out by the *Pegasus Research Consortium* on Hatice Cengiz's mobile phone, among others, found traces of the surveillance Trojan. Her mobile phone was infected only four days after the murder of her fiancé (Biermann et al. 2021). The same pattern can be seen among friends of the deceased and among Turkish investigators and officials involved in the case: notably Yasin Aktay, an Erdoğan confidant and acquaintance of Jamal Khashoggi, whom he considered an emergency contact with the Turkish government; Wadah Khanfar, the former managing director of Al-Jazeera television and a close friend of Khashoggi's; Irfan Fidan, the Turkish prosecutor leading the investigation into Khashoggi's murder; and Abdullah Khashoggi, one of his two sons. They were all targeted and monitored with *Pegasus*. It seems that the Saudi royal family wanted to know how much evidence there was of the crime and whether it could get away scot-free. In the end, MBS was held internationally responsible by the United Nations and the USA, among others, but the crime has still not been atoned for. The members of the murder squad were officially sentenced to prison in Saudi Arabia, but no details about the trials were made public, not even the names of the accused, or whether and how they are serving the sentences. While MBS hardly felt any consequences, NSO did. Internally, many staff members were horrified by the brutal political murder. A few weeks later, NSO used its 'kill switch' and deactivated the Saudi *Pegasus* licence. Not for very long, though.

Saudi Arabia was unlocked again as early as spring 2019, according to data the research consortium was able to analyse. Since then, the Saudi authorities have been allowed to continue spying with *Pegasus*; very likely the Israeli Government asked NSO for this permit (Biermann et al. 2021). Only after its publication was the renewed licence finally revoked in 2021; NSO lost a well-paying customer.

Mexico, Hungary, Azerbaijan, Morocco, and Saudi Arabia are just a few of the countries where *Pegasus* has been and is being abused, as the media consortium was able to prove. According to the report issued by the *Pegasus* research consortium, globally almost 200 journalists and many human rights activists are victims of this surveillance technique. Their cases have drawn a lot of attention to NSO. More and more revelations followed: Finnish diplomats were targeted, as well as Polish opposition politicians and US State Department employees. In Israel itself, the police also used *Pegasus* to spy on people from the business world, the media and politics, including the entourage of Prime Minister Benjamin Netanyahu, without the necessary court order. The list included Avner Netanyahu, one of his sons, Topaz Luk and Yonatan Urich, two advisors to the long-time head of state (Ganon 2022). Ironically, Netanyahu had personally lobbied for NSO several times and helped the company to market its product.

11. SCOPE OF SANCTIONS

The global attention had a significant impact, at least on NSO. As a result, a whole series of sanctions were imposed. Amazon announced that it would no longer tolerate the server infrastructure necessary for the infection on its cloud services called AWS. Amazon also deactivated all corresponding accounts that the company could identify (Cox 2021). The US government placed NSO on an embargo list because the company had developed and supplied spy software to foreign governments 'that have used this tool to maliciously surveil government officials, journalists, businesspeople, activists, academics and embassy staff'.[7] As a result, US companies can no longer do business with the Israeli firm very easily. Following Facebook's lead, Apple also instigated a lawsuit against NSO in November 2021 over allegations of misuse of its infrastructure in the US.[8] At the same time, Apple closed the security hole that NSO and

---

[7] US Industry and Security Bureau, Addition of Certain Entities to the Entity List, 4 November 2021, https://www.federalregister.gov/documents/2021/11/04/2021-24123/addition-of-certain-entities-to-the-entity-list.

[8] Apple, Statement of Claim against NSO before the Northern District of Columbia, https://www.apple.com/newsroom/pdfs/Apple_v_NSO_Complaint_112321.pdf.

another surveillance company had exploited to sneak into mobile phones with an update. Apple informed customers affected by this through a message on their phone (Biermann 2021b), making many more people aware of this practice of surveillance.

Will this change the global market for rental surveillance companies? The chance of this happening is rather slim. The interest in digital data, which has long determined and defined our lives, is too great. Before NSO, there were already two companies that were strong in this market segment and sold their spy products to many authoritarian regimes: *Hacking Team* from Italy and *FinFisher* from Germany. Both became known through a hacker calling himself Phineas Fisher, whose identity has remained hidden to this day. He had obtained and published data from both companies, making their business practices and clients public. Due to these disclosures, both companies no longer exist today. However, other companies such as NSO have emerged instead and now offer their monitoring products. All that can be achieved is more transparency for the industry and its business models.

Citizen Lab, the research of Amnesty International and the *Forbidden Stories consortium* may have achieved something if only to reveal *Pegasus*'s connection to regular clandestine surveillance methods. These are always introduced with the justification that they are necessary to solve and prevent the worst crimes. In the end, however, they morph into everyday tools to be used against any form of crime, whether a threat to society or not. This happens in stark contrast to the surveillance tools, which invade privacy so deeply and destroy so much trust that they have become a threat to democracy and social cohesion. One of the great merits of Edward Snowden was to prove to the world in 2013 that anyone can be the victim of clandestine spying, including a German Chancellor. The *Pegasus* research now verifies the same. Even those who decide to use instruments like *Pegasus* can realise how dangerous they are and how easily they can be abused. This at least offers a chance to negotiate future international restrictions on such spying tools.

REFERENCES

Amnesty International (2021), 'Forensic Methodology Report: How to catch NSO Group's "Pegasus"', veröffentlicht am 18. Juli, https://www.amnesty.org/en/latest/research/2021/07/forensic-methodology-report-how-to-catch-nso-groups-Pegasus/.

Amnesty International (2020), 'NSO Group Spyware Used Against Moroccan Journalist Days After Company Pledged to Respect Human Rights', 22 June, https://www.amnesty.org/en/latest/news/2020/06/nso-spyware-used-against-moroccan-journalist/.

Apple, Klageschrift gegen NSO vor dem Northern District of Columbia, https://www.apple.com/newsroom/pdfs/Apple_v_NSO_Complaint_112321.pdf.

Bateson, Melissa et al. (2006), 'Cues of being watched enhance cooperation in a real-world setting', in *Biology Letters* 22 November, 412–414 https://www.ncbi.nlm.nih.gov/pmc/articles/PMC1686213/.

Beaubien, Jason (2011), 'Mexico Busts Drug Cartels' Private Phone Networks', in *NPR*, 9 December, https://www.npr.org/2011/12/09/143442365/mexico-busts-drug-cartels-private-phone-networks?t=1643631088846.

Biermann, Kai (2020a), 'Die Absauger', in *Die Zeit* Nr. 27, https://www.zeit.de/2020/27/spionage-ueberwachung-nso-israel-Pegasus.

Biermann, Kai (2020b), 'Wie Marokko Kritiker einschüchtert', in *Zeit Online*, 10. Juli. https://www.zeit.de/politik/ausland/2020-07/marokko-amnesty-international-omar-radi-ueberwachung.

Biermann, Kai (2021a), 'Warum einer der Pegasus-Erfinder zum Aussteiger wurde', in Zeit Online, 7 October 2021 https://www.zeit.de/digital/datenschutz/2021-10/nso-gruender-niv-karmi-Pegasus-ueberwachungssoftware-entstehungsgeschichte-unternehmen.

Biermann, Kai (2021b), 'BKA hat NSO-Spähtrojaner bereits mehrfach eingesetzt', in *Zeit Online*, 7 September 2021, https://www.zeit.de/politik/deutschland/2021-09/spionagesoftware-Pegasus-bka-einsatz-nso-trojaner-israel.

Biermann, Kai, Geisler, Astrid, Stark, Holger & Venohr, Sascha (2021), 'Der Kontrollverlust', in *Die Zeit*, Nr. 30/2021, 22. Juli 2021, https://www.zeit.de/2021/30/nso-cyber-unternehmen-Pegasus-software-israel-spionage.

Cox, Joseph (2021), 'Amazon Shuts Down NSO Group Infrastructure', in *Motherboard*, 19 July, https://www.vice.com/en/article/xgx5bw/amazon-aws-shuts-down-nso-group-infrastructure.

Dvilyanski, Mike & Dvilyanski, Mike (2021), 'Threat Report on the Surveillance-for-Hire Industry', in *Meta*, 16 December, https://about.fb.com/news/2021/12/taking-action-against-surveillance-for-hire/.

Endres, Alexandra (2019), 'Der Mafiaboss ist verurteilt – der Drogenkrieg geht weiter', in *Zeit Online* vom 13. February, https://www.zeit.de/gesellschaft/zeitgeschehen/2019-02/el-chapo-drogenboss-joaquin-guzman-haft-mexiko-mafia-drogenkrieg.

Ganon, Tomer (2022), in *Calcalist*, 7 February, https://www.calcalistech.com/ctech/articles/0,7340,L-3928830,00.html.

'Gobernio Espia', Bericht der mexikanischen Bürgerrechtsorganisation R3D, 19 June 2017 https://r3d.mx/wp-content/uploads/GOBIERNO-ESPIA-2017.pdf.

Guarneri, Claudio (2021), 'Pegasus – Product Description'. NSO-Originalbroschüre.

Kahlweit, Cathrin et al. (2021), 'Big Brother Orbán', in *Süddeutsche Zeitung, Beilage v.* 19 July, p. 24.

Lewis, Paul (2021), 'Das sollte uns mehr als alles andere Angst machen', in *Zeit Online* v. 19 July, https://www.zeit.de/digital/2021-07/edward-snowden-spionage-software-Pegasus-handy-ueberwachung-diktaturen.

Ludwig, Kristiana & Munzinger, Hannes (2021), 'Unerwünscht und ausgeforscht', in *Süddeutsche Zeitung, Beilage,* 19 July, p. 25.

Marczak, Bill u.a. (2018), 'The Kingdom Came to Canada', in *Citizen Lab*, October, https://citizenlab.ca/2018/10/the-kingdom-came-to-canada-how-saudi-linked-digital-espionage-reached-canadian-soil/.

Panyi, Szabolcs (2021), '"A story like out of a spy movie", personal reports by two surveilled Direkt36 journalists', in *Direkt 36,* https://www.direkt36.hu/en/egy-kemfilmbe-illo-sztori-a-ket-megfigyelt-direkt36-os-ujsagiro-beszamoloja/.

von Randow, Gero (2021), 'Frankreichs Präsident Macron im Visier der Spione', in *Zeit. Online*, 20 July, https://www.zeit.de/politik/ausland/2021-07/spionage-frankreich-marokko-emmanuel-macron-handy-Pegasus-cyberwaffe-ueberwachung.

Rueckert, Phineas (2021), 'Pegasus: The new global weapon for silencing journalists' in *forbidden stories* , 18 July, https://forbiddenstories.org/Pegasus-the-new-global-weapon-for-silencing-journalists/.

Schulze, Matthias (2017), 'Going Dark? Dilemma zwischen sicherer privater Kommunikation und den Sicherheitsinteressen von Staaten', in *APuZ November*.

Stark, Holger (2021), 'BKA kaufte heimlich NSO-Spähsoftware', in *Zeit Online* 7 September, https://www.zeit.de/politik/deutschland/2021-09/spionagesoftware-Pegasus-nso-israel-bundeskriminalamt-kauf-innenauschuss-bundestag-unterrichtung.

Steiner, Peter (1993), 'On the Internet. Nobody Knows You Are a Dog', in *The New Yorker*, No. 69, 5 July, https://web.archive.org/web/20051029045942/http://www.unc.edu/depts/jomc/academics/dri/idog.html/.

Stempel, Jonathan & Culliford, Elzabeth (2021), 'Facebook can pursue malware lawsuit against Israel's NSO Group – US appeals court', *Reuters* 9 November, https://www.reuters.com/technology/facebook-can-pursue-malware-lawsuit-against-israels-nso-group-us-appeals-court-2021-11-08/.

US Industry and Security Bureau (2021), 'Addition of Certain Entities to the Entity List', 4 November, https://www.federalregister.gov/documents/2021/11/04/2021-24123/addition-of-certain-entities-to-the-entity-list.

17. Under what conditions do authoritarian social movements develop in Western societies?

Dieter Rucht

1. ON THE CATEGORY OF AUTHORITARIAN MOVEMENTS

Social movements can be conceived as mobilised networks of groups and organisations which, supported by a collective identity, want to bring about or prevent fundamental social change, primarily by means of public and collective protests (Rucht 1994: 76f.). This definition does not specify the ideological orientation of movements. However, structural and action-related formal elements are named, which allows movements to be distinguished from loose communication circles on the one hand and formal organisations on the other. The latter, including political parties, can certainly be part of movements.

In general usage, individual social movements are usually named based on their goals (for example, as a peace movement), their sponsorship (for example, as a women's movement) or their ideological orientation (for example, as a fascist movement). In addition, scholars also use analytical criteria to distinguish types of movements. These can refer to the basic strategic orientation (reform or revolution), the context of origin (*movements of affluence* versus *movement of crisis*), the preferred field of action (production or reproduction), the political orientation (left, liberal, right movements) and much more. The category of *authoritarian* movements, on the other hand, is addressed rather rarely in the literature and then mostly without in-depth explanations.

The adjective authoritarian, for which there is no semantically meaningful counter-term,[1] is used with regard to the characteristics and actions of staff, people (including movements), political systems (regimes) and entire societies.

1 Unlike pairs of terms such as egoistic vs. altruistic, in the case of authoritarian the only recourse is the formal linguistic negation of the term ("anti-authoritarian"). However, this categorisation, which is usually associated with a historically specific

The concept of authority must be clearly distinguished from authoritarianism,[2] as Frankenberg and Heitmeyer emphasise in their contribution to this volume. Furthermore, they register overlaps between populism, illiberalism and authoritarianism. Moreover, in line with the mainstream in political science, they argue for distinguishing authoritarianism from totalitarianism.[3] However, some of the characteristics that Frankenberg and Heitmeyer ascribe to authoritarianism (such as the all-or-nothing structure, the defence against "foreign infiltration", the tendency to violence) also characterise totalitarian thinking and action. It thus remains debatable whether totalitarianism should be understood as a qualitatively distinct concept alongside that of authoritarianism or as an extreme variant of authoritarianism. Empirically oriented political science draws the line between authoritarian and totalitarian systems based on a decisionistically set threshold. Political philosophy gives different answers. Under the impression of fascism and Bolshevism, it emphasised systematic terror and the readiness to destroy political opponents as characteristics of totalitarianism (Arendt 1955). Subsequent theorists of totalitarianism tended to detach the concept from this specific historical connection and to understand it in general terms as a system of (political) control that permeates all social spheres. I tend to treat authoritarianism as a generic term. Totalitarianism is then that variant which takes characteristics of authoritarianism to the extreme.

The core of authoritarianism rests the combination of two attitudes. The first assumes a *natural hierarchy* of social relations. From this follows the fundamental advocacy of inequality, of superiority and subordination, leadership and followership, command and obedience. Allegedly, inequality arises from human nature, resulting in a largely invariable gradient of abilities, achievements and rights.

The second basic attitude is the unquestioning self-assurance and *dogmatism* with which one's own ideological and moral positions are championed. This claim to absoluteness results in a tendency to refuse discourse, to reject relativising and pluralistic positions, to despise compromise, and often to be aggressive towards those who are different (e.g. migrants) and those who think differently (e.g. feminists). The forms of expression of authoritarianism are

---

anti-bourgeois educational concept, is of little help for my attempt at clarification with regard to social movements.

[2] The hallmark of authority "is unquestioning recognition on the part of those to whom obedience is demanded; it requires neither coercion nor persuasion" (Arendt 1970: 46). On the role of authority in a secular society, see also Frankenberg 2020: 55–85).

[3] As early as 1929, the constitutional lawyer Hermann Heller had distinguished between an authoritarian and a totalitarian dictatorship (Heller 1971: 515).

outlined below, first for individuals, then for political systems and finally for social movements.

(1) *Authoritarianism as a personal trait*: The characterisation of a person, group or action as "authoritarian" does not follow a generally binding standard in psychology and social psychology. Accordingly, the instruments for recording or measuring this characteristic as a personality trait vary. This is expressed in the coexistence of different scales.[4] The study on the authoritarian character by Adorno et al. (1950), which is primarily based on psychoanalytical assumptions and is thus narrow in scope, continues to point the way. More recent approaches, on the other hand, focus on the learning of authoritarian attitudes in a specific social context. This perspective also lends itself to the consideration of social movements.

Altemeyer's (1996) conception of authoritarianism, which he had already specified as "right-wing authoritarianism" (Altemeyer 1981), is aimed at personal attitudes, namely as a linkage of three clusters or "orientation reactions": authoritarian submissiveness, authoritarian aggression and conventionalism. However, the origin of these clusters remains largely unexplained. This is where Oesterreich (1996) comes in. He understands authoritarianism as a reaction to situations that make people insecure. His approach focuses less on existing attitudes, but rather on the experience of situations and the resulting behaviour, namely the "flight into security", the title of his book. This perspective seems to me to be particularly fruitful with regard to collective action as the central mode of identity formation and self-representation of social movements.

(2) *Authoritarianism as a characteristic of political systems*: Authoritarian systems are mostly spoken of when rulers usurp sprawling powers, undermine or disregard principles of separation of powers, violate civil and democratic rights, and use rigorous or even brutal measures to achieve their goals. Authoritarianism is at its core, albeit in varying degrees, anti-democratic and anti-pluralist. Its ultimate form is a dictatorial or totalitarian regime. Accordingly, in a categorisation such as that used in the Democracy Index,[5] authoritarian regimes are shown as a fourth category alongside complete democracies, incomplete democracies and hybrid regimes. In a similar classification, a distinction is also made between moderate and hard variants of autoc-

---

4 The fascism scale (F scale), which consists of nine dimensions, was developed in the early 1940s. It was followed by a range of other and partly more sophisticated scales.

5 The Economist Democracy Index, 25 February 2023. See https://thegeopolitics.com/ democracy -index -2023 -understanding -the -global -scenarios/ - accessed 10 October 2023.

racies.[6] Occasionally, however, and especially in public political discourse, an authoritarian system is also referred to if it only partially violates democratic principles, which in the above categorisation would correspond to the type of a deficient democracy (for example Hungary) or a hybrid regime (for example Bolivia).

(3) *Authoritarianism as a trait of movements*: The characterisation as an authoritarian movement can refer to its social objectives as well as concrete practices. It is obvious to apply the characteristic authoritarian in the attribution to staff, people, groups, and movements in a gradual sense. According to the understanding indicated above, authoritarianism combines the assertion of a natural social hierarchy with a dogmatic representation of certain values and views. If these two dimensions are visualised as intersecting axes with the poles of hierarchy versus equality and scepticism versus dogmatism, different and partly opposing movements can be located in a two-dimensional space (Figure 17.1). Authoritarian movements are marked in grey and black respectively. With the exception of left-wing populism, they are located in the upper right field. They find their extreme expression in fascist and religious fundamentalist movements. The ideological counterpart to these are libertarian-anarchist movements.

Movements that want to install or support an authoritarian regime can be regarded as clearly authoritarian. However, organisations and movements that relativise or reject egalitarian and pluralist principles in relation to their own structure can also be regarded as more or less authoritarian. On the one hand, this attitude can have a magnetic effect on appropriately disposed staff and people who therefore join such a movement. However, an authoritarian internal structure and communication can also cause movement supporters who are not initially authoritarian to gradually adopt authoritarian attitudes and patterns of action. Regarding authoritarian movements, a distinction should be made between (a) programme, (b) internal structures and modes of communication, (c) public appearances and (d) outcomes.

Fascist movements, radical right-wing movements but also some religious fundamentalist movements come closest to the ideal type of authoritarian movements, characterised by the triad of a corresponding concept of society, public appearance and hierarchical internal organisation and communication. Here, two components are intertwined: firstly, the willingness to follow or devote oneself to certain staff, people or institutions while at the same time devaluing people and groups that are considered inferior, execrable, culturally alien or unbelieving; secondly, the propagation of authoritarian concepts and practices of political order.

---

6 See https://www.demokratiematrix.de/ranking.

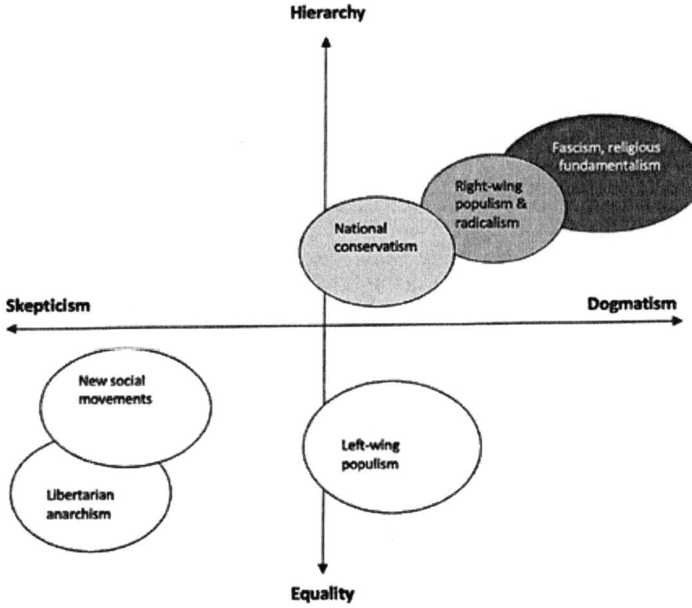

Source: Author.

Figure 17.1 Political-ideological positioning of social movements

A number of other movements fulfil these characteristics only in a weakened or partial form. More or less authoritarian features can also be found in some national-conservative movements. Likewise, some historical as well as contemporary radical-left movements exhibit authoritarian features and structures, especially insofar as they espouse Leninist, Trotskyist or Stalinist ideas. However, these groupings tend to endorse authoritarian patterns as merely temporarily or sectorally beneficial. Recall the formula of the dictatorship of the proletariat as a transitional stage to classless and egalitarian communism. Nevertheless, the thesis that authoritarianism is a genuine characteristic of the political left (Shapiro 2021) is untenable. Authoritarian patterns can also be found beyond radical political-ideological camps.[7] For example, an

---

7 In the mass psychology that flourished at the turn of the twentieth century (Le Bon, Sighele, Tarde), a distinction is made between leaderless and led masses. According to Robert Michels, leadership is universal and indispensable. The "incompetence of the masses ... forms the firmest anchorage of leader power" (Michels 1989: 83).

organisation like Greenpeace expresses its appreciation for a strong and tight leadership.

Of particular interest appear populist movements that are characterised by a systematically applied ambivalence with regard to authority. This is expressed in paradoxical labels such as "conformist revolt" or "authoritarian rebels". On the one hand, populists emphasise the homogeneity – and thus also the egalitarian structure – of the "people" in distinction from the "elites" who are perceived as self-referential and aloof. This results in the implicit or explicit demand for the abolition or abdication of the elites. On the other hand, right-wing populist groups are characterised not only by the desire for a strong and, if possible, charismatic leadership and, accordingly, their distance from the parliamentary system based on compromise, but also by the devaluation of social groups classified as inferior, such as migrants, ethnic minorities and "social parasites". Precisely because of their structural ambivalence, right-wing populist movements are probably the quantitatively most significant variant of authoritarian movements in Western societies. The strange combination of a postulate of equality and participation with the call for a strong hand appeals to different clientele groups; it also finds favour in the bourgeois centre. But it is also important to note the existence of left-wing populist groups[8] that have gained political majorities. Furthermore, some populist movements (e.g. Peronist movements) combine left-wing and right-wing ideas (Rossi 2013). From this follows that that the category of authoritarian movement is a broad one and should not be hastily equated with strong right-wing currents. Apart from extreme cases, a preliminary and general categorisation of movements as either authoritarian or non-authoritarian is therefore out of the question even if, in reality, the opposing extremes of totalitarian movements on the one hand and libertarian-anarchist movements on the other are to be found.

2. GENERAL CONDITIONS FOR PROTEST ACTIONS AND SOCIAL MOVEMENTS

No single-factor theory can do justice to the complex set of conditions that explain the emergence of social movements. Rather, diverse approaches associated with concepts such as structural strain, relative deprivation, resource mobilisation, collective identity and framing need to be integrated into a larger theoretical framework that links basic assumptions of action and systems theory and also includes factors at the micro, meso and macro levels (Rucht 2023). Examples of these factors are the strength of movement organisations

---

8 See Priest (2012). A slightly different terminology is used by Hall (1986), who distinguishes popular-democratic from authoritarian populism.

emphasised by John McCarthy and Mayer Zald, William Gamson's basic frames for mobilising movements (injustice, identity, agency), and Charles Tilly's (2006) WUNC formula, consisting of the components worthiness, unity, numbers and commitment. Partly drawing on Tilly's (1978) central variables for collective action (interests, organisation, opportunity, mobilisation), the following general conditional factors for the emergence of collective protests can be identified:

The indispensable raw material for (protest) action is the perception of a burden, a grievance or an injustice. This situation must be seen neither as self-inflicted nor as a fate, but as caused by people and in principle surmountable by people. This is linked to the imagination of a better state of affairs that is worth standing up for and fighting for together. Bert Klandermans (1988) proposed the term *consensus mobilisation* for this stage of opinion formation. However, in order for individuals to participate in concrete actions (Klandermans then speaks of *action mobilisation*), context-specific or situational barriers to participation must be overcome. These include material and other costs of participation (long access routes, bad weather, risks of protest) as well as the attractiveness of competing offers of action.

These impressions and experiences are not produced in their entirety in advance and individually to then guide and fuel collective action. Rather, they emerge and solidify in ongoing interactions in which existing as well as new impressions flow in and in which individual staff, people or organisations take on an impulse-giving or formative role. However, the aforementioned conditions only favour the potential for collective protest. Apart from spontaneous expressions of displeasure, a call is needed with the announcement of the purpose, place, time and sometimes also the concrete form of the protest. However, an actual protest may remain an isolated event. A larger campaign or even a social movement only develops when other preconditions are in place, which then lead to organisational consolidation and the formation of an identity as a social movement. These preconditions are essentially of a structural nature and can be located at the meso and macro levels.

A first factor is an interpretation of the problem that refers to structural causes and expands the circle of those (potentially) affected or addressed. In this way, the initial and central problem is declared to be a matter to which a reaction is expected from the political public, political decision makers and ultimately society as a whole. Large, potentially effective movements address a fundamental conflict of a certain social formation and thus point beyond the special interests of relatively small groups. In movements, such interpretations are usually further developed and possibly canonised by specialists (movement entrepreneurs, charismatic leaders, theoreticians, strategists, agitators).

A second factor that opens up a longer-term perspective is the presentation of a project that ultimately encompasses society as a whole and promises a better future. Such a project, which can include visionary or utopian moments, only finds wider acceptance if it can tie in with values, horizons of experience and communicative networks already present in larger groups. A societal project can offensively aim at a historically new form of social order, but it can also be defensively directed at restoring a – mostly glorified – past state. Habermas (1987: 393) thus distinguishes the "emancipatory potentials from potentials for resistance and withdrawal". The latter "aim at stemming formally organized domains of action for the sake of communicatively structured domains, and not at conquering new territory" (ibid). Together with the naming of causes and culprits, one's own mission and social designs for the future, such ideas aimed at society as a whole can crystallise into ideologies.

A third condition for the emergence of a social movement is the consolidation of communication, the creation of organisations and networks of an informal and/or formal nature, the development of mechanisms of will formation, decision-making and steering, including the ability to act strategically. In this process, collective identity must be strengthened, centrifugal tendencies of a movement must be avoided to let the movement emerge as a real or imagined unity. According to Tilly (1978: 62 f.), joint action in movements is facilitated by two factors. *Catness* (categoriness) refers to the degree to which a group conforms to ascriptive characteristics and forms a collective identity. *Netness* (networkness) refers to the density of the communicative network that directly or indirectly connects the potential agents. It proves advantageous if existing social relays (factories, schools, universities, etc.) can be used for processes of consensus and action mobilisation.

Fourthly, the strength, endurance and resilience of a movement is influenced, among other things, by *opportunity structures*, which are not limited to *political* opportunities. In addition, there is also the power, unity and strategy of the opponents as well as the attitude of third parties. In today's liberal democracies, the attitude of the mass media plays a key role as part of *discursive* opportunities. Movements that meet with unanimous and decisive rejection by the political public and the mass media have little chance of growth; at best they are able to stabilise as a marginal social phenomenon, in extreme cases in sect-like forms. On the other hand, movements that want to grow beyond their original nuclei require a certain social and ideological openness and flexibility to be able to both win new supporters and take account of changing contexts.

The conditions for the emergence and development of social movements are not identical with the factors that make the success or failure of movements likely. The latter would be the subject of a separate consideration. In general, it can be assumed that movements with a large, self-confident, unified and militant following have greater chances of success than movements with opposite characteristics. However, it is also true that, depending on the social context, the unity or division of elites and their counter-strategies, even relatively small movements can achieve success. There is also the possibility that a movement is strengthened rather than weakened by the interaction of a moderate and radical wing (positive *radical flank effect*). On the other hand, it cannot be ruled out that even large and united mass movements, as recently in Hong Kong and Belarus, can be effectively suppressed at least in the short and medium term.

3. CONDITIONS FOR THE EMERGENCE OF AUTHORITARIAN MOVEMENTS

The four general conditions of emergence mentioned above can be contextualised and concretised with regard to authoritarian protest acts and movements for micro, meso and macro levels.

1. The raw material of absolute and even more relative deprivation, which can be used for mobilisation with an affinity for authority, is present in a significant part of the population in Western societies. Communication in small everyday worlds as well as representative surveys prove the existence of latent as well as manifest dissatisfaction, frustration, fear of decline, insecurity and the experience of loss of control, which all tend to favour defensive reactions. In the Federal Republic of Germany, the potential for authoritarian consensus mobilisation is probably in the order of 15 to 25 per cent, depending on the time and the items of the respective survey. Using the Populism Index by Castanho et al. (2018), of twelve EU countries studied, Denmark, Austria, Germany and – most clearly – the Netherlands have below-average scores, while France, Spain and, above all, Greece have the highest scores (Kaltwasser/Vehrkamp/Wratil 2019: 114). With regard to some countries, there is talk of "populism as mainstream" (Bauer 2010: 15), or, generalising, of a "populist zeitgeist" (Mudde 2004). Recent reviews of the state of research agree that "right-wing populism is a phenomenon that is not only to be found on the margins of society" (Kohlrausch/Höcker 2020: 23). The now differentiated recording of (right-wing) populist attitudes also contains specific sets of questions that can be considered indicators of authoritarian personal value attitudes. However, a systematic inventory of corresponding attitudes in relation to the entire spectrum of authoritarian movements is still lacking, not to mention an analysis of these movements' internal structures and modes of communication.
2. One's own situation, subjectively experienced as unjust and unreasonable, is not interpreted as an individual fate but as a collective situation affecting a significant part or even the majority of the population. Protest groups and movements are the visible and activist expression of this

perception. In this context, the construction of a multi-layered collective identity is significant. It can be imagined as a linkage of concentric circles, ranging from the innermost circle of key activists to committed activists to adherents. Regarding the ensemble of these circles, movements tend to stylise themselves rhetorically and symbolically as a "community". De facto, however, authoritarian movements distance themselves from multipolar, decentralised and egalitarian structures. Instead, they advocate hierarchical patterns of relations in which leaders set the tone. In some authoritarian movements, a singular, nationally prominent leader does indeed emerge and, at least in phases, finds broad recognition in his or her own camp. In other phases or kinds of authoritarian movements, the juxtaposition and opposition of rival leadership figures prevents a hierarchical arrangement of different groupings and levels of action. Thus, even an authority-oriented movement may retain its status as a decentralised network without a coordinating centre. However, insofar as a movement-wide recognised central leader emerges who can underpin his or her claim to power organisationally and ultimately bring other movement segments under control, the movement character is lost, even though it may continue to be rhetorically invoked. If the former movement finally succeeds in "seizing power", often combined with the elimination of democratic mechanisms, organisations (including parties) and institutions, it enters the regime phase, as was the case with the NSDAP (the German Nazi-party) from 1933 onwards.

In the struggle for power as well as in the stage of successful exercise of power, authoritarian movements and their end products, which have coagulated into an apparatus, are anxious to stylize themselves as the authentic representation of the entire body of the people. Its allegedly natural and homogeneous interests are threatened by supposed special interests. Right-wing authoritarian movements present themselves as defenders of a community of culture and destiny with an ethnocentric or even *völkisch* slant. The difference between inside and outside is constitutive here. On the other hand, left-wing authoritarian movements, including left-wing populist movements, place the interest of the exploited class at the centre of their collective identity constructions. Instead of the opposition of inside and outside, their worldview is shaped by the large gap between the lower and the higher classes. In the version of Chantal Mouffe (2015), "left populism" is based on the opposition to the political and economic forces of neoliberalism.

3. If the actual or perceived deprivation is not interpreted as an inevitable fate or self-inflicted, it is obvious to identify other staff, people and groups as causers and culprits. In doing so, it is above all emotions that are addressed and stirred up. Protesters with authoritarian attitudes and

objectives typically name two main groups as culprits: on the one hand, the established elites, "those up there", who are perceived as powerful, privileged, self-referential and detached from the people; on the other hand, those who are seen as foreigners, unbelievers and those of a different faith, non-entitled or only allegedly disadvantaged and in need of protection. From the point of view of their critics, they all make illegitimate claims, be it for cultural recognition, political representation or material provision, thereby intensifying the competition for scarce material and other resources. Their own insecurity and experiences of a loss of control over anonymous powers and processes lead authoritarian actors to identify and discriminate against those groups that are located below their own position in the social hierarchy. Corresponding to the willingness to follow strong leaders is the urge to dominate outsiders and the weak.

In contrast to the interpretation of a disastrous present or future, authoritarian groups create the image of an organic order. This, of course, is not supposed to be established in the tough democratic-discursive struggle for majorities. Rather, it is assumed that it breaks through as the evident "will of the people", be it thanks to the instruments of direct democracy, be it through spontaneous acclamation, the use of a popular, strong-willed leadership equipped with considerable means of power, or through uncontrolled acts of violence.

4. Finally, envisaged joint protest actions must appear suitable and purposeful in their form, with authoritarian staff, people and groups showing little reluctance to break the rules. In both internal and external communication, those who are particularly loud and aggressive often set the tone. At the centre of their actions are ciphers such as unambiguity, courage, struggle, resistance and revolution.[9] In extreme cases, the law of the strongest should apply.

However, the form of an authoritarian *social movement* (as distinct from single collective protests or protest campaigns that are limited in terms of subject matter and time) only comes about when further factors are present that lead to a generalisation of the concerns and a consolidation of the structures.

[9] The term "Conservative Revolution", coined by the young Armin Mohler, was intended to set a demarcation line vis-à-vis National Socialism. At an advanced age, Mohler admitted the difficulty of this distinction (see Weiß 2017: 47). Nevertheless, the term found favour in New Right circles.

3.1 Micro Level

In concretising the general conditions mentioned above, the following prerequisites can be postulated for the type of authoritarian movements:

(1) Significant parts of a society must gain and spread the impression that something is fundamentally wrong with this society, i.e. that grievances and undesirable developments are structurally conditioned and, in this respect, also affect larger groups of society, if not society as a whole. Populist currents, according to Canovan (1999), feed on a collective experience of disappointment. As part of the structural problem, such movements, like authoritarian movements as a whole, see a pluralisation or polarisation of social and political forces – wanted and pursued by ruling elites – which must be overcome.

(2) Part of this agreement is the commitment to a common direction, the project of a viable society that can hold its own against external competitors. Patterns of thought of natural selection, of *survival of the fittest*, often come into play. As with a pack of wolves, strong leadership and a people that is as united behind its leadership are needed. The Nazi slogan "Führer befiel, wir folgen Dir" (Leader, command, we follow) is prototypical of this. The position of leadership figures is affirmed in rites and stagings, and criticism of them is branded as "treason" or heresy.

(3) These images and visions are partly borrowed as already existing mental building blocks from other contexts, modelled for the interpretation of the present, but partly also first established in ongoing communications and inserted into simple worldviews characterised by dichotomies.[10] This creates a mental framework for the interpretation of an initial problem together with its origins and causes. It is worth making sacrifices for the desired new or old order, not least for one's own mission as a movement that is historically necessary and legitimate in its aims and forms. It is no coincidence that the own group is often labelled as a movement, sometimes even in relation to regular parties, as the concept of a movement signals dynamism, strength and significant size.

---

[10] According to Dubiel (1986: 37), populist movements are, among other things, "defined by the fact that they have no theoretically oriented, comprehensive programme of their own, but merely organise group-, local- or situation-specific concerns". In my opinion, this does not apply to all populist movements.

3.2 Meso Level

At this level, already existing or newly emerging groups and organisations need to network. With the integration of already existing groups, *bloc recruitment* of many individuals is feasible. Authoritarian movements usually tend to form a very loose structure in which the individual components, possibly including parties, maintain their independence. With quite different thematic accentuation, they take up perceptions and moods of their mobilisation potential, strengthen and bundle them.

In authoritarian movements, individual leadership groups and leaders typically declare themselves to be the advocates of the common people, a social class, ethnicity, the people or the true religion. They name the sources and causes of social grievances and identify those responsible and guilty. Enemy images are propagated; emotions and above all aggression are stirred up (Koppetsch 2020: 55 ff.; Rosanvallon 2020: 56 ff). This applies equally to secular and religious authoritarian movements. In addition to this *diagnostic framing*, they also engage in *prognostic framing*, i.e. they propagate goals and conditions that need to be achieved. Also, they specify the steps required for this. Authoritarian movements, especially in the form of "authoritarian threat alliances [...] directed against open society and liberal democracy" (Heitmeyer et al. 2020: 18), call for self-empowerment and resistance. In recent times, some right-wing populist groups have appealed to a misinterpreted idea of civil disobedience or even a revolutionary rhetoric, while religious groups have revived the idea of a "holy war".[11] Thirdly, organisers of authoritarian movements encourage their followers to take action (*motivational framing*). If no self-organisation of the followers is to be expected, they name a concrete framework for action and create the organisational conditions for entire series of collective actions in various social arenas. Authoritarian movements are sometimes able to mobilise tens of thousands, occasionally hundreds of thousands, for demonstrations. Participation in violent protest actions is much lower, although they are not uncommon in some countries. These actions receive widely varying media attention. They are usually only recorded in rough statistical categories by the authorities but tend to be neglected in scientifically oriented research.

However, the build-up and development of an authoritarian movement remains narrowly limited if the structural opportunities are lacking or existing favourable opportunities, for example differences of opinion within the circle of political decision-makers or manifest wrong decisions, are not recognised and used. State authorities' attempts to contain authoritarian movements, but

---

11 On the history of this figure of thought, see Schreiner (2008).

also civic counter-mobilisation, can produce different results. The strength of the authoritarian movement can weaken due to stalling tactics or partial concessions; the movement can radicalise in view of its loss of numerical significance or split into a moderate and a radical branch; the frequent rivalries between different leadership figures who each claim strength and determination for themselves, can lead to the movement's self-paralysis. However, it is also conceivable that an authoritarian movement changes its goals and means by virtue of its own insight and/or to avert its loss of significance, i.e. gradually democratises and moderates itself.

3.3 Macro Level

At the macro level, authoritarian movements are not merely concerned with policies, but with the question of order and power per se. Existing democratic systems are portrayed as lukewarm, weak in decision-making, and compromise oriented. They should be replaced by a strong state and a correspondingly strong leadership. This leadership must assert the interests of the people, which are largely imagined as a homogeneous entity and therefore do not need an extensive network of intermediary groups and institutions. According to the motto "Whoever is not for us is against us", camp thinking and camp formation are promoted. Without further ado, third and independent actors, such as the entire "system media", the courts, the – partly state-supported – cultural sector, the "raunchy left-green milieu" (according to AfD leader Jörg Meuthen), are considered stooges or mouthpieces of the established forces. The question of power is not only understood as a political struggle for votes and for political offices, but also as a cultural battle (Terkessidis 1995), in which interpretive sovereignty over what is "normal" – for example in relation to education, sexuality, family and gender roles – is called for. The cultural essentialist position is usually associated with a transfiguration of tradition and history, the memory of heroic struggles that must be continued today. For example, speakers at Pegida events (a right-wing and racist group created in Dresden in 2014) not only invoked the legacy of the civil rights movements of the imploding GDR, but also recalled the defence against Turkish invaders in the 16th century as an act to protect the Christian-Jewish culture.

Macrosociological interpretations of the rise of authoritarian movements set different accents without necessarily contradicting each other. In a 1967 presentation on the new right-wing radicalism, Adorno (2019) named capitalism as the structural background, pointing to the concentration of capital, the threat posed to small and medium-sized enterprises by globally active corporations and the growing gap between rich and poor. At the same time, he also pointed to the factor of narcissistic mortification, in which the blame is not assigned to the systemic "apparatus" but to its critics.

Andreas Reckwitz sees in right-wing populism essentially a "*reaction* to the unfolding hegemony of the new liberalism", to the "paradigm of apertist-differential liberalism in its left-wing *and* economically liberal variety" (2017: 414). Philip Manow (2018), on the other hand, criticises the overhang of cultural interpretations and instead emphasises the economic roots and the connection between populism and capitalism, without, however, committing to a specific definition of populism. Several works by Klaus Dörre also point in the same direction (see his contribution in this volume and Becker/Dörre/Reif-Spirek 2018).

However, the fundamental dispute as to whether it is cultural, political or economic developments that are feeding current populism seems idle as long as only certain substantive characteristics or individual geographical variants of populism are used as evidence for one or the other position. In this respect, it seems reasonable to assume a multidimensional complex of causes. For example, Heitmeyer (2018) points out that in the emergence of authoritarian patterns and authoritarian movements, a combination of material status threats and the erosion of social integration modes (differentiated as social-structural, institutional-participatory and personal dimensions) play a central role in the overarching framework of "authoritarian capitalism". Schäfer and Zürn (2021: 82) interpret authoritarian populism as the manifestation of a new line of conflict as "a consequence of the globalisation that began in the 1980s and accelerated in the 1990s". In their view, at least in Western Europe, the contemporary basic conflict is between cosmopolitanism and communitarianism.[12] In addition to cultural factors, the authors also point to a number of political factors, which they summarise under the denominator of a "crisis of representation" and "alienated democracy" (ibid.: 89 ff.).

At first glance, it seems plausible to attribute the rise of authoritarian movements primarily to experiences of crisis. However, this assumption does not apply to all cases. Even National Socialism, whose electoral breakthrough was essentially fostered by the world economic crisis in 1929, had already emerged and gained strength in the phase of the "Roaring Twenties". Attention should therefore also be paid to more insidious causal processes, which can condense and overlap, sometimes only leading to manifest authoritarian mobilisation after a critical threshold has been reached.

In my interpretation of the structural causes of the rise of right-wing populism in recent decades, I pointed to three deep social currents at the inter-

[12] The naming of one pole as communitarianism seems ignores the attitude of leading representatives of communitarianism (for example, Charles Taylor, Michael Walzer, Amitai Etzioni), who do advocate cosmopolitan, pro-democratic and culturally liberal positions and in this respect have unmistakable intersections with cosmopolitanism.

section of which the driving core of this movement is located (Rucht 2018). This explanatory pattern also seems applicable to the broader phenomenon of authoritarian movements, although differentiations and extensions would be necessary for individual variants, such as religious fundamentalist but also left-wing authoritarian movements. These deep currents are relatively constant. They can explain the emergence and existence of a rather stable mobilisation potential, but not the cyclical ups and downs of shorter waves of mobilisation. The key words are the syndromes of (1) fear of material loss and social status decline, whereby the perception of relative deprivation plays a role (which can also explain why even people who are relatively well off economically follow populist interpretations), (2) political alienation between those in power and those governed, which is reflected in a loss of trust, (3) a cultural disorientation against the background of a pluralisation of values and lifestyles in the context of globalisation, transnational interconnections and migration movements, the emphasis on singularities, private morals and shifts in cultural power constellations. These deep currents also give rise to certain contents, so that the interpretation of right-wing populism as a mere *form* of the political (Müller 2016; Reckwitz 2017) or a "thin ideology" (Mudde 2004) seems overly narrow. I share the position of Schäfer/Zürn (2021: 64) that contemporary (authoritarian) populism also includes "a set of substantive political positions and ideas".

The anchoring and relative strength of these three deep currents varies significantly within the group of Western societies and presumably even more when other regions of the world are considered. However, the empirically relatively tangible existence of authoritarian regimes and parties is not in itself a good indicator that allows direct and valid conclusions to be drawn about the vitality and strength of right-wing populist or authoritarian movements in a given country. Firstly, authoritarian regimes may have come to power through purely military means or a coup d'état without a strong movement in the background. Secondly, the strength of authoritarian parties is determined not only by their endogenous potential, but also by the relative weakness of competing parties and the heterogeneity or fragmentation of social forces. Thirdly, contingent factors can also give authoritarian parties a strong position, at least temporarily, for example due to a massive political scandal or an acute state crisis. Fourthly, the relative independence or entanglement of authoritarian rulers, parties and movements must be taken into account. A charismatic leader can temporarily mask the organisational weakness of the party or movement that supports him or her. Likewise, the field of forces and the interrelations between an authoritarian party and an authoritarian movement must be considered. With regard to right-wing populism in Europe, there are indications that a relatively strong right-wing populist party correlates with a rather weak right-wing populist movement, since the latter already sees its concerns represented institutionally and therefore perceives its own extra-parliamentary mobilisation as less urgent. An example of this is France with its electorally significant *Rassemblement National* (formerly *Front National*). On the other hand, the strengthening of the AfD (*Alternative für Deutschland*) in Germany was accompanied by the intensification of extra-parliamentary activities of radical right-wing groups. Furthermore, another constellation is to be thought of: a strong movement with a correspondingly strong parliamentary arm, which even provides the government, as is currently the case in Hungary and Turkey.

It also needs to be explained why in some European countries, such as Portugal, Spain and Ireland, right-wing populist parties and movements were very weak and have only recently gained ground. The chilling reverberations of a dictatorial past in Portugal and Spain cannot provide a satisfactory answer since Greece had a similar past but since then a more continuous presence of right-wing populists and right radicals.

The reunified Federal Republic of Germany could be an instructive case to explain the emergence and development of a right-wing populist movement (with large overlaps to right-wing radicalism). Here we have a macro-experimental constellation, so to speak, which raises the question of why there are clear differences in the relative strength of right-wing populism in the East and West. After all, the political-institutional framework has been largely identical for more than three decades now. Moreover, the East and West had a common political and cultural past up to 1945. The more massive right-wing populism in the east of the country cannot be adequately explained by a four-decade authoritarian state system and the associated cultural imprints, mentalities and socialisation processes. Also, the finding that the different levels of right-wing populist and radical right-wing attitudes in the East and West[13] are equally found among the younger generations suggests that the experience of social and political disadvantage in the phase after reunification – and not GDR socialisation – favours right-wing radicalisation in the East Germany.

Nor does the absence of a culturally consequential anti-authoritarian 1968 movement in the GDR offer a sufficient explanation for the strength of right-wing populism and right-wing radicalism in the east of the Republic. Looking at other European countries, it is difficult to substantiate the assumption that a strong '68 movement in its aftermath proved to be a kind of bulwark

---

[13] One indicator of this is the approval ratings for the statement: "In the national interest, a dictatorship is the better form of state under certain circumstances." In 2018, 6.5 per cent of West Germans, but 13.1 per cent of East Germans agreed with this (Decker/Brähler 2018: 75). In the follow-up study of 2020, values of 3.3 per cent in the West and 11 per cent in the East were determined (Decker et al. 2020: 37).

against authoritarian tendencies or especially against right-wing populism. The case of Italy speaks against this. So does the French case where right-wing populism had already achieved a strong position with Poujadism before the student revolt. Moreover, the traces of a massive student revolt in France did not prevent the rise of the *Front National* as an important political player. On the other hand, there are countries such as Austria with a weak student movement in the 1960s but a strong right-wing populist movement in the recent decades. This example clearly speaks against the general assumption that right-wing populism is a delayed reaction to the cultural and political consequences of the student movement of the 1960s. These rather cursorily cited cases illustrate the complex interplay of diverse factors.

4. CONCLUSION

Whether the concept of authoritarian movements can be empirically substantiated and whether there is a typical constellation of conditions for the emergence of such movements cannot be conclusively demonstrated based on the above. The relatively abstract definition of the adjective "authoritarian" refers to a spectrum of movements that clearly differ in their ideological basis and political objectives (e.g. authoritarian movements with a secular or religious-fundamentalist orientation). Also, these movements are "authoritarian" to very different degrees – ranging from moderate authoritarian features to totalitarian objectives and means. Even the subgroup of populist movements shows great diversity, so that it is suggested to speak of populisms in the plural (Rosavallon 2020: 72). Whether, in addition to the highly general explanations for the emergence of social movements, a more concrete set of factors can also explain the emergence of all variants of authoritarian movements seems open to debate. We lack quantitative comparative data on both the explanatory variables and the movements as dependent variables, for instance with regard to their emergence and development trajectories. My explanatory offer is thus largely general and hypothetical in nature.

Notwithstanding these deficits, there is the impression that monocausal explanations do not do justice to the complexity of the subject matter. This applies, for example, to the connection between rapid social change and anomie (Emile Durkheim) with the consequence of authoritarianism, the connection between drive suppression and fascism (Wilhelm Reich), but also to more recent attempts to explain right-wing populist and radical right-wing movements. In some of these explanations, the factors for an authoritarian mobilisation potential are mixed up or confused with the factors that are decisive for the cyclical ups and downs of manifest action mobilisations. Explaining these, however, requires highly contextual and process-related and, moreover, comparative analyses that are not currently available. For almost every general assertion on the emergence and expansion of authoritarian movements, counterexamples can also be cited. Individual case studies run the risk of being burdened with inadmissible generalisations.

The three deep currents that seem to me to be central to explaining the rise of right-wing populist groups and mobilisations can also be significant for the broader category of authoritarian movements. Of course, this would then have to be examined for different variants in a comparative perspective. The specific profiles of types of authoritarian movements should not be blurred in favour of an overly diffuse conceptual container. Nor should direct conclusions be drawn about the strength of right-wing populist or radical right-wing movements or even the entirety of authoritarian movements from the easily tangible election results of right-wing populist or radical right-wing parties. Moreover, the interaction of extra-parliamentary and parliamentary authoritarian forces should be taken into account, which can follow the mode of a zero-sum game but also the mode of mutual reinforcement.

In addition to the comparison of authoritarian movements in similar as well as in strongly contrasting social contexts, two further dimensions of comparison should be included. The first is the comparison between right-wing and left-wing authoritarian movements. Both variants have, by definition, authoritarian internal structures, but differ in their respective justifications and socio-political designs. For right-wingers, authoritarian structures are not only the means but also the goal of systemic concepts of order. The rarer left-wing authoritarian movements accept authoritarian patterns for their organisational and communication structures but see in them rather a strategic lever for a transitional phase, in order to establish an egalitarian and in this sense non-authoritarian social order in the end. Empirically, however, there is a tendency into the opposite direction. Once left-wing authoritarian movements have seized power, authoritarianism becomes, at least de facto, the leading political currency for the system as a whole. Eloquent examples of this are Stalinist Russia, but also Nicaragua and Venezuela in recent decades.

Secondly, the far more difficult litmus test for a theory of the emergence of authoritarian movements would be the inclusion of religious fundamentalist movements in comparison to secular authoritarianism.

REFERENCES

Adorno, Theodor W., Frenkel-Brunswik, Else, Levinson, Daniel J. & Sanford, R. Nevitt (1950), *The Authoritarian Personality*, New York.

Adorno, Theodor W. (2019 [1967]), *Aspekte des neuen Rechtsradikalismus*, Berlin.

Altemeyer, Bob (1981), *Right-Wing Autoritarianism*, Winnipeg CA.

Altemeyer, Bob (1996), *The Authoritarian Specter*, Cambridge MA.

Arendt, Hannah (1970), *Elemente und Ursprünge totaler Herrschaft*, Frankfurt am Main.

Arendt, Hannah (1970), *Macht und Gewalt*, München.
Bauer, Werner T. (2010), *Rechtspopulismus in Europa. Vergängliches Phänomen oder auf dem Weg zum politischen Mainstream?* Bonn: Friedrich-Ebert-Stiftung. https://library.fes.de/pdf-files/id/ipa/07293.pdf.
Becker, Karina & Dörre, Klaus & Reif-Spirek, Peter (eds.) (2018), *Arbeiterbewegung von rechts? Ungleichheit – Verteilungskämpfe – populistische Revolte*, Frankfurt a. M./ New York.
Canovan, Margaret (1999), "Trust the People! Populism and the Two Faces of Democracy", in *Political Studies*, 47(1), 2–16.
Castanho, Silva, Andreadis, Ioannis, Anduiza, Eva, Blanuša, Nebojša, Morlet Corti, Yazmin, Delfino, Gisela, Rico, Guillem, Ruth, Saskia P., Spruyt, Bram, Steenbergen, Marco & Littvay, Levente (2017), "Public Opinion Surveys: A New Scale?", in Hawkins, Kirk A., Carlin, Ryan E., Littvay, Levente, Rovira Kaltwasser & Cristóbal (Hg.), *The Ideational Approach to Populism: Theory, Method and Analysis*, London, 150–178.
Decker, Oliver & Brähler, Elmar (eds.) (2018), *Flucht ins Autoritäre. Rechtsextreme Dynamiken in der Mitte der Gesellschaft*, Gießen.
Decker, Oliver, Kiess, Johannes, Schuler, Julia, Handke, Barbara, Pickel, Gert & Brähler, Elmar (2020), "Die Leipziger Autoritarismus Studie 2020: Methode, Ergebnisse und Langzeitverlauf", in Decker, Oliver & Brähler, Elmar (eds.), Autoritäre Dynamiken. Alte Ressentiments – neue Radikalität, Gießen, 27–87.
Dubiel, Helmut (1986), "Das Gespenst des Populismus", in Dubiel, Helmut (ed.), *Populismus und Aufklärung*, Frankfurt am Main.
Frankenberg, Günter (2020), *Autoritarismus. Verfassungstheoretische Perspektiven*, Berlin.
Habermas, Jürgen (1987), *The Theory of Communicative Action. Vol 2. Lifeworld and System: A Critique of Functionalist Reason.* Boston.
Hall, Stuart (1986), "Popular-demokratischer und autoritärer Populismus", in Dubiel, Helmut (ed.), *Populismus und Aufklärung*, Frankfurt am Main.
Heitmeyer, Wilhelm (2018), *Autoritäre Versuchungen. Signaturen der Bedrohung I*, Berlin.
Heitmeyer, Wilhelm, Freiheit, Manuela & Sitzer, Peter (2020), *Rechte Bedrohungsallianzen, Signaturen der Bedrohung II*, Berlin.
Heller, Hermann (1971 [1929]), *Europa und der Fascismus*, in ders., *Gesammelte Schriften*, Bd. 2, Leiden, 463–609.
Höcker, Linus M. & Kohlrausch, Bettina (2020), *Ursachen für rechtspopulistische Einstellungen. Ein Überblick über den Forschungsstand*, Hans Böckler Stiftung, Düsseldorf, https:// www .econstor .eu/ bitstream/ 10419/ 217253/ 1/ hbs -fofoe -wp -178–2020.pdf/.
Kaltwasser, Cristóbal Rovira, Vehrkamp, Robert & Wratil, Christopher (2019), *Europa hat die Wahl. Populistische Einstellungen und Wahlabsichten bei der Europawahl 2019*, Gütersloh.
Klandermans, Bert (1988), "The Formation and Mobilization of Consensus", in *International Social Movement Research*, Bd. 1, Greenwich CT, 173–196.
Koppetsch, Cornelia (2020), *Rechtspopulismus als Protest: Die gefährdete Mitte in der globalen Moderne*, Hamburg.
Lederer, Gerda & Schmidt, Peter (eds.) (1995), *Autoritarismus und Gesellschaft*, Opladen.
Manow, Philip (2018), *Die Politische Ökonomie des Populismus*, Berlin.
Michels, Robert (1989 [1911]), *Soziologie des Parteiwesens*, Stuttgart.

Mouffe, Chantal (2015) “Für einen linken Populismus”, in IPG Newsletter. https:// www .ipg -journal .de/ rubriken/ zukunft -der -sozialdemokratie/ artikel/ fuer -einen -linken-populismus-857/.
Mudde, Cas (2004), “The Populist Zeitgeist”, in *Government and Opposition*, 39 (4), 541–563.
Müller, Jan (2016), *Was ist Populismus? Ein Essay*, Berlin.
Nath S.S. Democracy Index (2023): Understanding the global scenarios. The Geopolitics. Published online 26 February 2023. https:// thegeopolitics .com/ democracy -index -2023-understanding-the-global-scenarios/.
Oesterreich, Detlef (1996), *Flucht in die Sicherheit. Zur Theorie des Autoritarismus und der autoritären Reaktion*, Opladen.
Priester, Karin (2012), Rechter und linker Populismus: Annäherungen an ein Chamäleon, Frankfurt am Main.
Rathkolb, Oliver (2011), “Neuer Politischer Autoritarismus”, in *Aus Politik und Zeitgeschichte* No. 44–45, Bonn, 56–62.
Reckwitz, Andreas (2017), *Die Gesellschaft der Singularitäten*, Berlin.
Rosanvallon, Pierre (2020), *Das Jahrhundert des Populismus. Geschichte, Theorie, Praxis*, Hamburg.
Rossi, Frederico M. (2013), “Peronism”, in Snow, David & della Porta, Donatella & Klandermans, Bert, eds, *The Wiley-Blackwell Encyclopedia of Social and Political Movements*. DOI: 10.1002/9781405198431.wbespm366.
Rucht, Dieter (1994), *Modernisierung und neue soziale Bewegungen. Deutschland, Frankreich und USA im Vergleich*, Frankfurt/New York.
Rucht, Dieter (2018), “Right-wing Populism in Context: A Historical and Systematic Perspective”, in Fitzi, Gregor, Mackert, Jürgen & Turner, Bryan S. (eds.), *Populism and the Crisis of Democracy*. Vol. 2: *Politics, Social Movements and Extremism*, London and New York, 67–84.
Rucht, Dieter (2023), *Social Movements: A Theoretical Approach*. Oxford.
Schäfer, Armin & Zürn, Michael (2021), *Die demokratische Regression*, Berlin.
Schreiner, Klaus & Müller-Luckner, Elisabeth (2008), *Heilige Kriege. Religiöse Begründungen militärischer Gewaltanwendung: Judentum, Christentum und Islam im Vergleich*, München.
Shapiro, Ben (2021), *The Authoritarian Moment: How the Left Weaponized America's Institutions Against Dissent*, New York.
Terkessidis, Mark (1995), *Kulturkampf. Volk, Nation, der Westen und die neue Rechte*, Köln.
Tilly, Charles (1978), *From Mobilization to Revolution*, Reading MA.
Tilly, Charles (2006), “WUNC”, in Schnapp, Jeffrey T. & Tiews, Matthew (eds.), *Crowds*, Stanford CA, 289–306.
Weiß, Volker (2017), *Die autoritäre Revolte. Die Neue Rechte und der Untergang des Abendlandes*, Stuttgart.

Index